The Self-Donation of God

The Self-Donation of God

A Contemporary Lutheran approach to Christ and His Benefits

Jack D. Kilcrease

WIPF & STOCK · Eugene, Oregon

THE SELF-DONATION OF GOD
A Contemporary Lutheran approach to Christ and His Benefits

Wipf & Stock
An Imprint of Wipf and Stock Publishers
199 W. 8th Ave., Suite 3
Eugene, OR 97401
www.wipfandstock.com

ISBN 13: 978-1-62032-605-3
Manufactured in the U.S.A.

Unless otherwise stated, scripture quotations are from the English Standard Version of the Bible. Please use standard language for this Bible translation.

This work is dedicated to my parents for all they have done for me, not least raising me in the Christian faith.

Also I want to thank my wife for her love and guidance.

Lastly, I would like to dedicate this book also to my dearly departed *doktorvator* Ralph Del Colle for his work with me and his guidance.

Contents

Contents

Foreword

Looking for a Unifying Principle

A THEOLOGIAN'S TASK IS developing a theology around a unifying theme that is descriptive of the entire theological enterprise and permeates all its parts. This is not unique to theology, but is required of particular philosophies and with most every other scholarly discipline. Without a discoverable unity any system disintegrates and becomes inaccessible to those attempting to come to terms with it. Before going any further, we can say that Dr. Jack Kilcrease is a theologian in every sense of the word. In the current state of theological affairs, no one idea or principle comes close to providing an umbrella under which what theologians do can be placed. In former days systematic theologians, who were simply known as theologians without further description of their special interest, pursued their tasks around traditional and widely held and known principles. Such was the case in the Reformation and post-Reformation era, when particular theologies, that later formed basis for the mainline denominations, arose and could be identified by one or two prominent themes. Each church tradition had a principle making it distinct from others and by which each one recognized itself as unique. One could not be confused with another. Lutheran theology was not Reformed and vice versa and so it was. The unifying principle of each tradition permeated every article of the faith and provided unity to the theological system. Lutherans saw justification as the core principle that surfaced in such doctrines as the sacraments and the ministry which existed for the sake of declaring the sinner righteous. So accepting the law's condemnation, they heard and believed the gospel and were relieved from the impending judgment of God and the fear it created. Reformed, Presbyterians, Congregationalist, and other groups rooted in the teachings of Ulirch Zwingli and John Calvin saw the center of theology in divine sovereignty, a doctrine that played itself out in what they said about the covenant as a contract between God and the believer that dare not be broken, providence and election. Methodism, not strictly a Reformation era phenomenon, was an eighteenth century reaction to Reformed doctrine of election and saw the impetus for salvation not in God's sovereignty but in the will of each human being, a precursor of the rationalism of the Enlightenment. Later holiness groups and today much of American Evangelicalism follows in what is commonly called the Arminian tradition enveloped in Methodism. Before the Reformation, Catholicism was a covering for various theological approaches, but the Council of Trent in reaction to the Lutheran doctrine of justification by faith insisted that works had a place alongside of faith. Some of these works that contributed to one's salvation were specifically religious ones like doing penance, making pilgrimages, and participating in the Mass. In resolving theological differences, the bishop of Rome had the last word. Around these doctrines Roman Catholicism took shape. For Protestant heirs of the Reformation the scriptures exercised this role, but the *sola scriptura* principle as it came to be known, multiplied differences and did not provide the hope from principle of unity. This would have to be found elsewhere.

The survival of classical principles that determined the faith of the churches emerging from the Reformation are heading towards extinction in identifying what mainline denominations confessed. Their confessions or more properly statements of what they believed have been gradually disintegrated by a centrifugal diffusion that has emptied the core of these older theological traditions. Some Lutherans and the Reformed remain steeped in their Reformation heritages and continue to be at odds with each other, just as Luther and Zwingli were, on such essential issues as God, the person and work of Christ, and the sacraments, but they are in an ever decreasing minority. Dr. Kilcrease reassesses these differences and finds that they are still valid in how Lutherans and Reformed differ from each other. Interest in historical differences does not consume the interest of theologians in the mainline churches, who are willing to let bygones be bygones. Similarly those who sit in the pews are unlikely to know or be concerned about the distinctive beliefs of their churches and how these churches came to believe what they do. Identifying a principle holding the church and its beliefs together is no longer a concern and in many, perhaps most, cases impossible. This has opened the door to an endless round of ecumenical alliances with each church selling its birthright. The ecumenical movement in bringing together churches that were historically opposed to each other is like a tire that has gradually lost air and has gone flat. Into this situation syncretism has found an entrance. A Shinto altar can be found in a prominent New York City cathedral and sacred symbols of non-Christian religions often adorn the walls of Christian sanctuaries. An annual Reformation Day celebration once served the purpose of saying that one's church was really different from those of others. This is less important today. Religious diffusion and diversity of principles are exacerbated by the rise and proliferation of churches that claim no denominational affiliation. More conservative churches may go under the banner of Bible churches and make a point of not being bound to one set of beliefs, life confessions, or official statements of any kind. Only the Bible demands their allegiance, so they say. On the other side of the ledger, community churches may not even make believing in the Bible a requirement. Membership is open to all those who reside in geographical proximity to their houses of worship. Both types of churches agree that the members can believe what they want. Locating a central theological core holding together these free standing congregations together is impossible, simply because there is none. What is believed in one year may not be believed in the next year and its members are not required to subscribe to any article of faith. Adherence to the Apostles' Creed is off limits even to Evangelicals who are committed to the Bible's inspiration and more likely to be open about their faith. They account for a good segment of the Protestant population. Congregations in mainline denominations with roots in the Reformation may not be able to identify the core of their belief. Allegiance to statements of faith is more a formality than theologically determinative. These churches have no constitutional-like documents to be referenced in cases of dispute.

Another factor in the disintegration of theological cores in churches and their theologies is the division of study of theology into the sub-disciplines of biblical, systematic,
historical and practical theologies. There is hardly a seminary, if any at all, that does not
have its faculty divided into departments for each of these subdisciplines. A seminary
or a university school of religion instructor is less likely to see him/herself as a theologian competent to handle the full range of theology. So one professor is a systematic
theologian, another a biblical scholar, still another an historian and finally the practical
theologian teaches how to get things done, a feature attractive to the American mind.
Each of these specialties can be further fragmented. One is not simply a New Testament
scholar, but a specialist in the Pauline epistles, the gospels, or even just one gospel. Rarely
does a scholar at a seminary or in a college's department of religion see him/herself as
competent to participate in the full entire range of the theological curriculum. Rarely
is one professor accredited to more than one department. Each one is a specialist in
one of the subdisciplines and finds kindred spirits not in his church tradition but in the
scholarly guild of his expertise. Faculty specializations are mirrored in curriculums. A
course of study is never simply theology, but biblical, systematic, historical, or practical theology. Deeper fragmentation is found in nondenominational and freestanding
seminaries where the professors represent different and contradictory traditions and
confessions. Even denominational owned or controlled colleges and seminaries engage
professors from theological traditions other than their own. Commitment to the beliefs
of the church supporting the school is not required of the faculty. In this virtually universally segmented theological environment, students in the seminary and those under-
taking a general study of theology of religion are often left to themselves to provide or
identify a unifying principle from among the various options presented to them. Pastors
coming out of any of these environments, even those with deep Reformation era roots,
are more likely to see themselves as preachers and practitioners of religion equipping
their congregations to do ministry. They see themselves as professionals and do not see
themselves as theologians prepared to teach even a minimum of the faith contained in
the creeds that in spite of the diversity in Western Christianity since the Reformation has
remained a unifying factor in offering a common Christian faith. A church's historical
traditions are no longer a factor to what the pastor preaches and how he interacts with
his parishioners. This segmenting of theology in mainline church seminaries is acceler-
ated by removing the study of religion from church controlled and supported colleges
and universities and giving it to state colleges and schools with self-perpetuating boards
of regents each accountable only to itself. In these instances historic positions of the
churches formulated in the Reformation and post-Reformation eras are no longer factors in the theological enterprise. Theological studies have seen further fractionalization
by the special interests of each scholar with the result that theology and religion faculties
of seminaries and universities have come to accept the wide diversity of views existing
among themselves and they make no attempt to articulate a unified understanding of a
common theological task and goal. Diversity is not new. After the Reformation the classical forms of Lutheranism, Calvinism, and Catholicism were represented in German
theological faculties, as they still are, and a general type of Protestantism once prevailed
in most American colleges and universities. Today throughout the Western world Islam,

Hinduism, and Buddhism have been given a place at the table where only the classical Christian view could once be found. One only has to go to the annual meetings of the American Academy of Religion and the Society of Biblical Literature to encounter these continuously multiplying possibilities of what presents itself as theology. For the sake of clarity, when the study of non-Christian options is placed on an equal plane with Christian ones, it would be better to speak of these scholarly endeavors as religious studies and thus reserving and restricting the word theology for the study of Christianity. In this definition of theology as a Christian enterprise, Kilcrease more than qualifies as a theologian.

Kilcrease does not see his task in proposing a unifying principle into the religious marketplace where ever newer options are continually being offered. Rather he sets forth for himself the task of locating a unifying principle for Christian theology. In *The Self-Donation of God: A Contemporary Lutheran Approach to Christ and Benefits*, he proposes that this unifying principle is Christology, specifically in the person of Jesus as prophesied in the Old Testament as the Christ and realized in the New. By providing a revelation of himself in the biblical narrative, God gives of himself and makes a commitment to its hearers. Revelation is a self-giving of God reflecting what he is in himself. As the title indicates Kilcrease is unabashedly Lutheran and thus not surprisingly he sees justification as the core doctrine; however, he expands his understanding of justification to include Christology as a prior, necessary, and fundamental corollary to justification. Strictly speaking, Christology is the chief doctrine and serves as the unifying principle of the entire biblical narrative from Genesis though Revelation. He writes from within the perspective of historic, confessional Lutheran theology, but he goes beyond setting forth the views of the sixteenth- and seventeenth-century Lutheran Orthodox and first offers a thoroughly biblical theology. Where required, he takes issue with the Lutheran fathers, but is convinced that they understood Christology as a unifying principle of the scriptures around which they developed their own theologies. A confessional theology that attempts to be at the same time biblical and confessional is caught between the Charybdis in being limited to long held historical positions that seemingly are not open to adjustment and the Scylla of biblical theological proposals that is practiced without confessional restrictions and cannot propose for itself definite goals. To the outside observer biblical studies can appear without purpose and so are more likely to create skepticism rather than engender faith. Let's put it another way. If some biblical studies are open ended with no prior intention of coming to once and for all conclusions, denominational studies begin and end with predetermined conclusions. Theological studies of the historic Reformation churches, including the Roman Catholicism ones, come to predictable outcomes. Methods of biblical studies are so varied, that with their multiple and varied conclusions, they are rarely, if ever, in agreement with one another. For Kilcrease Christology is the lodestone that allows biblical theology to be presented in the service of historical, confessional Lutheran theology and so he presents a principle that provides order to the theological task and a governing principle to biblical studies. Christology drawn from the biblical narrative is the unifying principle for the entire task of theology and so theological and confessional studies constitute one discipline.

Kilcrease sees the divine narrative as it holds the history of salvation together. Adam distances himself from the word by which he was created. He and his wife owe their creation and continued existence to God's gracious word, but Eve is not content to accept God's gracious offer and speculates about this word. By so doing this, she seeks to acquire divinity for herself and her husband and so nullifies the first narrative. To salvage the situation God offers himself in the history of redemption that then constitutes the content of the biblical narrative. Adam's role as prophet, priest, and king is inherited by Israel and comes to a climax in Jesus who is twice anointed, first in taking upon himself and the fulfilling the Old Testament offices of prophet, priest, and king, and more profoundly in being God's Son through the hypostatic union. God's self-giving of himself in the Old Testament in the glory residing in the tabernacle advances to the presence of the glory found in Jesus who as God's final temple replaces the one in Jerusalem. All of the New Testament shows Jesus as the fulfillment of the Old Testament, but each gospel and epistle does it in its own way. Rather than seeing Christ's atoning work as something in addition to the Old Testament, Kilcrease locates it in the Genesis creation narrative. Humanity's rejection of God as the giver of all good things leaves each human being in the predicament of having to rely on him/herself. In spite of its alienation from God, humanity continues to receive good things from God but does not recognize him as the giver. Since the old narrative that brought forth creation was rejected, God sets in place a new narrative, one of redemption; that is, the narrative of the new creation. Placed alongside of the old narrative that man rejected and brought death is the new narrative that was first given to Israel and then could be found completely in Jesus. Throughout the new narrative God is the speaker and the content. Jesus is assumed into the old narrative in which God's promise was transformed into condemnation. By being assumed into the old, Jesus transforms it into a new narrative promising salvation. In believing in this narrative the believer is not only justified, but is included in the narrative itself and receives Christ's righteousness. In the last chapters Kilcrease discusses Christology along traditional dogmatical lines that defined Lutheran theology from the Reformed kind. Mary's role in Christology is presented and contemporary understandings of her are analyzed for their acceptability. Kilcrease readdresses Reformed and Lutheran differences over the person and work of Christ, showing that the Lutheran understandings are the right ones. Not at issue is the *genus idiomaticum* between the two major Protestant traditions in assigning divine attributes to Christ's divine nature and the human ones to his human nature. Remaining in contention is whether all of Christ's actions can be assigned to the total person, so that the man Jesus can be regarded and worshiped as the world's creator, a doctrine to which the Reformed take strong exception. Also in contention is the *genus majestaticum*, the Lutheran belief that the human nature shares in all of the divine attributes. Since Christ is not two persons, but one divine person, the human nature is *anhypostasis*, that is, the man Jesus does not have a separate personality. This doctrine takes on meaning in the face of the critical biblical studies in their quests for the historical Jesus that ignore his claims to deity. Christ's full possession of who and what God is including his righteousness does not allow for either the Catholic and or the Reformed concepts of grace as a substance that can be quantitatively distributed. In hearing and listening to the narrative, believers are given all of what Christ is and has done. Grace, like justification, is declared. Kilcrease understands the role of Jesus as prophet, priest, and king as reflecting God's Trinitarian existence, an item not previously found in theology.

Since Christian theology is Christology, ideally any Christian dogmatics, especially one that offers itself as Lutheran, also should be thoroughly christological. In engaging Catholic and especially Reformed dogmatics, and adopting their outlines, Lutheran dogmatics has tended to deviate from their christological content and goal. Kilcrease works to overcome christological deficits in theology by presenting a truly biblical theology that is thoroughly christological. This is rarely done. He has done it and in so doing set a standard in showing how biblical and systematical theology should be one theology—Christology.

David P. Scaer
Professor of Biblical and Systematic Theology
Concordia Theological Seminary
Fort Wayne, Indiana

Acknowledgments

I WOULD LIKE TO thank a number of people and institutions for contributing to the publication of this book. I would like to thank John Pless and Mark Mattes for reading and endorsing this manuscript. I would like to thank David Scaer for agreeing to write the foreword of this work. Troy Neujahr also deserves special mention for having helped me with editing the work. I would also like to thank my wife and other family members for their encouragement and support that made it possible for me to write this book. Lastly, I would like to thank Luther Seminary and Calvin College library for providing me with the research materials necessary for the completion of this book.

Abbreviations

AE	Luther, Martin. *American Edition of Luther's Works*. 55 vols. Edited by Jaroslav Pelikan and Helmut Lehmann. Philadelphia and St. Louis: Fortress and Concordia, 1957–86.
ANF	*Ante-Nicene Fathers*. 10 vols. Edited by Alexander Roberts and James Donaldson. Peabody, MA: Hendrickson, 2004.
Ap	Apology to the Augsburg Confession
BF	*Summa Theologiae*. 60 vols. Blackfriars Edition. New York and London: McGraw-Hill, 1964–1973.
CA	Unaltered Augsburg Confession
CD	*Church Dogmatics*. Karl Barth. 4 vols. Translated by G. T. Thomason et al. Edinburgh: T. & T. Clark, 1936–77.
CT	*Concordia Triglotta: The Symbolical Books of the Evangelical Lutheran Church, German-Latin-English*. Translated and Edited by W. H. T. Dau et al. St. Louis: Concordia, 1921.
Ep	Epitome of the Formula of Concord
FC	Formula of Concord
ICR	*Institutes of the Christian Religion (1559)* of John Calvin.
LC	Large Catechism of Martin Luther
NPNFa	*Nicene and Post-Nicene Fathers*. 14 vols. Edited by Philip Schaff. First Series. Peabody, MA: Hendrickson, 2004.
NPNFb	*Nicene and Post-Nicene Fathers*. 14 vols. Edited by Philip Schaff and William Wace. Second Series. Peabody, MA: Hendrickson, 2004.
SA	Smalcald Articles of Martin Luther
SC	Small Catechism of Martin Luther
SD	Solid Declaration of the Formula of Concord
ST	*Summa Theologiae* of Thomas Aquinas
TR	*D. Martin Luthers Werke: Kritische Gesammtausgabe. Tischrede*. Weimar: Hermann Böhlau and H. Böhlaus Nachfolg, 1883–2009.

Abbreviations

WA   *D. Martin Luthers Werke: Kritische Gesammtausgabe.* Martin Luther. 120 vols. Weimar: Hermann Böhlau and H. Böhlaus Nachfolg, 1883–2009.

Chapter 1

Mediation in the Old Testament, Part 1

Approach to Scripture, Prophetic Mediation

Approach to Scripture

THE BIBLE IS THE Word of God (Rom 3:2; 2 Tim 3:16; 1 Pet 1:11; 2 Pet 1:21, v. 25).[1] It is absolutely truthful because of its inspiration by God the Holy Spirit.[2] For this reason, the orthodox Lutheran dogmaticians rightly called the prophets and apostles "amanuenses of the Spirit."[3] By proceeding in this manner, we stand firmly with one of the foundational documents of the Lutheran Reformation, the Formula of Concord in its affirmation that "We believe, teach, and confess that the sole rule and standard to which all dogmas together with all teachers should be estimated and judged are the prophetic and apostolic scriptures of the Old and New Testament."[4] Indeed, we can have no other starting point. Through God's election of Israel, he has chosen to make its life and traditions the medium of his law and promise. Just as Jesus Christ is the true and perfect Word of God from all eternity, so too he is present and active communicating himself infallibly to the people of God through the Word of the prophets and apostles. Indeed, the "testimony of Jesus is the spirit of prophecy" (Rev 19:10).[5]

In light of the fact that scripture centers on the promise of the gospel, we must insist on the reality of its truthful historicity. Although "literal religion" is frequently maligned as childish by our culture, the truth of the gospel presupposes the truthful historicity of the Bible. The "nonliteral" and therefore more "mature" reading of the Bible insisted upon by much of contemporary culture in fact denigrates Christianity into an incipit

1. Unless indicated otherwise, all biblical citations are drawn from the English Standard Version (ESV) translation of the Bible.

2. See Gerhard, *On the Nature*, 43–84; Hoenecke, *Evangelical Lutheran Dogmatics*, 1:403–505; F. Pieper, *Christian Dogmatics*, 1:193–265.

3. For the characterization of the writers of scripture as "Amanuenses" see Robert Preus, *Inspiration of Scripture*, 54; R. Preus, *Post Reformation Lutheranism*. This, it should be stressed (as Preus pointed out in his *Inspiration of Scri*pture, 71–73), does not mean a theory of "dictation."

4. FC Ep, Norm and Rule, par. 1; *CT* 777.

5. Luther writes: "All of Scripture is pure Christ" (*AE* 15:339).

religion of the law. It is infrequently acknowledged that Liberal Protestantism's legalism automatically follows from its antiliteralism. If the Bible only presents us with fanciful allegorical stories, then these narratives are capable of doing nothing other than giving us general moral truths. But, if scripture centers on God's promises which culminate in Christ, it must be the case that God has literally been faithful to his promises in the actual history of the world. To suggest that God's activities of promise making and fulfillment in scripture are mere allegories or legendary "sagas"[6] makes such promises about some other realm and not about the real, literal, historical world. If the scriptural world is not the real, literal, historical world, then what freedom can it give to sinners living in the real historical world? This means that the gospel-centered message of the Bible is inherently tied up with the truth of its history in which God makes his trustworthiness known.

Similarly, to admit that scripture could be untruthful in historical matters would also be to suggest that God's ultimate promise in the gospel could be an error. Even if we have considerable evidence of the central events of the crucifixion and the resurrection of Christ, admitting that scripture can error downgrades the certainty of these events to the level of "probable." Saying that the biblical documents can be untruthful is to say that their historical claims are to be believed with the same degrees of greater and lesser probability that all secular history possesses. Nevertheless, if we have full assurance of our salvation (as scripture tells us we do, Heb 10:19–20), then the events that underline those promises cannot merely be probable, but absolutely true. Indeed the nature of the faith does not allow Christians to confess that Christ "probably" died for their sins and "probably" rose for their justification. If that were the case, my assurance through Word and sacrament is also merely probable. But these things are not probable, but as Luther repeatedly states in the Catechisms, they are "most certainly true." They are most certainly true because God makes them known and guarantees them in his truthful written Word. Indeed, as Luther aptly states in the Large Catechism: "Because we know that God does not lie. I and my neighbor and, in short, all men, may err and deceive, but the Word of God cannot err."[7]

One could of course claim that only the "essential" facts of scripture need be true.[8] But this leaves open the question: how does one decide upon what is essential? Where does one draw the line between the essential and inessential? Furthermore, as we will argue below, if any fact is only meaningful and understandable within an entire narrative framework (in this case, the whole of the history of salvation centering on Jesus) how then can any facts be inessential to the truth of the gospel?[9] Indeed, all individual facts contribute to this narrative and for that reason none can be deemed inessential.

In light of this, our method of dealing with scripture in the following work will grow out of the claim that the Old and New Testaments are the utterly truthful, inspired Word of God centering on Jesus Christ as the incarnate eternal Word of God. Because

---

6. See Barth, *CD* 3.1:76–94. Karl Barth's term for a hazy area between myth and literal history.

7. LC 4; *CT* 747.

8. This seems to be the attitude of Paul Althaus. See Althaus, *Das Sogenannte Kerygma*. Also see the nineteenth–century version of this in Johannes von Hofmann, *Biblische Hermeneutik*.

9. Here we reject the critique of orthodoxy made in Prenter, *Creation and Redemption*, 87–92.

God is the author of scripture, God cannot be thought to contradict himself. Nor does he err.[10] Whereas modern liberal biblical scholars break the unity of scripture apart into contradictory traditions, we will read the scripture in a manner consummate with its own claims about itself and with the history of Christian interpretation prior to the Enlightenment.

Because God inspired the scriptures to speak his eternal Word Jesus through human words, we should not in our exposition of scripture shy away from the fact that the Old Testament is to be expounded christologically. This means that typological readings of the Old Testament are therefore completely appropriate. God's authorial intention expressed through the Old Testament authors was always to point ahead to Jesus Christ.[11] In keeping with this, we must also positively assert that the Old Testament is a book of predictive prophecy truly fulfilled in the manifestation of the Savior. Indeed, if Christ were not present in the Old Testament, it would be difficult to say Marcion was not correct after all.[12]

This does not mean that exegesis should hover somewhere above its concrete historical context. Rather, as we will argue below, it is a question of what contextualizes the history of salvation itself. Just as Jesus Christ is incarnate in the flesh of a particular people and within a particular historical situation, so too the Word of God as it is incarnate in the scriptures is mediated through the thought forms, history, and cultural structures common to the Ancient Near East and the Hellenistic world. If anything, this has been the main contribution of modern critical scholarship. Certain words, for example, mean different things within the context of different historical periods and are frequently used differently by various authors. At the same time, different biblical authors have unique emphases in their theology. Ecclesiastes is not Romans after all! The interpreter of scripture must be sensitive to this, and although some "proof-texting" is not entirely illegitimate, theologians must use it with care to the context of the overall book of scripture.

This means that we will expound the scriptures according to the *sensus literalis*, that is, the literal sense. This is by no means identical with the "literalism" or, perhaps even better, "letterism" as the Wittenberg Reformers were well aware. In his definition of the literal sense, Thomas Aquinas claimed that the literal sense was the meaning that God intended when he communicated the content of the Bible through the inspired authors.[13] Doubtless, the Reformers would not have disagreed with such a sentiment.[14]

---

10. For an excellent exposition of what inerrancy means and what it does not mean, see R. Preus, "Notes on the Inerrancy," 127–38. Preus notes that inerrancy as understood by the Lutheran scholastics does not mean crass literalism. Neither does it ignore historical context. What it does mean is that the Bible is truthful and trustworthy about what it teaches us.

11. This is why the hermeneutics of Lutheran orthodoxy insisted that the typological or "mystical sense" was actually part of the *sensus literalis*. See Dannhauer, *Hernenevtica Sacra*.

12. See von Harnack, *Marcion*.

13. *ST* 1a.1.1; *BF* 1:38. Aquinas writes:
   Quia vero sensus litteralis est, quem auctor intendit: auctor autem sacrae Scripturae Deus est, qui omnia simul suo intellectu comprehendit: non est inconveniens, ut dicit Augustinus XII Confessionum, si etiam secundum litteralem sensum in una littera Scripturae plures sint sensus.

14. See Frei, *Eclipse of the Biblical Narrative*, 18–37. Frei mainly deals with Calvin, but mentions

To show how the Reformers understood this intended meaning, we should turn to Luther's concept of scriptural clarity. Luther spoke about two kinds of clarity, external clarity and inner clarity.[15] The external clarity, claimed Luther, was the grammatical and hence historically accessible meaning of the text. Such a meaning was open to anyone. The inner clarity was the meaning of the Bible as it centered on Christ. Since one cannot understand Christ or see the unity of the Bible in him without the Holy Spirit (2 Cor 3) those who read the scripture without faith fail to grasp its true meaning. Conversely, it is also true that one will not understand the scriptures if one does not understand their mode of speaking and grammar, which are of course, historically conditioned.

We can therefore see what the *sensus literalis* is for Luther in light of Christ.[16] On the one hand God communicated himself in the concrete, contextual meaning of the text for the people to whom he addressed it through the prophets and apostles. At the same time, he intended that that meaning might also bear witness to Christ and ultimately drive people to him. Therefore the literal sense is the coming together of the external and internal clarity of the Bible, just as when we refer to the person of Christ in the concrete we speak about the unity of his two natures. The literal sense is not, as modern interpreters have often thought, the meaning of the text as we might want to construe it based on the limited circumstances of certain historical authors.[17] Rather, it is the harmony of the literal, grammatical meaning of the words of the Bible, together with the larger narrative of the history of salvation, culminating in and centering in Jesus Christ. This conception of the Bible is consummate with the Lutheran doctrine of the *genus majestaticum*,[18] wherein the divine nature (in analogy to the internal clarity) is not something separate from the human nature (in analogy to the external clarity), but rather communicates the fullness of itself through the external form of the human nature.

Modern liberal biblical scholars have failed to understand this and will doubtless protest that this does violence to the original intention of the authors. Of course, extreme versions of Christian exegesis (beginning with Origen and moving on into the Middle Ages) did do violence to the original meaning of the text by burying it under imaginative and often times fanciful Christian allegory.[19] The problem with all this was not that it attempted to read the Bible as a book about Jesus, but that it understood Jesus incorrectly. Allegorical reading tries to strip away the external meaning to find the Spirit hidden within. It gives us a Docetic Bible, in the same way that Protestant Liberalism

---

Luther as well. His point is that the *sensus literalis* is the simple grammatical meaning of texts harmonized with the location the divine author has placed it within a sequence of events in the large context of the history of salvation. Hence, mystical and typological senses of the Bible are not conceptualized as being in conflict with historical ones. Also see a good description of pre-critical typological interpretation in Eckhardt, *New Testament in His Blood*, 13–16.

15. *AE* 33:28.

16. This was the approach of the first Lutherans and the first Lutheran book exclusively devoted to hermeneutics. See Illyricus, *How to Understand*.

17. Frei, *Eclipse of the Biblical Narrative*, 66–104. Frei here describes the emergence of this sort of thinking.

18. Brenz, *Personali Vnione Duarum*; Chemnitz, *Two Natures*, 25, 217, 241–47. Also see Vainio, *Justification and Participation*, 136–40.

19. De Lubac, *Medieval Exegesis*.

gives us a Nestorian Bible. In this framework, the Bible effectively becomes a mere steppingstone to God hidden in his majesty, rather than God hidden in concrete written Word of the scripture.

The younger Luther recognized this and, beginning with his early commentaries on the Psalms (1513–1515) moved away from allegorical exegesis, insisting instead on the primacy of the *sensus literalis*. Nevertheless, he still interpreted the Psalms as having their ultimate reference in Christ.[20] Holding these two aspects of the text of scripture together, Luther grasped what Wolfhart Pannenberg has in our present situation emphasized, that any study of any historical event must occur within an overall framework. In a similar vein, Pannenberg has noted, events take on meaning in light of what they later give rise to.[21] For example, the meaning of the French Revolution can be more acutely realized in light of Soviet and Chinese revolutions than can be recognized merely by studying France in the late eighteenth century.[22] N. T. Wright has similarly noted that a Roman citizen who heard about the resurrection of Jesus and was unfamiliar with the prophecies of the Hebrew Scriptures would doubtless have regarded him as being something like a *Nero Redivivus*.[23] Not interpreting scripture in light of Christ ultimately leads to the application of an alien framework and context. It represents merely the imposition of a different framework on scripture, and not a neutral and scientific interpretation of scripture.

In point of fact, this is precisely what we are proposing that modern biblical scholars have done and continue to do. They impose an alien framework on scripture and thereby distort individual texts by interpreting them within that framework. One steeped in the history of modern biblical scholarship is bound to find this unsurprising in light of the fact that this tradition of interpretation begins with Baruch Spinoza and the revival of Epicurean thought in the early modern period.[24] Part of Epicureanism was the denial of divine design within the world (Epicurus followed the atomism of Democritus) and the rejection of supernatural revelation (the gods, claimed Epicurus do not interact with the world).[25]

For this reason, scripture is seen as the patchwork of the different writings of those involved in "priestcraft" (as later Rationalists frequently called it) cut and pasted together and edited by one great imposter as the final redactor. Since different writing styles can obviously be used by the same author and because none of the intermediate or ur-documents that supposedly made up whole biblical books have ever been found, the supposition of modern liberal biblical scholars that the Bible was produced in this way is almost entirely based on discerning the power-play present in the rhetorical violence of the various invented authors of the theoretical documents (Q, JEDP, etc.). By reading the Bible this way, liberal critics of the Bible seek to free themselves from the heteronomous

---

20. See S. Preus, *Shadow to Promise*.

21. Pannenberg, "Dogmatic Theses," 131–55.

22. See similar perspective in Steinmetz, "Miss Marple Reads the Bible," 15–26.

23. N. T. Wright, *Christian Origins*, 3:720.

24. See Harrisville and Sundberg, *Bible in Modern Culture*, 30–43. Also see S. Preus, *Spinoza and the Irrelevance*.

25. B. Russell, *History of Western Philosophy*, 240–52.

claims of these ancient authors and assert their autonomy against the text.[26] This kind of freedom of course (as we shall see later) is not real freedom. It is a defensive action of a creature bent by sin. Such phony autonomy seeks a defense against the accusation of the law present in the supposedly heteronomous claims of the text. The only freedom that can be real freedom is in Christ. By accepting that the Bible is truthful and centers on Christ, believers gain the true freedom that modern liberal biblical scholars seek through the destruction of biblical authority.

Epicureanism also automatically rules out the supernatural. This again is merely an *a prior* hermeneutical decision, and not something necessitated by the material itself. Rather than offer any hard evidence that the Hebrew prophets did not predict Jesus, they merely interpret the scriptures within a framework that does not view reality as centering on the christological. Indeed, not only is predictive prophecy ruled out of court, but there can be no divinely designed melody of salvation history. Any subtle connection between one event in scripture and another must be manufactured afterwards out of thin air. Any fulfillment of predictive prophecy must have been redacted after the event to fit the prophecy.[27] In reading modern biblical scholarship what one is amazed by time and again is how commentators get away with so much conjecture without offering a slightest bit of evidence. They also frequently present weak evidence or dismiss evidence devastating to their position.[28] Since their audience has been acculturated into the Epicurean assumptions about divine agency, they can simply build conjecture on conjecture. Those who challenge such practices (within and outside the academic world) are dismissed as "Fundamentalists" who worship a "Paper Pope." All this suggests that many exegetes are engaged in a covert theological agenda and not in neutral historical investigation as they attempt to claim. As was suggested at the beginning of this section, the theology they propose is one that needs scripture to be errant in order to bolster their religion of allegory (so that they might maintain their precious bourgeois autonomy against the peril of divine providence and miracle) and moralizing (so that in their autonomy they might continue their project of self-justification).

This being the case, we can observe that modern biblical scholarship with its supposed objectivity is simply another exegetical tradition with no more claims to neutral interpretation than that of traditional orthodox Christianity.[29] In fact, as we have seen, it has less of a claim than traditional Reformation hermeneutics. Though it insists on a privileged status as more neutral and rational, there is no evidence to demonstrate this. Recent scholars (none of whom can be characterized as "Fundamentalists") have argued that there is in fact a great deal of data that calls major aspects of the critical tradition

26. See Hart, *Beauty of the Infinite*, 1–3. Hart makes a similar observation about the Nietzschean interpretation of Christianity.

27. See Plantinga, "Sheehan's Shenanigans," 316–27. Plantinga makes the point that Christian faith will necessarily influence what is possible and impossible in historical reality. That so many interpreters do not acknowledge this fact is astonishing.

28. See for example Finkelstein and Silberman, *Bible Unearthed*.

29. John Milbank makes a similar point about sociology and modern political theory in relationship to Christian theology. See Milbank, *Theology and Social Theory*. Also see this critique of the modern liberal tradition in MacIntyre, *Whose Justice?*

into question.[30] Ultimately, much of the critical tradition has accomplished little but to rip the biblical texts away from their proper framework of divine inspiration and centeredness on Christ, and imposed an alien, Epicurean framework upon them.

This being the case, Christian interpreters of scripture should feel no obligation to adopt this framework. The fact that so many creedally orthodox Christians (mainly in mainline Protestant institutions) think that they are under this obligation at the present time demonstrates not the wealth of data contradicting traditional christological interpretation, but rather a loss of nerve on the part of Christianity faced with the rather paltry challenge of modern and postmodern Epicureanism.

This does not mean that they should reject insights from all scholars who use such critical methods. Many modern techniques of biblical scholarship (most notably biblical archaeology) have yielded a great deal of information about the original context of scripture. In fact, as the late Kurt Marquart has helpfully noted, no modern form of biblical criticism is in itself morally wrong or anti-Christian, rather it is how the technique is used.[31] When evaluating scholarship one should not ask whether the scholar uses these modern techniques, rather one should ask whether the scholar proceeds from orthodox Christian assumptions (truthfulness and Christ-centeredness of scripture) or from another framework (Epicurean, etc.).

To summarize our method and approach: Because this study works from the perspective of what the Bible says about itself (namely, that it is divinely inspired and centers on Jesus Christ) we will expound the whole Bible on the basis of its chief article, Jesus Christ and his redeeming work. This does not mean to ignore or smooth over the historical context of scripture, its variety of genres, or its diversity of theological vocabulary. What it means is to recognize the harmony and unity of the historical and theological meaning of scripture. Discovering and expounding the *sensus literalis* means correlating the historical, contextual, and grammatical meaning of texts with their overall center found in Christ. This is possible because God himself is the author of scripture and his intended meaning throughout his narration of the Bible is Jesus.

In terms of actual practice, our treatment of the Old Testament will recognize the analogical similitude between God's saving acts within Israel and his final saving act in Jesus in the form of typology. Since the same God is the agent of both, then both bare

---

30. See for example the wealth of data uncovered by modern biblical archaeology. Keller's *Bible as History* is somewhat of an older study and therefore has some problems, but is generally still good. Also see a more up-to-date version in K. A. Kitchen, *Reliability of the Old Testament*, 449–500. It should be born in mind that Kitchen is an Egyptologist and not a biblical scholar. His expertise is in the Ancient Near East and therefore he has more knowledge of the era than many modern biblical scholars. Kitchen observes that Wellhausen among the other founders of modern biblical scholarship insisted upon evolutionary models of the development of Israelite religion. He had no access to the majority of the evidence we have now which makes the historical claims of the Old Testament (though we might say scripture in general) seem very credible even without a prior commitment to scriptural inerrancy. Kitchen derides the fact that modern biblical scholars continue to hold onto the old, developmental models even with massive amounts of evidence contradicting them and validating the historicity of the Bible. Beyond the aforementioned studies of the Old Testament, we might mention N. T. Wright's demonstration of the historicity of the Gospels in his *Christian Origins*, and also Richard Bauckham's demonstration that the Gospels are eyewitness accounts in his *Jesus and the Eyewitnesses*.

31. Marquart, *Anatomy of an Explosion*, 113.

an irresistible relationship to one another and exist within a common framework of meaning and history. Similarly, we will not hesitate to assert that predictive prophecy does exist and that the prophets of the Old Testament did quite literally predict Jesus. If we accept God's power and providence, as well as the witness of the New Testament, we should not have any intellectual difficulty with this concept.

Furthermore, in order to respect both the diversity and unity of the scriptures, our method will be essentially synthetic. We will examine the content of the different books and strains of tradition in the Old Testament, and correlate their meaning with one another. Isaiah, for example, speaks of the Messiah using different terminology than does Jeremiah. He also describes different aspects of the Messiah's career. Nevertheless, both speak of the same Messiah and both have some commonalities in their predictions (a new covenant, forgiveness, etc.). Hence, both should be treated separately, while the results of exegesis for both can be correlated with one another in order to reveal a common witness to the truth.

In two opening chapters, our goal will be to expound common themes of mediatorship that emerged in the history of the Old Testament. This makes sense because the works of the Old Testament are addressed to a common audience (ancient Israel) over a long period of time. For this common audience there is a shared history, with a generally (though not completely) similar theological vocabulary. In discussing the New Testament in later chapters, we will divide our work up according to books or groups of books (i.e., Paul's epistles, Johannine literature, etc.). The New Testament writings are occasional writings to different audiences (i.e., Gentile and Jewish, etc.), with different shared histories (think Hebrews vs. 1 Corinthians vs. the Johannine epistles, etc.). Hence, although there is a unity of witness, there is a greater diversity of theological terminology (Paul vs. John, John vs. the Synoptic Gospels, etc.). For this reason, we will divide up the New Testament by groups of books and correlate their common witness to Jesus with one another.

Exile and Return

In order to understand Christ and his coming, we must first understand the history of salvation in the Old Testament that his advent presupposes. In the twentieth century, there were a number of attempts to posit a central theme or concept of the Old Testament. This has tended to take the form of the identification of an abstract concept or idea as a central theme. Notably, this identification of the organizing principle of the Old Testament with an abstract concept has been the method of both Walther Eichrodt and Gerhard von Rad. In Eichrodt's case, this was the "covenant," whereas for von Rad it was the significantly more fluid, yet equally problematic concept of "recitation."[32]

32. Eichrodt, *Theology of the Old Testament*; von Rad, *Old Testament Theology*. Beyond these two main approaches to Old Testament theology, see the following works: Anderson, *Contours of Old Testament*; Archer, *Survey of Old Testament*; Brueggemann, *Theology of the Old Testament*; Dempster, *Dominion and Dynasty*; Drane, *Introducing the Old Testament*; Goldingay, *Old Testament Theology*; R. Gordon, *Christ as made known*; Gunneweg, *Biblische Theologie*; R. Harrison, *Introduction to the Old Testament*; Hummel, *Word becoming Flesh*; Jacob, *Grundfragen Alttestamentlicher Theologie*; Kittel, *Handbuch der*

Instead of an abstract concept, we will choose a historical pattern. The pattern that we will identify as residing at the very heart of the history of salvation in the Old Testament is the theme "exile and return." This theme is not an arbitrary decision of one historical pattern among many, but rather stands as the very contours of the history of salvation as it is presented to us in the scriptures. The foundational events in Israel's story as recounted in both the historical and prophetic writings are in fact the redemption from Egypt and the settlement of Palestine. In the same way also, the preaching of Leviticus, Deuteronomy, the pre-exilic prophets, and the later experiences of the Babylonian exile certainly must also be viewed as reinforcing this historical and theological pattern of existence upon Israel's psyche. As we will observe, such a pattern prefigures the narrative of Christ's death and resurrection. From the perspective of confessional Lutheran theology this way of understanding the Old Testament is particularly important in light of the fact that both exile and return are the temporal manifestations of God's law and grace.

Moreover, Israel did not merely view exile and return as being a quirk of their particular national history, but the pattern of cosmic and human existence. The account of Genesis 2 begins with the creation of human beings (Gen 2:15–25) and their subsequent placement in the garden of Eden. Although we will later return to the wider significance of Eden for the Israelite cult, here it is sufficient to say that Eden is described as a place where humanity works the soil (Gen 2:15) and where the fertility of the earth is guaranteed. Furthermore, YHWH is directly present to the first humans and guarantees his favor to them by his glorious presence (Gen 3:8). Humanity sins by disobeying the divine command and by listening to the serpent, a false mediator of God's will ("Did God actually say . . . ?" Gen 3:10). This leads to the exile of Adam and Eve from the garden, which brings with it their removal from God's gracious presence and the guarantee of the fertility of the soil ("cursed is the ground because of you" Gen 3:17). They are also denied immortality (v. 19). As many interpreters have recognized, such a narrative is echoed in Israel's own story. G. K. Beale correctly observes the parallels between Adamic humanity and Israel in Genesis 2–3: "Israel, as representative of God's true humanity, also separated themselves from the divine presence and failed to carry the commission . . . Israel failed even as had Adam. And like Adam, Israel was also cast out of the 'garden land' into exile."[33]

If Genesis's primal history suggests that humanity exists in a state of universal exile, the Pentateuchal narrative of the election of the patriarchs suggests that Israel itself is the beginning of the restoration of the Adamic humanity. In describing the structure of the Genesis narrative, N. T. Wright observes:

Alttestamentlichen Theologie; Löhr, *Alttestamentliche Religions Geschichte*; Martens, *God's Design*; Möller, *Biblische Theologie*; Niditch, *Ancient Israelite Religion*; Perdue, *Collapse of History*; Rendtorff, *Canonical Hebrew Bible*; Riehm, *Alttestamentliche Theologie*; Schmidt, *Altes Testament*; Schofield, *Introducing Old Testament*; H. Schultz, *Die Offenbarungsreligion*; Stade, *Biblische Theologie*; Watts, *Basic Patterns*; Westermann, *Elements of Old Testament*; Youngblood, *Heart of the Old Testament*; Zummerli, *Grundriss der Alttestamentlichen Theologie*.

33. Beale, *Temple*, 120–21.

> Thus, at major turning-points in the story [the Pentateuchal narrative] Abraham's call, his circumcision, the offering of Isaac, the transition from Abraham to Isaac and from Isaac to Jacob, and the sojourn in Egypt—the narrative quietly insists that Abraham and his progeny inherit the role of Adam and Eve.[34]

Throughout Genesis, YHWH's promise to the patriarchs, (realized in the exodus and the conquest), is that he will multiply their descendants and give them dominion in the land of Canaan.[35] As Wright goes on to demonstrate, this status of Israel as the restoration of Adam and Eve comes across most strongly throughout the story because the dual promise of dominion in the land and of having many descendants directly parallels the promise made to the first man and woman at the end of the account of creation in Genesis 1: "And God blessed them. And God said to them, 'Be fruitful and multiply and fill the earth and subdue it and have dominion over the fish of the sea and over the birds of the heavens and over every living thing that moves on the earth'" (Gen 1:28).

The Pentateuchal narrative also reinforces the identification of Israel as the restoration of Adamic humanity in a number of other ways. The land that YHWH promises Israel is in some measure represented as a restoration of the pre-lapsarian blessing on the soil: "And Lot lifted up his eyes and saw that the Jordan Valley was well watered everywhere *like the garden of the Lord*" (Gen 13:10, emphasis added). For Israel, the restoration of the presence of God enjoyed before the Fall also occurs. We are told that YHWH's glory (*kavod*) traveled with Israel during the entire period of the exodus under the form of a cloud (Exod 40:36–38). When the tabernacle's construction was completed, a thick cloud filled the camp and the glory of YHWH descended into the tabernacle (Exod 40:34–35).

These descriptions of Israel's early history suggest several things. First, the narrative strongly implies that the tabernacle and the later temple are in a sense the restoration of Eden, wherein humans dwelled directly in God's gracious presence. In the same manner the promises to the patriarchs and the fecundity of creation are portrayed as a restoration of the true humanity. Secondly, these accounts imply that through entering into a covenant with the patriarchs, YHWH has pledged his own being to Israel as a pledge of his faithfulness. Indeed, to give an unconditional promise means always to give the self, because a promiser is logically tied to the enactment and fulfillment of the promise. The presence and the activity of the divine self now must conform to the situation of the one to whom the promise was made.

If then Edenic harmony and its restoration in the election of Israel means the renewal of creation and the self-donating presence of YHWH, then sin and its consequence of exile mean the very opposite of these goods. YHWH speaks to the Israelites through Moses and tells them that "if you spurn my statutes, and if your soul abhors my rules, so that you will not do all my commandments, but break my covenant . . . I will do this to you: I will visit you with panic, with wasting disease and fever that consume the eyes and make the heart ache. And you shall sow your seed in vain, for your enemies shall eat it" (Lev 26:15–16). Indeed, "I will discipline you again sevenfold for your sins." In the exile,

---

34. N. T. Wright, *Christian Origins*, 1:263.

35. Ibid., 3:720. Wright lists the example of Gen12:2, 17:2–8, 22:16, 26:3, 26:24, 28:3, 35:11, 47:27, 48:3.

"I will break the pride of your power, and I will make your heavens like iron and your earth like bronze" (vv. 18–19). The curses that we discover in Leviticus also suggest that there will be a loss of Israel's restored dominion in the land: "I will set my face against you, and you shall be struck down before your enemies. Those who hate you shall rule over you, and you shall flee when none pursues you" (v. 17). These curses are also well attested by the threats of the later prophets. Ezekiel, who was a priest, also places an emphasis on the loss of the divine presence. According to Ezekiel 10, the prophet fully realized the completeness of the judgment of the exile only when he had a vision of the divine glory leaving the temple (Ezek 10:18).

Nevertheless, in spite of the situation of exile and human sin, YHWH promises his continuing faithfulness to Israel. After the passages threatening judgment, we find passages in the same texts assuring Israel of God's continuing faithfulness to his promises made to the patriarchs. In spite of human sin, there would be eschatological renewal and the return from exile: "I will remember my covenant with Jacob and my covenant with Isaac and my covenant with Abraham" (Lev 26:42). St. Paul observes in Galatians 3:13–25, the Mosaic record demonstrates that the Abrahamic covenant of grace (or more properly, his "testament," as Paul puts it) precedes and in fact stands as separate from the Sinaitic covenant of law. In contrast to the Abrahamic testament of unilateral promise and blessings, the Sinaitic covenant entails a long list of demands and curses. The reception of the two covenants is different as well. Von Rad notes that Abraham is passive and asleep as he receives the unilateral covenant of grace (Gen 15). By contrast, we are told that the Israelites were called upon to actively receive and to perform the works of the Sinaitic covenant: "Moses came and told the people all the words of the Lord and all the rules. And all the people answered with one voice and said, 'All the words that the Lord has spoken we will do'" (Exod 24:3).[36]

Therefore, YHWH's dealing with Israel takes on a paradoxically dual character. On the one hand, God has pledged himself to Israel and will fulfill his promises to it in spite of every obstacle. On the other hand, the covenant of Sinai is equally valid and demands on the part of Israel a real heartfelt obedience to God's commandments. Both words from God are valid and therefore the unconditional nature of the former continuously comes into conflict with the conditional nature of the latter throughout the history of salvation. In the book of Hosea, the prophet enacts the sign of this paradoxical situation by marrying a prostitute (Hos 1, 3). As a sign of Israel's state of affairs, Hosea's marriage presupposes the validity of the covenant of the law, as well as God's unilateral and unconditional faithfulness to Israel. Israel is rightly imputed with sin for having broken the law by prostituting itself to the nations, but YHWH must remain true to his promise and remains "married" to Israel in spite of its apostasy.

The promise of YHWH to Israel throughout the prophetic literature is that ultimately God's own faithfulness will triumph over the impediments of human sin and divine wrath. Therefore, as early as the book of Deuteronomy (chapters 28–32), we have a promise of a second exodus and renewal of the divine-human relationship. Similar to

---

36. Von Rad, *Old Testament Theology*, 1:131.

the prophetic writings of Hosea, we have the promise of a second exodus wherein God will reestablish Israel's status (Hos 11–14).[37]

Isaiah 40–66 goes further and envisions a universal end to exile. God, who due to Israel's sin has withdrawn his personal presence from his people and his dwelling place Zion, is said to be returning through a miraculous desert highway (40:3–6). He will do this because he will forgive Israel's sin (40:2). Not only will Israel return to Zion, the city of YHWH's presence (Isa 44–45), but the Gentiles who also suffer the universal exile from God's presence will stream from the whole expanse of creation to worship the true God (Isa 45:23).

In the case of Ezekiel, God promises the prophet that he himself will follow the Jews into the exile he has enacted upon them and thereby stand in solidarity with them: "Therefore say, 'Thus says the Lord God: Though I removed them far off among the nations, and though I scattered them among the countries, yet I have *been a sanctuary to them* for a while in the countries where they have gone'" (Ezek 11:16, emphasis added). Later in the book, when there is a prophecy of the return from exile, restoration takes the form of a metaphorical resurrection from the dead (i.e., the restoration of the life and fecundity of creation, Ezek 37:1–14), the rebuilding of an elaborate eschatological temple (40–48), and return of the presence of God (37:27, 43:1–12). This time though, the presence of the divine glory is not just restricted to the holy of holies, but permeates the entire nation: "My dwelling place will be with them; I will be their God, and they will be my people. Then the nations will know that I the Lord make Israel holy, when my sanctuary is among them forever" (37:27). Beale in his study on chapters 40–48 of Ezekiel has demonstrated that the restored Jerusalem is itself not only a temple-city (i.e., a perpetual arena of the self-donating presence of God), but displays significant features that make it similar to the garden of Eden.[38]

The apocalyptic tradition, as embodied in the book of Daniel (though also in Isa 26 and a number of other Old Testament texts), continues this line of thought in seeing a restoration of creation through a resurrection of the dead: "And many of those who sleep in the dust of the earth shall awake, some to everlasting life, and some to shame and everlasting contempt" (Dan 12:2).[39] Here we may observe that Daniel posits a final restoration for some, (an eternal return from exile and reversal of the effects of the Fall as we have it in Genesis 3) and for others an infinite and eternal eschatological judgment (who will stay in an eternal state of exile). In this sense, God's promises of life and freedom to Israel are fulfilled and expanded.

This restoration does not merely extend to new and eternal bodily life. The presence of God will not just return to resurrected Israel, but the resurrected will share the glory of YHWH: "And those who are wise shall shine like the brightness of the sky above; and those who turn many to righteousness, like the stars forever and ever" (12:3). Walther Eichrodt makes a similar connection and observes: "The Daniel passage is unique in laying stress on the share in the divine light-glory, an image which is in any case entirely in keeping with the conception of God's new world as a revelation of the divine *kavod*

---

37. R. Harrison, *Introduction to the Old Testament*, 859.

38. Beale, *Temple*, 335–54.

39. R. Harrison, *Introduction to the Old Testament*, 1127–32.

[glory]."[40] Daniel 2 and 7 also envision the restoration of Edenic harmony and the return from cosmic exile in the form of the destruction of the idolater's demonic kingdoms, and their replacement by God's own kingdom. Much like in Genesis 1, where the humans made in God's image are given dominion on the earth, the Messiah is described in Daniel 7 as "one like a son of man" (v. 13) being given "dominion and glory and a kingdom" (v. 14). Moreover, as Beale has also noted concerning Daniel 2, the vision of the growing mountain which fills the entire creation is suggestive of the universalization of the Temple Mount and therefore the donation of divine presence to the whole creation.[41]

In summary, we therefore may observe throughout the Old Testament a pattern of exile and return, both in the understanding of Israel's own history, but also forming the background for creation and the eschton. This pattern of divine activity as we can observe is rooted in YHWH's dual relation with Israel as recorded in the historical accounts of the establishment of the law and gospel.

Mediators of the Promise: An Introduction

The first mediatorial figure of the Old Testament must be thought to be Adam. As we shall see, the Genesis account portrays Adam as prophet, priest, and king.[42] He possesses the universal dominion of kingship (Gen 1:28), he is placed over Eden as its ruling high priest (we will see evidence of this in the discussion of priestly mediation), and he was first to be given the Word of God (2:15–17). Nevertheless, he failed in his exercise of his mediatorial position and Israel was elected as the new carrier of the promise of universal redemption (3:15).

As previously noted, the Old Testament envisions creation and the history of salvation as existing within a matrix of exile and return. Within the pre-exilic history of Israel both the inspired prophets and the historians recognized YHWH's patient and persistent attempts to maintain his gracious promise to Israel. In particular, such a gracious purpose takes the form of YHWH's election of a series of mediatorial figures whose function it was to maintain the relationship between God and his people. Because of YHWH's own self-donation as Israel's God, he himself provided means of dealing with Israel's failure to fulfill the law through his appointed mediators. Throughout the Old Testament such mediators took the forms of prophets, priests, and kings. Since, as the Apostle Paul tells us, there is but "one mediator between God and men, the man Christ Jesus" (1 Tim 2:5), we must view these mediators as deficient in their roles as fulfillers of the law, but nevertheless efficient in prefiguring Christ. Their lack of success at resolving the tension between the law and the gospel creates the context wherein Christ enters the drama of history and fulfills all things.

It will be our thesis in this section that a pattern can be discerned in the function of the various mediatorial figures in the Old Testament traditions. First, mediators are consistently portrayed as representing both God and Israel. This represents both the unity of

---

40. Eichrodt, *Theology of the Old Testament*, 2:515.

41. Beale, *Temple*, 144–53.

42. See an interesting summary of their activity in Prenter, *Creation and Redemption*, 315–23.

the promise binding God and Israel together, as well as prefiguring the final unity of God and humanity through Christ, the God-man. God's ultimate faithfulness to his people and the whole cosmos will be to enter the field of battle himself as an individual Israelite. This hearkens back also to the *protevangelium*: "I will put enmity between you and the woman, and between your offspring and her offspring; he shall bruise your head, and you shall bruise his heel" (Gen 3:15). If the redeemer destroys the power of Satan, he must be divine, since humans after the Fall clearly remain under Satan's power.[43] Similarly, he must be human, because he is the "seed" of the woman and represents humans who are condemned to eternal death by God.[44] Thirdly, he must be born of a virgin since we are told that he is the woman's "seed," not the man's. As David Scaer notes, in the cultural understanding of the Ancient Near East, women did not have "seed" and thereby did not contribute to reproduction.[45] Therefore the "seed of the woman" is highly suggestive of virgin birth. Indeed such a birth represents a break with the previous dispensation of death (Rom 5; 1 Cor 15:42–56) and an inauguration of a new creation.[46]

Next, we must recognize that mediatorial figures were established to deal with Israel's sin. Mediators were regularly appointed by YHWH when Israel failed in a significant way to be the true humanity. This also in turn prefigures Christ's role as the one who overcame the curse of the law and made manifest God's purpose of grace towards sinners. The second aspect of mediation follows from the first, in that the mediator then

43. Gerhard agrees that the two natures are spoken of in the *protevangelium*:
Wherever the sacred writings of the Old Testament discuss the Messiah, they almost always explain the duality of the two natures and the unity of the person in the same place, lest people deny the duality of natures because of the unity of the person or claim that there are plural persons in Christ because of the duality of His natures. In the *protevangelium* (Gen 3:15), the promised Messiah is called "the seed of the woman," because, as true man, He was going to be born of the Virgin. To Him is attributed the bruising of the serpent's head, because, as true God, He was going to destroy with His divine power the kingdom of Satan and restore the good things that had been lost in the fall. (*On Christ*, 35)

44. The older Melanchthon (in the heat of battle against Osiander) summed up the reasons for the two natures well:
First, note that inasmuch as mankind fell into sin, the one to be punished and to pay the penalty had to be a man, but one without sin. Secondly, in order for the payment to be equal and even better, the one who pays is not simply a man or an angel, but is a divine person. Thirdly, no angel and no man could have borne the great burden of divine wrath against our sin. For that reason, the Son of God, who is omnipotent, out of immeasurable love and mercy toward men, laid upon himself this great wrath. Fourthly, no angel and no man is able to walk in the mysterious counsel of the divine Majesty. The Mediator prays for all men and especially for every petitioner, and the divine Majesty hears their desires, and then acts accordingly. All this pertains to an omnipotent person. In the Letter to the Hebrews, when only the High Priest enters into the *Sanctum sanctorum* (Holy of Holies), when only the High Priest, and no one else, is allowed to go into the secret altar in the temple, it means that only the Redeemer is to be in the secret counsel of divine Majesty, and wholly see and know the heart of the Father. Fifthly, no angel and no man might have conquered death and taken life again, for this belongs only to an omnipotent person. Sixthly, the Redeemer is to be a power [kräftig] within us; he bears and sustains our weak nature, beholds the hearts of all men, hears all sighs, prays for all, is and lives in the faithful, and creates in them new obedience, righteousness, and eternal life. All this pertains only to an omnipotent person; Immanuel, i.e. God *with* us and *in* us. (*Melanchthon on Christian Doctrine*, 33)

45. Scaer, *Christology*, 34–35. Luther also makes the same observation in *AE* 15:318–21.

46. See thorough discussion of the messianic nature of the *protevangelium* in Hengstenberg, *Christology of the Old Testament*, 1:17–30. Also see discussion in Leupold, *Genesis*, 1:163–70.

represents the fulfillment of the law on the part of Israel, as well as God's righteous maintenance of his promises to Israel through the fulfillment of the mediator. Christ is therefore mediator according to both natures, as the Formula of Concord states.[47]

Finally, the Old Testament explicitly understands God's election of mediators as possessing an ultimate fulfillment in the coming of a Messiah. Throughout the Old Testament, there are prophecies of the coming of one who will ultimately fulfill the various forms of mediation. Though these prophecies are diverse, the *protevangelium* spoken to our first parents unifies and frames these prophecies as all pointing to the manifestation of the work of Christ. Ultimately, Christ both recapitulates Adam and the history of Israel.

Prophetic Mediation

Within the Old Testament there is a significant amount of material concerning the work of prophetic mediators. Since Adam was the first to receive the Word of God, we must designate him as the first prophet. Nevertheless, below we will mainly focus our discussion on the prophet Moses in that he is exemplar and source of prophetic mediation throughout the Old Testament. All the later prophets call Israel back to the law and promise mediated to Israel by Moses. This choice is also fitting because the Bible views him as being a type of Christ in this capacity (Deut 18:18, Acts 7:37). Moses also exemplifies Christ in that his temporal exodus from Egypt prefigures Christ's leading humanity to a spiritual exodus from sin, death, the devil, and the law (1 Cor 5:7, 10; Heb 2–3). Beyond leading Israel out of Egypt, the major function of Moses's prophetic ministry is the fulfillment of Israel's vocation of receiving the Word of God, of which Christ being the true Word of God (John 1) is the final fulfillment.

Moses's role as mediator is best illustrated in the later chapters of the book of Exodus. Beginning in chapter 19, we are told after the long journey from Egypt that Israel came to the foot of Sinai. God calls Moses to the top of the mountain and tells him that he is going to come to the people in "a thick cloud" (Exod 19:9) (to conceal his glory) and then will speak with Moses. The purpose of such speech is so that "the people may hear when I speak with you, and may also believe you forever" (v. 9). When God's special presence finally descends onto the mountain, he does so in fire and smoke (v. 18). The people are warned to stay away lest they perish (v. 21). Moses and Aaron are then instructed to ascend the mountain. Before they can do so, God speaks the Decalogue from within the cloud (19:25—20:17). The people and the priests hear God's own voice reciting the words of the law and are completely terrified by both the sound and the visible manifestations of the divine glory. They cry out to Moses (who has apparently not ascended the mountain yet), "You speak to us, and we will listen; but do not let God speak to us, lest we die" (20:20). John Durham, commenting on this passage, states that Moses's response is best understood as suggesting that God has come to Israel in this manner in order to test them or give experience of his presence to them so that they

---

47. FC SD 3; *CT* 935.

will not sin.[48] In this way, the people have failed such a testing, and as Durham further comments, they have prefigured their future failure as God's people.[49]

A breach has therefore opened up between the holy God and his people dead in their sin. Moses moves into the breach created by their inability to receive the Word of YHWH. We are told that "The people stood far off, while Moses drew near to the thick darkness where God was" (20:21). In spite of the earlier instruction, Aaron is not reported to have entered into the thick darkness with him and Moses therefore becomes the sole mediator.[50] On the mountain, further instructions concerning the law are given (20:22—23:33) and Moses reports these commandments to the people who pledge themselves to obey the law (24:3).

There are several interesting aspects of mediation that we discover in this account. First, because of human sin, there is a necessary distance between the divine presence and humans. Israel cannot enter into the darkness of Sinai and receive the law, just as Adam could not stand in the presence of God once he had fallen into sin (Gen 3:8–10). Before the Fall, Adam and Eve were able to stand in the presence of God without fear. Israel cannot even bear the sound of the divine voice issuing from Sinai. For this reason, Moses as a mediator is necessary to represent Israel and do what Israel cannot do. The text of Exodus seems to make Moses an embodiment of Israel on several occasions. God refers to Israel as "my firstborn son" (Exod 4:22) and the name "Moses" means "a son" in Egyptian.[51] By divine power, he is able to bring YHWH and Israel together by fulfilling Israel's vocation in its place. That God called and established Moses as a mediator also means that the prophet represents God's own righteous faithfulness. He elects Moses to do what Israel cannot do. In this sense, Moses the mediator represents both God and Israel.

As the narrative of Exodus progresses there are several interesting developments in regard to Moses's mediatorship. The first development is in regards to the content of the Word of YHWH that he receives. Over the next ten chapters of Exodus, the pattern and accoutrements of the tabernacle are revealed. Before Moses is called to the mountain and the laws are given, YHWH tells the prophet that Israel is a "kingdom of priests and a holy nation" (19:6). Therefore all the works of the nation are the works of a priestly people and thereby a kind of liturgical service. The prior grace of God at having bound himself in the promise of grace to the patriarchs and having redeemed the people from Egypt is the presupposition of such service. The Ten Commandments themselves contain the preface: "I am the Lord your God, who brought you out of the land of Egypt, out of the house of slavery" (20:2). As a priestly people, Israel lives out the true human destiny of divine service as a response to prior divine favor given to them. In other words, their works of obedience are a liturgical activity in response to sheer divine love and grace. Israel is then a liturgical community in the truest sense. Prophetic mediation is then ordered to the establishment of priestly-liturgical worship of the one true Lord.

48. Durham, *Exodus*, 303.

49. Ibid., 304–5.

50. See comment in Houtman, *Exodus*, 78.

51. Dozeman, *Exodus*, 81. This does not contradict the statement earlier that he took the name because he was "drawn out" (Exod 2:10). The Egyptian name sounds like the Hebrew word to draw out.

The second development is the challenge to Moses's mediatorship. These challenges are ultimately counteracted by divine acts of approval in the form of theophanies. In chapter 24 of Exodus, after the people had agreed to follow the divine commandments, the elders of Israel ascend the mountain and have a partial vision of the divine glory or *kavod*. It must be explained here, in order to clarify our discussion below, what the Old Testament in general means by the *kavod* or the "glory of the Lord." Walther Eichrodt gives a helpful and compact definition of the *kavod* as the "reflected splendor of the transcendent God, a token of the divine glory, by means of which Yahweh declares his gracious presence."[52] Here Eichrodt emphasizes the two most important elements of the *kavod* as it is frequently used in relationship to God, namely, the *kavod* is a manifestation of the presence of God, and of divine luminosity. According to Eichrodt, *kavod* also has a second connotation of referring to a person's possession of riches, honor, and success. In other words, *kavod* can also mean glory, honor, or praise given or possessed by a person.[53]

In identifying the nature of the *kavod*, we will venture farther than Eichrodt. It must be recognized that the *kavod* does not merely refer to an attribute of God. Neither is *kavod* merely a metaphor for divine presence. Rather the Old Testament views the glory of the Lord to be something hypostatized. The *kavod* is often spoken of as God, but also separately as standing in relation to God (see Exod 33, Ezek 1–2). Some recognition of this fact continued in post-biblical Judaism. There is a manifestation of a continued belief in the distinction between God and his *kavod* in what Jewish scholar Alan Segal refers to as the "Heresy of the Two Powers" in rabbinic Judaism.[54]

This hypostatized divine presence of the divine glory is identical with the divine Word and Name, as Charles Gieschen has clearly shown.[55] The Name of God is YHWH, "I am what I am" (Exod 3:14) (or perhaps "I will be whom I will be"). We are told in Genesis 1 that the first word that God utters is "Let there be." Gieschen notes that many early Jewish interpreters of the text likely made a connection between the Word and the Name because they possess the identical verb "to be."[56] That there is an intentional connection in the biblical text itself and not just in the imagination of the later interpreters seems to be highly plausible insofar as God is identified throughout the Old Testament as both the creator and the initiator of the divine-human covenantal relationships. He "will be who he will be" because by his electing act he initiates his relationship both in the form creation and redemption. He thereby identifies himself with his redeeming and electing act and makes his reality known through it (for example see Exod 6:2–8, 33:19).

The Word and Name are therefore identical in that they have the same content of the divine reality and utterance. The Name is also identical with *kavod*, in that the tabernacle/temple is interchangeably described as the place of the dwelling of the glory

---

52. Eichrodt, *Theology of the Old Testament*, 2:32.

53. Ibid., 2:30. Eichrodt gives the examples of Gen 31:1; Isa 10:3, 66:12; Prov 49:17. Also see discussion in Collins, "Kabob," 2:577–87; G. Davies, "Glory," 2:401–3; Gaffin, "Glory," 507–11; E. Harrison, "Glory," 2:477–83; Huttar, "Glory," 287–88.

54. See Segal, *Two Powers in Heaven*.

55. Gieschen, *Angelomorphic Christology*, 103–7; Gieschen, "Real Presence of the Son," 105–26.

56. Gieschen, *Angelomorphic Christology*, 74.

of YHWH (Exod 40) and YHWH's Name: "He [Solomon/the Messiah] shall build a *house for my name*, and I will establish the throne of his kingdom forever" (2 Sam 7:13, emphasis added. Also see Deut 12:5, v. 11; 1 Kgs 5:5, 8:16; 2 Chr 6:5).[57] This identification is also made in Exodus by an act of poetic parallelism. When Moses is told he will see God's *kavod*, YHWH explains: "I will *make all my goodness pass before you* and will proclaim *before you my name 'The Lord.'* And I will be gracious to whom I will be gracious, and will show mercy on whom I will show mercy" (Exod 33:19, emphasis added).

Lastly, the entity designated as the "Angel of YHWH" is himself also identical with the *kavod*, the Name, and the Word. This can be shown studying a number of passages in the Old Testament.[58] The Angel of YHWH who appears in luminous manner on Mount Horeb, divulges and identifies himself with the divine Name in Exodus 3:2 and 3:14.[59] The Angel of YHWH is spoken of as a different "thou" to YHWH's "I," while also being the very presence of YHWH himself. YHWH will not go with Israel, but his angel will (Exod 33:3).[60] Nevertheless, the Angel of YHWH is identical with his Name and presence: "Pay careful attention to him [the Angel of YHWH] and obey his voice; do not rebel against him, for he will not pardon your transgression, *for my name is in him*" (Exod 23:21, emphasis added; also see 33:1).[61] In Isaiah 63:9, he is called "angel of his presence." In the book of Judges, Manoah remarks after the Angel of YHWH has announced Samson's birth and departed in the flame of a sacrifice: "we have seen God!" (Judg 13:22). His wife does not contradict him, but merely says that it has been for their good and not for ill (vv. 23–24). We see a similar situation in the narrative of Hagar's escape (Gen 16:7–13). As shall be observed later, some texts in the Old Testament also suggest that the Angel of the YHWH functions as a heavenly priest and king, who parallel Israel's earthly kings and priests. Later, we will see from the data of the New Testament that this figure is to be properly identified with the preincarnate Christ.[62]

57. See discussion of the relationship of the Name and Glory in McConville, "God's Name and God's Glory," 149–63.

58. The Angel of YHWH is mentioned in Gen 16:7–14, 19, 21:17–19, 22:11–18, 28:11–22, 31:11–13, 32:24–30, 48:16; Exod 3:1–7, 13:21, 14:19, 23:20–23, 33:14; Josh 5:13, 6:2; Judg 6:11–24, 13:3–23; Isa 63:8, 9.

59. Gieschen, *Angelomorphic Christology*, 53.

60. See discussion in Hengstenberg, *Christology of the Old Testament*, 1:126–28.

61. Gieschen, *Angelomorphic Christology*, 76.

62. Luther agrees:

> Thus it follows powerfully and irrefutably that the God who led the people of Israel out of Egypt and through the Red Sea, who guided them in the wilderness through the pillars of cloud and fire, who nourished them with heavenly bread, and who performed all the miracles Moses describes in his book, who also brought them into the land of Canaan and then gave them kings and priests and everything, is therefore God and none other than Jesus of Nazareth, the Son of the Virgin Mary, whom we call Christ our God and Lord . . . And, again, it is he who gave Moses the Ten Commandments on Mount Sinai, saying, "I am the Lord your God who led you out of Egypt; you shall have no other gods." Yes, Jesus of Nazareth, who died for us on the cross, is the God who says in the First Commandment, "I, the Lord, am your God." (*AE* 15:313–14)

Among modern interpreters, there is of course the aforementioned Charles Gieschen. The following theologians and exegetes (particularly of the Lutheran tradition) have taken this position on the Angel of YHWH: Hengstenberg, *Christology of the Old Testament*, 1:115–30; Hoenecke, *Evangelical Lutheran Dogmatics*, 2:170–73; Leupold, *Genesis*, 1:500–501. Hoenecke mentions the following Lutherans who

Having entered into the presence of the glory of the Lord, the elders return again to the camp, while Moses is called to again ascend to the heights of Sinai in order to see the pattern of the tabernacle and receive the instructions regarding priestly worship (Exod 25–31). Meanwhile, the Israelites come to doubt Moses's mediatorship and turn to Aaron for help. Aaron's solution is to cast a golden calf and announce to the camp: "These are your gods [or possibly 'your God'], O Israel, who brought you up out of the land of Egypt!" (32:4).

There is some debate among scholars regarding the function of the calf. First it should be observed that this event parallels an incident of the erection of two calf statues in 1 Kings 12:28 by Jeroboam the northern Israelite king. These calves are also credited with having led Israel out of Egypt and are viewed as an alternative to the temple in Jerusalem. As Cornelis Houtman points out, in the ancient Levant a rather significant number of deities were represented as a bull, including Baal and the Canaanite sky god El.[63] This of course leads to the question of whether the image is meant to represent the deity and mediate his presence or merely to be a pedestal or throne indicating the presence of the deity. Martin Noth takes the latter position; Houtman appears to lean towards the former position.[64]

Either way, both agree that this incident does not represent an apostasy in the sense of abandoning YHWH for another deity.[65] Beyond this cultural-religious background, the narrative context also helps us discern the function of the establishment of the calf. Moses has functioned previously throughout the narrative as the mediator, that is, as representative of the unity of God and Israel before both. He has nonetheless disappeared and therefore Israel is in need of a new mediator, a "replacement" of Moses as Rolf Rendtorff describes the situation.[66] Such a mediator must represent and mediate the presence of the deity to them. Hence, after having seen the luminous hypostatized glory of the Lord, they construct a golden calf, whose luminosity will imitate the divine *kavod*. They choose the image of the calf because their view of YHWH is very likely similar to

---

hold this view: Kahnis, *Lutherische Dogmatik*, 1:396–97, 399; Keil, *Bibelsk Commentar uber Genesis*, 126; Philippi, *Kirchliche Glaubenslehre*, 2:19, 194; Rohnert, *Dogmatik der Evangelisch-Lutherischen Kirche*, 145. Also, among older non-Lutheran interpreters, Gieshen ("Real Presence of the Son," 106) mentions the following: Alexander, *Isaiah*, 2:394; Borland, *Christ in the Old Testament*; T. Hanson, *Jesus Christ in the Old Testament*; Rhodes, *Christ Before the Manger*.

63. Houtman, *Exodus*, 626.

64. Houtman, *Exodus*, 624–26; Noth, *Exodus*, 247–48. It should be noted that older interpreters saw the golden calf as the Egyptian god Apis. See Keil and Delitzsch, *Pentateuch*, 222. We cannot agree with this option for several reasons. 1. It would be ludicrous for the Israelites to engage in an outright abandonment of YHWH after they had seen his destructive power against the Egyptians. 2. Aaron's statements on the matter suggest that the Israelites do not view themselves as abandoning YHWH: "behold the god[s] that brought [us] out of Egypt" (Exod 32:4). This would presuppose that they considered the calf a representative of YHWH and not a new god. YHWH had already previously identified himself and they were well aware of him as the one who brought them out of Egypt. One might object that if the Israelites had been in Egypt that they would be unfamiliar with western Semitic forms of religion. This is unfounded in that Egypt for much of the late Bronze Age controlled the Levant and influence between the two regions was significant. See discussion in Donald Redford, *Egypt, Canaan, and Israel*, 125–241.

65. Houtman, *Exodus*, 626.

66. Rendtorff, *Canonical Hebrew Bible*, 61.

that of the Canaanite's view of El.[67] Jethro states earlier in the narrative: "Now I know that the Lord is *greater than all gods*" (Exod 18:11, emphasis added). Statements like this suggest that they thought of YHWH as simply the highest God among the gods, much like El. Such a god would, like El, need a fitting mediatorial image that would reflect its power.

Trading an image for God himself makes sense in the logic of sinful Israel. As we have seen, Israel cannot stand the real presence of YHWH even when it is concealed. God proves uncontrollable to them when he speaks his law (19–20). Similarly, God's unilateral self-giving by his descent into the cult (which as we will see serves as a medium for the giving of his holiness to Israel) also proves that God cannot be manipulated. Rather, he graciously gives himself without human cooperation or merit (40). An imitation god keeps God at a safe distance or reduces God to one object among others. As a result, Israel's own conceit and self-justification can continue unabated.[68]

If we interpret the Israelites' action in this manner, then it is easy to view the next few chapters as functioning to reestablish the sole mediatorship of Moses. After the apostasy has been suppressed and Moses again takes control of the community, we are told that the prophet again communes with YHWH. He asks YHWH for a means to confirm his promise of grace and Moses's mediatorship: "Is it not in your going with us, so that we are distinct, I and your people, from every other people on the face of the earth?" (Exod 33:16). YHWH insists that he will bless the people. Moses asks that he be given a direct vision of the divine *kavod*: "Please show me your glory" (Exod 33:18). God tells him that he cannot do this directly, but that his "Name" (that is, his glorious presence) will pass before him as he stands in a cleft of a rock (v. 22).[69] Moses then sees (however indirectly) the divine *kavod* as YHWH proclaims his own glory. He is then instructed to chisel out the words of the law which he has previously destroyed and deliver them again to Israel. When he comes down from the mountain, he frightens the people because his face shines with the glory of the Lord (34:29–30). He must therefore cover his face as he reads the law to them. In contrast to the calf, Moses's face contains the real presence of YHWH and not an image. Martin Noth notes that (particularly in Ancient Egypt) the assumption of a face-covering after communion with a deity was a usual practice of the priestly caste. It effectively meant that "the priest assumes the 'face' of his deity and identifies himself with him."[70] Thomas Dozeman observes that although the name Moses only technically means "son," its use in other Egyptian names is typically integrated with a larger name of a god.[71] Therefore implicitly the name might be construed as meaning "divine son." This fact taken together with his luminous face suggests that Moses prefigures the glory incarnation of the true divine Son as manifested on the mountain of transfiguration (Matt 17:1–9, Mark 9:2–8, Luke 9:28–36).

Whereas the false mediator of the calf possessed a golden luminosity that imitated the divine *kavod*, Moses the true mediator possesses the true glory of God: "One might

67. Cross, *Canaanite Myth*, 3–60.

68. See similar critique of idolatry in Romans 1 in Paulson, *Lutheran Theology*, 74–78.

69. See *AE* 15:333–35. Luther interprets Exodus 33 in an appropriately Trinitarian manner.

70. Noth, *Exodus*, 267.

71. Dozeman, *Exodus*, 81–82.

say that the transfigured Moses, representative of YHWH, symbolized the presence of YHWH himself among Israel."[72] This glory is hidden glory, since he must cover his face when reading the law. Furthermore, Moses's action parallels the revelation of Exodus chapter 20 in that he conceals the divine glory in the same manner that YHWH did earlier. His mediation of the glorious presence is discerned by hearing and not by vision.

Lastly, it should be observed that Moses's glorious appearance seems to be connected with the concept of humanity we find in Genesis 1–3 and Israel in Exodus 19. He is the true image of God, because he is a human being and not an animal. As Genesis 1 teaches, it is humans and not animals (in contradistinction to the cultures surrounding Israel) that are the image of the deity (1:27–28).[73] He is also the true Israel because he has received the Word of the Lord. This is something that Israel ultimately could not do. If we also take the second connotation of *kavod* as meaning honor and personal glory, we can also observe that Moses fulfills the true liturgical vocation of Israel as a priestly nation to reflect the divine glory, as his doxology on the mountain demonstrates. His doxology is the giving of personal glory to YHWH in the form of praise. This interpretation is further bolstered by the fact that Moses is reported to have proclaimed cultic regulations and the pattern for the construction of the tabernacle in this state of luminosity, that is, regulations ordering the worship or the giving of honor to the true God (Exod 35–40).

Beyond being the representative of God and Israel before Israel, Moses also takes up the function of representing God and Israel before God. Returning again to the activity of Moses on Sinai before his reception of divine glory, we are told that YHWH informs Moses of the golden calf apostasy going on in the camp. God proposes to Moses that he annihilate the Israelites and make Moses into a great nation (32:10). Moses pleads with God to not destroy the Israelites and to "Remember Abraham, Isaac, and Israel, your servants, to *whom you swore by your own self*" (32:13, emphasis added). Here Moses stands before YHWH as both a representative of Israel, pleading with God concerning the sin of the people and as God before God by wielding God's own Word of grace against his Word of judgment. In this, he becomes a type of Christ's self-offering to and advocacy before the Father. After going down from the mountain and disrupting the apostasy, Moses again returns to the Lord and in a supreme act of mediation, offers his own life as a sin offering (32:31–32). This atoning mediation fails though because God declares in his anger that those who have sinned against him will pay with their own lives (v. 34). Moses shows himself to be inferior to Christ, whose self-offering was accepted by the Father. Neither is Moses himself ultimately saved from condemnation. According to Numbers, he is not allowed to enter the Promised Land because of an incident in which he abuses his role as mediator (Num 20:1–13). Much as the law cannot bring humanity into the rest of redemption (*vita passive*), Moses, the mediator of law, could not bring Israel into God's rest (Heb 2:16–19).

In subsequent Israelite history, prophetic mediatorship was also unsuccessful. In spite of this, we find the promise of the eschatological fulfillment of prophetic mediatorship throughout the Old Testament. In the farewell address of Deuteronomy 18, Moses

---

72. Houtman, *Exodus*, 733.

73. See a similar argument regarding the image of God and the golden calf in Fletcher-Louis, "God's Image," 85–88, 92–93.

prophesies of the coming of a prophet like himself, in whose mouth God will place his words (18:18). The book of Deuteronomy and the so-called Deuteronomistic history emphasize that God is present in his Word and in his Name, and therefore the implication is that this prophet will mediate the divine presence.[74] It also follows that this prophet must be greater than Moses and therefore must mediate the divine presence in an even greater manner than he did. If he were not greater, then Moses's mediation would have sufficed. Taking this reasoning one step further, we must posit that the coming of this prophet represents the coming of God himself. If Moses spoke with God "face to face" (Exod 33:11) and a prophet is measured by his closeness to God and his ability to mediate the divine (Num 12:6–8), then the only possibility for a greater revelation of God would be the coming of God himself.

Isaiah understands this coming of a prophet like Moses to be the coming of the Servant of YHWH, who is himself YHWH. We are first informed that the Lord himself is personally returning to Zion (Isa 40), thereby reversing the state of exile. This returning "glory" will be seen by "all flesh" (40:5). This returning presence is clearly identical with the Servant of the Lord. He is God's luminous glory in that he is a "light to the nations" (49:6). This description clearly parallels the universal manifestation of the *kavod* in 40:5. Furthermore he is described as the "arm of the Lord" (53:1, 63:12). He is also the "angel of the presence" sent to save (63:9).[75]

If Isaiah describes a new exodus, then there must logically also be a new Moses and a new Passover lamb. Just as Moses sprinkled Israel with the blood of the covenant (Exod 24:8), so the Servant will "sprinkle many nations" (Isa 52:15) and will not only establish a covenant, but himself will be a "covenant for the people" (42:6).[76] In light of the fact that the redeeming promise of grace ends the exile, which has occurred because of sin, this covenant can be none other than the new covenant spoken of by Jeremiah that eliminates sin.[77] God tells the prophet that the former covenant that he made with Israel after leading them out of Egypt was nonfunctional because of the unbelief and disobedience of the nation (Jer 31:31–32). Echoing Moses's own prediction in Deuteronomy 30:6 ("And the Lord your God will circumcise your heart and the heart of your offspring, so that you will love the Lord your God with all your heart and with all your soul, that you may live."), Jeremiah states that YHWH will make a new covenant (v. 31): "I will make with the house of Israel after those days, declares the Lord: I will put my law within them, and I will write it on their hearts" (31:33) and "for I will forgive their iniquity,

74. Eichrodt, *Theology of the Old Testament*, 2:41. In regards to the dwelling of the Name, Eichrodt notes Deut 12:5, 11, 14:23, 16:2; 1 Kgs 11:36, 14:21; 2 Kgs 21:4, 7. See Eichrodt's comments on the Word of YHWH in his *Theology of the Old Testament*, 71–75. Also see von Rad on the prophetic and Deuteronomistic conception of the Word in Eichrodt, *Theology of the Old Testament*, 2:80–99.

75. Note that this is one reading. The LXX version states: "not an ambassador, nor an angel, but he himself saved them." See discussion in Gieschen, *Angelomorphic Christology*, 116–19. Also see Barnes, "Veni Creator Spiritus," 4. Note that both authors consider the MT reading that we cite above to be the authentic one. Interestingly enough, Barnes comments that the rabbis treated the two readings as if they were identical.

76. Delitzsch, *Biblical Commentary*, 2:307–8. Delitsch also notes verbal similarities to the sprinkling of blood in atoning sacrifices.

77. Ibid., 2:179. Also see A. Pieper, *Exposition of Isaiah 40–66*, 187–88.

and I will remember their sin no more" (v. 34). Moses tried to place the law within the Israelites' hearts (Deut 6:6), but he could only demand and coerce them into imprinting it on themselves in an outward way (6:8–9). In the same manner, Moses established sin offerings (Lev 4:1—5:13, 6:24–30, 8:14–17, 16:3–22) and guilt offerings (Lev 5:14—6:7, 7:1–6), which could not ultimately cleanse the conscience (Heb 10:4). The result of this unatoned for sin would be exile, as Moses himself predicts in Deuteronomy 27–32. The word and works of the Servant will accomplish the end of exile, and therefore finally eliminate sin.

Moreover, the nineteenth-century Lutheran Old Testament scholar Ernst Hengstenberg, points out that the Servant does not merely mediate the covenant like Moses, but in fact is the covenant himself.[78] He can do this because he is the one who has become the new Passover lamb and true sin offering (Isa 53:5, vv. 7, 10).[79] He will for the sake of his people be "distressed" with their "distress" (63:9) (or possibly one could translate this as "afflicted" with their "affliction").[80] The Servant proclaims this universal Jubilee (Isa 61:2), based on the new covenant's forgiveness of sins (Jer 31:34) rooted in his own person and work.[81] Moses attempted to redeem Israel by doing this (Exod 32:31–32), but was unable.

78. Hengstenberg, *Christology of the Old Testament*, 3:221. Leupold makes a similar observation. See Leupold, *Isaiah*, 2:64–65.

79. Leupold, *Isaiah*, 2:229–31. Leupold agrees that this death is atoning, though he does not pick up on the Passover imagery.

80. Among older theologians, Nicolaus Hunnius interprets the verse as referring to the sufferings of Christ. See brief comment in Hunnius, *Epitome Credendorum*, 45. Also see Leupold, *Isaiah*, 2:342–43. Leupold understands these verses as referring to the exodus and not ahead to the incarnation.

81. Hengstenberg, *Christology of the Old Testament*, 3:351–53. Leupold agrees that this is a reference to Jubilee (*Isaiah*, 2:321).

Chapter 2

Mediation in the Old Testament, Part 2

Priestly and Kingly Mediation

Priestly Mediation

WITHIN THE HISTORY OF Exodus, priestly mediation arises through the prophetic mediation of the Word of God. The prophetic word both reveals the chosen status of the Levites and the practices in which they must engage. The occasion of the election of the Levites as the priestly caste occurs during Moses's reestablishment of order after Israel's apostasy to the golden calf. The Levites (Moses's own tribe) rally to support him and zealously exact vengeance on those who have fallen away from YHWH (Exod 25:32–39).[1] Our discussion of priestly mediation will nonetheless not begin with this narrative, but rather with the description of the nature of creation in Genesis 1–3. As we will see, these narratives served as foundational to priestly mediation.[2]

Recent scholarship on Genesis 1 has gradually come to recognize that it contains strong liturgical themes. Early in the twentieth century, much of the critical scholarship on Genesis 1 revolved around attempts to connect the chapter with the Babylonian epic, the *Enuma Elish*, and the ancient mythological motif of the *chaoskampf*.[3] Though parallels still continue to be recognized, critics have also come to appreciate the presence of significant cultic and liturgical themes as well.

P. J. Kearney's work has been particularly important for its recognition of these themes. Kearney has shown that there are not only strong verbal similarities between Genesis 1 and Exodus 25–32, but also that the seven days of creation directly correspond to seven speeches God made concerning the construction of the tabernacle in

---

1. See discussion in Hahn, *Kinship by Covenant*, 146–47. Hahn posits the interesting theory that because all firstborn sons were originally consecrated to YHWH, they served as priests in Israel prior to the golden calf incident. Afterwards, the Levites take over their position. Hahn then goes on to argue that this is why it is emphasized in the Epistle to the Hebrews that Christ is a firstborn son. In other words, he has restored by his life, death, and resurrection the original situation of Israel.

2. Much of the material in this section has previously appeared in my article, "Creation's Praise," 314–25.

3. See Gunkel, *Creation and Chaos*; Gunkel, *Genesis*. Also see Cross, *Canaanite Myth*, 77–144.

those chapters.[4] Similarly, although the Jewish scholar Jon Levenson has claimed that Kearney's interpretation is not entirely persuasive, nevertheless he thinks that it is impossible to deny that the accounts of creation and the tabernacle/temple share significant themes.[5] Levenson notes that in Exodus 40:2, the erection of the tabernacle occurs on the day of the vernal New Year, the same time Genesis tells us that Noah emerged from the ark into the new creation of the post-diluvium world.[6] Similarly, 1 Kings 6–7 emphasizes that Solomon's dedication of the temple occurred on the seventh month during the Feast of Tabernacles, a seven-day feast.[7] This would appear to suggest a connection with the seven days of creation.

Returning to Kearney's scholarship, the activities of each day of creation correspond to an aspect of the construction of the tabernacle. The tabernacle and the later temple are, therefore, intended to represent a microcosm of creation. Among the seven speeches establishing the tabernacle, the seventh speech concerns the Sabbath, directly paralleling God's own protological Sabbath rest. It stands to reason that if, as Kearney has shown, creation's formation directly corresponds to the erection of the tabernacle, then they must also serve the same purpose, that is, the worship of God. Evangelical scholar G. K. Beale generally agrees with Kearney and has argued that each major section of the temple/tabernacle represents a part of the created order.[8] In both the original tabernacle and the Solomonic temple, the basin of water represented the sea, the courtyard represented the land, while the holy place and holy of holies represented the starry and celestial heavens (or possibly Eden, in that it is the locus of divine presence). This theory is further bolstered by the fact that the curtains covering the holy place and the holy of holies were woven to resemble the sky (Exod 25), something also mentioned by Josephus concerning Herod's temple.[9] With Levenson, Beale also mentions the importance of the number seven in the liturgical calendar of Israel (notably the seven-day week and the forty-nine-year cycle of Jubilee) and in the imagery of the tabernacle.[10] He argues that the use of seven corresponds to the seven planets visible to the naked eye. In the tabernacle, the seven planets appear to be represented by the seven lamp stands.

The second chapter of Genesis continues the liturgical themes of the first chapter. The Old Testament scholar Gordon Wenham has argued for a strong connection between the garden of Eden as it is portrayed in the second chapter and the later Israelite cult. Wenham notes similarities between Eden and the temple/tabernacle such as the opening of both to the east and each functioning as the locus of the divine presence (Gen 2:15).[11] Wenham has also argued that the text's descriptions of Adam's activity in the garden possess verbal similarities with the ministrations of the priesthood elsewhere

---

4. Kearney, "Liturgy and Creation," 375–87.

5. Levenson, *Creation and the Persistence*, 83.

6. Ibid., 78.

7. Ibid.

8. Beale, *Temple*, 31–36.

9. See discussion in Beale, *Temple*, 46. Also see *Jewish War*, 5.5.4, in Josephus, *Works of Josephus*, 707.

10. Ibid., 35.

11. Wenham, "Sanctuary Symbolism," 19–37.

in the Pentateuch.[12] This means that the author of Genesis describes Adam and Eve's care for creation as a true act of grateful worship, making it a liturgical activity. In Wenham's commentary on Genesis, he also notes that Adam's reception of the first commandment in the garden parallels the storage of the book of the law in the Israelite tabernacle.[13] Adding to all this, Beale has noted the verbal similarities between the arboreal imagery in Genesis 2–3 and in the description of Solomon's temple in 1 Kings 6–7.[14] Jon Levenson has demonstrated the verbal parallels between the description of Eden and the Temple Mount, particularly in Ezekiel. Ezekiel 28:14 locates Eden on a mountain much like Zion.[15]

From these parallel descriptions we can discern a unity of purpose between creation and the Israelite tabernacle/temple. What has been partially realized in the Israelite liturgy is the restoration of the original creation. Creation is an immense tabernacle dedicated to divine worship. Israel, according to the Pentateuchal narratives, has taken up the position abdicated by Adam and Eve.[16] Israel is a liturgical community, a "priestly nation." Not only do Adam and Eve and all faithful Israelites worship and praise God as a result of God's creative Word, but there is some suggestion that the rest of the created order does as well. Each day of creation ends with the refrain, "And God saw that it was good." Such a phrase implies that as a temple of divine worship, creation reflects divine goodness back to God in a manner of almost personified thanksgiving ("glory" one might say) for having received itself from the divine Word. The praise of creation as a response to the gracious giving of the divine Word is a theme present elsewhere in the Old Testament (Isa 55:11–2).

The embodiment of divine graciousness and its echoed praise have other implications for the interpretation of Genesis 1–3. The fact that Adam and Eve are engaged in liturgical activities in Eden (mentioned above) also suggests how the shape of the divine image spoken of in Genesis 1:26 should be understood. The divine image is spoken of in connection with ruling over and maintaining creation (1:28), which, as we have observed, is a temple of divine presence. Wenham's interpretation of Adam and Eve's activity in Genesis 2 allows us to see liturgical themes throughout the entire text of Genesis 1–3. If, indeed liturgical service is a reflection of divine goodness and glory, it is an act of receiving and reflecting back divine glory. After all, *kavod* ("glory") has both the connotation of light (as in the divine light seen by Moses [Exod 33:18] and reflected by him in his luminous face in Exodus 34) and of praise.[17] If God is fundamentally glorious, then his image reflected in creation must be as well (Ps 19, Rom 1:19–21). Therefore, following Beale's thinking, it might be suggested that the first humans are portrayed as

12. Gordon Wenham mentions verbal parallels found in Num 3:7–8, 8:26, 18:5–6.

13. Wenham, *Genesis 1–15*, 64.

14. Beale, *Temple*, 23–29.

15. Levenson, *Creation and the Persistence*, 93.

16. This has also been suggested by N. T. Wright in his argument regarding the covenantal promise throughout the Pentateuch. There is a parallel between Adam and Eve's promise of fertility and dominion, and the same promise to Israel. See N. T. Wright, *Christian Origins*, 3:720. Wright lists the example of Gen 12:2, 17:2–8, 22:16, 26:3, 26:24, 28:3, 35:11, 47:27, 48:3.

17. Eichrodt, *Theology of the Old Testament*, 2:30–32.

priests presiding over the cosmic temple and reflecting divine goodness and glory back to God; this constitutes the embodied divine image.[18]

Hence, from the perspective of the Pentateuchal narratives (and much of the rest of the Old Testament), liturgical worship is built into the very structure of creation. God sends forth his gracious Word and Spirit (Gen 1:2–3, Ps 33:6), thereby bringing about the created order and communicating to it a reflection of his divine glory. As a great cosmic tabernacle, creation functions as an arena of embodied and reflected glory. This divinely established order reflects back to God his goodness and glory in a sacrifice of praise. In this protological order, humanity exemplifies this glory through its priestly ministrations in the maintenance of creation. Through these activities, they express the divine image of glory within them. The Israelite tabernacle/temple and its liturgy are merely restorations of this order among the particular worshiping community of the chosen people, who function as the new Adam and Eve.

Such sacrificial worship of praise carried out in Eden is restored and receives a more concrete form in the Israelite tabernacle. Israel, as we have seen, prefigures Christ and is called to be the image of the restored Adam. If the true human vocation is to preside over the tabernacle of creation as its true priestly ruler, then the Aaronic high priest must be the highest representative of the true humanity, Israel. Crispin H. T. Fletcher-Louis summarizes a lengthy list of ways in which the high priest embodies Adam and true humanity taken from both scripture and post-biblical Jewish commentaries:

> The High Priest is obviously a human being. He is the new Adam, wearing the garments that Adam lost on leaving Eden, doing what Adam failed to do in the temple-as-restored-Eden. He represents, or embodies the people of God, Israel (who are, in turn, the true humanity); wearing on his breastpiece and lapels the names of the twelve tribes of Israel (Exod 28:9–21). He brings humanity and Israel to God. He also brings the cosmos, the created world, to God since this is represented by his garments in its various parts.[19]

As a mediator and representative of Israel before God and Israel, the priestly mediator offered up thank-offerings as an expression of praise for God's graciousness in the form of his gifts of creation and redemption. This is the first major category of sacrifice that Leviticus discusses. Within this category, Leviticus gives the subdivisions of burnt of-ferings (Lev 1, 6:8–13, 8:18–21, 16:24), grain offerings (Lev 2, 6:14–23), and fellowship offerings (Lev 3, 7:11–34).

After the Fall, it is necessary for sacrifice to also take on the functions of confirming covenants and making atonement for sin.[20] "Gather to me my faithful ones, who made a covenant with me by sacrifice!" (Ps 50:5). These two functions are tied up with binding together two parties whose relationship has been broken. This takes the form of either binding by the promise of grace, or reconciling one party via an act of atonement. We will first discuss how covenantal sacrifice functions and then move onto the question of atoning sacrifice.[21]

18. Beale, *Temple*, 35.

19. Fletcher-Louis, "Jesus and the High Priest," 5.

20. On the concept of sacrifice in the Old Testament see K. Hanson, "Blood and Purity," 215–30.

21. Quell, "Diatheke," 2:113. Quell argues that covenants are solemn oaths that have the form of a

According to Scott Hahn, the sacrifices that establish a covenant function in such a way as to represent the content of the covenant, particularly in regard to the curses that would accompany it if not fulfilled.[22] Hahn posits this interpretation because he mainly (though not exclusively) understands the covenant sacrifices in light of the ancient practice of fealty oaths which also involved sacrifice. The biblical texts describe such sacrifices (often in a manner that directly parallels secular practice!) as occurring between YHWH and Israel/the patriarchs. Nevertheless, whereas the fealty oaths were about the subjection of the lesser party to the greater party (law), most of God's covenant sacrifices are concerned with the promise of blessing and redemption (gospel). Hence, they are more often meant to convey God's own subjection to Israel and not Israel's subjection to God. For this reason, it will be our argument that it is therefore fitting to read the symbolism of the sacrifice as prefiguring the ultimate fulfillment of redemption and grace that they promise. Reading scriptures, as it has been our method, we therefore must take the content of all covenants as being Christ. Indeed, as the Apostle Paul writes, Christ is the "yes" to all of God's promises (2 Cor 1:21). Therefore below we will observe how each covenant and covenantal ceremony points ahead to the advent of Christ.

From the very beginning of Old Testament history, covenants were established by an act of sacrifice. After the Fall, God covered Adam and Eve's shame by clothing them with the skins of animals (Gen 3:21). This occurs in connection with the promise of a redeemer (v. 15).[23] The redeemer will reestablish Adam and Eve in a state of life and freedom. He will cover their shame and he will return to them dominion over the animals (in that he will strike the head of the serpent in 3:15). It should not go unnoticed that one of the possible meanings of the Hebrew word *kap·pêr* (commonly translated as "atone") is to "cover."[24] This is also signified by the fact that animals are killed to make their clothing, suggesting (as it will become explicit in the Noahic covenant) that their dominion on the earth is being reaffirmed in their ability to kill animals.

---

specific covenantal ceremony:

> a. *bə·rît* "to cut" is used in summary description of the whole transaction recorded; b. there is a record of the divine attestation and the unalterable validity of the compact; c. more precise details are given of the mutual agreement; d. there is an oath in acknowledgment of the divine guaranteeing of correct intention; e. a sacrifice is offered; and f. the covenant brethren share a common meal. (Modified slightly; Hebrew and Greek letters transcribed into English.)

Also see Hahn, *Father Who Keeps*, 20–30. Hahn describes the difference between a covenant and a contract: 1. Covenants involve solemn oaths that curse those who break them, opposed to contracts that merely involve promises. 2. Covenants involve an exchange of persons. This is similar to what we have seen with the idea of self-donation being present in God's promises.

22. Hahn, "Broken Covenant," 428–29. Hahn thinks that the symbolism revolves around death. Perhaps, but that is not the only symbolism we will observe. Also see Hahn's aforementioned *Kinship by Covenant*. Beyond Hahn's own work, he helpfully provides the following contemporary bibliography (Hahn, "Covenant in the Old and New Testaments," 263–92): Baltzer, *Covenant Formulary*; Brueggemann, *Covenanted Self*; Cross, "Kinship and Covenant," 3–21; Dumbrell, *Covenant and Creation*; Faley, *Bonding with God*; McCarthy, *Treaty and Covenant*; McCarthy, *Old Testament Covenant*; McKenzie, *Covenant*; Mendenhall, *Law and Covenant*; Nicholson, *God and His People*; Perlitt, *Bundestheologie im Alten Testament*; Rendtorff, *Bundesformel*; Walton, *Covenant*; Weinfeld, "Covenant of Grant," 184–203; P. Williamson, *Abraham, Israel and the Nations*.

23. See *AE* 1:221–22. Luther makes a similar argument.

24. Milgrom, *Leviticus 1–16*, 1079–84.

This promise of deliverance of the whole of creation from the power of sin and its condemnation comes again in Genesis 8 and 9 in the form of the Noahic covenant. Prior to the flood Noah is told that he will be blessed by the promise of the *protevangelium* given to Adam and Eve, whereas the rest of the earth will perish: "But I will establish my covenant with you, and you shall come into the ark" (6:18).[25] In light of the fact that we are told of no other covenants than the one established with Adam and Eve in Genesis 3:15, we must assume that it is the same covenant as the *protevangelium*. After the flood, Noah makes a burnt offering (8:20). The burnt offering of animals is significant because it symbolizes the blessing of being given dominion over the animals in Genesis 1:28.[26] In effect, Noah and his sons are also given the same blessings that Adam and Eve receive: "Be fruitful and multiply and fill the earth. The fear of you and the dread of you shall be upon every beast of the earth and upon every bird of the heavens, upon everything that creeps on the ground and all the fish of the sea. Into your hand they are delivered" (Gen 9:1–2). God sets his "bow" in the sky, thereby establishing his promise of peace with every living creature (vv. 12–17).

The question nonetheless still remains as to how God will establish universal peace with his fallen creation. One must refer back to the promise of the coming "seed," which will reverse the effects of sin and make the establishment of universal peace possible. More specifically, Genesis 9 posits that God's promise of the "seed" for the restoration of universal dominion and life is given to Shem and his line (vv. 26–27). Shem will be blessed and Japheth will live in his tents. What this suggests is that Shem (the progenitor of the Semitic peoples) will finally reunite all creation in his universal reign and blessing. This includes the incorporation of the descendants of Japheth, who is the progenitor of the majority of the Gentiles.[27] Throughout the Old Testament, this coming of the messianic reign is anticipated in both Joseph's reign in Egypt (who has a coat of many colors like the rainbow and who reigns over both Egyptian Gentiles and Semites, see Gen 41–50).[28] It should also be observed that Solomon reigns over a kingdom of Israelites

25. Luther interprets the statement this way. See *AE* 2:70–73.

26. See argument in von Hofmann, *Der Schriftbeweis*, 1st ed., 2.1:143–50. Also see Hahn, *Kinship by Covenant*, 44–48. Hahn makes the interesting suggestion that animal sacrifice is also significant because it points to the destruction of idolatry. In other words, a great deal (in fact most) idol worship in the ancient world was directed to images of idols (see Rom 1:23). In Exodus, Moses tells Pharaoh that the children of Israel must take their livestock with them because sacrificial activity would offend the Egyptians (Exod 8:25–27). Hahn suggests that this occurred because the Egyptians worshiped these animals as gods. Later on, the Israelites worship a calf. On the Day of Atonement, a bull is sacrificed (Lev 16:3, 8). It is also strongly implied that they worship goats or goat gods of some sort (17:7). Two goats are offered up on the Day of Atonement (16:5).

27. The same passage condemns Ham descendants, most notably the Canaanites and the Egyptians who will be judged by God because of their wickedness. Nevertheless, Hagar the Egyptian later in Genesis is shown to be an inheritor of some of God's promises (though certainly not the promised seed as Muslims claim). Similarly, Isaiah 19:19 tells us that the Egyptians will eventually believe in the one, true God and that he will rescue them. Ultimately, as the Abrahamic covenant states and the prophets attest later on, all peoples of the earth will be blessed through Abraham and his descendants. Therefore, it appears that descendants mean those who follow his sin. Hence Ham's spiritual descendants are intended by Noah's curse. Likewise, it is obvious not all Israelites or descendants of Japheth are blessed, but only those who have faith. See Luther's argument to this effect in *AE* 2:174–86.

28. See comments in Peter Leithart, *House for My Name*, 64–65. Joseph also hearkens back to Adam,

and Gentiles (1 Kgs 1–11).[29] That Japheth will dwell in Shem's "tents" is suggestive of the participation of the Gentiles in the cult of the one God in the temple (originally a tent, the tabernacle) as is predicted in Isaiah 45.[30] This identification seems to be deepened by the fact that "Shem" means "Name," and the temple is a "house for My Name" (2 Sam 7:13).[31] In the New Testament, this is finally realized in Christ the true Temple (John 2:19–22) and his body the Church, the eschatological temple of God (Eph 2:11). Revelation 4:3 places this rainbow behind Christ and therefore sees Jesus as the ultimate fulfillment of God's promise of peace with creation.

Abraham's covenant must be thought of as a continuation of this promise, in that it reverses the curses of the Fall by making him a blessing to all nations (Gen 12:3). Abraham is also told that "kings shall come from you" (17:6).[32] We know from Genesis 49:10 that specifically an everlasting kingly line will come from Judah. This again represents a restoration of the promises made to Adam and Eve in Genesis 1. Such promises of restoration are partially fulfilled in the Davidic monarchy and finally fully fulfilled in the universal dominion of Christ (Pss 2, 110).

This covenant is confirmed in Genesis 15:9, when God tells Abraham to cut a series of animals in two and arrange them in two columns while at the same time leaving space between them. As many scholars have noted, there is evidence of this same covenant ceremony in the other cultures in the Ancient Near East, as well as the Old Testament.[33] According to many (but not all) of those who interpret the rite in this manner, the covenant ceremony referred to here consisted of the lesser party walking through the split animals and making an oath to the greater party (often a king) to the effect that they should be split in two just like the animals if they were to break the covenant. In contrast to how the covenant normally would have functioned, Abraham (clearly the lesser party) does not walk through the animals but rather falls asleep. God comes to him in a dream and promises him the land of Canaan. God's presence then appears in the form of a "smoking fire pot and a flaming torch" (Gen 15:17) and passes through the split animals. The covenant is then confirmed by God's own unilateral promise to die by being split in two if he fails to bless Abraham.[34]

This promise is confirmed again in Genesis 17 through the mark of circumcision. Circumcision is in sense a bloody sacrifice, insofar as it causes the male member to bleed.[35] The LXX more strongly emphasizes the bloody aspect of circumcision by

---

the protological priest-king and anticipates Christ, the eschatological priest-king. He not only reigns in Egypt, but he is married to the daughter of an Egyptian priest. See Gen 41:50.

29. See Leithart, *1 and 2 Kings*, 51–52.

30. Hahn, *Kinship by Covenant*, 98.

31. Kass, *Beginning of Wisdom*, 201.

32. See discussion in Hahn, *Kinship by Covenant*, 116–22.

33. Many interpretrs have acknowledged this. See Boice, *Genesis*, 118; R. Davidson, *Genesis 12–50*, 45; Gill, *Exposition of Genesis*, 271–72; Hamilton, *Book of Genesis*, 429–38; Hasel, "Meaning of the Animal Rite," 61–78; Leupold, *Genesis*, 1:480; Maher, *Genesis*, 102–4; von Rad, *Genesis*, 181; Van Seters, *Abraham in History*, 100–103; Westermann, *Genesis 12–36*, 228.

34. See argument in R. Davidson, *Genesis 12–50*, 45; Leupold, *Genesis*, 1:488–89.

35. R. Daly, *Christian Doctrine of Sacrifice*, 41–44.

translating a later passage dealing with the subject, Exodus 4:25 (which describes God's attempt to kill Moses for his tardiness in the circumcision of his son) in this way: "Behold the blood of the circumcision of my child."[36] This differs from the original Hebrew, which reads: "Surely you are a bridegroom of blood to me!" Since God's anger is abated by Moses's wife's action of circumcision, it appears that many Jews (or at very least the translators of the LXX) associated this and the blood of circumcision with propitiatory sacrifice.[37]

This makes a great deal of sense in that the act of circumcision is s sign of the coming final redemption in the Old Testament. Abraham is informed earlier that the covenant involves his "seed" (17:7, as it is found in the more literal translation of the KJV). Being that the same term is used in the *protevangelium*, and Abraham and his descendants are clearly the chosen agents to carry out this plan of redemption, we are clearly dealing with the same subject.[38] The coming seed will bless the nations by justifying and sanctifying them. Elsewhere in the Bible circumcision of the heart is a metaphor for the renewal of the mind and sanctification (Deut 10:16, 30:6; Jer 4:4). Therefore circumcision suggests new creation. It is performed on the eighth day (Gen 17:12). The eighth day is the day after the final seventh day of the original creation. Noah had eight people in the ark with him (6:9). Christ rose on the eighth day. Therefore the putting off of the flesh signifies a new and purified nature. For this reason, the sign of circumcision represents what the coming seed will accomplish.[39]

In an immediate sense, Isaac is the fruit of Abraham's body and therefore his "seed." While we might say that he does not represent the ultimate fulfillment (in light of Gal 3), Isaac still plays a role in the final confirmation of the Abrahamic covenant. In Genesis 22, after stopping Abraham from sacrificing Isaac, God speaks his promises to Abraham: "By myself I have sworn, declares the LORD, because you have done this and have not withheld your son, your only son, I will surely bless you, and I will surely multiply your offspring as the stars of heaven and as the sand that is on the seashore" (16–17). God then provides a ram caught in a bush as a sign that he will provide for the fulfillment of the promise of universal blessing: "and in your offspring shall all the nations of the earth be blessed" (v. 18).[40] Again, the promissory sign represents the content of the covenant. God will bless all nations through Abraham's seed being given over to death and returning to life (Heb 11:19). God will also work redemption by offering a substitute. This sign is also present in the Passover ritual where the lamb is substituted for the firstborn son (Exod 13:12–13).

---

36. Ibid., 42.

37. Ibid., 43.

38. Hengstenberg, *Christology of the Old Testament*, 1:53–56. Obviously the covenant between God and Abraham includes the coming of the "seed" that will bless all nations, but also the possession of the land and the many descendants. This is, quite literally, fulfilled in the exodus and growth of the nation in the Old Testament history. It is spiritually fulfilled in Christ through all who have faith becoming heirs to the promise (as Paul shows in Galatians and Romans) and through the possession of the new heavens and earth. The land of Israel is of course included within the whole of creation.

39. Leupold, *Genesis*, 1:520–21.

40. See discussion in Hahn, *Kinship by Covenant*, 123–30.

Beyond these examples, the idea of the death and resurrection of a beloved son also carries over into the other narratives in Genesis and the story of the Passover. These historical events serve as signs to the patriarchs that God is faithful to his promises to preserve the holy seed. In this manner, these narratives serve the same function as the promissory signs. Jon Levenson has drawn attention to the fact that there is an overall pattern of death and resurrection of a beloved son throughout Genesis.[41] Jacob goes to a far off land and returns to his family before his father's death (Gen 35:27). Joseph is sold into slavery and believed dead, but then is returned to his father Israel (formerly Jacob) in his old age (Gen 45). Although Levenson does not mention the exodus, the death and resurrection of the beloved son can be seen here as well. YHWH describes Israel as "my firstborn Son" (Exod 4:22). Slavery is a contradiction to their true creaturely status as God's viceroys in creation (Gen 1:26–28) and it is therefore a living death. The exodus means new life of God's firstborn son Israel.

Surveying this history of covenant sacrifice, the content of the divine promise that they represent becomes clear. These sacrifices point ahead to the promise of the covering of humanity's shame through sacrifice (Gen 3:21), the renewal of creation and universal peace through an act of sacrifice (8:20, 9:12–17), the restoration of human dominion and blessing (9:1–2), the promise of the death of God himself (15), the coming of the holy seed (17), a father offering his only son in the form of sacrifice (22), the offering of a substitute (Gen 22, Exod 13), and the death and resurrection of a beloved son (Gen 22, 35, 45, and the whole exodus narrative). Seen from the proper perspective of the New Testament, all these signs find their fulfillment and perfectly prefigure the person and work of Christ.

The Sinaitic covenant differs from the Abrahamic covenant in that it is a bilateral covenant, whereas the latter is a unilateral covenant (more appropriately, a testament, Gal 3:15–18). The covenantal ceremony clearly symbolizes this as well. We are told in Exodus 24:6–7 that Moses confirmed the Sinaitic covenant through the sacrifice of bulls. Half of the blood of the bulls was sprinkled on the altar (a sign of God's presence), while the other half was sprinkled on the people. If the life of the animal was in the blood, the sprinkling of the blood signifies the offering of one's life to live by the covenant.[42] Hahn also convincingly argues that the sacrifice of the bull is also significant because it represents what will happen to those who violate the covenant.[43]

As was previously noted in the introduction, the Abrahamic covenant stands in a kind of existential conflict with the Sinaitic covenant. The Sinaitic covenant is bilateral and therefore demands obedience on the part of Israel for its fulfillment. This means it demands the self-dedication and the self-giving of Israel to YHWH. The history of the Fall and the exodus narratives clearly demonstrate that Israel cannot do this. Furthermore, Deuteronomy 27–32 (after the Sinaitic covenant's restatement and renewal in the second generation) emphasizes the impossibility of the fulfillment of the covenant (without the circumcision of the heart, see 30:6) and plans for the covenant's obsolescence. The Abrahamic covenant, on the other hand, involves the self-donation of God

---

41. Levenson, *Death and Resurrection*, 55–143.

42. Noth, *Exodus*, 198.

43. Hahn, "Broken Covenant," 429.

and giving of the divine being to his people in the form of a promise. To engage in an act of unilateral promise is an act of self-donation. By making such a promise, God pledges his entire being to the task of fulfilling the terms of the promise. The biblical texts recognize this and therefore in making covenants (Gen 22:16) and sending forth his redemptive Word of grace (Isa 45:23), God repeatedly states: "I swear by myself." Particularly within the cultural context of the Ancient Near East, to swear by one's self is therefore to give the whole self over to curse and death, as we observed in the covenantal ceremony of Genesis 15.[44]

In Exodus 40, the self-donation of God in the confirmation of the promise also takes the form of the descent of the divine presence into the tabernacle. This descent of the divine *kavod* prefigures the incarnation. Therefore the New Testament and the church fathers rightly see the ceremonies of Leviticus (that center around this pre-Incarnation-incarnation) as being shadows of the work of Christ. In fact, as we will see, the New Testament identifies Jesus with the *kavod*, and therefore the preincarnate Christ is the agent who gives his righteousness to humanity before and after the incarnation. In this, God becomes present to Israel as a sign of his unilateral commitment to them by the giving of the divine being to them. By this action, God enables the cult, which as we will show below, is meant to channel his holiness to Israel. Giving his own holiness to Israel, YHWH acknowledges that his people do not possess holiness of their own.[45]

YHWH himself is holy and therefore gives his holiness to Israel, thereby making them holy: "I am the LORD who sanctifies Israel" (Ezek 37:28). As John Kleinig has shown, holiness is not a demand per se, in that it is not something humans produce or generate.[46] Rather, it is something God alone possesses: "The Lord alone is inherently and permanently holy. His holiness is his godliness, his nature, and his power as God. It is inseparable from him and his presence." For this reason, "Holiness is derived only from him. People and things borrow their holiness from their association with him at Mount Sinai and at the sanctuary."[47] Therefore, holiness is properly defined as God's otherness and godliness, including his righteousness and moral perfection.

Such a share in God's uncreated righteousness and glory is not generated by human activity, but rather is received passively. Humans of course can lose such a share in God's own holiness if they do not remain with the boundaries that God has established and consecrated: "Consecrate yourselves, therefore, and be holy, for I am the LORD your God. Keep my statutes and do them; *I am the Lord who sanctifies you*" (Lev 20:7–8, emphasis added). Violating God's commandments and opposing the proper boundaries of creation moves Israel out of the realm of God's holiness and into the realm of uncleanness. Becoming unclean causes Israel to be destroyed by God's holiness and unable to

---

44. See general discussion of divine swearing in the Abrahamic covenant in Hahn, *Kinship by Covenant*, 103–11.

45. For discussions of the divine presence in the temple, Charles Gieschen helpfully lists the following (Gieschen, "Real Presence of the Son," 108): Adams, "Present God," 279–94; Phythian-Adams, *People and the Presence*; Congar, *Mystery of the Temple*; Clements, *God and Temple*; Hummel, *Word Becoming Flesh*, 78–79; Terrien, *Elusive Presence*.

46. Kleinig, *Leviticus*, 4–13.

47. Ibid., 5.

participate in his holiness (Lev 10; 1 Sam 6; 2 Sam 6). God enacts the cult to maintain his promise of self-donating holiness to Israel. By participating in God's own holiness and not placing blocks in front of the flow of divine holiness, Israel maintains itself within the realm of the clean (holy and clean, and common and clean, as opposed to common and unclean).[48] This means primarily (as Kleinig has convincingly argued) avoiding idolatry and being weaned off of animistic modes of thought.[49] This way of understanding the divine-human relationship forms the first set of rationales for the ritual laws of the Pentateuch.

Expanding on Hahn's earlier suggestion regarding covenantal sacrifice, we can shed much light on the need for atoning sacrifice.[50] Atoning sacrifice prefigures the final new testament of forgiveness. Such a new testament represents the resolution in the tension between the Abrahamic and Siniatic covenants (Rom 3:25, 8:3–4). In effect, atoning sacrifice would be impossible if it were not for a prior commitment of God to Israel. It too represents the content of the two great covenants. It enacts the judgment of the Sinaitic code on a substitute in order to maintain the life of Israel promised in the Abrahamic covenant. It also represents God's own giving of an atoning sacrifice to Israel: "For the life of the flesh is in the blood, and I have given it for you on the altar to *make atonement for your souls, for it is the blood that makes atonement by the life*" (Lev 17:11, emphasis added). Moreover, atoning sacrifice represents and mediates the self-donation of God's own holiness to his people.[51]

Regarding the specifics of blood atonement, we should observe that this category of sacrifice comprised a number of different kinds of offerings: sin offerings (Lev 4:1—5:13, 6:24–30, 8:14–17, 16:3–22) and guilt offerings (5:14—6:7, 7:1–6).[52] Offerings for guilt involve the death of an animal, and just as in Genesis 3, humanity's disobedience resulted in their condemnation to death (Gen 3:19). All sin for Israel is tied up with the rejection of the creator who is the source of life. That all sin is ultimately sin against God is expressed most clearly in the fact that the first commandment recorded in Exodus is the prohibition of idolatry and apostasy (Exod 20:3). Hence, just as with regard to civil matters where Israel is to take an "eye for eye, tooth for tooth, hand for hand, foot for foot" (21:24), so too the rejection of God (the source of life) must result in death. In the book of Genesis it is not insignificant that animal sacrifice is first instituted in connection with God's authorization of *lex talionis*: "And for your lifeblood I will require a reckoning: from every beast I will require it and from man. From his fellow man I will require a reckoning for the life of man. Whoever sheds the blood of man, by man shall his blood be shed, for God made man in his own image" (Gen 9:5–6). The only way to

48. Ibid., 6.

49. Ibid., 4–6.

50. For a discussion of atoning sacrifice in Leviticus, see Balentine, *Leviticus*, 125–49; Bonar, *Book of Leviticus*, 300–20; Kiuchi, *Leviticus*, 32–46, 288–326; Levine, *Leviticus*, 100–117; Noth, *Leviticus*, 115–32; Radner, *Leviticus*, 284–99; Rooker, *Leviticus*, 211–37.

51. Hengstenberg, *Christology of the Old Testament*, 4:293–323. This was the approach of all pre-critical Christian orthodoxy, notably also Lutheran orthodoxy. See Franz, *Commentarius in Leviticum*. And also see J. Osiander, *Commentarii in Pentateuchum Pars Tertia*.

52. See very good discussion of sacrifice in Leithart, *House for My Name*, 87–95.

remedy sin is the substitution of life through the pouring of blood. This necessarily occurs through animal sacrifice, since as YHWH states, "the life of the flesh is in the blood" (Lev 17:11). For this reason, sacrifice for sin means a separation of blood from the flesh and not simply the death of the animal.

The choices of blood atonement and animal sacrifice are important for a number of other reasons. First, since blood contains life, it cries out and thereby gives a testimony. When Cain kills Abel, God tells Cain, "The voice of your brother's blood is crying to me from the ground" (4:10). Later the Epistle to the Hebrews tells us that Christ's blood also cries out and thereby "Jesus, the mediator of a new covenant, and to the sprinkled blood that *speaks a better word than the blood of Abel*" (Heb 12:24, emphasis added). Living blood therefore gives testimony of forgiveness that has been paid for. In the case of covenants, it also stands as a witness to the truthfulness of the divine promise.

Secondly, the choice of animals as sacrifices for sins (as opposed to, for example, grain offerings) is not arbitrary, but represents the restoration of human vocation in creation. As we noted earlier, the first real animal sacrifices by Noah coincide with the reiteration of the promises of dominion over creation given to Adam and Eve. In killing the animal, not only are the sins paid for by substitution, but humans are restored to their position of dominion in creation by being given the right and ability to kill the animals (Gen. 9:2). Where there is the forgiveness of sins, as Luther notes, there is also life and salvation.[53]

There has been some controversy whether or not these passages state that the blood actually atones for sin. John Kleinig comments on the grammatical construction in the passage above and states that the verse "presupposes that the life of the animal substitutes for the life of those who present the animal for sacrifice."[54] The meaning of the Hebrew word for "atone" (*kap·pêr*) here has frequently been disputed, since it is used differently in a number of other contexts in the Old Testament.[55] Nevertheless, it appears to have the very definite meaning of an atoning payment of sacrificial blood in the context of Leviticus.[56] Working from the varieties of meaning that the term has in other Old Testament books, liberal scholar Jacob Milgrom considers the best translations to be to "cover," "wipe away," or "smear" all of which have connotations of the removal of sin through cleansing blood.[57] Therefore, even if one were to accept this wider variety of meaning as applicable to the Leviticus usage (which as Kleinig points out, is very difficult to do), these usages still bear the connotation of propiatory sacrifice when read within the context of Leviticus and the larger Pentateuch's notion of *lex talionis*. In other

53. SC 6; *CT* 557.

54. Kleinig, *Leviticus*, 357.

55. Ibid., 117.

56. Ibid., 357.

57. Milgrom, *Leviticus1–16*, 1079–84. In spite of the connotations that Milgrom's translation suggests, he still considers the idea of the "sin offering" to be erroneous and theologically "foreign" (254) to Leviticus. He believes that the offering has nothing to do with personal guilt, but rather has the function of the "ritual detergent" of sacred space. Japanese scholar Nobuyoshi Kiuchi, who points to the fact that the texts of Leviticus are extremely clear that sin offerings are meant to cleanse from personal guilt, challenges this interpretation (held by several other scholars as well). See his masterful *Purification Offering*. Also see Kleinig, *Leviticus*, 117.

words, for Leviticus it is through blood and propiatory sacrifice that God "covers" and "wipes away" human sin. This is in fact really the only appropriate interpretation in that the text of Leviticus explicitly states that this is the function of the sacrifices and hence there can be little ambiguity that the term is meant to be understood this way. Therefore Kleinig concludes: "The legislation for the sin offering quite explicitly states its theological function. The Lord instituted this sacrifice for the performance of atonement and the reception of forgiveness from it."[58] Beyond this, there is also extra-biblical evidence that the sacrifices were understood this way. Josephus, who served as a priest in the Second Temple at the time of Jesus, quite explicitly understands the sacrifices as working atonement in this manner.[59] His remarks shed light not only on how sacrifice was understood in the priestly tradition passed down to him, but also how Jews in general and the New Testament authors in particular understood atoning sacrifice.

The propiatory and substitutionary nature of blood sacrifice is made even clearer by the consequences of sins that went unatoned. Sacrifice was a way of atoning for only some sins, but not others. Unintentional sins, though still worthy of death, could be atoned through substitutionary sacrifice. Intentional sins could not be atoned. Since all sin was worthy of death, intentional sins (no matter how trivial by the standards of human judgment) could only be met with capital punishment.[60] From this fact it is clear that in the sin offerings of Leviticus, forgiveness is not merely conveyed, retributive justice is also satisfied.

Other features of Israelite atonement theology should be recognized. Within Israelite cultic life, a wide variety of sacrifices (particularly sacrifices atoning for sin) also symbolically united in themselves both righteousness and sin. The Passover sacrifice (a substitutionary sacrifice for the life of the firstborn) was enacted by the sacrifice of a lamb without blemish, suggesting cultic and moral holiness. At the same time, the lamb was killed as a substitute of the firstborn male livestock and children of Israel, whom God insists must be ransomed: "you shall set apart to the LORD all that first opens the womb. All the firstborn of your animals that are males shall be the LORD's. Every firstborn of a donkey you shall redeem with a lamb, or if you will not redeem it you shall break its neck. Every firstborn of man among your sons you shall redeem" (Exod 13:12–13). Therefore, the lamb who united both purity and condemnation in itself served as the sacrifice to redeem the firstborn of Israel.

A similar pattern may be seen in the ritual of the Day of Atonement.[61] First, the high priest had to be pure before he was capable of administering the rite. In order to

---

58. Kleinig, *Leviticus*, 117.

59. *Antiquities of the Jews*, 7.13.4, in Josephus, *Works of Josephus*, 206. We read: "and he [David] built an altar, he performed divine service, and brought a burnt offering, and offered peace offerings also. With *these God was pacified, and became gracious to them again*" (emphasis added). Also see E. Sanders, *Judaism*, 106–7, 251–57. Sanders has some doubts about how much sacrifice was seen as propitiation, but adds some good facts to the discussion. Also see the older and somewhat outdated, but essentially correct assessment of the nature of sacrifice in Kurtz, *Der Mosaische Opfer*.

60. See discussion in Kleinig, *Leviticus*, 100, 123, 136, 119–20. For unintentional sins see Lev 4:2, 13, 22, 27. For intentional sins see Num 15:27–31. Though it is not clear how much in actual practice this was really carried out.

61. See discussions of the Day of Atonement in Hartley, *Leviticus*, 201–16; Kiuchi, *Leviticus*, 288–311;

gain this purity, he was instructed to sacrifice a bull for himself and his household (Lev 16:6). Nevertheless he must also be a sin bearer by placing his hands on the scapegoat and confessing the sins of Israel over the animal (vv. 20–22).[62] In this, the high priest unites both holiness and sin in his person. The two goats within the ritual also continue this pattern. One goat was sacrificed for the sins of Israel without having those sins pronounced over him. The blood of this animal made atonement for Israel by being placed upon the mercy seat, that is, the cover of the ark of the covenant in the holy of holies where the divine *kavod* is hidden within a cloud of incense (vv.15–17). The other goat, (the scapegoat who has the sins of Israel confessed over him) then escaped condemnation for sin, but at the same time was consigned to the oblivion of the wilderness thereby carrying the sins of the people with him (vv. 20–22). The two goats therefore represent both sin and purity united with one another.

That the high priest moves into the holy of holies through the blood of this goat on the Day of Atonement appears to lend further evidence to Fletcher-Louis's thesis that the high priest represents a new Adam. Though Fletcher-Louis does not make this direct connection, it could be suggested that just as Adam withdrew and "hid from the Lord God" (Gen 3:8) as a result of breaking the law, the high priest moves back into the representation of Eden (the holy of holies) and into the divine presence, through the fulfillment of the law. Interpreted in this manner, the ritual itself appears to be a representation of the end of universal exile. In enacting this ritual then, the high priest represents both Israel's sin and the actualization of its righteousness.

The high priest also represents the righteousness of God before God in having graciously enacted the cult to save his people from judgment. Fletcher-Louis states that "the high priest brings the one creator God to Israel and to the created world. He is the embodiment of God's Glory."[63] We may observe this first by looking at the high priest's consecration and clothing. The anointing oil consecrates the priest (Lev 8:10–13). It could very well be argued that this makes him glow in a similar fashion to the divine *kavod*. Also, much of the high priest's clothing is made out of gold which is again suggestive of divine glory. As Fletcher-Louis puts it, he wears "garments of glory."[64] He wears a golden diadem with the divine Name engraved on it (Exod 39:30).[65] He also wears a golden ephod (vv. 2–7). The ephod is particularly significant not only because it is

---

Kleinig, *Leviticus*, 327–353; Rodriguez, "Leviticus 16," 269–86.

62. See the following sources on the scapegoat: Westbrook and Lewis, "Who Led the Scapegoat?," 417–422; McLean, "Revision of Scapegoat Terminology," 168–73; Roo, "Was the Goat?," 233–42; Feinberg, "Scapegoat of Leviticus Sixteen," 320–33; R. Helm, "Azazel in Early Jewish Tradition," 217–26; Grabbe, "Scapegoat Tradition," 152–67.

63. Fletcher-Louis, "Jesus and the High Priest," 6.

64. Ibid.

65. The engraving on the diadem of the high priest in Exod 39 is typically translated as "Holy to YHWH." This disagrees with *Antiquities of the Jews*, 3.7.6, in Josephus, *Works of Josephus*, 90, and *Jewish War*, 5.5.7, in Josephus, *Works of Josephus*, 708. Josephus claims there that it is merely the Tetragrammaton that appears on the high priest's diadem. This discrepancy can be resolved by suggesting that the Exodus text might be translated as "the holy inscription: 'YHWH.'" J. E. Hodd has convincingly argued that Exodus should be interpreted in the direction of the later evidence from Josephus and other Jewish sources. See. Hodd, "Note on Two Points," 74–75.

golden (suggesting divine glory), but in the Ancient Near East, it is now generally agreed that ephods were originally coverings of idols or garments worn by deities.[66] The use of incense is also suggestive: "On the stage of the cultic microcosm he is the creator. He is the divine warrior, who is surrounded by clouds of incense (Exod 40:27, 34; 1 Kgs 8:10; 2 Chr 5:11; Lev 9:22–24, 16:12–13)."[67] Fletcher-Louis also mentions that he carries "fiery coals, dressed in garb that (according to Josephus B.J. 5:231, *Ant.* 3:184) symbolizes thunder and lightning, his garments sprinkled with the blood of God's victories (Exod 29:19–21; cf. esp. Isa 63:1–6, but also Deut 33:2–3; Judg 4–5; Ps 68:8–9, 18)."[68] His clothing then makes him, according to Fletcher-Louis, "the true idol, the image (Gen 1:26–27) of the one creator God . . . [he is effectively] . . . the "statue" of the living God."[69] Therefore, just as the statue or image of the deity in the Ancient Near East stood in the sanctuary (being representative of heaven), so Adam in the original creation and the high priest on the Day of Atonement stood in the divine sanctuary as the divine image.[70]

As God within the cosmic microcosm, the high priest's actions repeat the work of Genesis 1. Just as sin destroyed God's original order, so the sacrifice of the Day of Atonement within the cosmic microcosm renews creation. By purifying creation from sin, the high priest prefigured the eschatological renewal of God through the giving of his personal holiness through bloody sacrifice. The work of the Day of Atonement is also suggestive of the role of the divine warrior, who, much like the *protevanglium* promises, overcomes the negative effects of the serpent in creation. As we will see below, there is a significant connection between high priestly figures in Old Testament prophecy with the theme of the divine warrior.

Cosmological renewal is a theme elsewhere tied to sacrifice in the Old Testament. We should mention in passing, that Levenson has argued that the sacrifice of Passover is strongly tied to the reintegration of the created order.[71] Though he does not draw out all the implications of this, we might point out that the plagues of Egypt result in the systematic de-creation of that civilization through the different powers of nature. Such judgment culminates in the return of the Egyptians to watery depths of chaos in the Red Sea (echoing the original creation of Genesis 1 and the destruction of the first creation in Genesis 6–8), whereas the Israelites, freed through the substitution of the paschal lamb, are brought to Sinai. At Sinai they are established as the true worshiping community, and build the tabernacle, the microcosm of the original creation. This furthers reinforces Israel's identification as the true reconstituted humanity and suggests that the exodus was a recapitulation of creation.[72]

---

66. Fletcher-Louis, "High Priest as Divine Mediator," 188–89.

67. Fletcher-Louis, "Jesus and the High Priest," 6.

68. Ibid.

69. Ibid., 6–7.

70. Beale, *Temple*, 83. Beale makes a similar observation about divine kingship in the Ancient Near East. The divine king would stand for the living image of the god.

71. Levenson, *Creation*, 74–77.

72. See similar observations regarding the unity of cult and creation in Prenter, *Creation and Redemption*, 193–97.

The priestly mediation was not successful throughout the Old Testament. As early as the priesthood of Eli, the ministrations of the priests were condemned and it is prophesied that YHWH "will raise up for [himself] . . . a faithful priest, who shall do according to what is in my heart and in my mind. And I will build him a sure house, and he shall go in and out before my anointed forever" (1 Sam 2:35). Though this prophecy might find a preliminary fulfillment in God's choice of the line of Zadok later in the narrative, as we will see later in the writings of the New Testament (particularly Hebrews), there is recognition that the priesthood would need a final fulfillment and renewal by the Messiah.

Ultimately, the mediation of the priesthood could not hold off the exile. Furthermore, the priesthood could not by its own ministrations communicate holiness, but rather was dependent on God's presence and justifying power. Beyond the texts in Leviticus we have examined, in Zechariah 3, the Angel of YHWH purifies the high priest Joshua so that cult will be able to function. What this suggests is that the Angel of YHWH is present in (as the *kavod*) and enables the cult.[73] He is also a heavenly high priest in that he cleanses the earthly high priest from his sins. In the same manner that he functions as heavenly high priest, he also functions as a prophet speaking to the patriarchs (Gen 18, 22) and a heavenly king, leading the armies of YHWH (Exod 23, Josh 5, Dan 10).[74] Daniel 10:4 in particular suggests that the Angel of YHWH (who here is pictured dressed in the robes of a high priest) is at the same time the leader of YHWH's heavenly armies (Dan 10:20).[75] In this passage, the Angel of YHWH possesses the dual roles of a heavenly priest and king, also held by the mysterious "lord" of Psalm 110.

The heavenly high priest, the Angel of YHWH, also appears to be identical with the "one like a Son of Man" in Daniel 7. As Fletcher-Louis notes, the Son of Man must be a high priestly figure because he undoes all the impurity in creation (symbolized by the mixed animal breeds that come from the sea) by coming on clouds (reminiscent of clouds of incense that the high priest rides within upon entering the holy of holies on the Day of Atonement) while entering into the divine presence.[76] He is also given universal dominion (7:14) a prerogative of the Israelite king/Messiah described in Psalm 2:2, and a position held by the protological high priest Adam in Genesis 1:28. This figure must also be identified with the divine *kavod*, because he comes on the glory cloud, which is a sign of the glorious divine presence from elsewhere in the Old Testament (see Exod 40; 1 Kgs 7–8). Moreover, as a human figure he is pictured in an almost identical way to the vision Ezekiel has of the divine *kavod* in Ezekiel 1–2.[77] Again, all these prophetic visions bear a striking resemblance to the figure that appears in Psalm 110. Here the psalm refers to a

---

73. See Hengstenberg, *Christology of the Old Testament*, 3:283–89.

74. See discussion in Harstad, *Joshua*, 252–55. See also Hengstenberg, *Christology of the Old Testament*, 1:128. Hengstenberg connects this with Matt 26:53 where Jesus claims the role of being the leader of the heavenly hosts.

75. Steinmann, *Daniel*, 489.

76. Fletcher-Louis, "High Priest as a Divine Mediator," 169–74.

77. See Gieschen, *Angelomorphic Christology*, 80–89; Hengstenberg, *Christology of the Old Testament*, 3:75–76; Steinmann, *Daniel*, 490. Also see Mitchell, *Song of Songs*, 921–22, 944–61. Mitchell connects this figure with the angel of Rev 10, and suggests that both are Christ. Also see discussion of the christological nature of the Ezekiel vision in Hummel, *Ezekiel*, 1:49–50.

heavenly figure who is both the "lord" (v. 1) at the right hand of God and also a "priest forever after the order of Melchizedek" (v. 4).[78]

Not only does the Old Testament suggest that there is a parallel between the earthly high priest and a heavenly high priest who is the Angel of YHWH/*kavod*, but it predicts an eschatological fulfillment to priestly mediation. We are told in Numbers 25:13 that God has promised the Levites an eternal priesthood.[79] Nevertheless, the priesthood still is under the Sinaitic covenant and its curses. If so, then the whole of the priesthood's failure and sinfulness would logically disqualify them to possess a perpetual priesthood as it did with the house of Eli in 1 Samuel. To maintain the promise of eternal priesthood, God must act to purify creation and to make the priesthood function in a final eschatological act.

Such an implicit eschatological expectation becomes more explicit in the writings of the later prophets. In Malachi 3:3, we are told that God himself will come to purify the sons of Levi.[80] The text also tells us that God himself will come to his temple to purify it in the form of the Angel of the Lord: "Behold, I send my messenger [or "My Angel"], and he will prepare the way before me. And the Lord whom you seek *will suddenly come to his temple; and the messenger of the covenant* [or "Angel of the Covenant"] in whom you delight, behold, he is coming, says the LORD of hosts" (Mal 3:1, emphasis added).[81] This connects with the expectation of the return of God to Zion, found in Isaiah 40 and Ezekiel 37–39.[82] In Zechariah 3, we are told that the Angel of YHWH's purification of the high priest (v. 8) prefigures God's eschatological action of redemption: "I will remove the iniquity of this land in a single day" (v. 9).[83]

Descriptions of the actions of the eschatological high priest are scattered throughout the Old Testament in a variety of interconnected texts. As we have already noted, the Servant of YHWH in the later chapters of Isaiah is identified as the new Passover lamb, necessitated by the new exodus. He is, as we have also suggested, identified in chapters 49 and 63 with the Angel of YHWH and the *kavod*. This identification is deepened by the description of the Angel of YHWH in Isaiah 63:9 as possessing both robes soaked in blood (63:2) and the role of the divine warrior (vv. 1–5), much like Leviticus's portrayal of the high priest. As was previously noted, the Angel of YHWH is also said in Isaiah 63:9 to be afflicted with the afflictions of the people in order to redeem them. Isaiah then hearkens back to the time of the exodus and states that this same angel (as is clear from the text of the Pentateuch as well) guided and redeemed Israel in the first exodus. He is described as being "his [God's] glorious arm" (v. 12). This is identical with

---

78. See argument in favor of traditional messianic interpretation in Leupold, *Psalms*, 770–78. Also see discussions of Melchizedek in Fitzmyer, "Melchizedek," 63–69; McNamara, "Melchizedek," 1–31; Rooke, "Jesus as Royal Priest," 81–94.

79. One might ask how a promise of an eternal priesthood squares with Christ's own priesthood in the NT. Although Christ was not a Levite (Heb 7:14), all who are in him are eternally priests (1 Pet 2:9, Rev 5:10) and therefore Christ's eschatological priesthood fulfills this promise to the Levites who have faith in him as their eternal high priest.

80. Hengstenberg, *Christology of the Old Testament*, 4:172–75.

81. Ibid., 4:167–71.

82. Ibid., 4:162.

83. Leupold, *Zechariah*, 77–78.

the description of the Servant in Isaiah 53:1 as "the arm of the LORD." This wording therefore further identifies the sufferings of the Angel of YHWH and the Servant, and thereby positively demonstrates them to be the same figure. In the same way also atonement leads to a universal Jubilee. We are told that the Servant announces such a Jubilee in Isaiah 61 and that he will justify many in chapter 53.[84]

Isaiah 53, 61, and 63 find an intertextual echo in Daniel 7 and 9.[85] The *kavod* is described as functioning in Daniel 7 as a universal and heavenly high priest coming to God's throne to enact a universal Day of Atonement. If the Son of Man comes to God's throne, he must like the earthly high priest on the Day of Atonement possess an offering to make to God. Like the suffering Servant, he therefore implicitly makes "intercession for the transgressors" (Isa 53:12) by this offering. The Son of Man is also exalted to the divine throne in the same manner as the Servant, who after his sufferings has a "portion with the many" (v. 12). In light of the New Testament's identification (which we will examine below) and these striking parallels, we must posit that this text is suggesting that the Son of Man is the same person being spoken of in Isaiah 53 as the Servant.

Daniel 9 also describes these same themes of eschatological atonement and redemption. We are told: "Seventy weeks are decreed about your people and your holy city, to finish the transgression, to put an end to sin, and to atone for iniquity, to bring in everlasting righteousness, to seal both vision and prophet, and to anoint a most holy place" (Dan 9:24). Seventy "sevens" (or "weeks" as the KJV translates) represent the fulfillment of ten Jubilees (Lev 25). The number appears to suggest not an actual timeline, but rather symbolically conveys a supreme and definitive Jubilee.[86] The finality of this Jubilee is deepened by the statement that in this period there will be an "end of transgression" and the establishment of "everlasting righteousness." The agent of this transformation must be a divine and heavenly high priest (described as the Son of Man earlier), since God alone can bring "everlasting righteousness."[87] This also parallels the "year of the Lord's favor" of Isaiah 61 enacted by the Servant.

The seventy weeks (or as it is restated "sixty-two sevens and seven-sevens, i.e., sixty nine sevens, that is, a "seven" before ultimate fulfillment) will culminate in the coming of the "anointed one, a prince" (v. 25).[88] This prince or anointed one "will confirm a covenant with many" (v. 27), which will end sacrifice. The confirmation of this covenant is presumably tied up with a new order of redemption.[89] Because of the universal Day of Atonement and a supreme Jubilee, sacrifice for the sake of atonement will no longer

---

84. See discussion in Bergsma, *Jubilee from Leviticus to Qumran*, 198–203.

85. Keil, *Biblical Commentary on Daniel*, 270–75, 320–402.

86. See Collins, *Daniel*, 352; Hengstenberg, *Christology of the Old Testament*, 3:89–90. See Leupold, *Daniel*, 408–9. Leupold disagrees with the reference of Jubilee, but considers the numbers of seven and ten as emblematic of the highest perfection of divine work. Either interpretation fits with our insistence that it does not refer to literal time, but to the divine completion of redemption.

87. Hengstenberg, *Christology of the Old Testament*, 3:100–102.

88. Ibid., 3:117–21.

89. Hengstenberg, *Christology of the Old Testament*, 3:142–46; Steinmann, *Daniel*, 474–76. For an alternative view, see Leupold, *Daniel*, 431–32. Leupold holds that it is in fact the antichrist who is making the covenant in order to imitate Christ.

be necessary.[90] The anointed one is therefore also identical with the Servant who is a "covenant to the nations," the "Angel of the covenant" of Malachi 3, and the prophet like Moses of Deuteronomy 18. He is indeed like Moses, in that he also mediates a covenant. Lastly, since this covenant is tied up with "ending sacrifice" and bringing "everlasting righteousness" (i.e., forgiveness and sanctification), it must be thought to be identical with Jeremiah's new covenant. This parallel is further suggested by the fact that Daniel at the beginning of the chapter is reading a scroll of Jeremiah (v. 2). Part of God's promise to Jeremiah regarding the new covenantal order is that Israel will never lack a priestly mediator to stand before him (Jer 33:18). This finds fulfillment in the announcement that the anointed one "will be cut off and will have nothing" (Dan 9:26).[91] This again directly parallels the fate of the Servant of Isaiah 53 (who is also "cut off" v. 8), and implicitly the Son of Man of Daniel 7 (who as we saw, has an offering to offer the Ancient of Days). For this reason, the anointed one must be both the heavenly high priest, who is the Angel of YHWH/*kavod*, and the eschatological suffering Servant, who brings about a new covenant through his earthly vicarious suffering and death. In a word, this must be the "seed of the woman," whom we know to be Christ.[92]

Kingly Mediation

Walter Brueggemann has appropriately emphasized the need for a kingly mediator who arises within Judges and 1 Samuel as a response to the problem of military subjugation by neighboring civilizations.[93] Nevertheless, it must also be observed that this kingly mediation ultimately has the same goal in mind as the prophetic and priestly mediations. As Rolf Rendtorff accurately notes, the book of Judges presents us with a continuous cycle of Israel's apostasy to foreign gods and its subsequent conquest by the other peoples of the land.[94] Such apostasy, notes Rendtorff, also has the aspect of the failure of Israel in its vocation, that is, the conquest of Palestine to the end of the expulsion of false foreign gods.[95] The author of the book of Judges views the conquest by foreign peoples as the punishment for the failure on the part of Israel to live by the divine grace of election, and thereby act as a true worshiping community that destroys and expels idolatry.

This places the kingship as a response to the conquest of foreign powers in a new light. If conquest is the response to apostasy, then military success and the expulsion of hostile pagan peoples logically means the expulsion of idolatry and the establishment of the true worship. True worship is the vocation of Israel as a priestly nation. It also means to establish creation in true rest from their enemies, as many biblical texts emphasize.[96]

90. Hengstenberg, *Christology of the Old Testament*, 3:146–48.

91. See Keil, *Daniel*, 360–62; Steinmann, *Daniel*, 474–76. Also see Pitre, *Jesus, the Tribulation*, 51–62. Pitre holds this text to directly predict a suffering Messiah who atones for sin.

92. See comments in Keil, *Commentary on Daniel*, 354–55.

93. Brueggemann, *Theology of the Old Testament*, 601.

94. Rendtorff, *Canonical Hebrew Bible*, 101.

95. Ibid. Also see Exod 23:32, 34:12; Deut 7:1–5.

96. Exod 33:14; Deut 12:9–10, 25:19; Josh 1:13, 15, 11:23, 14:15, 21:44, 22:4, 23:1; 2 Sam 7:11–12; 1 Kgs 5:41, 8:56; 1 Chr 22:9.

Such a rest, as we shall see, prefigures the true and eternal Sabbath of the people of God at the eschaton.

The book of Judges also demonstrates the need within Israel for the institution of the monarchy with the oft repeated refrain that "everyone did as he saw fit" (Judg 21:25). If Israel could not receive the law or obey the law, then it must be necessary for the law to be enforced. Deuteronomy emphasizes that the king is subject to the rule of the revealed law of Moses. He must keep his own copy of the law and study it diligently (Deut 17:18–20). The so-called Deuteronomistic history characterizes the rule of any given king as either righteous or unrighteous to the extent that they enforce the worship of the true God. Solomon initially comes off well insofar as he who builds the temple. Early in 1 Kings he is described as an embodiment of divine wisdom. Similarly, Josiah, who is described in 2 Kings as the most righteous of all the later kings (2 Kgs 23:25) is the one who purifies the Israelite cult and nation from idolatry (vv. 24–25).

Initially 1 Samuel reports that YHWH is not pleased with the prospect of a king. This is because it represents a rejection of God's own divine kingship (1 Sam 8:7). It should be observed that this does not mean that God will not use the people's apostasy to his own ends. Similarly, Peter Leithart points out that this does not necessarily mean that God rejects the entire notion of kingship, as has frequently been asserted by liberal biblical scholars.[97] Deuteronomy, as we have previously seen, assumes that the Israelites will eventually have a king. It would appear then that God does not like the idea simply because the occasion for kingship shows their lack of trust in his gracious rule. Such rejection has come about not only because of Israel's apostasy, but also the failure of previous mediators to fulfill the law on Israel's behalf. Eli the high priest, who does not curb the corruption of his sons, is a prime example of this (2:12–36). Similarly, Samuel the prophet does not curb his sons' corrupt actions (8:1–2).[98] From 1 Samuel it is therefore clear that both priestly and prophetic forms of mediation have failed. Such failure has resulted in Israel's continuing apostasy.

Despite God's initial hostility to the idea of kingship, the author of 1 and 2 Samuel shows that God uses kingship in Israel as a means of mediating both his presence and will to Israel. In fulfilling this vocation, the kingly mediators of Israel are described as uniting and representing God and Israel, much like the prophetic and priestly mediators. David fights the battles of YHWH throughout 1 and 2 Samuel, and thereby disestablishes idolatry and establishes the true cult of YHWH. In this, David becomes a temporal embodiment of the Angel of YHWH, who is as we have seen, the primary agent of Israel's conquest (Exod 23, 33; Josh 5). In fact, on a number of occasions he is compared to an angel of God (1 Sam 29:9; 2 Sam 14:17, 19:27), although it is not entirely clear from the context whether or not the Angel of YHWH is meant. Nevertheless, such language is highly suggestive.

There are other parallels as well. David is also represented as wearing an ephod as he engages in a cultic dance before the ark of the covenant (2 Sam 6:14). This occurs as the ark is being brought to Jerusalem to be established as the basis for a unified royally led cult. As we previously noted, the ephod was a garment worn by deity. We are also told

97. Leithart, *Son to Me*, 71–72.

98. See discussion in ibid., 70–73.

later on that David's sons serve as "priests" (8:18 NIV has "royal officials").[99] In 1 Kings 3:4, we are told that Solomon engaged in priestly sacrifice. This connects David with the role of priest and therefore also binds him to the other associations that we noted throughout the Old Testament between priestly mediation and the Angel of YHWH/*kavod*. As we will see, many texts in the Old Testament appear to connect the king to the presence of YHWH with Israel.

Royal psalms, like 110, appear to strongly connect the Davidic monarchy with priestly mediation. A figure, referred to as "my lord" possesses a heavenly throne and the role of priest-king much like the mysterious figure Melchizedek spoken of in Genesis 14.[100] It would appear (as even some critical scholarship seems to suggest[101]) that this figure is associated with the Davidic king while at the same time possessing a heavenly throne and being an eternal priest.[102] As we saw in the last section, these characteristics are highly suggestive of the Angel of YHWH and therefore this Psalm appears to connect the Davidic king with him.

In keeping with these parallels, Scott Hahn convincingly argues that David under-stood himself as a new Melchizedek. He did not choose Zion as the location of his capitol by accident. Elsewhere in the Old Testament, Jerusalem is identified with Salem (see Ps 76:1–2), where Melchizedek was the priest-king.[103] We observed that David dressed in priestly garb when the ark (the seat of divine presence) was brought to Jerusalem.[104] We are also told that David feeds his guests "a cake of bread, a portion of meat, and a cake of raisins to each one" (2 Sam 6:19). Hahn argues that the second item, "a portion of meat" (frequently translated as "meats" based on how Vulgate understands the difficult Hebrew word,[105] though NIV and other translations have "dates") could better be translated as "wine."[106] If so, all this suggests that David meant to identify himself as a new Melchize-dek, who also feeds the people bread and wine (Gen 14:18). The bread and wine also connects David to the promises given to the patriarchs. The giving of bread and wine also hearkens back to Isaac's blessing to Jacob that God may give him "plenty of grain and wine" (Gen 27:28). This oracle is connected also to Isaac's prophecy to Jacob that "nations [will] bow down to you" (v. 29), which seems to be echoed in Genesis 49:8:12 and in Psalms 2 and 110.[107]

There is also a more direct connection between David and the Abrahamic narra-tives. Mount Moriah (the location of the Solomon's temple and David's capitol) was the place of God's confirmation of his promise to Abraham in the binding of Isaac (2 Chr

---

99. NIV translates this as "royal advisors" but some translators (notably the ESV) suggest "priests."

100. See discussion in Leupold, *Genesis*, 1:462–66; Leupold, *Psalms*, 770–78.

101. Kraus, *Psalms 60–150*, 346–47.

102. Hengstenberg, *Christology of the Old Testament*, 1:151.

103. Ibid., 190.

104. Ibid., 180, 190–91.

105. In the Vulgate 2 Sam 6:19 reads: "Et partitus est multitudini universae Israhel tam viro quam mulieri singulis collyridam panis unam et assaturam bubulae carnis unam et similam frixam oleo et abiit omnis populus unusquisque in domum suam."

106. Hahn, *Kinship by Covenant*, 180.

107. Ibid.

3:1).[108] Just as God told Abraham he would make his name great (Gen 12:2), he tells David the same thing (2 Sam 7:9).[109] Hahn notes here that we can observe a connection to and a preliminary fulfillment of the blessing of Shem, whose name means, "Name."[110] Shem is also told that Japheth (i.e., the Gentiles) will dwell in his tents (Gen 9:27). Solomon's kingdom includes both Israelites and non-Israelites (1 Kgs 9:20–21) and builds the temple as a house for God's Name. During the reign of Solomon, the Bible states that the "people of Judah and Israel were as numerous as the sand on the seashore" (1 Kgs 4:20), fulfilling God's promise to Abraham in Genesis 22:17. Indeed, this promise is itself made on Mount Moriah. This establishes David not only as heir of the Abrahamic testament, but also establishes the Abrahamic testament as a continuation of the blessing of Shem and the *protevangelium*. Just as the Abrahamic testament is meant for the blessing of the nations, so David exclaims after the oracle promising him an eternal house: "this is instruction for mankind" (7:19).[111] Hence, David's covenant fulfills the restoration of Adam's dominion and accomplishes Abraham's blessing of all nations.

Just as there is a connection between the promises given to David and Abraham, the narrative of 2 Samuel 24 connects David's sacrifice and establishment of the locale of the temple with the binding of Isaac. Just as the Angel of YHWH appeared to Abraham on Mount Moriah, so too he appeared in the same location to David in 2 Samuel 24 in connection to the plague resulting from David's census (2 Sam 24:16–17). Just as Abraham drew his knife to kill Isaac (Gen 22:10), so David sees the Angel of YHWH drawing his sword to strike down Jerusalem (24:16–17).[112] In the same manner that God gave a substitute to the patriarch (22:13–14), so too David offers himself as a substitute for the people (2 Sam 24:17).[113] Just as Abraham constructed an altar at that place (Gen 22:9), David did as well (24:18).

These connections are hardly coincidental. They clearly identify David and his descendants with the promises to Abraham sworn in this location. For this reason, the Davidic line also becomes the focus of God's plan for the restoration of Edenic harmony present in his promises to Abraham. The temple is, as we have noted, the new Eden. David and his descendants will reign over all creation like Adam, the protological priest-king. Finally, neither is it an accident that Golgotha is a hillock in the same area as Mount Moriah. The New Testament tells us that Jesus fulfilled the Abrahamic and Davidic testaments by the testament of his own body and blood communicated through bread and wine.[114]

David's preliminary fulfillments of the Abrahamic testament and the *protevangelium* find an even more sharp expression in the oracle of Nathan. David's son is to "build a house *for my Name*" (1 Sam 7:13, emphasis added). As we have previously noted, the divine Name and the temple were the means by which the presence of God was mediated

---

108. Ibid., 117.

109. Hahn, *Father Who Keeps*, 211.

110. Ibid.

111. Hahn, *Kinship by Covenant*, 119. Though this is how the ESV translates the text, it is also Hahn's preferred translation.

112. Ibid., 191.

113. Ibid., 191–93.

114. See comment and discussion in Hahn, *Lamb's Supper*, 14–28.

throughout the Old Testament.[115] This becomes even clearer in the description of the descent of the divine *kavod* into the Solomonic temple (2 Kgs 8:10–14). Much like God's presence in the tabernacle with a sign of his commitment and self-donation to Israel, God's personal presence in the temple meant a promissory guarantee of the Davidic testament. The Levitical and Deuteronomic codes do not (contrary to the claims of Wellhausen) anticipate the building of a temple.[116] Therefore the temple is specifically tied to the house of David. Just as David desired to build God a house, so God would make David a house (2 Sam 7).[117] We will observe the ultimate fulfillment of this in John's gospel when Jesus claims to be the true Temple (John 2:22). In this, God's fulfillment of his promise of an eternal "house" for David, and David's building of a house of the Lord coincide. God builds David's house through his preservation of the holy seed. He thereby makes David and his line a house for the dwelling of the divine glory in the form of the incarnation.[118]

In that he represents the divine rule and presence, the kingly mediator represents YHWH before Israel. He is, as he is addressed by YHWH in the royal enthronement hymn of Psalm 2, "my Son" (v. 7). Hans-Joachim Kraus claims that sonship in this context has a connotation of designating the Israelite king as an heir of the property of YHWH's creation.[119] As the embodiment of YHWH's universal reign, God states, "I will make the nations your heritage, and the ends of the earth your possession" (v. 8). Of course, Kraus may indeed be correct about the original use of the psalm (there is no way to verify this). Nevertheless, he has no explanation as to why the Israelite king should be promised the nations if in fact no Davidic king ever actually ruled all the nations or attempted to do so. In fact, what we must conclude is that these verses in their ultimate sense point ahead to an eschatological fulfillment in the Messiah.[120] The Messiah would

115. McBride, "Deuteronomic Name Theology."

116. Wellhausen, *Prolegomena*, 20–43. Wellhausen asserted (without any evidence) that the "tabernacle" was simply a code word in Leviticus for the Second Temple. Kitchen demonstrates that tent-shrine like the tabernacle were frequently used in the late second-millennium BC. Also, it was not too large for the Israelites to carry around in the desert (as many have claimed) because other peoples of the era carried around much larger tent-shrines. See Kitchen, *Reliability of the Old Testament*, 279–83. Also, Kitchen notes, Deuteronomy's statements prohibiting worship at sites other than where YHWH places his Name (Deut 16:6, etc.) does not necessarily designate the temple in Jerusalem (Jerusalem is never mentioned or implied!), but rather simply refers to a place God designates (*Reliability of the Old Testament*, 302). Even if it did designate Jerusalem, from the perspective of faith, this does not pose a problem in that God who knows the future can reveal things to the prophets. This only becomes a problem if one, due to their worldview, rejects rectilinear prophecy.

117. See similar argument in Leithart, *House for My Name*, 130–31.

118. This is Peter Leithart's insight in a personal conversation.

119. Kraus, *Psalms 1–59*, 132.

120. Augustine interpreted this purely messianically and suggested that the "today have I begotten you" was the today of eternity. See Augustine, *Expositions of the Psalms: Psalm 2:6*; *NPNFb* 8.3. He writes:
> Although that day may also seem to be prophetically spoken of, on which Jesus Christ was born according to the flesh; and in eternity there is nothing past as if it had ceased to be, nor future as if it were not yet, but present only, since whatever is eternal, always is; yet as today intimates presentiality, a divine interpretation is given to that expression, Today have I begotten You, whereby the uncorrupt and Catholic faith proclaims the eternal generation of the power and Wisdom of God, who is the Only-begotten Son.

In this he was followed by most of the western exegetically tradition.

be divine and therefore reign over all creation in an unrestricted way, not just Israel and the surrounding nations, as did the kingly mediators of the Old Testament.[121] This being said, we should not forget that an anticipation of this universal rule can be found in Solomon's reign. The Chronicler tells us that Solomon sat *"on the throne of the Lord"* (1 Chr 29:23, emphasis added). Peter Leithart also notes that he rides on a mule (1 Kgs 1:38), which being a beast of mixed stock is a "cherubic" animal similar to those that pull the chariot thrown of the divine *kavod* (see Ezek 1).[122] Lastly, both Solomon (1 Kgs 1:39) and David (1 Sam 16:13) are anointed with oil. In a similar manner to the priestly anointing that was discussed earlier, this suggests the glow of the divine glory.

Solomon not only embodies divine rule over all creation, but also divine creative activity. Much like Moses embodied the divine *kavod* when he spoke forth the tabernacle in seven divinely given speeches, so too Solomon is the builder of the temple, the cosmic microcosm. What is even more remarkable about this is how it creates a parallel between Solomon as the embodiment of divine wisdom (1 Kgs 3:7–13) and God's hypostatized Wisdom as it is described in Proverbs 8. This scripture describes holy Wisdom as an offspring of the deity (Prov 8:22–29). Solomon/Israelite king is described as God's Son (2 Sam 7:14, Ps 2:7) and as one that has also been begotten of God (Ps 2:7). Solomon is the builder of the temple (1 Kgs 6–8), the cosmic microcosm. God's hypostatized Wisdom is described as a "craftsman at his [God's] side" (Prov 8:30) in creation. Therefore, as the ultimate fulfillment of the Davidic testament, it is not for arbitrary reasons that the Apostle Paul identifies Christ as the hypostatized Wisdom of God (1 Cor 1:29, Col 1:16). It was therefore fitting that Christ was a carpenter (Mark 6:3) in that both Solomon and holy Wisdom are builders, and the Messiah is promised as one who will build God's house (2 Sam 7:13). Just as Christ in his preincarnate state as God's hypostatized Wisdom brought about creation, so he brings forth new creation through his incarnation, life, death, and resurrection (2 Cor 5:17). Solomon, as a type of Christ, prefigures his coming incarnation and divine creativity as the wise builder of the cosmic microcosm.

Beyond these connotations of divinity, there is (as has previously been mentioned) a prevalent use of the language of sonship in monarchic and messianic texts throughout the Old Testament: "I will be to him a father, and he shall be to me a son" (2 Sam 7:12–14).[123] Traditions describing the king as divine are by no means unprecedented within the environment of the Ancient Near East. Kraus has noted Egyptian and Mesopotamian parallels.[124] Eichrodt has pointed to Urgaritic examples.[125] This prevalence of divine kingship language should not surprise us in the least. In light of the *protevangelium's* promise of a divine Messiah that would renew creation, it would appear that many ancient peoples understood their divine kings as fulfilling this role.

Nevertheless, although the Israelite king embodies God's rule, he is not divine himself. Gerhard von Rad and Sigmund Mowickel emphasize that the Hebrew Scriptures do not designate the king as divine, but rather the king embodies the divine to the extent

---

121. Hengstenberg, *Christology of the Old Testament*, 1:150–52; Leupold, *Psalms*, 41–58.

122. Leithart, *1 and 2 Kings*, 32.

123. Hengstenberg, *Christology of the Old Testament*, 1:130–49.

124. Kraus, *Psalms 1–59*, 131.

125. Eichrodt, *Theology of the Old Testament*, 1:448.

that he is a representative of YHWH's rule.[126] The king is, as Walter Brueggemann notes, an Israelite among Israelites, standing under the authority of the law.[127] Kraus also observes that the formula of the public pronunciation of someone as one's own "Son" (such as in Psalm 2) was a common way of designating them as an heir by adoption in ancient law codes (he mentions the code of Hammurabi).[128]

Beyond its divine connotations, it should also be noted that the language of divine sonship meant the Israelite king represented the restoration of Adamic humanity. Israel is also referred to in Exodus as "my firstborn Son" (Exod 4:22). We also have seen that Genesis views Israel as a type of the ultimate fulfillment and restoration of human freedom and dominion. For this reason, the kingly mediators also stand as representatives of Israel before God and Israel.

Through the historical record of the Old Testament, this representative quality becomes clearer in that the nation fares as well as the behavior of its king allows. According to the accounts of the so-called Deuteronomistic history, Israel prospers during the righteous reigns of David, the younger Solomon, and Hezekiah (even if in this last case "prosper" means a last minute reprieve from destruction (see 2 Kgs 18–22). In the same manner, David's sins result in the punishment of the nation (2 Sam 24), just as the nation is punished because of the wickedness of the reign of Manasseh (2 Kgs 21:1–17).

This relationship is a two-way street, in that some kings also suffer for the sins of the nation. At the end of 2 Kings, during the reign of Josiah, though righteous, he was still cursed by God because of the previous sins of Manasseh and the people of Judah in general (2 Kgs 23:26–27). Although 2 Chronicles connects his death with disobedience to God (2 Chr 35:22), this is not incompatible with the account in 2 Kings. His death could represent both punishment for Manasseh and his own disobedience. In any case, Josiah is killed at Megiddo and the exile follows not far behind (2 Kgs 23:29–30). Therefore Josiah bears the nation's sin and thereby represents them before God and the nation. The king then stands as a sin bearer, much as we observed both Moses and the high priest doing earlier. This role of the Israelite king was also prefigured earlier in the history of Genesis, where Judah (David's forefather and the inheritor of an eternal kingship) offers himself as a substitute for his brother Benjamin (Gen 44:33).

For the Old Testament, God's promises to David (2 Sam 7) would find fulfillment in spite of human failings.[129] David's kingship is an eternal one and not dependent on obedience to the law. This promise was a fulfillment of Israel's prophecy to Judah that eternal kingship would come from his line (Gen 49:8–13).[130]

Just as Isaiah prophesies about the fulfillment of the prophet like Moses, he also predicted the fulfillment of the Davidic testament. The Davidic Messiah, much like the figures prophesied to fulfill priestly and prophetic mediation, takes on divine qualities. He is described as "Immanuel" (Isa 7:14), that is, "God with us."[131] In chapter 9, he is

---

126. Mowinckel, *He That Cometh*, 172; von Rad, *Old Testament Theology*, 1:320.

127. Brueggemann, *Theology of the Old Testament*, 606–7.

128. Kraus, *Psalms 1-59*, 131–32.

129. Hengstenberg, *Christology of the Old Testament*, 1:130–52.

130. Ibid., 1:57–98; Leupold, *Genesis*, 2:1176–85.

131. Delitzsch, *Biblical Commentary*, 1:220–23.

also described as giving those in darkness a "great light" (v. 2). This is more than reminiscent of the Servant of YHWH in chapter 49, who is therein described as a "light to the nations," a phrase we earlier connected to the manifestation of the divine *kavod*.[132] In Isaiah 42:7 the Servant's task is described as to "bring out the prisoners from the dungeon, from the prison *those who sit in darkness*" (emphasis added). In Isaiah 9 he is described as "Wonderful Counselor, Mighty God, Everlasting Father, Prince of Peace" (v. 6). The adjectives "Mighty" (*'êl gib·bō·wr,*) and "Everlasting" (which is one word in Hebrew with "Father," *'ă·ḇî·'aḏ*) are consistently associated with God elsewhere in the Old Testament.[133]

There also might be a connection between the Messianic figure of chapter 9 and the Angel of YHWH. The LXX translates the verse not as "Wonderful Counselor" but rather as the "Angel of Great Council."[134] There is little in the Hebrew text that would definitively suggest this translation. Nevertheless, Hengstenberg believes that the title "Wonderful" is a divine one, in that it parallels the name (or is a description of the name) of the Angel of YHWH in Judges 13.[135] If the translators of the LXX connected the use of the term in the two texts, it might mean that they thought that the messianic title was a reference to Judges 13, and therefore that the coming Messiah was identical with the Angel of YHWH.

This divine identity of the Messiah is suggested elsewhere in the prophets. Ezekiel describes the situation at the eschaton as thus: "My servant David shall be king over them, and they *shall all have one shepherd*" (Ezek 37:24, emphasis added). Earlier, God states that he will shepherd Israel: "I myself will be the shepherd of my sheep" (34:15). Though the text does not appear to explicitly teach a divine Messiah, what seems to be implicit is that because there is only one shepherd, God and the Davidic Messiah are a single subject.[136] It should also be noted that Ezekiel's prophecies of the Messiah are connected with the coming of a new covenant ("I will make with them a covenant of peace" 34:25, an "everlasting covenant" 37:26) and the divine act of cleansing from sin ("I [will] *cleanse you from all your iniquities*" 36:33, emphasis added), which in turn connect the texts to the prophecies of Isaiah 53, 61, Jeremiah 31, and Daniel 7, 9.

Moving on to Isaiah chapter 11, the Davidic Messiah is described as "a shoot from the stump of Jesse, and a branch from his roots shall bear fruit" (v. 1). This is very similar language to what we find elsewhere in the Old Testament. We read in Jeremiah 23 that the Davidic Messiah is also referred to as a "branch" (Jer 23:5). His name will be "The LORD Our Righteousness," which again suggests divinity. The language of "branch" and "shoot" is remarkably similar to that used in Isaiah 53: "For he grew up *before him like a young plant*, and like a *root out of dry ground*" (v. 2, emphasis added). The common

---

132. Leupold, *Isaiah*, 2:179–80. Leupold concludes that the Servant must be divine, in that he serves as a light to the nations in a way that only God could.

133. Hengstenberg, *Christology of the Old Testament*, 1:89–90. Also see Leupold, *Isaiah*, 1:185–86.

134. Daniélou, *History of Early Christian Doctrine*, 333.

135. Hengstenberg, *Christology of the Old Testament*, 2:37.

136. Hummel, *Ezekiel*, 2:1003–7. Dr. Hummel sees this as a prediction of the Davidic Messiah unification of the Church. Nevertheless, he also sees an ultimate fulfillment in Christ's theandric nature, in that he is a ruler who unifies divine and human rule.

wording of these passages suggests then that the "branch" is the same person as the Servant.[137] On a typological level as well, it also makes sense that the Davidic Messiah would be connected with the Servant, who acts as a new Passover lamb for a new exodus. Previously, in the case of Judah and Josiah, the Davidic line acted as a substitute for others. David and Solomon also engaged in explicitly priestly activities. Therefore the Davidic Messiah acting as a substitute for sin, and a new Passover lamb makes perfect sense.

The description of the "shoot" coming "out of dry ground" also might connect Isaiah 53 with Isaiah 7.[138] We are told in Isaiah 7 that "Immanuel" will be born of a virgin.[139] The figure of the Servant is also divine in that he is called "the arm of the Lord" (53:1). Ground that has not been watered might very well be a metaphorical way of talking about virginity. This not only connects the Messianic prophecies of Isaiah 7, 9, and 11 to the Servant songs, but also connects them to the *protevangelium*'s "seed of the woman."

---

137. A. Pieper, *Exposition of Isaiah 40–66*, 436. Also see argument in Block, "My Servant David, 17–56. Block makes the argument that the Servant is clearly a Davidic king.

138. See A. Pieper, *Exposition of Isaiah*, 436. Pieper disagrees and claims that "dry ground" refers to the political situation.

139. See a defense of this interpretation of Isaiah and its application to Christ in Gibbs, *Matthew 1–11*, 99–104; Hengstenberg, *Christology of the Old Testament*, 2:44–50; Leupold, *Isaiah*, 1:155–57; Niessen, "Virginity of the 'Almah," 133–50; Rydelnik, *Messianic Hope*, 152–54; E. Young, "Immanuel Prophecy," 97–124. Also see a Jewish defense of the word "*almah*" (virgin) in C. Gordon, "*Almah* in Isaiah," 106.

Chapter 3

Christology and Atonement in the New Testament, Part 1

The Christology of the Gospels

Introduction

JESUS CHRIST IS THE fulfillment of the entire Old Testament. He is the true mediator between God and humanity (1 Tim 2:5). He is the one who finally brought an end to universal exile brought by the fall of our first parents. This theme of exile and return, which we have traced throughout the Old Testament, will be important in our treatment of how the New Testament authors understood Jesus's atoning work as the final end to the universal exile of creation from its creator God. This would take the form of the return of divine presence, renewal of creation, and fulfillment of the law through eschatological judgment. In order to reverse the state of universal exile, we will observe that Jesus is God's own self-donation and entry into the story of Israel and humanity. As we saw in the previous chapters, God in his faithfulness elected mediators in the Old Testament period in order to fulfill the law and thereby represent himself in faithfulness to Israel. Mediators also served as an embodiment of Israel remaining faithful to him. Jesus is the true prophet, priest, and king, who fulfills God's own faithfulness by coming in the flesh. As an ultimate fulfillment of his faithfulness, God literally gives himself to Israel by donating his person to them. From within our nature, God finally wins a victory over sin, death, the devil, and the law, thereby enacting a true and everlasting testament of his love.

The Synoptic Gospels: Mark

In discussing the Synoptic Gospels, we will begin first with the shortest gospel, Mark.[1] Mark's gospel works from an alternating pattern of humiliation and exaltation. It is a

---

1. See the following commentaries: Alexander, *Gospel of Mark*; Carrington, *According to Mark*; Cranfield, *Gospel*; J. Edwards, *Gospel*; France, *Gospel of Mark*; Gould, *Critical and Exegetical Commentary*; Gnilka, *Evangelium nach Markus*; Grundman, *Evangelium nach Markus*; Hauck, *Evangelium des Markus*;

book of glory and of the hiddenness of glory *sub contrario*. In it, Jesus is the divine Son of God, the Son of Man, and the divine *kavod* come in the flesh to fulfill the pattern of exile and return prefigured in the history of Israel. He thereby forgives sins, renews creation, and overcomes demonic forces.

Mark begins his gospel with glory, by announcing his intention of informing his audience of the "Gospel about Jesus Christ, the Son of God" (Mark 1:1). In that Jesus brings a "gospel," he must necessarily be divine, for as Ben Witherington III comments:

> Only a god is really able to bring world-changing and lasting good news and benefaction and hope. Mark, then, from the outset, is announcing not merely a coming of a teacher or even just a human messianic figure (though that is part of the truth), but the epiphany or advent of a deity who will reveal himself in various and sundry ways during his time on earth.[2]

There are other indications of Jesus's divine glory throughout the gospel. Simon Gathercole has pointed to Jesus's citation of Psalm 110 in his question concerning whether the Messiah is David's Son or David's Lord (Mark 12:35–37). Though the Hebrew of Psalm 110:3 is notoriously difficult to translate, the LXX version of the text reads: "With you is the rule on the day of your power, in the radiance of your holy ones; *From the womb, before the morning star, I gave you birth*."[3] Read in light of the rest of the gospel, this definitely points to the divinity and preexistence of Jesus. Doubtless Mark's original readers would have read it this way, since they were probably most familiar with the LXX.

Martin Hengel has also suggested that Mark's use of Isaiah in 1:2–3 ("I send my messenger before your face, who will prepare your way") is highly suggestive of an inter-Trinitarian conversation before Jesus's earthly advent.[4] It should be noted that read against the background of Second Temple Jewish expectations of YHWH's return to Zion, Mark's use of the verse, "a voice of one calling in the desert, 'Prepare the way of the Lord, make straight paths for him,'" seems to suggest that he is indicating Jesus has come to fulfill that expectation.[5]

Hobbs, *Gospel of Mark*; Horne, *Victory According to Mark*; Huby, *Evangile selon Saint Marc*; Hunter, *Gospel*; Jeremias, *Evangelium nach Markus*; S. Johnson, *Commentary on the Gospel*; Juel, *Mark*; Keegan, *Commentary on the Gospel*; Keil, *Evangelien des Markus und Lukas*; Kilgallen, *Brief Commentary*; Lagrange, *Evangile selon Saint Marc*; Lamarche, *Evangile de Marc*; LaVerdiere, *Beginning of the Gospel*; Lenski, *St. Mark's Gospel*; Lohmeyer, *Evangelium des Markus*; G. Martin, *Gospel according to Mark*; Michael, *Am Tisch der Sünder*; Menzies, *Earliest Gospel*; Morgan, *Mark*; Moule, *Mark*; Nineham, *Saint Mark*; Riddle, *According to Mark*; Sabin, *Mark*; J. Schmid, *Evangelium nach Markus*; Schnackenburg, *Evangelium nach Markus*; Schanz, *Evangelium des Heiligen Marcus*; Schweizer, *Mark*; St. John, *Analysis of the Gospel*; Taylor, *Mark*; Trocmé, *L'Evangile selon Saint Marc*; Weidner, *Mark*; Wellhausen, *Das Evangelium Marci*; Witherington, *Gospel of Mark*; Wohlenberg, *Evangelium des Markus*; Wolff, *Mark*.

2. Witherington, *Gospel of Mark*, 69–70.

3. Gathercole, *Pre-Existent Son*, 236 (emphasis added). Also see the arguments for early high Christology in Bauckham, *God Crucified*; Hurtado, *How On Earth*; Hurtado, *Lord Jesus Christ*.

4. Hengel, *Four Gospels*, 95.

5. N. T. Wright, *Christian Origins*, 2:615–31. Also see an argument about this theme in Mark in Horne, *Victory according to Mark*, 14–24.

As a book of glory, Mark also emphasizes Jesus's role as the "Son of Man."[6] The Son of Man was understood by at least some of the Second Temple Jews to be the cosmic judge who would come at the end of time (for example in 1 Enoch 61–62, 64). As the cosmic judge, the Son of Man takes on the role held by the priests within the Levitical cult: "You must distinguish between the holy and the common, between the unclean and the clean" (Lev 10:10, also see 11:47). Because Jesus is the true advent of this figure, Mark indicates that he has the power to forgive sins on earth in the present (Mark 2:10) and will serve as the judge of humanity at the eschaton (13). Jesus makes his judgment available ahead of time to those who have received his word of forgiveness with faith.

Mark's glorification of Jesus in the first verses of his gospel is followed by his description of Jesus's entry into humiliation. Jesus goes to the Jordan and is baptized with sinners, thereby identifying himself with them. Being indistinguishable from the mass of sinful humanity, Jesus's glory is revealed when his Father testifies to it: "You are my beloved Son; with you I am well pleased" (1:11). Mark tells us that the heavens are "torn open" (*schizomenous*) and the Spirit in the form of a dove descends upon him. The violence of the term *schizomenous* seems to indicate the disruption of the normal structure of reality that had held sway in the Old Testament. God in his holiness had segregated himself from sinners in the tabernacle/temple. In the person of Jesus, he now identifies with them.

The Father's pronouncement of sonship echoes the royal Psalm 2, which designates the Israelite king as God's Son and promises him the nations as his inheritance.[7] Predictably, the revelation of this glory is followed by humiliation. Jesus is "driven out" (*ekballei*) into the wilderness (Mark 1:10, 12). The use of *ekballei* is particularly harsh. Elsewhere, Mark uses it to describe what happens to demons during exorcisms (1:39). Jesus, having identified with sinners, is now an object of condemnation much like demonic forces of the old creation that he is charged by the Father to destroy.

This opening sequence of alternation between humiliation and glory is repeated throughout the rest of the gospel. In fact, following this pattern S. Moyter has argued that there is an intentional literary *inculsio* that brackets the whole of the gospel.[8] The *inclusio* commences at Jesus's baptism (1:9–11) and ends at his death on the cross (15:36–39).[9] At Jesus's baptism, John is mentioned in connection to Elijah, the heavens are ripped open, and he is designated as the Son of God by the Father's voice. At his crucifixion, there is a mention of Elijah (15:35), the rending of the veil of the temple (the same Greek word is used), and a voice designating Jesus as the Son of God is heard, this time coming from the Centurion.[10] The *inclusio* that Moyter suggests seems to correspond well to what appears to be an intentional structural division in the book. The first half of the

---

6. This is a theme throughout the Gospels: Mark 2:27–28, 8:11–13, 8:31–32, 38, 8:38—9:1, 10:32–34; Matt 8:20, 12:8, 12:38–42, 13:37, 41–42, 16:27–28, 18:11, 20:17–19, 24:30, 25:31–32; Luke 6:5, 9:26–27, 9:58, 11:29–32, 18:31–34.

7. Nineham, *Saint Mark*, 61–62.

8. Motyer, "Rendering of the Veil," 155–57.

9. Though I cite other scholars with regard to this insight, the first person to direct me to this point was David Frederickson, professor of New Testament, Luther Seminary.

10. Also see comments in Leithart, *Four*, 153.

gospel is primarily concerned with Jesus's glory (hidden though it often is) and therefore culminates in the transfiguration. Conversely, the second half is primarily concerned with Jesus's abandonment and humiliation. For this reason, it fittingly culminates in his crucifixion.

After Jesus's return from the wilderness, he engages in a series of deeds of power. He heals, works exorcisms, and forgives sins. He is the mighty one who has come to bind the strong man (Satan) and plunder his goods (3:23–29). This narrative of Jesus's power culminates in the direct revelation of his glory in the transfiguration on Mount Tabor. In this event, Jesus reveals himself to be the hypostatized *kavod* that was encountered in the Old Testament by Israel. As Gathercole correctly notes, there is no indication that such glory is borrowed.[11] A further indication of this is the fact that he is accompanied by Elijah and Moses, both of whom (as Donald Juel observes) were witnesses to theophanies on mountains (Exod 33; 1 Kgs 19).[12] Lastly, he is encompassed with a thick cloud, which, as we have seen, is an Old Testament sign of God's presence (Exod 19:18). God's voice again pronounces Jesus to be his true Son and again thereby testifies to his glory as he did at the Jordan.

Jesus's glorification is now followed again by humiliation. This time his humiliation culminates in the Father abandoning him to the cross. This downward turn is expressed in other ways as well. In the second half of the gospel, Jesus does very few miracles and speaks a great deal about his coming crucifixion. After instituting the Lord's Supper, he travels to the garden of Gethsemane at the base of the Mount of Olives. The Mount of Olives is the pathway through which David fled Jerusalem when he was betrayed by Absalom (2 Sam 15:30). In the same manner, Jesus, the true king, is betrayed by Judas and his own nation. Jesus prays that he might have a reprieve from his destiny to suffer and die. The voice that came to him on the Jordan and at Tabor is now silent. Silence seems to indicate the Father has abandoned him. His faith in the Father's Word nevertheless remains strong. Jesus ultimately accepts the "cup" (Mark 14:36) that the Father gives him. According to David Scaer, it is most likely that the "cup" Jesus speaks of is an allusion to the "cup of wrath" spoken of in Isaiah 51:22 and Jeremiah 25:16.[13]

In Gethsemane, Jesus is arrested and taken to the Sanhedrin. Before the high priest, Jesus is initially silent as is proper to his identity as the Suffering Servant of Isaiah who "did not open his mouth" (Isa 53:7).[14] After a lengthy silence, he must finally answer the high priest regarding his identity: "Again the high priest asked him, 'Are you the Christ, the Son of the Blessed?' And Jesus said, 'I am, and you will see the Son of Man seated at the right hand of Power, and coming with the clouds of heaven'" (Mark 14:61–62). In other words, Jesus confesses that he is the human one and cosmic judge whose divine identity will be revealed when he shares the divine throne and glory cloud.[15]

The question has been frequently asked concerning whether Jesus's "I am" in this confession constitutes a claiming of the divine Name. Even if this were not the case,

11. Gathercole, *Pre-Existent Son*, 49.

12. Juel, *Mark*, 128.

13. Scaer, *Christology*, 79.

14. France, *Gospel of Mark*, 608.

15. See discussion of this interpretation of Jesus's confession in N. T. Wright, *Christian Origins*, 2:551.

Jesus's confession still constitutes a claim of divinity, as the high priest's accusation of blasphemy indicates (14:64). Gathercole notes that within later rabbinical circles the claim to have a heavenly throne was considered to be blasphemous because only God could claim to have such a throne. Therefore Jesus, in claiming to have a heavenly throne, was claiming to stand in the place of God.[16] It should also be noted that Jesus's description of the "Son of Man seated at the right hand of Power, and coming with the clouds of heaven," actually combines the Son of Man of Daniel 7 with Psalm 110's description of the Melchizedekiah priest-king.[17] As we have previously noted, both texts have strong messianic and theophonic connotations to them. These allusions and their connotations are only strengthened when read in the overall context of Mark's gospel.

After being condemned by both the Sanhedrin and Pilate, Jesus is led out to be crucified. His crucifixion scene possesses strong sacrificial imagery borrowed from the Old Testament and contemporary Judaism. Earlier in the gospel, Jesus asserts that he will serve "to give his life as a ransom for many" (10:45). Some have noted that the use of the word "ransom" (*lytron*) is similar to the description of the substitution of monies for the firstborn in the LXX version of Numbers 3.[18] Mark also tells us that Jesus is nailed to the cross at nine o'clock in the morning (15:25) and dies at three o'clock in the afternoon (v. 33). Arthur Just has noted that according to later Jewish tradition, sin offerings occurred in the Second Temple at exactly nine o'clock in the morning and three in the afternoon.[19] Similarly, Mark writes that they "crucified two robbers, one on his right and one on his left" (v. 27). The unusual emphasis that Mark places on the location of Jesus might have been intended to provide typological value. Jesus's location between the thieves seems to echo the Day of Atonement when both the blood and the divine presence hidden under the cloud of incense stood between the two cherubim on the ark of the covenant (Lev 16:15). Later, we will find similar uses of this typology in John's gospel and Paul's Letter to the Romans.

In the final moment of his crucifixion, Jesus cries out in the words of Psalm 22, "My God, my God, why have you forsaken me?" Much like in his pleading in Gethsemane, Jesus's cry to the Father is met with silence. Jesus's two cries to the Father (in Gethsemane and on the cross) parallel God's two pronunciations of him as his Son. The silence of the Father and the condemnation of the Son seem to contradict his earlier words. Nevertheless, Jesus's cry to the Father does not indicate the failure of his faith. What should be remembered is that all the Psalms were part of the temple liturgy and therefore are in a sense all concerned with the praise of God for his goodness.[20] Psalms of lamentation also assume the existence of and trust in divine grace. One does not lament if one does not consider God to be gracious and good. Lamentation is faith's response to appearances that contradict its trust in God's goodness and graciousness. Those who do not believe

---

16. Gathercole, *Pre-Existent Son*, 60–61. Also see similar arguments in Bock, *Blasphemy and Exaltation*; Timo Eskola, *Messiah and the Throne*. Beyond Gathercole's argument, Bock mentions that the challenge to the priesthood (representatives of God) would be viewed as blasphemy.

17. Fletcher-Louis, "Jesus and the High Priest," 21.

18. Ibid., 15.

19. Just, *Heaven on Earth*, 100.

20. Mowinckel, *Psalms in Israel's Worship*, 2–3.

God is good and gracious do not lament because the world is precisely as a nonexistent or malevolent deity would have it. Therefore, in his lamentation Jesus maintains his faith in God's Word to him, in spite of divine hiddenness and condemnation.[21]

Following Jesus's cry of lament, he dies and the curtain of the temple (probably the holy of holies) is torn (*eschisthē*) from top to bottom.[22] This parallels the ripping of the heavens at the beginning of the gospel not only because of the use of the same Greek word, but also because the curtain covering the holy of holies was at that time embroidered to represent the heavens.[23] Hence both represent a ripping of the heavens.

The significance of this ripping has often been debated by scholars. Frequently, the event has been interpreted to mean that sinners now have access to God.[24] In light of the fact that sinners were quite literally separated from God in the Old Testament by the veil, this interpretation seems to have much value. Donald Juel offers two other suggestions that are consistent with our earlier argument regarding the _schizomenous inclusio_. First, Juel claims that sinners are not only separated from God by the veil, but that God himself is segregated from sinners. The torn veil therefore signifies God's own willingness to identify with sinful humanity in the person of his Son.[25] The culmination of this is God's own death in solidarity with sinners on the cross. The moment this death occurs, the veil is torn and God's identification with sinners is complete.

Secondly, Juel also connects the ripping of the veil with the coming destruction of the temple, predicted in Mark 13. When the temple's curtain is torn, Jesus's prediction of the temple's coming destruction becomes a present reality.[26] People mock Jesus on the cross by asking if this is the fate of one who would have destroyed the temple (15:29). This is ironic for several reasons. First, Jesus only predicted the destruction of the temple (Mark 13); he did not actually threaten to destroy it. Mark insists all threats of destruction attributed to Jesus are false testimony (14:57–59). The mockery of Jesus is ironic for the second reason. His death on the cross causes the ripping of the veil and thereby begins the process of the temple's destruction. The one who appears weak, is, in fact, all-powerful, even on the cross.

The inauguration of the destruction of the temple also suggests that Mark believes Jesus has taken over the functions of the temple. The temple was a microcosm of creation and functioned as a means to renew creation. It was also the location where sin was forgiven by bloody sacrifice. Through his death, Jesus works as the forgiveness of sin by bloody sacrifice, and by his resurrection he renews creation.[27] The new creation that Jesus brings cannot exist alongside the old creation in some neutral fashion. Judgment of sin means the destruction of the old cult insofar as it represents the old creation. In this new creation, God overcomes his separation from sinners and therefore rips the old order to

---

21. For a similar argument see Bayer, "Toward a Theology of Lament," 211–20. Gerhard also suggests that Jesus was a hero of faith who was not defeated even in death (*History of the Suffering*, 265).

22. Lenski, *St. Mark's Gospel*, 722–23.

23. *Jewish War*, 5.5.4, in Josephus, *Works of Josephus*, 707.

24. For example, Schweizer, *Mark*, 354–55.

25. Juel, *Mark*, 225.

26. Ibid., 226.

27. Lenski, *St. Mark's Gospel*, 724.

pieces *chizomenous*). Similarly, the separation between Israel and the Gentiles is abrogated. Upon his death, Jesus is confessed by the Gentile Centurion to be the Son of God.

The Synoptic Gospels: Matthew[28]

Matthew begins his gospel by telling his audience about Jesus's human and divine identity. His divine identity is revealed in that the name "Jesus" means "God is our salvation."[29] Matthew's intention to identify with this name Jesus as divine is clear insofar as he then reports the angel's explanation of the name: "for he will save his people from their sins" (Matt 1:21). If Jesus is the agent of salvation, then he himself therefore must be God. If this were not enough, the evangelist then tells his audience that this fulfills the prophecy that a virgin will conceive and give birth to Immanuel, "God with us" (1:23).[30]

Throughout the gospel, Jesus reveals himself as the true savior God of Israel in five separate theophanies. First, in chapter 5, he promulgates the Word of God on a mountain (v. 1). Moses came down from the mountain and gave the Torah after speaking with God at the summit. Jesus stands on top of the mountain and directly promulgates the Word of God to the people as God himself. In chapter 17, Jesus is transfigured, which as we have noted in the last section, must necessarily represent a theophany. The third theophany occurs as Jesus stands on the Mount of Olives, where we are told that God's glory rested when it left the temple (Ezek 11:23). It is also the location where Zechariah prophesied that God will stand before the final battle that will destroy Jerusalem (Zech 14:4). This fits well with Jesus's discourse in this section, which describes the destruction of Jerusalem. He ends the discourse by saying "Heaven and earth will pass away, but my words will not pass away" (24:35) an echo of Isaiah 40:8: "The grass withers, the flower fades, but the word of our God will stand forever." The fourth theophany occurs on Golgotha as Jesus is crucified. The darkness and earthquakes that accompany his death are direct parallels with Amos's description (Amos 8:9) of the Day of the Lord, that is, God's own epiphany in judgment. It is also somewhat reminiscent of the coming of God to commune with Israel as seen in Exodus 20, wherein the old covenant was ratified. In keeping with this, Jesus's death ratifies the "new testament" in his "blood." The

---

28. See the following commentaries: Allen, *Critical and Exegetical Commentary*; Broadus, *Gospel of Matthew*; Bruner, *Matthew*; M. Davies, *Matthew*; Allison and W. Davies, *Saint Matthew*; Dickson, *Brief Exposition*; Erdman, *Matthew*; Fiedler, *Matthäusevangelium*; Fenton, *Saint Matthew*; Filson, *Saint Matthew*; France, *Gospel of Matthew*; Gaetcher, *Matthäus Evangelium*; Gibbs, *Matthew 1–11*; Grundmann, *Evangelium nach Matthäus*; Gundry, *Matthew*; Hagner, *Matthew*; Harold, *Gospel of Matthew*; Harrington, *Matthew*; Jerome, *Matthew*; Keener, *Gospel of Matthew*; Keil, *Evangelium des Matthäus*; Lagrange, *Evangile selon Saint Matthieu*; Lenski, *Matthew's Gospel*; Luz, *Evangelium nach Matthäus*; Michaelis, *Evangelium nach Matthäus*; Meier, *Matthew*; Nolland, *Gospel of Matthew*; Overman, *Church and Community*; Rienecker, *Evangelium des Matthäus*; T. Robinson, *Gospel of Matthew*; Sabourin, *St. Matthew*; Sand, *Evangelium nach Matthäus*; Scaer, *Discourses in Matthew*; Scaer, *Sermon on the Mount*; Schanz, *Evangelium des Heiligen Matthäus*; Schlatter, *Evangelist Matthäus*; J. Schmid, *Evangelium nach Matthäus*; Schniewind, *Evangelium nach Matthäus*; Staab, *Evangelium nach Matthäus*; Schweizer, *Evangelium nach Matthäus*; D. Turner, *Matthew*; Wiefel, *Evangelium nach Matthäus*; Witherington, *Matthew*; Zahn, *Evangelium des Matthäus*.

29. Harrington, *Matthew*, 35; Lenski, *Matthew's Gospel*, 49; Meier, *Marginal Jew*, 207.

30. Lenski, *Matthew's Gospel*, 54–55.

fifth and last theophany is on a mountain in Galilee after the resurrection, when Jesus commissions the disciples as they "worship" or "prostrated" (*prosekynēsan*) themselves before him (Matt 28:17). In this context, such an action can only be understood as divine worship.[31] Indeed, Jesus states, "All authority in heaven and on earth have been given to me" (v. 18). This means that Jesus transcends merely human dominion on the earth (Gen 1:28), and also possesses all authority in heaven, which according to his earlier statement in the gospel, is "God's throne" (Matt 5:35).

From this pattern, the question arises: why five theophanies? To begin to answer the question, it should be observed that Matthew's five theophanies parallel his five great discourses (5:3—7:27, 10:5–42, 13:3–52, 18:2–35, 23:2—25:46).[32] Dale Allison has observed Matthew's use of Mosaic typology.[33] If this is so, Jesus's five great discourses might represent the giving of a new Torah of law and promise. He also leads the new Israel out of the exile of sin and death, as we will see later.

Nevertheless, there also appears to be a deeper significance to the five discourses. N. T. Wright has noted that in Second Temple Judaism Torah was viewed in many circles as the living Word of God. It represented a means (particularly in Pharisaic circles) of entering into the divine presence, equal even to that of the temple.[34] If this is the case, then the parallel between the five theophanies and the five discourses makes sense. Jesus is the living Torah, and therefore the presence of God with Israel. He is not the one who merely speaks with God "face to face" (as Moses did), but is in fact the very presence of God. Gerhard Barth agrees, remarking, "The presence of Jesus in [Matthew's] the congregation is here described as analogous to the presence of the Shekinah . . . the place of Torah is taken by . . . Jesus; the place of the Shekinah by Jesus himself."[35]

In keeping with this, Matthew also describes the Name of Jesus as taking over the position of the divine Name in the Old Testament: "For where two or three are gathered in my name, there am I among them" (18:20). Charles Gieschen asserts that passages like these in the New Testament suggest that for early Jewish Christians the divine Name properly belonged to Jesus along with the Father.[36] Therefore, just as the temple was the location of the divine Name and presence in the Old Testament (2 Sam 7:13), Jesus as the divine Name and presence now takes over the position of the temple. For this reason, the Church is also the eschatological temple, because it is the locus of the divine presence. The Church is the place where Jesus's Name (i.e., presence) is manifest in Word and sacrament.[37]

In support of this reading, there is evidence that Matthew structures his gospel around an *inclusio* of Name and presence.[38] At the beginning of the work, Joseph is

---

31. Ibid., 1168.

32. David Scaer considers these to be highly significant for the structure of Matthew. See Scaer, *Discourses in Matthew*.

33. Allison, *New Moses*.

34. N. T. Wright, *Christian Origins*, 1:236–37.

35. G. Barth, "Matthew's Understanding," 135.

36. Gieschen, "Divine Name," 130–48.

37. See similar argument in Scaer, *Discourses in Matthew*, 157–99.

38. Ibid., 172.

informed that "you are to give him the name Jesus, because he will save his people from their sins" (Matt 1:21). Matthew then cites the prophecy of Isaiah: "they will call him Immanuel"—which means, "God with us" (v. 23). At the end of the gospel, the divine Name is repeated to the disciples: "make disciples of all nations, baptizing them in the name of the Father and of the Son and of the Holy Spirit" (28:19).[39] Again, the Name is linked to the divine presence: "And behold, I am with you always, to the end of the age" (v. 20).[40]

This makes Jesus's rejection as a prophet much more serious than those of the Old Testament. The final rejection of Jesus and the crowd's acceptance of Barabbas is in fact nothing short of the rejection of God's own person. Jesus is not just one of the prophets who possesses the Word of God, but the Word himself. As the parable of the vineyard indicates (21:33–40), Jesus is the culmination of the rejection of prophetic mediation. Again, much like the worship of the golden calf, such rejection seeks alternative false mediators, in this case in the form of Barabbas.[41] As an insurrectionist, Barabbas ("son of the father") also claims to be one who can bring the kingdom of heaven, the content of Jesus's new Torah of law and promise.[42] Nevertheless, even in their rejection of Jesus, God's faithfulness succeeds. At his trial, those who condemn him demand that "his blood be on us and on our children" (27:25). We are reminded of the fact that Jesus's own blood is that of the "testament" (26:28) and that the Servant of Isaiah, the new Moses, would sprinkle the nations (Isa 52:15), much like Moses did when he ratified the Sinaitic covenant in Exodus 24. In effect, their rejection of the promise of the gospel paradoxically means its ratification through his bitter, innocent suffering and death.[43]

As God returned to his people, Jesus is also the one who fulfills the Old Testament promises of rest. In recounting Jesus's genealogy and human origin, Matthew highlights that Jesus is a descendent of Abraham and of David (Matt 1:17). He thereby implicitly suggests that Jesus is a fulfillment of the Abrahamic and Davidic testaments, both of which promised rest from Israel's enemies. It should also be observed that in giving Jesus's genealogy, Matthew makes the number of generations symbolic of the eschatological rest that Christ brings. The evangelist tells us that there were forty-two generations between Abraham and Christ. The symbolism here appears to be associated with the numbers seven and six in the genealogy, in that the number forty-two is six times seven. Seven is of course the number of the original creation. Six would be the number

---

39. Gieschen, "Divine Name," 124–25.

40. Scaer, *Discourses of Matthew*, 202.

41. See discussion of the incident in the context of Matthew's gospel in Maccoby, "Jesus and Barabbas," 55–60; H. Rigg, "Barabbas," 417–56.

42. Leithart, *Four*, 90.

43. We offer this interpretation against the claim of many that this passage has to do with anti-Judaism (or anti-Semitism). See discussions in the following authors: Crossan, "Anti-Semitism," 189–214; Fitzmyer, "Anti-Semitism," 667–71; Gaston, "Messiah of Israel," 40; Harrington, *Matthew*, 388–93; Stanton, *Gospel for a New People*, 148–57. First, claiming the passage is anti-Semitic is absurd insofar as it is not only an anachronism (prior to the modern period, hatred of the Jews was for the most part not racial, but religious), but also the author and the gospel hero are both Jews. Secondly, Matthew does not portray Pilate tremendously well either (while he pretends to shuck responsibility, but ultimately allows an innocent man to die). Similarly, many of Jesus's negative statements about Gentiles are reported through the gospel. Ultimately, Matthew's polemic is not against the Jews as such, but against unbelieving humanity that rejects Christ. Jews who do not accept Christ are no worse than Gentiles who do the same.

of creation minus the extra day of Sabbath. This final "seven" is then inaugurated by the birth of Jesus. This seems to suggest that Jesus's forgiveness brings a new creation and a new Sabbath. Just as Christ is the eternal Word of God (i.e., the living Torah) who was the agent of the old creation, he stands at the beginning and enacts a new narrative of creation. In this regard, David Scaer has also pointed to the fact that the first words of the gospel are *BIBLOS geneseōs*, suggesting the beginning of a new Genesis.[44]

Jesus's life not only has the goal of a new Sabbath, but is also itself the presence of that Sabbath. Throughout the gospel, Matthew repeatedly introduces the theme of the messianic Sabbath. It should be noted that many Second Temple Jews held that when the Messiah came there would be an age of Sabbath paralleling the seventh day in Genesis 1.[45] Jesus brings the rest of this messianic Sabbath. He himself is the Sabbath and he offers rest: "Come to me, all you who are weary and burdened, and I will give you rest. Take my yoke upon you and learn from me, for I am gentle and humble in heart, and you will find rest for your souls. For my yoke is easy and my burden is light" (11:28–30).

What is the content of this rest though? If Jesus comes to complete the "seven" and "six" with the final "seven" of new creation, then his ministry is not only one of re-creation, but also Jubilee. By adding a final seven to the forty-two generations, we get forty-nine, the year of Jubilee in the Old Testament (Lev 25). This is a fulfillment of the eschatological Jubilee of Daniel 9. For this reason Jesus also tells his disciples to forgive their brothers "seventy times seven" (Matt 18:22), the number of Daniel's great Jubilee.[46] As the bringer of universal Jubilee, Jesus brings the true rest of the forgiveness of sins.

Jesus can offer this eschatological Sabbath rest because he is the true presence of God with Israel. He is the new and true Temple. Therefore his disciples enjoy the same perpetual Sabbath that the priests do: "have you not read in the Law how on the Sabbath the priests in the temple profane the Sabbath and are guiltless? I tell you, something greater than the temple is here" (12:5–6). Fletcher-Louis suggests that the rationale for this judgment on Jesus's part is the Second Temple Jewish belief that due to God's own presence in the temple, the priests enjoyed a perpetual Sabbath.[47] For this reason, priests could engage in labor on the Sabbath, because being always in the midst of perpetual Sabbath they would otherwise never do any work. If this is the case, it means that Christ himself is the new Temple and thereby also the presence of God with Israel. The Temple, as we recall, mediated both God's holiness and his forgiveness of sins to Israel. Jesus therefore does the same.

44. Leithart, *Four*, 118–20; Scaer, *Discourses of Matthew*, 123.

45. See 1 Enoch 93:2; Ezra 7:4, 12:34; 2 Baruch 24:1–4, 30:1–5, 39:3–8, 40:1–4; Jubilees 1:4–29, 23:14–31.

46. See different opinion in Harrington, *Matthew*, 269. Actually the phrase can be translated as either "seventy-seven" or "seven times seventy." Both have symbolic significance. On the one hand, "seventy-seven" is the number of times that Lamech states that he is avenged in Gen 4:24. If this is the case, Jesus's forgiveness counteracts human revenge and self-justification as embodied by Cain and his descendents. (See criticism of this reading in Lenski, *Matthew's Gospel*, 709–10.) Or it could be a symbolic representation of the age of Jubilee that Jesus brings as we suggested above. Both carry the same essential message of forgiveness in the new age.

47. Fletcher-Louis, "Jesus and the High Priest," 43–45. Fletcher-Louis makes substantially the same point about the Markan parallel text.

Jesus is not only the true presence of God with Israel, but also the true recapitulator of Israel. Peter Leithart has noted that not only do the words *BIBLOS geneseōs* that appear at the beginning of the book (as we noted earlier) identify it with the beginning of the Hebrew Scriptures, but Jesus's commission to the disciples in chapter 28 echoes Cyrus's commission for the restoration of Israel and the temple at the end of 2 Chronicles (the canonical end to Israel's history).[48] Jesus's ministry therefore encompasses and redeems the whole of Israel's history.

This reading is also validated by the fact that Jesus's ministry and life move through the stages of Israel's history. During his flight to Egypt as an infant, Matthew cites Hosea 11:1: "Out of Egypt I called my Son" (Matt 2:15). The passage in its original context literally describes Israel in the desert and therefore should not be confused with rectilinear prophecy. Nevertheless, the use of this passage typologically identifies Jesus with the true Israel. If Jesus is the true Israel, he must also follow their route of exile and return from Egypt.[49] He is not only the divine Son of God, but a "replacement" (to use Jeffrey Gibbs's term) for God's human son Israel (Exod 4:22, Hos 11:1).[50] Gibbs has highlighted this theme and observed that there is an obvious connection between this and Jesus's designation as the "Beloved Son" in Matthew's baptismal scene. This title does not come from Psalm 2 (as is commonly thought), but rather has a direct verbal parallel with the designation in the LXX version of Genesis 22 for Isaac and Jeremiah 31 (Masoretic text, chapter 38) for Israel.[51] Similarly, Austin Farrer has shown in his book, *The Triple Victory* that Jesus's temptations in the wilderness directly parallel those of Israel.[52] Jesus goes so far as to quote the verses that accompanied each act of apostasy by Israel in the wilderness, culminating in his rejection of the devil's insistence on receiving divine worship. Here Jesus overcomes where Israel fell to the temptation of worshiping the golden calf.[53]

Scaer has also highlighted Matthew's theme of the recapitulation and transcendence of Israel's history of mediation.[54] Jesus fulfills and transcends kingly mediation because, as he asserts, he is greater than Solomon (Matt 12:42, i.e., the greatest Israelite king). He fulfills and transcends prophetic mediation because he is greater than Jonah (v. 41). Finally, he transcends and fulfills both the Old Testament cult because he is greater than the temple (12:6).

Much as he recapitulated the exodus and wanderings of Israel in the desert, Jesus's ministry represents a reconquest of the land (this time from the power of the devil) by his exorcisms, healing, and the forgiving of sins. As Ernst Hegstenberg notes, Jesus identifies himself with the Angel of YHWH who participated in the original conquest of the land, by claiming that he is the commander of God's heavenly armies (Matt 26:53, echoing Joshua 5 and Daniel 10).[55] He finally is rejected like the prophets and suffers

---

48. Leithart, *Four*, 118–20.

49. Harrington, *Matthew*, 44; Lenski, *Matthew's Gospel*, 77–79.

50. Gibbs, "Son of God," 211.

51. Ibid., 213–16.

52. Farrer, *Triple Victory*.

53. Ibid., 61–73.

54. Scaer, *Christology*, 54–55.

55. Hengstenberg, *Christology of the Old Testament*, 1:128.

death on the cross as a sign of Israel's continuing exile. In this, he is the true king who bears the wrong doing of the people, like his ancestor Josiah. Indeed, as in Mark's gospel, Jesus is willing to drink the cup of wrath spoken of by the prophets of the Old Testament (Matt 26:42).[56] His resurrection then becomes an end of cosmic exile and his enthronement as the true king.

The Synoptic Gospels: Luke

In Luke's gospel, the emphasis falls on Jesus's prophetic ministry as the Servant of Isaiah and YHWH returning to Zion.[57] Luke's Christology is best summarized by the acclamation of the people in their response to Jesus's work: "A great prophet has arisen among us!" and "God has visited his people!" (Luke 7:16). By recording statements like this and others, Luke makes explicit the fact that he understands Jesus to be a fulfillment of the coming of the Servant, who, as we saw, Isaiah also identified with the return of YHWH himself.

The gospel is replete with evidence for this reading. When in chapter 2 Gabriel begins to announce Jesus's birth to Mary, he states: "The Lord is with you" (1:28). The coming of Jesus is therefore implicitly equated with the coming of God's presence. When informed that she will give birth to Jesus, Mary asks how this will be, in light of the fact that she is a virgin. The angel responds, "The Holy Spirit will come upon you, and the power of the *Most High will overshadow you*" (1:35, emphasis added). Arthur Just has demonstrated that this description (particularly the language of "overshadowing") directly corresponds to the description of the *kavod*'s descent into the tabernacle in the LXX's version of Exodus chapter 40.[58] In that she is the new dwelling place of the *kavod* come in the flesh, Elizabeth can very easily call her "mother of my Lord" (1:43). Leithart also notes that the overshadowing of Mary is reminiscent of the Spirit's hovering above the waters at the beginning of creation (Gen 1:2).[59] Later, Jesus's genealogy connects him with Adam, whom Luke also refers to as "the son of God" (Luke 3:38). By implication then, Luke seems to be suggesting to his audience that Jesus is the beginning of a new creation.

---

56. See Allison and W. Davies, *Saint Matthew*, 3:497; France, *Gospel of Matthew*, 1005; Hagner, *Matthew*, 783; Gundry, *Matthew*, 533; Keener, *Gospel of Matthew*, 683.

57. See the following commentaries: Bock, *Luke*; Bovon, *Evangelium nach Lukas*; Caird, *St. Luke*; Conzelmann, *Theology of St. Luke*; Craddock, *Luke*; Alexandria, *Saint Luke*; Danker, *Jesus and the New Age*; C. Evans, *Saint Luke*; Fendt, *Christus der Gemeinde*; Geldenhuys, *Gospel of Luke*; Gooding, *Luke*; J. Green, *Luke*; Hobbs, *Gospel of Luke*; L. Johnson, *Luke*; Just, *Luke*; H. Klein, *Lukasevangelium*; Lagrange, *Evangile selon Saint Luc*; Leaney, *Saint Luke*; Lenski, *St. Luke's Gospel*; Lieu, *Gospel of Luke*; Manson, *Luke*; I. Marshall, *Luke*; D. Miller, *Gospel according to Luke*; Morgan, *Luke*; P. Müller, *Lukas-Evangelium*; Plummer, *St. Luke*; Rengstorf, *Evangelium nach Lukas*; Rienecker, *Evangelium des Lukas*; Ringe, *Luke*; Schanz, *Evangelium des Heiligen Lucas*; Schlatter, *Evangelium des Lukas*; G. Schneider, *Evangelium nach Lukas*; Schweizer, *Evangelium nach Lukas*; Stuhlmueller, *St. Luke*; Summers, *Luke*; Tannehill, *Luke*; Tiede, *Luke*; LaVerdiere, *Luke*; Vinson, *Luke*; Julius Wellhausen, *Evangelium Lucae*; Wiefel, *Evangelium nach Lukas*; Zahn, *Evangelium des Lucas*.

58. Just, *Luke*, 1:69. Also see the same argument in Chemnitz et al., *Harmony of the Four Evangelists*, 118.

59. Leithart, *Four*, 59–60.

Luke's identification of Jesus with the Servant and *kavod* is reinforced when he is presented in the temple for circumcision. Just notes that if one adds up the weeks between Gabriel's confrontation of Zechariah in the temple (the angel, who is also the agent of revelation in Daniel 9) and Jesus's presentation at the temple, one gets the number seventy.[60] As we observed earlier, this is the number of the universal Jubilee of Daniel 9.[61] In connection to this, later Luke recounts Jesus's reading of Isaiah 61 in the Nazareth synagogue, where he himself makes the claim to be the Servant of that text (4:16–20).[62] Indeed, this announcement is keeping with Jesus's preaching of the kingdom of God. The coming of universal Jubilee was a common image of eschatological redemption in many of the texts of Second Temple Judaism.[63]

After Jesus is presented in the temple, Simeon makes the final identification between Jesus and the returning *kavod*/Servant in his song: "for my eyes have seen your salvation that you have prepared in the presence of all peoples, a *light for revelation to the Gentiles*, and for *glory to* [or 'of'] *your people Israel*" (Luke 2:30–32, emphasis added). This on the one hand represents an allusion to the Servant of 49:6 who is a "light to the nations," and also to the *kavod*. The later phrase, "the glory of your people Israel," is reminiscent of the description of the *kavod* in the LXX version of 1 Samuel 4:22.[64] When informed of her status as the mother of God, Mary's song of praise echoes that of Hannah, Samuel's mother, in 1 Samuel (compare 1 Sam 2:1–11 and Luke 1:46–55). This suggests that Jesus will be a prophet similar to Samuel. Nevertheless, in that he is God himself come in the flesh, Jesus's role is not merely one of continuation of prophecy, but also its fulfillment. As the final and universal prophet, Jesus is the "light to the nations."

This idea of Jesus as the "light" of revelation might also be present in Luke's prologue. Here Just notes the possibility of a non-Johannine reference to Jesus as the "Word of God" in the sentence: "those who from the *beginning were eyewitnesses and ministers of the word* have delivered them [the kerygma] to us" (Luke 1:2, emphasis added).[65] If "eyewitnesses" and "ministers" are the same people, then their witness is not to something, but to someone (i.e., the divine Word, Jesus). David Scaer agrees with this argument and observes that Luke's rhetorical use of this description of his sources makes little sense if the eyewitnesses are not the same as the ministers. If the ministers are not the same as the eyewitnesses, how would Luke's claim to rely on them validate his claims of authority for his gospel? Would he not simply be bearing witnesses to the fact that there are people who proclaim Jesus and not that his sources were those who were directly appointed to be eyewitnesses to him?[66]

---

60. Just, *Luke*, 1:58.

61. Collins, *Daniel*, 352; Hengstenberg, *Christology of the Old Testament*, 3:89–90.

62. See J. Green, *Luke*, 212; L. Johnson, *Luke*, 79; Lenski, *Luke's Gospel*, 252; Sloan, *Favorable Year of the Lord*; Sri, "Release from the Debt," 183–94; Strauss, *Davidic Messiah*, 219–43. We thank Edward Sri for directing us to many of these sources.

63. Bergsma, *Jubilee from Leviticus to Qumran*, 233–94, 298–301; Sri, "Release from the Debt," 189–90. We thank Sri for directing us to the Bergsma source.

64. See similar arguments in Just, *Luke*, 1:117–20.

65. Ibid., 1:36.

66. Scaer, "Doctrine of the Trinity," 329.

In further keeping with these divine designations, Just also suggests that Jesus applies the divine Name to himself on a number of occasions.[67] In teaching the disciples about humility, Just translates Jesus's remark about service as: "I AM in the midst of you as one who serves" (Luke 22:27).[68] Similarly, he translates the risen Jesus's self-identification to the disciples as, "I AM myself" (24:39). That Jesus would identify himself with the Name in these texts is coherent with Luke's previous identification of him with the *kavod* and Word.

Therefore, much like Matthew and Mark, Luke identifies Jesus with the fulfillment of God's presence with Israel in the Old Testament. Similar also to the other synoptic evangelists, Luke believes that Jesus continues to be present with his Church, particularly in the Lord's Supper. This is strongly indicated by his use of an *inclusio* of sacramental presence. At the beginning of the gospel, we are told that Jesus is born in Bethlehem, meaning "house of bread."[69] When Jesus is born, he is placed in a manger (2:7), that is, an animal's feeding trough. By implication then he himself is food from the very beginning of his existence. Throughout the gospel, Jesus perpetually eats with sinners, culminating in his institution of the Lord's Supper for the forgiveness of sins.[70] At the end of the gospel, we find him revealing himself in the "breaking of bread" (24:35).[71]

As God's returning glory, Jesus comes to fulfill his former promise to Abraham that he would bless the nations through his seed (1:55, 71–73).[72] As the "light to the nations" Jesus unites Jews and Gentiles by his lineage. To emphasize this point, Luke traces his lineage back to Adam, rather than merely to Abraham as does Matthew (3:23–37).[73] Even in his death, he is able to unite Jews and Gentiles. Herod and Pilate, who had previously been enemies, are made friends by later handing him over to the former for trial (23:12). Moving on into the book of Acts, the apostles incorporate the Gentiles into the people of God and thereby fulfill his promised blessings to the nations (Gen 12; Isa 45, 49).

This emphasis on Christ's prophetic office as the Servant of Isaiah does not preclude his occupancy of the offices of king and priest.[74] Robert Sloan observes that Jesus's role as the true king connects well with his announcement of Jubilee. This is because it in fact was the responsibility of kings in the Old Testament to announce the Jubilee.[75] Luke, like the other evangelists, also identifies Jesus with the Melchizekiah priest-king of Psalm 110 (Luke 20:40–45). In keeping with his priestly role, he is the Son of Man prophesied in Daniel (6:5, 9:26–27, 9:58, 11:29–32, 18:31–34). Beyond

---

67. See discussion in Just, *Luke*, 2:784, 792, 846–47.

68. Ibid., 2:846–47.

69. Ibid., 1:14.

70. Ibid.

71. See detailed discussion in Just, *Ongoing Feast*.

72. See the role of the fulfillment of the Abrahamic covenant in Luke-Acts in Robert Brawley, "Abrahamic Covenant Traditions," 109–32.

73. Though it should of course be noted that Matthew does include Gentile women in Jesus's genealogy.

74. See the connection between the Davidic and Abrahamic covenants in Luke-Acts, in Sabine Van den Eynde, "Children of the Promise," 470–82. We thank Scott Hahn in his piece, "Christ, Kingdom, and Creation," for directing us to this source.

75. Sloan, *Favorable Year of the Lord*, 58–67.

this, Jesus is David's son (Luke 3:31) and therefore the true fulfillment of the promises made to David, as Gabriel tells Mary (1:32–33). N.T. Wright has noted that much of Luke's use of language and narrative imagery suggests that he is intentionally echoing the LXX version of 1 and 2 Samuel.[76] Similar to David, Wright observes that Jesus wanders throughout the gospel as he awaits the kingdom promised to his mother at the beginning of the gospel (1:32–33).[77] Later in Acts, just as David is persecuted by king Saul of the tribe of Benjamin, Jesus's body, the Church, is persecuted by a man named Saul of the tribe of Benjamin (Acts 9:5–6, Phil 3:4–6).

As in the other gospels, Luke portrays Jesus as an exorcist and healer. This does not detract from Luke's description of Jesus as a new David, but rather shows how the Third Evangelist views Jesus's fulfillment of this role. Jesus's war for the kingdom is not with temporal enemies, but with Satan and the demonic forces of the old creation (Luke 11:20). After his disciples return with joy from battling the devil in Jesus's Name, Jesus exclaims "I saw Satan fall like lightning from heaven" (10:18). The devil, as the source of all evil, is the direct or indirect source of all disease and demonic possession. In combating these things therefore he is the one who Jesus and his disciples overcome through the power of the Holy Spirit.

Jesus's announcement of Jubilee and the forgiveness of sins also works against and finally defeats the devil. Though Satan is certainly the enemy of God, he is also an accuser of humanity in the heavenly court (Job 1:6–8, 2:1–7; Zech 3:1–10; Rev 12:10). In this sense, the devil maintains his power through his ability to accuse. Understood in this light, Jesus's forgiveness of sins and his sacrificial death are the true exercises of his office as king. Luke, it would appear, also envisions the Church throughout Acts as continuing this mission of Jesus to the ends of the earth. After the ascension, the apostles persist in Jesus's activities of preaching, teaching, celebrating the sacraments, and engaging in healings and exorcisms.

It has often been argued that Luke utterly lacks an atonement theology. Both Hans Conzelman and James D. G. Dunn have claimed that Luke has no understanding of Jesus's death as being sacrificial or directly redeeming.[78] Roy Harrisville, while acknowledging both Dunn and Conzelman's objections, counters their claim by citing Gerhard Fredrich, who points to Luke's report of the words of institution (Luke 22:19–20), and also Philip's reading of the Fourth Servant Song (Isa 53) with the Ethiopian eunuch (Acts 8:26–40).[79] We are also told that when Jesus begins his ministry he is "about thirty years" (Luke 3:23). This is the same age (according to Numbers 4:3) that priests began their service in the tabernacle/temple.[80]

---

76. N. T. Wright, *Christian Origins*, 1:379. Also see Bock, *Proclamation from Prophecy*, 293–94; Bruce, "Davidic Messiah," 7–17; Hahn, "Christ, Kingdom, and Creation," 113–38. We thank him in his aforementioned article for directing us to these sources.

77. N. T. Wright, *Christian Origins*, 1:380–81.

78. Conzelmann, *Theology of St. Luke*, 201; Dunn, *Unity and Diversity*, 17.

79. Harrisville, *Fracture*, 175–77.

80. Although for Levites this appears to have begun at age 25. See Num 8:24. There probably was about a five-year period of training.

More subtly, Jesus's fulfillment of priestly mediation is suggested by the fact that Luke chooses to begin and end his gospel in the temple (Luke 1:8, 24:52). This appears to mean that the entire story of Jesus has been bounded by and therefore finds its meaning in the temple. It also strongly implies that Jesus has fulfilled and taken over the function of the temple. This interpretation makes a great deal of sense in light of the data that we have earlier examined that suggests that Luke views Jesus as the returning *kavod*, as well as a final universal sacrifice for the forgiveness of sins. Through Word and sacrament, Jesus mediates God's presence, holiness, and the forgiveness of sins to the Church.

John's Gospel and Letters[81]

Much like Mark's gospel, John's gospel is one of glory and humiliation. John, nonetheless, works with these themes differently than Mark. As we observed earlier, Mark reveals Jesus's glory and humiliation through a pattern of alternation. John is much more comfortable describing Jesus's glory in a pattern of paradoxical disclosure and hiddenness. John describes Jesus as the one who makes his power and glory known by his act of humiliation. His humiliation is the very act of his exaltation. His veiling is the unveiling of his revelation.

John begins his gospel by telling his audience that Jesus is the true divine Word who spoke forth the original creation (John 1:1–4). Jesus is also the true glory of God. His light has shown in the darkness and triumphed over it (1:5). This also seems to suggest John's identification of Jesus with the Servant of Isaiah 49:6 who is a "light to the nations" in that he is "true light, which enlightens everyone, and is coming into the world" (1:9).[82]

As Rudolf Schnackernburg observes, John posits that Jesus is greater than Moses. Whereas Moses desired to see God, but was only allowed to do so indirectly, Jesus is God himself come in the flesh.[83] Indeed, as Charles Gieschen adds, Moses's revelation is of a lesser variety than that of Jesus, because Jesus has directly seen the Father as no one else has.[84] Whereas Moses only ascended to Sinai, Jesus has descended from heaven and will ascend there again: "no one has ascended into heaven except he who descended from heaven, the Son of Man" (3:13). As the true *kavod* himself, Jesus himself is the source of all glory. Moses's face merely reflected glory, but Jesus is the glory of God

81. Aquinas, *Gospel of St. John*; Beasley-Murray, *John*; J. Becker, *Evangelium nach Johannesm*; Bernard, *Gospel according to St. John*; de Boor, *Evangelium des Johannes*; R. Brown, *Gospel According to John*; R. Brown, *Gospel of John*; Bultmann, *Gospel of John*; Büchsel, *Evangelium nach Johannes*; von Burger, *Evangelium nach Johannes*; Calvin, *John*; Carson, *John*; Deutz, *Evangelium Sancti Iohannis*; Dodd, *Fourth Gospel*; Godet, *Evangelium Johannis*; Keil, *Evangelium des Johannes*; Koester, *Fourth Gospel*; Lagrange, *Evangile Selon Saint Jean*; Lincoln, *Saint John*; Lücke, *Evangelium des Johannes*; Luthardt, *Evangelium nach Johannes*; H. Meyer, *Handbook to the Gospel*; Mopsuestia, *Gospel of John*; Orback and Kirk, *Gospel of John*; J. Sanders, *Saint John*; Schanz, *Evangelium des Heiligen Johannes*; Schick, *Evangelium nach Johannes*; Schlatter, *Johannes*; Schnackenburg, *St. John*, vols. 1 and 3; J. Schneider, *Evangelium nach Johannes*; Schnelle, *Evangelium nach Johannes*; Schulz, *Evangelium nach Johannes*; Strathmann, *Evangelium nach Johannes*; Thulock, *Evangelio Johannis*; Vanier, *Drawn into the Mystery*; Wikenhauser, *Evangelium nach Johannes*; Wilckens, *Evangelium nach Johannes*; Zahn, *Evangelium des Johannes*.

82. Dodd, *Fourth Gospel*, 246.

83. Schnackenburg, *St. John*, 1:278.

84. Gieschen, *Angelomorphic Christology*, 273.

in person. Throughout his book, John reinforces Jesus's identity with the hypostatized *kavod* present in the Old Testament. At one point in the gospel, Jesus also chides the Jews for not listening to his voice (5:17–47) in the same manner that they would not listen to him when he spoke to their forefathers in the cloud on Sinai (Exod 20).[85]

John identifies himself as a true witness to this glory, just as Moses was on Sinai: "we have seen his glory, glory as of the only Son from the Father, full of grace and truth" (John 1:14).[86] Looking upon God in the flesh, the apostles have gained the same revelation as Moses. In seeing Jesus, Nathaniel is called a "true Israelite" (1:47) because the etymology of "Israel" in the first century among many Hellenistic Jews was "one who sees God."[87] Indeed, because the disciples have seen Jesus, they have also "seen the Father" (14:7). Since Jesus's revelation fulfills God's revelation to Moses, one might say that their revelation is of a greater variety: "For the law was given through Moses; grace and truth came through Jesus Christ. No one has ever seen God; the only God, who is at the Father's side, he has made him known" (1:17–18).

Jesus reveals his glory through his prophetic Word. This Word reveals Jesus's true identity in the midst of his outwardly humble form. Jesus testifies that he will be "lifted up" (3:14) and be glorified (17:1), both of which refer to his passion. Dying, Jesus will reveal his divine power to save and to condemn: "Father, the hour has come [of his passion]; glorify your Son that the Son may glorify you" (17:1). His actions not only reveal his own glory as the sole agent of redemption, but also glorify his Father: "I glorified you on earth, having accomplished the work that you gave me to do. And now, Father, glorify me in your own presence with the glory that I had with you before the world existed" (17:4–5).

At the hour of his death, Jesus's identity is paradoxically revealed. The inscription over his cross declares his true identity: "Jesus of Nazareth, King of the Jews." As Craig Koester correctly observes, this inscription stands as a prophetic proclamation in all three major languages of the Roman world (19:19).[88] This echoes Isaiah's insistence that the glory of the Lord would be seen by all flesh (Isa 40:5).[89] The paradox, that such glory is hidden, nevertheless remains. Such glory can only be perceived by those who believe the Word of God concerning Jesus: "Did I not tell you that if you believed *you would see the glory of God*?" (John 11:40, emphasis added).[90] It is, indeed, true that John does often talk about "seeing" the glory of revelation. But as the passages cited above demonstrate, this seeing is a spiritual seeing that is mediated through the auditory faculties. In point of fact, such spiritual seeing frequently stands in contradiction to ordinary physical vision: "Have you believed because you have seen me? Blessed are those who have not seen and yet have believed" (20:29).

---

85. Ibid., 274.

86. For discussions of the theme of glory in John see Caird, "Glory of God," 265–77; Cook, "'Glory' Motif," 291–97.

87. Gieschen, *Angelomorphic Christology*, 281.

88. Koester, *Fourth Gospel*, 203.

89. Dodd, *Fourth Gospel*, 246.

90. See Bauckham, *God Crucified*, 63–68.

Jesus's identity does not merely testify to the truth, but is the truth. For John, truth is a person, and not an abstract proposition. The truth is the content of Jesus's revelation. As the inscription above the cross makes clear, this truth is that Jesus is the true Messiah king who has come to redeem the world from sin, death, and the devil: "You say that I am a king. For this purpose I was born and for this purpose I have come into the world—to bear witness to the truth" (18:37). Jesus's kingship is tied up in his prophetic ministry of conquest through the Word. By his prophetic Word of truth he has come to destroy the devil who is the "prince of this world" and one whom he will make certain is "driven out" (12:31). The devil is a "liar" and a "murderer" (8:44) whom Christ counters with his "truth" (1:17) and "life" (v. 4). By this prophetic Word of salvation, he will ultimately redeem humanity and bring it to the Father.[91] This truth brings the freedom of the gospel: "you will know the truth, and the truth will set you free" (8:32).

Jesus's Word of redemption triumphs over Satan and the mangled old narrative of creation by enacting a new creation story. Just as he spoke forth the original creation, his prophetic Word of redemption will actualize the new creation. N. T. Wright observes: "John confronts his readers with a strange new Genesis."[92] Later, Wright argues that the pattern of John's gospel corresponds to the works and days of creation, and therefore the book represents a new narrative of creation:

> The large-scale outworking of this [Jesus's renewal of creation] can be seen in John's deliberate sequence of "signs." I believe that John intends his readers to follow a sequence of seven signs, with the water-into-wine story at Cana as the first and the crucifixion as the seventh. The resurrection of Jesus takes place, he is careful to tell us twice, "on the first day of the week," and I believe this is best interpreted as the start of God's new creation. On the Friday, the sixth day of the week, Jesus stands before Pilate, who declares "behold the man!" (19:5), echoing the creation of humankind on the sixth day of creation. On the cross Jesus finishes the work the Father has given him to do (17:4), ending with the shout of triumph (*tetelestai*, "it is accomplished," 19:30), corresponding the completion of creation itself. There follows, as in Genesis, a day of rest, a Sabbath day. . . . [therefore] Jesus' public career is to be understood as the completion of the original creation, with the resurrection as the start of the new.[93]

This act of recreation through the Word is also tied up with Jesus's identity as the fulfillment of the temple. As we saw in the previous chapter, the Old Testament authors saw creation as a vast temple dedicated to the worship of God. In the same manner, the Israelite cult was a restoration of the original creation. This means that Jesus's enactment of a "strange new Genesis" cannot be divided from his fulfillment of the temple and its sacrificial worship. Jesus's role as the fulfillment and re-creator of the cult/creation fits not only with his reality as the "Word made flesh," but also makes him the true son of David. As we should remember, God promised David that the Messiah would build the house for his Name (2 Sam 7:14).[94] Jesus's re-creation of the world was not only

91. Schanckenburg, *St. John*, 3:65.

92. N. T. Wright, *Christians Origins*, 1:411.

93. Ibid., 3:440.

94. See discussion in Hahn, "Temple, Sign, and Sacrament," 109–11.

prefigured in Solomon's construction of the temple (i.e., cosmic microcosm), but also in the building of the original creation by the preexistent Christ as Holy Wisdom (Prov 8). Solomon (as we previously argued) was therefore an image of the preexistent Christ, as well as a type of his redemptive work.

For this reason, Jesus is not only a prophet and king, but also a priest and a new temple. Jesus fulfills his messianic priesthood in a number of ways. First, John makes certain that his readers recognize that Jesus is the true Temple. Christ is the returning *kavod* of the Old Testament. He has returned to "tabernacle" among us (John 1:14).[95] Indeed "his body" (2:21) is the true Temple.[96] The temple of Jesus's body will be destroyed and raised up again (2:22–24). Hence, he not only mediates the presence of God, but he will also destroy the old creation and bring about a new creation through his sacrifice on the altar of the cross.

The second major aspect of Jesus's fulfillment of the temple cult in John is the fact that Jesus recapitulates the ritual festivals. Indeed, as Wright has shown, John structures Jesus's ministry around Israel's liturgical calendar.[97] Several other scholars have noticed this pattern as well.[98] According to John's reckoning, Jesus attends three Passovers (2:12–25, 6:4, 11:55—19:42), the festival of Tabernacles (7:2), and possibly Hanukah (10:22).[99] In this vein, Scott Hahn writes:

> We also see a dramatic identification of Jesus and the Temple in John 7–10:21. There, the backdrop is the festival celebrating the building of the Temple (Tabernacles), during which the priests daily poured out water from the Pool of Siloam on the altar steps and kept the Temple courts illuminated twenty-four hours a day in anticipation of the eschatological prophesies. In the midst of this, Jesus claims himself to be the true source of water and light, and brings light to a blind man through the waters of Siloam, thus supporting his claim to be the true Temple.
>
> In John 10:22–42, during the Feast of Dedication, which commemorates the re-consecration of the Temple by the Maccabees, Jesus describes himself as the one "consecrated" by the Father and sent into the world—that is, he calls himself the new sanctuary. In John 14:2–3, Jesus again refers to his "Father's House," a Temple reference alluding to John 2:16 and supported by other Temple references—the house with many "rooms" is probably the many-chambered Temple of Ezekiel 41–43; and the "place" (Greek: *topos*; Hebrew: *mâqôm*) he goes to prepare connotes the "sacred place" of the Temple. In the final analysis, this passage describes Jesus' departure to be prepared as a Temple wherein his disciples will "dwell."[100]

95. This is often translated as "dwelt," but many have noted that "tabernacled" is a more appropriate translation. See Koester, *Fourth Gospel*, 125. Also see discussion in Um, *Temple Christology*, 153–54.

96. See Coloe, *God Dwells With Us*; Frühwald-König, *Tempel und Kult*; Hahn, "Temple, Sign, and Sacrament," 107–43; Hoskins, *Jesus as the Fulfillment*; Kerr, *Temple of Jesus' Body*.

97. N. T. Wright, *Christian Origins*, 1:412.

98. Yee, *Jewish Feasts*; Daise, *Feast in John*; Mlakushyil, *Structure of the Fourth Gospel*. We thank Scott Hahn in his "Christ, Kingdom, and Creation" for directing us to these sources.

99. Hahn, "Christ, Kingdom, and Creation," 111.

100. Ibid., 114.

Jesus's fulfillment of Israel's cult not only takes the form of his recapitulation of its festivals, but also of its sacrificial worship. John the Baptist informs his listeners at the beginning of the gospel that Jesus is "the Lamb of God, who takes away the sin of the world!" (1:29). Raymond Brown notes that this description of Jesus is reminiscent of both the Suffering Servant and the paschal lamb.[101] These two echoes of the Old Testament fit together nicely insofar as we have seen that Isaiah envisions a universal Passover lamb to match his universal exodus. Jesus's identification with the paschal lamb is also shown by the fact that his death occurs during the festival of Passover. Later, it will be shown that other details of Jesus's passion reinforce his fulfillment of the Passover sacrifice.

Beyond the Passover sacrifice, there is much in John's narrative to suggest that Jesus is also the fulfillment of the Day of Atonement. In this regard, it should first be noted that the location of Jesus's betrayal in the garden of Gethsemane is significant. As George Beasley-Murray observes, John, like Luke, does not give us the specific name of the garden of Jesus's betrayal (although 18:1 strongly implies Gethsemane).[102] In other words, John appears to be interested in emphasizing the location of the beginning of Jesus's passion as simply a "garden." From the re-creation imagery used by John earlier, it is not unlikely to think that John intends his readers to think of this garden as a new Eden.

The second interesting thing about the location of Jesus's arrest is that it takes place at the base of the Mount of Olives. The Mount of Olives is not only the route through which David fled from Absalom (as we mentioned in our discussion of Mark), but it is also the location where Ezekiel saw the glory of the Lord resting when it left the temple (Ezek 11:23).[103] Read in this light, the Mount of Olives has become the real temple, since it is *de facto* the new holy of holies where the *kavod* has come to rest. As a result, the themes of both the true Temple and Eden come together in a remarkable way. The identification of Eden as the protological temple was, as Stephen Um demonstrates, by no means limited to the Old Testament, but was widely recognized in the literature of Second Temple Judaism.[104] If this reading of John's intention is correct, then John wishes to portray Jesus as the new Adam and the true high priest standing in the reconstituted garden-temple of Eden.

The location of the narrative within the true garden-temple then forms the context of Jesus's atoning actions. These actions draw a striking parallel with the liturgy of the Day of Atonement as it was possibly practiced during the time of Christ. First, let us examine the description of Jesus's arrest:

> Then Jesus, knowing all that would happen to him, came forward and said to them, "Whom do you seek?" They answered him, "Jesus of Nazareth." Jesus said to them, "*I am* he." Judas, who betrayed him, was standing with them. When Jesus said to them, "*I am* he," they drew back and fell to the ground. So he asked them again, "Whom do you seek?" And they said, "Jesus of Nazareth." Jesus answered, "I told you that *I am* he. So, if you seek me, let these men go." (18:4–8, emphasis added)

101. R. Brown, *Gospel According to John*, 62–63.

102. Beasley-Murray, *John*, 316.

103. The "mountain east of" the Temple Mount is the Mount of Olives.

104. Um, *Temple Christology*, 20–52.

Andrei Orlov has noted the significance of the fact that John mentions the divine Name "I AM" three times (though Jesus himself, of course, technically only speaks the divine Name twice, and only implies it in the Greek a third time) and has connected it with traditions in the Mishnah concerning the liturgy of the Day of Atonement.[105]

According to the Mishnah, after the high priest completed his ritual sacrifices of the bull and the goat meant for YHWH, he would confess the sins of the people over the scapegoat while reciting the following prayer:

> *O Lord*, your people, the house of Israel, has committed iniquity, transgressed, and sinned before you. Forgive, *O Lord*, I pray the iniquities, transgressions, and sins, which the people, the house of Israel, have committed, transgressed, and sinned before you, as it is written in the Torah of Moses, you servant, "For on this day shall atonement be made for you to clean you. From all your sins shall you be clean before *the Lord.*" (Yoma 6:2, emphasis added)[106]

There is an obvious parallel between this text and John's description of Jesus's arrest, the chief one being that there is a threefold repetition of the divine Name. Both the location of the recitation of this prayer and the reaction of the hearers is also highly suggestive. First, this prayer is spoken after the priest comes out of the holy of holies, which, as we have seen, is where John effectively places Jesus. He moves towards the people in the way that John described Jesus's moving towards the guards. The reaction of the guards directly parallels the description of the priest and people in the courtyard of the temple:

> And the priests and people standing in the courtyard, when they would hear the Expressed Name [of the Lord] come out of the mouth of the high priest, *would kneel and bow down and fall on their faces* and say, "Blessed be the name of the glory of his kingdom forever and ever.[107]

Despite these significant parallels, we must remain somewhat cautious regarding this interpretation in light of the fact that the Mishnah was compiled more than one hundred years after the writing of John's gospel (probably around AD 200).[108] These parallels are at least highly suggestive and fit well with the earlier scholarship that showed John viewed Jesus's ministry as tied up with the fulfillment of the Jewish liturgical calendar.

The rest of John's passion narrative offers other echoes and similarities with the Day of Atonement. If Jesus offers himself up in the temple-garden as the goat for YHWH, then he must also be cast out of the city like the scapegoat. For this reason he is crucified outside the city (19:17). Of course, the difficulty is that there were two goats, and only one Jesus. Since the goat for YHWH was killed in the temple and the scapegoat was cast out of the city unharmed, it might be argued that John combines the two events of bloody sacrifice and being cast out into a single one. In fact, John is careful to tell us that the place where Jesus was crucified also had a garden (i.e., in reminiscence of the

---

105. Andrei Orlov, professor of New Testament, Marquette University, personal conversation. I must also thank my classmate Arvid Nybroten for first alerting me to this literary parallel.

106. Neusner, *Mishnah*, 275.

107. Ibid. (emphasis added).

108. Neusner, *Mishnah*, xvi.

garden-temple) nearby: "Now in the place where he was crucified *there was a garden*" (19:41, emphasis added).[109]

There are other aspects of John's description that suggest that John means to imply that Jesus's blood is offered up in a garden-temple. The garden spoken of in 19:41 is ultimately where Jesus is buried. Later, on the day of resurrection when Mary Magdalene looks into the tomb where Jesus had been laid she sees "*two angels* in white, sitting where the body of Jesus had lain, *one at the head and one at the feet*" (20:12, emphasis added). Wright has observed that this strongly parallels the liturgy of the Day of Atonement wherein the blood of the first goat was placed on the mercy seat between golden images of the two cherubim on the cover of the ark.[110] Jesus's person is therefore the new mercy seat (*hilastērion*).

John's crucifixion scene itself also further reinforces this interpretation. As Jesus dies he cries out "*tetelestai*" a word frequently written on a paid bill in the Hellenistic world. [111] Indeed, Jesus is not just the victim on the Day of Atonement, but the priest. John also uses the word "*chitōn*" to describe the seamless garment that Jesus wears as he is brought to the site of crucifixion (19:23–24). This word is used in the LXX to describe the garment that the high priest wore on the Day of Atonement (see LXX Exod 28:4, Lev 16:4).[112]

Beyond parallels with the Day of Atonement, there are other hints in the passion narrative of the fulfillment of the Passover sacrifice. According to some, the piercing of Jesus's side hearkens back to the Passover lamb. Hans Urs von Balthasar cites the rabbinical legislation concerning Passover that prescribes that the blood of the slain Paschal lamb must be drained from the heart.[113] Schnackenburg argues that the passage regarding the piercing of Jesus's side must be interpreted as conveying that the soldiers intended to pierce his heart, since we are told that it is their goal to make certain that Jesus is dead.[114] Since Jesus is pierced through the heart and his blood is drained, he is the true "lamb of God which takes away the sin of the world" (John 1:29). While Jesus is dying, the vinegar given to him to drink is hoisted on a hyssop branch (19:29). This is the same branch used to smear the blood of the Passover lamb on the lintels of the houses during the exodus (Exod 12:22).[115] In other words, by his substitionary death, Jesus releases humanity from sin, death, and the devil just as the lamb served as the catalyst for the exodus from temporal bondage in Egypt.

After being pierced by the Centurion's spear, blood and water flow from Jesus's side (John 19:34). Following a long established patristic reading of this text, Oscar Cullman

---

109. I must again thank my classmate Arvid Nybroten for this insight and calling this passage to my attention.

110. N. T. Wright, *Christian Origins*, 3:668. Wright's suggestion is taken from Rowan Williams, *Christian Theology*, 186.

111. N. T. Wright, *John for Everyone*, 131.

112. Hahn, *Father Who Keeps*, 228.

113. Von Balthasar, *Mysterium Paschale*, 129. Von Balthasar is thinking of Mishnah Tamîd 4:2. See R. Daly, *Christian Doctrine of Sacrifice*, 41.

114. Schnackenburg, *St. John*, 3:289.

115. Hahn, *Father Who Keeps*, 228.

and Rudolf Bultmann have suggested that the flow of blood and water represent the sacraments of baptism and the Lord's Supper.[116] Another complementary reading of this symbolism might be that the blood and water represent John's final identification of Jesus with the temple and its cult. Hahn notes that we are told in Ezekiel 47:1–11 that living water would flow out of the eschatological temple. Read in light of this passage, it would appear that John is suggesting, yet again, that Jesus's body is the eschatological temple. The same author has also pointed to the rabbinic tradition that two streams, one of water and the other of blood (i.e., from the sacrifices), flowed out of the Second Temple.[117] As we observed earlier, the temple was the locus of God's glory in the Old Testament. From it he mediated his holiness to his people. Read from this perspective, John asserts that as the glory of God, Jesus now mediates that same holiness to the Church by his death and through the sacraments.

This scene also evokes more Edenic imagery as well. Christ lying dead on the cross is reminiscent of Adam asleep giving birth to Eve out of his side. This parallel has been frequently noticed throughout the history of exegesis.[118] In support of this reading, it should be observed that the crucifixion occurs on the sixth day of the week (the day of the creation of humanity) and that (as Wright noted above) Jesus has been identified as the true man (*ecco homo*, actually "human," "*anthrōpos*" John 19:5). Read in this light, John appears to be asserting that Jesus is the second Adam and does for the Church through Word and sacrament what Adam did for Eve. This interpretation is bolstered by J. Ramsey Michaels's observation that John possesses no description of ripping the veil of the temple.[119] If Jesus is the true Temple, then the piercing of his heart is the actual ripping of the veil. Therefore, much like the preincarnate Christ gave himself over to ancient Israel by his presence in the cult, he now gives himself to the Church through Word

116. Cullman, *Early Christian Worship*, 114–16; Bultmann, *Gospel of John*, 678. Also see Lincoln, *Saint John*, 479. Exegetically, this typological explanation of the passage appears to have begun with Augustine. He writes:

> Then came the soldiers, and broke the legs of the first, and of the other who was crucified with Him. But when they came to Jesus, and saw that He was dead already, they broke not His legs: but one of the soldiers with a spear laid open His side, and immediately came there out blood and water. A suggestive word was made use of by the evangelist, in not saying pierced, or wounded His side, or anything else, but opened; that thereby, in a sense, the gate of life might be thrown open, from whence have flowed forth the sacraments of the Church, without which there is no entrance to the life which is the true life. That blood was shed for the remission of sins; that water it is that makes up the health-giving cup, and supplies at once the laver of baptism and water for drinking. This was announced beforehand, when Noah was commanded to make a door in the side of the ark, Genesis 6:16 whereby the animals might enter which were not destined to perish in the flood, and by which the Church was prefigured. Because of this, the first woman was formed from the side of the man when asleep, Genesis 2:22 and was called Life, and the mother of all living. Genesis 3:20 Truly it pointed to a great good, prior to the great evil of the transgression (in the guise of one thus lying asleep). This second Adam bowed His head and fell asleep on the cross, that a spouse might be formed for Him from that which flowed from the sleeper's side. O death, whereby the dead are raised anew to life! What can be purer than such blood? What more health-giving than such a wound? (*Tracts on the Gospel of John*, 120.2; *NPNFa* 7:434)

117. Hahn, "Temple, Sign, and Sacrament," 114. Also see Kerr, *John*, 244–45.

118. See description in Schankenburg, *St. John*, 3:289.

119. Michaels, "Centurion's Confession," 102–9.

and sacrament. In contrast to the Israelite cult though, he now ceases to be segregated from them, but instead directly gives himself over to them in the means of grace.

By rising from the dead in a garden on the first day of the week, Jesus reveals himself as the new Adam and the divine agent of new creation. In the garden Mary mistakes him for the gardener (20:15), the vocation held by Adam prior to the Fall. In effect, Adam has returned to the garden and creation has begun anew. By faith (3:16), one enters into this new creation and is "born again" (3:3), this time of "water and the Spirit" (3:5), that is, through baptism. In this passage, we are reminded again of the original creation in which the Spirit hovered over the waters (Gen 1:2) and recognized the new act of creation that Jesus brings to us, mediated through Word and sacrament.

Chapter 4

Christology and Atonement in the New Testament, Part 2

The Christology of the Epistles and Revelation

The Epistles of Paul[1]

BEFORE WE DISCUSS THE Christology and atonement theology of the apostle Paul, we must first make clear the perspective from which we are going to engage in our subject. This is an important measure in light of a debate that is currently underway within Pauline studies between those who roughly stand in the tradition of the Reformation understanding of Paul's concept of the law and justification (notably, the late Ernst Käsemann, Peter Stuhlmacher, and less consistently by Simon Gathercole), and those who adhere to the somewhat loosely defined "new perspective" (James D. G. Dunn, E. P. Sanders, and anticipated by the late Krister Stendahl).[2] Whereas the former group (broadly speaking) holds that the gospel is distinguished from the law in the sense that it is a promise that brings about salvation rather than a demand, the later group considers the law to be either a cultural boundary marker designating those elected by grace (Dunn) or a means whereby those who are elected by grace maintain their election (Sanders). Paul's difficulty with the law then (according to the "new perspective") was not that it could not save, but rather that it was not an inclusive enough sign or marker

---

1. See the following studies of Paul's theology: Baird, *Paul's Message and Mission*; Baker, *Saint Paul and his Gospel*; Beker, *Triumph of God*; Betz, *Paulinische Studien*; Brox, *Understanding the Message of Paul*; G. Bornkamm, *Paulus*; Drane, *Paul, Libertine or Legalist?*; Dubose, *Saint Paul*; Dunn, *Theology of Paul*; Freed, *Apostle Paul*; Feine, *Saint Paul*; Fitzmyer, *According to Paul*; Furnish, *Theology and Ethics in Paul*; Garvie, *Studies of Paul*; Grollenberg, *Paul*; Hafemann, *Paul, Moses*; Hultgren, *Paul's Gospel and Mission*; Knox, *Saint Paul's Gospel*; Kuss, *Paulus*; Lindemann, *Paulus*; Longenecker, *Studies in Paul*; R. Martin, *Reconciliation*; Martyn, *Theological Issues*; Moe, *Apostle Paul*; Penna, *Paul the Apostle*; Prat, *Theology of Saint Paul*; Schelkle, *Paulus*; Schnelle, *Apostle Paul*; Schoeps, *Paulus*; Simar, *Theologie des Heiligen Paulus*; Jeremias, *Schlüssel zur Theologie des Apostels Paulus*; Söding, *Wort vom Kreuz*; Wansbrough, *Theology in Saint Paul*; Whiteley, *Theology of Saint Paul*.

2. Käsemann, *Commentary on Romans*; Stuhlmacher, *Paul's Letter*; Gathercole, *Where is Boasting?*; Dunn, *Theology of Paul*; Dunn, *New Perspective on Paul*; E. Sanders, *Paul and Palestinian Judaism*; E. Sanders, *Paul, the Law*; Stendahl, *Paul among Jews*.

to designate those who were elected by grace, whereas faith was (Dunn).[3] Or, Paul shared the perspective of late Second Temple Judaism and the early rabbinic circles that entry into the covenant occurred by grace, but had to be maintained through obedience (what Sanders refers to as "covenantal nomism"[4]). In this section, we cannot fully debate or engage adequately the questions raised by the "new perspective" at any length. Nevertheless, we will disclose beforehand that our exposition will stand in the tradition of Reformation's reading of Paul.

The best place to begin in explaining Paul's conception of Christ and his work is the sharp distinction he makes between law and promise: "For the letter kills, but the Spirit gives life" (2 Cor 3:6). At the beginning of Romans, Paul argues that Jews and Gentiles are both under the law because both have had the law revealed to them. In Romans 1:18–20, Paul follows the liturgical understanding of humanity and creation that we encountered in the Old Testament. Though this is unmistakable, Dunn is also likely correct to suggest that Paul also draws upon language of Stoic natural theology here, whereas Stuhlmacher also notes similarities with Jewish wisdom theology.[5] The created order reflects divine glory, and therefore human beings made in the divine image of glory should see that glory and reflect it with trusting praise. The Gentiles do not do this, but instead engage in idolatry (Rom 1:23). Though the Jews have had the law directly revealed to them in the Sinaitic covenant, they are equally disobedient and faithless to God (2–3). In this sense, the Sinaitic covenant is not a special law, but rather making explicit what is implicit in creation. In that both Jews and Gentiles are unable to obey the law, the creation and the written code become a medium through which both are cursed. In this, divine wrath is made manifest against the whole of the human race.

For this reason, no one can in fact claim to be righteous (Rom 3:9–18) because no one functions correctly in their roles as creatures. No one has trusted in God as the source of good and thereby glorified him: "For there is no distinction: *for all have sinned and fall short of the glory of God*" (3:22–23, emphasis added). To refuse to reflect divine glory is therefore to lose the image of divine glory. This reading is agreed with by Peter Stuhlmacher who cites the Apocalypse of Moses in order to demonstrate that Second Temple Jews (along with Paul) thought of the Fall as consisting of the loss of divine glory.[6]

Like many Jewish apocalypticists of the first century, Paul believed that this situation could only be expected to come to a climax in a universal eschatological judgment (Rom 2:16). If Paul had held to the typical Jewish apocalyptic perspective, wherein only those who held to the covenant by performing the works of Torah would be vindicated (with the possible exception of a few righteous Gentiles), he would necessarily have concluded that no one could be rescued from this coming judgment.[7] If he had taken this stance, the apostle would not have been the only Jew of this era to come to this

---

3. Dunn, *Theology of Paul*, 461–532.

4. Sanders, *Paul and Palestinian Judaism*, 422–23.

5. Dunn, *Romans 1–8*, 58–59; Stuhlmacher, *Paul's Letter*, 44.

6. Stuhlmacher, *Paul's Letter*, 58.

7. For descriptions of the various eschatological scenarios see N. T. Wright, *Christian Origins*, 1:299–338.

conclusion. The author of 4 Ezra reached such a conclusion.[8] Nevertheless, unlike 4 Ezra, Paul believed that God had triumphed in Jesus. This redemption meant the overcoming of the curse of the law through the power of the divine promise of the gospel: "But now the righteousness of God has been manifested apart from the law, although the Law and the Prophets bear witness to it" (Rom 3:21). Indeed this redemption came by "Christ Jesus, whom God put forward as a *propitiation by his blood*, to be received by faith" (3:24–25, emphasis added). In this, God maintained his faithfulness to both to the law revealed at Sinai (and nature) and to his promise to Abraham to bless all nations through his seed: "This was to show God's righteousness, because in his divine forbearance he had passed over former sins. It was to show his righteousness at the present time, so that he might *be just and the justifier of the one who has faith in Jesus*" (3:25–26, emphasis added).[9]

Even if Israel and the rest of humanity had been faithless to God through their unwillingness to give God his proper glory, God himself was by no means faithless to his unilateral promises of grace: "sin increased, grace abounded all the more" (5:20). Humanity's faithlessness only served to show God's even greater faithfulness and solidarity (3:1–8). As we observed in our treatment of the Old Testament, every failure on the part of Israel led to God increasing his faithfulness to his promise to Abraham.[10] Therefore every mediator was an embodiment of God's own deepening solidarity with his people in the face of their failure to fulfill the law. For this reason we will suggest that Käsemann's interpretation of the "righteousness of God" (1:17) as God's own "salvation creating power" best fits with Paul's argument in Romans and Galatians.[11] It is the righteousness whereby God brings about eschatological redemption based on his prior promise to Abraham. Because of this faithfulness, God shares his own alien righteousness with sinners through Jesus Christ (1:16–17, also see Gal 3:6–9, v. 17; Phil 3:4–11).[12]

God's own righteous solidarity with Israel and humanity has therefore come to a climax in the atoning work of Jesus. His death not only fulfilled the righteous demands of the law's curse, but it was the final seal and confirmation of the promise made to Abraham. God's righteousness in his faithfulness to humanity was so great that he gave up his own Son to maintain his promise: "If God is for us, who can be against us? He who did not spare his own Son but gave him up for us all, how will he not also with him graciously give us all things?" (Rom 8:31–32).

For Paul, Jesus is the embodiment of divine righteousness made manifest apart from the law. Jesus is the divine Son of God (Rom 9:5; 1 Cor 1:24, 2:8, 8:6; Phil 2; Col 1:15, 2:3, 2:9; Eph 4:9–10; Titus 2:13), through whom God had made all creation (1 Cor

---

8. E. Sanders, *Paul and Palestinian Judaism*, 409–19.

9. Franzmann, *Commentary on Romans*, 71–72.

10. See discussion in the following: Bruce et al., *Epistle to the Galatians*, 168–74; Cole, *Epistle of Paul to the Galatians*, 84–112; R. Johnson, *Letter of Paul*, 74–102; Lenski, *St. Paul's Epistles to the Galatians*, 156–58; Lightfoot, *St. Paul to the Galatians*, 133–64; Ridderbos, *Epistle of Paul*, 129–42; Schreiner and Buchanan, *Exegetical Commentary on Galatians*, 256–59.

11. Käsemann, *Commentary on Romans*, 21–33.

12. See different exegetical theories concerning the "righteousness of God" in Heliso, *Pistis and the Righteous One*.

8:6; Col 1:15–21).[13] He was sent forth by God in the final decisive battle for creation. As God's glorious and self-donating presence, Jesus was with Israel in the desert as the Angel of YHWH (1 Cor 10:1–10).[14] Jesus is not only the true divine Son of God, but he is also the promised Davidic Messiah (Rom 1:3).[15] He is also the Melchizedekiah priest-king (1 Cor 15:25).[16] He is the second and true Adam (Rom 5; 1 Cor 15) and therefore (in light of the Pentateuch and first-century Jewish thought), the true Israel and the true humanity.[17]

For this reason Jesus is the true fulfillment of Old Testament mediation. He is the embodiment of God's willingness to manifest his commitment to his people by giving them mediators who represent his own righteous adherence to his promises. As the fulfillment of this history, he is God himself come in person to fulfill the law in all the ways that neither Israel nor its mediators could. Christ fulfilled and overcame the curse of the law by becoming a curse for humanity: "Christ redeemed us from the curse of the law by becoming a curse for us—for it is written, 'Cursed is everyone who is hanged on a tree'" (Gal 3:13, also see Rom 8:2–4). Through becoming a curse, he destroys the curse. By dying he swallowed up death in victory (1 Cor 15:54).

In describing how Jesus became a curse, Paul uses the language of Old Testament sin offerings and substitutionary death. Christ is the fulfillment of the Passover sacrifice, wherein God gave a substitute for the firstborn of Israel and as a result brought about a new liturgical community (1 Cor 5:7).[18] In his death on the cross, he was "made sin" (2 Cor 5:21), which as many interpreters have noted is a direct verbal parallel of the LXX's description of the sin offerings of Leviticus.[19] He was a fulfillment of the Day of Atonement, because he became for us the *hilastērion* (Rom 3:25). Stuhlmacher notes that it is without question that any first-century reader familiar with the LXX would have recognized Paul's verbal allusion.[20] From this Paul's meaning is clear: Jesus is God himself present in the

13. Richard Bauckham demonstrates that in 1 Cor 8:6 where Paul reworks the Shema to include Jesus within the identity of the one God. See Bauckham, *God Crucified*, 37–40.

14. Gathercole, *Pre-Existent Son*, 29–30; Gieschen, *Angelomorphic Christology*, 325–29. There is of course a textual variant here, but Gieschen makes a convincing argument for Paul saying that the Israelites rebelled against "Christ."

15. See discussion in the following: Boice, *Romans*, 39–42; Bruce, *Epistle of Paul*, 72; Cranfield, *Romans*, 5–6; Gill, *Epistle of Paul*, 8–9; Haldane, *Commentary on Romans*, 29–30; Hodge, *Commentary on the Epistle*, 26–27; Jewett, *Romans*, 103–8; J. Murray, *Epistle to the Romans*, 5–9; Osborne, *Romans*, 29–32; Plumer, *Commentary on Paul's Epistle*, 34–37; J. Stott, *Romans*, 49–51.

16. Paul applies Psalm 110:1 to Jesus. See discussion in the following: Barrett, *First Epistle to the Corinthians*, 358–59; Conzelmann, *First Epistle to the Corinthians*, 272–73; T. Edwards, *First Epistle to the Corinthians*, 417–18; Godet, *St. Paul's Epistle*, 361–63; Grosheide, *First Epistle to the Corinthians*, 366–68; Hodge, *First Epistle to the Corinthians*, 331; Holladay, *First Letter of Paul*, 203–4; McFadyen, *Epistle to the Corinthians*, 214–15.

17. See N. T. Wright, *Climax of the Covenant*, 18–35, 57–62, 90–97. See Christ's role as the second Adam in Lenski, *First and Second Epistles to the Corinthians*, 663–67; Lockwood, *1 Corinthians*, 566–73.

18. See Barret, *First Epistle to the Corinthians*, 128–29; Conzelmann, *First Epistle to the Corinthians*, 98–99; Holladay, *First Letter of Paul*, 73–74; Lenski, *First and Second Epistles to the Corinthians*, 220–22; Lockwood, *1 Corinthians*, 171–77.

19. Schreiner, *Romans*, 403. Also see comments in Dunn, *Romans*, 422; Käsemann, *Commentary on Romans*, 216–18.

20. Stuhlmacher, *Paul's Letter*, 58. See other interpretations along this line: Griffith-Jones, *Gospel*

hiddenness of bloody and atoning sacrifice. Just as in the Old Testament, where hidden in the darkness of the temple the preincarnate Christ was manifest as the divine *kavod* and channeled his personal holiness to Israel through the medium of the bloody and atoning sacrifice, so too now he does so again at the end of the ages through his self-offering and atoning sacrifice on the cross, by giving his own personal righteousness to those who have faith (Rom 1:17, 3:25; 1 Cor 5:21; Phil 3:9). Just as his glorious presence was concealed in the holy of holies, he is now hidden under a form of sin, death, and weakness. Because of this, he is an affront to all human wisdom and sinful pretensions, yet he is the source all true wisdom and righteousness before God (1 Cor 1:18–31).

Jesus's redemptive work culminated in his resurrection from the dead. This victory not only destroyed the power of death, but establishes a new humanity. Christ has recapitulated Adam (Rom 5; 1 Cor 15), and by his divine power established a new narrative of creation in which the law has been fulfilled and brought to its proper end: "For Christ is the end of the law for righteousness to everyone who believes" (Rom 10:4). In baptism (Rom 6), we are incorporated into Christ's new narrative of creation and thereby conformed to that narrative sequence of his death and resurrection (vv. 5–8). Just as Christ took our place and "became sin," so too we take on his reality of new creation. There is then a "happy exchange" between the believer and Christ (to use Luther's phrase).[21] In this, Christ is imputed with human sin and humans are imputed with Christ's righteousness.

Because in Christ's new narrative of creation the law has been fulfilled for the believer, the believer is now free from the dominating power of sin (7:1–6) and is thereby transformed through the Spirit (8:4). Indeed, the law created an oppositional relationship in that "our sinful passions, [were] aroused by the law" (7:5). In the new narrative of creation, the law has been fulfilled and taken away. The sinful nature therefore dies through the Spirit's incorporation of the sinner into the body of Christ through faith. As a result, the "requirement of the law . . . [is] fulfilled in us" (8:4). The requirements are met in us because the law is fulfilled by faith, for: "whatever does not proceed from faith is sin" (14:23). Out of this faith flows works of love (Gal 5:6). The Christian's life comes from faith active in love and thereby becomes a "living sacrifice" (Rom 12:1) of praise for the gift of grace.

According to Paul, 66–67; Lenski, *Paul's Epistle to the Romans*, 254–59; Moo, *Epistle to the Romans*, 231–36; J. Murray, *Epistle to the Romans*, 117–18; Nygren, *Commentary on Romans*, 156–59; Schreiner, *Paul*, 234–36; Tholuck, *Epistle to the Romans*, 110. Also see discussion of Paul's formula and its relationship to the Day of Atonement in Ben Ezra, *Impact of Yom Kippur*, 197–203. There is of course a well-known argument about the term in twentieth-century New Testament scholarship. See Dodd, "ΙΛΑΣΚΕΣΘΑΙ," 352–60. See the masterful counter argument in Morris, "Use of ilaskesthai," 227–33. Also see other articles relating to the debate: Nicole, "Hilaskesthai Revisited," 173–77; Nicole, "C. H. Dodd and the Doctrine of Propitiation," 117–57. In the debate whether or not to translate the verse as "propitiation" or "expiation," the former is to be preferred for the linguistic reasons Morris described. "Propitiation" also properly describes the work of Christ insofar as it renders satisfaction to God's wrath without removing the object of that wrath (i.e., Rom 7). Ultimately though, the "mercy seat" translation is to be considered the best. Paul not only could have expected his audience to recognize the literary allusion to the Day of Atonement (i.e., Stuhlmacher's claim), but he views Jesus as encompassing the whole reality of the mercy seat. Jesus for Paul is both God's righteous hidden presence fulfilling his promises and also a propitiation of God's justice. Through such sacrifice, he channels his personal holiness of the new people of God. Therefore Luther rightly translated the word as "*Gnadenstuhl*."

21. *AE* 31:351.

The humanity that receives itself from God's gracious Word of new creation can only live in such a way as to offer up a continuous doxology for God's goodness.

All of Jesus's work in the establishment of God's kingdom will result in the universal transformation of creation into the true Tabernacle of divine presence and praise: "in heaven and on earth and under the earth . . . every tongue confess that Jesus Christ is Lord, to *the glory of God the Father*" (Phil 2:10–11, emphasis added). In this he is the true God and the true creature who reflects divine glory back to God, as a sacrifice of praise for divine graciousness. Jesus is the true divine *kavod*, the luminous image of God.[22] Indeed believers have seen the "glory of God in the face of Jesus Christ" (2 Cor 4:6). In our resurrection, we will be conformed fully to the resurrected image of the Son. As a result, we will fulfill the true meaning of creation by reflecting such glory in its fullness: "with unveiled face, beholding the glory of the Lord, are being transformed into the same image from one degree of glory to another. For this comes from the Lord who is the Spirit" (3:18).

The Catholic Epistles[23]

In the Catholic Epistles, direct references to Jesus are quite sparse. The Epistle of James only mentions Jesus twice (1:1, 2:1), Jude mentions him four times (1:1, 4, 17). Neither epistle says very much about his person or work. James does refer to Jesus as the "glorious Lord" (2:1) (or perhaps better translated, "the Lord of glory").[24] This would suggest an identification of Jesus with the hypostatized *kavod* to which many of the other New Testament authors identify with Jesus.[25] Similarly, one textual variant in Jude identifies Jesus with the Angel of YHWH who redeemed Israel from Egypt: "Now I want to remind you, although you once fully knew it, that *Jesus, who saved a people out of the land of Egypt, afterward destroyed those who did not believe*" (Jude 1:5, emphasis added).[26] This

---

22. See Belleville, *Reflections of Glory*.

23. Achtemeier, *1 Peter*; Barclay, *Letters of John and Jude*; Bauckham, *Jude, 2 Peter*; Bigg, *St. Peter and St. Jude*; Boring, *1 Peter*; Brosend, *James and Jude*; Cantinat, *Les Épîtres de Saint Jacques et de Saint Jude*; Cedar, *James, 1, 2 Peter, Jude*; Craddock, *First and Second Peter and Jude*; Cranfield, *I and II Peter and Jude*; Fronmüller, *Epistle General of Jude*; Fuchs and Reymond, *La Deuxieme Epitre de Saint Pierre*; Hartin, *James, First Peter, Jude, Second Peter*; Harvey and Towner, *2 Peter and Jude*; Hillyer, *1 and 2 Peter, Jude*; Horrell, *Epistles of Peter and Jude*; Gardiner, *Last of the Epistles*; G. Green, *Jude and 2 Peter*; J. Green, *1 Peter*; Keil, *Petrus und Judas*; J. Kelly, *Epistles of Peter and Jude*; Kraftchick, *Jude, 2 Peter*; Lenski, *Epistle to the Hebrews and the Epistle of James*; Lilje, *Petrusbriefe und der Judasbrief*; Manton, *Epistle of Jude*; McKnight, *1 Peter*; Michaels, *I Peter*; Moo, *2 Peter and Jude*; Neyrey, *2 Peter, Jude*; Perkins, *First and Second Peter, James, and Jude*; Plumptre, *General Epistles*; E. Richard, *1 Peter, Jude, and 2 Peter*; Roos, *Kurze Erklärung der Zween Briefe*; Rushton, *First Peter*; Saarinen, *Pastoral Epistles*; Scaer, *James*; Schelkle, *Petrusbriefe und der Judasbrief*; Senior and Harrington, *1 Peter, 2 Peter, and Jude*; Turner et al., *Jude*; Vögtle, *Judasbrief*; Witherington, *Letters and Homilies*; Wohlenberg, *Erste und Zweite Petrusbrief*; Wolff, *Epistle of Jude*.

24. Lenski, *Epistle to the Hebrews and the Epistle of James*, 563.

25. Also see Scaer, *James*, 27. Scaer also suggests that the greeting at the beginning of the epistle that is usually translated as "James, a servant of God and of the Lord Jesus Christ" could be translated as "servant of Jesus Christ, who is both God and Lord."

26. Fossum, "Kyrios Jesus as the Angel of the Lord," 226–43; Gathercole, *Preexistent Son*, 36–43.

again follows already established patterns of New Testament Christology that we have studied.

First Peter says a little bit more, even if the main issue of these epistles remains Christian moral conduct. In the first Petrine epistle, there are references to Jesus as the true Passover lamb (1 Pet 1:19). The payment for the redemption of the Church was not with precious metals, but rather with the blood of Jesus (1:18). The metaphor of the redemption of a slave is used to explain the effects of Christ's substitutionary death.[27] Jesus is also described in terms echoing Deuteronomy's curse on criminals and the Servant of Isaiah: "he himself bore our sins in his body on the tree, that we might die to sin and live to righteousness. By his wounds you have been healed" (2:24). Release from the debt and burden of sin frees the people of God to be a priestly people and the eschatological temple (2:4–10), a pattern of theological reasoning that we have seen previously in our study.

The Revelation of St. John[28]

The book of Revelation centers on Jesus Christ as both the author and object of the Church's liturgical activity. By his death and resurrection Jesus Christ has actualized a new creation and determines his bride the Church as a new creation by freeing her from sin, death, and the devil. He thereby actualizes her as a creature capable of reflecting his glory through a sacrifice of praise. This occurs when humanity is recreated in the Divine Service through Word and sacrament. Nevertheless, as the book of the seven seals reveals, the divine act of redemption has a corresponding act of judgment. By his opening the book of the testament (the book of the seven seals), God in Christ unleashes divine judgment on the dark forces of the old creation and their addiction to false worship. He also redeems his Church so that the message of judgment becomes glad tidings to the earthly and heavenly Church.

Revelation begins with John encountering the risen Jesus (Rev 1:7–8, 13, 19–20) on the "Lord's Day" (1:10), probably Sunday, the day of liturgical worship in the early Church.[29] Jesus is dressed in the garb of a high priest and is described as being one like

---

27. Michaels, *1 Peter*, 63–64.

28. Much of the material in this section has previously appeared in my article, "Creation's Praise," 314–25. For sources on Revelation, see the following: Bauckham, *Book of Revelation*; Beale, *Book of Revelation*; Beasley-Murray, *Book of Revelation*; I. Beckwith, *Apocalypse of John*; Boer, *Book of Revelation*; Bonsirven, *L'Apocalypse de Saint Jean*; Brighton, *Revelation*; Brütsch, *La Clarté de l'Apocalypse*; Buchanan, *Book of Revelation*; Caird, *Revelation of St. John*; Charles, *Revelation of St. John*; Chilton, *Days of Vengeance*; Corbin, *Book of Revelation*; Cory, *Book of Revelation*; Court, *Myth and History*; Cox, *Apocalyptic Commentary*; Chytraeus, *Auslegung der Offenbarung Johanni*; Dean, *Book of Revelation*; Düsterdieck, *Revelation of John*; Glasgow, *Apocalypse Translated and Expounded*; Heidt, *Apocalypse*; Hobbs, *Cosmic Drama*; Hoeksema, *Behold, He Cometh*; P. Hughes, *Book of the Revelation*; Ketter, *Apokalypse*; Ladd, *Revelation of John*; Loenertz, *Apocalypse of Saint John*; Lupieri, *Apocalypse of John*; Milligan, *Book of Revelation*; Mounce, *Book of Revelation*; Müller-Jurgens, *Apokalyps*; F. Murphy, *Fallen is Babylon*; Newell, *Book of the Revelation*; Newbolt, *Book of Unveiling*; Prigent, *L'Apocalypse de Saint Jean*; Risisi, *Alpha und Omega*; Schick, *Apokalypse*; Sena, *Apocalypse*; Stuart, *Commentary on the Apocalypse*; Torrey, *Apocalypse of John*; Weidner, *Revelation of St. John*.

29. Beale, *Temple*, 203.

the "Son of Man," who has received universal dominion.[30] In chapter 5, Jesus is further described as "the Lion of the tribe of Judah" (referring to the messianic prophecy of Gen 49:9–10) and as a "lamb" "as though it had been slain" (5:5–6) (a priestly image borrowed from the exodus narratives). In this, Christ is portrayed as a second Adam. Adam, as we have seen, is portrayed by Genesis as the protological high priest, just as Christ is the high priest and progenitor of a new creation. According to Genesis, creation is inherently liturgical; therefore, with a new creation comes a new liturgy of creation (Heb 7:12). This fact alerts us both to Jesus's identity and the liturgical nature of the book as a whole.

This new liturgy centers on the worship of the risen and ascended Jesus. When John enters heaven (Rev 4:4), he discovers representatives of the people of God (the twenty-four elders, possibly representing the twelve tribes of Israel and the twelve apostles) worshiping God the Father and Jesus (4:4) in the power of the sevenfold Spirit (probably a reference to the sevenfold gifts of the Spirit, Isa 11:1–2).[31] They do so along with symbols of the creation. The four living beasts before the divine throne (Rev 4:6–8) are likely symbols of the zodiac and therefore images of the starry heavens.[32] Jesus is portrayed as possessing a throne in a manner similar to the hypostatized divine *kavod* in many other contemporary Jewish apocalypses.[33] In this, Revelation is clear that Jesus is the divine *kavod,* who had occupied the earthly tabernacle and temple from Exodus 40 to Ezekiel 10, and has now come again (Isa 40) to "tabernacle" among us (John 1:14–15).

For John then, the object of the liturgy of the Church is no different than that of Israel. Jesus, who was the *kavod* worshiped and encountered in the midst of Israel in the tabernacle and temple, is now the incarnate one dwelling in the midst of the Church through Word and sacrament.[34] The only difference is that whereas the old covenant restricted access to the holy of holies, Jesus has now torn the veil of the temple (Matt 27:51, Mark 15:38, Luke 23:45–46) and has given the Church direct access by way of his presence in Word and sacrament. This is a restoration of Eden, where humanity had direct access to God, but was ultimately expelled. Even when God dwelt in the midst of Israel in the Old Testament, he could only be directly approached on the Day of Atonement by the high priest (Lev 16). Jesus has now not only been exalted to the right hand of God, but in a special sense also dwells in the midst of and within believers through Word and sacrament. In this, the exile from the divine presence that occurred from Genesis 3 onward has been reversed via the Divine Service. Each Divine Service is a sharing of Jesus's heavenly presence. It frees the believer to participation in the act of heavenly worship. Implicit in John's vision is the claim that every Divine Service is also a restoration and completion of creation, as well as the actualization of heaven on earth, and therefore, its final eschatological goal.

30. Fletcher-Louis, "Jesus and the High Priest," 26.

31. For various alternatives see F. Murphy, *Fallen is Babylon,* 181–82.

32. Chilton, *Days of Vengeance,* 158–60.

33. F. Murphy, *Fallen is Babylon,* 176–77. There is an interesting parallel between the throne-room in Revelation and the throne-room in 1 Enoch 14.

34. See argument in Kleinig, *Leviticus,* 4–13.

Jesus is praised as one who has freed the Church by the shedding of his blood to be a true liturgical community, a "kingdom and priests" (Rev 5:10). The intention here appears to echo and fulfill Isaiah 61's description of the final destiny of the restored Israel. As "kings" (as some manuscripts have it, notably the *Textus Receptus*) or "a kingdom" they are "lords of all" and as "priests" they are "servants of all."[35] This freedom has occurred through the substitionary death of Jesus, typologically described as the true Passover lamb. The Passover lamb is itself the substitutionary victim that freed Israel to come out of exile. Leaving exile, Israel gained the land of Canaan and partially restored the dominion that Adam had had over the whole creation (Gen 1:28). The Church, united with Christ through faith, has now received the whole creation again: "The one who conquers, I will grant him to sit with me on my throne, as I also conquered and sat down with my Father on his throne" (Rev 3:21). Similarly, Israel itself became a "priestly nation" (Exod 19:6) both prefiguring the restored liturgical humanity of the Church and looking back to the original role of Adam in the garden as the protological high priest. The Church has come out of the true exile of spiritual alienation from God and thereby entered into the eternal homeland of the restored humanity.

Though it would appear that the Divine Service has already conformed the people of God to the true eschatological goal of creation, the temporal world still stands under the sway of demonic forces. The Lamb who sits at the "right hand" of God (an intertextual echo of Ps 110:1) is given a scroll with seven seals that he alone can open. In the first century AD any scroll sealed seven times represented a "will" or "testament."[36] The Lamb is worthy to open it because he was slain and his blood is the catalyst for the giving of the redeeming testament of the gospel. As we shall see, the opening of this testament (the gospel of the forgiveness of sins and eternal life) results in the re-creation of the world. Nevertheless, it also leads to the judgment and destruction of the old creation, much like God's promise to Abraham in Genesis 15 led to the judgment of Egypt and Canaan (Gen 15:16). In the same way, in baptism, the promise not only creates a new person in Christ, but also drowns the old Adam or Eve (Rom 6).

---

35. Luther uses this description of the freedom of a Christian and makes specific reference to the wording of the *Textus Receptus* in this verse. See *AE* 31:343.

36. Zahn, *Introduction to the New Testament*, 393–94. With slightly modified letters whereby the Greek is transcribed into English, Zahn writes:

> The word *Biblion* tself permits a great many interpretations, but for the readers of that time it was designated by the seven seals on its back beyond the possibility of mistake. Just as in Germany before the introduction of money-orders, everyone knew that a letter sealed with fives seals contained money, so the most simple member of the Asiatic Churches knew that a βιβλίον made fast with seven seals was a *testament*. When the testamentor dies the testament is brought forward, and when possible opened in the presence of the seven witnesses who sealed it; i.e. unsealed, read aloud, and executed. The making of a will assumes that the death of the testamentor lies in the future, while its opening and execution imply that his death has taken place. But, as is well known, the Christian of earliest times, although mindful of the fact that God does not die (Heb. ix. 16 f.) and that *omne simile claudicate*, does not hesitate to imagine the property supposed to belong to God, to His Son, and to His Church, and the entrance of the Church into possession of it, under the figure of inheritance (heritage and inheriting), and accordingly, to compare the assurance of these properties on God's part with a testamentary disposition.

Also see Beasley-Murray, *Book of Revelation*, 121; Brighton, *Revelation*, 107; Chilton, *Days of Vengeance*, 166; Court, *Myth and History*, 55–56.

It should also be noted that the fellowship of the earthly and heavenly Churches with the Lamb in the throne room scene contains overtones that imply the celebration of the Lord's Supper.[37] In the institution narratives in the New Testament (Matt 26:26–28; Mark 14:20–25; Luke 22:19–20; 1 Cor 11:20–26), Jesus himself characterized his death as a means for the forgiveness of sins. His death thereby enacts the new "covenant" or "testament" (*diatheke* is used in secular Greek for testaments or wills and in the LXX for covenants) through his body and blood.[38] In his death, Jesus is able to "will" his own life and righteousness to the Church and thereby enter into a new relationship with humanity. The Lord's Supper is a tangible giving of this testament and the visible sign of the ratification of the testament in his blood. The redeemed can be certain that this sacrifice has been offered for them because God himself in Christ donates his own person to us in the form of his sacrificed body and blood (to sacrifice in the Old Testament is to drain the blood, thereby separating body and blood, see Lev 17: 11–14). Similarly, just as by eating that Adam had fellowship with the serpent and fell into sin at the tree of the knowledge of good and evil, by eating the lamb sacrificed on the altar and the tree of the cross, the Church now reenters its fellowship with God who is present in his body and blood. In light of the fact that Revelation pictures the whole Church engaged in heavenly fellowship with the Lamb as he opens his testament, there appears to be more than a small suggestion that this describes the Church's unity through the Lord's Supper.

If the word of the testament is rejected, it can also be a destructive force of judgment (Matt 10:15; 1 Cor 11:27–32). Because of this, the seven seals opened by the Lamb not only result in the redemption of the new creation, but also in the destructive judgment of the old. It is difficult, as Richard Bauckham notes, to directly identify any of the judgments unleashed by the opening of the seven seals with any particular historical events.[39] Nevertheless, John appears to see the pretentions of fallen humanity as manifested in the prevalence of emperor worship under the *Pax Romana*. However, this embodiment of the spirit of antichrist in John's time does not exclude his manifestation in other forms. As the Epistle of John notes: "many antichrists have appeared" (1 John 2:18).

John describes Satan as being thrown down from his place in the heavenly court (where he serves as chief prosecuting attorney, much as in Zech 3 and Job 1–3) by the blood of the Lamb who has atoned for sin (Rev 12:7–9). Due to his loss of power, he seeks to make war against the Lamb and the true liturgical community through the organs of religion and state. The war of Christ and his people with Satan is portrayed with the image of the conflict between the seed of the woman and the dragon/serpent (12).[40] The imagery of strife between the "Son of Man" and the serpent/dragon represents the culmination and fulfillment of the *protevangelium* (compare Gen 3:15 and Rev 12).

---

37. See one example of interesting Eucharistic reading of Revelation in Hahn, *Lamb's Supper*.

38. See Quell, "Diatheke," 2:107–20. Luther made a great deal of this. See *AE* 36:35–57. Also see description of Luther's position on this matter in the following sources: Althaus, *Theology of Martin Luther*, 375–82; Croken, *Luther's First Front*, 73–87; Köstlin, *Theology of Luther*, 1:393–94; Lohse, *Martin Luther's Theology*, 134–36; Sasse, *This is My Body*, 82–89; Schwarz, "Last Supper," 198–210; Vajta, *Luther on Worship*, 39–49.

39. Bauckham, *Book of Revelation*, 20–22.

40. See discussion of this conflict in Bauckham, *Climax of Prophecy*, 174–98.

The beast and his community are the antithesis of the Lamb and his community. Not only does the image of the beast suggest a mangling of the divine image through idolatry (most ancient idolatry took the form of the worship of animals, i.e., those who worship beasts become bestial through their false worship), but it also describes an ethos counter to the testament of the gospel.[41]

The false community and "the beast" (Rev 13) are described as "Babylon" throughout the book. The use of "Babylon" for John evokes several intertextual echoes. First, much as Babylon was the source of Israel's greatest exile and the destroyer of Israel's temple, the universal world system of evil (presently manifest in the Roman emperor and the false worship of his cult) seeks to make the cosmic exile persist and to destroy the eschatological temple, the Church (Eph 2:20–22).[42] Babylon is thus a community that seeks to destroy creation by stifling and rejecting of the purpose of creation, namely the glorification of God. Similarly, as G. K. Beale notes, Babylon is associated with the tower of Babel. Just as "ancient Babylon attempted to link earth to heaven through self-glorifying pride (Gen 11:1–9) . . . latter-day Babylon would 'pile-up' her sins 'high as heaven.'"[43] We might go a step further than Beale and suggest that whereas ancient Babel once attempted to exalt itself into heaven, the Lamb is one who comes down from heaven and gives himself over to the service of his people. This self-surrender makes the Lamb worthy to receive worship (Rev 5:9–10). For this reason, we must see Babel as the antithesis of the tabernacle and temple. Whereas God established the temple and its true worship, humans established the tower of Babel. Whereas the temple represented the descent of God in solidarity with his liturgical community (Exod 40:34–35; 1 Kgs 8:10), Babel represented the attempted self-exaltation and divinization of humanity. In this sense, the true worship, brought about by the gospel, centers on the action of God for humanity and stands in contradistinction to the false worship of the beast and Babel, which centers on human self-exaltation.

After a lengthy series of judgments, Christ leads his heavenly armies to conquer the nations by the prophetic Word of God. John explicitly gives Jesus the title "Word of God" (Rev 19:13). We are also told that Jesus wears a "robe dipped in blood" (19:11–16) much like the earthly high priest. The description of Christ in this passage also echoes the portrayal of the Angel of the Lord in the LXX version of Isaiah 63.[44] The description of the Angel of the Lord wearing a robe "dipped in blood" (i.e., from the blood of his sacrifices) implies a status as a heavenly high priest (this also seems to be implied by Zechariah 3). John's suggestion here appears to be that just as the high priest prefigured Christ's expiation of sins, he also prefigured his office as the divine warrior. The high priest reenters God's presence in the holy of holies (i.e., the new Eden) on the Day of Atonement in order to cleanse Israel from its sin, thereby reversing Adam's defeat by the serpent.[45] In this, John sees the high priest as prefiguring Jesus's victory over the serpent, which had

41. See description in Beale, *We Become What We Worship*.

42. If this book were written at the time of Domitian, then Rome would also be the destroyer of Israel's temple as well as making it the new Babylon.

43. Beale, *Book of Revelation*, 1119.

44. See Gieschen, *Angelomorphic Christology*, 246–52.

45. See argument about this ritual in Fletcher-Louis, "God's Image," 93.

led Adam into sin and removed him from God's direct presence. Christ is, therefore, the true heavenly high priest, because through the expiation of sins he has defeated the chaos serpent (Isa 27:1), that is, the devil, and thereby inaugurated a new creation. As the result of the decisive victory against his temporal opponents and the devil, Christ reigns for a figurative thousand years (Rev 20:1–6). Ultimately, it is through the proclamation of Word and sacrament that Christ conquers and reigns. After the final judgment, the new heaven and new earth are established.

The new heavens and new earth recapitulate Eden and the temple. The New Jerusalem is described as an "arboreal temple-city."[46] We are also told that this new creation is the culmination of Christ's atoning work. Just as he had surrendered himself to the Church as its priest-king in his eschatological battles and atoning work, so too at the end of all things he finally gives his entire being over to the new creation in order that it might be a tabernacle of his presence: "Behold, the dwelling place of God is with man. He will dwell with them, and they will be his people, *and God himself will be with them as their God*" (21:3, emphasis added). Again, John writes: "And I saw no temple in *the city, for its temple is the Lord God the Almighty and the Lamb*" (21:22, emphasis added). In this, based on God's own self-donation of grace through Christ, the new creation is completed by his establishment of the heavenly Jerusalem where there is no distinction between the city and the temple. All existence delights in the presence of God and is devoted to the liturgy of God and the Lamb. The protological existence of creation is restored and surpassingly glorified in its eschatological fulfillment.

The Epistle to the Hebrews[47]

We have saved our discussion of the Epistle to the Hebrews until the end of this chapter because of its intense focus on the questions of both Christology and atonement. For this reason, the Epistle to the Hebrews in many ways represents a recapitulation of the themes that we have observed throughout our study. Hence, it is fitting that we treat it last.

---

46. Beale, *Temple*, 23.

47. Aquinas, *Epistle to the Hebrews*; Attridge, *Epistle to the Hebrews*; Barclay, *Epistle to the Hebrews*; Braun, *An die Hebräer*; R. Brown, *Christ Above All*; Bruce, *Epistle to the Hebrews*; A. Davidson, *Epistle to the Hebrews*; Delitzsch, *Commentar zum Briefe an die Hebräer*; Ebrand, *Der Brief an die Hebräer*; Ellingworth, *Epistle to the Hebrews*; Erdman, *Epistle to the Hebrews*; Gerhard, *Commentarius super Epistolam ad Ebraeos*; Goodspeed, *Epistle to the Hebrews*; Grässer, *An die Hebräer*; O. Green, *Epistle of Paul the Apostle*; Hagner, *Hebrews*; Hegermann, *Der Brief an die Hebräer*; Hérings, *L'Epitre aux Hebreux*; Hewitt, *Epistle to the Hebrews*; Hillmann, *Der Brief an die Hebräre*; P. Hughes, *Epistle to the Hebrews*; Keil, *Commentar über den Brief an die Hebräer*; Kent, *Epistle to the Hebrews*; Kurtz, *Der brief an die Hebräer*; Kuss, *Der Brief an die Hebräer*; Laubach, *Der Brief an die Hebräer*; Michel, *Der Brief an die Hebräer*; Montefiore, *Epistle to the Hebrews*; Moses and Henderson, *Epistle to the Hebrews*; McConnell, *Epistle to the Hebrews*; McDonald, *Epistle to the Hebrews*; Moffatt, *Epistle to the Hebrews*; Moll, *Epistle to the Hebrews*; Neil, *Epistle to the Hebrews*; Patterson, *Epistle to the Hebrews*; Pfeiffer, *Epistle to the Hebrews*; Plumer, *Epistle of Paul*; Rendall, *Epistle to the Hebrews*; Riggenbach, *Der Brief an die Hebräer*; T. Robinson, *Epistle to the Hebrews*; Royster, *Epistle to the Hebrews*; Schierse, *Der Brief an die Hebräer*; A. Seeberg, *Der Brief an die Hebräer*; Strobel, *Der Brief an die Hebräer*; Tholuck, *Commentarie öfwer Brefwer till Hebreerna*; Weiss, *Der Brief an die Hebräer*; Westcott, *Epistle to the Hebrews*; R. Williamson, *Epistle to the Hebrews*.

The epistle begins by highlighting the finality of the Jesus's office as mediator. Although God spoke through the prophets to Israel, he has now in a final and definitive way spoken in the person of his Son (Heb 1:1–2). Implicitly, the author suggests that Jesus is superior to Moses, because Moses only reflected the divine glory in his face, whereas Jesus is the "radiance of the glory of God" (1:3; i.e., he is the hypostatized *kavod*. Similarly, Moses was merely a servant over the house of God, whereas the Son is the builder of the house of God (i.e., the eschatological temple, the Church).[48]

The Son's revelation is the final, definitive, and superior fulfillment of prophetic mediation, because he is God himself speaking directly to humanity (1:2).[49] This does not mean that Christ's revelation contradicts the previous divine revelations. As Charles Gieschen demonstrates, the author describes Jesus in such a manner as to identify him with the Angel of YHWH in the Old Testament and thereby the agent of revelation in both testaments.[50] Nevertheless, all previous revelations pointed to or prefigured the redemption that Jesus would bring about. By contrast, Jesus's own revelation is identical with the presence of that redemption. It points ahead to nothing, but is the omega point of the Old Testament. Hence, in relationship to the prophetic mediation of the Old Testament, the Son's mediation is the "*telos*, the goal and ultimate meaning of all that preceded."[51]

That God has come to redeem in the person of his Son is fitting for a number of reasons. The Son is a fulfillment of all of God's promises. In making the promise of redemption to Abraham, God found nothing greater than himself by which to swear (6:13–16, echoing Genesis 22 and Isaiah 45). Having immutably pledged himself, God himself must be the agent of the fulfillment of his own redemptive purpose by becoming Jesus, dying on the cross, and entering into heaven as the great eternal high priest (6:17–20).[52] Furthermore, it is also fitting that the agent of creation be the agent of redemption, insofar as redemption is a fulfillment of creation: "For it was fitting that he, for whom and by whom all things exist, in bringing many sons to glory, should make the founder of their salvation perfect through suffering. For he *who sanctifies and those who are sanctified all have one source*" (Heb 2:10–11, emphasis added).

As the fulfillment of all mediation, Jesus is not only the final and definitive prophet, but also the true king and the great high priest. Throughout the early chapters, the author makes clear that Christ is the true kingly mediator (1:2–4) by applying the royal psalms and God's promises to David to him (1:5).[53] At the same time, Jesus is the true priestly mediator who "provided purification for sins" (1:3). As we will discuss below, this identification mainly grows out of the historical events of the crucifixion and the author's interpretation of Psalm 110. It is interesting to note that Jesus himself used this psalm to describe his identity. Later, Paul and John (in Revelation) did likewise.[54] Though we

48. Hagner, *Hebrews*, 59–60. See Heb 3:1–6. Also see Attridge, *Epistle to the Hebrews*, 104–5.

49. Bruce, *Epistle to the Hebrews*, 1–3.

50. Gieschen, *Angelomorphic Christology*, 295–303.

51. Hagner, *Hebrews*, 22.

52. Hahn, *Kinship by Covenant*, 326.

53. Bruce, *Epistle to the Hebrews*, 11–17.

54. See larger discussion of the New Testament's usage of the psalm in Bateman, "Psalm 110:1 and the New Testament," 438–53.

do not have time to go into detail regarding messianic expectation at the time of Christ, it suffices to say that this description of the fulfillment of the messianic hope is in some ways quite different than what many Jews held in the first century.[55] Consequently, the author writes in part to explain to his (presumably) mostly Jewish-Christian audience how Jesus's fulfillment of the messianic hope was the appropriate one.

In order to argue the appropriateness of Jesus's eschatological fulfillment of mediation the author engages in a highly typological reading of the Old Testament (see his summary of this approach in 10:1). Using a brilliant intertextual argument (that has been described as a "Midrashic hook-word" [*hypotassein*] method), the author demonstrates that the people of God are on an exodus from the world of transitory existence and sin, to the eternal rest of God's heavenly kingdom (3–4).[56] The author reasons that the people of God must in fact have an eschatological "rest" (God's eternal rest, typologically represented by the Sabbath rest of Genesis 2 and the temporal rest of the Holy Land) because many other references by God to his "rest" in the Old Testament (LXX) do not correspond to or find their fulfillment in either the Sabbath or Israel's settlement of the Holy Land.[57] For example, David in Psalm 95 promises a "rest" and he wrote long after the seventh day of creation and the conquest of Canaan.[58] This "rest," argues the author, must therefore be God's eternal rest (4:6–12).[59] This "rest" is available in the present to the Church through repentance and faith (vv. 9–13), and will find its fulfillment in heaven. Jesus is the one who brings the Church into this eschatological rest by giving it rest from its "works" (4:10), for example the "dead works" of the law (9:14). It should at this point be observed that the belief that the Messiah has come to give an eschatological rest is highly consistent both with the expectation of Second Temple Judaism, and with Jesus's own claims about himself found in the Synoptic Gospels (Matt 11:28).

Just as the Sabbath day and the exodus were typological of the reality of the eschatological rest given by Christ, so too Jesus's priesthood was typologically prefigured in the Levitical priesthood (Heb 8). The author shows that according to Exodus 25, Moses was given a pattern for the building of the tabernacle from a heavenly pattern. Consequently, it is logical to assume that it reflected a heavenly priesthood and temple that transcends Aaron's earthly priesthood (8:5).

---

55. For a summary of these expectations see the following: Charlesworth, "Concept of the Messiah," 188–218; Charlesworth, "Jewish Messianology to Christian Christology," 225–64; Charlesworth, *Messiah*; Charlesworth, *Qumran-Messianism*; Collins, *Scepter and the Star*; C. Evans and Flint, *Eschatology, Messianism*; Fitzmyer, *One Who is to Come*; W. Green, "Introduction: Messiah in Judaism," 1–13; Hess, *Israel's Messiah*; Lenowitz, *Jewish Messiahs*; Neusner, *Messiah in Context*; Neusner et al., *Judaisms and their Messiahs*; Zetterholm, *Messiah in Early Judaism and Christianity*.

56. D'Angelo, *Moses in the Letter*, 69. Scott Hahn agrees and makes reference to D'Angelo's findings in his *Kinship by Covenant*, 289–90. Hahn also directs us to: Guthrie, "Hebrews' Use of the Old Testament," 271–72; R. Thurston, "Midrash and 'Magnet' Words," 22–39. All of these articles give an excellent background on the subject.

57. Hagner, *Hebrews*, 70–71.

58. Hahn, *Kinship by Covenant*, 306.

59. See discussion of the logic of these chapters in the following: Attridge, "Let Us Strive to Enter That Rest," 279–88; Oberholtzer, "Kingdom Rest," 185–96.

This heavenly priesthood was that of Melchizedek, the priest-king of Genesis 14 and Psalm 110.[60] In Psalm 110 in particular, God makes an oath to the mysterious kingly figure ("my lord"), promising that he is eternally a priest (Ps 110:4). If the Levites had represented an adequate priesthood, asks the author, why then did God establish another priesthood later with an oath? Furthermore, notes the author, God did not make an oath when he established the Levitical covenant in Numbers 25:

> And it was not without an oath. For those *who formerly became priests were made such without an oath,* but this one was *made a priest with an oath* by the one who said: The Lord has sworn it, he will not change his mind "You are a priest forever." (Heb 7:20–21, emphasis added)[61]

This oath is significant not only because it provides a contrast between the two priesthoods, but because it ties into the author's earlier observation that the gospel is God's own pledge of himself (i.e., God swearing by himself). Whereas God's establishment of the Levitical priesthood was always bilateral and therefore dependant on the proper performance of priestly duties (its establishment was prompted by the zeal of Phineas and was often lost due to the unrighteousness of certain priests, most prominently Eli and his sons), Jesus's priesthood was founded on God's immutable purpose to save: "[Jesus] has become a priest, *not on the basis of a legal requirement* concerning bodily descent, but by the *power of an indestructible life*" (7:16–17, emphasis added).

Empirically speaking, the Levitical priesthood due to its finitude and sin could not work redemption. In fact, suggests the author, it was never meant to: "For on the one hand, a former commandment is set aside because of its weakness and uselessness (for the law made nothing perfect); but on the other hand, a better hope is introduced, through which we draw near to God" (7:18–19). By contrast, Jesus as God's own self-donation could perform this task of bringing about eternal righteousness and redemption by an immutable promise: "We have this as a sure and steadfast anchor of the soul, a hope that enters into the inner place behind the curtain, where Jesus has gone as a forerunner on our behalf, having become a high priest forever after the order of Melchizedek (6:19–20).

The author adduces other arguments connecting Melchizedek and Christ. He notes that the Pentateuch does not mention the lineage of the former and therefore describes him as "without father or mother or genealogy, having neither beginning of days nor end of life, but resembling the Son of God he continues a priest forever" (7:3). Many commentators have connected this statement to the rabbinical interpretative principle: "*Quod non in thora, non in mundo*" ("what is not in Torah, is not in the world").[62] Hahn

---

60. See the following discussions of Melchizedek in Hebrews: Fitzmyer, "Further Light on Melchizedek," 245–67; Fitzmyer, "'Now This Melchizedek,'" 221–43; Fitzmyer, "Melchizedek," 63–69; Horton, *Melchizedek Tradition*, 152–88; Hurst, *Epistle to the Hebrews*, 52–60; Longenecker, *Studies on Hermeneutics*, 187–223; J. Marshall, "Melchizedek in Hebrews," 339–42; Mason, *You are a Priest Forever*; Rothschild, *Hebrews As Pseudepigraphon*, 182–84; Rooke, "Jesus as Royal Priest," 81–94.

61. Hahn, *Kinship by Covenant*, 305.

62. See Attridge, *Epistle to the Hebrews*, 190; Bruce, *Epistle to the Hebrews*, 156–60. Scott Hahn argues that this goes back to the Strack-Billerbeck commentary on the New Testament and that it is not a genuine rabbinical interpretive technique. See Hahn, *Kinship by Covenant*, 300. Hahn mentions Billerbeck's commentary and cites Strack and Billerbeck, *Kommentar zum Neuen Testament*, 3:694.

suggests that not only is this interpretative principle a scholarly construct, but that the author's real point is to suggest that both Jesus and Melchizedek were both legitimate priests, yet lacked a priestly lineage. This reading makes a great deal of sense, not least because the author of Hebrews clearly does think that Jesus had a mother and father, and also a genealogy. Indeed, he mentions Jesus's descent from Judah in 7:14. Nevertheless, Jesus does not have a priestly lineage and therefore his priesthood does not depend on right of birth within the Old Testament legal order, but rather on the Father's oath and promise recorded in Psalm 110.

Not only is the Melchizedekiah priesthood superior for these logical and scriptural reasons, but it was recognized as such by the patriarchs. Abraham recognized the superiority of Melchizedek's priesthood when he paid a tenth of his plunder taken in a military expedition to him. Levi, the progenitor of the Levitical priesthood, was still in the loins of Abraham, and therefore, reasons the author, he could be figuratively thought of as having paid a tithe to Melchizedek (7:7–10).[63] If this is the case, obviously Melchizedek and his priesthood are superior to that of Levi and Aaron. The Levites received a tenth from all of Israel (Num 18:26), and thereby proved their superior vocation. In the same way, Melchizedek, whom the Levites gave a tenth, must indeed be superior to them.[64]

As a superior high priest to Aaron, Jesus can meet the needs of humanity by working a final and definitive eschatological redemption. The sacrifices of the Levitical priesthood were demonstrably ineffective because they needed to be offered continuously (10:1–3, 11). By contrast, Jesus offered up himself as an atoning sacrifice only once and thereby conclusively destroyed the power of sin (10:12).[65] Similarly, the Levitical high priest was a mere human being and a sinner. Consequently he had to offer sacrifices for himself as well as for the people (9:7). In a word, he was not a proper savior, but rather one in need of a savior. It is of course true that Jesus was also a human being. Nonetheless, this gave him an ability to sympathize with human sufferings and temptation. As we have previously noted, Jesus was also the glorious divine person through whom the world was created (1:1–3). In his person he united perfect man and the eternal God, so he could overcome such temptation (2:17–18) and thereby break the power of sin, death, and the devil (vv. 14–15). Similarly, as a single theanthropic subject, he could transcend the imperfections of the previous sacrifices by offering up a single and eternal sacrifice that would stand eternally before the Father and cleanse the consciences of believers (9:14).[66]

The author connects the sufferings of Jesus to the whole of his earthly life, not merely his death on the cross. In 2:18, the author describes Jesus's suffering as being constituted by the temptation to fall into sin. His overcoming of this temptation followed from his perfect faith: "let us run with endurance the race that is set before us, looking

---

63. Lenski, *Epistle to the Hebrews and the Epistle of James*, 215–21.

64. Bruce, *Epistle to the Hebrews*, 133–49.

65. Ibid., 198–240.

66. See the following discussions of sacrifice in Hebrews: Brooks, "Perpetuity of Christ's Sacrifice," 205–14; Dunnhill, *Covenant and Sacrifice*, 227–38; W. Stott, "Conception of 'Offering,'" 62–66; Swetnam, "Sacrifice and Revelation," 227–34; J. Thompson, "Hebrews 9," 567–78; Vanhoye, *Our Priest is Christ*; Vanhoye, "Esprit éternal et feu du sacrifice en He 9,14," 263–74; N. Young, "Gospel according to Hebrews 9," 208–9.

to Jesus, the founder and perfecter of our faith, who for the joy that was set before him endured the cross, despising the shame, and is seated at the right hand of the throne of God" (12:1–2). Attridge comments: "Thus the faith that Christ inaugurates and brings to perfect expression is not the content of Christian belief, but fidelity and trust that he himself exhibited in a fully adequate way and that his followers are called upon to share."[67] Indeed the author asserts that Jesus trustingly expected the joy of resurrection and exaltation. This faith stood in contrast to his empirical experience of abandonment (5:7–8). Faith must trustingly hope against vision because: "faith is the assurance of things hoped for, the conviction of things not seen" (11:1). Without faith it is impossible to be righteous because: "without faith it is impossible to please [God]" (11:6). In this way, Jesus, though he was the eternal Son of God "learned obedience through what he suffered. And being made perfect [that is, as a perfect source of salvation], he became the source of eternal salvation to all who obey him" (5:8–9).[68]

Because Jesus trusted in his own vindication and exaltation, he was able to freely offer himself up to the Father for the sins of humanity. Thereby he became "the mediator of a new covenant, so that those who are called may receive the promised eternal inheritance, since a death has occurred that redeems them from the transgressions committed under the first covenant" (9:15). The establishment of a new testament through bloody sacrifice was necessary because "without the shedding of blood there is no forgiveness of sins" (9:22). As an act of his total theanthropic person, Jesus's sacrifice was a perfect and eternal sacrifice: "[Christ] *through the eternal Spirit offered himself* without blemish to God, purify our conscience from dead works to serve the living God" (9:14, emphasis added).[69] As the eternal mediator of the new testament, Jesus has entered heaven (the true Tabernacle) through his own blood, just as the earthly high priest entered the holy of holies through the blood of "goats and bulls" (9:23–24). The reference to the entering of the holy of holies, and to the "blood of goats and bulls" suggests that the author views Jesus's sacrifice as being the fulfillment of the Day of Atonement, much like several other authors of the New Testament that we have previously examined. In heaven, Jesus eternally "appear[s] in the presence of God on our behalf" (9:24) as our righteousness.

The fact that he is an eternal high priest also makes it possible for Jesus to fulfill the third function of sacrifice in the Old Testament, namely the sealing of a covenant or testament (9:15).[70] Jesus has, by his cleansing of humanity from sin, established a *diatheke*:

---

67. Attridge, *Epistle to the Hebrews*, 356.

68. Hagner, *Hebrews*, 82.

69. Lenski, *Epistle to the Hebrews and the Epistle of James*, 298–99.

70. Quell, "Diatheke," 2:107–20; Gielesser, "Appendix: Diatheke," 531–40. Gielesser notes that although *diatheke* in Hellenistic literature generally has the meaning of a last will and testament, the LXX always translates the Hebrew word for covenant as *diatheke*. There are nonetheless "covenants" (bilateral agreements) and "testamental covenants" (unilateral agreements). Since the covenant Jesus enacts is unilateral and connected with his death, it is proper to think of as a "testamental covenant." Furthermore, as we shall see, both Revelation and Hebrews explicitly understand the new covenant inaugurated by Jesus as being a *diatheke* in the sense of a last will and testament. Nevertheless, it seems that "will" is a part of the Hebrew meaning of the term. After all, as we have seen, covenants were almost always confirmed with blood. In that blood signifies life, it means that the covenant partner commit their entire existence, that is they donate their own being, to the promise. In the same manner, when a person dies, he donates his own goods and also the meaning that comes with them to those whom he writes his will to address.

"For where a will is involved, the death of the one who made it must be established. For a will takes effect only at death, since it is not in force as long as the one who made it is alive. Therefore not even the first covenant was inaugurated without blood" (9:16–8). One could also translate "a will is in force only when somebody has died" as "for a covenant is confirmed over the dead."[71] If translated in this manner, the author would be referring to the Old Testament practice of covenants/testaments being confirmed by bloody sacrifice. Theologically speaking, either translation would encompass the author's clear intentions. As we earlier noted, to enter into a covenant/testament is to pledge the self to the other. This happened both unilaterally and bilaterally in the Old Testament period. In this case though, testament or "will" is probably a more faithful translation to the author's intention. Like last wills or testaments (and unlike many covenants of the Old Testament!) the promise that Jesus has established is unilateral rather than bilateral. Previously, the author argued that Jesus has unilaterally given and pledged himself to the Church. He is the fulfillment of the self-donating act whereby God pledged his own being to Abraham by "swearing by himself." In this sense, his death can be understood not only as an offering of himself to the Father, but the establishment of the inheritance of the Church to which he has "willed" his life and righteousness, thereby bringing it into the eternal Sabbath rest.

As a result of this great redemption, the Church is now the eschatological house of God (i.e., the new Temple).[72] The Church is in no way separated from God's living presence, but has direct access to it through Christ. Not only is Jesus the true priest-king, but he is also the gracious presence of God with the people of God. His body is itself the new tabernacle: "Therefore, brothers, since we have confidence to enter the holy places by the blood of Jesus, by the new and living way *that he opened for us through the curtain,* [i.e., the curtain covering the holy of holies] *that is, through his flesh*" (10:19–20, emphasis added). Through Jesus, the Church has already proleptically entered into God's rest, the true, heavenly Mount Zion (12:18–21). Therefore the Church offers up a continuous living sacrifice of praise in response to Christ's redeeming power (13:11–16).

Furthermore, the designation of Israel (Exod 4:22) and the Davidic king (2 Sam 7, Ps 2) as "the son of God" within covenantal contexts is suggestive of testamental connotations built into the Hebrew use of the concept of covenant. "Son" always means in the ancient world one who inherits. Also see Scott Murray who adds: "The Study of the word bǝ·rît in the Old Testament shows that it has a very broad meaning that included both covenantal and testamentary tones" ("Concept of *diatheke*," 59). He goes on to write: "The translators of the Septuagint deliberately chose the word *diatheke* to translate bǝ·rît because it best conveyed the rich content of the concept in the Old Testament. They made this choice based on their knowledge of the Hellenistic use of the word *diatheke*" (60). The quote is slightly modified by the transliteration of Hebrew and Greek words into English. For options see the following: Attridge, *Epistle to the Hebrews*, 253–56; Dunhill, *Covenant and Sacrifice*, 123–34, 149–87; Gardiner, "On *diatheke* in Hebrews 16, 17," 8–19; Swetnam, "Suggested Interpretation of Hebrews 9, 15–18," 373–90; Hahn, "Broken Covenant," 416–36; Koester, *Hebrews*, 418, 424–26; Long, *Hebrews*, 99; Omanson, "Superior Covenant," 361–73; Pfitzner, *Hebrews*, 131; Vos, *Teaching of the Epistle*, 27–48.

71. J. Hughes, "Hebrews," 45.

72. Beale, *Temple*, 293–309.

Chapter 5

The Mystery of the Person of Christ, Part 1

Creation and the Fall

Introduction

NOW THAT WE HAVE discussed the biblical data, we will now move to our doctrinal appropriation of it in the form of a dogmatic description of the person and work of Christ. We will operate from the perspective of the creedal tradition of the ancient Church as embodied by the first six ecumenical councils and the confessional tradition of the Evangelical Lutheran Church.[1] In doing this, we regard the dogmatic definitions of Christ and his work present in scripture as the norming norms of our description (*norma normans*), whereas the aforementioned creeds and confessions are a normed norm (*norma normata*). This does not of course mean that we take them any less seriously. In our dogmatic construction we hold without reservation to the doctrinal teachings of the Lutheran Confessions (*quia* subscription). Nevertheless, we must distinguish between the fountain of truth (the scriptures) and the stream (the creeds and confessions).

In investigating the dogma of the person and work of Christ, we recognize that the articles of the faith are utterly mysterious and not subject to the limitations of human reason or a closed system of thought. There is of course an inner logic to the truth of the faith (*analogia fidei, typus doctrinae, regula fidei*) and scripture must be interpreted on this basis.[2] The brightest passages (*sedes doctrinae*) that teach dogma must mutually

---

1. Bente and Dau, *Concordia Triglotta*. We have specifically chosen to use the *Concordia Triglotta* over newer editions of the Book of Concord. For justification of this practice see the following article: Ziegler, "New English Translation of The Book of Concord," 145–65. Also see Gerhard: "The third [kind of unity of the Lutheran Church] is *symbolic unity*, a unity which we embrace by common consent the doctrine contained in the symbolical books of our churches: in the Augsburg Confession and the Apology of the same, in the Luther's catechisms, in the Smalcald Articles, and in the Formula of Concord. If anyone refuses to give his name to this, we do not recognize him as a brother in the matter of faith and confession" (*On the Nature*, 523). It is mentioned in the footnote that The Treatise on the Power and Primacy of the Pope is not mentioned because at the time it was viewed as being an appendix to the Smalcald Articles.

2. See discussion in Robert Preus, "How is the Lutheran Church?," 187–89. Also see in the same collection, "Hermeneutics of the Formula of Concord," 232–35.

interpret each other and illuminate the more opaque.[3] Nevertheless, this does not mean that every antinomy may be logically smoothed out. Similarly, a focus on the *sedes doctrinae* does not reduce our doctrinal claims to a series of proof texts.[4] Rather, the *sedes doctrinae* represent a clear perspective wherein one is able to see the true inner analogy of different portions of scripture.

Moreover, the theological realism with which we are going to approach the articles of the faith in no way reduces the mysterious nature of divine truth. Each article of the faith is an unfathomable mystery (*mysterium fidei*). As John Klenig notes, a mystery as it is described in the Bible (particularly in Paul's later epistles), is a thing that we know to be true, but cannot comprehend how it is true.[5] This is not only because the ultimate object of the articles of the faith is the Triune God (who preexists and infinitely transcends our creaturely reason), but because in our fallen state we find the truth of God to be counter to our unbelieving orientation towards the world. Even our own sin, as we will see, is a great and utterly unfathomable mystery.

We will first discuss the person of Christ and then move to his work. This way of proceeding is in accordance with the practice of traditional dogmatics and represents a convenient means of organizing the theological task. Nevertheless, much like the two natures, the person and work of Christ can be considered from two distinct perspectives: in the concrete (i.e., as they stand in their actual relationship to one another) or in the abstract (i.e., merely considered in themselves). Considered in the abstract, Christ's person and work may indeed be separated as two distinct things. Christ is a person with certain ontic properties, regardless of his actions. Considered in the concrete though, the person and work of Christ constitute a singular phenomenon. As we will see, created being is narratively constituted. My being derives its reality from my individual story as it subsists within the larger narratives of the old and new creations. In the same manner, Christ's timeless and transcendent divine person incorporates into itself (*enhypostasis*) the reality of his humanity. Because of the preceding history of Adam and Israel, the humanity of Christ from the moment of its conception stands in solidarity with human nature in general. This human nature has been previously determined by the narratives of creation and the Fall, and therefore Christ, as true man and true God must deal with these realities. Conversely, because Christ's human nature is at his conception also free of sin and contains within it God's infinite and creative divine life (*genus majestaticum*), it also possesses within its reality the pattern of a new redemptive narrative. This new narrative will be actualized in Jesus's incarnation, life, death, and resurrection. Hence, viewed in their totality, the two natures are constituted by the dynamic event of the coming of the Son of God into creation and assuming the total fallen narrative of human existence. In doing this, Jesus overcomes this mangled narrative by the counter-narrative

---

3. Here I refer to the "seat" of doctrine. That is, those passages that are grammatically clear and that form the doctrinal basis of the *regula fidei*. See discussion of the *sedes* and the *loci* method in Richard Muller, *Post-Reformation Reformed Dogmatics*, 1:177–81. See also R. Preus, *Post-Reformation Lutheran Dogmatics*, 1:35, 1:44–49.

4. Scaer, "Doctrine of the Trinity," 326. Scaer has frequently made this charge, though it does not seem fair to the sources in every case.

5. Kleinig, *Grace Upon Grace*, 57.

of his death and resurrection. This narrative constitutes Christ's redemptive work. Therefore, viewed in their concrete totality, one could say in a sense that the person is the work and the work is the person. Oswald Bayer characterizes Luther's understanding of the person and work of Christ in accordance with this: "Christ nature is his work—Christ work is his nature."[6] Similarly, as Regin Prenter notes the Greek patristic theologians (notably Athanasius) in discussing the person of Christ never developed a separate treatise on his work.[7]

The Context of the Person and Work of Christ: The Mystery of Created Being

Before discussing the details of the person of Christ and his work, we must properly set the stage for the drama of redemption. Christ's person and work are not abstract propositions, but manifest themselves within the context of the created order. To understand who Jesus Christ is, we must first briefly investigate the nature of creation and sin. Creation and sin form the presupposition of the advent of Christ, in that, without creation or sin the person and work of Christ would be utterly meaningless and unnecessary.

According to the Luther scholar Kenneth Hagen, Luther differed profoundly from the theological tradition (he particularly mentions Anselm) that preceded him because he was interested in the concrete actuality of God's work, rather than speculations about how "fitting" it might be for God to undertake.[8] It is for this reason that Luther described his method of exposition in the Galatians commentary as *enarratio*. *Enarratio* means getting the message out into the public sphere as to what God has actually done.[9]

In a similar vein, Oswald Bayer describes Christian theology as occupying a place suspended between "metaphysics and mythology."[10] On the one hand (states Bayer), Christian theology is concerned with an infinite God, who transcends all creaturely existence.[11] On the other hand, Christian theology also deals with a concrete, historical narrative of Jesus, in which the eternal God comes to his creation. Such a historically embedded event affects the eternal and infinite God's relationship to the created realm.[12] Nevertheless, God is not swallowed up into the finitude of the story of redemption. He does not metamorphose into a mythological character (like Zeus among the other gods of Greece) that somehow reacts to and competes alongside other characters within it. Similarly, the story of Jesus as a concrete historical event does not give rise to the "free

---

6. Bayer, *Martin Luther's Theology*, 232. This is also an observation by Congar, "Regards et réflexions sur la christologie de Luther," 3:457–86.

7. Prenter, *Creation and Redemption*, 368.

8. Hagen, "Luther on Atonement-Reconfigured," 256.

9. Ibid.

10. Bayer, *Theology the Lutheran Way*, 8.

11. Ibid.

12. Ibid., 9.

rein" of mythological fantasy.[13] It cannot be changed; it is a historical event that determines who we are and God's relationship to us.[14]

In effect (implies Bayer), theology is essentially incarnational and ecclesial. It is about God's real presence within the history of salvation through the incarnation of the Word, the scriptural authority, and the sacraments. The recognition of the significance of this history is not a private affair, but happens in the context of the corporate history and worship of the people of God. Furthermore, it cannot be understood apart from the Church's own communal practice of the proclamation of Jesus Christ in Word and sacrament.[15]

This gives us significant insight as to how to proceed. Theology is necessarily narrative in that God's act of creation and redemption takes on a narrative form. This narrative is recorded in the Bible, which Luther fittingly refers to as the "divine *Aeneid*."[16] Calling the Bible the "divine *Aeneid*" is important for several reasons. First, the *Aeneid* was the national epic of the Roman people. It gave them a story that informed them as to their place in history and their praxis as the rulers of the ancient world. Secondly, it was a story about Aeneas, the progenitor of the Roman people and therefore of Rome's universal dominion. In much the same way, the story of God's activity as creator and redeemer inform the reality of the Church. Similarly, the narrative of creation and salvation given in sacred scripture is the story of the establishment of God's universal kingdom.

In that it is a narrative, creation is the product of the act of narration. As Bayer correctly describes it, creation is a narrative of God's "effective address" to his creatures.[17] God's Word creates and determines creation by his address. His Word calls creation into being, judges it, and redeems it, thereby establishing new creation. Our creaturely existence is therefore determined by and subsists in the divine address within the dynamic narrative of creation. Creation is a dynamic narrative that is ever being spoken forth by the divine narrator.[18]

Working from this perspective, we are given a clearer basis for understanding creation, sin, and ultimately the person and work of Christ. Beginning with creation, if we

13. Ibid.

14. Ibid.

15. Ibid., 86–93. Hence modern historical criticism's misguided anti-supernaturalist reading of the Bible is partially the result of a failure to take into account the fact of benefits of Christ given to the people of God in the Divine Service. Read in light of the fact of actual event of proclamation, the Bible cannot be evaluated as a fanciful made-up history or mythology, but rather as the literal historical basis of what happens in Word and sacrament in the Divine Service. Acceptance of the truth of the *pro me* of the gospel present in Word and sacrament directly implies the literal and inerrant truth of scripture.

16. Ibid., 41. Luther is quoting Statius according to Bayer. The quote is taken from Mattes and Silcock's translation of *WA TR* 5:168n7.

17. See Bayer, *Martin Luther's Theology*, 101–5; Bayer, "Creation as History," 253; Bayer, "God as Author of My Life History," 437–56; Bayer, "Poetological Doctrine of the Trinity," 43–58.

18. Robert Jenson has taken a similar narrative approach. See Jenson, *Story and Promise*; Jenson, "How the World Lost Its Story," 19–24; Jenson, "Can We Have a Story?," 16–7. One of his difficulties though is that he assumes that God's own being is conditioned by salvation history. This is false in that not only is God immutable, but this would deny his reality as creator by claiming his creatures possess possibilities alien to his own being. Another helpful approach and one that has partially inspired our own can be found in Hans Urs von Balthasar, *Theo-Drama*.

assume that creation draws its being from its story, it is logical to infer that creation could only gain its reality by being created as a story. This story then informs and determines the essence and activity of created beings. All subsequent created beings are determined in their essence by the primal narrative of creation. For this reason, the claim that it can be considered mythological or even "sagic" (Barth) is utterly false.[19] If the narrative of creation given to us by Genesis 1–3 is not literally true, then it possesses no ability to determine us ontologically and consequently is meaningless.[20]

If creation's essence is determined by narrative, what sort of narrative is creation? From what we observed in our exegesis in the first chapter, the Bible considers creation to be essentially rooted in the liturgical. In our earlier exegesis of the Old Testament, we have also observed how the structure of the tabernacle also mirrors the structure of creation. In that both time and space within creation is dedicated to divine liturgy, creation's chief purpose is to glorify God (Rom 1, Phil 2). Creation is therefore a liturgical narrative of divine glorification.

Because creation subsists through God's effective address, creatures are created words of God. They are created words brought into being through the uncreated eternal Word of God. They are also masks (*larva Dei*) through which God acts and addresses his intelligent creatures. As Paul asserts: "For his [God's] invisible attributes, namely, his eternal power and divine nature, have been clearly perceived . . . in the things that have been made" (Rom 1:20).[21] These created words are means through which God promises all good things to his creatures: "You may eat . . ." etc. As words from God, they have the character of both law and gospel. They are gospel in that they are spoken forth freely and graciously by an act of fiat without any effort on the part of the creature. They are law insofar as these words give a structure and logos of being within which creatures necessarily act. This structure serves to channel the creature's response of praise for being given all good things by God's unmerited favor.

This giving and receiving of glory is in fact rooted in the Trinitarian life of God. God is by nature a gracious giver and a self-donator in his eternal being. His acts of giving in time are therefore rooted in his prior nature as a self-communicating giver in eternity. The Father eternally gives his entire being to the Son (John 1:1–5, Heb 1:1–5) and creates all things to the end of glorifying him (John 8:54, 17:5; Phil 2:9–11). The Father is infinite and therefore he may give of himself infinitely in the begetting of the Son and yet remain himself. Due to their infinite glory in eternity, the Son and the Father are free to

---

19. *CD* 3.1.43.

20. In other words, to say that creation is in fact rooted in the free giving of the Triune God by an act of fiat, responded to by a glorious liturgy of creation (as Gen 1–3 says) and then to say (as these same theologians do) that this is a metaphor for creation dragging itself up by its own bootstraps, by way of nature red in tooth and claw, is utterly incoherent. If evolution were true, it would not merely be "the way God creates" (as mainline Protestants and most Catholics claim), rather it would be a total reversal of what creation is about. It would be to make creation about self-creation through doing (*autopoesis*, i.e., self-deification through the works of the law), rather than free reception by God's act of giving. It would in fact contradict the very nature of the gospel and the nature of God (Triune), which is based on giving. See David Scaer's critique of the idea of Genesis 1–3 as allegory in his "Problems of Inerrancy and Historicity," 21–25.

21. See argument in Paulson, *Lutheran Theology*, 73.

fully give of their being in the dual procession of the Spirit (Gal 4:6). In his incarnation and earthly life, the Son is free to give all glory to the Father (Matt 11:25, John 17:1–5). In time, the Father then exalts the Son and the Spirit glorifies the Father through creation's worship of the Son (John 16:4, Gal 4:6, Phil 2:9–11, Heb 13:15, Rev 4–5).[22]

In creating humanity, God gives men and women his own image (Gen 1:26–27). The question as to what constitutes this image has been hotly debated throughout the history of Christian thought.[23] Lutherans have historically confessed the divine image to be the original righteousness and holiness lost in the Fall.[24] This interpretation must be considered accurate based on biblical evidence from the description of sanctification being a restoration of the *imago Dei*: "put on the new self, which is being renewed in knowledge after the image of its creator" (Col 3:10, also see Eph 4:24).[25]

Nevertheless, it is important to flesh out this definition of the *imago Dei* by the observation that the divine righteousness is not an abstract quality, but something that possesses a concrete existence within a relational framework. God's own character as God is on the one hand defined by his reality as the free lord and sovereign of all reality. Nonetheless, it is also defined by his relational, self-donating life eternally actualized as the Trinity. These two aspects of God's being are in fact interconnected. Because the Father lacks nothing, he can give all in his eternal generation of the Son. The Son, in turn, can give the totality of his being in the procession of the Holy Spirit. Put succinctly: God is the free lord of all, yet at the same time an eternally self-donating servant. Hence, the divine image consists in the same things that in *Freedom of a Christian* Luther identifies as being the defining characteristics of the righteousness of faith.[26]

In light of this insight regarding the relational nature of the *imago Dei*, we can better understand the passages that deal with it in the early chapters of sacred scripture. In Genesis chapter 1 we read: "God blessed them. And God said to them, 'Be fruitful and multiply and fill the earth and subdue it and have dominion over the fish of the sea and over the birds of the heavens and over every living thing that moves on the earth'" (Gen 1:28). It should be observed that in the first section of the verse we are told that

22. See similar description in von Balthasar, *Theo-Drama*, 4:323–27. Also see Leithart:

To put it another way, the trinitarian life is a rhythm of self-giving and return within the life of God. Trinitarian life is a life given over and returned as glorified life. The Father loves and submits to the Son, and the Son to the Father, and the Son to the Spirit, and so on. But this self-giving of one Person to the others is always met with a return gift: the Father's gift of Himself to the Son is met with the Son's gift of Himself to the Father. "Self-sacrifice" is met with a returning of the self gift that eternally and ever refreshes and renews the triune fellowship. Gift and return, we might say, are simultaneous in the life of God, since the Father who gives the Son in the Spirit is in the Son who returns the gift to the Father in the same Spirit. There is not even a moment of "stasis" or death, since "resurrection" life is offered back from the moment the original life is offered. (*Deep Comedy*, 89)

23. See description in Hefner, "The Creation," 1:330–33.

24. See Ap 2; CT 109; AE 1:162. Also see Baier, *Compendium Theologiae Positivae*, 1:143–61; Chemnitz, *Loci Theologici*, 2:185; Chytraeus, *Summary of the Christian Faith*, 50; Hoenecke, *Evangelical Lutheran Dogmatics*, 2: 317–27; Gerhard, "Image of God," 32–33; Koehler, *Summary of Christian Doctrine*, 50–51; Krauth, *Conservative Reformation*, 379; J. Mueller, *Christian Dogmatics*, 205–9; F. Pieper, *Christian Dogmatics*, 1:515–26.

25. See Graebner, *Outline of Doctrinal Theology*, 58.

26. See AE 31:344.

the subsequent statement is to be characterized as an act of "blessing" (*way·bā·rek*). In other words, God's Word to them in the second half of the verse (which has the ring of a commandment) only makes sense if one assumes that it is also a promise and act of blessing. While being given the task of "subduing" the earth, they are promised that they possess the ability to subdue and thereby are given freedom of dominion. In telling them to multiply, God also implicitly promises that he will guarantee their life, that is, their fertility. Hence, the word that God addresses to the man and the woman, and which determines their status as the *imago Dei* within creation is one of both law and gospel.

The same pattern can be observed in Genesis 2. As Bayer has observed, the first statement of God to Adam is one of promise: "*You may surely* eat of every tree of the garden" (2:16, emphasis added).[27] The man is also given dominion in the garden and the ability to cultivate it (v. 15). Only after this word of promise does God prohibit the eating of the tree of the knowledge of good and evil. Hence, the divine image is then a relational image, established by God's initiative in giving his gracious Word of promise. It must be as such since the eternally relational God aims at making humanity after "our image" and "our likeness" (Gen 1:26). Humans are free lords of all that God has created and, therefore, they are free to submit to God and each other as perfect servants.

For this reason, it is important to recognize that the original righteousness of the *imago Dei* is rooted in righteousness of faith. As creatures, Adam and Eve passively receive themselves through God's gracious Word. Faith is a receptive organ[28] and the life of faith is the *vita passiva,* wherein life and freedom are passively received from the bounty of God's goodness in creation and redemption.[29] Sin is therefore by definition the opposite of this. As Paul observes "whatever does not proceed from faith is sin" (Rom 14:23). So too we read in the Epistle to the Hebrews: "without faith it is impossible to please him [God]" (Heb 11:6). Luther echoes these sentiments in the Genesis commentary by stating: "Unbelief is the source of all sins; when Satan brought about this unbelief by driving out or corrupting the Word, the rest was easy for him."[30]

Such faith glorifies God, which is the central purpose of creation (Phil 2:9–10). After all, *kavod* ("glory") has both the connotation of light and praise.[31] If God is fundamentally glorious, then his image reflected in humans must be as well (Rom 3:23). This understanding of the *imago Dei* fits well with Luther's concept of the righteousness of faith found in *Freedom of a Christian*. Because Adam and Eve are perfect and believe in God's Word, they glorified God by their trust in his Word:

> It is a further function of faith that it honors him whom it trusts with the most reverent and highest regard since it considers him truthful and trustworthy. There is no other honor equal to the estimate of truthfulness and righteousness with which we honor him whom we trust. Could we ascribe to a man anything greater than truthfulness and righteousness and perfect goodness?[32]

27. Bayer, "Worship and Theology," 149.

28. F. Pieper, *Christian Dogmatics,* 2:423–24.

29. Bayer, *Martin Luther's Theology,* 42–43.

30. *AE* 1:147.

31. Eichrodt, *Theology of the Old Testament,* 2:30–32.

32. *AE* 31:350.

Peter Brunner similarly observes:

> As God created man in His image, He created a creature in which His own reality, glory, might, and beauty are reflected within the boundaries implicit in the creatureliness of the foremost creature. The special feature of the mirrored image, by which this creature is distinguished from the reflection of the divine essence in the other earthly creatures, consists in the fact that man became an "I" through God's fatherly address. . . . the reality of God, reflected mutely and unconsciously, as it were, in nonhuman earthly creatures, is perceived, recognized, acknowledged, and returned to the Creator with thanks and adoration. . . . Man cannot be God's image without the immediate, adoring word of acknowledgement, of gratitude, of glorification addressed to the Creator. Without the prayer and laudation, man would not be the mirror of God's glory, would not be a man.[33]

In discussing God's Word to the first humans, we must address the question of the function of the law prior to the Fall. According to some Lutheran theologians, one cannot speak of the law prior to the Fall in that law is exclusively tied to condemnation.[34] It should also be observed that Luther's own position on the nature of the law has been much disputed.[35] Though we cannot engage in a lengthy debate on this subject, it is important below to establish a working concept of the law and its function in the pre- and post-lapsarian world based on the scriptures as properly understood by Luther and the Lutheran symbols. This question is important to our task, insofar as it will help us describe the shape of Christ's redemption from the condemnation of the law.

In describing Luther's concept of the nature of the law, we will primarily follow the Erlangen theologian and Luther scholar Theodosius Harnack. In his interpretation of Luther, Harnack helpfully makes the distinction between the "office" and "essence" (*Amt und Wesen*) of the law. In the present age of sin and death, it is the office of the law to accuse and condemn sinners through the mediums of God's created masks (*larva Dei*).[36] Nevertheless, the law is also a positive good that expresses the eternal will of God (*lex*

---

33. Brunner, *Worship in the Name of Jesus*, 36. Also see Scaer, "Man Made in the Image of God," 20–35.

34. This is the logic of Gerhard Forde's position. See Forde, *Law-Gospel Debate*, 180–87. Forde defines the law as "a general term for the manner in which the will of God impinges on Man" (194). Obviously there is no threatening or impinging on humanity prior to the Fall. See A. Pieper "Law is not made for the Righteous Man," 2:80. Pieper writes: "To do the will of God was his very nature and delight. Therefore he did not feel God's will to be 'law.' But when man fell into sin, he cast God's will out of his inner nature, out of his desires and wishes; and he placed this will in opposition to himself, as being to himself, as being no longer his own but a strange will . . . and so he made it into the 'law' for himself . . . therefore it is sin that changed God's moral will into *law*." Pieper's point is not that God lacked a moral will prior to the Fall or that he did not expect humans to obey it. Rather, he identifies "law" with a threatening demand (as does Forde) and therefore this can only been a phenomenon after the Fall. The command not to eat from the tree of the knowledge of good and evil was not a demand or even part of God's general moral will, since it was a special commandment given to a willing subject. If one is willing, then, Pieper's logic goes, no request can function as demand.

35. See Forde, *Law-Gospel Debate*, 81–120, 150–200.

36. *AE* 26: 95. Luther writes in the Galatians commentary of 1531–1535: "the whole creation is a face or mask of God."

aeterna) for human beings.[37] Hence, the law is not to be defined as a purely negative phenomenon, but rather becomes negative merely due to sin.

This distinction appears to work well on certain texts, most notably Luther's *Antinomian Disputations*. Here, Luther is clear that the law is God's eternal will ("the Decalogue is eternal").[38] In saying this, Luther does not mean that God's demand for our obedience continues even after the law has been fulfilled in us. Rather, in the same breath he is careful to note that the law becomes "empty" (*lex vacua*) when it is fulfilled. Hence, he distinguishes the law's reality as the eternal will of God from the "office of the law," which is "whatever shows sin, wrath, and death."[39] These passages appear to vindicate Harnack's "essence/office" distinction.[40] Read in this manner, Luther's position in these passages stands in total agreement with the Formula of Concord.[41]

For this reason, the law is not something purely negative and has an existence apart from sin. We find this claim in Luther's Genesis commentary, where he discusses the

37. See T. Harnack, *Luthers Theologie*, 1:368–401. Robert Schultz has argued that Harnack's view might be based on some faulty understandings of certain statements of Luther and in one case an inaccurate translation. See R. Schultz, *Gesetz und Evangelium in der Lutherischen Theologie des 19*, 142. Schultz is well known for his work as a partisan in the great LC-MS civil war of the 1970s. For critique of Schultz (among others) see Scaer, "Law Gospel Debate," 156–71. And also by the same author, "Law Gospel Debate in the Missouri Synod Continued," 107–18. Based on the evidence that we will see below, there is at very least a strong suggestion that Luther did make such a distinction. In any case, even if he did not systematically between "essence" and "office," it seems at least that these two things are at very least conceptually the distinction in his thinking. Luther for example, did not use christological terminology such as "*genus majestaticum*" either, but conceptually he affirms what Chemntiz and Lutheran orthodoxy meant by these terms.

38. Luther, *Only the Decalogue is Eternal*, 75. See Nestingen, "End of the End," 200–201. Nestingen claims that Luther's statement refers to the eternal restoration of creational relationships: "The law signifies the restoration of the defining relationships of life: the first commandment, with the second and third, in relation to God; the remaining commandments in relation to the neighbor and the earth. These are the relationships of redemption, of the hope of faith. Consequently, Luther insists, they are eternal: they never end." This is not a plausible interpretation of this statement for three main reasons. First, Nestingen (following Forde) wrongly conflates "law" with "vocation." Nevertheless, this cannot be in that the existence of our creational vocations does not automatically dictate how we carry them out. That X office exists does not mean that one is aware of what one should do with the office. Luther assumes this as well in the Catechism in that he does not instruct people to enter into certain creational relationships, but already assumes they exist and must be regulated by the commandments. Secondly, the relationships we have with God and creation do in fact end at the Last Judgment and therefore are not eternal. After the Last Judgment Christ will rule and therefore there will be no need of civil government. We will "see God"; consequently, we will not need the preaching of the Word or the office of ministry. We will neither "give in marriage nor be given in marriage"; therefore marriage and the family will also cease. Luther fully expected this (as we shall see below) and therefore it is impossible to place this interpretation on these words. Lastly, Luther from the context is clearly referring to the law as God's will for his creatures. He is not talking about creational relationship (i.e., vocation and structures) but how those vocations and structures are to be enacted and preserved by obeying God's will for them. What actually appears to be going on is that Nestingen here is attempting to uphold Forde's rejection of *lex aeterna*.

39. Luther, *Only the Decalogue is Eternal*, 80 (emphasis added).

40. See similar reading of Luther in Paulson, *Lutheran Theology*, 222–25.

41. FC SD 3; *CT* 935, in which Luther states that "the eternal, immutable righteousness of God, [is] revealed in the Law." FC SD 5; *CT* 955, which quotes Luther's statement in the *Antinomian Disputations* approvingly: "Anything that preaches concerning our sins and God's wrath, let it be done how or when it will, that is all a preaching of the Law."

existence of law before the Fall. The Reformer insists that the claim that the law did not exist prior to the Fall is "full of wickedness and blasphemy."[42] He goes on to note in the same passage that it would be impossible for the Fall to have occurred without law since a commandment that does not exist cannot be violated.[43] We observe here again, that these statements stand in perfect agreement with the later affirmations of the Formula of Concord regarding pre-lapsarian human existence.[44]

When speaking about the function of the law before the Fall, Luther specifically asserts in the Genesis commentary that in this state of innocence there was still a need for commandments. This was because faith needed a medium into which it could channel its fruits.[45] Tilling the soil and guarding the garden would have been performed as "play and joy."[46] Similarly, according to Luther, the command of not eating from the tree of the knowledge of good and evil would have been used as an act of worship and devotion: "Only this He [God] wants: that he [Adam] praise God, that he thank Him, that he rejoice in the Lord, and that he obey him by not eating from the forbidden tree."[47] The Reformer goes on to speculate that the tree itself was not a single tree, but more like a grove of trees that could have served as a chapel.[48] He further suggests that Adam and his descendants would have gathered together and Adam would have preached on the divine Word given to him that prohibited the consumption of fruit from the tree.[49]

The point is that although the law as the will and command of God existed prior to the Fall (we should not be squeamish about using the term "law," as some have been), it functioned in an utterly different manner. In that humans were willing subjects and had God's law written on their hearts, the law prior to the Fall did not function as external coercive demand. Demand always presupposes the need to self-justify by producing what is lacking. As we can observe from the narrative of Genesis, there is no Decalogue given to Adam and Eve.[50] Being creatures created in the perfect righteousness of faith,

42. *AE* 1:108. It should of course be noted that Peter Meinhold claimed that the Genesis commentary was compromised by Melanchthonian influences, particularly on the issue of the law. See Meinhold, *Genesisvorlesung Luthers und ihre Herausgeber*, 44–52. Surveying Meinhold's work, this partially has to do with a perception among scholars of that generation that there was a profound theological difference between Luther and Melanchthon. Certain scholars attempt to continue to maintain this view of Luther and Melanchthon and of the Genesis commentary (see Nestingen, "End of the End," 195–205; Nestingen, "Luther in Front of the Text," 186–94). Mickey Mattox has shown that Meinhold's position is inaccurate in that it relies on an "abstract set" of alleged differences between Luther and Lutheran orthodoxy and not clear textual evidence. It would therefore appear that the text we possess (with minor additions) is representative of the theology of the mature Luther. See Mattox, *"Defender of the Holy Matriarchs,"* 265–66.

43. *AE* 1:108.

44. FC Ep 6; *CT* 805: "For even our first parents before the Fall did not live without Law, who had the Law of God written also into their hearts, because they were created in the image of God."

45. See comment in Bell, "Man is a Microcosmos," 171. Also here we agree with the opinion of Bernd Wannenwetsch, "Luther's Moral Theology," 125.

46. *AE* 1:103.

47. Ibid.

48. *AE* 1:105.

49. *AE* 1:106.

50. See similar observation in Scaer, "Law and Gospel in Lutheran Theology," 30.

they would have simply fulfilled all the commandments spontaneously. Nevertheless, they were still given specific and special commands as external means of worshiping God (*cultus Dei*).

One objection to this interpretation might be that God promised death to the violator of the commandment (Gen 2:17). Although this is true, it does not mean that the commandment functioned as a demanding threat. Rather it would be more appropriate to characterize it (as David Scaer has) as a boundary marker that told Adam and Eve what would happen if they stood outside the relationship of grace.[51] In other words, since they already stood in the circle of righteousness, the threat of death merely explained the consequence of stepping outside of it. Leaving it, any attempt at obeying the law in order to facilitate reentry would become a futile attempt at self-justification (Gal 2:18).

Neither is this inconsistent with Luther's talk (strongly emphasized by theologians like Gerhard Forde) of the law becoming "empty" (*lex vacua*) in heaven among the angels and the beatified: "Where sin ceases, there law ceases, and to that degree sin ceases, to that degree law ceases, so that in the future life the law ought to completely cease, because then it will be fulfilled."[52] Forde is correct that law cannot condemn or demand anything from those in heavenly existence who are free from sin (1 Tim 1:9). Nevertheless, law did exist as a positive commandment prior to the Fall (both Luther's commentary and Genesis itself are quite clear about this) and therefore it is important to explain why Luther thinks in terms of cessation of the law for the righteous in heaven, while positing its existence for the righteous prior to the entry of sin.

Though we cannot venture an answer based on an exhaustive study of Luther's works within this context, it would appear from a reading of the Genesis commentary that Luther's talk of law ceasing in heaven must be understood against the background of his belief in the eventual translation of Adam and Eve into God's presence in heaven. For Luther, the primal state of innocence was an intermediate state between the sinfulness of post-lapsarian existence and the blessedness of heaven. At a future point, humanity would have entered into heavenly bliss and would have thereby enjoyed God's eternal rest.[53] Luther's interpretation (and much of the patristic and medieval tradition before him) has strong support in texts like Hebrews 3–4. Paul also implicitly supports this inference, in his remark that Adam's pre-lapsarian earthly body was only a preliminary stage to the eventual reception of a spiritual body (1 Cor 15:45–46).

Therefore it may be inferred that before the Fall commandments were given in order to regulate creation prior to the final consummation.[54] In a preliminary sense,

51. Ibid.

52. Forde, *Law-Gospel Debate*, 182; quoting from his translation of *WA* 39.1:431, 6–7.

53. *AE* 1:104:
   But the church was established first because God wants to show by this sign, as it were that man was created for another purpose than the rest of the living beings. Because the church is established by the Word of God, it is certain that man was created for an immortal and spiritual life, to which he would have been carried off or translated without death after living in Eden and on the rest of the earth without inconvenience as long as he wished.

54. *AE* 1:106:
   This outward place, ceremonial word, and worship man would have had; and later on he would have returned to his working and guarding until a predetermined time had been fulfilled, when he would have been translated to heaven with the utmost pleasure.

humans enjoyed this heavenly rest through the *vita passiva* in the inner person, whereas the external person needed divine commands to channel their gratitude towards God through specific external acts in the temporal world. By contrast, in the final state of consummation there is no need of commandments such as "be fruitful and multiply" since people at the resurrection "neither marry nor are given in marriage" (Matt 22:30). Similarly, in the final state there would be no need for the command to preach the Word of God, since all will see God "face to face" (1 Cor 13:12).[55]

Sin: Re-Narration, False Mediation, and Unbelief

Now that we have dealt with the nature of the original creation and place of humans within it, we will move on to a discussion of the Fall and the nature of sin. As we have previously seen, for Luther, Adam and Eve were created in compliance with God's law and standing within his favor. Therefore, in giving the commandment not to eat from the tree of the knowledge of good and evil, God established the primal *cultus Dei*. Obedience to such a command expressed the gratitude of faith, whereas disobedience would necessarily represent unbelief in God's gracious goodness.

Beyond this, according to Luther, by giving the commandment not to eat from the tree God also established the office of ministry. In Genesis 2:15–17, Adam is given the Word of God prior to the creation of Eve. As the Reformer observes, since the text does not indicate that God repeated the Word to the woman, it follows that Eve as a hearer of the Word from Adam functioned as the first Church, whereas her husband occupied the role of the first minister of the Word.[56] This is the same situation that prevails in the Church of the New Testament, where all possess the priesthood (as Eve did in her role as a caretaker of the cosmic tabernacle), but some are specifically selected to publically exercise the office of ministry.[57]

In light of this situation, the serpent brings about sin through a twofold strategy. First, and most importantly, he directs Eve away from the external Word of God to speculations about God's hidden being and intentions above and beyond his revealed will. Secondly, in keeping with this, the serpent encourages Eve to abandon the divinely established office of ministry for his alternative mediation. It is seldom noted among theologians and commentators that Genesis 3:6 indicates that Adam was present for the entire dialogue between Eve and the serpent, yet apparently did nothing. Hence the originating sin did not consist merely in the abandonment of the Word of God, but it was also the failure to properly exercise the office of ministry.

55. In a sense, we are arguing that the logic of two kinds of righteousness hold even in the pre-lapsarian situation. In other words, law-gospel is better understood within the framework of two kinds of righteousness. See Arand, "Two Kinds of Righteousness," 417–439.

56. *AE* 1:105: "Adam alone heard it [the command not to eat from the tree of the knowledge of good and evil], he later informed Eve of it. If they had not fallen into sin, Adam would have transmitted this single command later to their descendants." Also see Scaer, "Ordaining Women?," 83–85.

57. See discussion in Marquart, *Church and Her Fellowship*, 103–20; Walther, *Church and Ministry*, 161–76, 198–212, 219–88.

According to Luther, the process of Eve's apostasy from the external Word begins the moment she answers the serpent's initial question. In quoting God's command, the woman adds the word "*perchance*" to the command: "*perchance* lest we die" (Gen 3:3, emphasis added).[58] Luther suggests that Satan's deception has already begun to work on Eve. If Eve only believes that they will "perchance" die, then she is speculating about God's hidden intention behind his Word. In other words, according to Luther's interpretation of the Hebrew, Eve's response betrays her doubt as to whether or not the threat will actually be carried out.

Having directed the woman away from God's Word to speculate about God's hidden intentions above his Word, the serpent sets himself up as a new mediator: "Satan imitates God. Just as God had preached to Adam, so he himself also preaches to Eve . . . Therefore just as from the true Word of God salvation results, so also from the corrupt Word of God damnation results."[59] Eve has, in Luther's estimation, become the first enthusiast.

In order to understand this aspect of Luther's reading of the history of the Fall, we turn to the background to Luther's understanding of the nature of theological knowledge and the divine-human relationship. We will begin by discussing Luther's early work, the *Heidelberg Disputation* (1518). Though it is debatable how significant this disputation is for Luther's later theology, it is a convenient starting point for describing the evolution of the Reformer's contention (found in the Genesis commentary and the Smalcald Articles in their fully developed form) that the essence of human sin is the search for God apart from the external Word.

In the *Heidelberg Disputation*, Luther distinguishes between two different sorts of theologians: theologians of glory and theologians of the cross.[60] Regarding the theologian of glory, Luther writes:

> That person does not deserve to be called a theologian who looks upon the "invisible" things of God as though they were clearly "perceptible in those things which have actually happened" [Or the more correct translation: "things that are made."][61] (Rom 1:20; cf. 1 Cor 1:21–25). This is apparent in the example of those who were "theologians" and still were called "fools" by the Apostle in Rom 1:22. Furthermore, the invisible things of God are virtue, godliness, wisdom, justice,

58. *AE* 1:155.

59. *AE* 1:147.

60. See these books on the subject: Althaus, *Theology of Martin Luther*, 25–35; Althaus, *Die Christliche Wahrheit*, 126, 129–30; Anthony, *Cross Narratives*, 1–105; Deutschlander, *Theology of the Cross*; Eckermann, "Luthers Kreuzestheologie," 306–17; Forde, *On Being a Theologian*; Koppperi, "Theology of the Cross," 155–72; Köstlin, *Theology of Luther*, 1:284–86; von Loewenich, *Luthers Theologia Crucis*; McGrath, *Luther's Theology of the Cross*; Modalsli, "Heidelberger Disputation," 33–39; Nestingen, "Luther's Heidelberg Disputation," 147–54; Ngien, *Suffering of God*; Prenter, *Luther's Theology of the Cross*; Sasse, "Theology of the Cross," 35–45; Vercruysse, "Luther's Theology of the Cross," 523–48.

61. Marquart, "Luther and Theosis," 195. This is a strange translation not only because it is grammatically incorrect and because it is obviously a quote from Rom 1:20 (which is cited), but because as Marquart points out, it makes no sense in terms of Luther's obvious intention. The cross and the empty tomb obviously are things that "actually happen" and Luther is urging them as sources of revelatory knowledge. Marquart suggests that this translation choice is probably the result of the influence of mid-twentieth-century existentialism.

> goodness, and so forth. The recognition of all these things does not make one worthy or wise.[62]

In other words, the theologian of glory looks to God apart from his Word and speculates about him through the created order by analogy. By observing and identifying with God's hidden power and glory as it is manifested in the temporal realm, the theologian of glory believes that he or she may enter into fellowship with God through embodying that glory.

The background of this polemic is an attack on Aristotelian philosophy, a subject that Luther was trained in and which he mentions derisively in passing.[63] According to Aristotelian epistemology all human knowledge is a kind of intellectual vision. To simplify things only slightly, in the act of knowing, objects imprint themselves on the human mind in the form of intellectual vision.[64] As a result, the more one contemplates an object, the more one's intellect will become like it. Logically then, this would also be true of God as well. The more one contemplates God in his glory, perceived through the glorious aspects of the visible creation, the more God's own reality would imprint itself upon the human mind. Similarly, according to Aristotle's ethics, virtues come about through performing external acts corresponding to virtue. One's external and visible "doing" of virtue results in "being" virtuous.[65] Hence, the more one engaged in acts of righteousness the more similar one would become to God in his righteousness.

Throughout the high and later Middle Ages the influence of Aristotle on Latin theology was substantial to say the least. Luther lumped together these various medieval theologians who drew heavily on Aristotle and attacked them rather violently in his earlier *Disputation against Scholastic Theology* (1517).[66] With this background in mind, we can easily observe exactly what Luther means by the theology of glory. A theologian of glory is a person who tries to know God through his visible forms of glory and righteousness. In order to have fellowship with this God, he or she attempts to embody this glory and righteousness through knowing and doing. It is this contention that Luther condemns.[67]

---

62. *AE* 31:52.

63. *AE* 31:57.

64. See Aristotle, *De Anima* 3.4–8, 201–11. Also see Copleston, *Medieval Philosophy*, 297–332. Lastly, see Robert Jenson's description of this in the scholastic tradition and its relation to Luther in "Luther's Contemporary Theological Significance," 282–83.

65. See Aristotle, *Nicomachean Ethics*.

66. *AE* 31:3–16. Also see Eckermann, "Aristoeleskritik Luthers," 114–30; Mühlen, "Luther's Kritik am scholastischen Aristotelismus in der 25," 40–65.

67. *AE* 31:57–58:

> The love of God does not find, but creates, that which is pleasing to it. The love of man comes into being through that which is pleasing to it. The second part is clear and is accepted by all philosophers and theologians, for the object of love is its cause, assuming, according to Aristotle, that all power of the soul is passive and material and active only in receiving something. Thus it is also *demonstrated that Aristotle's philosophy is contrary to theology* since in all things it seeks *those things which are its own and receives rather than gives something good.* The first part is clear because the love of God which lives in man loves sinners, evil persons, fools, and weaklings in order to make them righteous, good, wise, and strong. Rather than seeking its own good, the love of God flows forth and bestows good. Therefore sinners are "attractive" because they are loved;

Note that there is no suggestion here on Luther's part that the theologian of glory does not have (from a purely epistemic perspective) a valid knowledge of God: "Yet that wisdom is not of itself evil, nor is the law to be evaded; but without the theology of the cross man misuses the best in the worst manner."[68] Rather, his criticism is that by attempting through their activity to echo the divine being in their knowing and doing, the theologian of glory sought deification. They abuse the knowledge of God's glory, which they possess and through it become conceited.[69]

By contrast, the theologian of the cross holds to the flesh of Jesus where God is hidden in sufferings:

> The manifest and visible things of God are placed in opposition to the invisible, namely, his human nature, weakness, foolishness. The Apostle in 1 Cor 1:25 calls them the weakness and folly of God. Because men misused the knowledge of God through works, God wished again to be recognized in suffering, and to condemn "wisdom concerning invisible things" by means of "wisdom concerning visible things," so that those who did not honor God as manifested in his works should honor him as he is hidden in his suffering (*absconditum in passionibus*). As the Apostle says in 1 Cor 1:21, "For since, in the wisdom of God, the world did not know God through wisdom, it pleased God through the folly of what we preach to save those who believe." Now it is not sufficient for anyone, and it does him no good to recognize God in his glory and majesty, unless he recognizes him in the humility and shame of the cross. Thus God destroys the wisdom of the wise, as Isa 45:15 says, "Truly, thou art a God who hidest thyself." So, also, in John 14:8, where Philip spoke according to the theology of glory: "Show us the Father." Christ forthwith set aside his flighty thought about seeing God elsewhere and led him to himself, saying, "Philip, he who has seen me has seen the

---

they are not loved because they are "attractive": For this reason the love of man avoids sinners and evil persons. Thus Christ says: "For I came not to call the righteous, but sinners" (Matt 9:13). This is the love of the cross, born of the cross, which turns in the direction where it does not find good which it may enjoy, but where it may confer good upon the bad and needy person. "It is more blessed to give than to receive" (Acts 20:35), says the Apostle. Hence Ps 41:1 states, "Blessed is he who considers the poor," for the intellect cannot by nature comprehend an object which does not exist, that is the poor and needy person, but only a thing which does exist, that is the true and good. Therefore it judges according to appearances, is a respecter of persons, and judges according to that which can be seen, etc. (emphasis added)

68. *AE* 31:55. This was actually a fairly typical Occamist stance on reason's relationship to God. See Ngien, *Suffering of God*, 22.

69. *AE* 31:53:

That wisdom which sees the invisible things of God in works as perceived by man is completely puffed up, blinded, and hardened. This has already been said. Because men do not know the cross and hate it, they necessarily love the opposite, namely, wisdom, glory, power, and so on. Therefore they become increasingly blinded and hardened by such love, for desire cannot be satisfied by the acquisition of those things which it desires. Just as the love of money grows in proportion to the increase of the money itself, so the dropsy of the soul becomes thirstier the more it drinks, as the poet says: "The more water they drink, the more they thirst for it." The same thought is expressed in Eccl 1:8: "The eye is not satisfied with seeing, nor the ear filled with hearing." This holds true of all desires. Thus also the desire for knowledge is not satisfied by the acquisition of wisdom but is stimulated that much more. Likewise the desire for glory is not satisfied by the acquisition of glory, nor is the desire to rule satisfied by power and authority, nor is the desire for praise satisfied by praise, and so on, as Christ shows in John 4:13, where he says, "Everyone who drinks of this water will thirst again."

Father" (John 14:9). For this reason true theology and recognition of God are in the crucified Christ, as it is also stated in John 10 (John 14:6) "No one comes to the Father, but by me." "I am the door" (John 10:9), and so forth.[70]

Luther's point here is clear. Whereas the theologian of glory tries to become like God through activity and vision, the theologian of the cross becomes a receptive and hearing creature through word of the cross. There is nothing attractive about the crucified Jesus (Isa 53:2). Neither does his visible manifestation in weakness and condemnation give him the appearance of the almighty God, who is defined by his attributes of glory, power, and righteousness.

In the same way that God is hidden in Jesus, the righteousness of the person of faith is hidden. The person of faith holds to God's own external judgment of them over against their own internal judgment of themselves. To the theologian of glory, who operates with the conceit of self-judgment of vision, the repentant person of faith lacks attractiveness of works and glory. By openly and humbly admitting their sins, they reveal themselves to be maximally unattractive and therefore unworthy of God's justifying verdict. Nevertheless, from God's perspective (*coram Deo*) they are humble and receptive as true creatures should be.[71] Contrary to Aristotle, it is receptivity and passivity, and not external deeds of virtue that stand as righteousness *coram Deo*. This is because the theologian of the cross sees that his or her works are of no avail in light of cross.

Secondly, their knowledge of Christ comes by hearing and not by vision, that is, the "preaching" of the cross mentioned in the citation of Paul. Luther's point here is not that God's being becomes transparent in the cross. This is a mistake commonly made by modern proponents of the theology of cross.[72] Rather, Luther insists that God is completely and wholly present in the cross, yet utterly "hidden in . . . suffering."[73] We know and believe that God is there because we heard Jesus's testimony.

All this presupposes a division of the human knowledge of God through vision and hearing. Later in the Galatians commentary of 1531–1535 Luther writes: "Thus faith is a sort of knowledge or *darkness that nothing can see*. Yet the Christ of whom faith takes

---

70. *AE* 31:52–53.

71. See discussion in Bayer, *Martin Luther's Theology*, 106–14.

72. The most glaring examples of this are Moltmann, *Crucified God*; Jüngel, *God as the Mystery of the World*. The major problem with recent so-called modern theologies of the cross is that they want to claim that the knowledge of God given in the cross can form a basis for the criticism and revision of classical theism. This is particularly true of Moltmann who insists that we can predicate suffering, passion, and mutability to the divine being because of the cross. In turn, Moltmann argues, we can then correspond to this suffering and solidarity with the oppressed through secular leftist political activism (what Gerhard Forde has referred to as a "negative" theology of glory). This entirely misses Luther's point, in that contrary to these thinkers, he is claiming that the divine attributes posited by classical theism are valid. The cross conceals these attributes of power and glory in order to humble us. If we could see the divine being through the cross, then for Luther the cross would lose its paradoxical character. It would be a matter of vision and not faith. In the same way, our proper response to the cross should not be the animation of political activism (though in the kingdom of the world this is certainly not bad), but rather the passivity of faith. In other words, Luther's point is exactly the opposite of these modern appropriations. See a good critique of Moltmann in Eckhardt, "Luther and Moltmann," 19–28. Also see criticisms of both Moltmann and Jüngel in Mark Mattes, *Role of Justification*, 23–56, 85–117.

73. *AE* 31:52–53.

hold is sitting in this darkness as God sat in the midst of darkness on Sinai and in the temple."[74] The Word tells us that all righteousness, glory, and power are hidden in Jesus and perceived only through hearing of faith. In the *Bondage of the Will* (1525), Luther further states that God always acts under the form of his opposite: "thus when God makes alive he does it by killing, when he justifies he does it by making men guilty, when he exalts to heaven he does it by bringing down to hell."[75] The creature does not have, as in the Aristotelian epistemology, a partial intellectual vision of God made transparent by analogy. Rather, one has a word and promise which stand in contradiction to God's visible manifestation: "Thus God hides his eternal goodness and mercy under eternal wrath, his righteousness under iniquity. This is the highest degree of faith, to believe him merciful when he saves so few and damns so many, and to believe him righteous when by his own will he makes us necessarily damnable."[76] This apparent contradiction humbles reason and destroys all human moral pretentions.[77] In light of this realization Luther comments: "I myself was offended more than once, and brought to the very depth and abyss of despair, so that I wished I had never been created a man, before I realized how salutary that despair was, and how near I was to grace."[78] For this reason, faith and receptivity to the divine Word are the proper stance of the creature in relation to divine hiddenness.

We find much that connects this description of the divine-human relationship to the narrative of the Fall. Eve was attracted to the prospect of gaining hidden divine wisdom (Gen 3:6) and thereby becoming "as God" through her actions. The desire for hidden divine wisdom, that is, to have the "knowledge of good and evil" is central to the project of self-justification and deification. Rather than listening and trusting in God's own external verdict of "very good" and his commandment "do not eat," Eve like the theologian of glory seeks to hold divinity and wisdom within herself. She wishes to become "as God" and thereby exalt herself as powerful and glorious.

In harmony with Luther's early insistence that God only manifests his grace in the tangible Word, is his later condemnation of enthusiasm. Luther's attack on enthusiasm began with his conflict with Andreas Karlstadt, the Zwickau prophets, and Thomas Müntzer, in the early 1520s.[79] Much as Luther had insisted earlier in the *Heidelberg Disputation* on finding God hidden solely in the tangible flesh of the crucified Jesus, he

74. *AE* 26:129–30 (emphasis added).

75. *AE* 33:62.

76. Ibid.

77. *AE* 33:61. Luther states that God hides for the sake of "the humbling of our pride" in order that we might come to recognize "the grace of God."

78. *AE* 33:190.

79. See Althaus, *Theology of Martin Luther*, 40–42, 375–76, 382–92; Bayer, *Martin Luther's Theology*, 246–47; H. Bornkamm, *Luther's World of Thought*, 188; Brecht, *Martin Luther*, 2:146–95; Gritsch, *Martin*, 57, 72, 83, 144–45; Kittelson, *Luther the Reformer*, 195–213; Köstlin, *Theology of Luther*, 2:21–28, 220; Lohse, *Martin Luther's Theology*, 141–51; Marius, *Martin Luther*, 398–402; Maurer, *Kirche und Geschichte*, 1:103–34; Oberman, *Luther*, 61, 64, 66, 317; Prenter, *Spiritus Creator*, 247–305; Schwiebert, *Luther and His Times*, 225, 449, 538, 542, 546–48, 604, 615. This stance continued through his career. We read in the Galatians commentary of 1531–1535: "I avoid all speculations about the Divine Majesty and take my stand in the humanity of Christ" (*AE* 26:39).

now emphasized the need to look for God not in the utterances of those who claimed the intangible Spirit, but rather to seek him in the tangible means of grace. Later in the Smalcald Articles (1537) Luther would comment that he saw very little daylight between the enthusiasts, the Pope, and the serpent in the garden of Eden.[80] All took up the office of ministry without a proper call, drawing people away from those who exercised ministry with a proper call. All claimed the ability to know God's hidden will and drew people away from external Word.[81] In this, Luther posits that enthusiasm and unbelief are the originating sin. The "Schwärmerei" (as Luther referred to them) were essentially of the same stripe as the theologians of glory that he had mentioned in 1518.[82] Without recourse to the Word, they claimed to have bridged the gap between God hidden in his majesty and themselves.[83] Just as the theologians of glory conceitedly sought to hold within themselves power, glory, and righteousness, so too the heavenly prophets and the Pope had "swallowed the Holy Spirit, feathers and all."[84] As a result, they claimed the

---

80. SA 3:8; *CT* 495–96. Luther writes:

All this is the old devil and old serpent, who also converted Adam and Eve into enthusiasts, and led them from the outward Word of God to spiritualizing and self-conceit, and nevertheless he accomplished this through other outward words. Just as also our enthusiasts [at the present day] condemn the outward Word, and nevertheless they themselves are not silent, but they fill the world with their pratings and writings, as though, indeed, the Spirit could not come through the writings and spoken word of the apostles, but [first] through their writings and words he must come. Why [then] do not they also omit their own sermons and writings, until the Spirit Himself come to men, without their writings and before them, as they boast that He has come into them without the preaching of the Scriptures? But of these matters there is not time now to dispute at greater length; we have elsewhere sufficiently urged this subject. In a word, enthusiasm inheres in Adam and his children from the beginning [from the first fall] to the end of the world, [its poison] having been implanted and infused into them by the old dragon, and is the origin, power [life], and strength of all heresy, especially of that of the Papacy and Mahomet. Therefore we ought and must constantly maintain this point, that God does not wish to deal with us otherwise than through the spoken Word and the Sacraments. It is the devil himself whatsoever is extolled as Spirit without the Word and Sacraments. For God wished to appear even to Moses through the burning bush and spoken Word; and no prophet neither Elijah nor Elisha, received the Spirit without the Ten Commandments [or spoken Word]. Neither was John the Baptist conceived without the preceding word of Gabriel, nor did he leap in his mother's womb without the voice of Mary. And Peter says, 2 Pet 1:21: "*The prophecy came not by the will of man; but holy men of God spake as they were moved by the Holy Ghost.*" Without the outward Word, however, they were not holy, much less would the Holy Ghost have moved them to speak when they still were unholy [or profane]; for they were holy, says he, since the Holy Ghost spake through them.

81. See CA 5; *CT* 45. Melanchthon writes:

That we may obtain this faith, the Ministry of Teaching the Gospel and administering the Sacraments was instituted. For through the Word and Sacraments, as through instruments, the Holy Ghost is given, who works faith; where and when it pleases God, in them that hear the Gospel, to wit, that God, not for our own merits, but for Christ's sake, justifies those who believe that they are received into grace for Christ's sake. They condemn the Anabaptists and others who think that the Holy Ghost comes to men without the external Word, through their own preparations and works.

82. See "Against the Heavenly Prophets in the Matters of Images and Sacraments," in *AE* 40:144–223.

83. *AE* 40:149. Against Karlstadt he writes: "For [even] if Christ had been given and crucified for us a thousand times, it would all be for naught had not the Word of God come and distributed it to us and given it to me as a gift and said: 'You shall do this, take and have it for yourself.'"

84. *AE* 40:83.

ability to judge "good and evil" apart from and even against the external Word through the power of the intangible Spirit.[85]

Hence, in both his earlier theology and his later thought, Luther contended against the fallen human impulse to ascend to an intangible God. The promise of the gospel must be consistently understood as an act of self-donation. By becoming present in a concrete word of promise, God tangibly and unilaterally surrenders his being to faith through the means of grace.[86] If we understand the underlying logic of Luther's position in this way, the gospel goes hand-in-hand with a strong concept of the incarnation (God's surrender of his very being to humans) and the means of grace. Receptivity to God's concrete self-donation is in fact the essence of the life of faith.

By contrast, the life of sin and unbelief is necessarily bound up with the human search for the intangible and unbound God. Encountered as the unbound by his promise of grace, God is utterly threatening.[87] In this situation, God is not my tangible object; rather I am his. Consequently, the enthusiast who has chosen to look for God in the sphere of the intangible, where God is not bound by his promise of self-donation, must enter into an unending project of self-justification like the theologian of glory. This project necessitates continuing to hold onto the delusion of secret, divine knowledge in one's own heart (i.e., "the Spirit," the "knowledge of good and evil," etc.), rather than listening to the external Word. The external Word always places God in his proper relationship to the human creature by revealing God as either law (destroying the pride and emptying the creature) or gospel (filling the creature by his grace, after he or she has been emptied). The enthusiast must ignore all this and hold onto their conceit of self-judgment. Otherwise their project of self-justification and deification would crumble. Such self-judgment is the only means of defense against God hidden in his majesty and terrifying omnipotence that crushes all human conceit.[88] By claiming the right to judge themselves, they claim the ability to oppose their own judgment to God's.

Returning to the Genesis commentary, Luther suggests essentially the same thing regarding Satan's act of temptation. The serpent directs Adam and Eve away from the tangible word of grace, to the hidden being of God. The serpent claims that God above and outside of his Word does not wish them well. God, claims the serpent, is trying to withhold divinity from humans: "For God knows that when you eat of it your eyes will be opened, and you will be like God, knowing good and evil" (Gen 3:4–5).[89] In his act of false mediation, the serpent effectively re-narrates reality as it was established in the earlier chapters of Genesis. Whereas in Genesis 1–2, God establishes humanity in life

85. See good description of this topic in Luther in Paulson, *Luther for Armchair Theologians*, 108–16, 161–67.

86. This emphasis of the tangibility of the means of grace and the act of revelation are stated in some interesting ways in Luther's writings. In the Genesis commentary, he defends the anthropomorites, stating: "When God reveals Himself to us, it is necessary for Him to do so through some such *veil or wrapper* and say: 'Look! *Under this wrapper* you will be sure to *take hold of Me*.' When *we embrace the wrapper*, adoring, praying, and sacrificing to God there, we are said to be praying to God and sacrificing to Him properly" (*AE* 1:15, emphasis added).

87. See comments in Forde, *Theology is for Proclamation*, 15. Forde rightly comments that the hidden God is "unavoidably wrathful."

88. See similar observations in Forde, "Work of Christ," 2:66.

89. *AE* 1:158.

and freedom through his gracious Word of promise, the false mediator Satan substitutes a false word that narrates reality as not rooted in grace.[90] Rather than freely given, the good must be grasped at. Grasping logically follows from speculation about God's intentions apart from his Word. When humans stand before the abyss of the hidden and unbound divine will, they have no other recourse but to attempt to oppose and control God by their self-justification.

By leaving the sphere of grace, humans enter into the sphere of law, wrath, and hiddenness. Just as they were in their pre-lapsarian existence determined by God's Word of grace, so now they are determined by his condemning Word of law. Werner Elert correctly describes the life-form of human beings addressed by condemning command as "nomological."[91] By "nomological," Elert means that humans in their fallen state are under the constant assault of the law and divine condemnation.[92] Such a demand for self-justification drives humans all the more into sin. Indeed, as Paul tells us: "for apart from the law, sin is dead" (Rom 7:8). Luther makes the similar observation that when God confronted Adam, he did so with his condemning Word of law and therefore Adam had no other recourse but to engage in self-justification.[93] In effect, he is bound to continue to claim that he holds in his own heart the true knowledge of good and evil over against God's external Word. But for Adam to claim himself as righteous is blasphemy because by such a claim he makes God a liar.[94] "If we say we have not sinned, we make him a liar, and his word is not in us" (1 John 1:10–11).

Indeed, self-justification and unbelief have been Adam and Eve's heritage to the human race. Being bound to the curse of self-justification, all humans are either despairing libertines or Pharisaic legalists.[95] The Pharisaic legalists try to justify themselves by their superabundant moral achievement. Nevertheless, the call to moral achievement only exacerbates sin. If I am called to achieve righteousness, I am called to produce something that is lacking. As we noted earlier, Adam and Eve prior to the Fall were in a state of original integrity and therefore the law was a channel, not a demand. It did not demand what was lacking since they were created in a state whereby they were already in compliance with God's eternal will.[96] But in the state of sin, where righteousness is lacking, the law's demands prove that we are unrighteous and we cannot produce what

90. See excellent description of this in Jüngel, *Justification*, 136–37.

91. Elert, *Law and Gospel*, 28.

92. Also see Elert, *Christian Faith*, 30–67. Elert correctly describes human existence under sin as inherently contradictory. On the one hand, humans live a self-centered existence (*Mittelpunktsdasein*), while constantly being confronted by the other and the demand to justify themselves. This informs the human creature that they are not the center of existence, yet also drives them more and more towards self-justification. Also see an excellent description of the need of sinners to self-justification in Jüngel, *Justification*, 5–8.

93. *AE* 1:77–78.

94. *AE* 1:77–79.

95. FC Ep 5; *CT* 803:

> As to the revelation of sin, because the veil of Moses hangs before the eyes of all men as long as they hear the bare preaching of the Law, and nothing concerning Christ, and therefore do not learn from the Law to perceive their sins aright, but either become presumptuous hypocrites [who swell with the opinion of their own righteousness] as the Pharisees, or despair like Judas.

96. Scaer, "Law and Gospel in Lutheran Theology," 30.

we do not have. As Paul states: "For if I rebuild what I tore down, I prove myself to be a transgressor" (Gal 2:18).

Practically, then, this self-justification means two things. First, that if I am actively trying to establish my own righteousness then I am not trusting in God as the source of the good. This makes me a sinner, since Paul states: "everything that does not proceed from faith is sin" (Rom 14:23). Secondly, this lack of passivity and trust means to be involved in a project of self-deification.[97] If I am trying to produce my own righteousness, then logically I am trying to create myself by my own actions (*autopoesis*).[98] Since only God is the creator, this action logically means self-exaltation to the status of divinity. I am in effect trying to reverse the proper relationship between God as agent of the good and myself as its passive receiver of it. In this scenario, I produce the good and God passively receives it. In effect, I have now placed myself in the role of the creator and God as the creature.

Humanity may also have an opposite reaction to condemnation of the law. This reaction is the one that has ruled Western thought and culture since the Enlightenment. It begins as a Promethean libertinism and ends in despair, as twenty-first-century America and Europe are quickly discovering in their long hangover from Modernism. It is the impulse to reject the demand and claim that any demand stifles the actualization of the self and its freedom. Here again, because the human subject operates under the belief that God is not *pro nobis*, I must dislodge him from his lofty position and take up the mantle of divinity myself.

In this situation, the assertion of divine authority simply confirms the divine threat to my being and thereby baits on the desire to secure myself by coveting God's divinity: "Do not covet," it made him wish to covet all the more: "sin, seizing an opportunity through the commandment, produced in me all kinds of covetousness. For apart from the law, sin lies dead" (Rom 7:7–8). After Satan has told Eve that God is not on her side, he then told her that she may become as God by eating (Gen 3:5). In that all creatures are God's masks (*larva Dei*), the atomistic individual of the post-Enlightenment world sets himself or herself to work attacking God in his masks. In attempting to demythologize institution after institution (morality, Church, State, etc.), the human subject under the power of sin tries to gain freedom by silencing the law. In postmodern thought, we are told that the individual will not really be free unless even the very concept of the self is eliminated.

But through these obfuscations the power of the law and the cycle of self-justification cannot be broken. As Bayer has pointed out, the modern or postmodern individualist's stance toward the world can only result in more bondage.[99] The individualistic antinomianism of modernity and postmodernity is ironically quite legalistic. If I labor without God's promise guaranteeing my life from the beginning, my existence is not secure. I am enslaved to the need to engage in activity to create myself and secure my own life. I exist under the constant threat of failure and therefore I remain perpetually bound to the task of self-justification with no end in sight.

---

97. See Jüngel, *Justification*, 136–69.

98. See R. Hütter, "(Re–) Forming Freedom," 120.

99. Bayer, "With Luther in the Present," 1–16.

We might also add to Bayer's observation that any potential actualization of the self through one's own activity will be utterly meaningless without a Word of God to judge the quality of one's work. The rejection of God's judgment of the law merely means its reassertion in a new form. Such judgment is annihilating. If one does not work, then it is meaningless and if one does work it is meaningless. Ultimately, the condemnation of meaninglessness leads to despair under the judgment of the law. Indeed, "the wages of sin is death" (Rom 6:23). The realization of this condemnation leads to despair because there is no escape.[100]

From the perspective of the human subject, unbelief recreates God. It ultimately makes him untrustworthy because it seeks him where he has not bound himself to grace. As Luther states in the Great Galatians commentary (1531–1535) faith "is something omnipotent."[101] It is omnipotent because it determines one's relationship with God. If approached outside of his Word is unbelief, God can only be experienced as condemning. Whereas creation once served as a medium of God's gracious address, it now becomes a medium of his terrifying judgment. As Gustaf Wingren comments, human existence becomes a "continual foretaste of the Last Judgment."[102]

Hence, by believing Satan's counter-narrative, Adam and Eve have mangled the original narrative of creation. This being said, sin and bondage do not cancel the original narrative of creation. Creation remains in its essence determined by the original narrative of grace. Indeed, God continues to graciously sustain "the universe by the word of his power" (Heb 1:3). Hence, all things continue to subsist in their original goodness: "For everything created by God is good, and nothing is to be rejected *if it is received with thanksgiving*" (1 Tim 4:4, emphasis added). For this reason, the authors of the Formula of Concord were justified in their rejection of Flacius's heresy (or more accurately his overstatement).[103] Every moment of creation is a recapitulation of the original story of the seven days. Every moment of human existence is defined by God's gracious giving of the good in spite of sin (Matt 5:45).[104] Nevertheless, because of unbelief, humans do not

---

100. Gerhard Forde correctly observes that antinomianism is "fake theology" because the law cannot be escaped by merely erasing its condemning effects. Forde, "Fake Theology," 215.

101. *AE* 26:277.

102. Wingren, *Creation and Law*, 174. Also see *AE* 1:170:
"After their conscience had been convicted by the Law, Adam and Eve were terrified by the rustling of a leaf . . . We see it to be so in the case of frightened human beings. When they hear the creaking of a beam, they are afraid that the entire house may collapse; when they hear a mouse, they are afraid that Satan is there and wants to kill them." Indeed, "by nature we have become so thoroughly frightened that we fear even the things that are safe."

103. FC SD 1; *CT* 859–881; FC Ep 1; *CT* 779–85. For sources on Flacius and his misstatements regarding original sin, see the following: Arand et al., 201–11; Bente, *Historical Introductions*, 144–45; Dorner, *History of Protestant Theology*, 1:370–83; González, *History of Christian Thought*, 3:124–25; Klann, "Original Sin," 115–17; Kolb, *Bound Choice*, 118–20; Kolb, "Historical Background to the Formula of Concord," 29–33; Kordić, "Croatian Philosophers IV," 229; O. Olson, "Matthias Flacius," 87; Pelikan, *Christian Tradition*, 4:142–44; Preger, *Matthias Flacius Illyricus*, 2:310–412; O. Ritschl, *Dogmengeschichte des Protestantismus*, 2:430–54; Schaff, *Creeds of Christendom*, 1:271–74; R. Seeberg, *Text-Book of the History of Doctrines*, 2:367–69; Twesten, *Matthias Flacius Illyricus*, 20–22; Vogel, "On Original Sin," 126–31.

104. SC 2; *CT* 543:
I believe that God has made me and all creatures; that He has given me my body and soul, eyes, ears, and all my limbs, my reason, and all my senses, and still preserves them; in addition thereto,

give thanks, but rather abuse the good.[105] Indeed, that sin is sin demonstrates that the original narrative of creation has not been canceled. In other words, if God did not give the good then there would be nothing for unbelief and ingratitude to sin against.

That human nature can be in revolt against its own essence is utterly mysterious. It is absurd to reason and beyond our capacity to understand. Nevertheless, through the explicit teaching of scripture and ultimately in the cross (wherein our total nature in Christ is condemned before our very eyes) this great mystery is revealed to us. As a great mystery the power of sin can only be countered by an even deeper mystery; that of the incarnation and the death of God himself.

From this contradiction in human existence, we can come to understand what the Apostle Paul means by being "in Adam" (1 Cor 15:22). In Romans 5 and 1 Corinthians 15, the apostle describes our reality as being established by Adam's narrative. We are trapped in this narrative because of our hereditary corruption (*peccatum haereditarium, erbsüde*).[106] Despite the variations of our individual life-narratives, every moment of them echoes and is determined by the original corruption of Adam's narrative. As in the case of Adam, every moment of our existence is passively received through grace (Matt 5:45) and nevertheless we do not reflect God's glory. As a result, the *imago Dei* within us is utterly destroyed.[107] For us to be redeemed, we need an act of God's omnipotent Word to speak us forth a new narrative of creation.

---

clothing and shoes, meat and drink, house and homestead, wife and children, fields, cattle, and all my goods; that He provides me richly and daily with all that I need to support this body and life, protects me from all danger, and guards me and preserves me from all evil; and all this out of pure, fatherly, divine goodness and mercy, without any merit or worthiness in me; for all which I owe it to Him to thank, praise, serve, and obey Him. This is most certainly true.

105. See discussion in Jüngel, *Justification*, 141–44.

106. CA 2; *CT* 43–45:

Also they teach that since the fall of Adam all men begotten in the natural way are born with sin, that is, without the fear of God, without trust in God, and with concupiscence; and that this disease, or vice of origin, is truly sin, even now condemning and bringing eternal death upon those not born again through Baptism and the Holy Ghost. They condemn the Pelagians and others who deny that original depravity is sin, and who, to obscure the glory of Christ's merit and benefits, argue that man can be justified before God by his own strength and reason.

Also see SA 3:1; *CT* 477–79; FC SD 1–2; *CT* 859–915; FC Ep 1–2; *CT* 779–839.

107. *AE* 1:63:

This is My [God's] image, by which you are living, just as God lives. But if you sin, you will lose this image, and you will die.

Ap 2; *CT* 109:

And Scripture testifies to this, when it says, Gen. 1:27, that man was fashioned in the image and likeness of God. What else is this than that there were embodied in man such wisdom and righteousness as apprehended God, and in which God was reflected, i.e., to man there were given the gifts of the knowledge of God, the fear of God, confidence in God, and the like?

FC SD 1; *CT* 863:

That original sin (in human nature) is not only this entire absence of all good in spiritual, divine things, but that, instead of the lost image of God in man, it is at the same time also a deep, wicked, horrible, fathomless, inscrutable, and unspeakable corruption of the entire nature and all its powers.

Chapter 6

The Mystery of the Person of Christ, Part 2

The New Narrative of Creation

The New Narrative of Creation

ACCORDING TO THE GENESIS narrative of the Fall, God counteracts human sin through a sermon of both law and gospel. Self-justification *coram Deo* (Gen 3:10–13) must be met with condemnation and judgment. Humanity's attempt at self-justification is an obvious failure in that it only results in condemnation. Not only are Adam and Eve convicted of sin, but they also lose their dominion through their enslavement to the ground and loss of life (3:18–19). By his curse, God also extinguishes the self-giving relationship between man and woman (v. 16). He who once freely gave to humanity now becomes a condemning and demanding God. From the perspective of fallen humanity, he becomes a new kind of God in a manner alien to his original relationship to them (*opus alienum*).[1] In this regard, Werner Elert writes, quoting Luther: "For it goes against His 'nature' exactly as sin, which compels Him to wrath, 'because' he [Luther] adds, 'thus the wickedness of men compels' (*cogente ita malicia hominum*)."[2]

In spite of this condemnation, God also speaks forth a second word, that is, the Word of the gospel. This countermove is possible because the law does not exhaust God's will. Although the law is God's holy will and God cannot deny himself (2 Tim 2:13), it is only one aspect of his will. God's being and will encompass and transcend the law and therefore the law does not exhaust it. God acts within creation, as we have seen, under different masks (*larva Dei*). Some masks are of law, and others are of the gospel. Although God binds himself to act according to the law and the gospel within these masks, he may "shuffle" them as he chooses in accordance with his hidden electing

---

1. Elert, *Structure of Lutheranism*, 212. Elert writes: "Yes, because God, by means of the revelation of Christ, lets one look into His heart, Luther can say that the 'alien work' (*opus alienum*) goes 'against His nature' (*contra naturam suam*)." In modern Luther scholarship Karl Holl was the first to recognize the distinction in Luther between God's alien and proper work. See Holl, *Gesammelte Aufsätze*, 1:75–77, 3:562–67.

2. Elert, *Structure of Lutheranism*, 212.

will.[3] As Luther writes in *The Bondage of the Will*: "But God hidden in his majesty neither deplores nor takes away death, but works life, death and all in all. *For there he has not bound himself by his word, but has kept himself free over all things.*"[4] Indeed, that God is an electing and free God is shown in that his proper name is "I will be who I will be" (Exod 3:14, personal translation). God more clearly explains this to Moses when he proclaims his name before him on Sinai: "I will make all my goodness pass before you and will proclaim before you my name 'The LORD.' ['I will be who I will be'] *And I will be gracious to whom I will be gracious, and will show mercy on whom I will show mercy*" (33:19, emphasis added).[5]

Therefore, God's wrathful and gracious activities in creation cannot be reduced to the structure of the law.[6] God does not merely judge noncompliance with the law, but propagates the human species in such a way as to spread original sin to each and every person.[7] Each person, without choosing to be so, is a sinner from their conception (Ps 53:5) and object of divine wrath. Furthermore, despite the universality of original sin, the law of wrath and judgment is not applied evenly. Jacob and Moses were attacked by God for no discernible reason. The generation of Israel that was exiled to Babylon can hardly be thought to be worse than the generation that entered Canaan. In a word, although all are fallen and wicked, and therefore deserving of death and eternal condemnation, some suffer condemnation and others do not. Within scripture, this mysterious reality of election is particularly emphasized in the books of Job and Jonah.

In that human beings are bound to self-justification, they wish the law to exhaust God's will (*opinio legis*). They wish to control God with the law and thereby protect themselves from the fact that God is utterly free, unbound, and electing. They therefore invent false images of God wherein he is subordinate to the larger reality of the law. Such images of God seek to domesticate him. According to these ideas, the existence of God still allows for free will. He is not identical to the terrible power of fate, but rather the overseer of a vast system of law.[8] Within this clean and neat system, all humans are given the opportunity to pull themselves up by their moral bootstraps.

Nevertheless, this concept of God is a false idol. God hidden in his majesty is utterly free, unbound, and sovereign. Although from the perspective of fallen humans this fact is terrifying beyond comprehension, from the perspective of faith this is the greatest comfort. That God's will transcends the law also means that his choice to elect and save need not be based on the law and human obedience to it. Though in saving humanity he will have to deal with the problem of the law (in that it is his eternal will!), the law does not determine his purpose to save.

Therefore, after he has convicted humanity of sin and cursed them, God nonetheless reasserts himself as a gracious giver and enters again into his *opus proprium*. As the unbound God, God is free to oppose the relationship of condemnation under which

3. Forde, *Theology is for Proclamation*, 17.

4. *AE* 33:140 (emphasis added).

5. Forde, "Work of Christ," 2:65.

6. Paulson, *Lutheran Theology*, 66.

7. Ibid., 149–50. Also see *AE* 33:174–77.

8. *AE* 33:189.

he himself has placed humanity. Just as God had with his previous act reestablished himself as the lord of humanity by asserting the law, he now reestablishes himself as the servant of humanity by way of the *protevangelium*: "I will put enmity between you and the woman, and between your offspring and her offspring; he shall bruise your head, and you shall bruise his heel" (Gen 3:15). Here God donates himself to Adam and Eve through promise.[9] The solution to humans' attempt to become God is for God to lower himself to become human. In a word, he reasserts himself in an even more profound way as the self-donating God. Nevertheless, because he has already become one who condemns, he must oppose his own act of condemnation. In his self-donation, he must subject himself to his creatures in such a manner as to enter into their own condemnation in order to defeat it.

In doing this, God establishes a counter-narrative to the mangled narrative of the original creation. In order for creation to be redeemed, its story once mangled by sin must be spoken forth again in order to establish a new narrative of creation. As we have observed, creation receives its essence from its narrative. Like the old narrative, this new narrative is formed by the pattern of God's effective address of law and gospel. Nevertheless, whereas the old narrative succumbed to the curse of the law, the new narrative will be the story of the eternal triumph of divine grace. In order to achieve this, the eternal Word of God became flesh in order to enter into the curse of the law as a new Adam. Fulfilling and destroying that curse by his divine power, he may speak forth a new creation in the power of his resurrection. It is fitting that he undertook this role, in that it was he himself who spoke for the first creation.[10]

This counter-narrative does not mean the abandonment of God's original plan for his creation. In that neither God's being, nor his intention change (Num 23:19, Mal 3:6, Heb 13:8), the new narrative of creation is in its essence no different than the original narrative of creation.[11] Before the Fall, Adam and Eve were given the promise of life and

---

9. See Bayer, *Living By Faith*, 53. Bayer writes: "God's being is [a] gift and promise as he gives himself wholly and utterly to us."

10. For the fittingness of the incarnation as a countermove on God's part, see Chemnitz et al., *Harmony of the Four Evangelists*, 67–68. They write:

> However, John draws us especially to that consideration that through the Word all things were made and that through Him man before the fall man was made after the image of God. This he does to show that the work of redemption and justification of fallen man was so great that no created thing could have accomplished it, but that the person of the divinity through whom man had at first been created after the image of God had to come into the flesh. And He had to come into the flesh in such a way as to show that He alone through whom lost mankind had originally been created could recreate or repair it; that He alone in whom was the beginning the light and life of men could free them from darkness and death and restore them to life; that He alone who is the substantial image of God and the only-begotten Son of the Father could restore in us the image of God and cause us to be adopted into sonship with God. Furthermore, that we may be sure that the blessings of Christ, our Redeemer and Mediator about whom the Gospel preaches, have been validated for us before God and are firm against all the gates of hell; therefore in his introduction [to his Gospel] John says first that the Word, through whom all things were made and in whom were the light and life of man in the beginning, has become our Redeemer and Savior in such a way that the faith of our salvation does not lie in some created thing outside of God, for "Cursed be him who trusts in man and makes flesh his arm." (Jer 17:5)

11. We assert this in contradistinction to the position taken by Robert Jenson. See Jenson, *Systematic Theology*, 1:66. Jenson writes: "The biblical God is not eternally himself in that he persistently

freedom (Gen 1:28, 2:15–17). After the Fall, they were given the same promises through the *protevangelium*'s prophecy of the destruction of the power of Satan by the seed of the woman (3:15). Insofar as this entails the resurrection of death and the renewal of all creation (Isa 26, 66; Dan 12; 1 Cor 15; Rev 20–22), this not only means the release from sin, but also the fulfillment of the original goal and purpose of creation, that is, to enter into heavenly rest. Therefore, Jesus will also bring creation into that eternal rest prefigured by the Sabbath (Heb 2–4, Rev 20–22).[12]

---

instantiates a beginning in which he already is all he ever will be; he is eternally himself in that he unrestrictedly anticipates an end in which he will be all he ever could be." Scripture obviously teaches the opposite, that God is immutable. Jenson's concept of history as providing possibilities for God's being that he does not possess in and of himself is utterly absurd and contradicts God's reality as creator. Creation's being is derived from its own story, but God's is immutable and eternally himself. He is the speaker who speaks forth the narrative of creation. He himself incorporates the narrative of creation into himself (*enhyposthesis-anhypostheis* Christology), but he in himself is immutable and is not defined by the narrative in his eternal life. Jenson's persistent claim that traditional Christian orthodoxy's belief in divine immutability is based in Platonism and does not take into consideration many passages of scripture or the very nature of the gospel. Though the church fathers obviously used Platonism, whether they derived the idea of immutability from it and simply imposed it upon the Bible is rather questionable. Without immutability, the biblical gospel cannot be an absolute promise because God could very well change his mind about it. Lastly, Jenson does not actually escape the trap of philosophical metaphysics. Jenson's move is simply to substitute Hegelian and Heideggerian metaphysics for those of the Platonic. See critiques of Jenson's position in Hart, *Beauty of the Infinite*, 160–66; F. A. Murphy, *God Is Not a Story*. The Roman Catholic theologian Hans Urs von Balthasar rightly criticizes this sort of thinking in Moltmann and other modern Hegelians. See von Balthasar, *Theo-Drama*, 4:320–28. According to von Balthasar, God who is not immutable and transcendent is swallowed up in the power or nothingness and the world process. Since he does not present redemptive possibilities to the world that transcend the world, he is a mythological being who is subject to being destroyed by them himself. This is why all talk of divine mutability is pure nonsense and blasphemy. Luther makes a similar point in *Bondage of the Will*. If God were mutable and did not reign with absolute foreknowledge, any of his promises would be subject to revision. See *AE* 33:37–44.

12. We follow a similar line of reasoning regarding Christ's recapitulation of humanity found in Lutheran theologians such as Thomasius, *Christi*, 2:216–18; Wingren, *Gospel and Church*, 95–101. Despite his fairly disastrous teaching regarding *kenosis*, Thomasius does a relatively good job integrating substitutionary atonement with recapitulation. In the history of Christian thought, Irenaeus of Lyons originally expounded the doctrine of recapitulation. See Irenaeus, *Against the Heresies*, 3.18; *ANF* 1:448. He writes:

Therefore, as I have already said, He caused man (human nature) to cleave to and to become, one with God. For unless man had overcome the enemy of man, the enemy would not have been legitimately vanquished. And again: unless it had been God who had freely given salvation, we could never have possessed it securely. And unless man had been joined to God, he could never have become a partaker of incorruptibility. For it was incumbent upon the Mediator between God and men, by His relationship to both, to bring both to friendship and concord, and present man to God, while He revealed God to man. For, in what way could we be partaken of the adoption of sons, unless we had received from Him through the Son that fellowship which refers to Himself, unless His Word, having been made flesh, had entered into communion with us? Wherefore also He passed through every stage of life, restoring to all communion with God. Those, therefore, who assert that He appeared putatively, and was neither born in the flesh nor truly made man, are as yet under the old condemnation, holding out patronage to sin; for, by their showing, death has not been vanquished, which reigned from Adam to Moses, even over them that had not sinned after the similitude of Adam's transgression. Romans 5:14. But the law coming, which was given by Moses, and testifying of sin that it is a sinner, did truly take away his (death's) kingdom, showing that he was no king, but a robber; and it revealed him as a murderer. It laid, however, a weighty burden upon man, who had sin in himself, showing that he was

Three Contrasts

Even though it is in essence the same, the new narrative of creation differs from the old in its execution. This is true in three respects. First, the new narrative of creation must undo the effects of sin on the old creation. This means that the new narrative of creation incorporates the old creation within itself, while neutralizing its harmful effects of the Fall. This incorporation is analogous to the *enhypostasis-anhypostasis* Christology of the fifth ecumenical council, accepted both by the Lutheran confessors and scholastics.[13] In this description of the relationship between Christ's two natures, Christ's divine person (*hypostasis*) incorporates into itself (*enhypostasis*) a unit of human nature (*anhypostasis*) but not a human person. In other words, Christ's human nature subsists in the already existing person of the Son of God, who is the true subject of the incarnation. So likewise, by analogy, Christ's new narrative of creation assumes the existence of and incorporates into itself the old narrative of creation. Nevertheless, as the proper *hypostasis* of creation, it neutralizes and drains that old narrative of its independent reality. Though it continues to subsist as an actual reality, it nonetheless becomes a subplot of the overarching narrative of redemption actualized by Christ.

Christ assumes the old narrative of creation by entering into its story and identifying himself with its fallen reality. He assumes Mary's flesh (Gen 3:15, Isa 7:14, Matt 1:18, Luke 1:26–35) and accepts the imputation of human sin (Isa 53:3–8; 2 Cor 5:9; 1 Pet 2:14). As an individual Israelite, Christ assumes the particularity of that identity and therefore the burden of Israel's national sin, as it is expressive of universal human sin. Christ does not erase these realities, but incorporates them into his being and narrative.[14] He fulfills the law which condemned humanity, he does not simply abandon it (Matt 5:17). Christ does this because the law is God's word and will, to which he is faithful.[15] Hence, within the gospel, the law is contained and fulfilled (Rom 3:31, 10:4). This is why the Lutheran scholastics called Christ's act of atonement an event that "mixed" together justice and

---

liable to death. For as the law was spiritual, it merely made sin to stand out in relief, but did not destroy it. For sin had no dominion over the spirit, but over man. For it behooved Him who was to destroy sin, and redeem man under the power of death, that He should Himself be made that very same thing which he was, that is, man; who had been drawn by sin into bondage, but was held by death, so that sin should be destroyed by man, and man should go forth from death. For as by the disobedience of the one man who was originally moulded from virgin soil, the many were made sinners, Romans 5:19 and forfeited life; so was it necessary that, by the obedience of one man, who was originally born from a virgin, many should be justified and receive salvation. Thus, then, was the Word of God made man, as also Moses says: God, true are His works. Deuteronomy 32:4. But if, not having been made flesh, He did appear as if flesh, His work was not a true one. But what He did appear, that He also was: God recapitulated in Himself the ancient formation of man, that He might kill sin, deprive death of its power, and vivify man; and therefore His works are true.

13. Chemnitz, *Two Natures*, 30, 68–72. Also see Schaller, *Biblical Christology*, 49–52. See fifth ecumenical council in Grillmeier, *Christ in Christian Tradition*, 341, 387, 402–10, 419–62, 463; Meyendorff, *Christ in Eastern Christian Thought*, 38–40, 59–64; Pelikan, *Christian Tradition*, 2:29–30. For the text of the fifth ecumenical council see Denzinger, *Sources of Catholic Dogma*, 85–90.

14. See von Balthasar, *Theology of History*, 51–60.

15. See description of the Lutheran scholastic's views on this subject in Haikola, *Studien zu Luther*, 8–13. Also see H. Schmid, *Doctrinal Theology*, 232–34, 511.

mercy (*temperamentum justitiae et misericordae divinae*).[16] Because God is faithful to that which has come before, he always incorporates his previous Word and works into his new act. Likewise, Christ takes natural bread and communicates his body and blood through it. He also takes natural water and communicates his Spirit through it.[17] The old creation is encompassed by and becomes the vehicle of new creation.

In the same manner, God's temporal promises to Israel are typological of the final fulfillment in Christ of God's purposes for creation. Since Christ is "yes" to all of God's promises (2 Cor 1:21), he incorporates and fulfills these promises in himself. In fact, he is the true fulfillment to all creation and scripture, in that he "unite[s] all things in him[self], things in heaven and things on earth" (Eph 1:10). For this reason, Johann Gerhard is correct to assert that all the prophets and patriarchs were types of Christ and his redemption.[18] According to Hebrews, God's promises to Israel of temporal dominion were typological of the final heavenly resting place of the people of God (Heb 3–4). In John's gospel Jesus is described as the fulfillment of all the Old Testament realities when he is called the true Lamb of God (John 1:29), the true Temple (2:19), the true manna (6:51), and so forth. Paul agrees, stating that the realities and institutions of the old covenant were a mere shadow of Christ (Col 2:17). In this, we reject the teachings of the various millenarian groups present throughout Church history in their false belief that Christ's role is to serve Old Testament realities (i.e., a temporal kingdom of Israel, actual renewal of temple worship and sacrifice, etc.). In opposition to all this, we stand with Reformers, the majority of the later church fathers, and the New Testament, in asserting that Old Testament realities should always be viewed as shadows of Jesus and his ultimate fulfillment of all of God's promises.[19]

The fact that Old Testament realities are typologically fulfilled in Christ does not of course exclude their rectilinear fulfillment as well. God's promises to Israel of temporal dominion (Gen 12, 15, 17, etc.) are fulfilled in Christ's universal dominion in which Christians are lifted up to sit enthroned in Christ (Eph 2:4–6). Because of this, Paul in Romans asserts that Abraham was not merely promised dominion in the land of Israel, but to reign in the whole of creation (Rom 4:13). In a similar fashion, Christians are all priests of God (Isa 61:6; 1 Pet 2:4; Rev 5:10) in that they are united with Christ the great high priest (Heb 9:11–15). Through this, God has fulfilled the promises made to the Levites in Numbers 25, of an eternal priesthood.

In saying this, we posit that there is a certain kind of continuity between the law and the gospel, between the old creation and new creation. This stands in contradistinction with the way of speaking popularized by a group of theologians known as the "Radical Lutherans" who insist that there is "no continuity" between these realities.[20] In stating our disagreement with this group's manner of speaking, we must clarify that we do not

16. Elert, *Structure of Lutheranism*, 110.

17. See Scaer, "Sacraments as an Affirmation of Creation," 241–63.

18. Gerhard, *On Christ*, 30–33.

19. See the argument in Scaer, "Lutheran Viewpoints," 4–11.

20. Based on the manifesto by Forde, "Radical Lutheranism," 3–16. See Mattes, "Beyond the Impasse," 278. Mattes writes: "there is no continuity between old and new beings. This is because the new being lives from faith in Jesus Christ alone." Also see the same argument in Forde, *Justification by Faith*.

reject the reality that they are attempting to explicate, but merely with the terminology whereby they are attempting to explicate it. When the Radical Lutherans state that there is "no continuity," they mean that there is no neutral, middle ground between the self under the power of sin and unbelief, and new person of faith.[21] Similarly, they mean to say that our life under sin is not an inadequate or preparatory stage to be completed by the life of faith. With this, we can hardly disagree. Faith in the gospel means a total reorientation of the self and its relationship to God. The life of faith means one's redemptive incorporation into the new narrative of creation that is utterly counter to the old one of sin, death, and law.

Similarly, for this reason, the old creation and the law do not possess an "actualizing self-potential before God" as in, for example, the Thomistic tradition.[22] The flesh of Mary possesses no imminent potentiality to become the human nature of the Son of God. Similarly bread, wine, and water do not contain a potentiality to function as sacraments. Neither does the law have the potentiality to become the gospel. All these things are dependent on God's act of new creation, into which they are incorporated. Nevertheless, the new creation does not eliminate these things. Rather it is the proper *hypostasis* that the *anhypostasis* of old creation comes to subsist in.

In a word, this the problem with the Radical Lutherans' use of the language of "no continuity." It gives the impression that the entity of the old creation is somehow negated by the new. But if redemption means total annihilation and recreation, what is left to be redeemed in the new creation? Indeed, if the old creation is merely negated and replaced by the new, then there is in fact no object of redemption. Again, we cannot disagree that the old creation does not escape a total divine judgment. That judge neutralizes the power of sin and law, thereby making the old creation passive and prepared for God's act of new creation. Nevertheless, the Bible constantly speaks of the old creation being the object of divine redemption (John 3:16). The language of "no continuity" suggests that nothing is actually redeemed, merely replaced. Replacement rather than redemption presupposes a different God than the one manifest in the gospel. The God of the gospel is absolutely faithful to his Word and works, and this includes the old creation. Of course, Radicals Lutherans do not hold that God is faithless or that he negates his own creation. Nevertheless, in spite of their good intentions, their unfortunate choice of language tends to give this false impression.[23]

In that the new narrative of creation presupposes the old, Christ as the second Adam does not merely reestablish himself in the original position of humanity, but rather must overcome the power of the fallen creation (Rom 5; 1 Cor 15).[24] In order

21. See comments in Paulson, *Luther for Armchair Theologians*, 20–21.

22. Mattes, "Beyond the Impasse," 288. See description of Thomistic tradition in Maritain, *Integral Humanism*, 291–308.

23. Luther himself comments in *The Disputation Concerning Man* (1536): "Therefore, man in this life is the simple material of God for the form of the future life. . . just as the whole creation which is now subject to vanity [Rom 8:20] is for God the material for its future glorious form" (*AE* 34:140). Also see Thielicke, "The new man is not a creation out of nothing. This is a miracle of change. He is made out of the existing material of the old man" (*Evangelical Faith*, 1:202).

24. See Gerhard, *On Christ*, 142. Gerhard sides with Aquinas (against Scotus): "For that reason, because Scripture everywhere indicates the sin of the first man as the reason for the Incarnation, it is

to do this he had to be both divine and human. In that the Fall of the original creation hinged on the destruction of the relationship between the creator God and his created image, in his person Christ must reconcile the two parties by uniting them.

As true God (*vere Deus*) Christ alone can speak forth a new creation.[25] Likewise, as God, he alone can forgive sin committed against his person and make infinite atonement.[26] Simultaneously, Christ as true man (*vere homo*), can represent other human

---

more fitting to say that it was as a remedy for sin." He goes on writing:

> Contrast Adam as the source of sin and death to Christ as the source of righteousness and life (Rom 5:12, 1 Cor 15:45, 47) . . . Represent this very thing with types, parables, and comparisons. If there had not been a flood, the ark would not have been built (Genesis 6). If the fiery serpents had not struck the Israelites because of their sin, the bronze serpent would not have been lifted up (Numbers 21). If the storm had not developed at sea, Jonah would not have been hurled off the ship (Jonah 1). If the servants of the king had not been rejected, the son would not have been sent (Matthew 21). If the sheep and the coin had not been lost, the lamp would not have been lit to look for the coin nor would the shepherd have gone off to look for the wandering sheep. (*On Christ*, 142)

25. "As *God* Christ is at work in begetting and creating in others the life which they themselves do not possess. Adam did not have the power to create even in his God-appointed state of purity" (Wingren, *Gospel and Church*, 97). We read similarly: "Since the dominion of death and the destruction of human life arose in man's disobedience and yielding to temptation, Christ brings His creative power to bear at the critical point when He forgives sins. His divinity was to be seen in his earthly life in His forgiving of men their sins" (96).

26. FC SD 3; *CT* 935:

> For even though Christ had been conceived and born without sin by the Holy Ghost, and had fulfilled all righteousness in His human nature alone, and yet had not been true and eternal God, this obedience and suffering of His human nature could not be imputed to us for righteousness. As also, if the Son of God had not become man, the divine nature alone could not be our righteousness. Therefore we believe, teach, and confess that the entire obedience of the entire person of Christ, which He has rendered the Father for us even to His most ignominious death upon the cross, is imputed to us for righteousness. For the human nature alone, without the divine, could neither by obedience nor suffering render satisfaction to eternal almighty God for the sins of all the world; however, the divinity alone, without the humanity, could not mediate between God and us. But, since it is the obedience as above mentioned [not only of one nature, but] of the entire person, it is a complete satisfaction and expiation for the human race, by which the eternal, immutable righteousness of God, revealed in the Law, has been satisfied, and is thus our righteousness, which avails before God and is revealed in the Gospel, and upon which faith relies before God, which God imputes to faith.

Also see *AE* 26:33:

> In addition, it follows that our sins are so great, so infinite and invincible, that the whole world could not make satisfaction for even one of them. Certainly the greatness of the ransom—namely, the blood of the Son of God—makes it sufficiently clear that we can neither make satisfaction for our sin nor prevail over it. . . . But we should note here the infinite greatness of the price paid for it. Then it will be evident that its power is so great that it could not be removed by any means except that the Son of God be given for it. Anyone who considers this carefully will understand the one word "sin" includes the eternal wrath of God and the entire kingdom of Satan, and that sin is no trifle.

See Chemnitz as well: That the divine nature "does not turn away from the suffering but permits the human nature to suffer and die, yet strengthens and sustains it so that it can endure the immeasurable burden of the sins of the world and the total wrath of God, thus making those sufferings precious before God and saving the world" (*Two Natures*, 216). Later we read that the human nature would not have represented a sufficient payment for the sins of the world because "there would not have been an adequate ransom . . . for sin and God's wrath, which are boundless evils. For this reason, therefore, the price is so great and the merit of the suffering and death of Christ [so great] that it is the propitiation for the sins of the whole world" (148). "The creature by itself could not have borne the enormous burden of the wrath

beings by fulfilling the role of the original Adam. He thereby recapitulates humanity by fulfilling and transcending Adam's role in the original creation. Having described the nature of his person in this manner, it is important to clarify that we do not wish to divide up the work of redemption between the two natures. In that they are divine and creative acts, Christ's recapitulation of humanity is a work of his divine person. Nevertheless, this redemptive act clearly occurs in, under, and with Christ's humanity.

As we observed in the first chapter, this redemption occurs in a preliminary sense in the history of Israel. Israel was given the same promises as Adam and Eve and was elected to fulfill the same role in creation. Nevertheless, Israel's history stands in a precarious position between the new narrative of creation spoken forth in the *protevangelium* and the old narrative of creation. Israel is placed under the law and gospel. As Israel continuously fails to fulfill its role as prophets, priests, and kings, God elects substitutes for them. Because Israel cannot fulfill the role of prophet (Exod 19), Moses is elected. Because they cannot fulfill their role as a priestly nation (Exod 32) the Levites are elected. Because Eli and his sons (and later Samuel and his sons, see 1 Sam 8:2–3) could not lead Israel, first Saul and then David are elected to be kings. Because all these mediators fail, Israel must go into exile. This exile itself was merely a recapitulation of Adam and Eve's own exile. Just as they were driven east out of the garden (Gen 3), so Israel is driven east out of the garden land (Gen 11). In the end, Israel as a new representative of humanity fails as their protological counterparts did before them. Being "in Adam" their wills remain bound and they must play out his script.

Nevertheless, within Israel's history the new narrative of God's self-donating grace also appears. God promises Israel that he will bless all nations through them (Gen 15, 17, 22). In order to fulfill this promise, God's self-donating grace must manifest itself in greater and greater degrees as Israel's sin increases. Indeed, as Paul writes: "where sin increased, grace abounded all the more" (Rom 5:20). From the beginning, God had promised a final and universal deliverer (Gen 3:15). When blessing Israel, God promised his own self to them. He did this both by his self-maledictory oath (Gen 15), as well as his repeated acts of swearing by himself (Gen 22, Isa 45). Therefore, the giving of God's grace to Israel also meant the literal giving of God's own being to Israel. Specifically, this manifested itself in the presence of God through his Name, his Word, his *kavod*, and as the Angel of the Lord.[27] This presence with Israel would be fulfilled by the incarnation.[28]

This self-donating presence dwelt with Israel throughout the Old Testament and revealed God's faithfulness to Israel in ever-greater degrees as Israel failed. It is only after the incident with the golden calf that the *kavod* comes to dwell with Israel in the tabernacle. His goal in dwelling in the tabernacle is to give Israel a share in his holiness

---

of God which was owed for the sins of the entire world" (ibid.).

Lastly, see Wingren: "The power of His divinity to destroy the dominion of the law is effective even in his humiliation, for His humiliation is obedience that puts an end to the law and to wrath" (*Gospel and Church*, 96–97).

27. See similar argument in Jenson, "Bible and the Trinity," 329–39.

28. See Jenson, *Systematic Theology*, 1:141. Jenson correctly remarked that Christ is already present as the "narrative pattern in the history of Israel."

through the medium of the sacraments of the old covenant.[29] He must do so because Israel is sinful and is in need of his holiness. God gives sacramental signs that prefigure the final fulfillment of the law and the gospel in his own sacrifice on the cross (Matt 17:1–9; Mark 9:2–8; Luke 9:28–36; John 1:14; 2 Cor 4:6).

Likewise, God's hypostatized presence with Israel also exemplifies and fulfills the roles of its earthly mediators. As we observed earlier, the role of the mediators presupposes sin and the need to create a substitute to overcome the curse of the law. Hence, in a preliminary sense God's presence serves as Israel's substitute. As the one present in the Levitical cult and mediating his holiness to Israel, he takes on the role of priest. This reality was reflected in the high priest's garments, which designated him as both the divine warrior and the second Adam. Furthermore, the earthly high priest not only served as an image and representative of God's glorious presence in the cult, but was a counterpart to the Angel of YHWH, who is described as functioning as a heavenly high priest (Ps 110, Zech 3:1–10, Dan 10:4). Beyond functioning as the great high priest, the presence of God with Israel fulfilled the role of prophet and king as well. As the Angel of YHWH, he speaks prophetically to Abraham throughout Genesis. We are also told that this same figure is the one who addressed Moses in the burning bush and in the tabernacle. Likewise, the Angel of YHWH also functions in the role of a heavenly king by participating in Israel's conquest of the land and later protects it from foreign invaders (Exod 31, 33; Josh 5; 2 Kgs 19; Dan 10).

Ultimately, the ever-increasing manifestation of God's solidarity with Israel found its apocalyptic fulfillment. The harshest preachers of judgment and exile (Jeremiah, Ezekiel, Isaiah) also contain the greatest promises of restoration. In Ezekiel, as YHWH sentences Israel to be overthrown by the dark power of exile, he himself agrees to go into exile with them: "I have been a sanctuary for them in the countries where they have gone" (Ezek 11:16). Indeed, for this reason the promise of the later prophets is of God's own personal return to Zion. In the apocalyptic tradition God promised that he would finally overthrow all opposition to his rule (Dan 2, 7) and would finally restore his people to life, even giving them a share in his glory (Dan 12).[30] He himself would also finally return and dwell with his people forever (Isa 40, Ezek 40–48).

Throughout the Old Testament, this same pattern of redemptive solidarity can also be observed with regard to God's presence in his Name. As we have previously seen, the divine Name is identical with God's hypostatized presence. The tabernacle/temple is a "house for my name" (2 Sam 7:13). God gives Israel his Name in Exodus 3 at the same time of the revelation of their redemption. By giving his Name to Israel, he unilaterally binds his reality to their fate. His Name is exalted through the exodus and redemption of Israel (Exod 9:16). Likewise, his Name is cursed among the nations when Israel sins (Ezek 36:20). Ultimately, YHWH will redeem Israel not for their sake, but for the sake of his Name (v. 22). There will be a final moment of universal reconciliation where all the nations recognize his Name and will give true worship (Isa 45:23).

---

29. See discussion in Baier, *Compendium Theologiae Positivae*, 2:421–33.

30. Eichrodt observes: "The Daniel passage is unique in laying stress on the share in the divine light-glory, an image which is in any case entirely in keeping with the conception of God's new world as a revelation of the divine *kavod* [glory]" (*Theology of the Old Testament*, 2:515).

This coincides with the promise to Abraham (Gen 12:2). Since God has in fact tied himself to Israel, the exaltation of his name through the unity and true worship of all the nations must logically be connected to Israel's own exaltation. Before the election of Abraham, the one who receives the blessing of the coming "seed" (which eventually came down to Abraham) was Shem (9:26–27). Shem's name literally means "Name."[31] Abraham is an inheritor of God's promise to Shem to bring about the reconciliation of the Gentiles (suggested by 9:26–27), and is told that his name will be "great" (12:2). All the nations will be blessed and reconciled in him (22:18). This promise directly parallel's God's statement in Isaiah 45 that the exaltation of his Name would coincide with the reconciliation of the nations. Elsewhere, David (as the representative Israelite) is told that his name will be made great: "I will make for you a great name, like the name of the great ones of the earth" (2 Sam 7:9). This will come about because God will establish the eternal throne of the Messiah. David states in his prayer in response to the oracle: "this is the instruction of all mankind" (7:19). He goes on to prophecy that by fulfilling his promise, God's Name will also be exalted among the nations (7:26).

In other words, by way of the exaltation of David's seed and name (which embody the destiny of Israel) God's own Name will be exalted, thereby fulfilling his promises to Adam, Eve, and Abraham about the coming "seed." In this, the exaltation of Israel and of YHWH's Name merges into a single reality, that is, a single person. In the christological hymn of Philippians 2, Paul insists that this single person is Jesus. It is Jesus, the Davidic Messiah (Rom 1:3) and the seed of Abraham (Gal 3:16), who by his exaltation has gained "the name that is above every name" (Phil 2:9). In this, the prophecy of YHWH's exaltation in Isaiah 45 has been fulfilled and superimposed on Isaiah 53's description of the Servant's suffering and exaltation. The author of the Epistle to the Hebrews likewise states that Jesus: "After making purification for sins, he sat down at the right hand of the Majesty on high, having become as much superior to angels *as the name he has inherited is more excellent than theirs*" (Heb 1:3–4, emphasis added).

As we can observe, this merger of Israel and YHWH into a single person occurs because of the need for redemption from the curse of the law. In Jesus, YHWH gave himself over to Israel as promise in such a totalizing fashion that he became an individual Israelite. He himself must now stand under the curse of exile with Israel and undergo the attacks of sin, law, death, and the devil. This totalizing act of self-donation coincides with a totalizing event of judgment. It is, therefore, not surprising that the prophets (culminating in John the Baptist) announce the coming of the great and terrible Day of the Lord. Such a day will be a time of both redemption and destructive wrath (see particularly Mal 3:2; Isa 61:2, 63; Matt 3; Mark 1; Luke 3). God's ultimate self-giving, therefore, means standing in total solidarity with those upon whom this eschatological judgment falls as a substitute for sin. As we observed at the beginning of chapter 3, the work is the person and the person is the work. Christ's person is constituted by the dynamic event of God's ultimate self-donation and his total judgment of sin.

The second aspect of the new narrative of creation is that it must be characterized as an apocalyptic war against the devil.[32] This follows from what we have observed in

31. Hahn, *Kinship by Covenant*, 98.

32. Gerhard writes:

describing the first aspect of the new narrative of creation. As a result of God's Word being distorted by the devil, the original narrative of creation had been damaged and humankind fell into sin. Therefore, a reestablishment of the right relationship between God and humans must also mean the destruction of the power of the devil. For this reason, Gustaf Wingren is most correct when he states: "The Bible's theme is the conflict of God and the devil."[33] Indeed, the story of the Bible is in fact summarized in the *protevangelium*. The New Testament is clear about this: "The reason the Son of God appeared was to destroy the devil's work" (1 John 3:8). Furthermore, this theme is present throughout the Bible even when Satan is not mentioned by name. Indeed, there are many false mediators, just as there are many "so-called gods in heaven or on earth" (1 Cor 8:5). Similarly, there are "many antichrists" (1 John 1:18). A multitude of false mediators present themselves throughout the history of Israel in the form of false prophets and pagan gods. All these are manifestations of Satan, insofar as all forms of false mediation are rooted in his power. At the climax of Israel's history, Jesus enters creation and finds himself opposed by Satan. In parallel to Christ's fulfillment of the history of true mediation, Satan as the supreme false mediator sums up the history of false mediation in himself. Hence, it is impossible to describe the work of Jesus in the New Testament without reference to his defeat of the devil.[34]

Christ defeats the devil by his atonement and forgiveness of sins. There is a great deal of biblical support for the view that Satan's power is derived from human sin. Without sin, he would be unable to rule over humanity. He is often pictured as an accuser in the heavenly court (Job 1:6–8, 2:1–7; Zech 3:1–10; Rev 12:10). In fact, the word "Satan" can mean "adversary" or even "accuser" in the original Hebrew.[35] For this reason, he is not only the enemy of God, but an instrument and manifestation of God's wrath against sin. By fulfilling the law and neutralizing the wrath of God, Christ therefore also defeats Satan.

The defeat of the devil means defeat of all the demonic forces of the old creation; that is, sin, law, death, and hell. We call these "demonic," because they not only ultimately have their origin in Satan, but like him they assume a position within creation after the Fall of determining the meaning and value of human existence contrary to God's original intention.[36] By Christ overcoming the law and wrath, and by giving eternal life, he returns freedom to temporal life by taking away the power of the demonic to determine it.

The principal fruit of the Incarnation is *the healing of our nature*. . . No other medicine [than the Incarnation] could heal the lethal wounds of our soul. Our first parents were seduced through the serpent (Gen. 3:2). He was not just a *natural serpent*, but in him hid the *serpent of hell* who injected the lethal poison of sin in them. The expulsion of the this poison and the healing of our corrupt nature did not require a common nature but the sort to be prepared for us from the divine and human natures of Christ. Through his extreme malice the devil had infected the nature of man; therefore God wished to show us His immense goodness in healing us. The devil had expended all his craft in seducing man; therefore God applied His greatest wisdom prepared a medicine for our fall. (*On Christ*, 145)

33. Wingren, *Living Word*, 42.

34. Against the position of Friedrich Schleiermacher and the Liberal Protestant tradition in general. See Schleiermacher, *Christian Faith*, 161–70.

35. J. Russell, *Devil*, 189.

36. See Tillich, *Systematic Theology*, 3:102–6. Tillich correctly observes that the demonic encompasses all finite things that seek to claim for themselves the status of the divine and therefore enslave

Christ's defeat of Satan is intimately tied to his recapitulation of Adam and Israel. The New Testament repeatedly draws parallels between Jesus's success against Satan with Adam/Israel's failure and sin. In the Synoptic Gospels, Jesus overcomes the devil's temptation in the desert and thereby triumphs where Israel failed.[37] Whereas Israel had food in the wilderness and yet fell into sin, Jesus surpasses Israel by remaining sinless while eating and drinking nothing (Luke 4:2). Whereas Adam fell in a green and lush garden, Jesus overcame the devil in a harsh wasteland. Christ's conflict with Satan culminates in the cross where he works the forgiveness of sins and thereby ends the dominion of the devil. In this, the cross becomes a new tree of the knowledge of good and evil, as well as a new tree of life. As the former, Christ overcomes the temptation to abandon his vocation on the tree of the cross, where Adam did not. As the later, the cross becomes a means of eternal life. Just as the sacramental fruits attached to the tree of life preserved eternal life (Gen 3:22), so too the body of Christ attached to the tree of the cross becomes food that gives a share in eternal life (John 6:51).[38]

Our discussion of the defeat of Satan leads us to the last aspect of the new narrative of creation, that is, the fulfillment of God's promise of heavenly rest. As we noted earlier, in the original creation the Sabbath was typological of God's eternal rest which humanity would eventually enter into. Before the Fall, humans enjoyed this rest in a preliminary fashion. Living the *vita passiva* of perfect faith, the inner person possessed a foretaste of heavenly rest. By contrast, the external person worked within creation and patiently awaited the coming of eternal rest. After the Fall, humans were not only cut off from entry into the heavenly rest, but were placed in a relationship of demand and self-justification before God, thereby removing the foretaste of heavenly peace. Similarly, Adam and Eve were instructed that they must now toil because of the curse of sin (Gen 3:17–19). It is prophesied that Cain, after killing his brother Abel, would not rest but would remain a restless wanderer on the earth (4:12). Ultimately, all these curses were expressions of nomological existence, in which no one can find rest from their works.

Within the history of Israel, God gave preliminary signs of the entrance into heavenly rest that Christ would establish. God gave the land of Palestine as a type of the heavenly country (Heb 3–4) and promised that he would give his people rest from their enemies.[39] He provided this rest in different ways through the work of prophets, priests, and kings. He promised forgiveness through the prophets (Isa 40; Jer 31, 33; Ezek 36–37). He worked forgiveness through the Levitical cult and also gave types of the coming translation of humanity into a heavenly existence. The ritual of the Day of Atonement presented the high priest entering into a type of heaven and/or Eden. This was not only a sign of the reversal of sin, but was also a type of Christ's ascension and fulfillment of the true destiny of humanity (Heb 4, 9–10).[40] Lastly, God gave rest from Israel's enemies

---

human life. Nevertheless, this does not exclude or consign to mythology (as Tillich would) the existence of real supernatural demonic forces.

37. See Farrar, *Triple Victory*.

38. Krauth, *Conservative Reformation and Its Theology*, 585–89.

39. See examples in Exod 33:14; Deut 12:9–10, 25:19; Josh 1:13, 15, 11:23, 14:15, 21:44, 22:4, 23:1; 2 Sam 7:11–12; 1 Kgs 5:41, 8:56; 1 Chr 22:9.

40. See exegetical argument in Chilton, *Paradise Restored*, 34, 44.

through kings and other military leaders, in particular David (2 Sam 7:11–12). Solomon is also a type of Christ in this regard. Not only are we told that he enjoyed rest from all of Israel's enemies (1 Kgs 5:41, 8:56), but that he established the temple as a type of God's heavenly presence and rest (7–8).

These earthly mediators were only able to engage in their activities because God enabled them through his hypostatized presence. The prophets were given revelation through the *kavod*/Angel of YHWH (Gen 18, 22; Exod 3, 33; Ezek 1–2). The priests were given access to the holiness of YHWH donated to Israel through the cult. Kings and other military leaders were given the ability to drive foreigners from the land because of the agency of the Angel of YHWH (Exod 31, 33; Josh 5). In the New Testament, the activity of the heavenly and the earthly mediators became one in Jesus Christ.[41]

In his earthly ministry Jesus became the rest of the people of God. He is in his person the eschatological temple and the new creation. This is the case because he himself is the returning glory of God prophesied by the Old Testament. In Daniel, God promised to universalize the temple, his presence, and rest within the whole of creation (Dan 2:35). In John's gospel, Jesus claims to be the eschatological temple (John 2:12) and is described as the returning glory (1:14). He takes up the function of the temple by glorifying God through his works and by offering up true sacrifice (1:29). Revelation sees the final fulfillment of all this in the new heavens and new earth: "Behold, the dwelling place of *God is with man. He will dwell with them*" (Rev 21:2–3, emphasis added) and again "I saw no temple in the city, for its temple is the Lord God the Almighty *and the Lamb*" (21:22, emphasis added).

The Synoptic Gospels also view Jesus as the returning *kavod* of Isaiah 40 (Matt 3, Mark 1, Luke 3). In Matthew, Jesus is greater than the temple (Matt 12:6) because he is not only the final sacrifice, but the personal presence of YHWH that will give eternal rest (11:29–30). He is greater than Solomon (12:42) because he will defeat Israel's true enemy, Satan (12:22–29). Finally, Jesus is greater than Jonah and all the prophets (12:39–41), because he alone knows the Father fully:

> At that time Jesus declared, "I thank you, Father, Lord of heaven and earth, that you have hidden these things from the wise and understanding and revealed them to little children; yes, Father, for such was your gracious will. All things have been handed over to me by my Father, and no one knows the Son except the Father, and no one knows the Father except the Son and anyone to whom the Son chooses to reveal him. (Gen 11:25–27)

Because of this, he can show the Father's true heart and thereby give the eternal rest of justification. As he also declares in the same passage: "Take my yoke upon you, and learn from me, for I am gentle and lowly in heart, and *you will find rest for your souls*. For my yoke is easy, and my burden is light" (11:29–30, emphasis added).

The rest that Christ brings is the free word of the gospel. Free from the compulsion of self-justification, the people of God receive in Christ complete rest from the works of the law: "for whoever has entered God's rest *has also rested from his works* as God did from his" (Heb 4:10, emphasis added). They become "fellow heirs with Christ" and will

41. Scaer, *What Do You Think of Jesus?*, 96.

indeed "be glorified with him" (Rom 8:17). They will even "become partakers of the divine nature" (2 Pet 1:4).[42]

Out of gratitude for this freedom, the Church praises God and the Lamb in the heavenly temple, as the book of Revelation describes (Rev 5–6). With a new creation, therefore, comes a new liturgy of creation. We are told that the Lamb and his army of martyrs stand on Mount Zion (implicitly as the new temple) and sing "a new song" (14:3). Heavenly rest gives rise to eternal heavenly praise. The temporal liturgy of the Church is integrated into the eternal praise of the heavenly hosts.

---

42. *AE* 26:247. Luther writes of the person of faith in the Galatians commentary of 1531–1535: "The one who has faith is a completely divine man, a son of God, the inheritor of the universe."

In discussing what the goal or end of the incarnation is, Gerhard writes:

> However, because God wished out of His immense mercy to turn our disgrace and misery away from us, to join us to Himself again, and to restore to our possession the goodness that was lost, He used this manner and means: that He personally united His Son with our nature that we might in turn be joined to God through Him who touches us by kinship and nearness of the human nature. (*On Christ*, 144)

Gerhard then goes on to cite Irenaeus:

> Because of His immense love, the Son of God became what we are, to perfect us to be what He is.
> He became a partaker of our nature to make us sharers in the divine nature. (ibid.)

Hence Gerhard views the true goal of the incarnation as being what the patristic theologians referred to as *theosis*.

Chapter 7

The Mystery of the Person of Christ, Part 3

The Name of Jesus, the Virgin Birth, and the Gender of Christ

The Name "Jesus Christ"

As sacred scripture testifies, the name of "Jesus" was given to Messiah by a revelation from God to his mother and father (Matt 1:21, Luke 1:33). In addition, he was revealed to be God's Christ by his resurrection from the dead (Rom 1:3). Because the name "Jesus Christ" is therefore divinely sanctioned, it is necessary to explain, insofar as it is the task of dogmatic theology to give expression to the articles of the faith as they are presented in the Word of God. As we shall see, the name of Jesus reveals his office and person as the anointed God-man tasked with redeeming the whole creation.

In the historical accounts of the birth of Jesus that we possess from the New Testament, both of Jesus's human parents are given specific instructions to name him "Jesus" (Matt 1:21, Luke 1:33).[1] The name Jesus itself means "God is our salvation."[2] In Matthew's gospel, this is connected to his mission by the angel's statement to Joseph that "you shall call his name Jesus, *for he will save his people from their sins*" (Matt 1:21, emphasis added). Matthew cites one of the messianic texts of Isaiah, which promises redemption through the child born of a virgin (Isa 7:14), whose name is "God with us."[3] "God with us" as we have examined in our discussion of the *kavod*/Angel of YHWH in the Old Testament is highly suggestive of God's own saving presence. His saving presence goes ahead of Israel into the land as the Angel of YHWH and conquers (Exod 31, 33; Josh 5). This makes sense in the context of the Gospels, because Jesus's proclamation is primarily of God's kingdom and his own work in establishing it. Much as it was the Angel of the Lord's presence (the preincarnate Christ) who established Israel in their temporal kingdom, so Jesus will lead a new exodus and establish the Church in a heavenly kingdom (Heb 3–4). He can do this because he is "God with us" and "God our salvation." The fact that "Jesus" is simply the Greek form of the Hebrew "Joshua" also draws these connections to

---

1. For a defense of the historicity of the infancy narratives see Paul Maier, *In the Fullness of Time*, 3–96.

2. Meier, *Marginal Jew*, 207; Chemnitz et al., *Harmony of the Four Evangelists*, 179–81.

3. Gerhard, *On Christ*, 6.

conquest and exodus.[4] As Johann Gerhard observes, Joshua is a type of Christ, who was the earthly agent of the conquest of the land of Palestine, much like the Angel of YHWH was the heavenly agent. He thereby prefigures Christ's victory and the Church's exodus into the eternal kingdom of heaven.[5]

The name "Christ" is a Greek translation of the Hebrew word "Messiah," meaning "anointed one."[6] As Gerhard notes, the kings and priests of the Old Testament prefigured the "anointings" that Christ received. In that the Messiah was to be a fulfillment of all the mediators of the Old Testament, he alone is most truly the anointed one that the others pointed ahead to. Hence, in Old Testament prophecy he is often referred to not as king or priest, but simply as the "anointed one" (Ps 2:2, Isa 53:1, Dan 9:25). Christ himself was not anointed with physical oil, but with the "oil of gladness" (taken from Psalm 45:7 and applied directly to Jesus in Heb 1:9), that is, according to Gerhard, the Holy Spirit (that he possesses without measure, John 3:34) and also the fullness of divine glory that Christ possesses according to his human nature (Matt 28:18; Col 2:3, v. 9).[7]

This explanation of Christ's anointing is not a typological-prophetic excess on Gerhard's part—something he was occasionally prone to do. Rather in the biblical texts themselves there is much to support this reading. First, as we observed in earlier chapters, the Old Testament priests and kings received an anointing with oil in order to imitate the divine *kavod* and his presence with Israel. This also accounts for the high priest's golden garb. As we also saw, all these figures represented a unity between God and Israel/humanity. They therefore also prefigure the communication of divine glory to humanity in Christ. As the divine person of the Son, Christ possesses this divine self-communication in its fullness. Being anointed twice, Christ demonstrates his superiority to the kings and priests, who were only anointed once. Also, a dual anointing is suggestive of his dual occupancy of the office of king and priest, which Christ obviously possesses as well (Ps 110, Heb, etc.). It should of course be noted that Christ's anointing as priest and king does not negate Christ's office as prophet as his use of Isaiah 61 in Luke 4:14–21 demonstrates. Christ's prophetic office is contained in these other two anointings in that it was the role of priests to teach the people, and kings like David prophesied.

Secondly, these two anointings are directly revealed in the Gospel record of Christ in two separate and important coronation scenes. First, at his baptism, Jesus is visibly anointed with the Holy Spirit in the form of a dove. The words "you are my son" bears much similarity to Psalm 2, which is a hymn of royal coronation both prefiguring and prophesying the anointing of the Messiah. This anointing with the Holy Spirit was dramatically shown at Christ's baptism in his public descent in the form of a dove. Although Jesus publically received the Spirit at his baptism, this was by no means the beginning of his possession of it. As the Gospels suggest, Christ's baptism is merely his public coronation. It does not bestow upon him what he did not previously have any more than a prince receives what he did not previously have by right of birth at his coronation. As

4. Gerhard, *On Christ*, 9; Chemnitz et al., *Harmony of the Four Evangelists*, 180; Meier, *Marginal Jew*, 206–7.

5. Gerhard, *On Christ*, 7.

6. Ibid., 13.

7. Ibid., 14.

the Second Person of the Trinity, Christ is also a source of the Holy Spirit's procession (Gal 4:6). According to his humanity, Christ possessed the Holy Spirit from the moment of his conception, which occurred by power of the Spirit (Matt 1:18, Luke 1:35). Hence it is proper to describe Christ as being anointed with the Spirit from the moment of the incarnation, because the Spirit is the agent and mediator of the incarnation. He unites Christ's divinity to his humanity, thereby breathing divine life and enlightenment into Christ's humanity (Isa 11:2, 61:1; Luke 4:16–21).

The second revelation of Christ's anointing occurs at the transfiguration (Matt 17:1–9, Mark 9:2–8, Luke 9:28–36). It is important to observe that in this scene God repeats the sonship language of the coronation psalm. In the same event, Jesus manifests in his flesh the glory that is properly his as the Son of God. He is, after all, accompanied by the two figures (Elijah and Moses) who had theophanies on mountains in the Old Testament. Moses saw the divine *kavod*, Elijah heard the divine Word. As we have previously observed, both God's Word and glory are viewed as being hypostatized by the Old Testament authors and identified with Jesus by the New Testament authors. As Simon Gathercole notes, there is no suggestion in the Gospel narratives of the transfiguration that Jesus's glory is something borrowed.[8] It is fully communicated to his flesh. The admonition "listen to him" identifies the word of Jesus with the Word of God that Elijah heard. The transfiguration is therefore the full revelation of God's glory in the flesh of Christ and that his human word is in fact God's own Word.

In that he is anointed with the "oil of gladness," he is an embodiment of the gospel itself. The gospel is the unilateral self-donation of God. It is the good news that God in Christ has totally and completely surrendered himself to sinful humanity. He holds nothing of himself back, but gives himself fully to humanity in an act of total self-communication. In this, he is also the image of redeemed humanity. Adam and Eve were made to receive God's own eternal rest (Heb 3–4). Humanity is made to the end of receiving God's own glory (Rom 8:30) and to become partakers in the divine nature (1 Pet 1:4).

For these reasons, the name "Jesus Christ" used throughout the New Testament properly summarizes the person and work of the Messiah. He is "Jesus," that is, God come in the flesh to be our savior. He is "Christ" the "anointed one" who because of the unity of his person is anointed with the Holy Spirit and the fullness of divine glory, in order that he might fulfill the offices of all the anointed ones of the Old Testament as the true prophet, priest, and king.

Born of a Woman: The Virgin Birth and the Gender of Christ

The Evangelical Lutheran Church has always affirmed the creedal statement concerning Jesus Christ: "who for us men, and for our salvation, came down from heaven, and was incarnate by the Holy Ghost of the Virgin Mary, and was made man [*Homo Factus Est*]."[9] The alternative Liberal Protestant view, that Jesus was born in a natural manner

---

8. Gathercole, *Pre- Existent Son*, 49.

9. *CT* 30–31. Also see CA 3; *CT* 45. We read:

   Also they teach that the Word, that is, the Son of God, did assume the human nature in the womb

and that the Gospel accounts are merely fictional, is sub-Christian and not worthy of consideration as a possibility.[10]

The biblical *sedes* for this teaching are clear, notably Isaiah 7:14, Matthew 1:18–23, and Luke 1:34–36. Matthew draws special attention to the prophecy of Isaiah 7:14. Although it is frequently argued that this verse only refers to a "young woman," several scholars have demonstrated that the word does mean "virgin" as the authors of the LXX had translated it from the original Hebrew.[11] In fact, that the pre-Christian Jewish translators of the LXX favored this rendering strongly suggests that it is a correct representation of the Hebrew.[12] Even the Jewish scholar Cyrus Gordon has argued that the Hebrew word ("*almah*") does in fact mean virgin.[13]

This interpretation of the word "*almah*" recommends itself on several counts. First, although the word is used infrequently in the Old Testament, every woman to whom it is applied is in fact a virgin.[14] In Song of Song 6:8 the term specifically distinguishes women who are neither queens nor concubines of the great king, but will someday be elevated to that status. If these women engaged in sexual intercourse with the king, then they would at the very least be accorded the status of concubines.[15] Proverbs 30:19 is one controversial verse where the term is used. Here the author speaks of the "way of a man with an *almah*." Though it has often been asserted that this refers to sexual intercourse, in the larger context (which discusses "four wonderful and incomprehensible things") this reading does not make sense. Michael Rydelnik rightly suggests that this refers to the attraction exerted over men by virgin maidens, rather than the sex act.[16] After all, considered by itself, the latter is a matter of simple mechanics and hardly a "wonderful and incomprehensible thing."

Beyond the linguistic arguments, the context of Isaiah 7:14 is highly suggestive of the traditional Christian reading of *almah*. Ahaz is told by Isaiah that "the Lord himself will give you a sign" through the birth of "Immanuel." If an ordinary birth is referred to here and not a virgin birth, it is difficult to see how this would function as a sign. In other words, if Isaiah merely refers here to a "young woman," then this would not be a miraculous sign, since as a rule young women give birth all the time.

---

of the blessed Virgin Mary, so that there are two natures, the divine and the human, inseparably enjoined in one Person, one Christ, true God and true man.

Also see SA 1:4; CT 461; LC 2; CT 683; SC 2; CT 545; FC SD 8; CT 1017; FC Ep 8; CT 821.

10. See Spong, *Born of a Woman*. Spong makes the absurd claim that the Gospel accounts of Jesus's birth are "Midrash" by which he means they are metaphorical legends. This is not even a correct use of the term Midrash, which in actuality is a Jewish interpretative/literary form that expands on existing biblical stories and does not aim at inventing new ones from scratch. See critique of Spong in N. T. Wright, *Who Was Jesus?*, 65–93.

11. See Gibbs, *Matthew 1–11*, 99–104; Hengstenberg, *Christology of the Old Testament*, 2:44–50; Leupold, *Isaiah*, 1:155–57; Niessen, "Virginity of the 'Almah," 133–50; E. Young, "Immanuel Prophecy," 97–124.

12. Hindson, *Isaiah's Immanuel*, 67–68.

13. C. Gordon, "*Almah* in Isaiah 7:14," 106. It is frequently claimed that *betulah* is the technical term for virgin. But this cannot be uniformly true because Joel 1:8 refers to a *betulah* weeping for her husband.

14. Rydelnik, *Messianic Hope*, 152–54.

15. Ibid., 154.

16. Ibid.

Going beyond these typical and obvious *sedes*, David Scaer notes that in at least one of the textual variants of the Gospel of John (1:13, which we will briefly discuss below), there is also a suggestion of virgin birth.[17] Also, as we have previously noted, the New Testament teaching of virgin birth represents the fulfillment of Genesis 3:15, where we are told of the coming of the "seed of the woman." Within Ancient Near Eastern culture, the women do not have "seed" and therefore such a phrase is highly suggestive of virgin birth.[18]

Although it has been popular among theologically liberal circles to do so, it is incorrect to argue that the doctrine of the virgin birth is unique to Matthew and Luke. According to this theory, because John and Paul do not directly mention Jesus's virgin birth they did not believe in it. Conversely, according to this theory, Matthew and Luke thought Jesus was a mere human and therefore needed to explain how Jesus could be God's Son. Therefore they invented the virgin birth (independently!) as an explanation.[19] John and Paul believed in the preexistence of Christ and therefore did not need a virgin birth to explain Christ's filial relation with God.[20]

This theory is problematic for several reasons. First, as we have shown in chapter 2, the overwhelming evidence is that Matthew and Luke did believe that Jesus was God. In fact, Matthew directly says this when quoting Isaiah's prophecy that Christ would be "God with us" (Matt 1:23). As we also noted, this reading is supported by the *inclusio* of divine presence within the Gospel.[21] That the virgin birth is directly connected to Christ's divinity in Matthew was recognized by the early Jewish Christian heresy of the Ebionites. Although they used Matthew's gospel, they removed the section that spoke of the virgin birth because they understood it to directly teach his divinity.[22] Similarly, as Arthur Just notes, Luke describes Mary as the new location of the *kavod* in terms reminiscent of the LXX version of Exodus 40.[23] Hence, the virgin birth is not part of an alternative ascending Christology, but rather is part and parcel of a high, divine, descending Christology.

Moving onto the teachings of St. John and St. Paul, we have already mentioned the textual variant in John 1:13. This variant describes the birth that does not come through the "will of man" as being that of Christ's and not the believer's. We of course do not know if this textual variant preserves the original reading, but it is at least highly suggestive. Regarding the Pauline witness, it should be observed (with Scaer again) that in Galatians 4:4 Paul says merely that Jesus was "born of a woman" and not a "woman and a man."[24] Within this context there was no reason not to say that Christ was sim-

---

17. Scaer, *Christology*, 39.

18. Ibid., 35. Luther also makes the same observation in *AE* 15:318–21.

19. Dunn, *Christology in the Making*, 51; Pannenberg, *Jesus*, 141–58.

20. For the popular position that John and Synoptics have conflicting Christologies see the following: R. Brown, *New Testament Christology*; Fredrikson, *From Jesus to Christ*; Theissen, *Religion of the Earliest Churches*.

21. Scaer, *Discourses in Matthew*, 172.

22. Scaer, *Christology*, 37. Also see Theissen and Merz, *Historical Jesus*, 53.

23. Just, *Luke*, 1:69.

24. Scaer, *Christology*, 34.

ply "made man" or just "born." Paul appears to rather deliberately go out of his way to emphasize that Christ was "born of a woman" alone. Indeed, in the Judaism of the period inheritance came through the father (contrary to later practice) and it would have been fitting for Paul to mention Christ's human father at this point as the basis of his messianic identity as the son of David.[25] Furthermore, in using the phrase "born of a woman" Scaer also suggests that we might be hearing an echo of the *protevangelium* and its implicit reference to virgin birth.[26]

In any case, even if one does not find these textual arguments convincing, it would be odd for John and Paul not to possess a belief in the virgin birth for a number of other reasons. Not only did they share a common incarnational theology with Matthew and Luke (who taught the virgin birth), but the virgin birth stands in perfect coherence with their other teachings. First, throughout the Pauline epistles and John's writings, Jesus is described as God's Son alone. He is never really referred to as Joseph's son or spoken of as having a human father. Moreover, if Jesus had two fathers, his references to "my Father" throughout the Johnanine witness would become strangely ambiguous; to which father would Jesus be referring? Therefore, claiming that Jesus had both a biological and divine father lacks coherence with both witnesses' claims about who Jesus is. Ultimately, if we accept the claim that Paul and John did not hold to the doctrine of virgin birth, we would have to posit that both shared a rather strange theology wherein the Son of God had somehow intervened at an opportune moment of human copulation. Since there is no trace of any theology like this in their respective witnesses or in later patristic theology, this seems highly unlikely.[27] Lastly, this position stands in total contradiction to the monergistic theologies of grace taught by both. After all, the new spiritual birth that Christ brings occurs "not of blood nor of the will of the flesh nor of the will of man, but of God" (John 1:13). If this is how believers gain spiritual birth, then it would be an odd inconsistency if the Son of God was born from "the will of man." This can also be said regarding Paul's teaching as well.

But if John and Paul did believe in the virgin birth, why did they not directly mention it? There are very likely several reasons. First, many of the writings of the New Testament (particularly Paul's) are occasional and do not deal with every article of the faith. Since it appears that the Synoptic Gospels were widely circulated at an early date (as David Scaer, Martin Hengel, and Richard Bauckham have convincingly argued) it is likely that they would have assumed their audiences were already familiar with the doctrine via other writings or simple contact with the apostolic *kerygma* by way of oral teaching.[28] Hence there would have been no reason to directly mention it.

---

25. Ibid., 34–35.

26. Ibid., 35.

27. See summary of early Christologies in Norris, *Christological Controversy*.

28. Scaer, *Discourses in Matthew*, 29–32, 85–150. Also see Bauckham, *Jesus and the Eyewitnesses*, 290–319; Bauckham, "For Whom Were the Gospels Written?," 9–48; Hengel, *Four Gospels*, 96–116. Of course, these authors do not agree how early. But the point still stands that in a written form the *kerygma* existed alongside Pauline and Johannine teachings and that the New Testament writings were interpreted in light of one another.

Secondly, as N. T. Wright has noted, that although the virgin birth is an important doctrine, it is not at the very heart of the New Testament gospel. Good Friday, Easter, and Pentecost are in fact more central to the New Testament's saving message than is Christmas.[29] Consequently, the preaching of Paul and John emphasize Jesus's saving acts on the cross and the empty tomb, while not emphasizing the nativity.

Wright further notes that when we turn to Matthew and Luke, the doctrine is only taught in a few verses.[30] Hence even in the Gospels that directly teach the doctrine, there would appear to be a conscious attempt to downplay it.[31] The reason for this seems to be quite clear. After all, as we have observed in chapter 2, it is the purpose of Luke to portray Jesus as an incarnation of YHWH's hypostasized *kavod*, the Servant of Deutro-Isaiah, and the new David. Luke is very likely writing what (according to Arthur Just) is a catechism for Gentiles.[32] An overemphasis on such a doctrine might make his formerly pagan audience (with their lingering memories of heroes as physical offspring of the gods) begin to think of Jesus as a pagan demi-god.

Matthew might very well have faced similar challenges with his Jewish audience. In the first-century context, there is significant evidence that certain Jews of this period (notably those who read Enochic literature, including the sect at Qumran) misread the story of the "sons of God" copulating with the "daughters of men" in Genesis 6 and thereby constructed a fantastic notion that sexual intercourse between fallen angels and human women had led to the insemination of a race of giants.[33] Matthew probably did not wish to emphasize the virgin birth because this might create associations within the minds of some of his Jewish contemporaries between Jesus and supernatural human-angel hybrids.[34]

On an apologetic note, in light of these concerns it is therefore hard to see why Matthew or Luke would have invented the doctrine of virgin birth. In fact, if it were not for their inspiration by the Holy Spirit, their immediate impulse might have very well been to suppress the event as embarrassing. After all, there is no suggestion from the Second Temple Jewish texts we possess that there was a widespread belief that the Messiah would be born of a virgin.[35] Consequently, a virgin birth would not ultimately make much of a difference in arguing that Jesus was the Messiah and in fact might very well be detrimental to that claim if their audience (in the aforementioned ways) got the wrong idea.

Neither, in light of the aforementioned concerns, does the idea that the virgin birth was invented to cover up Jesus's illegitimacy seem plausible. This claim has a long history,

---

29. N. T. Wright, "Born of a Virgin?," 171.

30. Ibid.

31. Ibid., 175–78.

32. Just, *Luke*, 1:4–20.

33. For example, see 1 Enoch 6–11. Jubilees (very likely written in the second century BC) also seems to assume that angels are capable of sexual reproduction. See Jubilees 15:26–27.

34. Theissen, *Religion of the Earliest Churches*, 175. Theissen finds the virgin birth odd in light of Matthew's Jewish orientation.

35. A survey of rabbinic, Qumranic, and psedepigraphic literature will yield nothing in this regard. See Vermes, *Jesus the Jew*, 129–59, 192–222.

in that the early rabbis and the ancient anti-Christian philosopher Celsus promoted it.[36] Both the former and the latter claimed that Jesus is the illegitimate son of a Roman solider named Panthera (or sometimes transcribed as Pantera), which is possibly a corruption of *parthenos*, the Greek word for "virgin."[37] The linguistic similarity between the two words makes the claim sound extremely suspicious, even apart from the perspective of Christian faith.

Another idea popular among some Liberal Protestants is that Jesus was the product of a rape and that the virgin birth was a means of covering up this crime.[38] Doubtless if either this scenario or the one discussed above was the case, the generation of the myth of the virgin birth would help little and rather be viewed by persons with even an ounce of incredulity as representing an absurd form of special pleading. In fact, if the goal of the Gospel writers were a cover-up, would not legitimacy and a normal birth simply be an easier lie to tell? Why go to the trouble of inventing a supernatural birth that might sound all the more implausible? This fact, combined with the obvious lack of emphasis by the Gospel writers on the reality of the virgin birth (something they might have been more sanguine in promoting if the intention was a cover-up!) leads us to conclude that neither scenario is even remotely a plausible option.

Beyond the scriptural data, which clearly teaches the virginity of Mary at the time of Jesus's conception, there is the issue of the extrabiblical tradition of her perpetual virginity (*semper virgo*).[39] As it is well known, the perpetual virginity of Mary was taught widely in the early Church, some claim as early as St. Ireneaus in the late second century.[40] Luther, Zwingli, Calvin, and the later Lutheran scholastics also supported the doctrine.[41] Protestant Reformers and scholastics mainly drew their arguments in favor of Mary's perpetual virginity from St. Jerome's work, *Against Helvidius*. This teaching continues to be upheld by the Roman Catholic Church to this day.[42]

In light of the New Testament witness, the doctrine faces several challenges. First, in the Gospels Jesus clearly possesses brothers and sisters (Matt 12:46, 13:55–56; Mark 3:31–34; Luke 8:19–21; John 2:12). Other objections have been raised on the basis of verses such as: "but [Joseph] *knew her not until* she had given birth to a son" (Matt 1:25,

---

36. Tabor, *Jesus Dynasty*, 59–73. Tabor believes that it is a reason to take the idea seriously. Origen, *Contra Celsus*, 1.28, 32, 38; *ANF* 4:408, 410, 412–13.

37. Origen, *Contra Celsus*, 1.28, 32, 38; *ANF* 4:408, 410, 412–13.

38. See Schaberg, *Illegitimacy of Jesus*, 29–61.

39. See the following recent articles on the topic from within American Lutheran circles: C. Hogg, "Ever-Virgin Mary," 36–39; Scaer, "Semper Virgo: Pushing the Envelope," 24–28. Also by the same author: "Semper Virgo: A Doctrine," 15–19. Scaer has a negative assessment of the doctrine on similar historical and theological grounds that we shall present below. Hogg positively argues for the doctrine, particularly on extra-scriptural grounds and on the need for catholicity. Unsurprisingly, Hogg has since abandoned confessional Lutheranism and is now an Eastern Orthodox priest.

40. See Irenaeus, *Against the Heresies*, 3.21; *ANF* 1:454. This text is often cited, though it appears to be somewhat ambiguous.

41. *AE* 22:23, 22:214–15, 24:107, 43:40, 45:199, 206, 212–13; Zwingli, "Friendly Exegesis," 2:217, 275; Calvin, *Harmony of Matthew*, 1:107, 1:83, 2:215; Chemnitz et al., *Harmony of the Four Evangelists*, 150–52; F. Pieper, *Christian Dogmatics*, 2:307–9.

42. *Catechism of the Catholic Church*, 126–27.

emphasis added). Verses like this seem to suggest that Joseph did have sexual intercourse with Mary after Christ was born.

To these objections, Jerome responded with a number of arguments. Regarding the issue of brothers and sisters, he argued that within their biblical idiom the words "brothers" and "sisters" could also mean cousins or even countrymen.[43] Others have argued that these brothers and sisters were merely children from a previous marriage of Joseph. In that Joseph does not appear in later stories concerning Jesus's ministry (unlike Mary), it is possible that there was a considerable age difference between him and his wife. If this is so, then Joseph could have had an earlier marriage that produced "brothers" and "sisters" for Jesus. Regarding the "not until" of Matthew 1:25, Jerome claimed that this was merely a temporal statement, similar to "before he repented, he was cut off by death."[44] Of course, the person in question never did repent and consequently saying "before" does not mean that they eventually repented.

In evaluating Jerome's argument, it should be taken into consideration that his main goal here was not simply to vindicate a fondly held tradition of the early Church. Helvidius had claimed that virginity was no better than matrimony and children in the eyes of God.[45] To prove this, he stated that if Mary as one "blessed among women" had occupied both the estates of virginity and matrimony, both must be equally good. To counter this claim and validate his understanding of the superiority of virginity, Jerome did his best to vindicate the tradition.

Although Luther and the majority of the Lutheran tradition prior to the Enlightenment held to the doctrine of the perpetual virginity, Lutheran theology must be wary of accepting this idea for several reasons.[46] The first difficulty is the lack of scriptural support. Although we do not have the space here to engage in a thorough examination of every passage that Jerome cites, for the sake of argument let us posit that all of his exegesis is essentially correct. Even if we grant this, his arguments do not positively vindicate the tradition on the basis of scripture. Jerome's argumentation style is rather ad hoc. What he suggests is that the word usage of scripture provides sufficient ambiguity, thereby leaving room for the tradition. If one accepts that this ambiguity exists and therefore the possibility that the texts can be read in such a way as to not exclude perpetual virginity, the exegete can take the next step by reading the text in light of the extrabiblical tradition. Nevertheless, as is apparent, if one was not motivated by the imperative of the extrabiblical tradition and was simply left to make a decision for or against the doctrine on the basis of scripture alone, it is difficult to see how the conclusion would be reached that Mary always remained a virgin. In essence, the difficulty is that the exegetical method employed here allows a nonbiblical tradition to not merely shed light on a passage in scripture, but rather to determine that content of scripture. This is not acceptable in light of the Reformation principle of *scriptura sui interpres*.

---

43. Jerome, *Against Helvidius*, 16; *NPNFb* 6:341.

44. Jerome, *Against Helvidius*, 4; *NPNFb* 6:335.

45. Jerome, *Against Helvidius*, 22–24; *NPNFb* 6:344–46.

46. We must say "wary." We in no way mean to suggest that those who accept said doctrine are heretics.

The second difficulty with Jerome's position is that it is motivated by a belief that virginity is more meritorious in God's eyes than marriage. Jesus certainly does praise virginity for those who can accept it (Matt 19:3–12). Paul also considers virginity to be a higher estate than marriage (1 Cor 7:8–9, 27, 32–35, 38), but nevertheless insists that this does not negate the goodness of other vocations (1 Cor 7:7). The bottom line is that the apostle considers the state to be better for practical reasons and does not hold that one estate is more meritorious than another (1 Cor 7). Finally, it is important to recognize that God only commands unmarried persons not to engage in sexual intercourse. By contrast, he positively commands those who are married to do so (Gen 1:28). Since God placed Mary in a married vocation, it would have been in violation of God's original commandment if she had permanently rejected any possibility of ever having sexual intercourse with her husband.

This brings us to one of the most puzzling aspects of the doctrine of perpetual virginity. Namely, if Mary decided to remain a virgin perpetually, where did she get the idea? There is no indication in scripture that she was commanded by God to do so. The idea that she did so of her own accord without a Word from God suggests a sort of enthusiasm on her part. This would have been rather inconsistent with her faithful hearkening to the Word of God spoken to her by the angel (Luke 1). One might also pose the question of what purpose the maintenance of virginity within marriage might serve. It is easy to see what both Jerome and the Latin tradition in general's argument in this regard might be; if virginity means a greater degree of self-denial, it can function as an act of supererogation.[47] In contrast to this, Evangelical Lutheran dogmatics posits on the basis of scripture that no vocation can be considered meritorious (Luke 17:7; 1 Cor 7). All are justified by faith and all serve an equally important function in the one body of Christ (Rom 12; 1 Cor 12).

This brings us to the two most important points regarding the virgin birth from the perspective of Lutheran dogmatics. First, Christ's virgin birth means that he represents a new creation and a break with the dispensation of death (1 Cor 15) brought by Adam. This break is what forms the basis of Paul's discussion of original sin and the new creation inaugurated by Christ in Romans 5. Just as the first Adam was created by an act of fiat, so too is the second Adam.[48] Of course, whereas Adam was taken out of the ground, the new Adam is taken from the flesh of Mary and thereby incorporates within himself the fallen human narrative of sin and death in order to redeem it. Nevertheless, the virgin birth represents a new beginning. Secondly, in regards to the inner unity and coherence of the faith, the virgin birth stands as an important corollary of the *sola gratia*. As we noted above, John makes pains to state that the Christian's new spiritual birth occurs "not of blood nor of the will of the flesh nor of the will of man, but of God" (John

47. See for example, Tertullian, *Exhortation to Chastity*.

48. See Anslem, "Virgin Conception and Original Sin," 165–211. This is essentially Anselm's argument. Nevertheless, it is developed in a somewhat more incoherent and unbiblical manner. Anselm claims that it was to guard against original sin. Following the medieval tradition in general and Anselm in particular, Luther agrees with this reasoning. See *WA* 12:403. Though of course God could very well have made certain that Christ had not contracted original sin without the mechanism of virgin birth. Also, part of the assumption appears to be that the male is the sole generator of human life, which is biologically false and is not taught by scripture.

1:13). If indeed salvation comes by grace, then it is not fitting that the Messiah's birth would come about by anything other than an act of grace rather than by human effort.[49]

It is important to observe that ecumenical disagreements as to the status and nature of Mary reveal quite important differences regarding the doctrine of grace. Most notably (as both Herman Sasse and Karl Barth have observed), the Roman Catholic understanding of Mary mirrors their compatibalistic concept of grace.[50] According to the Catholic Catechism, the Virgin Mary was herself conceived without sin (described as being "born redeemed") and was filled with supernatural grace, both created and uncreated.[51] This makes her capable of participating in the work of redemption through her cooperation with divine grace.

The description of Mary being "full of grace" originates from the translation of Luke 1:28 in the Vulgate which reads, "*et ingressus angelus ad eam dixit ave gratia plena Dominus tecum benedicta tu in mulieribus.*" The words "*gratia plena*" ("full of grace") is the translation of the Greek "*kecharitōmenē*," which does not mean "full of grace" but "highly favored" (compare with usage in Eph 1:6). In light of the fact that medieval and modern Roman Catholics understand "grace" to denote a supernaturally infused predicate inhering in the human subject capable of making it pleasing to God,[52] it is easy to see how theologians of that tradition came to view Mary as they did. Put succinctly, the Greek text locates grace as divine favor external to the person (*extra nos*), whereas the Latin makes it a quality internal to Mary. If one's relationship with God is based on the degree to which one has become pleasing to God through the power of grace, then Mary as one "full of grace" must be maximally so.

The difference between the account of the annunciation in the original Greek New Testament and the Vulgate (and how this translation was appropriated) illuminates the difference between Roman Catholic and Evangelical Lutheran understanding of grace. From the Roman Catholic perspective grace is given so that we might correspond to God's expectations and thereby gain salvation. Although "justification" (translated in the Vulgate Romans 3:28 as "*iustificari*," [i.e., to "make righteous," rather than to "judge righteous," "forgive," or "vindicate" as "*dikaiousthai*" (justification in the original) means in New Testament and LXX Greek][53]) cannot properly speaking be merited, salvation

---

49. Elert makes this point in his *Christian Faith*, 208. Also see Scaer, *Christology*, 35.

50. Sasse, "Liturgy and Confession," 299–316. Also see *CD* 1.2.143–46.

51. *Catechism of the Catholic Church*, 123–24:
   To become the mother of the Savior, Mary "was enriched by God with gifts appropriate to such a role." The angel Gabriel at the moment of the annunciation salutes her as "full of grace." In fact, in order for Mary to be able to give the free assent of her faith to the announcement of her vocation, it was necessary that she be wholly borne by God's grace. Through the centuries the Church has become ever more aware that Mary, "full of grace" through God, was redeemed from the moment of her conception . . . The "splendor of an entirely unique holiness" by which Mary is "enriched from the first instant of her conception" comes wholly from Christ: she is "redeemed, in a more exalted fashion, by reason of the merits of her Son." The Father blessed Mary more than any other created person "in Christ with every spiritual blessing in the heavenly places" and chose her "in Christ before the foundation of the world, to be holy and blameless before him in love."

52. *Catechism of the Catholic Church*, 483–86.

53. McGrath, *Iustia Dei*, 12–16. Also see Preuss, *Justification of the Sinner*, 30. As Preuss points out, the term is used thirty-eight times in the New Testament and every usage is forensic.

itself can and must be.[54] Catholics use the term "justification" to mean moral regeneration that occurs in baptism through the reception of created and uncreated grace, not exclusively to denote the imputation of righteousness for the sake of Christ. Nevertheless, salvation is not conceived in crass Pelagian terms (as many Protestants have charged), but in terms of a compatibalism between divine grace and human choice. If humans had no power to contribute to their salvation by cooperating with grace, then nature would be defective and God would lack his glory as creator. If they did not need grace, the work of Christ and the supernatural power of God would be unnecessary, and again, God would lack his glory as redeemer.

The merit of those who are redeemed is in a sense a participation in the merit of Christ, since Christ is casually responsible for their meritorious behavior.[55] Grace then is viewed as being inherently participatory insofar as its aim is to activate human agency. One of the major problems faced by this model of grace is the historicity of salvation. In other words, if salvation has already occurred and is complete as a previous historical event, one is powerless to contribute anything to said event. Rather, as a saving event in the past, it can only be recognized and trusted in passively. Hence, participation with regard to grace utterly breaks down.

For Roman Catholic theology, the two main solutions to this problem are the sacrifice of the Mass and the Marian doctrines. All creedally orthodox Christians acknowledge that salvation has occurred because of the incarnation, death, and resurrection of Christ. According to Catholic dogma, in the Mass, the believer not only receives grace, but also participates in Christ's death and self-offering to the Father irrespective of time and space.[56] One is effectively taken back in time to the crucifixion so that one might have the opportunity to be offered up with Christ.[57] Through this the tension between the participatory nature of grace and the historical distance of the crucifixion is solved.

Similarly, the Marian doctrines resolve the tension between participatory nature of grace and fiat nature of the historical event of the incarnation. The Roman Catholic claim is in effect that although individual believers cannot participate in the actual event of the incarnation, one person did, namely Mary. Mary is for this reason the "Queen of Heaven" and the "highest of all creatures."[58] Like the believer who participates in their own redemption through the reception of grace (created and uncreated), so too Mary, being "full of grace," was born "redeemed" from original and actual sin. For this reason,

54. *Catechism of the Catholic Church*, 481–83.

55. Ibid., 487: "The Charity of Christ is the source of all merits."

56. Ibid., 343–45.

57. Although the idea of the identification between sacrifice of the Mass and that of the cross has long been firmly present in Roman Catholicism, the idea of how this is the case, that is, through the cessation of time and space, was invented in the twentieth century by the German monk Odo Casel. He took the idea from his study of Greek mystery cults. He assumed like the *religionsgeschichtliche schule* that influenced him, that Christianity was a syncretistic religion that had drawn on the pagan and Gnostic currents of its Hellenistic environment. The advantage of the Christian Mass over the mystery cults was that the Christian Mass actually worked as a vehicle of self-transcendence into the divine mystery, whereas the pagan version did not. See Casel, *Mystery of Christian Worship*. See critiques of Casel and the liturgical movement in general in Oliver Olson, "Contemporary Trends in Liturgy," 110–57; O. Olson, "Liturgy as Action," 108–13.

58. See discussion in *Catechism of the Catholic Church*, 252–53.

she was able to actively participate in the work of redemption. Indeed, because of this she is the unique mediatrix of grace and worthy of *hyperdulia*, that is, veneration that is not quite true worship ("*latria*," that is true worship, is reserved for God alone).[59] She is, then, the model of the graced human subject participating in redemption.

Of course the difficulty with all this is the total lack of attestation from the New Testament or even early Christian tradition, a point particularly emphasized in Karl Barth's own discussion.[60] As we noted, the actual Greek text of the first chapter of Luke utterly contradicts the traditional Roman Catholic reading of it. In fact, what appears to be the case is that the genesis of Marian doctrines occurred partially because the text was badly translated and therefore misunderstood. It is therefore highly unusual that the present Catholic Catechism continues to cite the words "full of grace" as a biblical basis, despite the fact that modern Roman Catholic scholars and theologians acknowledge the original Greek text. One suspects that they might invoke the theory of the development of doctrine.[61] But even if the Evangelical Lutheran Church accepted the legitimacy of the idea that the articles of the faith can be developed beyond their annunciation in the biblical authority, it is difficult to see how the Greek text of Luke has any relationship to the later Roman Catholic Marian doctrines. Put another way, development presupposes a trajectory that is already present in the evolving subject. Since the original text teaches that Mary is an ordinary woman highly favored by God, and not a supernaturally superior human (the opposite of the former), it is hard to see how the former teaching could logically imply the latter.

Beyond the brute facts of scripture and extra-scriptural doctrinal history, Mariolatry violates the scriptural and Reformation principle of *sola gratia*. Roman Catholics would doubtless protest that Mary could only serve as the mediatrix of salvation because of divine grace. Nevertheless, this response presupposes the Roman Catholic definition of grace as a supernaturally infused quality, rather than as divine favor. Ultimately, Roman Catholic Marian teaching presupposes that there must in effect be something on our side (i.e., Mary, a human perfected by divine grace) before God can act in our favor (i.e., bring about the incarnation). For the biblical authority and the Reformers, the opposite is the case. God unilaterally acts on behalf of sinners because of his loving kindness, and not because he finds something attractive already present on our side.

That the Reformation understanding of grace holds in the case of Mary is demonstrated not only by the narrative of the annunciation, but by other passages in scripture as well. First, Mary declares in the Magnificent, "my spirit rejoices in God my Savior" (Luke 1:47). If Mary did indeed rejoice in God as her savior, then she needed a savior. But if she was not subject to original and actual sin, then this statement would be false. Furthermore, scripture teaches that all persons are fallen and subject to original sin. Paul (among others) asserts several times that "all have sinned" (Rom 3:23). If that is so, then logically the predicate "all" (which Paul and the other New Testament writers qualify in relationship to Christ alone) would also apply to Mary. Lastly, Mary died and as scripture clearly teaches "the wages of sin is death" (Rom 6:23). If she died, then she must

59. Lumen Gentium, 66, in *Sixteen Documents*, 175–76.

60. *CD* 1.2.143–46.

61. Newman, *Development of Christian Doctrine*. Also see Congar, *Meaning of Tradition*.

have been subject to sin (a point made by Gregory of Rumini against Duns Scotus).[62] The Roman Catholic Church acknowledges this fact and claims that Mary was assumed into heaven after her death with little explanation as to why she died.[63]

Official Roman teaching is cognizant of the first objection and has stated (echoing the reasoning of fourteenth-century theologian Duns Scotus[64]) that preservation from original and actual sin constitutes being "redeemed in a more exalted fashion" by the merits of Christ than the rest of the human race.[65] Nevertheless, this is not cogent reasoning in light of the fact that they are positing that Mary as a concrete subject never actually in need of a savior, since she would in reality never have been subject to original sin. The entire position seems to hinge largely on the acceptance of a Realist ontology and not from anything implied by the truths found in scripture itself. From this perspective of Realism, (which Subtle Doctor would have accepted a version of, and which continues to implicitly predominate in Catholic thinking through the influence of Thomism), Mary participates in and represents the universal of human nature that is subject to original sin, even if she as an individual is not.[66] Hence her birth without original or actual sin is an act of redemption from the degraded state of the universal of humanity. Again, such reasoning clearly lacks a basis in scripture, and is rather rooted in later metaphysical assumptions.

The second problem with the Marian doctrines from the Evangelical Lutheran perspective is that it promotes enthusiasm. In Catholic teaching, Mary gained her preservation from sin and therefore her redemption apart from the Word through the Immaculate Conception.[67] In the same way, the Pope (and the Roman magisterium in general) insists that he possess holiness and teaching authority on the basis of the Spirit by virtue of a divine office.[68] By contrast, in Luke's account Mary trusts in the angel's Word that tells her that God is favorable to her (Luke 1:38). In connection with his rejection of enthusiasm, Luther held that Mary had conceived through the hearing of the Word in faith (*conception per aurem*).[69] The text itself clearly vindicates this view: "And Mary said, 'Behold, I am the servant of the Lord; *let it be to me according to your word*.' And the angel departed from her" (Luke 1:38, emphasis added). Similarly, the Evangelical Lutheran claims that the Church is always sinful and therefore must trust in an alien righteousness (*iustitia aliena*) external to it. It always needs God as "savior." Therefore

---

62. Oberman, *Harvest of Medieval Theology*, 290.

63. *Catechism of the Catholic Church*, 252.

64. Oberman, *Harvest of Medieval Theology*, 289.

65. *Catechism of the Catholic Church*, 124.

66. See ibid., 123–24. The discussion in the section of the Catechism of the Roman Church does not state this reason explicitly, but it is very strongly implied by the talk of Mary's "redemption" and her relationship to Eve and the rest of the human race. Also, see Medieval discussions on the question of universals in Copleston, *Medieval Philosophy*, 136–56.

67. *Catechism of the Catholic Church*, 123–25.

68. See Luther's critique in SA 3:8; *CT* 495–96.

69. *WA* 23:185. The Lutheran scholastics did as well. See Chemnitz et al., *Harmony of the Four Evangelists*, 120.

the true Church hearkens to the Word of God and lives the *vita passiva* through the external Word and the means of grace alone.

If this is the case, then Evangelical Lutheran dogmatics should both register its approval and also disapproval of the tradition going back to Irenaeus that Eve is to be interpreted as the antitype of Mary.[70] The idea can be theologically dangerous if one understands it in a synergistic fashion. Talk of Mary as "Coredemptrix" in popular (though not yet official) Catholicism, suggests that humanity in Mary plays its part, God in Christ plays his part, and together salvation is wrought. This is of course not acceptable in light of *sola gratia* and *sola Dei gloria*.

More appropriately, Lutheran theology can accept that there is a parallel between Eve and the Church, of which Mary is part. As we observed earlier, the Gospel of John sees Jesus as a second Adam, giving birth to the new Eve (the Church) out of his side through blood and water, that is, the sacraments (John 19:33–35; 1 John 5:6–8). Indeed, Paul also teaches that the relationship between man and woman in the old creation finds its fulfillment in Christ and the Church (Eph 5:33). This is why Paul not only states that the Church is the bride of Christ, but also the body of Christ (Rom 12:5; 1 Cor 12:12–27; Eph 3:6, 5:23; Col 1:18, v. 24). In other words, the Church receives and possesses everything it has from the substance of Christ himself. Just as Christ surrendered his body on the cross and through the means of grace (particularly the Lord's Supper) to create the Church, so Adam surrendered his body in a deathlike state to create Eve (Gen 2:22). Christ as the true man, who received the fullness of divine glory, was thereby capable of surrendering all to the other. Adam received the whole creation (1:28) and therefore was capable of surrendering himself by giving his body to create Eve. For this reason, Eve and the Church are dependent then on an act of unilateral self-donation by one who possesses all.

This typology is one of the reasons why modern Feminist theologians' insistence on the mere "humanity" of Christ at the expense of his masculinity, must be rejected.[71] It is of course not wrong to emphasize that as a human being Jesus can represent and reconstitute the humanity of both men and women. It is ontologically inaccurate to divide men and women in such a way as to make them into alien species. Human nature is human nature, whether it is male or female. On the other hand, there is no generic humanity and men and women possess different roles.[72] Christ is not an amorphous pretemporal human being.

---

70. Irenaeus, *Against the Heresies*, 3.22; *ANF* 1:455. See *Catechism of the Catholic Church*, 125.

71. See E. Johnson, *Consider Jesus*, 97–110. For examples of Feminist theology see the following authors: M. Daly, *Amazon Grace*; M. Daly, *Beyond God the Father*; M. Daly, *The Church and the Second Sex*; M. Daly, *Gyn/Ecology*; M. Daly, *Pure Lust*; M. Daly, *Outercourse*; M. Daly, *Quintessence*; E. Johnson, *Church Women Want*; E. Johnson, *Consider Jesus*; E. Johnson, *Friends of God and Prophets*; E. Johnson, *Quest for the Living God*; E. Johnson, *She Who Is*; E. Johnson, *Truly Our Sister*; E. Johnson, *Women, Earth, and Creator Spirit*; E. Johnson, *Who Do You Say that I Am?*; McFague, *Body of God*; McFague, *Life Abundant*; McFague, *Metaphorical Theology*; McFague, *Models of God*; McFague, *New Climate for Theology*; McFague, *Speaking in Parables*; McFague, *Super, Natural Christians*; Ruether, *America, Amerikkka*; Ruether, *Church Against Itself*; Ruether, *Gaia and God*; Ruether, *Integrating Ecofeminism*; Ruether, *Sexism and God-Talk*; Ruether, *Goddesses and the Divine Feminine*; Ruether, *Wrath of Jonah*.

72. Von Balthasar, *Theo-Drama*, 5:290. Von Balthasar writes: "The man-woman relationship is thus shown to be an ultimate one. All attempts to overcome it in the direction of an androgynous primal being or a sexless first man must be dismissed."

Rather he is a concrete individual male, existing in context of the narrative of the old and new creation. Within this narrative, the destiny of the human race has been determined by the relationship between male and female (i.e., Adam and Eve).

Therefore an emphasis upon the masculinity of Christ is important in order to correctly identify Christ in his role as the new and true Adam. In this role, he is the true minister of the Word and the true self-donating originating human. As we noted earlier, ministry is a male prerogative because Adam was given the Word of God and Eve was not.[73] Christ takes on the true role of Adam and surrendered himself for his bride the Church. Adam did not confront the serpent who tempted his bride (Gen 3:6) and the universal ruin of humanity ensued. By contrast, Christ himself confronted Satan and surrendered himself to redeem his bride the Church. By recognizing the role Christ's masculinity plays in redemption, we also thereby meet the Feminist concern regarding oppressive patriarchy. As exemplar, Christ's masculinity does not promote male oppression, but self-surrender.

This typology is also evident in the Gospel narratives of the resurrection as well. As the true male minister of the Word, Christ instructs the women in the garden (a new Eden) who are witnesses of his resurrection to tell his male disciples that he is going to Galilee (Matt 28:10). The women, unlike Eve (who rejected the Word of God), believe him. Upon hearing the Word of God from the women, the male disciples do not believe it and therefore, in a sense, reverse Adam who believed his wife. In spite of this, their own ministry is reaffirmed and they eventually do believe (Matt 28, Acts 1–2).

From this, we should observe two things. First, we are shown that true ministry properly belongs to men, since the male disciples were the ones who received instruction during the forty days following the resurrection. Nevertheless, the male disciples' faithlessness demonstrates that ministry does not rest on their native capacities (male or otherwise). Rather, by their abandonment of Christ and their initial incredulity to his Word, we are taught that Christ is the one who is present in them and therefore validates their ministry in spite of their sin. He alone is the true minister of the Word and the true recapitulator of Adam. In regard to their preaching, Jesus says: "The one who hears you hears me, and the one who rejects you rejects me, and the one who rejects me rejects him who sent me" (Luke 10:16).[74] Ministry belongs to him properly, and to them (and us) only secondarily.

Christ is truly the one who "unite[s] all . . . things in heaven and things on earth" (Eph 1:10). For this reason, he not only recapitulates the male, but also the female. Since the female is derived from the male (Gen 2:22), it is possible for the male to recapitulate

73. "Adam alone heard it [the command not to eat from the tree of the knowledge of good and evil], he later informed Eve of it. If they had not fallen into sin, Adam would have transmitted this single command later to their descendants" (AE 1:105). Also see Scaer, "Ordaining Women," 83–85.

74. Luther writes: "We are not willing to give them room or yield to this metaphysical and philosophical distinction, as it was spun out by reason—as though man preaches, threatens, punishes, gives fears and comforts, but the Holy Ghost does the work; or a man baptizes, absolves, and hands out the supper of the Lord Christ, but God purifies the heart and forgives sin. Oh no, absolutely not! But we conclude thus: God preaches, threatens, punishes, gives fear, comforts, baptizes, hands out the Sacrament of the Altar, and absolves Himself" (L. Green, "Philosophical Presuppositions," 29, quoting from WA TR 3:673 [no. 3868 Lauterbach Text], L. Green's translation).

the female. Again, human nature is human nature. Man and woman are not alien species. Nevertheless, male and female do differ in their originating relationship and therefore in their roles. In the case of Jesus, just as Eve was derived from Adam by an act of divine fiat, so too he was derived from his mother Mary by an act of divine fiat in the virgin birth. In this, there can be observed something of a chiastic structure of the history of salvation. The second Adam is derived from a female, just as the first female was derived from the first male. Consequently, although Christ was not female or hermaphroditic, he does take upon himself the role of the female thereby recapitulating her as well.

This can also be observed from his place within the Godhead. Paul in one passage compares the relationship between the Father and Son to that of male and female:

> But I want you to understand that the head of every man is Christ, *the head of a wife is her husband*, and *the head of Christ is God*. For man was not made from woman, but woman from man. Neither was man created for woman, but woman for man. Nevertheless, in *the Lord woman is not independent of man nor man of woman; for as woman was made from man*, so man is now born of woman. And all things are from God. (1 Cor 11:3, 8–9, 11–12, emphasis added)

The word "head" (*kephalē*) as many have noted, may also be translated as "source."[75] In this context, it would appear that Paul means it in both senses. He is, on the one hand, insisting on male headship by appealing to the protological relationship between man and woman, while at the same time insisting that this headship/source relationship mirrors that of the inner life of the Trinity.[76] Therefore, just as the woman is born from the man's side, so too the Son is eternally born from the Father.

Hence, the protological relationship of the female to the male reflects the eternal relationship of self-donation within the Godhead. The Father's own eternal self-surrender in his act of begetting makes Christ's own self-surrender to the Father possible. As we have seen in our discussion of Ephesians 5, this is also true for the woman in relationship to the man within Christian marriage. Because of this self-surrender, the Father is glorified and obeyed by the Son (John 17:1). The Son is not obedient to the Father because he is inferior (much as women are not inferior to men), but because, in an eternal act of self-surrender, the Father has given the fullness of his being and glory to the Son (Heb 1:3) thereby freeing him for total self-surrender.

In eternity, Christ takes over the position of the woman in the first creation by receiving all from the Father's being. He extends this relationship into time by becoming incarnate and living as a receptive hearer of the Word. By listening to and trusting in the Word of the Father in his state of humiliation, Christ overcomes the woman's disobedience by fulfilling her role in creation as a hearer of the Word. Because of this, the Father glorifies and loves the Son (Phil 2:9–11). In eternity, as in time, the Father and the Son are united by their self-surrendering love through the procession of the Holy Spirit. The Spirit brings glory to them both (John 14, Phil 2). Likewise, in the state of integrity, Adam expresses the divine righteousness of faith not only in his self-giving to the woman, but also in his glorification of the woman: "This at last is bone of my bones and flesh of my

---

75. See brief discussion in Holladay, *First Letter of Paul*, 139–40.

76. Both von Balthasar and Karl Barth also make these observations. See von Balthasar, *Theo-Drama*, 2:365–84, 3:283–92; *CD* 3.1:183–91.

flesh; she shall be called Woman, because she was taken out of Man" (Gen 2:23). As a result, the original creation's narrative of male and female is incorporated, recapitulated, and redeemed in Christ's new narrative of creation.

Chapter 8

The Mystery of the Person of Christ, Part 4

The Genus Idiomaticum *and the* Genus Apotelesmaticum

Brief Ontological Prolegomena

NOW THAT WE HAVE spoken about the occasion of the Word becoming flesh, it is our purpose to explore the communication of attributes (*communicatio idiomatum*) as they are set down in scripture and expounded upon in the Lutheran symbolic writings. The truth of the communication of attributes cannot be discovered by human reason. That eternal and infinite God could become human and thereby communicate his infinite glory to humanity, is an utterly unfathomable mystery. In light of this, we are to confess its truth and not fully comprehend it.

Although the scriptures witness to the two natures in Christ and the communication of attributes, much of the terminology used among the church fathers and the Lutheran confessors/scholastics to describe this blessed union has been developed out of the Greek philosophical tradition. In particular, certain conceptualities are borrowed from Greek substance ontologies that have been used to construct the familiar formulas of classical Trinitarian and christological theology. Broadly speaking (since we are of course talking about several philosophical traditions here) substance ontology assumes that there is a sort of essence in things that determines what they are and persists over time. The essential reality of an individual subject (substance) does not change over time, while certain predicates do. So for example, classical Trinitarian theology talks about one divine substance (*ousia*) and three persons (*hypostasis*). By this, the Nicene Fathers meant that there is something that makes God-God. And so, the claim goes, all three persons have this "something" and are united with one another as a single entity with one single essence while remaining distinct in their subsisting relations as persons. So too, Christ has all the essential attributes that determine one as human (a human nature or *physis*) and also has what it is to be God (a divine nature or *physis*) united in a single divine/human subject. As a subject, Christ subsists as a divine and human person over time, and this does not change, even if he gets older, grows in wisdom, and dies. Substance language is then (broadly understood) as realistic language. It insists that our language and cognitive perception has access to real entities and the essential nature of those entities.

Modern theology (beginning with Schleiermacher, whom we will discuss below) has generally been uncomfortable with these categories of thought. This has been the case for several reasons. One objection comes from the Liberal Protestant historian of dogma Adolf von Harnack. Von Harnack derided the church fathers for their use of philosophical categories taken from Platonism, Stoicism, and Aristotelianism. He viewed this as being essentially the downfall of Christianity. The intellectualizing tendency, the use of which these philosophical traditions represent, degraded Christianity into an abstract philosophical belief system from its pristine origin as a religion of the heart.[1] In essence, then, for von Harnack, true Christianity is tied up with ethical uprightness ("brotherhood of man" and "fatherhood of God") and the interior experience of the divine that does not need theological abstractions such as the incarnation or the Trinity.

Regarding von Harnack's treatment of the church fathers, much research has shown that his thesis is not accurate. The newer scholarship has demonstrated that as a result of theological debates and Church-usage, much of the Greek philosophical terminology that the church fathers borrowed was significantly redefined.[2] In fact, sometimes the terminology was modified quite radically in light of the newness present in the biblical teaching. In this vein, Luther in some of his later writings spoke similarly of the "new language" (*nova lingua*) of faith.[3] In speaking of the *nova lingua*, the Reformer noted that words take on new meaning through the events of revelation. Quiddities like "divinity" and "humanity" are mutually exclusive in normal (or philosophical) language, but when we come to discuss the incarnation they are not.

Adding to this point historically, the patristic scholar Robert Wilkens has also noted that the Church was in fact instrumental in developing its own unique grammar for dealing with christological and Trinitarian realities.[4] Ultimately, such language (and the ontological presuppositions that came with it) developed in debates because of interaction with the biblical texts. Such debates were of course influenced by Greek philosophical presuppositions, but as the discussions progressed many of these presuppositions were greatly changed by interaction with the biblical material or even eliminated.

Nevertheless, even with the downfall of classical Protestant Liberalism in the early twentieth century, these objections have remained, especially among Existentialist theologians. On one level, some criticism of the use of these categories can be valid. Any theological category can be abused and understood in an overly reified manner. We of course cannot know in an ultimate sense the essence of God, or even for that matter

---

1. See von Harnack, *History of Dogma*, 1:14–23; von Harnack, *Das Wesen des Christentums*. Werner Elert's last theological-historical project was to critique von Harnack's position. See his *Der Ausgang der Altkirchlichen Christologie*. This was also largely Jaroslav Pelikan's argument in his monumental history of doctrine. See Pelikan, *Christian Tradition*, 1:1. Instead of the history of degrading Hellenization, Pelikan helpfully describes the history of doctrine as, "What the church of Jesus Christ believes, teaches, and confesses on the basis of the word of God: this is Christian doctrine."

2. This has been demonstrated by the following works: R. Hanson, *Search for the Christian Doctrine*; Ayres, *Nicaea and Its Legacy*; Davis, *First Seven Ecumenical Councils*.

3. *AE* 38:241–42.

4. Wilkens, "Church's Way of Speaking," 27–31.

humanity itself. Indeed, God himself is a mystery, as are all the teachings of the faith. As John Kleinig notes, scripture defines a mystery as a thing one knows to be true, yet cannot explain how it is true.[5] God always speaks to us under the covering or of his creatures (*larva Dei*). We can only listen to him and trust that he is who claims to be. At best, our conceptual knowledge of *Deus ipse* is analogical and indirect, "through a glass darkly" as the Apostle Paul puts it. We are told to confess the faith, not fully comprehend its content. It is difficult to see how the church fathers, medieval theologians, or Reformers would have denied this.

Beyond these valid objections, we might also add that substance ontology becomes dangerous when the essence of things is viewed as something independently determining them apart from God's own sustaining power. From the perspective of Christian orthodoxy, ultimately the reality of any creature is rooted outside itself in God's speech act. *Creatio ex nihilo* and *continua* mean that creatures are radically de-centered and subsist in God's act of creative narration.[6] As we observed earlier, because this divine speech is itself narrative, quiddities do not possess their reality as something abstract and independent of their relationship with other entities, but within the dynamic narrative of creation and redemption as it is established by the Word of God. Understood in this light, it is correct to say that individual substances do persist over time, but not because of something centered and independent within them. Rather, because of God's creative and sustaining Word outside of them. We observed how this is the case in our discussion of Genesis 1, and later with regard to Christ's new narrative of creation.

Therefore, in spite of the ways that substance language can be abused, it does not mean that we must discount such language. When used responsibly, such language can be part and parcel of a healthy theological realism. In fact, a rejection of such language opens the door to an irresponsible and unfaithful theological anti-realism. For example, it should not go without notice that the complaints regarding substance language and ontology are the loudest from those theologians who stand in the stream of tradition coming out of Kant and Existentialism. In Kant's philosophy, there is a general lack of confidence that the human subject can actually know entities in themselves ("*ding-an-sich*").[7] Consequently, according to Kant, we can reasonably talk about the effects of things on us and thereby gain some intimations of their reality. Ultimately though, we cannot really know things as they are. This massively undermines epistemic and theological realism, and tends to lead to a theological solipsism.

---

5. Kleinig, *Grace Upon Grace*, 57.

6. Bayer writes: "The criterion for truth is provided by this event [the happy exchange], in which Jesus Christ takes another person's place with a propitiatory death, on the basis of which *theology, concerning both premodern metaphysics of substance and the modern metaphysics of subject, can be evaluated only critically*, since these approaches to life do not permit one to think in a way that looks beyond the self and to find my identity outside myself" (*Martin Luther's Theology*, 235). In other words, both the Christian doctrine of creation and redemption insist that the being of any creature is to be found outside themselves in God's Word. This will become important in our next chapter.

7. Kant, *Critique of Pure Reason*, 74, 87, 149, 172–73. See critique of modern Kantian epistemology in theology in Paul Hinlicky, *Paths Not Taken*, 43–86. Helmut Thielicke has traced back the theology consciousness to Descartes. See comments in Thielicke, *Evangelical Faith*, 1:38–64.

Kant's epistemology is one of the major contributing factors to the tradition of modern theology as we know it. The Reformed theologian Friedrich Schleiermacher was the first person to consistently apply Kant's epistemology to the task of dogmatic theology.[8] Schleiermacher's dogmatic theology is one of consciousness.[9] God is posited as an ontologically real entity, but this is established on the basis of an inference from the effect of God on human consciousness.[10] Christ's relationship to God is explained by the fact that as a perfect human being he had a perfect consciousness of God, and therefore he was capable of communicating this consciousness to us.[11] Because the foundation of theological judgment is the interior experience of divine sovereignty mediated through Jesus ("a feeling of absolute dependence"), the Trinity is a meaningless and speculative concept. Even if God were a Trinity, it would have no specific echo in human consciousness and consequently be unknowable. Hence, within the structure of Schleiermacher's *Glaubenslehre*, the Trinity is ultimately consigned to a final appendix where its truth is very seriously questioned, if not utterly dismissed.[12] One can find similar attempts at making the ground of all theological propositions about human existential states in twentieth-century theologians like Rudolf Bultmann and Gerhard Ebeling.[13]

Though it would of course take an entire volume (if not more) to fully critique the position of these theologians, it is important that we give a brief outline of a response to theological anti-realism. We must particularly do this in regard to modern theology's propensity to question the possibility of realistic language about God and creation. It is

---

8. See the following works by Friedrich Schleiermacher, *Brief Outline of the Study of Theology*; Schleiermacher, *Christmas Eve*; Schleiermacher, *Christian Faith*; Schleiermacher, *Introduction to Christian Ethics*; Schleiermacher, *On Religion*. See brief comment in T. Kelly, *Theology at the Void*, 15. Kelly writes:

> *This is the key to the appeal to human experience in the defense of religion.* He will try to reimagine and ground religion *within a Kantian construct.* Whatever objective data are dealt with by the mind are experienced through the forms and *concepts conferred by the subject.* But Schleiermacher goes even further by grounding his method in the human experience of God that occurs *in the interiority of the subject and is accessible through simple reflection on the fact of existence.* This becomes the *comprehensive principle* by which religion is redefined. It is this appeal to inner experience that made Schleiermacher's apology for religion so effective. (emphasis added)

9. Schleiermacher, *Christian Faith*, 5–9.

10. Ibid., 12–18.

11. Ibid., 355–475.

12. Ibid., 738–51.

13. See the following work by Bultmann and Ebeling: Bultmann, *Alte und der Neue Mensch*; Bultmann, *Begriff der Offenbarung im Neuen Testament*; Bultmann, *Beitrage zum Verstandnis der Jenseitigkeit Gottes*; Bultmann, *Drei Johannesbrief*; Bultmann, *Erforschung der Synoptischen Evangelien*; Bultmann, *Evangelium des Johannes*; Bultmann, *Geschichte der Synoptischen Tradition*; Bultmann, *History and Eschatology*; Bultmann, *Jesus and the Word*; Bultmann, *Jesus Christ and Mythology*; Bultmann, *Primitive Christianity in Its Contemporary Setting*; Bultmann, *Second Letter to the Corinthians*; Bultmann, *Theologie des Neuen Testamentes*; Ebeling, *Dogmatik des Christlichen Glaubens*; Ebeling, *Einfuhrung in Theologische Sprachlehre*; Ebeling, *Evangelische Evangelienauslegung*; Ebeling, *Frei aus Glauben*; Ebeling, *Geschichtlichkeit der Kirche*; Ebeling, *Kirchengeschichte als Geschichte der Auslegung der Heiligen Schrift*; Ebeling, *Luther*; Ebeling, *Luthers Seelsorge*; Ebeling, *Lutherstudien*; Ebeling, *Nature of Faith*; Ebeling, *Problem of Historicity in the Church*; Ebeling, *Psalmenmeditationen*; Ebeling, *Study of Theology*; Ebeling, *Theologie und Verkündigung*; Ebeling, *Truth of the Gospel*; Ebeling, *Das Wesen des Christlichen Glaubens*; Ebeling, *Wort Gottes und Tradition*; Ebeling, *Wort und Glaube*.

important to do this in light of our prior commitments to the Christian doctrine of creation and redemption in Jesus Christ. Ultimately such commitments are necessary for a proper discussion of the article of the communication of attributes within the hypostatic union. The divine person and the human nature must be understood as real realities with real and understandable properties. Otherwise, any talk of exchange or interplay between them is meaningless.

The main issue appears ultimately to be modern and postmodern skepticism about the reliability of human perception and of language as a vehicle of truth. That is to say, recent Western culture has become anti-realist in its orientation towards the world because of a lack of faith in harmony between word and world.[14] Following this tread, modern theology has had a great deal of difficulty in making realistic claims about God and his work in salvation history. This is partially due to a lack of faith in the historical reliability of the Bible (beginning in the eighteenth century[15]) and the resultant need to find a second source of authority (i.e., human consciousness). Furthermore, in light of what we have seen in our very cursory discussion of Schleiermacher, another aspect of the move to Liberalism was a lack of faith in the ability of realistic propositional language to make true statements about God. This is mainly because human language ultimately cannot carry the freight of reality in any realistic sense. With this, the articles of the faith and any sense of authority (beyond generalized corporate feelings of a given religious community) melt away.[16] In fact, the articles of the faith simply become an arbitrary linguistic grid wherein the same perceptions of transcendental realities shared across many cultures become thematized.[17] This would appear to account for a great deal of the doctrinal relativism and religious universalism present in the mainline Protestant denominations in the United States.

Anti-realism is the original sin of modern theology (as it was of Kant's philosophy) because it entails a lack of faith in God the creator who connects word and world. If we trust in God as our creator, then we must accept that he loves and sustains creation even now, as the Large Catechism teaches.[18] If this is the case, then as faithful Christians we

14. The Jewish scholar George Steiner makes this observation about postmodern philosophy in general. See Steiner, *Real Presences*.

15. See discussion in Frei, *Eclipse of the Biblical Narrative*, 86–104; Harrisville and Sundberg, *Bible in Modern Culture*, 30–62.

16. Bayer writes: "In neo-Protestantism of the Kantian variety, this *pro me* [Luther's insistence that the Word of God is always addressed to us individually] has been and continues to be misused as a methodological principle, in order to eliminate anything that is objective concerning what faith believes, and to characterize faith as that which happens to each one individually" (*Martin Luther's Theology*, 131–32).

17. See description of this paradigm in George Lindbeck, *Nature of Doctrine*, 32–34.

18. LC 2:1; *CT* 681:

> But what is the force of this, or what do you mean by these words: I believe in God, the Father Almighty, Maker, etc.? Answer: This is what I mean and believe, that I am a creature of God; that is, that He has given and constantly preserves to me my body, soul, and life, members great and small, all my senses, reason, and understanding, and so on, food and drink, clothing and support, wife and children, domestics, house and home, etc. Besides, He causes all creatures to serve for the uses and necessities of life, sun, moon, and stars in the firmament, day and night, air, fire, water, earth, and whatever it bears and produces, birds and fishes, beasts, grain, and all kinds of produce, and whatever else there is of bodily and temporal goods, good government, peace, security. Thus we learn from this article that none of us has of himself, nor can preserve, his life

must accept that in spite of our fallen nature, the human language has not been utterly destroyed as a truth-medium. Humans are still capable of knowing the truth and speaking the truth (this being part of civil righteousness), even if this does not help them achieve salvation. This is true even when language distorts reality, as for example in the use of racist or sexist language. In these cases, there is a real reference to something in our concrete experience of reality (i.e., for people of different skin colors or genders). Hence, although faith in God the creator compels us to accept the premise that our perceptions and our language can carry the freight of reality, due to the power of sin they do not do so infallibly. For this reason, our realism cannot be naïve realism but rather a critical one.

Because human language is fallen, yet functional, we can accept the terms "essence" and "substance" as a way of describing how our language corresponds to real entities in the world. For example, human language recognizes that cats are cats, and dogs are dogs. There is something about cats that makes them cats and our language identifies that and mediates that reality to us. The same is true of individual substances: our language recognizes that the identity of certain entities persists over time irrespective of the change of certain predicates. Our ability to recognize this and use our language to portray it is something guaranteed to us by God the creator, who is the good author of our language and its harmony with the world. In fact, since all human beings do use such language casually, they implicitly assume a God who connects word and world. Without such a deity who is the author of both human language and the world that it portrays, it is hard to know how or why our words should correspond to things in reality. Even if they did, there would be no way of discerning this fact. Because of our faith in God the creator, we find it justifiable then to follow something close to the "common-sense realism" tradition of Thomas Reid and Alvin Plantinga.[19]

Instead of trusting in the preservation of God the creator, much recent theology shares the false starting point of modern philosophy of basing truth on the autonomous self and its interior consciousness of the truth. This approach is the very definition of original sin. It is an outright rejection of faith in God the creator as the truthful author of language and the world. In light of the fact that the human subject is inherently unstable

nor anything that is here enumerated or can be enumerated, however small and unimportant a thing it might be, for all is comprehended in the word Creator.

Also see Ratzinger, *Introduction to Christianity*, 26. The pope states well the Christian commitment to philosophical realism: "Ever since the Prologue to the Gospel of John, the concept of *logos* has been at the very center of the our Christian faith in God . . . the God who is *logos* guarantees the intelligibility of the world, the intelligibility of our existence, the aptitude of reason to know God . . . and the reasonableness of God, even though his understanding infinitely surpasses ours and to us may so often appear to be darkness."

19. See the following works by Thomas Reid: *Powers of the Human Mind*; Reid, *Inquiry into the Human Mind*; Reid, *Lectures on Natural Theology*. See Alvin Plantinga, "Is Naturalism Irrational?," 72–96. Plantinga notes that only by recognizing that God is the creator and designer of our senses, can we accept a realistic concept of our language and sense knowledge. Also see Plantinga, *Faith and Philosophy*; Plantinga, *God and Other Minds*; Plantinga, *God, Freedom, and Evil*; Plantinga, *Nature of Necessity*; Plantinga, *Warranted Christian Belief*; Plantinga, *Warrant*; Plantinga, *Warrant and Proper Function*. One can also find a fine Lutheran example of this sort of thinking in Dennis Bielfeldt, "Luther's Late Trinitarian Disputations," 59–130.

and fallible as an entity, making this the starting point of our epistemic endeavors is like trying to levitate by pulling on one's suspenders. Beginning with my own consciousness and autonomy, and afterwards moving outward from there will ultimately lead me to affirm nothing but my own autonomy. Anything that is not "me" is a boundary and boundaries are intrinsically detrimental to autonomy. Hence acknowledging anything that is not "me" places an epistemic demand upon me against which I must protect myself. This is the voice of the law, and I, as a self-justifying sinner cannot accept its voice. In order to maintain my autonomy, I must reject this voice and be skeptical about everything. This degenerates very quickly into the oldest heresy of our first parents, enthusiasm and its attending self-justification.

Faith in God the creator (reestablished by the power of the gospel of redemption), by contrast, understands the world as a gift from God who frees us, and does not enslave us. Because he richly provides for us, the existence of the other is not a threat to our reality. Such an attitude is essential for a realistic concept of the world and human capacity to know it through language. Ultimately, for there to be a real world, where semantically real statements are capable of representing it, then there must be a true and living God who organizes its structures and makes it capable of being known.[20] He does this all through his pure grace.

The Genera of Confessional Lutheran Christology: The Genus Idiomaticum and Apostelestamaticum

Having discussed the questions of Christ's birth, gender, and that nature of the theological language used to describe the incarnation, we now proceed with a discussion of the communication of attributes. The communication of attributes (as we have previously noted) is the surrender of God to humanity in the self-donation of the gospel. Because God-in-Christ surrenders himself in the form of his unilateral promise, he concretizes this promise in the form of giving his full reality to the human Jesus through the communication of idioms within the hypostatic union.

In light of our confessional commitments, we will work in this section from the perspective of the Formula of Concord's threefold genera of the communication of attributes. Although our guide for this exposition of the Bible will be the aforementioned confessional documents, we will primarily rely on the lengthier explanation of the three genera by Martin Chemnitz in his work *De Duabus Naturis in Christo* (*The Two Natures in Christ*).[21] We will of course also make frequent references to biblical material in order to demonstrate that our fathers in faith have been true to God's revelation.

As a theologian, Martin Chemnitz was an evangelical-catholic. He believed that the Great Tradition of the ancient Church had been more or less pure, and that later

---

20. This is one of the reasons why science cannot give a proper account of itself without reference to Judeo-Christian theism, and therefore, scientific atheism is an absurdity. See the extended argument in McGrath, *Scientific Theology*.

21. Chemnitz, *Two Natures*. Much of the material in this chapter and the next will appear in a similar (but not identical) form within an article for Lutheran Quarterly on the hypostatic union in Chemnitz and Thomas Aquinas, that will published sometime in 2013.

medieval innovations had corrupted the ancient creedal faith.[22] For this reason, he finds very little fault with the first six ecumenical councils and gives a preliminary outline of both the definitions and terminology for describing the incarnation that are found in both the patristic authors and the early church councils.[23]

Chemnitz therefore begins his discussion with an affirmation of the ancient creedal tradition of the Church as biblical. Following the first through fourth ecumenical councils, Chemnitz states that Jesus is true God and true man in one person (or *hypostasis*).[24] In spite of the insistence by modern liberal interpreters, we have demonstrated that this is without a doubt the consistent teaching of the whole Bible. Within this union of divine and human natures, neither nature is mixed with or transmuted into the other. Both natures retain their essential integrity, while neither nature can be spoken of alone except by abstraction. All these propositions represent the logical implication of the aforementioned teaching of duality of Christ's natures in the Bible. If it were not so, Christ would become a hybrid incapable of bringing about the salvation that the New Testament ascribed to him. Namely, he could not represent other human beings and atone for sin. As only half God or a mixed God, neither could he fulfill the Father's infinite righteousness, defeat the devil, or overcome death thereby renewing creation.

Following the third and fifth ecumenical councils, Chemnitz explains that we must think of the Logos as the subject of the incarnation. The divine person of the Logos incorporates an impersonal human nature (*anhypostasis*) into his own preexistent hypostasis (*enhypostasis*).[25] It is the person of the Logos who is born to the blessed virgin through his human nature and therefore it is proper to call her the "Mother of God" (*Theotokos*, following the third ecumenical council).[26] This doctrinal statement is thoroughly biblical in that when Mary visits Elizabeth, the latter is filled with the Holy Spirit and explicitly refers to Mary as "mother of my Lord" (Luke 1:43).[27] "Lord" (*kyriou*) in

---

22. See good discussion of Chemnitz's appropriation of the church fathers in Carl Beckwith, "Martin Chemnitz's Use of the Church Fathers," 271–90. Also see by the same author: "Martin Chemnitz's Reading of the Fathers," 231–56.

23. Chemnitz, *Two Natures*, 29–37.

24. Ibid., 83, 113, 131, 172–73, 221, 383. For discussions of Chalcedon see J. Kelly, *Early Christian Doctrines*, 339–42, 406; Pelikan, *Christian Tradition*, 1: 263–66; Meyendorff, *Christ in Eastern Christian Thought*, 12–16; Urban, *Short History of Christian Thought*, 74–75, 88–89, 91, 93–94, 98–100. For these individual councils see Heinrich Denzinger, *Sources of Catholic Dogma*, 26, 34–36, 49–57, 60–64.

25. Chemnitz, *Two Natures*, 68–72. For the text of the fifth ecumenical council see Denzinger, *Sources of Catholic Dogma*, 85–90. See discussion of the fifth ecumenical council in Grillmeier, *Christ in Christian Tradition*, 341, 387, 402–10, 419–62, 463; Meyendorff, *Christ in Eastern Christian Thought*, 38–40, 59–64; Pelikan, *Christian Tradition*, 2:29–30.

26.   Chemnitz, *Two Natures*, 208–10. For the text of the third ecumenical council see Denzinger, *Sources of Catholic Dogma*, 49–57. See discussion of the third ecumenical council in J. Kelly, *Early Christian Doctrines*, 328, 331, 341; Pelikan, *Christian Tradition*, 2:260–61, 329–30; Urban, *Short History of Christian Thought*, 86, 322.

27. SD 8; *CT* 1023:
> On account of this personal union and communion of the natures, Mary, the most blessed Virgin, bore not a mere man, but, as the angel [Gabriel] testifies, such a man as is truly the Son of the most high God, who showed His divine majesty even in His mother's womb, inasmuch as He was born of a virgin, with her virginity inviolate. Therefore she is truly the mother of God, and nevertheless remained a virgin.

this context is not merely a polite address (as it of course can be in others), but rather is meant to serve as a translation for YHWH as it does throughout the LXX.[28] This is consistent with Luke's earlier identification of Jesus with YHWH. As we have noted, in the annunciation, Luke describes Mary as being the new location of the presence of the *kavod*.[29]

In Christ, states Chemnitz (again, following the fifth ecumenical council), the human nature is not properly speaking a person or *hypostasis*, but is rather *anhypostasis*. Chemnitz explains that Christ's human nature is not a person, but rather "one particular individual unit (*massa*) of human nature."[30] This does not mean that the human nature lacks anything that is essential to being human. This includes a proper *hypostasis*, since it possesses one through its unity with the subject of the Logos himself. Rather what it lacks is any independent subsistence as an individual human being.[31]

Though sacred scripture does not explicitly use this terminology, it must be considered a conceptually accurate way of speaking in light of the fact that the Bible speaks of the Logos as the subject of the incarnation. It is the man Jesus who consistently speaks of himself as one who existed before Abraham (John 8:58) and who also had glory with the Father before the world began (17:24). In many other locations in scripture, we are told that Christ is the creator of the world (John 1:3, v. 10; 1 Cor 8:6; Col 1:16–17; Heb 1:2). In these passages, there is no suggestion of Christ's human nature (which is of course a creature and not preexistent) being an agent of the original creation. There are also many explicit statements about the person of Logos taking on flesh at a certain point in time (John 1:14, Gal 4:4). For this reason the biblical material demands that we speak of human nature as nonpersonal.

Moreover, such a theological judgment also stands in coherence with the biblical insistence upon monergism (John 15:5; 1 Cor 12:3; Eph 2:5, 8). It is Christ as a divine subject who is the acting agent of our salvation working through his human nature. It is not a quasi-independent or preexistent human subject cooperating with God the Son. Furthermore, in that the human nature finds its center of identity outside of itself in the person of the Logos, Christ prefigures the ecstatic nature of Christian existence. The person of faith finds their reality outside of themselves in God's gracious address and in the love for the

---

Luther states in *On the Council and the Church* (1539) regarding the biblical basis of the third ecumenical council:

> This council too did not establish anything new in faith, as we said above, but only defended the old faith against the new notions of Nestorious . . . this article was in the church from the very beginning and was not newly established by the council, but was preserved through the gospel or Holy Scripture, for it is written in Luke 1[:32] that the angel Gabriel announced to the Virgin Mary that of her would be born "the Son of the Most High." And Elizabeth, "Why is this granted to me, that the mother of my Lord should come to me?" (*AE* 41:105)

28. Tuckett, *Christology and the New Testament*, 19–22.

29. Just, *Luke*, 1:69.

30. Chemnitz, *Two Natures*, 30.

31. Hence, we reject the Liberal Protestant tradition's criticism that the fifth ecumenical council's *enhypostasis-anhypostasis* Christology destroys Christ's human nature. See examples in Dorner, *System of Christian Doctrine*, 3:216; Schleiermacher, *Christian Faith*, 402–3. Also see a Neo-orthodox rejection, with the same unfounded criticism in Dietrich Bonhoeffer, *Christ the Center*, 81.

neighbor: "We conclude, therefore, that a Christian *lives not in himself, but in Christ and the neighbor*. He lives in Christ *through faith*, and in his *neighbor through love*."[32]

Finally, Chemnitz accepts the teaching of the sixth ecumenical council that Christ possesses two wills.[33] This does not mean that Christ has two centers of identity or consciousnesses that are potentially in conflict with one another. Rather, what is meant is that Christ lacks nothing that is essential to human nature, including a human will. As Maximus the Confessor pointed out during the Monothelite controversy, if Christ indeed did lack anything that is essential to human nature, it would be impossible for him to redeem other humans.[34] This again stands in accord with the teaching of scripture regarding Christ's full humanity (Heb 2:17).[35]

Positing two wills also brings us to the question of the temptation and impeccability of Christ.[36] As is evident from the Bible, Jesus in Gethsemane asks for a reprieve from his mission of death (Matt 26:36–46, Mark 14:32–42, Luke 22:39–46). There are of course other instances of temptation presented in the New Testament (Matt 4:11, Mark 1:12–14, Luke 4:1–13, Heb 2:14–18). Regarding Christ's temptation in Gethsemane, obviously the divine nature always willed death, whereas Christ's flesh wished for a possible reprieve because of its natural and reasonable fear of torture and death. One should say "natural" and "reasonable" because human nature prior to the Fall was naturally created so as to have an aversion to death and suffering. Otherwise God's threat of death for eating from the tree of the knowledge of good and evil would have been meaningless (Gen 2:17). Similarly, when Jesus was tempted in the desert by Satan with the possibility of eating, he had a natural and uncorrupted sense that bread would be desirable. It is also correct to say that neither universal dominion (given to Adam in Genesis 1 and offered by Satan to Jesus) nor the public demonstration of divine grace and love (offered by Satan in his suggestion that Jesus might throw himself down from the temple) are evils in and of themselves. The aforementioned temptations become evil when human desire for them expresses a rejection of God's will. As we saw earlier, this desire is rooted in unbelief in God's trustworthiness and goodness. After the Fall, such unbelief is an intrinsic corruption in human nature. Hence, the feeling of temptation for fallen humans is always tied up with the will to sin, whereas for Jesus or for Adam before the Fall it need not necessarily be so.

Therefore, when we say that Jesus was tempted we do not thereby mean that he felt the desire to violate God's will. This is evident from his statement in the midst of the prayer in Gethsemane: "not as I will, but as you will" (Matt 26:39). In other words, in spite of his natural desire to avoid death (the feeling of temptation), he trusted in God

32. *AE* 31:371 (emphasis added). Oswald Bayer also describes Christian existence as being "enhypostatized" by the Word. See Bayer, *Theology the Lutheran Way*, 53.

33. Chemnitz, *Two Natures*, 233–39. For the text of the sixth ecumenical council see Denzinger, *Sources of Catholic Dogma*, 113–15. For discussion of the sixth ecumenical council see George Ostrogorski, *History of the Byzantine State*, 127; Pelikan, *Christian Tradition*, 2:70–75.

34. See discussions of Maximus the Confessor in Andrew Louth, *Maximus the Confessor*; Meyerdorff, *Christ in Eastern Christian Thought*, 42–43, 99–115; Pelikan, *Christian Tradition*, 2:8–36; Thunberg, *Microcosm and Mediator*; J. Williams, "Pseudo-Dionysius and Maximus the Confessor," 193–99.

35. See interesting discussion in Bulgakov, *Lamb of God*, 74–88.

36. F. Pieper, *Christian Dogmatics*, 2:76–77.

and was always willing to be obedient to him. For this reason, the doctrine of the two wills helps explain how Christ's sinlessness coheres with the reality of his temptations (Heb 2:14–8).

Lastly, it should be understood that positing two wills in Christ does not violate the unity of his person. In fact, it properly describes both his personal unity and his full entrance into a mission of solidarity with humanity. As Athanasius suggests, it was the will of the divine nature that the human nature might experience temptation in order to redeem humanity.[37] Hence, the experience of temptation does not violate the human nature's unity with the divine person. Where Adam and Israel succumbed to satanic temptation, Christ persisted and thereby redeemed by his obedience. In the same manner, Gethsemane is the beginning of the culmination of the human experience of God's judgment against sin. Because human redemption occurs as a result of Christ's experiencing the abandonment of the Father and the curse of sin, it was God's own will that he might enter into the temptation of despair and persevere. It therefore also goes without saying that as a part of this divine plan Christ could never have succumbed to these temptations and thereby violate his mission. In that Jesus is God himself in the flesh it would be illogical for him to have violated the will of his divine person. Hence, although there are two wills in Jesus, they are always in harmony within a single subject of the Logos.

---

37. Athanasius, *Four Discourses Against the Arians*, Discourse 3, 26.34; *NPNFb* 4:412–13. He writes: And that one may attain to a more exact knowledge of the impassibility of the Word's nature and of the infirmities ascribed to Him because of the flesh, it will be well to listen to the blessed Peter; for he will be a trustworthy witness concerning the Saviour. He writes then in his Epistle thus; "Christ then having suffered for us in the flesh 1 Peter 4:1." Therefore also when He is said to hunger and thirst and to toil and not to know, and to sleep, and to weep, and to ask, and to flee, and to be born, and to deprecate the cup, and in a word to undergo all that belongs to the flesh, let it be said, as is congruous, in each case "Christ then hungering and thirsting for us in the flesh;" and saying "He did not know, and being buffeted, and toiling for us in the flesh;" and "being exalted too, and born, and growing in the flesh;" and "fearing and hiding in the flesh;" and "saying, If it be possible let this cup pass from Me Matthew 26:39, and being beaten, and receiving, for us in the flesh." and in a word all such things "for us in the flesh." For on this account has the Apostle himself said, "Christ then having suffered," not in His Godhead, but "for us in the flesh," that these affections may be acknowledged as, not proper to the very Word by nature, but proper by nature to the very flesh. Let no one then stumble at what belongs to man, but rather let a man know that in nature the Word Himself is impassible, and yet because of that flesh which He put on, these things are ascribed to Him, since they are proper to the flesh, and the body itself is proper to the Saviour. And while He Himself, being impassible in nature, remains as He is, not harmed by these affections, but rather obliterating and destroying them, men, their passions as if changed and abolished in the Impassible, henceforth become themselves also impassible and free from them for ever, as John taught, saying, "And ye know that He was manifested to take away our sins, and in Him is no sin 1 John 3:5." And this being so, no heretic shall object, "Wherefore rises the flesh, being by nature mortal? And if it rises, why not hunger too and thirst, and suffer, and remain mortal? For it came from the earth, and how can its natural condition pass from it?" since the flesh is able now to make answer to this so contentious heretic, "I am from earth, being by nature mortal, but afterwards I have become the Word's flesh," and He "carried" my affections, though He is without them; and so I became free from them, being no more abandoned to their service because of the Lord who has made me free from them. For if you object to my being rid of that corruption which is by nature, see that you object not to God's Word having taken my form of servitude; for as the Lord, putting on the body, became man, so we men are deified by the Word as being taken to Him through His flesh, and henceforward inherit life "everlasting."

Explaining with precision the relationship between two natures was particularly necessary of the polemical situation of the sixteenth century. The specific occasion for Chemnitz's treatment of the communication of attributes was a series of debates that broke out between the Lutheran and Reformed communions regarding Christology and its relationship to the Lord's Supper. Zwingli and Calvin's rejection of the substantial presence of Christ according to his human nature in the Lord's Supper was partially rooted in their distinctive understanding of the hypostatic union. In accordance with Chalcedon, Reformed theologians correctly asserted that humanity and divinity are unchanged in their essential qualities by the incarnation. From this, they drew the implication that because human nature is essentially and immutably circumscribed, Christ's flesh and blood could not become substantially present in the Lord's Supper. Since Christ is seated at the right hand of God, due to its spatial limitations, it could not become present at the church altar.[38] These christological claims had differing implications for various Reformed authors. For Zwingli it meant that only a symbolic interpretation of the Lord's Supper was allowable.[39] For Calvin and Bucer a spiritual presence of Christ was considered an acceptable interpretation of the words of institution.[40]

Within the ranks of the Wittenberg reformation itself, the older Melanchthon and his followers remained more agnostic as to the mode of Christ's presence. Paralleling this development, in the 1540s and 1550s, Melanchthon came to argue that Christians need only trust that the person of the Son is present in the Lord's Supper. Implicitly this seemed to suggest that the mode of presence (bodily or purely spiritual) was irrelevant. Many of Melanchthon's later followers were considerably more explicit in their rejection of bodily presence and thereby earned the name "Crypto-Calvinist."[41]

Chemnitz and the conservative or "Gnesio-Lutherans" sought to reject both schools of Reformation thought by reasserting Luther's understanding of the communication of attributes and the Lord's Supper.[42] In *The Two Natures in Christ*, Chemnitz sets out to systematize Luther's scriptural insights regarding the communication of attributes.[43]

---

38. Dorner, *Doctrine of the Person of Christ*, 4:116–40; González, *History of Christian Thought*, 3:84, 3:149–53; Hägglund, *History of Theology*, 256, 264–65; Pelikan, *Christian Tradition*, 4:158–89; Thomasius, *Christi*, 1:520–37; J. Willis, *History of Christian Thought*, 3:31.

39. George, *Theology of the Reformers*, 144–58; R. Olson, *Story of Christian Theology*, 406–8; Placher, *History of Christian Theology*, 189–90; Potter, *Zwingli*, 304–5; Rilliet, *Zwingli*, 228–31; Stephens, *Theology of Huldrych Zwingli*, 218–59; J. Willis, *History of Christian Thought*, 3:30–32.

40. See discussion in Gerrish, *Grace and Gratitude*, 157–90; McDonnell, *John Calvin*, 223–27, 348–52. Also see classical study of the subject in John Nevin, *Mystical Presence*. Regarding Bucer also see discussion in Greschat, *Martin Bucer*, 70–78.

41. Melanchthon's description of the Lord's Supper in his second-to-last edition of *Loci communes* is conspicuously missing any direct affirmation of the real presence. See Melanchthon, *Melanchthon on Christian Doctrine*, 217–23. Also see discussion in Arand et al., *Lutheran Confessions*, 227–49; Fraenkel, "Ten Questions concerning Melanchthon," 146–64; Manschreck, *Melanchthon*, 229–48; Quere, *Christum Cognescere*; J. Richard, *Philip Melanchthon*, 178–80, 242, 361; Rogness, *Melanchthon*, 131–35. It should be noted that Rogness is not entirely convinced that Melanchthon really rejected the real presence.

42. See discussion in Arand et al., *Lutheran Confessions*, 231–36; Bente, *Historical Introductions*, 183–84; Gritsch, *History of Lutheranism*, 91–95; J. Preus, *Second Martin*, 174–77.

43. See a summary of Luther's Christology in the following sources: Althaus, *Theology of Martin Luther*, 179–218; Anthony, *Cross Narratives*, 106–54; Congar, "Regards et réflexions sur la christologie

The systematization of these distinctions does not represent a merely abstract intellectual exercise, but is motivated by a desire to clarify the nature of Christ and his benefits. As the Finnish Reformation scholar, Olli-Pekka Vainio comments: "for Chemnitz, *communicatio idiomatum* is first and foremost a soteriological concept."[44] To explain his position, Chemnitz divides the biblical statements regarding the communication of attributes into three genera: the *genus idiomaticum*, the *genus apotelesmaticum,* and the *genus majestaticum.*[45]

The first genus Chemnitz terms the *genus idiomaticum.*[46] This is a genus that very likely could be agreed upon by most post-Chaceldonian Christians and bears within itself the clarifications of both the third and fifth ecumenical councils. According to this genus, the properties of both natures are to be attributed to the total theandric person of Christ when considered in the concrete. In other words, because the Logos possesses a human nature in the unity of its person, it is proper to attribute all the attributes of humanity to him.[47] Conversely, one may say the same thing regarding the human nature as it exists within the hypostatic union. This genus does not concern each nature considered in abstraction (that is, considered in itself apart from the hypostatic union), but rather in the concrete unity of the incarnation.

The scriptures frequently speak in this manner. For example, we are told that Jesus Christ is the "same yesterday and today and forever" (Heb 13:8). It is obviously a property of the divine nature to be eternal and immutable and not the human nature. Nevertheless the single theanthropic subject "Jesus Christ" is described as being eternal and immutable. Similarly, Matthew's citation of Isaiah's prophesy that the child born

---

de Luther," 3:457–86; Dorner, *Doctrine of the Person of Christ*, 4:53–115; Hinlicky, *Luther and the Beloved Community*, 31–65; Janz, *Westminster Handbook to Martin Luther*, 19–22; Juntunen, "Christ," 59–79; Kolb, *Martin Luther*, 110–17; Lienhard, *Luther*, 153–248; Lohse, *Martin Luther's Theology*, 219–31; Sasse, *This is My Body*, 148–61; Steiger, "Axle and Motor of Luther's Theology," 125–58; Siggins, *Martin Luther's Doctrine of Christ*, 191–243.

44. Vainio, *Justification and Participation*, 136.

45. See summary in J. Preus, *Second Martin*, 266–76.

46. FC SD 8; *CT* 1027:

First, since in Christ two distinct natures exist and remain unchanged and unconfused in their natural essence and properties, and yet of both natures there is only one person, hence, that which is, indeed, an attribute of only one nature is ascribed not to that nature alone, as separate, but to the entire person, which is at the same time God and man (whether it is called God or man). But in hoc genere, that is, in this mode of speaking, it does not follow that what is ascribed to the person is at the same time a property of both natures, but it is distinctively explained what nature it is according to which anything is ascribed to the person. Thus the Son of God was born of the seed of David according to the flesh, Rom 1:3. Also: Christ was put to death according to the flesh, and hath suffered for us in, or according to, the flesh, 1 Pet 3:18, 4:1.

See also Baier, *Compendium Theologiae Positivae*, 2:45–51; Chemnitz, *Loci Theologici*, 1:114; Hoenecke, *Evangelical Lutheran Dogmatics*, 3:85–87; Hunnius, *Epitome Credendorum*, 102–3; L. Hütter, *Compendium Locorum Theologicorum*, 2:923, 2:24–27; Gerhard, *On Christ*, 180–205; Graebner, *Outline of Doctrinal Theology*, 108–9; Koehler, *Summary of Christian Doctrine*, 90–91; Luthardt, *Kompendium der Dogmatik*, 201; J. Mueller, *Christian Dogmatics*, 273–75; Lindberg, *Christian Dogmatics*, 216–17; von Oettingen, *Lutherische Dogmatik*, 2.2:83; Philippi, *Kirchliche Glaubenslehre*, 4.1:258; F. Pieper, *Christian Dogmatics*, 2:152–223; Schaff, *Creeds of Christendom*, 1:319; Schaller, *Biblical Christology*, 65–68; H. Schmid, *Doctrinal Theology*, 313–14.

47. Chemnitz, *Two Natures*, 173–74. See discussion in J. Preus, *Second Martin*, 267–68.

would be "God with us" (Matt 1:23) witnesses to this genus. In the opposite direction, the "Son of Man" (i.e., Christ's humanity, whatever its other apocalyptic connotations may be) is spoken of as both eternal and the subject of the incarnation (Matt 22:42–43, John 6:62). These are not merely ways of speaking, but rather refer to the fact that Jesus Christ is a single theandric subject.

The second category, the *genus apotelesmaticum*, represents the communication of activities between the two natures within the hypostatic union.[48] Due to the concrete unity of the person of Christ, it is possible to say that when the man Jesus died, the Logos died. This is true, even though when considered in the abstract God the Son can neither die nor suffer.[49] Conversely, it is also possible to state that the man Jesus made the world even though the human nature of Christ did not always exist.[50] Indeed, both Hebrews 1 and John 1 ascribe creation to the single subject of Christ. This does not abrogate the integrity of either nature. The genus merely pertains to the concrete and not the abstract. Neither nature is transmuted into the other.

Moreover, it should be observed that this genus is not a uniquely Lutheran innovation, but simply a more systematic outworking of the scriptural teachings presented in the third and fifth ecumenical councils. The third ecumenical council asserted that Mary is the *Theotokos*, the God bearer. This does not mean that Mary somehow generated the divine substance (a mistake made by some modern Protestant Evangelical critics). Rather it means that the act of being born (which occurs to the humanity alone when considered in the abstract) pertains to the total theandric person in the concrete. If Christ is a divine subject with a human nature (as proclaimed by the fifth ecumenical council) then anything done or suffered by that subject in either nature must logically be

---

48. FC SD 8; *CT* 1031:

> Secondly, as to the execution of the office of Christ, the person does not act and work in, with, through, or according to only one nature, but in, according to, with, and through both natures, or, as the Council of Chalcedon expresses it, one nature operates in communion with the other what is a property of each. Therefore Christ is our Mediator, Redeemer, King, High Priest, Head, Shepherd, etc., not according to one nature only, whether it be the divine or the human, but according to both natures, as this doctrine has been treated more fully in other places.

See also Baier, *Compendium Theologiae Positivae*, 2:70–75; Chemnitz, *Loci Theologici*, 1:113; Hoenecke, *Evangelical Lutheran Dogmatics*, 3:99–102; Hunnius, *Epitome Credendorum*, 103–4; L. Hütter, *Compendium Locorum Theologicorum*, 2:927–28; Gerhard, *On Christ*, 288–97; Graebner, *Outline of Doctrinal Theology*, 110–12; Koehler, *Summary of Christian Doctrine*, 92–93; Lindberg, *Christian Dogmatics*, 225–26; Luthardt, *Kompendium der Dogmatik*, 204–5; J. Mueller, *Christian Dogmatics*, 284–86; von Oettingen, *Lutherische Dogmatik*, 2.2:83; Philippi, *Kirchliche Glaubenslehre*, 4.1:276–88; F. Pieper, *Christian Dogmatics*, 2:243–70; Schaff, *Creeds of Christendom*, 1:319; Schaller, *Biblical Christology*, 79–80; H. Schmid, *Doctrinal Theology*, 315–16.

49. Chemnitz, *Two Natures*, 215–30.

50. Luther writes in *AE* 41:103–4:

> Consequently Christ is God and man in one person because whatever is said of him as man must also be said of him as God, namely, Christ has died, and Christ is God; therefore God died—not the separated God, but God united with humanity . . . [similarly] whatever is said of God must also be said of man, namely, God created the world and is almighty; the man Christ is God, therefore the man Christ created the world and is almighty. The reason for this is that since God and man have become one person, it follows that this person bears the *idiomata* of both natures.

attributed to the total person.[51] Otherwise, Christ would be two separate subjects, and no real incarnation could properly be thought to have taken place.

As Chemnitz recognizes, this genus has significant implications for the doctrine of atonement. Because each nature participates in all actions of the other, the act of redemption "pertains to the person of Christ not according to either the divine or the human nature alone but to both. And the person in carrying out these works possesses activities or operations in both natures and not only in one."[52] In each act, both natures play their role. Vainio comments: "[The] *genus apotelesmaticum* illustrates that one nature is not passive when the other performs some deed, but works in co-operation with it."[53] Hence, Chemnitz writes that the divine nature "does not turn away from the suffering but permits the human nature to suffer and die, yet strengthens and sustains it so that it can endure the immeasurable burden of the sins of the world and the total wrath of God, thus making *those sufferings precious before God and saving the world*."[54]

Earlier in the text, Chemnitz made the participation of the divine person in the sufferings and death of the human nature integral to his understanding of how and why atonement is possible. In part echoing Anselm, Chemnitz posits that the human nature alone "would not have been an adequate ransom . . . for sin and God's wrath, which are boundless evils. For this reason, therefore, the price is so great and the merit of the suffering and death of Christ [so great] that it is the propitiation for the sins of the whole world." Due to the infinity of divine law and wrath, Christ had to be a divine person because "*the creature by itself could not have borne the enormous burden of the wrath of God* which was owed for the sins of the entire world."[55] Put succinctly then, the death of Christ must be the death of God himself in order to pay adequately for the infinite debt of sin. The divine person may be properly said to die through the human nature and thereby satisfy the righteous demands of the law. As we will see below, here Chemnitz stands in direct continuity with Luther.[56]

In holy scripture we find much support for the unity of Christ's agency. It is God's Son who is the subject sent into the flesh to be born (Gal 4:4). It is God's Son who has died for the sins of the whole world (Matt 20:28; John 4:10; 1 Cor 15:3; Gal 1:4; Eph 5:2; 1 Tim 2:5–6). It is the Lord of glory who was crucified (1 Cor 2:8) and the author of life

---

51. See *AE* 41:100. Luther writes:

Mary suckled God, rocked God to sleep, prepared broth and soup for God, etc. For God and man are one person, one Christ, one Son one Jesus, not two Christs, not two Sons, not two Jesuses; just as your son is not two sons, two Johns, two cobblers, even though he has two natures, body and soul, the body from you, the soul from God alone.

52. Chemnitz, *Two Natures*, 217.

53. Vainio, *Justification and Participation*, 137. Also see description and discussion in J. Preus, *Second Martin*, 267–68, 273, 289.

54. Chemnitz, *Two Natures*, 216 (emphasis added).

55. Ibid., 148 (emphasis added).

56. For discussions of Luther's view of atonement see the following sources: Althaus, *Theology of Martin Luther*, 201–23; Aulén, *Christus Victor*, 107–8; H. Bornkamm, *Luther's World of Thought*, 156–75; Elert, *Structure of Lutheranism*, 106–26; Forde, "Work of Christ," 2:47–65; Hinlicky, *Luther and the Beloved Community*, 66–138; Janz, *Westminster Handbook to Martin Luther*, 8–10; Kolb, *Martin Luther*, 118–124; Pinomaa, *Faith Victorious*, 46–57; Lohse, *Martin Luther's Theology*, 223–28; Watson, *Let God Be God!*, 116–25.

who was killed (Acts 3:15).[57] It is "God's own blood" that has paid for our sins (Acts 20:28).[58] Indeed this is necessary, because, as David tells us no mere human being is capable of paying for sin (Ps 49:7–9).[59]

The Epistle to the Hebrews also tells us that Christ's priesthood (his work on the cross) came by the "power of an indestructible life" (Heb 7:16). As a divine person, Jesus is able to stand before the Father eternally and thereby (unlike the earthly high priest) infinitely satisfy the law: "The former priests were many in number, because they were prevented by death from continuing in office, but he holds his priesthood permanently, *because he continues forever*. Consequently, he is able to save to the uttermost those who draw near to God through him, since *he always lives to make intercession for them*" (Heb 7:23–25, emphasis added). In a similar vein, elsewhere the author of Hebrews states that Christ offered himself up "through the eternal Spirit . . . without blemish to God" in order to "cleanse" our consciences (Heb 9:14). Hence, Christ's human nature was not offered alone, but was offered up through his divine nature (the "eternal Spirit") to the Father. By this he cleanses consciences; something God alone can do, since all sin is ultimately directed against him (Ps 51:4).

It might be objected that the phrase "eternal Spirit" refers to the Holy Spirit, which Christ possessed "without measure" (John 3:34). Nevertheless, unlike in many English translations, there is no definite article in the Greek and therefore the best and simplest understanding of the text is that this phrase refers to the eternal divine person and not the Holy Spirit.[60] Ultimately then, all these passages bear witness to the fact that as a single theandric subject, Christ is the agent and the mediator of salvation according to both his natures.[61]

The teaching concerning the unity of Christ's agency and mediatorship was a highly important issue during the period of the composition of the Formula of Concord. This is mainly because of the heresies introduced into the Lutheran Church by Andreas Osiander and Francisco Stancarus.[62] Nevertheless, the problem goes back much farther in the

---

57. See *AE* 41:105.

58. Though this translation is disputed, generally early Lutherans followed it. See Luther's comments on it in *AE* 41:105–6. Even if we accepted a different translation, our case for the genus would not fall apart.

59. See brief comment on this verse in Chemnitz, *Examination of the Council of Trent*, 499.

60. Lenski, *Epistle to the Hebrews and the Epistle of James*, 298–99.

61. FC SD 3; *CT* 935.

62. See the following sources on Andreas Osiander and his controversy: Bente, *Historical Introductions*, 152–59; Dorner, *Doctrine of the Person of Christ*, 4:107–15; Dorner, *History of Protestant Theology*, 1:353–69; González, *History of Christian Thought*, 3:114–18; Hamann, "Righteousness of Faith before God," 137–62; Kolb, "Historical Background," 36–41; Lawrenz, "On Justification," 149–74; McGrath, *Iustia Dei*, 213; O. Olson, "Matthias Flacius," 86; Pelikan, *Christian Tradition*, 4:150–52; Preger, *Matthias Flacius Illyricu*, 1:205–98; A. Ritschl, *Christian Doctrine of Justification and Reconciliation*, 214–33; O. Ritschl, *Dogmengeschichte des Protestantismus*, 2:455–88; Schaff, *Creeds of Christendom*, 1:271–74; R. Seeberg, *Text-Book of the History of Doctrines*, 2:369–74; Strehle, *Catholic Roots of the Protestant Gospel*, 73–78; Vainio, *Justification and Participation in Christ*, 95–118. Also see A. Osiander, *Von dem Einigen Mittler Jhesu Christo*. See the follow sources on Stancarus: Bente, *Historical Introductions*, 159; Vainio, *Justification and Participation in Christ*, 106–9; G. Williams, *Radical Reformation*, 854–55, 883–85, 999, 1106.

history of the Latin tradition. At least since the Tome of Leo (though probably extending even to Augustine), western Christology has had a problematic tendency towards dividing the agency of Christ.[63] By contrast, the early Alexandrian tradition emphasized the unity of the divine-human agency in Christ.[64] For example, in *On the Unity of Christ*, St. Cyril writes:

> Such things [hunger, suffering, etc.] would not be at all fitting to the Word, if we considered him nakedly, as it were, not yet made flesh or before he had descended into the self-emptying. Your thoughts are right on this. But once he is made man and emptied out, what harm can this inflict on him? Just as we say that the flesh became his very own in an economic appropriation according to the terms of the unification. So he is "made like his brethren in all things except sin alone. (Heb 2:17)[65]

Again, the patriarch states:

> In my opinion it is the height of absurdity, as I have already said, to find fault with the Only Begotten, when he did not disdain the economy and become flesh, and accuse him of having militated against his own glory by choosing inappropriately to suffer in the flesh. My good friend, this is a matter of the salvation of the whole world. And since on this account he wished to suffer, even though he was beyond the power of suffering in his nature as God, then he wrapped himself in flesh that was capable of suffering, and revealed it as his very own, so that even the suffering might be said to be his because it was his own body which suffered and no one else's. Since the manner of economy shows to choose both to suffer in the flesh, and not to suffer in the Godhead (for the self-same was at once God and man) then our opponents surely argue in vain and foolishly debase the power of the mystery, when they think they have made a worthy synthesis.[66]

63. See discussion in the following: Dorner, *Doctrine of the Person of Christ*, 3:86–92; G. Evans, "Eutyches, Nestorius, and Chalcedon," 246; Hägglund, *History of Theology*, 98; J. Kelly, *Early Christian Doctrines*, 334–38; Pelikan, *Christian Tradition*, 1:263–64; H. Rahner, "Leo der Große, der Papst des Konzils," 1:323–39; R. Seeberg, *Text-Book of the History of Doctrines*, 1:268 –70.

64. See interesting discussion in Galtier, "Saint Cyrille d'Alexandrie," 1:345–87.

65. Cyril of Alexandria, *Unity of Christ*, 107.

66. Ibid., 117–18.

The later Greek patristic tradition (much like the Lutheran[67]) followed Cyril in emphasizing the unity of divine and human agency in Christ.[68] Standing at the end of the development of Greek patristic Christology, John of Damascus states:

> For His flesh did not suffer through the divinity in the same way that the divinity *acted through the flesh*, because the flesh served as an instrument of the divinity. So, even though from the first instant of conception *there was no divisions whatsoever of either form, but all the actions of each form at all times belonged to one Person*, we nevertheless in no way confuse these *things which were done inseparably* . . . Christ acts through each of His natures and *in Him each nature acts in communion with the other*.[69]

By contrast, Leo (the bishop of Rome in the mid-fifth century) in his letter regarding the christological controversy that had erupted in the East (first between Nestorius and Cyril, and later due to the heresy of Eutyches[70]) took a different tact. Instead of emphasizing the unity of Christ's agency, the Western patriarch emphasized the duality of his operations to the point of giving the impression that it was possible to divide them

67. See observations in Lienhard, *Luther*, 341; Lohse, *Martin Luther's Theology*, 228–29. Also see Yeago, "Bread of Life," 257–79. Yeago writes: "Luther certainly knew the main lines of the Neo-Chalcedonian Christology from the *Sentences* of Peter Lombard, who cites John of Damascus at considerable length, and in his more technical writing in Christology shows himself thoroughly conversant with its conceptual subtleties. For our purposes, it will be sufficient to note that Luther's Christological priorities, as outlined above, are precisely those of the whole Cyrilline tradition. Luther's insistence on the inseparability and co-inherence of the two natures locates his Christology squarely in this succession; the doctrine of the deified and life-giving flesh of Christ is the unmistakeable signature theme of the Cyrilline tradition" (269). Again he writes: "The Christology on which Luther's theology of faith . . . depends is . . . identical with Patristic orthodoxy, as articulated at Nicaea, Ephesus, Chalcedon, and II Constantinople. Luther's loyalty to the catholic dogmatic tradition is not something extrinsic to his evangelical message, arising perhaps from a conservative temperament. On the contrary, apart from the context of catholic dogma, Luther's evangelical convictions make no sense whatsoever. In fact, we must go further and say that this distinction is ours, not his: for Luther, catholic dogma *itself* provides the substance of his distinctively 'evangelical' theology" (257). Yeago is probably correct that Luther never read Cyril. On the other hand, it is very hard to tell whether he received Cyril's theology through Peter Lombard's citations of John of Damascus. Peter does not really use said citations in order to construct a Cyrillian Christology or give much emphasis to the unity of the person of Christ. He, like almost all Western theologians, constructs a Leonine Christology. In other words, reading the *Sentences* and observing which citations are selected, one does not really get the impression of John as being a sort of champion of the unity of Christ. In any case, almost every theologian in the Middle Ages was exposed to the same text-book, and did not come up with a Cyrilian Christology. Historical influence is obviously very difficult to show, but it will be our suggestion below that Luther's christological emphasis might be due primarily to his concept of the self-donating character of promise. An alternative explanation comes from Graham White, *Luther as Nominalist*, 213–99. Although many authors have described the Moderni as having a quasi-Nestorian Christology, White shows that there is much continuity with Luther's later position. Some of this continuity perhaps points in the direction of a greater appreciation of the unity of Christ's person than the earlier tradition. Of course, much more research will have to be done on this question in the future and it is indeed premature to make a judgment now.

68. See modern example of this in Bulgakov, *Lamb of God*, 247–60.

69. *Orthodox Faith*, 3.15, in John of Damascus, *Saint John of Damascus*, 311 (emphasis added).

70. Dorner, *Doctrine of the Person of Christ*, 3:51–83; G. Evans, "Eutyches, Nestorius, and Chalcedon," 243–47; Hägglund, *History of Theology*, 89–106; J. Kelly, *Early Christian Doctrines*, 310–33; McGuckin, *St. Cyril of Alexandria*; Pelikan, *Christian Tradition*, 1:226–77; N. Russell, *Cyril of Alexandria*, 31–64; R. Seeberg, *Text-Book of the History of Doctrines*, 1:261–65; Tillich, *History of Christian Thought*, 79–90.

into distinctly human and divine acts: "For each form does what is proper to it with the co-operation of the other; that is the Word performing what appertains to the Word, and the flesh carrying out what appertains to the flesh. One of them sparkles with miracles, the other succumbs to injuries."[71] Though it is perfectly correct to recognize a duality of operations within the person of Christ in the abstract, it is as we have seen problematic to do so in the concrete. Statements like the one above are problematic because they give undue emphasis to the duality of the operation of the two natures. Thereby they denigrate the integrity and unity of the person. As the first part of the statement makes clear, Leo does not intend to divide the person of Christ. This being said, there is no sense for Leo that the two natures operate in and through one another in the concrete. He describes them as two quasi-separate subjects cooperating with one another.[72]

Later Western theologians such as Anselm of Canterbury, Peter Lombard, and Thomas Aquinas continued to operate within the tradition of Leo.[73] According to these

---

71. Leo the Great, *Letter 28*, 4; *NPNFb* 12:41. Leo goes on to write:
GOD in that "in the beginning was the Word, and the Word was with GOD, and the Word was GOD;" man in that "the Word became flesh and dwelt in us." GOD in that "all things were made by Him, and without Him was nothing made:" man in that "He was made of a woman, made under law." The nativity of the flesh was the manifestation of human nature: the childbearing of a virgin is the proof of Divine power. The infancy of a babe is shown in the humbleness of its cradle: the greatness of the Most High is proclaimed by the angels' voices. He whom Herod treacherously endeavours to destroy is like ourselves in our earliest stage: but He whom the Magi delight to worship on their knees is the LORD of all. So too when He came to the baptism of John, His forerunner, lest He should not be known through the veil of flesh which covered His Divinity, the Father's voice thundering from the sky, said, "This is My beloved Son, in whom I am well pleased." And thus Him whom the devil's craftiness attacks as man, the ministries of angels serve as GOD. To be hungry and thirsty, to be weary, and to sleep, is clearly human: but to satisfy 5,000 men with five loaves, and to bestow on the woman of Samaria living water, droughts of which can secure the drinker from thirsting any more, to walk upon the surface of the sea with feet that do not sink, and to quell the risings of the waves by rebuking the winds, is, without any doubt, Divine. Just as therefore, to pass over many other instances, it is not part of the same nature to be moved to tears of pity for a dead friend, and when the stone that closed the four-days' grave was removed, to raise that same friend to life with a voice of command: or, to hang on the cross, and turning day to night, to make all the elements tremble: or, to be pierced with nails, and yet open the gates of paradise to the robber's faith: so it is not part of the same nature to say, "I and the Father are one," and to say, "the Father is greater than." For although in the LORD Jesus Christ GOD and man is one person, yet the source of the degradation, which is shared by both, is one, and the source of the glory, which is shared by both, is another. For His manhood, which is less than the Father, comes from our side: His Godhead, which is equal to the Father, comes from the Father.

72. See good critique of Pope Leo I in Robert Jenson, *Systematic Theology*, 1:130–33; Paulson, *Lutheran Theology*, 94–96.

73. Anselm, *Cur Deus Homo?*, 2.28, in *Scholastic Miscellany*, 177. Anselm writes:
No man besides him ever gave to God, by dying, what he was not necessarily going to lose at some time, or paid what he did not owe. But this man freely offered to the Father what he would never have lost by any necessity, and paid for sinners what he did not owe himself.
As we can see, the accent here falls heavily on the activity of the human nature. We will briefly examine Anselm's atonement theology in the next chapter. See Lombard, *Sentences*, 3:81–84. Also see discussion in Dorner, *Doctrine of the Person of Christ*, 3:16–17; Roseman, *Peter Lombard*, 118–43. See *ST* 3a. 26, 1–2; *BF* 50:206–13. Aquinas writes:
Respondeo dicendum quod in mediatore duo possumus considerare, primo quidem, rationem medii; secundo, officium coniungendi. Est autem de ratione medii quod distet ab utroque extremorum, coniungit autem mediator per hoc quod ea quae unius sunt, defert ad alterum. Neutrum autem horum potest convenire Christo secundum quod Deus, sed solum secundum quod

theologians, Christ was mediator only according to his human nature, since it was that nature alone that had died and had been offered up in the work of atonement.[74] Though they all agree that the human nature could not have performed its task apart from the divine person, they nevertheless overwhelming emphasized the human agency of Christ in a manner that gave the impression that it was a quasi-independent agent of redemption.

Particularly in Aquinas's Christology, the medieval/Roman Catholic teaching that grace activates human agency is given full expression. According to his general description, the Angelic Doctor posits that the human nature of Christ possesses the ability to work salvation because of a special ontic bond with the Second Person of the Trinity and because it has a superabundance of created and uncreated grace. The impression of divided agency (noted above) is unabated by the fact that the *enhypostasis-anhypostasis* Christology is endorsed.[75] On the contrary, the union of the two natures is compared to union of grace that occurs between God and believers, although it is claimed that the former union is much closer and in fact surpasses the latter.[76] When discussing the

---

homo. Nam secundum quod Deus, non differt a patre et spiritu sancto in natura et potestate dominii, nec etiam pater et spiritus sanctus aliquid habent quod non sit filii, ut sic possit id quod est patris vel spiritus sancti, quasi quod est aliorum, ad alios deferre. Sed utrumque convenit ei inquantum est homo. Quia, secundum quod est homo, distat et a Deo in natura, et ab hominibus in dignitate et gratiae et gloriae. Inquantum etiam est homo, competit ei coniungere homines Deo, praecepta et dona hominibus exhibendo, et pro hominibus ad Deum satisfaciendo et interpellando. Et ideo verissime dicitur mediator secundum quod homo.

See discussion of Aquinas's Christology in the following: B. Davies, *Thought of Thomas Aquinas*, 321–38; Dorner, *Doctrine of the Person of Christ*, 3:29–39; Farrell, *Companion to the Summa*, 203–48; Glenn, *Tour of the Summa*, 351–57; Gratsch, *Aquinas' Summa*, 235–38.

74. This idea appears to go back as far as Augustine. See Augustine, *City of God*, 11.2; *NPNFa* 2:206. Augustine writes:

For this is the Mediator between God and men, the man Christ Jesus. For it is as man that He is the Mediator and the Way. Since, if the way lieth between him who goes, and the place whither he goes, there is hope of his reaching it; but if there be no way, or if he know not where it is, what boots it to know whither he should go? Now the only way that is infallibly secured against all mistakes, is when the very same person is at once God and man, God our end, man our way.

In fairness to Augustine and the later tradition, their intention appears to be anti-Arian. In other words, it seems to be implicit in their position that they do not wish to characterize the Logos as a lesser go-between bringing together God and the world.

75. *ST* 3a. 4, 2–3; *BF* 48:120–25:

Ad primum ergo dicendum quod huiusmodi locutiones non sunt extendendae, tanquam propriae, sed pie sunt exponendae, ubicumque a sacris doctoribus ponuntur; ut dicamus hominem assumptum, quia eius natura est assumpta; et quia assumptio terminata est ad hoc quod filius Dei sit homo. Ad secundum dicendum quod hoc nomen homo significat naturam humanam in concreto, prout scilicet est in aliquo supposito. Et ideo, sicut non possumus dicere quod suppositum sit assumptum, ita non possumus dicere quod homo sit assumptus. Ad tertium dicendum quod filius Dei non est homo quem assumpsit; sed cuius naturam assumpsit.

76. *ST* 3a. 2, 9–10; *BF* 48:72–79. Aquinas comments regarding the greatness of the union in saying: Respondeo dicendum quod unio importat coniunctionem aliquorum in aliquo uno. Potest ergo unio incarnationis dupliciter accipi, uno modo, ex parte eorum quae coniunguntur; et alio modo, ex parte eius in quo coniunguntur. Et ex hac parte huiusmodi unio habet praeeminentiam inter alias uniones, nam unitas personae divinae, in qua uniuntur duae naturae, est maxima. Non autem habet praeeminentiam ex parte eorum quae coniunguntur." He also asserts that the Incarnation is a union of grace similar (though not identical to God's union with believers) in stating: "Respondeo dicendum quod, sicut in secunda parte dictum est, gratia dupliciter dicitur, uno modo, ipsa voluntas Dei gratis aliquid dantis; alio modo, ipsum gratuitum donum Dei. Indiget

worship of Christ, Aquinas claims that Christ's flesh can be worshiped in the concrete unity of the incarnation much like a robe can be honored along with the king who is wearing it.[77] The problem with this analogy is that whereas Christ's humanity subsists in the person of the Logos, a king's robe does not subsist in his person but is rather an independent entity. Aquinas then goes a step further and reveals that when considered in the abstract, the human nature cannot really be worship (*latria*) at all, but can only be venerated (*dulia*).[78] That is to say, Christ's human nature possesses no more exalted status than that of the glorified saints.

In describing the work of Christ, Aquinas's accent falls heavily on the description of Christ's human psychology. Christ's soul was capable of giving the highest obedience because it was replete with created and uncreated grace.[79] His speculative intellect always

---

autem humana natura gratuita Dei voluntate ad hoc quod elevetur in Deum, cum hoc sit supra facultatem naturae suae. Elevatur autem humana natura in Deum dupliciter. Uno modo, per operationem, qua scilicet sancti cognoscunt et amant Deum. Alio modo, per esse personale, qui quidem modus est singularis Christo, in quo humana natura assumpta est ad hoc quod sit personae filii Dei. Manifestum est autem quod ad perfectionem operationis requiritur quod potentia sit perfecta per habitum, sed quod natura habeat esse in supposito suo, non fit mediante aliquo habitu. Sic igitur dicendum est quod, si gratia accipiatur ipsa Dei voluntas gratis aliquid faciens, vel gratum seu acceptum aliquem habens, unio incarnationis facta est per gratiam, sicut et unio sanctorum ad Deum per cognitionem et amorem. Si vero gratia dicatur ipsum gratuitum Dei donum, sic ipsum quod est humanam naturam esse unitam personae divinae, potest dici quaedam gratia, inquantum nullis praecedentibus meritis hoc est factum, non autem ita quod sit aliqua gratia habitualis qua mediante talis unio fiat.

77. *ST* 3a. 25, 2; *BF* 50:188–90:
Respondeo dicendum quod, sicut supra dictum est, honor adorationis debetur hypostasi subsistenti, tamen ratio honoris potest esse aliquid non subsistens, propter quod honoratur persona cui illud inest. Adoratio igitur humanitatis Christi dupliciter potest intelligi. Uno modo, ut sit eius sicut rei adoratae. Et sic adorare carnem Christi nihil est aliud quam adorare verbum Dei incarnatum, sicut adorare vestem regis nihil est aliud quam adorare regem vestitum. Et secundum hoc, adoratio humanitatis Christi est adoratio latriae.

78. *ST* 3a. 25, 2; *BF* 50:191:
Alio modo potest intelligi adoratio humanitatis Christi quae fit ratione humanitatis Christi perfectae omni munere gratiarum. Et sic adoratio humanitatis Christi non est adoratio latriae, sed adoratio duliae. Ita scilicet quod una et eadem persona Christi adoretur adoratione latriae propter suam divinitatem et adoratione duliae propter perfectionem humanitatis.

79. *ST* 3a. 7, 1; *BF*, 49:6:
Respondeo dicendum quod necesse est ponere in Christo gratiam habitualem, propter tria. Primo quidem, propter unionem animae illius ad verbum Dei. Quanto enim aliquod receptivum propinquius est causae influenti, tanto magis participat de influentia ipsius. Influxus autem gratiae est a Deo, secundum illud Psalmi, *gratiam et gloriam dabit dominus*. Et ideo maxime fuit conveniens ut anima illa reciperet influxum divinae gratiae. Secundo, propter nobilitatem illius animae, cuius operationes oportebat propinquissime attingere ad Deum per cognitionem et amorem. Ad quod necesse est elevari humanam naturam per gratiam. Tertio, propter habitudinem ipsius Christi ad genus humanum. Christus enim, inquantum homo, est mediator Dei et hominum, ut dicitur I Tim. II. Et ideo oportebat quod haberet gratiam etiam in alios redundantem, secundum illud Ioan. I, *de plenitudine eius omnes accepimus, gratiam pro gratia*. Ad primum ergo dicendum quod Christus est verus Deus secundum personam et naturam divinam. Sed quia cum unitate personae remanet distinctio naturarum, ut ex supra dictis patet, anima Christi non est per suam essentiam divina. Unde oportet quod fiat divina per participationem, quae est secundum gratiam. Ad secundum dicendum quod Christo, secundum quod est naturalis filius Dei, debetur hereditas aeterna, quae est ipsa beatitudo increata, per increatum actum cognitionis et amoris Dei, eundem scilicet quo pater cognoscit et amat seipsum. Cuius actus anima capax non erat, propter differentiam naturae. Unde oportebat quod attingeret ad Deum per actum fruitionis

enjoyed the highest vision of the divine substance possible (*visio beatific*).[80] Because of these gifts of divine grace, he was capable of becoming mediator by his obedient death. This mediatorship, as we noted above, is exercised according to his human nature alone.[81]

Ultimately, the concept of Christ presented by Aquinas greatly divides his person and work. Such a division mirrors Aquinas's compatiblistic conception of human agency's relationship to divine grace.[82] In other words, Christ's humanity (much like Mary in later Catholic teaching) stands as the exemplar of nature cooperating with grace in order to achieve the end of salvation. Aquinas envisions redemption as a process wherein nature gains grace as a predicate of its being. By this augmentation, nature develops its own grace infused agency in such a manner as to be able to gain salvation by its own merit.[83]

---

creatum. Qui quidem esse non potest nisi per gratiam. Similiter etiam, inquantum est verbum Dei, habuit facultatem omnia bene operandi operatione divina. Sed quia, praeter operationem divinam, oportet ponere operationem humanam, ut infra patebit; oportuit in eo esse habitualem gratiam, per quam huiusmodi operatio in eo esset perfecta. Ad tertium dicendum quod humanitas Christi est instrumentum divinitatis, non quidem sicut instrumentum inanimatum, quod nullo modo agit sed solum agitur, sed tanquam instrumentum animatum anima rationali, quod ita agit quod etiam agitur. Et ideo, ad convenientiam actionis, oportuit eum habere gratiam habitualem.

80. *ST* 3a. 7, 4; *BF* 49:14, 16:

Sed contra est quod dicitur Heb. XI, quod *fides est argumentum non apparentium*. Sed Christo nihil fuit non apparens, secundum illud quod dixit ei Petrus, Ioan. ult., *tu omnia nosti*. Ergo in Christo non fuit fides. Respondeo dicendum quod, sicut in secunda parte dictum est, obiectum fidei est res divina non visa. Habitus autem virtutis, sicut et quilibet alius, recipit speciem ab obiecto. Et ideo, excluso quod res divina non sit visa, excluditur ratio fidei. Christus autem in primo instanti suae conceptionis plene vidit Deum per essentiam, ut infra patebit. Unde fides in eo esse non potuit.

81. *ST* 3a. 26, 2; *BF* 50:212:

Ad tertium dicendum quod, licet auctoritative peccatum auferre conveniat Christo secundum quod est Deus, tamen satisfacere pro peccato humani generis convenit ei secundum quod homo. Et secundum hoc dicitur Dei et hominum mediator.

82. This tendency in Catholic Christology has continued to the present. Karl Rahner divides the person of Christ even more than does Aquinas. He describes Christ as God's perfect "self-communication" and the perfect "human response." Christ is not seen as God's own unilateral self-donation, but as divine and human mutual self-donation. We are left with a hyper synergism and a divided Christ who amounts to little more than a human subject somehow attached to the Second Person of the Trinity. In reading Karl Rahner, one often feels that they are reading Schleiermacher in Roman Catholic garb. See discussion of Christology in K. Rahner, *Foundations of Christian Faith*, 178–322. Assuming that their position is a correct understanding of Chalcedon, and not simply a highly problematic interpretation of it based on Leo's inappropriate division between the two natures, some Roman Catholic thinkers have attacked Luther. See Ratzinger, *Principles of Catholic Theology*, 260–61. Ratzinger (now Pope Benedict XVI) writes that Luther's monergism fails to appreciate a proper (i.e., Leonine) understanding of Christology. The two natures doctrine when properly understood should promote a bilateral movement of the human subject's free will being activated by divine grace:

The result [of making the Eucharist about forgiveness, and not personal sacrifice to God through Christ] was not only the banishing from the liturgy of the context of *communio*, the constitutive element of the Church, but also the obfuscation of the *two-sidedness of the Chalcedonian Christology, which not only knew Christ as the God who descended to earth and in whom God accepted man, who, in the God-man, became capable of responding to God precisely as man* and, in Christ, could again become sacrifice." (emphasis added)

In other words, the incarnation is not just God's unilateral self-donation to humanity; it is also humanity's cooperative movement towards God.

83. See summary in Joseph Wawrykow, "Grace," 192–222.

Likewise, Christ's human nature is given the ability by its unique bond with the Second Person of the Trinity to bring about and mediator salvation.

The tendency to divide the agency of Christ persisted in the Western Christendom and its tradition and found strong support at the time of the Reformation in the writings of Ulrich Zwingli, Francisco Stancarus, and Andreas Osiander. In the case of Zwingli, this division of christological agency finds its most prominent expression in the concept of *alloeosis*.[84] For Zwingli, *alloeosis* functioned as a hermeneutic rule whereby biblical texts were divided up on the basis of whether they described the actions of Christ's human or divines natures. For example, texts where Christ healed people were deemed to be speaking about his divine nature alone. Texts where Christ was born, ate, suffered, and died were deemed to refer merely to his human nature. This sparked bitter criticism from Luther, which we will discuss below. To their credit, later Reformed theologians broke with Zwingli and accepted a much stronger conception of the unity of Christ's agency.[85] In this they followed Calvin, who agreed with Lutherans that Christ should be considered mediator according to both natures.[86]

A similarly problematic interpretation can be found in the writings of Francisco Stancarus in the 1550s. As odd as it may seem, although Stancarus supported the Reformation, he continued to be enamored with the theology of the older scholastics (*via antiqua*) rather than the Reformers themselves.[87] Because this was the case, he was more inclined to follow the older Latin tradition in its claim that Christ was mediator according to his humanity alone.[88]

This brings us to one of the most prominent Lutheran heretics of the sixteenth century, Andreas Osiander. Historically, Osiander has been remembered for propagating the opposite heresy of that proposed by Stancarus.[89] That is to say, whereas Stancarus claimed that Christ was the mediator of redemption according to his human nature alone, Osiander claimed that Christ saved through the infusion of his divine nature and righteousness into believers. In this sense, the divine nature became the mediator of salvation, apart from the work of the human nature. The authors of the later Formula of Concord remembered Osiander (although they did not directly mention him by name)

---

84. See Huldrych Zwingli's own discussion of the concept in Zwingli, "Friendly Exegesis," 2:319–22. Also see Baur, *Zwinglis Theologie*, 2:425, 460, 473, 484–510; Dorner, *Doctrine of the Person of Christ*, 4:134–40; Hägglund, *History of Theology*, 243–44; Locher, *Zwingli's Thought*, 173–76; Potter, *Zwingli*, 43, 305, 312–13, 336; O. Ritschl, *Dogmengeschichte des Protestantismus*, 3:108–22; R. Seeberg, *Text-Book of the History of Doctrines*, 2:321, 324; Stephens, *Theology of Huldrych Zwingli*, 112–17. Also see Luther's polemic against this concept in *AE* 37:206–14, 230–36.

85. Heppe, *Reformed Dogmatics*, 445–46.

86. *ICR* 2.14.2–3, in Calvin, *Institutes of the Christian Religion*, 1:484–87.

87. Vainio, *Justification and Participation*, 107n57.

88. Arand et al., *Lutheran Confessions*, 220–21, 225–26; Bente, *Historical Introductions*, 159; O. Ritschl, *Dogmengeschichte des Protestantismus*, 2:325, 475, 482; R. Seeberg, *Text-Book of the History of Doctrines*, 2:374; Vainio, *Justification and Participation*, 107–9.

89. Arand et al., *Lutheran Confessions*, 217–27; Bente, *Historical Introductions*, 152–59; Dorner, *Doctrine of the Person of Christ*, 4:107–15; Dorner, *History of Protestant Theology*, 1:353–69; González, *History of Christian Thought*, 3:114–18; Hamann, "Righteousness of Faith before God," 137–62; Hirsch, *Theologie von Andreas Osiander*, 172–202; Kolb, "Historical Background," 36–41; Lawrenz, "On Justification," 149–74; Schmauk and Benze, *Confessional Princinple*, 599–600.

mainly for his rejection of a purely forensic doctrine of justification. Instead of basing all righteousness on Christ's work, claimed the authors, Osiander had taught that through our personal sanctification humanity could become acceptable to God.[90]

In recent years this interpretation has been challenged by a number of scholars. For example, Olli-Pekka Vainio has suggested an alternative interpretation to the traditional reading of Osiander. Although Osiander's position seems radically different than that of Stancarus, claims Vainio, a closer reading of Osiander suggests that the two may be less far apart than one thinks. According Vainio, it is unclear whether or not Osiander believed that the works produced by the indwelling of Christ counted towards one's relationship with God, as Chemnitz and Melanchthon charged that they did.[91] Stephen Strehle has similarly observed that even Joachim Mörlin, (one of the bitterest critics of Osiander) thought that Melanchthon's accusations of works righteousness were essentially baseless.[92] In examining the documents themselves, Vainio states that there is some ambiguity regarding the role of works,[93] but in certain passages Osiander appears to suggest that they ultimately do not affect one's relationship to God.[94] Vainio writes: "When Osiander speaks about God acting wrongly if he reckons as righteous someone who is not righteous *in re*, he does not refer to human properties but to God, who is the justifying righteousness through faith."[95]

Secondly, according to Vainio, Osiander's rejection of a purely forensic justification was mainly the result of his inability to accept communication of attributes in a manner commensurate with the Lutheran tradition. Osiander held that the divine substance was not communicable and therefore he utterly disavowed Luther's understanding of the communication of activities between the two natures. Because of this, he taught that Christ had died only according to his human nature and that this was sufficient for the forgiveness of sins.[96] Although forgiveness was a positive condition for the release of divine grace, in and of itself, it was not sufficient to reconcile humanity with God.[97] Rather, forgiveness does not mean that we can stand as positively righteous before God. Christ's death and obedience to God was merely human righteousness, which was always based on the performance of the law.[98] The sort of righteousness that would ultimately avail before God was divine righteousness, a predicate of God's personal reality alone.[99] God could only recognize humanity as righteous by looking at his own eternal and immutable

---

90. FC SD 3; *CT* 917–37.

91. Vainio, *Justification and Participation*, 105–6. Also see Strehle, *Catholic Roots of the Protestant Gospel*, 73–75.

92. Strehle, *Catholic Roots of the Protestant Gospel*, 74.

93. Vainio, *Justification and Participation*, 101–2.

94. Ibid., 102.

95. Ibid.

96. Stehle, *Catholic Roots of the Protestant Gospel*, 76–78; Vainio, *Justification and Participation*, 99.

97. Vainio, *Justification and Participation*, 100.

98. Ibid., 102.

99. Strehle, *Catholic Roots of the Protestant Gospel*, 75–78; Vainio, *Justification and Participation*, 102.

righteousness dwelling in them.[100] Hence, justification consisted not only of the imputation of the forgiveness of sins won by the death of Christ's human nature, but also of the indwelling of his infinite and eternal divine righteousness.[101] According to Vainio, the christological implications of this position are clear: "What Christ does is therefore separated from who Christ is."[102]

The Wittenberg reformation's response to these various challenges developed over time and found its final form in the confessional statements of the Formula of Concord. In the 1520s, Luther rejected Zwingli's teaching regarding the duality of Christ's agency in redemption, by noting that it was clearly necessary for God's infinite and eternal righteousness to be satisfied by God's own death. Luther writes in the *Confession Concerning Christ's Supper* (1528):

> Beware, beware, I say, of this alloeosis, for it is the devil's mask since it will finally construct a kind of Christ after whom I would not want to be a Christian, that is, a Christ who is and does no more in his passion and his life than any other ordinary saint. For if I believe that only the human nature suffered for me, the Christ would be a poor savior for me, in fact, he himself would need a Savior. In short, it is indescribable what the devil attempts with this alloesosis.[103]

In the Galatians Commentary (1531–1535), Luther is even clearer:

> In addition, it follows that our sins are so great, so infinite and invincible, that the whole world could not make satisfaction for even one of them. Certainly the greatness of the ransom—namely, the blood of the Son of God—makes it sufficiently clear that we can neither make satisfaction for our sin nor prevail over it *. . . But we should note here the infinite greatness of the price paid for it.* Then it will be evident that its power is so great that it could not be removed by any means except that the Son of God be given for it. Anyone who considers this carefully will understand the one word "sin" includes the eternal wrath of God and the entire kingdom of Satan, and that sin is no trifle.[104]

Finally, in *On the Council and the Church* (1539), Luther writes in the midst of another polemic against Zwingli:

> We Christians should know that if God is not on the scale to give it weight, we, on our side, sink to the ground. I *mean it this way: if it cannot be said that God died for us, but only a man, we are lost; but if God's death and a dead God lie in the balance, his side* goes down and ours goes up like a light and empty scale. Yet he can also readily go up again, or leap out of the scale! *But he could not sit on the scale unless he had become man like us,* so that it could be called God's dying, God's martyrdom, God's blood, and God's death. For God in his own nature cannot die; but now that God and man are united in one person it is called God's death when the man dies who is one substance or person with God.[105]

---

100. Vainio, *Justification and Participation*, 99.

101. Ibid., 98–99.

102. Ibid., 99.

103. *AE* 37:209–10.

104. *AE* 26:33 (emphasis added).

105. *AE* 41:103–4 (emphasis added).

Luther's point here is clear. One must recognize a communication of activities between the two natures in order to posit an adequate atonement for sin. God's own infinite person is the only thing that can counteract God's own infinite wrath and judgment. The divine person of the Son works through the human nature to achieve this by his death on the cross. By entering into solidarity with humanity and the law of condemnation, God the Son becomes capable of representing other human beings on the "scale" of divine justice.

A generation later, the negative response to Stancarus was more muted, though still real. Melanchthon was the first to take up of the task of answering him, though unfortunately his response reveals a somewhat underdeveloped Christology.[106] Melanchthon stated that Stancarus was wrong in claiming that Christ was mediator and redeemer only according to his humanity. What Stancarus was not taking into account was that Christ not only needed to atone for sin (which was primarily, though not exclusively, the work of Christ's humanity), but to defeat death and the devil (primarily the work of Christ's divine nature).[107] Melanchthon's response is inadequate because it lacks a systematic development of how the two natures relate to one another in the work of redemption. Reading his treatment, there is little emphasis on the fact that the divine nature acts through the human nature in order to redeem. This makes sense, in that a reading of his various editions of *Loci Communes* reveals that Melanchthon generally seems to have regarded the communication of attributes to be merely verbal.[108]

Melanchthon's criticism of Osiander was mainly directed at his false understanding of justification in relation to sanctification.[109] It fell to Flacius to give a more thorough critique to Osiander's false understanding of the work of Christ. Flacius did not explicitly develop the theme of the communication of attributes as did Chemnitz. Nevertheless,

---

106. Vainio, *Justification and Participation*, 108–9.

107. Ibid., 108. This is also reflected in Melanchthon's explanation of the work of Christ in his later editions of *Loci Communes*. See Melanchthon, *Melanchthon on Christian Doctrine*, 33. The older Melanchthon (in the heat of battle against Osiander) summed up the reasons for the two natures well:

First, note that inasmuch as mankind fell into sin, the one to be punished and to pay the penalty had to be a man, but one without sin. Secondly, in order for the payment to be equal and even better, the one who pays is not simply a man or an angel, but is a divine person. Thirdly, no angel and no man could have borne the great burden of divine wrath against our sin. For that reason, the Son of God, who is omnipotent, out of immeasurable love and mercy toward men, laid upon himself this great wrath. Fourthly, no angel and no man is able to walk in the mysterious counsel of the divine Majesty. The Mediator prays for all men and especially for every petitioner, and the divine Majesty hears their desires, and then acts accordingly. All this pertains to an omnipotent person. In the Letter to the Hebrews, when only the High Priest enters into the *Sanctum sanctorum* (Holy of Holies), when only the High Priest, and no one else, is allowed to go into the secret altar in the temple, it means that only the Redeemer is to be in the secret counsel of divine Majesty, and wholly see and know the heart of the Father. Fifthly, no angel and no man might have conquered death and taken life again, for this belongs only to an omnipotent person. Sixthly, the Redeemer is to be a power [kräftig] within us; he bears and sustains our weak nature, beholds the hearts of all men, hears all sighs, prays for all, is and lives in the faithful, and creates in them new obedience, righteousness, and eternal life. All this pertains only to an omnipotent person; Immanuel, i.e. God *with* us and *in* us.

108. See brief discussion in Hinlicky, *Luther and the Beloved Community*, 60–62; Vainio, *Justification and Participation*, 108–9.

109. Stehle, *Catholic Roots of the Protestant Gospel*, 74.

it could be said that he did so implicitly.[110] Flacius's main focus was on development of the concepts of active and passive righteousness of Christ. He writes in his *Concerning Righteousness vs. Osiander* (1552):

> The justice of God, as revealed in the Law, demands of us, poor, unrighteous, disobedient men, two items of righteousness. The first is, that we render to God complete satisfaction for the transgression and sin already committed; the second, that we thenceforth be heartily and perfectly obedient to His Law if we wish to enter life. If we do not thus accomplish this, it threatens us with eternal damnation. And therefore the essential justice of God includes us under sin and the wrath of God . . . Therefore the righteousness of the obedience of Christ, which He rendered to the Law for us, consists in these two features, viz., in His suffering and in perfect obedience to the commands of God.[111]

Whereas Osiander had suggested that our righteousness before God was divided between Christ's human nature (forgiveness) and his divine nature (positive righteousness), Flacius emphasized the fact that humanity is justified both positively and negatively before God through Christ's activity as a single theandric subject. Christ's divine person works positive righteousness in and through his human nature's obedience. The divine person dies to satisfy the infinite judgment of the law through the man Jesus. In other words, who Christ is could not be divided from what he did.

Flacius's approach not only coheres with Luther's opposition to Zwingli, but what we observed earlier in the biblical texts regarding the nature of God's holiness and sacrifice. As John Kleinig points out, holiness is something that God alone possesses and transmits to the people of God through his presence in the sacrificial cult. The propiatory sacrifice that God sanctions, provides, and accepts serves as a medium whereby Israel receives participation in God's holiness and moral perfection. From the beginning, righteousness was always a gift from God and therefore an *iustitia aliena*. Likewise, we observed that both Paul and John identify Jesus with the mercy seat, upon which the blood of the second goat and the divine presence rested. Hence, God transmits his righteousness to the Church through the medium of Christ's substitutionary sacrifice on the cross. Just as God's holiness was not something transmitted apart from the sacrifice and its propiatory qualities in the temple in the Old Testament, likewise within the Church, God's righteousness is not transmitted apart from human nature and activities of Jesus.

The authors of the Formula of Concord concluded with Flacius that Christ should be understood to be mediator and redeemer according to both natures. His total theandric person had been obedient to the law (active righteousness) and suffered sin's negative consequence on our behalf (passive righteousness):

> For even though Christ had been conceived and born without sin by the Holy Ghost, and had fulfilled all righteousness in His human nature alone, and yet had not been true and eternal God, this obedience and suffering of His human nature could not be imputed to us for righteousness. As also, if the Son of God had not

110. Vainio, *Justification and Participation*, 116n96. Also see Haikola, *Gesetz und Evangelium*, 172–76.

111. H. Schmid, *Doctrinal Theology*, 354. Also see discussion in Haikola, *Gesetz und Evangelium*, 318–23; A. Ritschl, *Christian Doctrine of Justification and Reconciliation*, 219–21, 226–29.

become man, the divine nature alone could not be our righteousness. Therefore we believe, teach, and confess that the entire obedience of the entire person of Christ, which He has rendered the Father for us even to His most ignominious death upon the cross, is imputed to us for righteousness. For the human nature alone, without the divine, could neither by obedience nor suffering render satisfaction to eternal almighty God for the sins of all the world; however, the divinity alone, without the humanity, could not mediate between God and us.[112]

Thus neither the divine nor the human nature of Christ by itself is imputed to us for righteousness, but only the obedience of the person who is at the same time God and man. And faith thus regards the person of Christ as it was made under the Law for us, bore our sins, and in His going to the Father offered to His heavenly Father for us poor sinners His entire, complete obedience, from His holy birth even unto death, and has thereby covered all our disobedience which inheres in our nature, and its thoughts, words, and works, so that it is not imputed to us for condemnation, but is pardoned and forgiven out of pure grace, alone for Christ's sake.[113]

Though we will save our detailed discussion of the active and passive righteousness of Christ for the locus on the work of Christ, the important thing to recognize at this point is the doctrine's relationship to the communication of activities within the hypostatic union. In other words, if Vainio's interpretation of the debate between Flacius and Osiander is correct, then the doctrine not only has the value of explaining the shape of Christ's vicarious fulfillment of the law, but originated as a way of defending the unity of Christ's personal agency. For this reason, among others, this doctrine is necessary and important for upholding the scriptural teaching regarding the unity of Christ's personal agency.

112. FC SD 3; *CT* 935.
113. FC SD 3; *CT* 937.

Chapter 9

The Mystery of the Person of Christ, Part 5

The Communication of Attributes:
The Genus Majestaticum *and Its Defense*

The *Genus Majestaticum*

THE LAST AND MOST controversial genus of the communication of attributes is the *genus majestaticum*.[1] Chemnitz lists this genus last after his discussion of the *genus apotelesmaticum*. By contrast, the Lutheran scholasticism of the seventeenth century typically reversed the order between the *genus majestaticum* and the *genus apostelesmaticum*.[2] The likely reason for this is that it made for an easy transition from the locus on the person of Christ to the locus on the work of Christ.[3]

---

1. FC SD 8; *CT* 1041:

    We, therefore, hold and teach, in conformity with the ancient orthodox Church, as it has explained this doctrine from the Scriptures, that the human nature in Christ has received this majesty according to the manner of the personal union, namely, because the entire fullness of the divinity dwells in Christ, not as in other holy men or angels, but bodily, as in its own body, so that it shines forth with all its majesty, power, glory, and efficacy in the assumed human nature, voluntarily when and as He [Christ] wills, and in, with, and through the same manifests, exercises, and executes His divine power, glory, and efficacy, as the soul does in the body and fire in glowing iron (for by means of these illustrations, as was also mentioned above, the entire ancient Church has explained this doctrine). This was concealed and withheld [for the greater part] at the time of the humiliation; but now, after the form of a servant [or exinanition] has been laid aside, it is fully, powerfully, and publicly exercised before all saints, in heaven and on earth; and in the life to come we shall also behold this His glory face to face, John 17:24.

    See also Althaus, *Die Christliche Wahrheit*, 448–53; Baier, *Compendium Theologiae Positivae*, 2:52–70; Chemnitz, *Loci Theologici*, 1:113; Hoenecke, *Evangelical Lutheran Dogmatics*, 3:89–99; Hunnius, *Epitome Credendorum*, 104–7; L. Hütter, *Compendium Locorum Theologicorum*, 2:928–32; Gerhard, *On Christ*, 203–87; Graebner, *Outline of Doctrinal Theology*, 109–10; Koehler, *Summary of Christian Doctrine*, 91–92; Lindberg, *Christian Dogmatics*, 217–24; Luthardt, *Kompendium der Dogmatik*, 201–4; J. Mueller, *Christian Dogmatics*, 275–83; von Oettingen, *Lutherische Dogmatik*, 2.2:83–85; Philippi, *Kirchliche Glaubenslehre*, 4.1:260–76; F. Pieper, *Christian Dogmatics*, 2:152–242; Schaff, *Creeds of Christendom*, 1:319–28; Schaller, *Biblical Christology*, 68–78; H. Schmid, *Doctrinal Theology*, 314–15.

2. For an example of this see Gerhard, *On Christ*, 203–98.

3. Gerhard seems to do this by transitioning from a discussion of the *genus apostelesmaticum* to the offices of Christ.

The *genus majestaticum* posits that Christ's humanity possesses by communication the fullness of divine attributes when considered in the abstract.[4] Chemnitz describes the genus thus: "so that when we speak of these matters in the schools we can be correct not only in calling Christ a man or saying that the Son of Man makes alive, but also we can then rightly speak in the abstract or in abstract language of the assumed nature as being united with the Logos. We can say that the flesh of Christ, which is united with the Logos, makes alive and that the blood of Christ cleanses from sin."[5] Vainio comments that "the third genus . . . refers to the supernatural gifts and attributes Christ's human nature receives in the hypostatic union. Since God's attributes and essence are inseparable, these supernatural gifts and attributes are God's essence."[6]

Gerhard observes that there was a difference between Lutheran theologians of the second generation as to whether one should speak of the glory of God communicated to Christ's human nature in the abstract.[7] Some thought it was proper (notably Chemnitz and Johannes Brenz) others did not (notably Tileman Heshusius).[8] Gerhard comments that this was ultimately a logomachy and not based on any substantive disagreement about the genus. Some claimed that considering the human nature in the abstract entailed thinking of only the essential attributes of his humanity. Therefore, since it was improper to say that divine attributes had been communicated to the human essence (this would entail the heresy of Eutyches, condemned by the fourth ecumenical council), it was not permissible to say that such glory had been communicated to the human nature in the abstract. Others disagreed and stated when a person considers the human nature of Christ in the abstract one must always think about it as it exists in the context of the hypostatic union. To be more exact, because the human nature is *anhypostasis*, it has never existed and never will exist, except in the concrete unity of the person of the Logos. It therefore follows that it must always be thought of as possessing the fullness of divine glory, because even when considered in the abstract the human nature was still the human nature of the Logos. This latter answer seems more satisfactory for of number reasons. First, terminologically speaking, it creates space for a clearer linguistic distinction between the *genus majestaticum* and the *genus idiomaticum*. Secondly, as we shall see below, it more closely replicates the Bible's own manner of speaking about Jesus. This being said, it should be observed that the other position is technically speaking not incorrect, simply less terminologically precise.

In insisting on the full communication of glory to Christ's humanity, it should be observed that Chemnitz is not positing transmuting of humanity into divinity. Throughout the sixteenth and seventeenth centuries (as it is at present in many circles) this was a common charge of those among the Reformed communions who rejected this genus. As we noted earlier, both Calvin and Zwingli claimed that there was no communication of glory to Christ's humanity and therefore his body was confined to heaven.[9] From

---

4. Chemnitz, *Two Natures*, 241–47. See lengthy discussion in J. Preus, *Second Martin*, 267–76.

5. Chemnitz, *Two Natures*, 32.

6. Vainio, *Justification and Participationst*, 141.

7. Gerhard, *On Christ*, 277–79.

8. Ibid.

9. *ICR* 4.17.29–31, in Calvin, *Institutes of the Christian Religion*, 2:1398–1403; Zwingli, "Friendly

their perspective, since Lutherans believed that Christ possessed the fullness of divine glory and could exercise that glory by being present in many places at once (most notably in the Lord's Supper) they must logically believe in the transmutation of Christ's humanity into his divinity. Working from Chemnitz's definitions, it is easy to observe that this charge is utterly without merit. The Lutheran claim is not that human essence is somehow mixed with the divine nature. Rather, the human possesses divine glory by communication within the personal union brought about by the incarnation.

Gerhard further develops this point. Using the terminology of Aristotelian metaphysics, he observes that human nature neither possesses the attributes of divinity according to substance or as an accidental quality.[10] Instead, he states, the attributes of divinity are communicated to the human nature "personally." This is the logical result of the structure of subsisting relationships in the Trinity. The Father differs by the Son not in essence (which would be Arianism), nor in an accidental quality (there are no accidental qualities in God, because his essence is identical with his existence). Rather, the Father differs from the Son because of the subsisting relationship of begotteness. The Son therefore possesses the divine attributes by virtue of the fact that he is a divine person begotten by the Father. Hence, the attributes of the divine nature are communicated to the man Jesus "personally," because he subsists in the person of the Son who receives them eternally from the Father.[11] Put succinctly, the predicates of the divine being are proper to the man Jesus in time, because they have always been his in eternity as a divine person.

Returning to the *Two Natures*, to further emphasize that the *genus majestaticum* does not posit a transmutation of humanity into divinity, Chemnitz uses a number of analogies. Among the more fitting ones, he cites the simile of fire communicating itself to metal: "fire communicates itself totally, with all its attributes, to heated iron"[12] By being heated, metal is not transformed into fire. Nonetheless, considered in itself the glowing and the heat do become real qualities of the metal. A similar analogy can be found in the communication of the attributes of the soul to a body.[13] Through the union of body and soul, the body takes on the qualities of the soul (i.e., it becomes animated) while not in fact being transmuted into something else.

These similes are largely taken from the Greek patristic authors, who more than the Latin theologians (standing under the influence of Leonine Christology) emphasized the communication of glory. In agreement with Chemnitz and Luther, Cyril of Alexandria states in his *On the Unity of Christ*:

> If the flesh that is united to him, ineffably and in a way that transcends thought or speech, did not become the very flesh of the Word, directly, then how could it be understood as life-giving? He himself says: "I am the living bread which has come down from heaven and gives life to the world. If anyone should eat

---

Exegesis," 2:250–52.

10. Regarding substance see *Metaphysics*, 1.1–3, in Aristotle, *Metaphysics*, 1–4. Regarding the description of accidents see *Metaphysics* 1.4, in Aristotle, *Metaphysics*, 4–6.

11. Gerhard, *On Christ*, 272–73.

12. Chemnitz, *Two Natures*, 309.

13. Ibid., 161.

of this bread he shall live forever, and the bread which I shall give is my flesh for the life of the world" (Jn 6:52, 33). But if it is the flesh of a different son than him, someone appropriated by him in a conjunction of relationship, called to an equality of honor as a grace, then how can he call this his own flesh if he is ignorant of all deceit? And how could the flesh of anyone else ever give life to the world if it has not become the very flesh of Life, that is of him who is the Word of God the Father?[14]

Again, the patriarch writes:

There was no other way for the flesh to become life-giving, even though by its own nature it was subject to the necessity of corruption except that it became the very flesh of the Word who gives life to all things. This is exactly how it accomplishes his own ends, working by his own life-giving power. There is nothing astonishing here, for if it is *true that fire has conversed with materials which in their natures are not hot, and yet renders them hot since it so abundantly introduces to them the inherent energy* of its own power, then surely in an even greater degree the Word who is God can introduce the life-giving power and energy of his own self into his very own flesh. We can see that this is his very own flesh since he is united to it unconfusedly and unchangeably and in a manner he alone knows.[15]

Finally, the later Greek patristic author John of Damascus writes in *The Orthodox Faith*:

This [the union of God and humanity in Christ] was by no transformation of nature but by union through dispensation, the hypostatic union, I mean, by which the flesh is inseparably united to God, the Word, and by the mutual indwelling of the natures such as that *we also speak of in the case of the heating of steel.*[16]

Having defined the genus, Chemnitz offers a series of highly convincing exegetical arguments in favor of it.[17] Here we will examine a number of texts our author mentions, and offer a few of our own. We will start with the narratives of Christ's resurrection, which offers ample testimony regarding the genus. After his resurrection, Christ speaks of his humanity in the abstract saying: "all authority in heaven and on earth has been given to me" (Matt 28:18).[18] The analogy of faith tells us that this authority was not given to him according to his divine nature (which always possessed it from eternity, see John 1:1–3, Heb 1:1–4), but to his human nature, which began to possess and exercise the fullness of his divine glory in time. In this text, Christ speaks of the manifestation of that glory which took place after his resurrection. This is abundantly clear from the narratives of resurrection, which portray Jesus as remaining a physical being who can eat (Luke 24:30, 41–42) and be touched (John 20:24–29), while at the same time being capable of appearing and disappearing at will (Luke 24:31) and walking through walls (John 20:19).[19] In these narratives, Christ's humanity simultaneously retains its essential

14. Cyril of Alexandria, *On the Unity of Christ*, 131.

15. Ibid., 132–33 (emphasis added).

16. *Orthodox Faith*, 3.16, in John of Damascus, *Saint John of Damascus*, 316 (emphasis added).

17. Ibid., 334.

18. FC SD 8; *CT* 1047.

19. Luther used arguments of Jesus's uncircumscribed presence against Zwingli:
    This [Christ's definitive presence] was the mode in which the body of Christ was present when

qualities, while participating in the infinite possibilities of the divine person. Moreover, as it is apparent from a reading of the Gospels, although such glory was suspended and hidden prior to his resurrection, its presence can definitely be felt throughout Jesus's earthly life. A significant number of Christ's miracles occur because of his human touch (Mark 5:28–34), or (in one case) even by contact with his saliva (John 9:5–6). Therefore it cannot be denied that the New Testament teaches that Christ's divinity is present and active in humanity.

It is interesting to note that Calvin had a very hard time dealing with texts when attempting to justify his rejection of the *genus majestaticum*. In one of its weakest sections of the final edition of *The Institutes of the Christian Religion* (1559), Calvin writes:

> They object that Christ went forth from the closed sepulcher [Matt 28:6] and went in to his disciples through closed doors [John 20:19]. This gives no more support to their error. For just as the water, like a solid pavement, provided Christ with a path as he walked on the lake [Matt 14:25], so it is no wonder if the hardness of the stone yielded at his approach. Yet it is more probable that the stone was removed at his command, and immediately after he passed through, returned to its place. And to enter through closed doors means not just penetrating through solid matter but opening an entrance for himself by divine power, so that he suddenly stood among his disciples clearly, in a wonderful way, although the doors were locked.[20]

The major problem with Calvin's reasoning is that the texts plainly do not say what he claims. His argument is purely predicated on the assumption that human nature can only exist in a circumscribed manner and that there is no communication of divine glory to the man Jesus. Since the resurrection accounts contradict this, he must go back and explain them away in a rather ad hoc fashion.

In light of this full communication of glory, divinity is not something that merely exists alongside Christ's humanity, but rather is present in, and through it. As Gerhard Forde describes it, Christ the man "does God to us."[21] Paul in agreement with this asserts that in Christ the "whole fullness of deity dwells bodily" (Col 2:9)[22] and we can see the "glory of God in the face of Jesus Christ" (2 Cor 4:6). Christ the man also possesses

---

he came out of the closed grave, and came to the disciples through a closed door, as the gospels show. There was no measuring or defining of the space his head or foot occupied when he passed through the stone, yet he certainly had to pass through it. He took up no space, and the stone yielded him no space, but the stone remained stone, as entire and firm as before, and his body remained as large and thick as it was before. But he also was able, when he wished, to let himself be seen circumscribed in given places where he occupied space and his size could be measured. (*AE* 37:216)

20. *ICR* 4.17.29, in Calvin, *Institutes of the Christian Religion*, 2:1400.

21. "In the language of act the divinity of Jesus consists in the fact that precisely through his suffering, death, and resurrection, *he does God to us*" (Forde, *Theology is for Proclamation*, 102). We agree of course that Christ's concrete activity "does God." Nevertheless, as we noted in our earlier discussion of substance language and ontology, we are deeply uncomfortable with moving away from the language of substance into an existialistic anti-realism, into which Forde, for all his good intentions, has a strong tendency to drift.

22. See discussion in Deterding, *Colossians*, 93–95, 101–3; Lenski, *St. Paul's Epistles to the Colossians*, 99–101.

infinite divine wisdom because "[in him] are hidden all the treasures of wisdom and knowledge" (Col 2:2–3).[23] The possession of this glory means that as a man Jesus can do only what God can do, forgive sins and work salvation. Indeed, "the blood of Jesus his Son cleanses us from all sin" (John 1:7).[24] Ultimately, because of his redeeming divine power, Christ's humanity is capable of bringing about a "new creation" (1 Cor 5:17).

Lastly, it should be observed that although the divine nature communicates its attributes to the human nature in the abstract, the reciprocal does not occur. As Gerhard states, the attributes of the Logos can be communicated to a finite human nature without contradicting its essential characteristics.[25] Human nature is not contradicted by taking on the attributes of divinity. Rather, as explained above, it simply augments attributes it already possesses (heated metal analogy, body and soul, etc.). The reverse cannot be said to be the case. If the Logos took on the attributes of humanity in the abstract, it would be reduced to finitude and thereby contradict its essential nature.

Furthermore, Gerhard also notes that human nature cannot communicate its own qualities to the divine nature because it is *anhypostasis* and is not the subject of the Incarnation.[26] Because the divine person preexists the human nature and subsists in itself, the divine nature in the abstract can be contemplated quite apart from the human nature and its attributes. Since the human nature is not a person and the Logos does not subsist in it, it follows that it cannot take on its attributes by way of personal communication.

In light of all this, we stand in opposition to the teaching of the nineteenth-century Neo-Lutheran theologian Gottfried Thomasius who advocated a reciprocal communication.[27] In fact, to account for this, he added a fourth and final genus, the *genus kenoticum* or *tapeinoticum*.[28] This genus lacks biblical support and does not cohere with the analogy of faith for the reasons mentioned above. Moreover, such a supposition implicitly assumes that God in his infinite glory cannot communicate himself to the finite. Consequently, he must modify his being in some way to make possible his translation into the finite. Seen from this perspective, these accounts of the incarnation represent a wholesale rejection of the Lutheran *capax*. Nevertheless, we will address many of the questions that Thomasius raised in a later chapter under the locus on *kenosis*.

---

23. Deterding, *Colossians*, 83, 84–85; Lenski, *St. Paul's Epistles to the Colossians*, 84–89.

24. FC SD 8; *CT* 1035:

> The Scriptures speak not merely in general of the Son of Man, but also indicate expressly His assumed human nature, 1 John 1:7: The blood of Jesus Christ, His Son, cleanseth us from all sin, not only according to the merit [of the blood of Christ] which was once attained on the cross; but in this place John speaks of this, that in the work or act of justification not only the divine nature in Christ, but also His blood per modum efficaciae (by mode of efficacy), that is, actually, cleanses us from all sins.

Also see Gerhard, *On Christ*, 224–25.

25. Gerhard, *On Christ*, 276–77. Also see discussion in F. Pieper, *Christian Dogmatics*, 2:229–35.

26. Gerhard, *On Christ*, 276–77.

27. Thomasius, *Christi*, 1:409–23. Also see a discussion of Gottfried Thomasius in Beyschlag, *Erlanger Theologie*, 14–19, 24–26, 29–31, 83–85, 93–98; L. Green, *Erlangen School of Theology*, 133–49.

28. See D. Brown, *Divine Humanity*, 232–33.

The Genus Majestaticum: Implications, Defense, and the Tangible God

The *genus majestaticum* has been a significant bone of contention between the Lutheran and Reformed confessions for the previous five centuries.[29] Below, we will not only defend the doctrine, but also discuss its significant implications to properly understanding the gospel and the other articles of faith. Below we will advance the argument that the *genus majestaticum* as the total and unilateral self-donation of God to the humanity of Jesus coheres with the biblical and confessional Lutheran prioritization of the gospel over the law.

Historically, one strategy that Reformed theology has used to combat the exegetical arguments of Lutheranism is the principle, "the finite is not capable of the infinite" (*finitum non capax infiniti*).[30] From the Lutheran perspective, this principle does not have a scriptural basis, but is rather rooted in the assumptions of fallen human reason. In some respects, it could be argued that this represents an over reification of the idea of the human substance that we rejected in our ontological prolegomena. The Reformed theologians, it would seem, have an *a prior* and exhaustive knowledge of what it is possible for human nature to do and not to do. In light of these concerns, one major polemical argument advanced by Lutheran theologians, is that Reformed Christology is rooted in a crass rationalism. As attractive as this critique might be, we must not jump ahead of ourselves and rush to a judgment. In responding to any theological position, one must thoroughly investigate the reason behind it before dismissing or rejecting it. In order to do this, below, we will briefly examine the basis upon which the Reformed advance the principle of *finitum non capax infiniti* and reject the *genus majestaticum*.

Taken from a historical and philosophical perspective, one might find the reason for the Reformed *non capax* in the theological antecedents of the southern Reformation. Richard Muller has shown that many of the Reformed theologians of the first generations were trained in the *via antiqua*, which taught that there was a continuity between human and divine reason.[31] In particular, it should not go unnoticed that Zwingli was a student of Thomas Wyttenbach, a representative of the *via antiqua* at the University of Basel.[32] By contrast, Luther attended the University of Erfurt where he learned the *via moderna*, with its characteristic emphasis on the discontinuity of human and divine rationality.[33]

29. For sources beyond Zwingli and Calvin's aforementioned rejections of the Lutheran concept of the communication of attributes, see the following: Berkhof, *Reformed Dogmatics*, 324–27; Heppe, *Reformed Dogmatics*, 439–47; Hodge, *Systematic Theology*, 2:405–19.

30. See discussion in Muller, *Christ and the Decree*, 20. See also Oberman, "'Extra' Dimension," 245–54.

31. Muller, *Post-Reformation Reformed Dogmatics*, 1:360–406.

32. Baur, *Zwinglis Theologie*, 1:19–26; Potter, *Zwingli*, 18–19, 111, 150; Stephens, *Theology of Huldrych Zwingli*, 6, 23–25, 222–23. Stephens notes the predominance of sources from the *via antiqua* in Zwingli's library. Although he also knew the *via moderna* as well. Also see Bolliger, *Infiniti Contemplatio*. Bolliger traces the origins of the Zwinglian/Reformed *non capax* to Realism and the *via antiqua*.

33. See good discussions in the following: Althaus, *Theology of Martin Luther*, 16–19, 31–33, 51–53, 64–71, 123–25, 387–90; Bayer, *Martin Luther's Theology*, 157–62, 174–76; S. Becker, *Foolishness of God*;

Nevertheless, even if one were to agree with the southern Reformers regarding the continuity of divine and human rationality, it is difficult to see how the principle of *finitum non capax infiniti* could still be justified. Taken simply from the perspective of human reason, the principle is in fact contradictory. In order to see how this is the case, it is important to observe what is really meant by the Lutheran *capax*. Put simply, the Lutheran *capax* is not really about the native capacities of the finite, but about the infinite God. The Lutheran claim is that infinite God is capable of communicating himself to the finite and that the finite is capable of receiving this communication because of the capacities given to it by the same infinite God. Hence the Swedish Lutheran theologian Gustaf Aulén has suggested that a better slogan might be "*infinium capax finiti.*"[34] Seen from this perspective, the Lutheran teaching does not entail positing a sort of intrinsic capacity of creation for infinite self-transcendence, in the manner that we might perhaps find in later German Idealism.[35] Rather, the accent falls exclusively on the capacities of the sovereignty and power of the infinite creator God. For this reason, the denial of the Lutheran *capax* does not somehow keep creaturely capacities within their own proper range, but rather denigrates divine power and sovereignty.

Understood from this perspective the Reformed *non capax* is simply illogical. As David Scaer has noted, if the infinite were not capable of communicating itself to the finite it would by definition not be infinite.[36] That is to say, if the infinite is truly infinite, then it must logically contain an infinite number of possibilities and one of these possibilities must be communicating itself to the finite. Beyond the logical incoherence of the Reformed position, the principle actually undermines what it seeks to achieve, that is, a proper respect for the ontological distance between God and his creatures. Rather than safeguarding the glory of God, it does exactly the opposite by limiting his power.

Perhaps a more reasonable argument and one more coherent with the analogy of the faith, is the Reformed claim that the communication of glory contradicts the basic nature of God and humanity as it is presented in the Bible. Considered from the perspective of his power and glory, God cannot be idolatrously brought down the level of creatures and thereby transformed into an easily controllable object of human religious machinations.[37] Typically Reformed theologians read the Chalcedonian definition of

---

Gerrish, *Grace and Reason*; Köstlin, *Theology of Luther*, 2:75, 114, 134, 195; Lohse, *Martin Luther's Theology*, 196–207.

34. Aulén, *Faith of the Christian Church*, 57. We must nonetheless be critical of Aulén for assuming that said slogan in fact transcends the impasse between the Reformed and Lutheran claims on the subject. Elert makes a similar judgment regarding the ability of the infinite to communicate itself to the finite. See Elert, *Christian Faith*, 210.

35. *CD* 4.2, 82–83. Karl Barth wrongly attributes German Idealism's deification of the finite to Lutheranism. A more credible source might be found in the influence of Spinoza.

36. David Scaer, personal conversation.

37. Hinlicky, *Luther and the Beloved Community*, 98. Hinlicky rightly observes that for Luther idolatry is not so much in God being brought down to the created image or object (as it is for the Reformed starting with Karlstadt), but in self-trust. This way of construing the differing understandings of idolatry is borne out by the historic division between the Reformed and Lutherans regarding the numbering of the Ten Commandments. Whereas the Reformed have made the prohibition of images a separate commandment, Luther included it within the first commandment. Luther in his explanation of the commandment is quite specific that having a God is a matter of having an object of trust. He has

Christ's two natures as "being neither separated nor confused" in light of their emphasis on the inherent distance between God and his creatures.[38] From this they draw the conclusion that although Christ is a single subject, no real communication of glory can be received by the human nature. If it could, the biblical definition of God and humanity would be abrogated. God would cease to be sovereign, powerful, and utterly different than creation. He would in effect be brought down to the level of his creatures, and become another object in the world capable of manipulation. Likewise, Christ's divinized humanity would make it possible to idolatrize creatures.

Nevertheless, this definition of the relationship between God and his creation does not exhaust the Bible's description of it. God is of course utterly different than his creatures insofar as he is infinitely greater than them. At the same time though, the God of the Bible is also by nature a self-communicating and self-donating God. He is, as we have seen, Triune and therefore subsists in an eternal event of self-communication. God the Father possesses all and therefore he eternally communicates himself in the begetting of the person of the Son (John 1:1–5, Heb 1:1–5). Possessing all, the Son eternally donates himself to the Father in the form of the procession of the Holy Spirit (Gal 4:6). In his eternal love for the Son, the Father does likewise and therefore also eternally breathes forth the Holy Spirit (John 14:16).

The biblical God's identity as self-communicating and relational also stands in coherence with his role as creator. A God, who is by nature neither relational nor self-donating, would in fact not set about creating a world to which he could relate. Conversely, a God who is by nature relational and free for the other, is also free to create the world and relate to it. Since creation passively receives itself from God through his act of fiat, the divine-creature relationship is primarily one of grace rather than law. Creatures are at their deepest ontic level receivers of the good and only derivatively doers of the good. Creation *ex nihilo* forces us to acknowledge that receiving is logically prior to doing (Matt 7:17). Luther himself describes nature as one that is essentially giving:

> These are the three persons and one God, *who has given himself to us all wholly and completely*, with all that he is and has. The Father *gives himself to us*, with heaven and earth and all the creatures, in order that they may serve us and benefit us. But this gift has become obscured and useless through Adam's fall. Therefore the Son himself *subsequently gave himself and bestowed all his works*, sufferings, wisdom, and righteousness, and reconciled us to the Father, in order that restored to life and righteousness, we might also know and have the Father and his gifts.[39]

If we take into consideration the articles of the Trinity and creation, then the incarnation and the work of Christ stand in dramatic coherence with God's nature and prior works. The *genus majestaticum* therefore does not contradict the essential nature of God and humanity, because God is an eternal communicator of his goodness, and it is the role of creation to receive all his goodness. The communication of the fullness of his

---

little to say about spiritual worship vs. the worship of images. To observe this contrast in approaches, see LC 1:1; *CT* 581–93, with Ursinus, *Commentary of Zacharias*, 517–36.

38. Denzinger, *Sources of Catholic Dogma*, 60–62.

39. *AE* 37:366 (emphasis added).

glory is simply the fulfillment of all this. The word of the gospel describes the response of God's self-donating goodness to the problem of sin. As we observed earlier, the new narrative of creation begins with God's self-donation to Adam and Eve in the form of the *protevangelium*. This new word of the gospel counteracts the condemnation of the law and begins the reestablishment of the original and natural relationship of grace. As the history of Israel and the condemning effects of the law progressed, God's self-donating grace manifested itself in more and more concrete ways, until finally God gave himself over so completely to humanity that he became human.

Hence the Lutheran *capax* also means that the infinite God has made finite creatures in such a way that they are capable of receiving the fullness of his goodness. This is in fact their destiny as receptive beings. Moreover, if, as the Reformed tradition (and the western Leonine tradition in general) posits, God did not fully donate himself to humanity, then reconciliation could not have taken place. In other words, since God's relationship to humanity apart from his self-donation is law, hiddenness, and wrath, failure to utterly surrender himself to humanity would have only served to maintain his negative relationship of law.

In fact, this is precisely the problem that the Reformed have with the *genus majestaticum*. Since the Reformed assume that the divine-human relationship is rooted in law, God must be thought of primarily as transcending all things temporal. If he did not, he would become a tangible object of human beings, idolatry would ensue, and the law relationship would dissolve. This law-oriented relationship with creation requires a certain distance between God and humanity, which unilateral and unbounded self-donation in the incarnation on God's part (*genus majestaticum*) would abrogate. For this reason God must not completely surrender himself to humans. Incarnation is necessary, but in it God must still hold something of himself back (*extra calvinisticum*). To use a spatial metaphor, he must continue to stand at a distance from humanity and command them. Simultaneously, humans must possess a proper distance from God so that they might move towards him through their grace-induced submission.

In reading *The Institutes of the Christian Religion*, it cannot be doubted that Calvin's theology fundamentally prioritizes the law over the gospel. It does so by making it abundantly clear that the gospel exists for the sake of the law. The Genevan theologian of course shares the Lutheran concept of forensic justification, defending it against the likes of none other than Osiander.[40] Nevertheless, although for Calvin faith is a receptive trust, it is not exclusively so.[41] Rather, it is also obedience to the sovereign call of God's electing grace.[42] The gospel itself is not a sheer promise, but rather also contains within itself the command to repent.[43] Earlier in *The Institutes*, Calvin makes the *sensus divinitatis* and natural man's recognition of his distance from his creator paradigmatic for his understanding of the divine-human relationship.[44] This is borne out by the fact

---

40. ICR 3.11.5–13, in Calvin, *Institutes of the Christian Religion*, 1:729–44.

41. ICR 3.2.6–7, in Calvin, *Institutes of the Christian Religion*, 1:548–52.

42. ICR 3.2.6, in Calvin, *Institutes of the Christian Religion*, 1:549. Calvin writes: "Paul defines faith as *that obedience which is given to* the gospel" (emphasis added).

43. ICR 3.3.1, in Calvin, *Institutes of the Christian Religion*, 592–93.

44. ICR 1.1.1–3, 1.2, in Calvin, *Institutes of the Christian Religion*, 1:1–2, 1:35–43. See discussion in

that this natural relationship of law finally reasserts itself in the redeemed. Calvin describes the third use (and not the second!) as the main use of the law.[45] Hence, unlike the Lutheran prioritization of the second use (therefore giving the law an office ordered towards grace), Calvin's insists on the primacy of the third use, thereby demonstrating that he considers God's grace to be ultimately ordered to the law. Having received forgiveness, elect and enlightened humans are able to see God's distance from them, feel small, and submit unconditionally to his authority.

Later Reformed scholasticism deepened Calvin's understanding of law as being foundational to the divine-human relationship by positing a pre-lapsarian "covenant of works."[46] In contrast to Luther, the Reformed scholastics thought of the law as being the original and most basic relationship between God and humans.[47] The distinction between pre- and post-lapsarian existence was merely that in the former humanity was able to possess and maintain a relationship based on obedience to the law, whereas in the latter they were unable to do so because of the corruption of original sin. The Reformed orthodox of course rejected the idea that God was a debtor to humanity.[48] Nevertheless, they insisted that eternal life and fellowship with God was something that humanity would have earned had the Fall not occurred.[49] Hence the command not to eat of the forbidden fruit was not primarily a means of divine worship for grace already received (as in Luther's Genesis commentary), but rather a test to see if humanity was worthy of the reward of eternal life.[50]

Returning to Calvin, it is clear that this understanding of the divine-human relationship under law is reflected in his Christology as well.[51] Throughout his writings,

---

P. Helm, *John Calvin's Ideas*, 209–45.

45. For discussion of the second use of the law see *ICR* 2.7.9–10, in Calvin, *Institutes of the Christian Religion*, 1:357. It should be noted, that we are using the Lutheran numbering here. Calvin reverses the order of first and second uses of the law. For the third use, see *ICR* 2.7.12–13, in Calvin, *Institutes of the Christian Religion*, 1:360–62. See discussion in Edgar, "Ethics," 320–46.

46. Heppe, *Reformed Dogmatics,* 281–300. For scholarship on covenant of works in Reformed scholastics see the following: Fischer, "Augustinian and Federal Theories," 355–409; Muller, "Covenant of Works, 175–89; Karlberg, *Mosaic Covenant*; Karlberg, "Reformed Interpretation of the Mosaic Covenant," 1–57; Lems, "Covenant of Works," 13–18; Lillback, "Ursinus' Development," 247–88; McGiffert, "From Moses to Adam," 131–55. We thank Richard Muller in his essay "The Covenant of Works" for directing us to these sources. Also see a modern Reformed discussion (both positive and negative evaluations) of this notion in the following: Bavinck, *Reformed Dogmatics*, 2:550, 567–73, 576–79, 587–88; J. Brown, *Systematic Theology of John Brown*, 192–225; Buswell, *Systematic Theology*, 1:309–12; Bosma, *Reformed Doctrine*, 91–95; van Genderen and Velema, *Concise Reformed Dogmatics*, 394–96; Grudem, *Systematic Theology*, 516–18; Hoeksema, *Reformed Dogmatics*, 214–26; Hodge, *Systematic Theology*, 2:217–22; Rushdoony, *Systematic Theology*, 1:376–79.

47. See Heppe, *Reformed Dogmatics*, 249–50. Heppe notes the contrast between later Lutheran scholastics and the Reformed on this issue. In contrast to the Reformed, the Lutherans followed Luther in positing that Adam did not need to work to achieve righteousness by his actions.

48. Heppe, *Reformed Dogmatics*, 282–83.

49. Ibid., 281–91.

50. Ibid., 292–94.

51. See discussion of Calvin's Christology in the following sources: K. Barth, *Theology of John Calvin*, 125, 263, 328–29; DeVries, *Jesus Christ in the Preaching of Calvin*; Edmondson, *Calvin's Christology*; P. Helm, *John Calvin's Ideas*, 64–65, 68–70; Jansen, *Calvin's Doctrine*; Muller, *Christ and Decree*, 27–38;

Calvin is unrelenting in his attempt to distance the two natures from one another. While accepting the *genus idiomaticum* and the *genus apotelesmaticum*, he struggles in the face of contrary biblical evidence (notably the appearance of the resurrected Jesus and the words of institution) to deny the *genus majestaticum*.[52] In a similar vein, Calvin posits the theory of the Lord's Supper, wherein human beings ascend to Christ in heaven through the Holy Spirit.[53] For Calvin, Christ's body being finite cannot come down to us, so the elect must come up to him. More importantly though, Calvin states that it is beneath Jesus's high estate and dignity to come down to merge with finite sinners.[54] Christ must be master, and humanity must submit to him in a manner worthy of his glory. In a word, for Calvin there must be a sufficient distance between God and humans for the law to work as the basis of their interaction. If God surrendered himself and became vulnerable as humanity's enfleshed object, then the law would cease as an existential relationship.

This way of thinking through the christological question also pervades later and less orthodox Reformed thinkers. In order to round off our discussion of the structure of Reformed Christology, we now briefly turn to the extremely influential twentieth-century Reformed theologian Karl Barth.[55] Although Barth is not a Calvinist per se (as Richard Muller has noted Calvinism is notoriously hard to define[56]), his system nonetheless maintains the basic structural priorities one finds in Calvin and Reformed scholasticism. As was noted above, one of these priorities is the utter and complete rejection of the *genus majestaticum* in favor of the *extra calvinisticum*.[57] This latter concept refers to the idea that there exists a *logos asarkos* alongside the *logos ensarkos* after the incarnation.[58] In other words, the divine being does not allow itself to become completely tangible in identifying with the humanity of Christ, but continues to retain something of its otherness and intangibility alongside and outside his flesh.

Niesel, *Theology of Calvin*, 110–19; Parker, *Calvin*, 64–77; Peterson, *Calvin's Doctrine*; Thomas, "Mediator of the Covenant," 205–25; Tylanda, "Christ the Mediator," 5–16; Tylanda, "Controversy on Christ the Mediator," 131–57; Van Buren, *Christ in Our Place*; D. Willis, *Calvin's Catholic Christology*; Witte, "Christologie Calvins," 3:487–529; Zachman, "Image of God in Calvin's Theology," 46–52.

52. *ICR* 4.17.29, in Calvin, *Institutes of the Christian Religion*, 2:1400; *ICR* 4.17.20–27, in Calvin, *Institutes of the Christian Religion*, 2:1382–95.

53. *ICR* 4.17.31–33, in *Calvin, Institutes of the Christian Religion*, 2:1403–8.

54. *ICR* 4.17.32, in *Calvin, Institutes of the Christian Religion*, 2:1404. Calvin ends his discussion of the real presence by telling us that he simply does not think it fitting for us to consume Christ. It would rob him of his glory: "I reject only absurd things which appear to be . . . *unworthy of Christ's heavenly majesty*" (emphasis added).

55. See the following sources for Karl Barth's Christology: Berkouwer, *Triumph of Grace*, 89–149; Busch, *Great Passion*, 86–95, 99–105, 199–218; Bromiley, *Theology of Karl Barth*, 175–238; Chapman, *Theology of Karl Barth*, 27–34; Hunsinger, *Disruptive Grace*, 131–47; Jenson, *Alpha and Omega*, 21–145; Jüngel, *Barth-Studien*, 233–45; Kantzer, "Christology of Karl Barth," 25–28; Mangina, *Karl Barth*, 115–42; D. Mueller, *Karl Barth*, 96–139; D. Mueller, *Karl Barth's Doctrine of Reconciliation*; Torrence, *Karl Barth*, 15–16, 20–22, 47–49, 71–72, 169, 176–77, 200, 202, 206, 234–36; Waldrop, *Karl Barth's Christology*. For a fairly good Lutheran critique of Barth's Christology see Forde, "Consequence of Lutheran Christology," 69–88.

56. Richard Muller, personal conversation.

57. *CD* 1.2.167–70; *CD* 4.1.180.

58. See discussion in Rohls, *Reformed Confessions*, 102–7.

Barth found the Lutheran *genus majestaticum* highly problematic, to say the least. He would not accept any communication of divine glory to the man Jesus.[59] Nevertheless, in order to make up for this deficit of divine glory, Barth (in a similar manner to Reformed scholasticism) settles on the concept of the *communicatio gratiarum*.[60] There is, claims Barth, a "total and exclusive determination of . . . [Jesus's] human nature . . . by the grace of God."[61] According to this concept, although the humanity of Jesus lacks divine glory, it possesses a superabundance of creaturely perfections, much like Aquinas's superabundance of created grace.[62]

The christological concept of the *communicatio gratiarum* is partially rooted in the Reformed scholastic distinction between communicable and incommunicable attributes of God.[63] Put succinctly, the older Reformed theologians held that God could communicate his wisdom and moral perfections to his creatures through their created similitude to his being (*analogia entis*), whereas his qualities of glory (omnipotence, etc.) could not be communicated. If these later attributes could be communicated, God would transmute creatures into himself and absurdity would result. When applied to Christology, such a concept also had the advantage of being able to explain the harmony between Jesus's morally perfected will and the divine person of the Son, without recourse to a real communication of glory within the hypostatic union posited by the Lutherans. In a similar manner to Aquinas as well, it presupposes a description of the humanity of Jesus as a quasi-independent agent, given the ability to act in harmony with the divine nature due to its augmentation by divine grace.[64] Therefore as we will see below, the primary function of the *communicatio gratiarum* for Barth is to describe the activation of the obedience of Christ's human nature in correspondence to his divine nature. Such a capability adheres in the human nature's created perfections and is not the result of the divine nature's deification of the human nature's will.

Barth views Jesus Christ as an image and actualization of the covenant between God and humanity. Christ is the "Real man" and the true "covenant-partner of God."[65] This covenant is decidedly bilateral, rather than unilateral. Therefore like Aquinas's nature cooperating with grace, Christ the man is exemplar of spontaneous human submission to divine sovereignty under the determination of divine grace. Within this bilateral struc-

---

59. *CD* 4.1.143. Also see brief discussion in *CD* 4.2.82–83.

60. See lengthy discussion in *CD* 4.2.91–115.

61. *CD* 4.2.88. Also see discussion in Jones, *Humanity of Christ*, 117–82.

62. Heppe, *Reformed Dogmatics*, 434–38. It should of course also be born in mind that the Lutheran scholastics never denied that Christ had an abundance of created gifts. They simply insisted that he also possessed the divine glory.

> Now it is indeed correct and true what has been said concerning the created gifts which have been given and imparted to the human nature in Christ, that it possesses them in or of itself. But these do not reach unto the majesty which the Scriptures, and the ancient Fathers from Scripture, ascribe to the assumed human nature in Christ. (FC SD 8; *CT* 1033)

63. Heppe, *Reformed Dogmatics*, 60–64; Muller, *Post-Reformation Reformed Dogmatics*, 3:223–36.

64. Pannenberg, *Jesus*, 314. Pannenberg expresses doubts that Karl Barth operates with a Christology that can give a plausible account of ontic unity between the two natures. The unity of the person of Christ in Barth's theology, according to Pannenberg, is merely a description of a "deed" of the two natures acting together in the same event (i.e., the life of Jesus).

65. *CD* 3.2.203.

ture, Christ's divinity moves towards humanity via the exercise of the priestly office,[66] whereas his humanity ascends towards God via his kingly office.[67] In the sequence of Jesus's life, the priestly office corresponds to his *kenosis* and crucifixion, whereas the kingly office manifests itself in the resurrection. As a result, the covenant is actualized because the man Jesus properly corresponds to and echoes the series of God's decrees by his human activity.

As can be observed, in Barth's Christology the accent falls heavily on Christ's grace-induced human agency cooperating with the divine person, rather than on the unity of the divine subject with the *anhypostatic* humanity.[68] In all fairness to him, Barth consistently emphasizes that redemption is the action of the single theandric subject. Nevertheless, much like Calvin, through his denial of the *genus majestaticum* Barth intentionally opens up conceptual space between the two natures within which the law can continue to function.

Turning to the Christian life, Barth posits that the relationship of redeemed humanity to God corresponds to and echoes the covenant relationship that has been actualized in Jesus Christ. In a similar (though not identical) manner to Calvin, Barth claims that the grace of election is ordered to the law.[69] This is because God's electing grace first intervenes and makes a relationship ordered by the law possible.[70] It is for this reason that Barth takes Calvin's concept of the primacy of the third use of the law to the extreme and actually argues that the sequence of law-gospel should be reversed to gospel-law.[71] The believer is to engage in an "act of responsibility, offering himself as the response to the Word of God, and conducting, shaping and expressing himself as an answer to it. He is, *and is man, as he does this*."[72] For this reason, the gospel is not the end of law's determination of the divine-human relationship, but rather its beginning. Grace's aim is fundamentally to activate human agency and place it in the right direction. Humanity is ultimately defined by "willingly corresponding to the claim laid upon us by the Word of God."[73] As a result (echoing both Aristotle and Aquinas), creation's essence is not to be found in receiving, but rather in doing. In one of the later volumes of *Church Dogmatics*, Barth very bluntly states regarding this ontic determination that "the statement 'I am' demands further explanation. It means: '*I do*.'"[74] As can clearly be observed, the believer's role in the covenant of grace corresponds to the humanity of Jesus as it is determined by divine grace and called upon to echo the divine will through its temporal activity.

The Lutheran alternative to all this is that of the freedom of the gospel, grounded in the total divine self-donation of Christ. The freedom of the gospel is founded on the

66. *CD* 4.1.142–43.

67. *CD* 4.2.4.

68. *CD* 2.2.94–194.

69. *CD* 3.4.32–46. See Busch, *Great Passion*, 152–75.

70. *CD* 3.4.32–46.

71. K. Barth, "Gospel and Law," 71–100.

72. *CD* 3.2.175 (emphasis added).

73. *CD* 3.2.181.

74. Ibid. (emphasis added). For a good summary of how Barth views divine and human agency see Hunsinger, *How to Read Karl Barth*, 185–224.

exchange of realities between Christ and the believer. Just as God communicates himself fully to the humanity of Jesus (*genus majestaticum*), so too Jesus on the cross gives himself fully and unilaterally to humanity to be received by faith. In this, he holds nothing back, but gives them his glory and righteousness in exchange for their sin.

Luther in his treatise *Freedom of a Christian* (1520) reflected this understanding of the gospel in his teaching that the "incomparable benefit of faith is that it unites the soul with Christ as a bride is united with her bridegroom."[75] Just as a bridegroom surrenders his very body, his bride, so too, Christ donates himself to humans through faith. The full self-donation of God to the believer in Christ is called, the "happy exchange" (*der fröhlicher wechsel*):

> Accordingly the believing soul can boast of and glory in whatever Christ has as though it were its own, and whatever the soul has Christ claims as his own. Let us compare these and we shall see inestimable benefits. Christ is full of grace, life, and salvation. The soul is full of sins, death, and damnation. Now let faith come between them and sins, death, and damnation will be Christ's, while grace, life, and salvation will be the soul's; for if Christ is a bridegroom, he must take upon himself the things which are the bride's and bestow upon her the things that are his.[76]

In contrast to the Reformed position, for the believer the law ends *coram Deo*. There is no bilateral movement of grace and human agency's correspondence to grace. Rather, there is a unilateral movement of Christ's self-donation to humanity. This is not an abrogation of the claims of the law. Christ does not leave the law unfulfilled, but rather enters into the law and fulfills it in order to save the believer from its condemnation. That is essential to the exchange. Nevertheless, the gospel ends the law as a means of divine-human interaction (Rom 10:4). The gospel is not ordered towards a better law or more law, but towards freedom from the law for its own sake: "For freedom Christ has set us free" (Gal 5:1).

Moreover, the end of the law does not mean that Christians may reject God's commandments. Luther states that the free Christian is not only "lord of all," but also "servant of all."[77] *Coram mundo*, the Christian serves his or her fellow human being and continues to operate within the boundaries established by the law. Nevertheless the self-donation of the Christian life is only possible because *coram Deo* they have received all from God in Christ. Having received all, they no longer need to grasp at God's divinity (*ambitio divinitatis*).[78] Possessing all righteousness from God, neither do they have to justify themselves.[79]

75. *AE* 31:351.

76. *AE* 31:351.

77. *AE* 31:344.

78. See Luther's comments in *WA* 27:504. Also see observation in Jüngel, *Entsprechungen*, 190–92.

79. See Paulson, *Luther for Armchair Theology*, 142–43. Paulson puts it well:
Luther is even willing to pause for a minute and talk about Christ's body being wherever Christ is—and that means everywhere present! Of course, this makes human reason and its bluff, free will feel "crowded out of the world." In other words, human reason that lusts for self-justification through imaginary free will, is "crowded out" of the world when it recognizes that Christ is all-present "for you." If the gracious God found in the flesh of Jesus reigns and is present everywhere, the human person loses all their power to establish themselves before God by their good works.

For this reason, the Lutheran response to the problem of idolatry is the opposite of the Reformed. Idolatry does not come about by finding God's reality in created means, but in self-trust. As we have previously seen, God wishes to be known through visible and created means he has established. He wishes to make himself into something tangible and trustworthy that faith can hold on to. As we saw, Adam and Eve looked for God above created means and fell into sin. To remedy this, God entered into our flesh as deeply as possible in order to refocus humanity's attention away from his hidden being toward his presence in the man Jesus. Only by God surrendering himself completely in the incarnation and the cross can the real idolatry of self-justification end. In the revelation of the cross, both the illusion of the possibility of self-justification and the need for such activity is removed. Only by God making himself a tangible object through the communication of the fullness of his glory to the man Jesus, can faith truly have an object to hold on to. By contrast, the Reformed approach can only lead human beings, fearful of God's majesty and intangibility, to strive even more greatly to protect themselves against God hidden in his majesty. Lacking concrete realities to hold on to, through a practical synergism human subject is left to grasp at signs of election.

For this reason, the full communication of God's glory to the man Jesus is at the very heart of the Lutheran understanding of the gospel. In this regard, it is interesting to observe that, at least according to Oswald Bayer's reconstruction, Luther came to his realization of the nature of the gospel (the so-called "Reformation breakthrough") by way of the recognition of God's own self-donating presence in the words "I absolve you" (*ego te absolve!*).[80] In other words, just as the flesh of Jesus is identical with the presence of God (*genus majestaticum*), so too the word of absolution that Jesus entrusted to the Church is identical with his own presence forgiving the sinner. In this, both the question of election and of God's attitude towards the sinner thereby ceased to be an issue. God's own electing power and forgiveness was identical with the word of absolution. Thereby the certainty of faith and Christian freedom are grounded in the sacramentality of the Word and the *communicatio idiomatum*.

If Bayer's reconstruction is to be believed, then Luther's breakthrough was rooted in the reality we find in Jesus's own self-understanding and ministry as we have described it earlier. As it should be recalled, Jesus's self-description as the "Son of Man" is significant in light of the use of the title in Second Temple Judaism. Though there is of course much debate about the title's usage, a large amount of the literature of the period (1 Enoch 61–62; 4 Ezra 11–13; 2 Baruch 39), as well as the Gospels themselves (particularly Matt 25) identify the Son of Man with a cosmic judge who will come at the end of time in order to meet-out judgment regarding both salvation and damnation: "The Father judges no one, but has given all judgment to the Son . . . And he has given him authority to execute judgment, because *he is the Son of Man*" (John 5:22, 27, emphasis added).[81]

There is no distance from this incarnate God within which they can use their free will in order to move towards him. They can only accept in faith that Christ is all-present and gracious *pro nobis*.

80. Bayer, *Martin Luther's Theology*, 52–53; Bayer, *Promissio*, 240–41.

81. For discussion of the meaning of the title see the following: Borsch, *Christian and Gnostic Son of Man*; Borsch, *Son of Man in Myth and History*; Burkett, *Son of Man*; Fitzmyer, "New Testament Title," 143–60; Gieschen, "Name of the Son of Man," 238–49; Hare, *Son of Man Tradition*; Hooker, *Son of Man in Mark*; Tödt, *Son of Man*.

It is hard to tell how widespread this expectation was, nevertheless, it appears to have existed in some quarters of Second Temple Judaism.[82] What is peculiar about Jesus's self-designation as the Son of Man is that he comes in the midst of history, rather than at its end. As Matthew 25 shows, his present advent in judgment does not exclude a future one. Rather what this does suggest is that Jesus's own present judgment about salvation and damnation was a proleptic realization in the midst of history of the final judgment. Therefore, just as Luther had realized that he could rely on the word of absolution in the present, so people who believed in Jesus's Word came to realize that they could be certain of God's final verdict.

Jesus made his verdict known in a number of ways. In some cases, he simply told people that their sins are forgiven. In other cases he combined his word of absolution with a common meal or healing. Ultimately though, he used his redeeming Word to elect a community (i.e., the Church) of those who will be vindicated in the coming kingdom. Hence, Jesus's own presence and word are identical with God's own presence and word. There was no "likeness and unlikeness . . . a partial correspondence and agreement" between God's eternal Word and his human word.[83] Rather his human word is identical with the divine Word, because he is God in the flesh. Being in contact with the man Jesus is identical with being in contact with God.

Jesus himself passed on this word of grace to his disciples. In both Matthew and Luke, Jesus gives his Word to the apostles and commissions them to preach eschatological salvation and judgment. Contained in the word of proclamation is the presence of his very being. He himself is both judge and comforter who acts through their word: "Whoever receives you receives me, and whoever receives me receives him who sent me" (Matt 10:40). Because of his sacramental presence in the Word, there is no ambiguity where one stands in relationship to him: "one who hears you hears me" (Luke 10:16). Rejection of Jesus's redemptive Word causes one to stand under divine judgment: "And if anyone will not receive you or listen to your words, shake off the dust from your feet when you leave that house or town. Truly, I say to you, it will be more bearable on the Day of Judgment for the land of Sodom and Gomorrah than for that town" (Matt 10:14–15).

This continues in the life of the Church. Later in the Gospel history we are told that the presence of Jesus's name in the midst of those gathered together (the Divine Service) is identical with the presence of Jesus himself: "where two or three are gathered in my name, there am I among them" (18:20). In this, Jesus's Name takes on the role of God's own Name (his hypostatized presence with Israel), and each liturgical gathering becomes a realization of the eschatological temple/tabernacle ("house for my name" 2 Sam 7:13). Hence, designation of the Church as the body of Christ throughout the New Testament (1 Cor 12:12–14, 27; Eph 4:12, 5:23; Col 1:18, 24, 2:19) makes a great deal of sense insofar as Christ is himself the new temple/tabernacle (John 1:14, 2:21).

---

82. Like Schweizer, some have assumed that the expectation of the coming Son of Man was quite close to universal in Second Temple Judaism. This is not likely. Schweitzer probably made this judgment due to his limited engagement with Jewish apocalyptic texts. The number of apocalyptic texts that had been translated into German in the early twentieth century was relatively small. See Schweitzer, *Quest for the Historical Jesus*, 237–49.

83. *CD* 2.1.225.

By the end of the Gospel histories, how this name is to be proclaimed among the "two or three" is clarified. Not only are the disciples given the ability to forgive in the name of Jesus, they are also given Jesus's name in the form of the sacraments. In Matthew 28:19, they are commissioned to baptize in the Triune name (which includes that of Jesus). Before his death, Jesus confirms his new testament of forgiveness, by offering them his own body and blood (to which his Name is also attached!) to consume (Matt 26:26–29). As we observed earlier, Jesus's presence at common meals directly mediated the divine presence of forgiveness to those who ate with him. This is now fulfilled in Jesus's giving an even greater share in himself than was possible in the aforementioned common meals. He does so by literally giving the sacrificed substance of his being on which they are to masticate. This flesh and blood is something living (John 6:53–58).[84] It is not a dead sign, but a living divine promise that this sacrificed flesh and blood pleads for them before the Father. By this saving bodily presence, they are both forgiven and assured of forgiveness. By Christ's real presence, they taste the Lord and know that he is good (Ps 34:8). Conversely, much like Jesus promises that those who rejected his presence in the preaching of the apostles would be destroyed (Matt 10:14–15), so Paul tells us that those who disbelieve his promise and treat the Lord's Supper as ordinary food will suffer divine judgment (1 Cor 11:27–32).

Indeed, no one can donate themselves to another in any greater way than to literally give their body over to the other. For example, in marriage both husband and wife seal the marriage by the literal giving of their physical substance to the other in the sexual act. Indeed, this is why fornication and adultery sows distrust. If prior to marriage, I give my ultimate pledge of myself to another for the sake of a pleasant evening, then how will the pledge of myself mean anything to my eventual spouse? Similarly, adultery is disturbing precisely because the ultimate pledge is given to the spouse and then indiscriminately to another. With a removal of the assurance of the ultimate gift of the self, the whole relationship is called into question.[85]

Ultimately, the picture that the New Testament presents of Jesus and his establishment of the Church makes very little sense without the *genus majestaticum*. There can be no distance between God's redeeming presence and Jesus's humanity. Otherwise, the saving divine presence and forgiveness that Jesus mediates would be utterly incoherent. Likewise, the promises of Jesus's presence, rule, or mediation also logically presuppose the absolute omnipresence of Christ's humanity.[86] Because all of the divine attributes are

---

84. FC SD 8; *CT* 1035:

> Thus in John 6:48–58 the flesh of Christ is a quickening food; as also the Council of Ephesus concluded from this [statement of the evangelist and apostle] that the flesh of Christ has power to quicken; and as many other glorious testimonies of the ancient orthodox Church concerning this article are cited elsewhere.

85. Jenson, *Systematic Theology*, 2:92.

86. Baier, *Compendium Theologiae Positivae*, 2:60–68; Hoenecke, *Evangelical Lutheran Dogmatics*, 3:90–92; Gerhard, *On Christ*, 227–43; Graebner, *Outline of Doctrinal Theology*, 109–10; Jenson, *Systematic Theology*, 1:203–6; Koehler, *Summary of Christian Doctrine*, 91–92; Krauth, *Conservative Reformation*, 456–517; Lindberg, *Christian Dogmatics*, 221–24; J. Mueller, *Christian Dogmatics*, 282–83; von Oettingen, *Lutherische Dogmatik*, 2.2:84–85; Prenter, *Creation and Redemption*, 345–48; F. Pieper, *Christian Dogmatics*, 2:173–214; O. Ritschl, *Dogmengeschichte des Protestantismus*, 4:70–106; Schaff, *Creeds of Christendom*, 1:32–38; Schaller, *Biblical Christology*, 72–73; Schmauk and Benze, *Confessional*

communicated to the human nature in the hypostatic union, Luther and the Lutheran symbolic writings maintain that Christ is omnipresent according to both natures.

This is in keeping with the unity of the incarnation. Indeed, as Franz Pieper correctly observes, John tells us that "the Word became Flesh" (John 1:14). This means the whole Word, and not merely his presence in one circumscribed place (*extra calvinisticum*) became incarnate.[87] As Luther shows, if this was not the case, Christ would in fact be two persons:

> Our faith maintains that Christ is God and man, and the two natures are one person, so that this person may not be divided in two . . . [therefore] if he is present naturally and personally wherever he is, then he must be man there, too, since he is not two separate persons but a single person. Where this person is, it is the single, invisible person, and if you can say, "Here is God," then you must also say, "Christ the man is present too." And if you could show me one place where God is and not the man, then the person is already divided and I could at once say truthfully, "Here is God who is not the man and has never become man." But no God like that for me![88]

As a single theandric subject, Jesus Christ is present and reigns at all times and places. As we have seen above, the Gospels tell us that from the time of the incarnation onward, it is incumbent upon us to look for God only in the humanity of Christ and not in an

---

Principle, 770–816; H. Schmid, *Doctrinal Theology*, 332–37. Werner Elert and Herman Sasse assert that the Formula of Concord only teaches the potential omnipresence of Christ's human nature (multivolipresence), rather than its actual omnipresence. See Elert, *Structure of Lutheranism*, 231–32; Sasse, *This is My Body*, 268–79. On the other hand, Edmund Schlink and Philip Schaff consider the Formula of Concord to teach omnipresence, though in a rather unsystematic manner that uses language of and confuses the difference between Chemnitz and Brenz on the issue. See Schlink, *Lutheran Confessions*, 191; Schaff, *Creeds of Christendom*, 1:321. Also see Arand et al., *Lutheran Confessions*, 249–53. According to Arand, Kolb, and Nestingen, the authors of the Formula of Concord moderated Brenz's Christology, while affirming its basic content. They also note in passing (280) that Hesshius (who only accepted the multivolipresence) expressed reservation about the perceived validation of Luther and Brenz's Christology by the Formula. Franz Pieper and Wilbert Gawrisch agree that the Formula does teach the absolute omnipresence of Christ according to his humanity. See Gawrisch, "On Christology," 229–54; F. Pieper, *Christian Dogmatics*, 2:166–214. The author of this book is inclined to agree with Pieper and Gawrisch. That the authors of the Formula of Concord agree with Luther on this point is particularly clear in that they approvingly quote Luther's defense of the omnipresence of Christ's humanity on the basis of the unity of the person. See FC SD 8; *CT* 1045. They also state it themselves quite clearly when they remark in FC SD 8; *CT* 1025: "But now He does, since He has ascended, not merely as any other saint, to heaven, but, as the apostle testifies [Eph 4:10], above all heavens, and also truly fills all things, and being everywhere present, not only as God, but also as man."

87. F. Pieper, *Christian Dogmatics*, 2:206. Also Jesus states to Nicodemus: "And no man hath ascended up to heaven, but he that came down from heaven, *even the Son of man which is in heaven*" (John 3:13 KJV, emphasis added). There is a textual variant here, present in the *Textus Receptus* and some early manuscripts. Though this reading was excluded from the Nestle-Aland thirty-seventh edition, it seems that it was unjustifiably so. According to the textual commentary on their decisions, the group making the decision admitted that there were a class of early manuscripts bearing witness to this reading, but they preferred the shorter reading. See Metzger, *Textual Commentary*, 203–4. Certainly, shorter readings are in many cases to be preferred. Nevertheless, for later patristic Christology, the insistence in the passage on the omnipresence of Christ's human nature would appear to be difficult enough reading, that it should be preferred as a reading.

88. *AE* 37:218.

abstract, fleshless deity (*Deus nudus*).[89] As an act of total self-donation, God the Son wills to be only the man Jesus at all times and all places. Indeed as Luther states: "You can say very correctly of the Man [Jesus]: That is God and there is no other God beside him."[90]

Jesus's omnipresent reign in his earthly life is fulfilled by his Ascension. As Paul puts it, "he who descended is the one who also ascended far above all the heavens, *that he might fill all things*" (Eph 4:10, emphasis added). In that it is in the flesh of Jesus that God has become a saving presence, that presence cannot be absent from the means of grace. His sacrificed body and blood continue to be present with it in the Lord's Supper, as he himself was present to sinners in his earthly ministry. The Lord's Supper would be a poor and wretched thing if it were not an improvement over Jesus's common meals with sinners at which he was bodily present. Through the means of grace, the omnipresent and glorified Christ continues to exercise his office of prophet in the midst of the congregation of the elect. It is the man Jesus who promises to be present among the "two or three" gathered (Matt 18:20), because as one who has received "all power in heaven and on earth" he is with the Church even unto the "end of the age" (28:20).

After the ascension, Jesus not only continues to exercise his prophetic office, but also his offices as priest and king. Throughout the New Testament we are told that he stands at the right hand of God.[91] As Luther notes, the phrase "right hand of God" is synonymous with God's power and glory in the Old Testament (Exod 15:6; Ps 16:8, 77:10, 98:1, 109:31; Isa 48:13, 62:8).[92] If we follow Luther's interpretation, Christ's presence at the right hand of God has several implications. First, because the phrase is used in the New Testament in reference to Psalm 110, Christ's presence at the right hand of God identifies him as one with authority as the Melchizedekiah priest-king. Secondly, because this place of authority is everywhere, Jesus is present at all places and all times interceding for humanity. Indeed, Jesus's omnipresent intercession meets the needs of humanity because God is the omnipresent judge of sin. Therefore by his omnipresent intercession, Christ secures the Church's life and salvation. Thirdly, because of his righteous mediation of grace and mercy, he also reigns everywhere as king for those who love God (Ps 110:1; Rom 8:28; 1 Cor 15:25).[93] His omnipresent rule according to his

---

89. *AE* 1:12–16, 5:42–49. See similar (though somewhat problematic) argument in Jenson, "Where the Body Went," 216–24.

90. *AE* 15:305.

91. Ps 110:1; Matt 22:44, 26:64; Mark 12:36, 14:62, 16:19; Luke 20:42, 43, 22:69; Acts 2:33–34, 5:31, 7:55–56; Rom 8:34; 1 Cor 15:25; Eph 1:20, 2:6; Col 3:1; Heb 1:3, 1:13, 8:1, 10:12–13, 12:2; 1 Pet 3:22; Rev 3:21.

92. *AE* 37:46–49, 55, 63–66, 101–2, 136–37, 144–45, 178–80. Also see Gerhard, *On Christ*, 220; FC SD 8; *CT* 1025:

> Yet this [the omnipresence of Christ's human nature] occurred not in an earthly way, but, as Dr. Luther explains, according to the manner of the right hand of God, which is no fixed place in heaven, as the Sacramentarians assert without any ground in the Holy Scriptures, but nothing else than the almighty power of God, which fills heaven and earth, in [possession of] which Christ is installed according to His humanity, realiter, that is, in deed and truth, sine confusione et exaequatione naturarum, that is, without confusion and equalizing of the two natures in their essence and essential properties. (FC SD 8; *CT* 1025)

93. FC SD 8; *CT* 1025:

human nature will finally culminate in the coming of his kingdom of glory, whereby he will be seen simultaneously by everyone on earth (Matt 24:23–28, Luke 17:24, Rev 1:7).[94]

Finally, although Christ possesses the glory of omnipresence he does not exercise it in a uniform manner. In the *Two Natures*, Chemnitz outlines five essential modes of presence.[95] These five are a finer categorization of the three modes of presence (local, definitive, repletive) found in the discussion of the issue in the Formula of Concord. These three categories reflect Luther's own description of Christ's presence.[96] The Reformer's own categorization of these modes was based on the earlier medieval scholastic tradition's discussion of the biblical material.[97]

The first presence is his local presence that is natural to the substance of Christ's humanity. We are told in scripture that Jesus went from place to place in Palestine and that during the three days between his death and resurrection his human body was locally present in a tomb. This presence is by no means negated by Christ's exercise of his other modes of presence, since he retained his essential attributes of circumscription according to his humanity while exercising other ones. The second mode of presence is termed "definitive." This term is used to describe Jesus's presence after his resurrection. According to this mode, the man Jesus walked through walls and disappeared and appeared at will during the forty days with his disciples. In this mode of presence, Christ transcended the normal modes of circumscribed human reality, while at the same time manifesting himself at a specific time and place. The third mode of presence is Christ's "repletive" presence. This is the presence whereby Christ is present to all creatures in an incomprehensible manner. Due to its possession of all divine attributes, Jesus's humanity is able to exercise this third presence as he chooses.[98]

But now He does, since He has ascended, not merely as any other saint, to heaven, but, as the apostle testifies [Eph 4:10], above all heavens, and also truly fills all things, and being everywhere present, not only as God, but also as man [has dominion and] rules from sea to sea and to the ends of the earth; as the prophets predict, Ps 8:1,6; 93:1f; Zech 9:10, and the apostles testify, Mark 16:20, that He everywhere wrought with them and confirmed their word with signs following.

Also see Gerhard, *On Christ*, 227–29.

94. It should be born in mind that this does not exclude Christ's exercise of his local presence. Nevertheless, if we take the promise of the scriptures literally, Christ's repletive presence is required for every eye to see him.

95. Chemnitz writes:

I therefore distinguish also between these kinds of presence: in the first place He walked on the earth, in the second He appears in heaven in glory, in the third he is present in the Supper with bread and wine, in the fourth He is present in the whole church, and in the fifth He has all creatures present with Him in a sense. (*Two Natures*, 448–49)

96. *AE* 37:215–18.

97. Sasse, *This is My Body*, 48–49.

98. See FC SD 7; *CT* 1005–7.

Chapter 10

The Mystery of the Work of Christ, Part 1

Doctrines of Atonement, Gnosticism,
and the Offices of Christ

Introduction

JESUS IS THE ETERNAL Word of God (Gen 1, John 1). Just as he once spoke forth creation in the beginning, in the midst of history he now speaks forth a new creation in and through his humanity and its temporal activity. Specifically, he does this by recapitulating creation through the exercise of his office as king, priest, and prophet. The significance of these offices is that they represent the original offices and vocations of Adam and Israel. In that the first Adam and later Israel failed to exercise these offices in accordance with God's Word of law and promise, Christ himself must take up the vocation and fulfill it himself. As God's own eternal Word and the second Adam, Jesus Christ is the true minister of the Word and the "Shepherd and Overseer of . . . souls" (1 Pet 2:25). By enacting his vocation, he ends the tyranny of the demonic forces of the old creation by the fulfillment of the judgment of the law and actualizes a new creation through a new Word of promise.

Although some theologians (notably Werner Elert and Wolfhart Pannenberg) have criticized this schema of the threefold office (*triplex munus*) first introduced into Lutheranism by Johann Gerhard, it is necessary for understanding the work of Christ.[1] First,

---

1. See Gerhard, *On Christ*, 318–31. Gerhard notes that one could simply designate Christ as priest and king, since it was also the office of the priest to teach the people according to Levitical law. This is in keeping with the earlier tradition of Lutheran dogmatics that tended to designate Christ as priest and king, but not prophet. See Luther's treatment in his commentary on Psalm 110 in *AE* 13:225–338 and Leonard Hütter, *Compendium Locorum Theologicorum*, 2:933–35. Also regarding Luther's treatment of the offices of Christ, see Siggins, *Martin Luther's Doctrine of Christ*, 48–64. It appears to be the case that Gerhard received the idea of the threefold office from Calvin. See *ICR* 2.15.1–6, in Calvin, *Institutes of the Christian Religion*, 1:494–503. Also see brief remarks in Hägglund, *History of Theology*, 313. The medieval scholastic and patristic traditions do not appear to have used this schema for the work of Christ. The only precedent for Calvin's use of the schema (beyond its presence in the scriptures themselves!) is a remark found in Eusebius. Eusebius writes: "all [three] [of the prophets, priests, and kings of the Old Testament] refer to the true Christ, the divine Word, who is the only High Priest of the universe, the only King of all creation, and the only Archprophet of the Father" (*Church History*, 1.3, in Eusebius,

as we have shown in our extensive exegesis in the preceding chapters (which we will not repeat here), the threefold office of Christ is thoroughly biblical and is not something arbitrarily imposed on the text of Sacred Scripture. In fact, as we have seen, this schema is used repeatedly not in just a few biblical texts, but is pervasive throughout the New Testament and prophetic writing of the Old Testament. Because of its presence in the Old Testament, the Second Temple Jewish expectation of multiple Messiahs to fulfill these multiple offices makes a great deal of sense.[2] Secondly, because Christ fulfilled the threefold office given to Israel and Adam, the threefold office is also useful for emphasizing the unity of God's works within the new and old creations. Just as God established human vocation in the beginning with Adam as the protological prophet, priest, and king, so too he elected prophets, priests, and kings in biblical Israel. Through the prophets he promised a coming Messiah who would fulfill all these roles and that creation would be renewed through him. Finally God sent forth his Son to fulfill these vocations and bring about redemption. Recognizing this unity of divine agency in creation and redemption is useful for staving off the ever-present threat of latent Marcionism.[3]

Lastly, humanity is redeemed by Christ's fulfillment of the law through his active and passive righteousness. The law is not an abstract standard, but is fulfilled by human moral agents within concrete vocations within the created order. Therefore in order for the law to be fulfilled, Christ had to take up the human vocations as it had been established at the beginning of creation. Since the law is in fact identical with God's desired structure for the created order, fulfillment of the law by Christ as a divine-human

---

Church History, 28). Elert thinks it somewhat arbitrary to pick "prophet, priest, and king" to describe the offices of Christ, since the Bible also uses other titles. See Elert, *Christian Faith*, 225–28. This misses the point that we have observed earlier that not only does the Bible prophecy that the Messiah will fulfill these roles and the New Testament sees Christ as fulfilling them, but that they represent the concrete shape of human vocation in the state of integrity. Christ does not fulfill the law in some sort of abstract way, but recapitulates Adam as the true minister of the Word. Also see Pannenberg, *Systematic Theology*, 2:443–46; Pannenberg, *Jesus*, 208–24. Pannenberg makes the claim that because Jesus's death was not something that he willed or planned, it cannot be considered an act of self-offering. Similarly, Jesus did not regard himself as a king. For this reason both the kingly and priestly offices are not valid interpretations of his mission. Lastly, although Jesus did see his mission in continuity with the Old Testament prophets, he was unlike them in that he did not predict or reveal this thing or that thing, but was rather concerned with the coming of God and his kingdom. As we shall demonstrate in later sections, the claim that Jesus did not regard himself as the Davidic Messiah or that he did not view his death as a propitiation for the sins of the world is demonstrably false in light of clear historical evidence. This is true in spite of oft repeated statements of liberal and moderate theologians to the contrary. For this reason, all of Pannenberg's criticisms are utterly invalid.

2. See discussion in Grabbe, *First Century Judaism*, 66–70; Chester, *Messiah and Exaltation*, 191–296.

3. See Elert, *Christian Faith*, 225–28. Beyond Elert's strong aversion to what he considers the arbitrariness of the schema of prophet, priest, and king, he thinks it wrong to understand the New Testament work of Christ in light of the Old Testament offices. It is of course correct that one should always give interpretive priority to the New Testament over the Old. Nevertheless, the New Testament, as we have seen in our very extensive exegesis, understands Christ to have fulfilled these offices. Furthermore, Elert's aversion to understanding Christ in terms of the Old Testament seems in many ways to correlate to the general discomfort towards seeing continuity between Judaism and Christianity in nineteenth and early twentieth-century German Protestant scholarship. The most notable example is Harnack's advocacy of Marcion as the only true interpreter of Paul. See A. Harnack, *Marcion*.

agent is identical with the renewal and recreation of the world. Since the old structure of creation was mangled, it was necessary to recreate the world by a re-actualization of its original narrative and structure. If Christ were merely a man, his activity of fulfilling the law could not do this. Humans are not capable of creating anything by their actions, even if performed in obedience to God's will. Nevertheless, since the activity and presence of the humanity of Jesus are identical with the divine person of the Logos, his human actions in fulfillment of the law were infused with divine power and glory. By this human obedience, he did what only God could do and renewed creation. In order to accomplish this, Christ took over and fulfilled the offices of Adam, the protological prophet, priest, and king.[4]

In that Christ's offices are meant to overcome Adam's primal failure, their exercise is conditioned by the reality of sin.[5] For this reason, the question of the exercise of Christ's offices is intrinsically connected to the nature of atonement and reconciliation. In order to clarify the form that atonement must take, we will briefly review the three main motifs of atonement as the Swedish Lutheran theologian Gustaf Aulén has schematized them in his book *Christus Victor*.[6] These three main motifs are: The conquest motif, the substitution motif, and the revelational motif.

Our goal in reviewing the three atonement motifs has a dual purpose. First, by reviewing the motifs we wish to recognize that each possesses a biblical basis. This is true, even if some variations on the general motif might be unscriptural. For example, Origen's "ransom" theory of atonement is unbiblical, even though it is properly classified as a variation on the conquest motif. Nevertheless, the Bible validates the conquest motif by portraying Christ as the conqueror of sin, death, and the devil. Similarly, in scripture Christ is also the one who makes atonement for sin (substitution motif) and reveals the true heart of the Father (revelational motif), even if there are problems with how these motifs have been appropriated in the history of Christian thought.

Secondly, because scripture teaches that reconciliation is affected by the exercise of Christ's offices, and because each office is characterized by the fulfillment of one aspect of atonement, when properly understood each office of Christ correlates to an atonement motif. As king, Christ conquers sin, death, and the devil. As priest he renders satisfaction to the Father, and as prophet confirms a new testament in his blood. By recognizing the full scope of the biblical understanding of atonement, we come to fully appreciate the necessity of the biblical doctrine of the threefold office of Christ.

---

4. We follow a similar line of reasoning regarding Christ's recapitulation of humanity found in Lutheran theologians such as Thomasius *Christi*, 2:216–18; Wingren, *Gospel and Church*, 95–101. Despite his fairly disastrous teaching regarding *kenosis*, Thomasius does a relatively good job integrating substitutionary atonement with recapitulation.

5. We favor the classical Lutheran insistence that the incarnation would not have happened if it were not for the fact of sin. This is in agreement with the contention of the larger stream of the Christian tradition to be found in Athasius, Augustine, Anslem, Aquinas, Luther, Melanchthon, Chemnitz, Calvin, and Zwingli. In this we stand against Irenaeus, Duns Scotus, Osiander, Schleiermacher, Barth, and Jenson, to name only a few. Scripture consistently construes Christ's mission this way (see Gal 4:4; 1 John 3:8). The alternative is merely speculation of the uninteresting variety.

6. Aulén, *Christus Victor*. Though Aulén's model is not satisfactory in every respect, it remains a helpful shorthand for broad similarities between different Christian thinkers.

In reviewing the history of the doctrine of the atonement, the first motif that we will discuss is that of conquest, or (as Aulén describes it), the "classical" motif.[7] By motif, Aulén does not mean a complete, precisely delineated doctrinal concept that is universally agreed upon by a group of theologians in all its details. Rather for the Lundesian school of Lutheran thought (of which Aulén was a part) a "motif" describes an image or general orientation of a class of thinkers in how they answer a central doctrinal question of the faith.[8] In the case of the first motif, Aulén groups together a number of theologians who have a great deal of theological divergence among them.

For example, with this category Aulén places Irenaeus of Lyons, who described Christ as a second Adam and recapitulator of creation.[9] As a second Adam, Christ freed humanity by overcoming the destructive elements of the old creation. He fulfilled this task by entering into the stages of creation's development and persevering where humanity had previously failed.[10] Within the same motif, Aulén places Origen of Alexandria, who posited that Christ redeemed by serving as a divine ransom.[11] On the cross, Jesus was given over to the devil in exchange for the human race. The devil, not knowing Jesus was God, accepted the ransom and released humanity from his power. After three days under Satan's dominion, by his divine power Christ overcame the devil and rose from the dead as a victorious conqueror.[12] As can be observed, although there is a wide divergence between these two descriptions of the work of Christ, the central thrust of the conquest model remains the same: Jesus, the divine savior, who enters into creation in order to rescue it from the power of demonic forces (sin, death, the devil, etc.).

7. By "classical" Aulén means that this was the earliest and most pervasive motif of atonement in Christian antiquity.

8. Aulén was part of the Lundesian school of Lutheran thought in the early part of the twentieth century and therefore shares goals with its founder, Anders Nygren regarding the idea of motif research. For all its rationalistic problems and many historical inaccuracies, it did do much interesting work. For a description of the concept of motif and the goal of motif research, see Nygren, *Agape and Eros*, 27–40. For the historical environment and the rationale for motif research, see also Arne Rasmusson, "Century of Swedish Theology," 131–38.

9. Aulén, *Christus Victor*, 16–35; Dorner, *Doctrine of the Person of Christ*, 1:303–26; González, *History of Christian Thought*, 1:157–70; Grant, *Irenaeus of Lyons*; Hägglund, *History of Theology*, 43–51; von Harnack, *History of Dogma*, 2:27–29, 230–318; J. Kelly, *Early Christian Doctrines*, 147–49; Lawson, *Biblical theology of Saint Irenaeus*; Minns, *Irenaeus*; Nielsen, *Adam and Christ*; Osborn, "Irenaeus of Lyons," 121–26; Osborn, *Irenaeus of Lyons*; Pelikan, *Christian Tradition*, 1:75–76, 149–50; Quasten, *Patrology*, 1:287–314; R. Seeberg, *Text-Book of the History of Doctrines*, 1:124–25; Steenberg, *Irenaeus on Creation*; J. Willis, *History of Christian Thought*, 1:93–106; Wingren, *Man and the Incarnation*.

10. For a relatively short and very easy-to-read summary of Irenaeus's position, see Ireneaus of Lyons, *On Apostolic Preaching*.

11. Aulén, *Christus Victor*, 38, 49, 51.

12. See a full account of Origen's system in Origen, *On First Principles*. For sources on Origen and his system see the following: Crouzel, *Origen*; Daniélou, *Origen*; Dorner, *Doctrine of the Person of Christ*, 2:104–49; de Faye, *Origen and His Work*; González, *History of Christian Thought*, 1:186–227; Greggs, *Barth, Origen, and Universal Salvation*; Hägglund, *History of Theology*, 63–68; A. Harnack, *History of Dogma*, 2:319–80; Küng, *Great Christian Thinkers*, 41–68; McGuckin, *Westminster Handbook to Origen*; Neve, *History of Christian Thought*, 89–91; Pelikan, *Christian Tradition*, 1:38; Quasten, *Patrology*, 2:37–100; Rowe, *Origen's Doctrine of Subordination*; Tillich, *History of Christian Thought*, 55–63; Trigg, *Origen*; Tzamalikos, *Origen*; R. Williams, "Origen," 132–42; J. Willis, *History of Christian Thought*, 1:143–58.

The conquest motif was the chief model of redemption in the early Church and was used by most of the Greek patristic theologians. Over time it became more and more elaborate. Athanasius's theology of atonement is an apt example of this. In his short work *On the Incarnation of the Word*, he argues that the incarnation occurred in order to overcome the fetters that had held humanity back from its own movement towards participation in the divine life (*theosis*).[13] In order to accomplish this, God the Logos entered the human story, deified his assumed humanity and defeated death and the devil.[14] The form the Messiah's death had taken was necessary because "the devil, the enemy of our race, having fallen from heaven, wanders about in the lower atmosphere." Therefore, "it was quite fitting that the Lord suffered this death . . . being lifted up he cleared the air of the malignity both of the devil and of demons of all kinds . . . and made a new opening of the way up into heaven."[15]

For Athanasius, this was not the only reason for the Lord's death. In Jesus's death, the curse of death had been exhausted: "all being held to have died in him, the law involving the ruin of men might be undone (insofar as its power was fully spent in the Lord's body, and had no longer holding ground against men, his peer)." Beyond this, Athanasius also understood Jesus's death as a sacrifice of sin: "by offering unto death he himself had taken as an offering and sacrifice free from stain, straightway he put away death from all his peers by offering an equivalent."[16] Hence, as can be observed, the model of conquest does not exclude substitution. Nevertheless, the substitution motif is for Athanasius a subplot in a larger drama of God's conquest of death and the devil.

Elaborations on these same themes continued to be the main overture in the later Byzantine theologies of Maximus the Confessor and John of Damascus.[17] In the theol-

---

13. See Athanathius, *De Incarnatione Verbi Dei*, 4, in *Christology of the Later Fathers*, 58. Here we read:

> So that, if they kept the grace and remained good, they might still keep the life in paradise without sorrow or pain or care, besides having the promise of incorruption in heaven; but that if they transgressed and turned back, and became evil, they might know that they were incurring that corruption in death which was theirs by nature, no longer to live in paradise, but cast out of it from that time forth to die and to abide in death and in corruption.

Athanasius also states:

> But men, having despised and rejected the contemplation of God, and devised and contrived evil for themselves. . . , received the condemnation of death with which they hand been threatened; and from thenceforth no longer remained as they were made, but were being corrupted to their devices; and death had mastery over them as king. (59)

14. See Athanathius, *De Incarnatione Verbi Dei*, 13, in *Christology of the Later Fathers*, 67–68. Again we read:

> Whence the Word of God came in his own person, that as he was the image of the Father, he might be able to create afresh the man after the image. . . .Whence he took, in natural fitness, a mortal body, that while death might in it be once for all done away, men made after his image might once more be renewed. None other, then, was sufficient for this need, save the image of the Father.

15. Athanathius, *De Incarnatione Verbi Dei*, 25, in *Christology of the Later Fathers*, 80.

16. Athanathius, *De Incarnatione Verbi Dei*, 9, in *Christology of the Later Fathers*, 63.

17. Meyendorf, *Christ in Eastern Christian Thought*, 137–40. Regarding Maximus and his thought, also see the following works: Dorner, *Doctrine of the Person of Christ*, 3:228–36; González, *History of Christian Thought*, 2:76–106; Hägglund, *History of Theology*, 103; Louth, *Maximus the Confessor*; Pelikan, *Christian Tradition*, 2:8–36; Thunberg, *Microcosm and Mediator*; J. Williams, "Pseudo-Dionysius and

ogy of the former, it was Adam's task not only to reach deification, but also to resolve various dualities within creation (the divergence between male and female, heaven and earth, etc.) that had been left unresolved by God in his initial creation.[18] Having fallen into sin and under the dominion of the devil, Adam was unable to perform this task.[19] Through his work of salvation, Christ was not only victorious over the demonic forces of the old creation, but also dualities that Adam failed to resolve.[20]

Similarly, according to John of Damascus, even in the garden of Eden, it had been the vocation of the human race to ascend toward the divine life and by so doing to bring the whole creation into union with God's being.[21] To do this it was necessary for Adam to strive for deification: "And so it was necessary first for man to be tested, since one who is untried and untested deserves no credit. Then when trial had made him perfect through his keeping of the commandment he should thus win incorruptibility."[22] Satan interfered by tempting Adam with offer of divine knowledge too early in the process of deification: "[the devil] tempted that wretched man with the very hope of divinity."[23] In spite of his emphasis on Christ's conquest of the power of the devil, in describing Jesus's death, the Damascene specifically rejects Origen's interpretation of a ransom paid to the devil ("God forbid that the Lord's blood should be offered to the tyrant!"[24]). Instead, in a fashion similar to Athanasius, emphasized that Jesus overcame the devil by suffering the curse suffered by humans under sin: "He appropriated our curse and dereliction and such things as are not according to nature, not because He was or had been such, but because He took on our appearance and was reckoned as one of us. And such is the sense of the words, 'being made a curse for us.'"[25] Jesus is the savior of the human race in that he completed human destiny by overcoming the demonic forces of the old creation and ascended into a heavenly existence.[26] By receiving Jesus's flesh and blood in the Lord's Supper, Christ's nature passes into the composition of the body and soul of the recipient.[27] Through this sacrament the believer shares in Jesus's victory and receives a share in his divinity.

Maximus the Confessor," 193–99. See description of John of Damascus in the following: González, *History of Christian Thought*, 2:201–4; Hägglund, *History of Theology*, 103–5; von Harnack, *History of Dogma*, 4:264–67, 301–3; Louth, *St. John Damascene*; Pelikan, *Christian Tradition*, 2:130–31; R. Seeberg, *Text-Book of the History of Doctrines*, 1:285–87; J. Willis, *History of Christian Thought*, 2:29–30.

18. Meyendorff, *Christ in Eastern Christian Thought*, 137.

19. Ibid.

20. Ibid., 137–39.

21. Louth, *St. John Damascene*, 117–43.

22. *Orthodox Faith*, 2.30, in John of Damascus, *Saint John of Damascus*, 265–66. Again we read in the same passage:

> He (who) had been created half way between God and matter should be freed from his natural relationship to creatures and united to God by keeping the commandment, then he was to be permanently united to God and immutably rooted in the good.

23. Ibid.

24. *Orthodox Faith*, 3.27, in John of Damascus, *Saint John of Damascus*, 332.

25. *Orthodox Faith*, 3.25, in John of Damascus, *Saint John of Damascus*, 330–31.

26. Louth, *St. John Damascene*, 144–78.

27. *Orthodox Faith*, 4.13, John of Damascus, in *Saint John of Damascus*, 361:

> [In the Lord's Supper it] is Christ's body and blood entering into the composition of our soul

Having reviewed the major elements and proponents of the conquest motif, we now turn to the substitution motif. Starting with Tertullian in the third century, Latin theologians began to emphasize the idea of Christ's death as a form of meritorious substitution, while still holding onto elements of the conquest motif.[28] The predominance of this doctrinal motif developed along with the Latin system of penance and merit, drawing heavily on the concept of "supererogatoria."[29] According to this concept, an individual by certain acts could make themselves worthy of higher merits before God through following the divine law more rigorously than was actually necessary. This could take the form of the maintenance of virginity, the seeking martyrdom, or fasting.[30] Tertullian himself was a strong proponent of such a view, as well as the idea that Christ's death had been a substitution for sin. Although Tertullian appears never to have believed that merit from the acts of the faithful could be transferred from one person to another, his student Cyprian, came to hold such an opinion and promoted it among his contemporaries.[31]

By the eleventh century, Latin Christianity had developed an elaborate system of merit and penance under the influence of the aforementioned theories, as well as certain concepts borrowed from Germanic law. Due to this fact, it is easy to see why Latin Christianity finally began to move away from the conquest motif, in that slavery to Satan now took a back seat to the problem of the debt of sin. Anselm of Canterbury represents the first theologian in the west to develop a concept of atonement that consciously de-emphasized the idea that Jesus's primary function was the destruction of demonic forces.[32] In some of the early passages of what is probably his best-known work, *Cur Deus Homo?*, he vigorously attacked the idea that the devil exercised any kind of rights over the human race: "As for saying that he [Jesus] came to conquer the Devil for you, in what sense do you dare assert that? Does not the omnipotence of God reign everywhere? How then did God need to come down from heaven to defeat the Devil?"[33] Instead, following the old Latin idea of merit and its transferability, Anselm argued that Christ himself had, by dying on the cross, performed an act of unprecedented supererogation: "No man besides him ever gave to God, by dying, what he was not necessarily going to lose at some time,

---

and body without being consumed, without being corrupted. . . . When we are purified by it we become one with the body of the Lord and with His Spirit, and we become the body of Christ.

Again in the same passage he states:

It is called participation [the Lord's Supper] because through it we participate in the divinity of Jesus. (361)

28. Aulén, *Christus Victor*, 82.

29. See *On Penance* 2 in Tertullian, *Treatises on Penance and Purity*, 16–17.

30. Aulén, *Christus Victor*, 82.

31. Ibid.

32. Aulén, *Christus Victor*, 84–92; Deme, *Christology of Anselm of Canterbury*, 175–208; G. Evans, "Anselm of Canterbury," 94–101; Forde, "Work of Christ," 2:20–25; Hägglund, *History of Theology*, 167–74; A. Harnack, *History of Dogma*, 6:54–81; Gasper, *Anselm of Canterbury*, 144–73; Gollnick, *Flesh as Transformation*; González, *History of Christian Thought*, 2:158–67; D. Hogg, *Anselm of Canterbury*, 157–88; Pelikan, *Christian Tradition*, 3:106–8, 116–17, 139–44, 210–11; J. Rigg, *St. Anselm of Canterbury*; A. Ritschl, *Christliche Lehre*, 1:31–47; R. Seeberg, *Text-Book of the History of Doctrines*, 2:60–70; J. Willis, *History of Christian Thought*, 2:85–94.

33. Anselm, *Cur Deus Homo?*, 1.6, in *Scholastic Miscellany*, 107.

or paid what he did not owe. But this man freely offered to the Father what he would never have lost by any necessity, and paid for sinners what he did not owe himself."[34]

This was necessary because the human race, having fallen into sin, could in no way merit its own salvation. If disobedience occurs and God is robbed of honor, then logically something greater must be given back for the sake of compensation. This is impossible, though. Since all rational creatures owe God absolute allegiance, explained Anselm, any act of obedience performed by such creatures would be only giving what was already owed. Consequently, acts of obedience could by no means make up for past acts of disobedience: "Every inclination of the rational creature ought to be subject to God . . . This is the debt angels and humans owe to God. No one who pays it sins."[35]

In order to bring about salvation, someone would have to pay this debt who himself did not owe it. Because Jesus was God, he did not owe the debt. Furthermore, Jesus could pay the debt incurred by fallen humans because he himself was greater than the whole of creation: "If he is to give something of his own to God, which surpasses everything that is beneath God, it is also necessary for him to be greater than everything that is not God."[36] On the other hand, being true man he was capable of paying the debt owed by other humans. Living a perfect life, Jesus was not obligated to die in the manner of other fallen humans.[37] Therefore, by dying, when it was unnecessary for him to do so, Jesus gained an infinite treasury of merit from God that he could in turn credit to the human race.

Anselm's theology does not of course exhaust the description of the substitution motif. In contrast to Anselm's description of Christ's vicarious death as meritorious, the Reformers and Protestant scholastics described Christ's work both as meritorious action and as a punishment for sin.[38] As previously noted, Flacius developed the categories of "active" and "passive" righteousness to describe this twofold form of substitution.[39] Later, we will discuss and explore the implications of understanding substitution in this manner. It should nevertheless be observed that although the Reformers and Protestant scholastics deviated from Anselm in many details, there remain important structural continuities between their positions.

---

34. Anselm, *Cur Deus Homo?*, 2.28, in *Scholastic Miscellany*, 177.

35. Anselm, *Cur Deus Homo?*, 1.11, in *Scholastic Miscellany*, 119. Also see 1.21, in *Scholastic Miscellany*, 139: "Therefore, you do not make satisfaction unless you repay something greater than that for the sake of which you were obliged not to commit the sin."

36. Anselm, *Cur Deus Homo?*, 2.5, in *Scholastic Miscellany*, 150.

37. Anselm, *Cur Deus Homo?*, 2.18, in *Scholastic Miscellany*, 179. We read:
Thus when the Lord Jesus willed to endure death (as we have said), because he had the right either to suffer or not to suffer, he ought to have done what he did, because he willed what ought to be done, and yet he was not obliged to do it, because there was no debt involved. For in his human nature (since he himself was God and man), from the time he became man, he received from the divine nature, which is different from the human, the right to claim as he had all that he possessed so completely from himself, and was so perfectly self-sufficient, that he neither owed any recompense to anyone else nor needed to give in order to have something repaid to him.

38. See H. Schmid, *Doctrinal Theology*, 342–70; Heppe, *Reformed Dogmatics*, 448–81.

39. H. Schmid, *Doctrinal Theology*, 354.

The last motif is the revelational or moral influence theory of atonement.[40] This motif was first developed by Abelard in the twelfth century.[41] According to Abelard, the killing of the Son by human beings would result not in the expiation of sin, but would rather cause an even greater sin than that of Adam's. God in Christ therefore did not die in order to atone for sin, but instead in order to demonstrate his love for humanity. This communication of love would lead to reciprocal love on the part of the human race. A form of this motif was promoted in the early modern period by the Socinians.[42] In the Socninian version, Jesus mainly serves as an exemplar of moral virtue by his death. Such an example was meant to influence the human race to engage in virtuous behavior. Modern Liberal theologicians, notably Friedrich Schleiermacher and Albrecht Ritschl have also promoted various versions of the revelational motif.[43] The essence of this motif is that God in Christ communicates his truth to humanity in an effective way, and thereby transforms them by it.

Having examined the three main motifs, there is a need in our development of the doctrine of atonement to systematically integrate them. As we have seen, this is the case because of the presence of all three in the biblical authority. This truth is recognized in the Lutheran symbolic writings themselves, which regularly describe all three aspects of Christ's work with a special emphasis on the first two motifs.[44] Luther's contribution to the Book of Concord particularly bears this out. Although we cannot enter into the often-heated debate regarding the exact nature of Luther's understanding of atonement, his treatment of the work of Christ in the Small and Large Catechisms exemplifies an integration of the motifs.[45] The Reformer writes in the Small Catechism:

> I believe that Jesus Christ, true God, begotten of the Father from eternity, and
> also true man, born of the Virgin Mary, is my Lord, who has redeemed me, a
> lost and condemned creature, *purchased and won [delivered] me from all sins,*

40. Aulén, *Christus Victor*, 133–42.

41. See Abelard, "Epistle to the Romans," 276–87. Also see summary in the following: Aulén, *Christus Victor*, 95–98; Bromiley, *Historical Theology*, 185–88; González, *History of Christian Thought*, 2:167–74; Hägglund, *History of Theology*, 167; Kaiser, *Doctrine of the Atonement*, 42–53; A. Ritschl, *Christliche Lehre*, 1:48–54; R. Seeberg, *Text-Book of the History of Doctrines*, 2:70–73.

42. Socinus, *Racovian Catechism*, 297–320. Also see Dorner, *Doctrine of the Person of Christ*, 4:249–65; González, *History of Christian Thought*, 3:264, 279; A. Harnack, *History of Dogma*, 7:139–67; Pelikan, *Christian Tradition*, 5:197–98; O. Ritschl, *Dogmengeschichte des Protestantismus*, 4:278–83; J. Willis, *History of Christian Thought*, 3:145–46.

43. One of the better examples can be found in Rashdall Hastings, *Idea of Atonement*. See also A. Ritschl, *Christliche Lehre*, 3:364–455; Schleiermacher, *Christian Faith*, 425–75.

44. For a discussion of the work of Christ in the Lutheran symbols see the following sources: All-beck, *Studies in the Lutheran Confessions*, 67–69; Fagerberg, *New Look at the Lutheran Confessions*, 117–21; Grane, *Confessio Augustana*, 31–36; Lehmann and Pöhlmann, "Gott, Jesus Christus, Wiederkunft Christi," 57–63; Little, *Lutheran Confessional Theology*, 16–23; R. Preus, *Theology of Concord*, 40–48; Schlink, *Lutheran Confessions*, 83–88; Schmucker, "Person and Work of Christ," 68–106.

45. For a discussion of the work of Christ in Luther, see the following sources: Althaus, *Theology of Martin Luther*, 201–23; Aulén, *Christus Victor*, 107–8; H. Bornkamm, *Luther's World of Thought*, 156–75; Elert, *Structure of Lutheranism*, 106–26; Forde, "Work of Christ," 2:47–65; Hinlicky, *Luther and the Beloved Community*, 66–138; Janz, *Westminster Handbook to Martin Luther*, 8–10; Kolb, *Martin Luther*, 118–24; Lohse, *Martin Luther's Theology*, 223–28; Paulson, *Lutheran Theology*, 96–113; Pinomaa, *Faith Victorious*, 46–57; Watson, *Let God Be God!*, 116–25.

from death, and from the *power of the devil*, not with gold or silver, but with *His holy, precious blood and with His innocent suffering and death*, in order that I may be [wholly] His own, and live under Him in His kingdom, and *serve Him* in everlasting righteousness, innocence, and blessedness, even as He is risen from the dead, lives and *reigns to all eternity*. This is most certainly true.[46]

In the Large Catechism, he writes:

For when we had been created by God the Father, and had received from Him all manner of good, the devil came and led us into disobedience, sin, death, and all evil, so that we fell under His wrath and displeasure and were doomed to eternal damnation, as we had merited and deserved. There was no counsel, help, or comfort until this only and eternal Son of God in His unfathomable goodness had compassion upon our misery and wretchedness, and came from heaven to help us. *Those tyrants and jailers, then, are all expelled now, and in their place has come Jesus Christ, Lord of life, righteousness, every blessing, and salvation*, and has delivered us poor lost men from the jaws of hell, has won us, made us free, and brought us again into the favor and grace of the Father, and has taken us as His own property under His shelter and protection, that He may govern us by His righteousness, wisdom, power, life, and blessedness. Let this, then, be the sum of this article that the little word Lord signifies simply as much as Redeemer, i.e., He who has brought *us from Satan to God, from death to life, from sin to righteousness, and who preserves us in the same*. But all the points which follow in order in this article serve no other end than to explain and express this redemption, how and whereby it was accomplished, that is, how much it cost Him, and what He spent and risked that He might win us and bring us under *His dominion*, namely, that He became man, conceived and born without [any stain of] sin, of the Holy Ghost and of the Virgin Mary, that He might overcome sin; moreover, that He suffered, died and was buried, that *He might make satisfaction for me and pay what I owe, not with silver nor gold, but with His own precious blood*. And all this, in order to become my Lord; for He did none of these for Himself, nor had He any need of it. And after that He rose again from the dead, swallowed up and devoured death, and finally ascended into heaven and assumed the government at the Father's right hand, so that the devil and all powers must be subject to Him and lie at His feet, until finally, at the last day, He will completely part and separate us from the wicked world, the devil, death, sin, etc.[47]

In the treatments above, Luther interprets the biblical materials in a very similar manner to some of the Greek Fathers. As we observed earlier, theologians like John of Damascus and Athanasius emphasized Christ's death as both a means of defeating demonic forces and (somewhat more mutedly) as a substitute for sin. In this regard, we agree with Aulén that what we find in Luther is a return to the theology of the early Church, even if we do not agree with every aspect of his interpretation of the Reformer.[48] Perhaps it might be speculated (although this cannot be proven), that having studied Peter Lombard at length in his student days, that Luther's description owes much

46. SC 2:2; *CT* 545 (emphasis added).

47. LC 2:2; *CT* 685, 687 (emphasis added).

48. Aulén, *Christus Victor*, 1–22. Since Luther so strongly emphasizes the substitution motif, it is difficult to positively place him in the category of conquest as Aulén would like.

to the Master of Sentences who also worked to integrate the different motifs.[49] Neither (contrary to Aulén's assertion) was the multidimensional nature of atonement entirely lost during the period of Lutheran orthodoxy.[50] As Robert Preus has shown, the defeat of death and the devil also played an integral role in the treatment of atonement in such Lutheran scholastic figures as Andreas Quenstedt.[51] Considered in light of his continuity with the previous tradition, Luther's integrative understanding of the redeeming work of Christ is both highly biblical and ecumenical.

Perhaps some might object that a discussion of the prophetic office is missing from Luther's description of atonement. Although it is of course true in that Luther's main emphasis is on the priestly and kingly work of the Messiah, he obviously does not deny that Christ engaged in prophetic activity. In one Easter sermon, the Reformer remarks that Christ's resurrection would have been meaningless had it not been preached.[52] Rather it is more likely that Luther sees the objective element of the work of Christ (defeating demonic forces and atoning for sin) as being properly discussed in the second article, whereas the subjective appropriation and communication of that work is properly discussed in the third article along with the Church and the means of grace. Of course the third article could not function without the prophetic activity of Christ. As the Reformer states elsewhere in the Catechisms, the means of grace were prophetically authorized by Christ's dominical command.

This brings us to our second point regarding the importance of the integrative model of the work of Christ. As Luther's treatment demonstrates, there is a unity of the prophetic work of the Holy Spirit in the third article with the kingly and priestly work of Christ in the second article. Such an observation allows us to focus our vision and recognize that the threefold office and the threefold work of reconciliation represent a unification of God's Triune agency in creation and redemption. Jesus, being both the true man and also the creator and redeemer God, necessarily "unite[s] all things . . . in heaven and things on earth" (Eph 1:10) in himself. As true God, he redeems and renews creation by becoming true man. He is the true fulfillment of the whole narrative of creation and redemption, and therefore the focal point and embodiment of the works of the whole Trinity.

Because the threefold office and action of reconciliation expresses the unity of Triune agency in creation and redemption, each office and work of reconciliation corresponds to a person of the Trinity. By defeating the devil in spiritual combat, Christ recapitulates the office of king and thereby establishes the freedom lost by Adam in the Fall. This office correlates to the role of the Father within the Godhead, who although he does not somehow dominate the Son and the Spirit (as is taught in the heresy of subordinationism), is the fount of divinity and therefore the originating source of all divine sovereignty. As priest, Christ offers up praise with his earthly life and also a propitiatory sacrifice that will satisfy divine wrath. This corresponds to the Son, who eternally receives all from the Father and therefore in an eternal priestly act, returns himself to

49. Lohse, *Martin Luther's Theology*, 45–47. Also see discussion in Lombard, *Sentences*, 3:72–92.

50. Aulén, *Christus Victor*, 128–33.

51. R. Preus, "Vicarious Atonement," 78–97.

52. Luther, "Easter Sunday Afternoon," 131.

the Father in the procession of the Holy Spirit. Lastly, by his revelation of Father, and his establishment of the new testament in his blood, Christ fulfills the role of prophet. This corresponds to the Holy Spirit, who is the agent of revelation and the unity of the Father and the Son, just as he unites God and his Church. All God's actions *ad extra* are performed by the Trinity as a single agent (*opera Trinitatis ad extra sunt indivisa*).[53] Consequently, although it is the Son alone who became incarnate, he expresses the reality of the whole Trinity.[54]

That Christ's work embodies the whole Triune economy not only gives us a clearer picture regarding the identity of the Messiah, but it also helps us avoid the Gnostic account of redemption that has often plagued the history of Christian thought. While Gnosticism is notoriously hard to define, there nevertheless appears to be a number of common features that are present across the variety of systems that stand within this classification.[55] Gnosticism was a heresy of the early patristic era, which taught that creation was the result of a lesser deity who was either evil or incompetent.[56] This deity was often identified with the God of the Old Testament.[57] The human person was divided between a spiritual-divine nature, which it had received from a higher and transcendent, purely spiritual god, and a physical body, that the spiritual nature had come to inhabit after a pre-temporal fall/cosmic accident.[58] Having come under the domination of matter and the lesser god of creation, humans were generally (though not always exclusively) viewed as being hapless victims of forces beyond their control.[59] Jesus was not a real physical man, but rather a phantom who rescued humanity from the lesser god by disclosing secret knowledge of their real identity as true divine children of the transcendent spiritual god.[60] By accepting this knowledge, human beings were able to shuck their physical nature, and ascend to the spiritual realm.[61]

In light of the themes that we have already developed in the previous chapters, it is clear and obvious Gnosticism is simply a variation on the heresy of our first parents, namely enthusiasm. The Gnostic rejects his or her status as a creature and rather wishes to be seen as a frustrated divine being. They reject the external Word of the creator God

---

53. See Luther's discussion in *AE* 15:302.

54. To find a similar approach to the one we have adopted here, see Robert Sherman, *King, Priest, and Prophet*.

55. See the following treatments: Bianchi, *Le Origini Dello Gnosticismo*; Churton, *Gnostics*; Couliano, *Tree of Gnosis*; Dunderberg, *Beyond Gnosticism*; Filoramo, *History of Gnosticism*; Haar, *Simon Magus*; Hanratty, *Studies in Gnosticism*; Grant, *Gnosticism and Early Christianity*; van Groningen, *First Century Gnosticism*; Jonas, *Gnostic Religion*; King, *Gnostics and Their Remains*; Lacarriere, *Gnostics*; Luttikhuizen, *Gnostic Revisions of Genesis*; Logan, *Gnostics*; Logan, Gnostic Truth and Christian Heresy; Mansel, *Gnostic Heresies*; Marjanen, *Was there a Gnostic Religion?*; M. Meyer, *Gnostic Discoveries*; Pagels, *Gnostic Gospels*; Perkins, *Gnostic Dialogue*; Perkins, *Gnosticism and the New Testament*; Petrement, *Separate God*; Roukema, *Gnosis and Faith*; Rudolph, *Gnosis*; Carl Smith, *No longer Jews*; Wilson, *Gnostic Problem*.

56. Rudolph, *Gnosis*, 74–84.

57. Ibid., 79.

58. Ibid., 92–93.

59. Ibid., 100–101, 104–5.

60. Ibid., 118–21, 144–52.

61. Ibid., 171–89.

that tells them of their sinful and creaturely status, and rather rely on the inner word of the secret spiritual messenger. Adam sought to hold the knowledge of good and evil in his own heart. In a similar manner, the gnostic holds the secret knowledge of his or her divine origin and the path to the transcendent created world within themselves. This knowledge becomes a tool of self-justification against the threatening and accusing Word of the creator God, whom the gnostic has become deluded into believing is not the real god after all. The word of the gospel is also rejected insofar as the gnostic holds the possibility of salvation from within him or herself and therefore needs no external word of redemption.

For this reason, properly recognizing the full scope of Christ's work as encompassing and focusing the whole creed helps us repudiate the gnostic temptation. First, as we observed earlier, Christ's recapitulation of Adam and Israel achieves for us the necessary connection between the two Testaments, as well as the unity of the articles of creation and redemption. Disintegration of the God of the New Testament from that of the Old is a hallmark of the gnostic system in general and its Marcionite variant in particular.[62] This has become a significant problem in many forms of modern theology, which are eager for the New Testament to be maximally discontinuous with God's previous dealings with humanity.[63] The complaint of many theologians is that if this were not the case, then the New Testament would lack a proper "novelty."[64] Nevertheless, such "novelty" is not consistent with the faithfulness of God as it is expressed in the proclamation of the gospel. A God who has not been faithful to his original creation or to his promises to the people of Israel cannot be thought to be the self-donating God of the incarnation and the New Testament. The true disruption and novelty is the word of the gospel as it disrupts the demanding word of the law. The gospel is not a new era, but a promise and an act of redemption. The fulfillment of this promise in the era of the New Testament is not a disruption of the old dispensation, but a fulfillment of the promises made in that era.

Moreover, much of this interest in "novelty" and in the God of redemption at the expense of the God of creation, is based on the assumption (becoming prominent in modern theology, beginning with Schleiermacher) that the basis of theology is not the word of the Bible (which encompasses the whole history of God's faithfulness in both creation and redemption), but rather the enthusiastic experience of redemption. As a result, the experience of the God of redemption trumps or mutes the relationship of the believer to the God of creation. This propounds a *de facto* Marcionism.[65] In this scenario,

---

62. Some historians of dogma would of course not classify Marcionism as a form of Gnosticism. Here we do so insofar as it shares the basic structural similarities of other forms of Gnosticism. We cannot debate at length whether this technically makes Marcion fall within the range of Gnosticism.

63. Elert, *Christian Faith*, 225–28.

64. Prenter, *Creation and Redemption*, 61.

65. Though Schleiermacher does discuss creation in the *Glaubenslehre*, he makes this discussion dependent on redemption (see Schleiermacher, *Christian Faith*, 142–56). Furthermore, since Christianity is the experience of redemption brought about by Jesus it has nothing to do with the Old Testament. He therefore proposes its removal from the canon (see Schleiermacher, *Christian Faith*, 608–11). In spite of Barth's castigation of Schleiermacher for his anthropocentrism, his preference for supralapsarianism over infralapsarianism makes him equally guilty of subordinating creation to redemption (see *CD* 2.2.127–45).

not only does theology degenerate into an enthusiastic-anthropocentric discourse, it also fails to recognize that the new narrative of creation is a recapitulation and fulfillment of the old creation.[66] As we have previously emphasized, this unity is necessary because without it we cannot proclaim the faithfulness of God which is at the heart of the gospel. The gospel, when properly understood brings the human person back to his or her original status as a hearing creature.

From this it should also become clear that the disintegration of creation and redemption tends to lead to a form of enthusiasm by positing that God operates apart from the mediums of creation. By contrast, Lutheran dogmatics has always taught that God always operates redemptively from within the realities of the original creation, namely physical and visible means of grace. Such incorporation represents divine faithfulness to the original creation. Indeed such faithfulness is the foundation of both the incarnation and the sacramental mediation of God's promises. Because God is faithful to his original works, he incorporates them into his eschatological work of redemption.[67]

Similarly, an overemphasis on any one office of Christ at the expense of the others can lead to a form of gnostic-enthusiasm. Since each office uniquely expresses and corresponds to the unified agency of the Trinity in creation and redemption, denigration or overemphasis of any one office naturally leads to the gnostic disintegration of God the creator from God the redeemer.

For example, an overemphasis on the kingly office of Christ at the expense of his role as priest and prophet, can lead to the aspect of the gnostic account that suggests that humans are hapless victims of the structures of creation. Jesus must rescue his creation by his use of force and power. This is particularly evident in modern Feminist and Liberationist theology.[68] Liberation theology and Feminist theology simply replace the old demonic rulers of the gnostic universe (typically called "Archons") with modern social and economic forces.[69] Jesus's role in this theory of redemption is to enlighten the oppressed and lead them to liberation by conquest of these forces by superior power. Excluding Jesus's office as great high priest, Feminist and Liberationist theologies view disenfranchised groups as hapless victims of the "system." Hence they are not guilty

---

66. See critique in Wingren, *Creation and Law*, 12–14; Wingren, *Theology of Conflict*.

67. See David Scaer's argument in "Baptism and the Lord's Supper," 37–59.

68. For examples of Feminist theology see the following authors: M. Daly, *Amazon Grace*; M. Daly, *Beyond God the Father*; M. Daly, *Church and the Second Sex*; M. Daly, *Gyn/Ecology*; M. Daly, *Pure Lust*; M. Daly, *Outercourse*; M. Daly, *Quintessence*; E. Johnson, *Church Women Want*; E. Johnson, *Consider Jesus*; E. Johnson, *Friends of God and Prophets*; E. Johnson, *Quest for the Living God*; E. Johnson, *She Who Is*; E. Johnson, *Truly Our Sister*; E. Johnson, *Women, Earth, and Creator Spirit*; E. Johnson, *Who Do You Say that I Am?*; McFague, *Body of God*; McFague, *Life Abundant*; McFague, *Metaphorical Theology*; McFague, *Models of God*; McFague, *New Climate for Theology*; McFague, *Speaking in Parables*; McFague, *Super, Natural Christians*; Ruether, *America, Amerikkka*; Ruether, *Church Against Itself*; Ruether, *Gaia and God*; Ruether, *Integrating Ecofeminism*; Ruether, *Sexism and God-Talk*; Ruether, *Wrath of Jonah*. For some sources on Liberation theology see the following: Berryman, *Liberation Theology*; Gutiérrez, *Theology of Liberation*; Gutiérrez, *We Drink from Our Own Wells*; Mahan and Richesin, *Challenge of Liberation Theology*; Petrella, *Future of Liberation Theology*; Sigmund, *Liberation Theology at the Crossroads*; Christian Smith, *Emergence of Liberation Theology*; De La Torres, *U.S. Theologies of Liberation*.

69. For discussion of Archons, see Rudolph, *Gnosis*, 172–75. Also see an attempt to combine *Christus Victor* with Liberationism in Maimela, "Atonement in the Context of Liberation Theology," 261–69.

and therefore have no need for atonement. The movement towards self-justification is complete. Status as a disenfranchised person *coram mundo* translates into righteousness *coram Deo*.

The same tendency can be observed elsewhere, particularly in the antinomianism of American mainline Protestantism. As of late, many American mainline Protestants have attempted to free humanity from God's law and the structures of creation through the promotion of homosexual marriage and women's ordination. The created roles determined by human embodiment are to be shucked in favor of the autonomous freedom of the divine, disembodied self. The divine, disembodied self can justify its claims of bourgeois autonomy against the demands of the created order and the God of the Bible by appealing to a "new thing," which the Spirit is doing in leading the voting assembly of a given denomination.[70] It is not tremendously surprising that among these denominations, Feminist and Liberation theology are also very popular and that there is a significant antagonism towards the concept of substitutionary atonement. Regarding the latter, for many in the American mainline, God's holy demand in the law has ceased to be a condition of salvation and therefore the payment of the debt of sin is superfluous. With this, the God of created distinction and law is rejected, and the gnostic myth is upheld.[71]

On the other end of the spectrum, contemporary American Evangelicals with their strong emphasis on Christ's role as priest, tend to downplay or misfocus their understanding of Christ's work as king and prophet. This too leads to a kind of Gnosticism. On one level, a strong emphasis on Christ's role as propitiator is of course important, particularly in light of its general rejection within modern theology. Nevertheless, Evangelicals tend to disintegrate the office of priest from that of king, and view Christ's work of propitiation as an abstract debt repayment. In other words, unlike in the treatments we have reviewed in the New Testament, the church fathers, and the Lutheran Confessions, the debt that humanity owes to God is only tenuously connected with creation's bondage to demonic forces. Rather, the language of popular Evangelicalism generally conceptualizes the debt of sin as an abstract sum held for repayment in a heavenly bank with little to do with temporal human bondage.

This unfortunate lack of clarity in Evangelicals' interpretation of Christ's priestly office has several effects on its popular theology. First, having disintegrated the debt of sin from the sway of sin, death, and the devil (all of which enslave the human will as a result of the debt of sin) they find it possible to hold an Arminian account of the freedom of the will. This description of human agency is imbued with a strongly gnostic account of the divine-human relationship. Within this account, the will is understood as something hermetically sealed from the casual order and therefore is utterly free. This lack of relatedness to the casual order can only mean a lack of contingency on outside forces. Since in fact the only thing that lacks dependency on the casual order is God himself, this account of redemption makes the human will something divine. Hence, the gnostic idea of the divine self is the logical implication of the popular Evangelical account of the freedom of the will. Likewise, the Evangelical description of faith is one

---

70. The author of this work has received this answer on a number of occasions when speaking with mainline Protestants about their acceptance and support for homosexual behavior.

71. See critique of Liberal Protestant Gnosticism in Lee Philip, *Against the Protestant Gnostics*.

of a decision to accept a certain sort of revealed heavenly knowledge (i.e., the knowledge of Christ's repayment of debt on one's behalf). This bears an interesting resemblance to the gnostic description of the secret knowledge brought by the heavenly messenger to the secret divine self.

This concept of faith also becomes self-justifying insofar as the person who has made their decision for Jesus can stand before God and others with the conceit of having performed the one good work that God demands. For this reason the popular American Evangelical concept of faith is utterly different than that of the Evangelical Lutheran. For the former, faith is an acceptance of a kind of abstract knowledge, and not a trust in the promises of God concretely presented in Word and sacrament. The reception of God's promises from the Lutheran perspective is tied up in freedom from sin, death, and the devil, "for where there is forgiveness of sins, there is also life and salvation."[72] As a result, God's effective Word is absolutely necessary to overcome the bondage of the will. Hence, the Arminian account of redemption also denigrates the work of Christ's prophetic office as well, because it denies the efficacy of the means of grace. This shifts power from the divine creative Word, to the divine, *autopoetic* self.[73]

To the extent that popular American Evangelical theology does discuss the kingly office of Christ, the description is misfocused. Instead of locating Christ's power to overcome the devil and death in his crucifixion, resurrection, and continuing presence in the Church via Word and sacrament, many strains of American Evangelicalism focus on Christ's defeat of the devil either through earthly political programs or on the elaborate and fanciful eschatological scenarios of Millenarianism.[74] Both these orientations toward the establishment of Christ's kingdom on earth assume that Christ's victory over demonic forces is in some sense incomplete and therefore needs to be augmented in some way. Similarly since the divine Word is ineffective, it would appear that proponents of such views assume that there is a need for the use of raw power, whether this occurs through the exertion of political coercion or by Christ's overwhelming of the antichrist at the battle of Armageddon. Again, the secret knowledge of the end (mediated through fanciful readings of Ezekiel, Daniel, and the book of Revelation) and redemption of the spiritually innocent from evil world forces (the United Nations, European Union, etc.) reflects a basically gnostic outlook.[75]

---

72. SC 6; *CT* 557.

73. For a description of *autopoesis* see R. Hütter, "(Re–) Forming Freedom," 120.

74. It should be observed that Millenarianism among Jews is thought by many modern scholars to have degraded into Gnosticism. See discussion in Pelikan, *Christian Tradition*, 1:83. This makes perfect sense insofar as claiming that one has received secret knowledge of the end and its positive outcome for innocent covenant-keepers oppressed by the Gentiles (Jewish Apocalypticism) and is not so far off from the claim that one has received secret knowledge of how to escape the temporal rule and oppression of the Archons into a higher spiritual realm (Gnosticism).

75. Another interesting aspect of the way Arminianism damages the biblical account of atonement is in its descent into a kind of Manichaeism. If the will of angels and humans is ultimately an omnipotent force that can overcome God, then obviously it represents a second God. Hence, Pelagianism oddly turns into Manichaeism. For an interesting example of Arminianism descent into Manichaeism, see Boyd, *God at War*; Boyd, *Satan and the Problem of Evil*; Boyd, *Is God to Blame?*

Lastly, certain modern theories of atonement (observed chiefly in Socinianism and Protestant Liberalism) have emphasized the prophetic office of Christ over the priestly or kingly. This again tends to play into the gnostic myth by making Jesus's sole function to be one who reveals a special sort of knowledge about God. The gnostic redeemer addresses the creature's inner moral faculties. Giving the knowledge the proper moral law, he redeems the creature's inner moral nature, while abandoning the body to sin, death, the devil, and the curse of the law. In effect, then, there is no need for him to redeem creation from demonic forces or fulfill the law. This redemption is one that is utterly spiritualistic since it is concerned merely with the salvation of the inner, spiritual self through correct knowledge, and not with the created order.

Trinitarian Taxis, Adamic Recapitulation, and the Structure of the Threefold Office

Within the *loci* concerning Christ's offices, Lutheran theologians have tended to order the offices primarily according to their temporal succession. In other words, following the accounts found in the Gospel histories, these theologians have observed that the early ministry of Jesus was primarily concerned with teaching and thereby corresponded to his office as prophet. This was followed by the end of his earthly life, where he offered himself as a sacrifice to the Father and thereby exercised his priestly office. Lastly, Jesus was resurrected and exalted. Logically this corresponds to his office as king.

There is of course nothing wrong with this way of ordering the offices of Christ. At worst perhaps the false impression might be given that each office is clearly identifiable with a stage of Christ's ministry, although it does not appear that this was the goal of these treatments. This is not an entirely satisfactory account of the offices though in that such a treatment ignores the reality of their inner interdependence. For example, in light of the doctrine of Christ's active and passive righteousness (held by all these theologians), one cannot logically exclude the earthly life and prophetic ministry of Jesus from the exercise of his office as priest. Similarly, during his state of exaltation, all agreed that Christ intercedes for sinners in the presence of the Father and thereby also exercises his office as priest.

Therefore, several observations should be made about the ordering of the offices of Christ. First, although the traditional order is clearly not incorrect, properly understood it represents a succession of periods in which one office simply characterized Christ's activity more than others. This may be thought of in analogy to the nature of Triune agency, wherein one person of the Trinity may be characterized by a specific action *ad extra* more than others (Father-creation, Holy Spirit-revelation, etc.). Nonetheless, each action *ad extra* necessarily involves all three persons (the Father creates the world through the Son in the power of the Spirit). This is not only true because of the unity of the divine essence, but also because of the mutual indwelling (what the Greek fathers called *perichoresis*) between the three persons: "I am in the Father and the Father is in me" (John 14:11). Secondly, it should be recognized that Christ's exercise of certain offices is dependent on other offices. In Christ's prophetic ministry, for example, he would not have the ability to forgive sins without his priestly office wherein he paid for the sins that he forgives. Similarly, the exercise of his priestly office is dependent on the royal freedom of his person, which he possesses as a result of his kingly office.

As a result, we may say that there is a sort of *perichoresis* between the offices of Christ. The exercise of one office involves the exercise of the other two. Because this mutual involvement arises from the fact of an order of dependency (noted above), we will suggest that a far more appropriate basis for discussing the threefold office is their proper *taxis*. In Trinitarian theology, the term *taxis* refers to the order among the persons of the Godhead (i.e., the Father begets the Son, the Son and Father breath forth the Spirit, etc).[76] In some contexts it can also refer to their order in the temporal economy, but for our purposes here we will primarily use the term in relationship to the immanent rather than the economic Trinity.

As we observed earlier, each office is expressive of the individual person of the Trinity. Because of the personal communication of the divine person of the Son to the human nature within the hypostatic union, the human nature's actions (the exercise of the threefold office) function within and represent a temporal manifestation of the eternal dynamism of the Logos's eternal relationship to the Father and the Spirit. The *taxis* of the offices therefore directly embody and manifest the *taxis* of the Trinitarian life of God through the temporal work of redemption. In this, the human nature's redemptive work does not merely echo these relationships, but rather because of the unity of the incarnation these eternal relationships function in and through the human nature in time. In that Christ's fulfillment of the law is the reestablishment of the image of God in humans, it is fitting that his earthly work embodies the ecstatic life of the Trinity.[77] Moreover, in this manner, *missio* is rooted in *processio*, without collapsing the latter to the former as is so often the case in modern post-Hegelian Protestant dogmatics.[78]

Operating from the perspective of *taxis*, we begin first with the Father, the fount of divinity (*fons totius divinitatis*), and the manifestation of this role in the office of king. As the Son of the Father, the Logos inherits all that is the Father's in an eternal event of generation. Christ's human nature as *anhypostasis* is incorporated into that eternal event of reception of the fullness of divine glory by the Logos. The communication in time of the fullness of divine glory to the human nature (*genus majestaticum*) therefore must be properly understood as the humanity's participation in the eternal event of the Logos's reception of himself in the act of begetting. As a result, the humanity of Jesus not only receives the fullness of divine glory, but the fullness of divine sovereignty in creation: "The LORD said to me, 'You are my Son; today I have begotten you. Ask of me, and I will make the nations your heritage, and the ends of the earth your possession'" (Ps 2:7–8).[79]

Just as the Father is the fount of divinity and all divine sovereignty, the kingly office is the fount of the priestly and prophetic. Being free lord of all, the Son is thereby

---

76. See brief comments in Gunton, *Promise of Trinitarian Theology*, 197–98.

77. See similar approach in von Balthasar, *Theo-Drama*, 2:646, 3:516–20.

78. Again, von Balthasar takes a similar approach throughout his *Theo-Drama*. Not only are Jenson, Pannenberg, Moltmann, and Jüngel guilty of this collapse of *processio* into *missio*, but many Roman Catholics also move in this direction. Much of this can be attributed to Karl Rahner's celebrated axiom that the "economic Trinity is the immanent Trinity." See K. Rahner, *Trinity*, 21–24.

79. See Luther's comments on these verses in *AE* 12:41–61.

eternally capable of returning himself fully to the Father in the eternal procession of the Spirit. This corresponds to Christ's priestly office, wherein the man Jesus participates in the eternal act of procession by offering up his life, that is his "life breathe" (the biblical description of life given and received, see Gen 2:7) to the Father. Luke describes Jesus's priestly act on the cross in this manner: "Jesus called out with a loud voice, 'Father, into *your hands I commit my spirit.*' When he had said this, *he breathed his last*" (Luke 23:47, emphasis added). Jesus is capable of returning all to the Father because he possesses all. The giving up of Jesus's human spirit in the exercise of the priestly office cannot be separated from the eternal return of the Son's Spirit to the Father, because of the communication of actions within the hypostatic union (*genus apotelesmaticum*). For this reason, his humanity's return of its spirit to the Father is united to the Son's eternal return of himself to the Father in the procession of the Holy Spirit.

As we have seen, the Son's reception of all from the Father from eternity (kingly office) results in his freedom to return all to the Father (priestly office) through procession of the Spirit through the Son (*ex Patre per Filium procedit*). In an identical fashion, as the eternal object of the Father's self-donation and love, the Son also received the procession of the Holy Spirit from the Father from eternity. In time, the expression of this dual procession (*filioque*) is not only enacted in the Son's offering himself up to the Father by way of his active and passive obedience through his assumed humanity, but also in the Father giving the Son the Spirit "without measure" (John 3:34). In the Gospel histories, the visible manifestation of this occurs in his conception, his baptism, his revivification, and his resurrection. The Spirit is of course given to the Son in his conception, just as he is eternally given to the Son in his eternal act of begetting. In the same way, the Spirit is given again by the Father to the Son at his baptism because he is "well pleased" (Mark 1:11) first with the Son's active obedience, and later his passive obedience (John 10:17). The fulfillment of this positive response to this self-offering of the Son in the form of the twofold obedience is his revivification and resurrection in the power of the Spirit (Rom 8:11; 1 Pet 3:18). From this perspective, we can come to understand that the dual anointing of the Son's humanity with the "oil of gladness" (Ps 45:7 [i.e., the glory of the Son and the Spirit]) is in fact a participation of the human nature in the eternal event of begetting and the procession within the life of the Trinity.

Hence, the content of the Spirit's reality is the mutual love and self-offering of the Father and the Son. In time, this mutual love and self-offering operates through the dynamic unfolding of the Son's active and passive righteousness. Therefore, just as the *taxis* of the Spirit is the result of the love of the Father and the Son in eternity, the prophetic office of Christ is the result of the Son's offering of himself to the Father through his human nature and the Father's affirmation of it. The content of Christ's prophetic ministry is dependent on his having won forgiveness through his priestly office, since his message is one of forgiveness and universal jubilee. The Father approves of this proclamation, and therefore anoints and raises the Son, thereby validating his message. By offering himself up, the Son receives the inheritance of the eternal testament that he shares with us through the ministry of the gospel made effecteve by the agency of the Spirit (Isa 61:1–3, Matt 11:28, Rom 8:17, Rev 5:1–10).[80] In the narratives of the Gospels, it should

80. David Scaer offers a briefer version of this Trinitarian basis of atonement. He writes:

be noted that the offering up of Christ's life-breath to the Father (Luke 23:47) results in his "breathing" the promise of the gospel in the power of the Holy Spirit onto his disciples: "he breathed on them and said to them, 'Receive the Holy Spirit. If you forgive the sins of any, they are forgiven them; if you withhold forgiveness from any, it is withheld'" (John 20:22–23).

Christ is not only true God (*vere Deo*), but he is also true man (*vere homo*). For this reason the *taxis* of his threefold office also intersects with his recapitulation of Adam and Israel. As we earlier observed, Adam's pre-lapsarian *imago Dei* of divine righteousness possesses its basis in the *imago Trinitatis*. Divine righteousness as it is reflected in the *imago Dei* is the righteousness of faith ("lord of all") exercised in the earthly vocation of love ("servant of all").[81] This reflects the inner life of the Trinity, which is constituted by infinite power and glory expressing itself in an eternal event of self-donation in the

---

Atonement and God's trinitarian existence are distinct, but the former is the most perfect expression of the latter. In the moment of the atonement God is revealed as the Father who offers up the Son and in reciprocal action the Son offers himself up to the Father. In this sacrificing and being sacrificed, the eternal giving and receiving between the first and second persons of the Trinity is seen. Also within the innertrinitarian life the Father gives of himself in love by eternally begetting the Son, and the Son responds to the Father with eternal love. All this is revealed in the atonement. Within the trinitarian life the Spirit proceeds from the Father and the Son (*filioque*) and the Father is the eternal source of the Son and the Spirit, so the Spirit is the goal and conclusion of the trinitarian life. The atonement, which is characterized by the Father's sacrifice of the Son in which the Son sacrifices himself to the Father, is the source of the Spirit's ability to create faith so that in hearing the gospel of the atonement believers find themselves accepted by the Father and sacrifice themselves for others. In this way the trinitarian life and the act of atonement are seen in the lives of Christians. In our being presented by Christ as sacrifices to God, the effects of the atonement are seen in our lives (Rom 12:l). Before the Son offered himself as atonement to the Father, he was the Spirit of Christ who spoke through the prophets of what God was going to do. Now through an accomplished atonement the one who has always proceeded from the Son has become in the moments of the cross and resurrection the Spirit of Jesus testifying to what God has accomplished in these events. The holiness which characterized the trinitarian life is extended to sinners in the gospel to create faith. So the Spirit shares in the holiness of the Father through the Son and by his presence in the preaching of Christ's death and resurrection appropriates this holiness to believers so that before God they become saints, that is, holy ones. From their eyes the veil is removed and they see God as Father, Son, and Holy Spirit. The one who is the eternal completion of the Trinity and brings the creative chaos to a glorious completion now completes the work of the Father and the Son in justifying sinners. Thus the Matthean formula Father-Son-Holy Spirit is not isolated dogma but a commentary of the cross event by and in which God makes atonement. ("Flights from the Atonement," 205)

Luther makes similar observations about temporal manifestation being rooted in immanent subsisting relations:

The Holy Spirit proceeds physically, the same who proceeds in eternity and is neither born nor Son. And thus the Father remains of himself, so that all three Persons are in majesty, and yet in such a manner that the Son has his Godhead from the Father through his eternal immanent birth (and not the other way around), and the Holy Spirit has his Godhead from the Father and the Son through eternal immanent proceeding. The Son shows his eternal birth through his physical birth, and the Holy Spirit shows his eternal proceeding through his physical proceeding. Each of them has an external likeness or image of his internal essence. (*AE* 24:292–93)

And again:

Therefore it was indeed fitting that the middle Person was physically born and became the Son, the same who was born beforehand in eternity and is Son, and that it was not the Father or the Holy Spirit who was thus physically born and became as Son. (*AE* 34:218)

81. *AE* 31:344.

form of generation and procession. Adam, who possesses all (king), is able to give of himself fully over to God's will (a "sacrifice of praise" Rom 12:1–2, Heb 13:15–16) and in the begetting of Eve (i.e., a priestly action; compare with John 19:31–37). Because of his begetting of Eve, he is able also to lovingly surrender himself over to her in his function as prophet, in that he is the first minister of the Word and Eve the first Church.[82] As the beginning of the restoration of God's purpose for creation, the people of Israel enjoyed the restoration of Adam's office of prophet, priest, and king during distinct, yet overlapping stages of their history. Since Christ's action recapitulates Israel's history (which in turn echoes that of Adam), the *taxis* of his offices logically reverse the stages of failure of mediation in ancient Israel.

As we have observed at the beginning of chapter 1, failure at each stage of Israel's history led to the calling of a distinct exercise of one of the threefold offices. This occurred in order to counteract the effects of the failure of mediation at an earlier stage. These stages of development represented the unique dynamics of the interplay of law and gospel in the history of Israel. The giving of new forms of mediation expressed the divine will to not only hold Israel to the law, but due to the divine promise of redemption also provides them with substitute mediators to overcome their failings. Similarly, in recognizing this fact, we should of course not reify these offices too much, in that those who exercised these offices often took up aspects of the other offices as well (Abraham, Moses, David, and Solomon performed sacrifices, David dressed as a priest, the Levitical priests taught and prophesied, etc.). In spite of this, as we observed in chapter 1, the Old Testament gives us both distinct stages of the establishment of these offices which coincides with the failure of others.

The first office was the prophetic office, established with the *protevangelium*, and was exercised in Israel's early history in particular by Abraham and Moses. The failure of prophetic mediation resulted in the establishment of the priestly caste, as can be observed in Exodus 33. The priestly caste's failure (Eli and his sons, and the loss of the ark of the covenant) ultimately resulted in the establishment of kingly mediation (i.e., the Davidic monarchy and the establishment of the Jerusalem Temple). As the recapitulator of Adam and Israel, Christ embodies this history in that the successive stages of his life directly parallel the stages of Israel's history (first prophet, then priest, and then king).

Conversely, because the *taxis* of his offices (discussed above), Christ also logically reverses the stages of Israel's decline into the temporal hell of exile (Dan 3:16–27). Because of his royal freedom as king (last stage), Christ is able to be a true priest (second stage) and is therefore capable of confirming a testament of forgiveness in his blood as prophet (first stage). In this regard, Christ continues the chiastic structure of salvation history that we observed earlier in his being generated from the flesh of Mary as Eve was generated from Adam.

As we observed at the beginning of chapter 1, Israel's history echoes Adam's history of sin and exile. Israel is a microcosm of the macrocosm of human history. Therefore, because Christ follows the pattern of Israel's history (while at the same time inverting it),

---

82. "Adam alone heard it [the command not to eat from the tree of the knowledge of good and evil], he later informed Eve of it. If they had not fallen into sin, Adam would have transmitted this single command later to their descendants" (*AE* 1:105). Also see Scaer, "Ordaining Women," 83–85.

he possesses a status before the Father both as a representative of the true humanity and as the false humanity. He sums up both Adam and Israel by not only fulfilling these offices, but also at the same time suffering the punishment for their failure. Thus he stands both for the sin of humanity and for the righteousness that should have belonged to humanity. By this priestly act, his death stands as the confirmation of the new testament in his blood. In giving this new word of grace, he thereby reestablishes humanity in its original role as passive receivers of God's Word.

Ultimately, Jesus is only capable of doing this because he is the true and faithful God, who in his self-donation to Israel throughout the Old Testament in the form of the *kavod*/Angel of YHWH served as the true heavenly mediator thus enabling all the earthly mediators to function in their roles. Eventually, due to his supreme grace and faithfulness, he entered into Israel's history and merged the offices of the heavenly and earthly mediators in his person. For this reason, Israel's history is unique in that it not only represents a recapitulation of Adam's Fall (as in a sense all national histories do), but also is the prefiguration and the final establishment of the one, true mediator, Jesus Christ.

Chapter 11

The Mystery of the Work of Christ, Part 2

Christ's Office as King and The Nature of Kenosis

Office of Christ: The Kingly Office

BECAUSE OF THE *TAXIS* of Christ's threefold office discussed in the last chapter, we will begin our discussion of the threefold office with the regal (*munus regium*).[1] Jesus is the true Davidic king (Matt 1:1, 9:27, 15:22, 20:30, 20:31, 21:9, 21:15; Luke 1:32, 1:69; Rom 1:3; Rev 3:7, 5:5, 22:16.) who fulfills God's promises to David (2 Sam 7; Ps 2, 89, 110). As the true Davidic king, he is the restorer of humanity's place within the original creation, as well as the fulfiller of the Abrahamic testament and its promise of universal blessing.[2]

The fact that Jesus is a descendent of David, and therefore the true inheritor of the promise of the Davidic testament, is clear from the genealogies provided for us by Matthew and Luke. The question of whether Jesus was a literal descendant of David is in fact not a trivial one, but rather concerns God's faithfulness to his promises. If the Messiah was not David's son, then we cannot understand the God of the New Testament to be a faithful fulfiller of his promises. This would place the promise of the gospel itself into question. Therefore, the issue of Christ's literal descent from David cannot be papered over with the typical Liberal Protestant shrug and appeal to the post-Enlightenment fact/value split.

Due to the extreme skepticism characteristic of many of the practitioners of the historical-critical method, the genealogies of the New Testament have been under fire since the eighteenth century. Nevertheless, contrary to popular scholarly belief, the Gospel genealogies contain much to recommend themselves on purely historically grounds.

---

1. See discussion in Baier, *Compendium Theologiae Positivae*, 2:128–33; Hoenecke, *Evangelical Lutheran Dogmatics*, 3:217–27; L. Hütter, *Compendium Locorum Theologicorum*, 2:934–35; Gerhard, *On Christ*, 320–21; Graebner, *Outline of Doctrinal Theology*, 148–54; Koehler, *Summary of Christian Doctrine*, 118–21; Lindberg, *Christian Dogmatics*, 285–94; Luthardt, *Kompendium der Dogmatik*, 247–54; Martensen, *Christian Dogmatics*, 315–29; J. Mueller, *Christian Dogmatics*, 314–18; von Oettingen, *Lutherische Dogmatik*, 2.2:276–95; Philippi, *Kirchliche Glaubenslehre*, 4.2:345–51; F. Pieper, *Christian Dogmatics*, 2:385–96; Schaller, *Biblical Christology*, 190–210; H. Schmid, *Doctrinal Theology*, 370–76.

2. Hahn, *Kinship by Covenant*, 176–237.

This would be true even if they were not guaranteed to us by the fact of their inclusion in the utterly truthful Word of God.

The first aspect that recommends them historically is the probability that Jesus would be descended from David. David after all had many descendants, not least as a result of his and his sons' prodigious harems. For this reason, a rather large number of people in ancient Israel could have very credibly claimed descent from him. That knowledge of this descent would also be accessible is equally plausible. It has also been noted by many, that Second Temple Jews scrupulously maintained their own genealogical records in both oral (mostly among peasants) or in written forms (among elites).[3] Josephus also reports that prior to the destruction of Jerusalem in AD 70 the Jews maintained a large store of public genealogical records.[4] If the Synoptic Gospels were written prior to 70 (as the ending of Acts and the lack of references to the destruction of the Temple as a past event suggest[5]) then it is not unreasonable to think that the Evangelists might have had access to these records.

We may also go further. As Gerd Theissen has rightly noted, Jesus's family was extremely prominent in the early Church, and therefore can be considered the source of the New Testament's assertion that Jesus was of Davidic descent.[6] Paul calls Jesus the "son of David" (Rom 1:3) and he clearly knew Jesus's relatives as both Galatians and Acts demonstrate.[7] If that is the case, then Jesus's family must have claimed descent from David. Going beyond Theissen, we might suggest that if Jesus's relatives did claim descent from David, they must have maintained some sort of genealogical records and these records could very well have been disseminated within the early Church. Such dissemination would have been a useful tool against those who contested Jesus's claims to be the true Davidic Messiah.

Theissen also urges that historical skeptics must recognize that it is highly unlikely that Davidic descent would be something that Jesus's family or the early Church would generate after the fact.[8] There were a variety of messianic expectations in first-century Judaism and not all of them made it necessary for the Messiah to be of Davidic descent.[9] Likewise, there were major disadvantages to claiming descent from David insofar as it might make one the object of intrigue by Roman officials fearful of messianic upstarts. As an example of this, Eusebius shares with us that Jesus's nephews were harassed by Domitian (it is claimed that Domitian ordered the execution of all of David's descendants) when he discovered that they held their uncle to be the true Davidic king and the ruler of the universe.[10] Although we do not have the space to debate the histori-

---

3. K. Hanson and Oakman, *Palestine in the Time of Jesus*, 58.

4. *Life of Flavius Josephus*, 1.1, in Josephus, *Works of Josephus*, 1. Josephus states that for his lineage, he has looked in the "public" records. Also see comment about Jewish genealogy records in *Against Apion*, 1.7, in Josephus, *Works of Josephus*, 775–76.

5. See arguments in favor of this line of reasoning in J. Robinson, *Redating the New Testament*.

6. Theissen and Merz, *Historical Jesus*, 194.

7. Ibid.

8. Ibid., 195–96.

9. Ibid., 196.

10. Ibid., 194. Theissen is specifically referring to *Church History*, 3.19–20, in Eusebius, *Church*

cal merits of this account, in light of Roman history it can hardly be doubted that this represents a plausible response on Jewish messianic claims. For this reason, Pannenberg is incorrect to assert that Jesus could never have conceived of himself as the Davidic king.[11] The historical evidence presented to us in the New Testament and elsewhere clearly shows his family (and therefore he) were quite self-conscious of being heirs of the Davidic monarchy.[12]

Perhaps an issue that is more troubling in approaching the question of Jesus's descent is the apparent disagreement between Matthew and Luke's genealogies. This problem is by no means insoluble and has been addressed in a number of ways. The beginning of a solution might come by recognizing that Matthew's genealogy has obvious and rather wide gaps in it. The intention of these gaps (as we suggested earlier) was to highlight Jesus's role as the agent of a universal Sabbath and Jubilee. Nevertheless, although Matthew's theological goal was somewhat symbolic, it was not fictive. Hence, appealing to Matthew's theological motives in structuring his genealogy in a particular way does not absolve us from dealing with the problem of genealogical contradictions with Luke.

The most common solution to this difficulty has been to suggest that Matthew and Luke's gospels each represents a separate parent's genealogy.[13] Perhaps Matthew gives Jesus's ancestry through Joseph and Luke through Mary. This division is suggested by the fact that the two evangelists focus on a particular parent in their recounting of the infancy narrative. All things considered, this is probably the best solution to the problem and interestingly, it was also Luther's approach.[14]

There are nonetheless a number of objections against this view as well. The first and most common is that both genealogies appear to trace Jesus's descent through Joseph. On the surface, it would appear that neither traces Jesus's ancestry through Mary. As J. Stafford Wright has argued, this problem may be solved by the fact that in ancient Judaism childless or sonless marriages often resulted in legal transference of sonship.[15] There are also a number of examples of this occurring in the Old Testament (1 Chr 2:34, Ezra 2:61).[16] Hence, it could be plausibly suggested that Mary's family might very well have lacked sons and that Joseph was named her father's legal heir. The fact that a lack of sons

---

History, 108–9. This story has obvious apologetic value as well. Domitian is assured by Jude and Jesus's other relatives that their uncle's kingdom will not dawn until the end of the world and therefore is no threat to his. This does of course not mean that the story is untrue. Indeed, even if it is untrue, it does express the attitude of the Romans to pretenders to the throne and therefore is of value in our argument.

11. Pannenberg, *Systematic Theology*, 2:443–46; Pannenberg, *Jesus*, 208–24.

12. Theissen and Merz, 196. They write:

So we must reckon with the possibility that the family of Jesus in fact claimed Davidic descent. The expectation that the Messiah must come from Davidic family could have played a role in the environment of Jesus and in the origin of his "charisma."

13. This is the solution suggested by the following: Chemnitz et al., *Harmony of the Four Evangelists*, 93–109; Just, *Luke*, 1:163–70; Lenski, *St. Luke's Gospel*, 218–19.

14. *WA* 53:579–648.

15. J. Wright, "Virgin Birth," 3:662.

16. See comments on the 1 Chronicles verse in R. Klein and Krüger, *1 Chronicles*; 101. We must thank Mr. Glenn M. Miller for directing us to these resources and the Stafford Wright article as well.

in a family is a common enough phenomenon in any culture makes this an extremely plausible solution.

Some might also object that this solution suggests that both parents were descendants of David. At first glance this might be considered unlikely. Nevertheless, this in fact fits well with historical data that we possess concerning Second Temple Judaism. Historical research has shown that during the Second Temple period most Jewish marriages tended to be among close relatives.[17] Scholars have also noted that much of the pseudepigraphal literature of this period (the book of Jubilees being the chief example) strongly encourages marriage with close kin.[18] The presence of this cultural practice in this literature suggests that endogamy was considered to be the ideal.[19] If Mary and Joseph were therefore anything like their contemporaries, it is highly likely that they were closely related and therefore both descendants of David.[20]

Having dealt with the historical issues surrounding Christ's regal office, we will now examine its theological implications in greater detail. Christ's kingly office not only means the fulfillment of God's faithfulness to David, but reestablishment of his own proper reign of grace within creation. This takes a paradoxical form of his self-subjection to David by his immutable promise of kingship. Such self-donation to David culminates in God actually becoming the Davidic king himself. In this, God's reign is established by its first being renounced.

As we have seen, Israel's act of apostasy led to their military defeat at the hands of the Gentiles. Israel, believing a lack of king was in fact the problem (instead of sin), requested a human ruler from God. God's response to their apostasy was one of law and gospel. Having his sovereignty and graciousness rejected (1 Sam 8:7), God punished Israel's apostasy by giving them the very thing that they desired. Through this, they would come to recognize that earthly kings abuse their authority and thereby prove themselves to be faithless (8:10–18). God by contrast maintains his fidelity to both his words of law and promise. It should always be remembered that like the rest of Israel, the king was also subject to the law (Deut 17:14–20). For this reason, Israel's kings were ultimately condemned along with the rest of the people.

Nevertheless, God not only condemned the apostasy of Israel and her earthly kings, but also made the exile an occasion of his grace. God's judgment throughout Israel's history was met with a simultaneous and corresponding act of grace. God therefore used the Israelite monarchy as the medium of his universal plan of redemption. Through the Davidic testament, God brought about the fulfillment of his universal purpose of redemption in spite of the faithlessness of David and his descendants.

17. K. Hanson and Oakman, *Palestine in the Time of Jesus*, 31–34.

18. Ibid., 32–33.

19. Ibid.

20. Though this was the ideal, this does not exclude the fact that marriages sometimes appear to have occurred among people who were not close kin. See K. Hanson and Oakman, *Palestine in the Time of Jesus*, 34–36. The Herodians for example married into the Hasmoneans in order to legitimize themselves. Therefore, it is not unlikely that Mary's cousin Elizabeth could have married outside the kin group within a Levitical, non-Davidic clan.

In the exile, God disestablished the Davidic line in an annihilating act of judgment. Conversely, in Jesus Christ, he subjected himself to David's line in an ultimate act of grace. As we have previously noted, the speech-act of unconditional promise is an act of self-donation. God's promise to David meant that he donated himself to David to the extent of becoming David's son. That is to say, through the hypostatic union he literally communicates himself to David's own flesh. In this, God is faithful to his two words of law and gospel. God in Christ fulfills the law by being perfectly obedient and suffering the punishment due to humanity's apostasy. Christ, the faithful God, also fulfills his promises to David by restoring one of his progeny to the throne by his obedience. In this, he fulfills the promise to the whole of creation made in the *protevanglium*. Therefore by his subjecting himself to David and surrendering his right to be Israel and creation's king, God established his reign over both. The movement of God's own self-subjection to humanity finds its final culmination in the incarnation, humiliation, death, and exaltation of Jesus: "who, though he was in the form of God, did not count equality with God a thing to be grasped, but made himself nothing, taking the form of a servant" (Phil 2:6–7).

Jesus's office as king is the root office and the basis of his work as the redeemer of creation. Through this office, he fights the Father's apocalyptic war against sin, death, the law, and the devil. As we shall see below, he conducted this war through his offices of priest and prophet. His office as king (and his other offices) was publically validated by an external divine call. As the second Adam and true minister of the Word, Jesus counteracted the enthusiasm of our first parents by his reliance on the sure Word of scripture and on his own public call by the Father in the power of the Spirit. What the Augustana says regarding the office of ministry with the Church is also true of the supreme minister of the Word: "they teach that no one should publicly teach in the Church or administer the sacraments unless he has been regularly called."[21] Indeed, Jesus did not receive his office (as Luther described that of the enthusiasts) "in some corner."[22] Rather, beginning with the revelation of his identity to his parents, Jesus's office is validated throughout his earthly life (at his baptism, his transfiguration, etc.) by God's Word of revelation concerning him.

Christ's regal office is not only validated by his external call during his temporal life, but also with his fulfillment of the scriptures. Luther states in his commentary on Psalm 110 that Christ's office as the true priest-king rests on the sure oath of God referred to in verse 4 of the Psalm.[23] In other words, Christ's office as priest-king rests on promises (Ps 110:4, Heb 7:21) that occurred even before his birth. We of course also made the same point earlier regarding Christ's Davidic descent. By fulfilling the scriptures, Christ directs humanity, bound to enthusiasm, back to the concrete Word of God: "Scripture cannot be broken" (John 10:35), "Today this Scripture has been fulfilled in your hearing" (Luke 4:21), "the Scriptures . . . bear witness about me" (John 5:39), "scripture must be fulfilled" (Mark 14:49 NIV), etc.

---

21. CA 5; *CT* 49.

22. *AE* 26:19.

23. *AE* 13:307.

In contrast to this, Jesus's opponents rested their own authority on a self-appointed office and thereby revealed themselves as false mediators. In particular, the Pharisees were self-appointed lay teachers of the law, having taken over the teaching function from the office of the Levites (Lev 10:8–10, Deut 33:10).[24] At the time of Christ, the priests themselves lacked the mandate of the external word. The chief priests of Jesus's time were mostly of the Hasmonean clan,[25] although God had told Ezekiel that it was the Zadokites who should serve in this role after the Babylonian exile (Ezek 48:11). Lastly, the Romans, who had violently taken over the eastern Mediterranean for their own profit, stood as a false parody of true governance. Although it is also true that God established them as rulers and they were useful for holding together order (Rom 13:1–5), their abuses of the office of ruler echoed that of Adam's sinful failure. In this, Christ's true office as prophet, priest, and king stands in contrast to false prophets (Pharisees), priests (Hasmoneans), and kings (Romans).

Excursus: Kenosis: Christ as the Agent and Exemplar of Christian Freedom[26]

Early in the seventeenth century, a controversy broke out between representatives of the Saxon and Swabian Lutheran Churches regarding the *communicatio idiommatum* and its relationship to the two states of Christ (humiliation and exaltation). Historians of dogma commonly refer to this conflict as the Crypto-Kenotic controversy.[27] The question of the controversy regarded the implications of the *genus majestaticum* for the earthly life of the human Jesus. This issue directly relates to the question of the exercise of Christ's kingly office that we have been discussing, since Christ is king according to his humanity not only because he is of David's flesh, but because he possesses the fullness of divine glory.

Saying that Christ possesses God's own glory, and therefore a divine kingly dignity as a man, does not resolve the question of how that glory was exercised. If Christ does have all these things, as Lutheran theologians recognized, there must be a distinction made between the two states (humiliation and exaltation) in which Christ exercised

---

24. E. Sanders, *Judaism*, 380–451.

25. Ibid., 22–25.

26. Althaus, *Die Christliche Wahrheit*, 451–55; Baier, *Compendium Theologiae Positivae*, 2:75–90; Hoenecke, *Evangelical Lutheran Dogmatics*, 3:105–29; L. Hütter, *Compendium Locorum Theologicorum*, 2:932–33; Gerhard, *On Christ*, 298–318; Graebner, *Outline of Doctrinal Theology*, 113–26; Koehler, *Summary of Christian Doctrine*, 97–99; Lindberg, *Christian Dogmatics*, 227–37; Luthardt, *Kompendium der Dogmatik*, 205–14; Martensen, *Christian Dogmatics*, 289–92; J. Mueller, *Christian Dogmatics*, 287–94; von Oettingen, *Lutherische Dogmatik*, 2.2:100–134; Philippi, *Kirchliche Glaubenslehre*, 4.1:124–31, 256–69, 366–86; F. Pieper, *Christian Dogmatics*, 2:280–310; Schaller, *Biblical Christology*, 86–88; H. Schmid, *Doctrinal Theology*, 376–407. Much of this section is based on the following article: Kilcrease, "Kenosis and Vocation," 21–34.

27. Dorner, *Doctrine of the Person of Christ*, 4:281–306; O. Ritschl, *Dogmengeschichte des Protestantismus*, 4:180–92; Schaff, *Creeds of Christendom*, 1:294–96; H. Schmid, *Doctrinal Theology*, 390–92; Thomasius, *Christi*, 1:579–610.

his divine glory differently.[28] That is to say, positing the *genus majestaticum* raises the additional question: If Christ did possess this divine glory from the moment of his conception, how does one understand the presence of death, suffering, and ignorance in his earthly life? The two sides of the controversy answered this question differently.

The Saxon-Kenotic theologians claimed that Christ had partially suspended the use of his divine glory. Nevertheless, he did not totally renounce it, but occasionally exercised his divine power in the form of miracles and prophecy (total renunciation is an idea foreign to orthodox Lutheranism and arose in certain heretical strains of nineteenth-century Neo-Lutheranism).[29] Furthermore, argued the Kenotic party, Christ according to his human nature, did not exercise his divine rule over the universe during his state of humiliation, while maintaining it according to his divine.[30] In his state of exaltation, Christ had begun to exercise his divine rule according to both natures.

The opposing position of the Swabian-Cryptocist theologians claimed that Jesus had in fact merely "concealed" (*krypsis*) his glory and used his divine attributes secretly during his state of humiliation.[31] Still, they were willing to say that he had renounced use of his divine glory in the capacity of his sacerdotal office. Nevertheless, this was the exceptions and not the rule.[32] Cryptocists claimed that because of the unity of his person, Christ in his state of humiliation had not renounced the exercise of his universal dominion according to his human nature. This, they argued, would have divided the person of Christ.[33] The question was eventually resolved largely in favor of the Saxons in 1624 by the *Deciso Saxonica*.[34] The Saxon-Kenotic view (with some modifications) subsequently became the more favored view in Lutheran theological history.[35]

In this section, it will be our purpose to revisit these issues and attempt to transcend the debate between the two sides. On the one hand, we will agree with the Saxon position regarding Christ's use of his divine attributes in his state of humiliation. The New Testament portrays Christ as using his divine attributes on various occasions, while renouncing their use a significant amount of the time. One could say that this was a "concealment" in a certain sense (in that he still possessed them), but properly speaking, Christ must be thought as having suspended their use. Conversely, we will agree with the Swabians, that Christ did not abandon his universal dominion in his state of humiliation. Rather, paradoxically, it is Christ's universal dominion that makes him free and able to renounce the use of certain divine attributes in obedience to the will of the Father. In this, Christ becomes both the author and model of subsequent Christian freedom and vocation. Just as Luther insisted that the Christian can be the "servant of all," because he

28. H. Schmid, *Doctrinal Theology*, 376–407.

29. Gottfried Thomasius being the chief example of this. See dicsussion of him in Beyschlag, *Erlanger Theologie*, 14–19, 24–26, 29–31, 83–85, 93–98; L. Green, *Erlangen School of Theology*, 133–48. See brief summary of Thomasius's position in Thomasius, *Christi*, 2:411–12.

30. H. Schmid, *Doctrinal Theology*, 390–91.

31. Ibid., 391–92.

32. Ibid.

33. Ibid., 391.

34. Ibid., 393.

35. Ibid.

is the "free lord of all,"[36] so too Christ exercises his lordship within his earthly life by suspending the full use of his glory. As one who possesses the "form of God" he is free to take on the "form of a servant" (Phil 2:6–7).

In order to make our case for this understanding of *kenosis* and the self-understanding of Christ, we must examine the texts of the New Testament that deal with the subject. We begin with the *locus classicus* of the doctrine of *kenosis*, the Christ hymn of Philippians 2. The hymn begins by Paul stating that although Christ was in or possessed the "form of God" he did not "count equality with God a thing to be grasped" or as some (including NRSV) translate it, "something to be exploited." Gerald Hawthorne has also suggested "ground for grasping,"[37] whereas Peter O' Brien has suggested "something to be used for his own advantage."[38] N. T. Wright favors this latter translation and has argued very convincingly that Paul is here contrasting Jesus's proper and self-giving use of his power to pagan Hellenistic kings.[39] We cannot, of course, enter into the debate concerning the exact translation of the phrase here. Nevertheless, what seems to be clear is that a great many translators and exegetes of merit seem to think that the phrase means that although Christ possessed all the power and glory of divinity, he did not use such glory for himself or for his own advantage.[40]

Before we enter into a discussion as to how Christ used or did not use such sovereignty, we must first explore the meaning of the phrase "the form of God." Lutherans have historically understood this to be a reference to the *genus majestaticum*.[41] In order to see the reason for this interpretation, we turn to Johann Gerhard's exegesis of the passage which is representative of the larger tradition.[42] First, Gerhard notes, that the hymn describes the action of "Christ Jesus," that is, the human nature considered in the abstract. He is spoken of as "Christ" in connection to his human nature, in that the name means "anointed," something that clearly did not occur to the *logos asarkos* before the Incarnation.[43] We ourselves might add that this is supported by the fact that on the very few occasions that Paul speaks of Christ's preincarnate state, he does not typically speak of the subject "Christ Jesus," but rather of the "Son" (Rom 8:3, Gal 4:4). Gerhard goes on to point out that the *logos asarkos* does not possess the "form of God" but rather is God.[44] In that Paul has already indicated that he is talking about the "anointed one" (the human nature in the abstract), who possessed the "form of God" (rather than "was

---

36. *AE* 31:344.

37. Hawthorne, *Philippians*, 98.

38. O'Brien, *Epistle to the Philippians*, 202–3.

39. N. T. Wright, "Harpagmos," 321–52.

40. Also see the following commentators who have reached similar conclusions: B. Thurston and Ryan, *Philippians and Philemon*, 81–82; Fee, *Paul's Letter to the Philippians*, 206–10; Bockmuehl, *Epistle to the Philippians*, 129–31; Hendriksen, *Exposition of Philippians*, 104–6; Lightfoot, *St. Paul's Epistle*, 109–11.

41. See Gerhard, *On Christ*, 301–2; H. Schmid, *Doctrinal Theology*, 383.

42. See examples in H. Schmid, *Doctrinal Theology*, 376–407.

43. Gerhard, *On Christ*, 305.

44. Ibid., 301–2.

God" as he states in Rom 9:5[45]), he seems to be referring to the humanity of Christ in itself. Christ's humanity possesses the "form of God" because it possesses the fullness of divine glory.

Gerhard goes on also to observe that the didactic intention of Paul would be meaningless if we did not think he was talking about the human nature in itself. The apostle wishes the Philippians to consider the visible manifestation of Christ as their model for behavior.[46] Therefore, it is not the *logos asarkos* that he is bidding them to imitate, but rather Christ's visibly manifest humanity.

We might also add that Jesus's state of humiliation is described as his taking the "form of a slave." When his exaltation is referred to in verses 9–11, Paul no longer describes him as a "slave," but rather says that he has received the name "*KYRIOS*." "*KYRIOS*" is of course the LXX translation of the divine name YHWH.[47] In the Bible (as we discussed at length earlier), the divine Name is the divine reality and presence. The temple is the location of the divine presence and, therefore, is a "house for my name" (2 Sam 7:13; 1 Chr 22:10). To receive the divine Name is to receive the fullness of divine glory or to manifest it. This nicely parallels Jesus's own statement in Matthew 28:18: "All authority in heaven and on earth has been given to me." Since Paul has already told us that Christ possesses the fullness of divine glory ("form of God"), the glory spoken of here is one that was suspended so that it might later be manifested (compare with similar verses Heb 1:1–4).

In light of Paul and the rest of the New Testament's emphasis on the resurrection of the body as a real physical event, taking on the "form of the slave" cannot refer to becoming human. That is to say, if the taking of the form of a "slave" referred the preincarnate *logos asarkos* becoming human, then his exaltation and reception of the name "Lord" would logically mean the removal of his humanity. Conversely, some might surmise that becoming a servant would mean the removal of his divinity, a position that Gottfried Thomasius came close to.[48] Instead, Paul's delineation of the two states conveys

---

45. For a defense of this controversial reading of Romans 9:5 see Witherington, *Paul's Narrative Thought*, 112–13.

46. Gerhard, *On Christ*, 300–301.

47. Tuckett, *Christology and the New Testament*, 19–22.

48. Essentially, Thomasius thought that the Philippians hymn applied to the *logos asarkos*, rather than the position of Luther, the Confessions, and scholastic orthodoxy, that the hymn applies to the *logos ensarkos*. This did not mean that the divine nature had been abrogated, but rather that it only maintained its "absolute attributes" (the moral ones, [i.e., goodness and holiness, etc.]), while shucking the "relative attributes" (omnipotence, etc., see Thomasius, *Christi*, 1:411–12, 467–69) only to have them restored later in his state of exaltation (see Thomasius, *Christi*, 1:331). Thomasius considered certain attributes in God to be „relative" because God's relationship to the world evoked them. Another part of Thomasius's justification for this move was his insistence that because the Second Person of the Trinity was not a nature or essence, but rather a person, he could conceivably lose certain attributes while remaining God. Lowell Green rightly views Thomasius's intentions as orthodox, but ultimately disastrously rationalistic and heterodox. See Green, *Erlangen School of Theology*, 139–48. We thank Dr. Green for directing us to the key passages in his writing in which Thomasius develops his kenoticism. In light of this correct judgment, we must utterly reject his position. After all, the God of the Bible does not change (Mal 3:6, Heb 13:8) and therefore he cannot shuck his divine attributes at will. Much of the logic of Thomasius's position appears to be rooted in nineteenth-century developmentalism. For other examples of radical *kenosis* and developmentalism, see Gess, *Christi und Werk*, 3:345–410. Gess taught an even more radical

the differing usages of the "form of God" imparted to the flesh. As is clear from his other writings and the rest of the teaching of the New Testament, he is not describing a transmutation of divinity into humanity, followed by the transmutation of humanity into divinity.

From this it appears that Christ's slavery in the hymn means two things. First, when Paul describes the law, he describes people who are under the law as slaves (Gal 3:23, 4:1–7). This suggests Paul is saying that Christ became a slave to the law on our behalf and, therefore, to the Father. Indeed, he tells us that Christ was "born of a woman, born *under the law*, to redeem those under the law, that we might receive the full rights of sons" (Gal 4:4, emphasis added). Secondly, Paul is claiming that we are now free because Christ is our slave. Humans are slaves under sin and the law, and Christ has exchanged that position with them and made them sons and coheirs with him through faith (Rom 8:15–17). Conversely, our freedom makes us capable of now being "slaves of Christ" (Eph 6:6), that is, doers of the law. Hence, Paul is not actually advocating the loss of divine power and glory in and of itself. Rather he is discussing Christ's use of his power and glory in obedience to the Father and in service to humanity. Since this service depends on him suffering death, obviously it also involves some suspension of divine glory, but this is not Paul's main subject. Rather he is contrasting the use of divine glory as for itself, (namely as "something to be exploited") and its redemptive use on behalf of humanity.

Since Paul describes the Christian life throughout his letters as existing in this dialectic of freedom and servitude, we may be confident in light of the first verse of the passage that he is suggesting this is also the case with the kenotic life of Christ: "have in you the same mind as was in Christ Jesus." In other words, Jesus Christ, who possesses all of God's glory (that is the "form of God") was therefore free from servitude, just as the Christian who is now Christ's own coheir. Because of his freedom as a true Son of the Father, he is able to give himself in service to his people and to the Father. His possession of glory leads to his ability to suspend it and to die. If he had lacked the fullness of glory, there still might have been something for Jesus to grasp at. But possessing all, he can give all. Suspension then becomes a kind of use. Christians who are free sons of the Father are now also free in the same way to take on the "form of a servant."

Following a similar line of reasoning, Luther agrees with this interpretation, and makes Christ (with whom the Christian becomes a single subject through faith) both the agent and exemplar of Christian freedom. In *Freedom of a Christian* (1520), Luther writes:

---

kenosis, wherein the divine nature simply lost all of its attributes and was reduced to the finitude of the human nature. This reduced Logos replaced the human soul in Christ (Gess, *Christi und Werk*, 3:358–64). Another view that strongly relied on the concept of developmentalism was that of I. A. Dorner, *System of Christian Doctrine*, 3:283–380. Dorner claimed that the incarnation was not an immediate and complete event that occurred in the conception of Jesus by Mary. Rather, it was a gradual process of the Second Person of the Trinity melding into a single subject with the human Jesus. This process was completed at the resurrection. In more recent times, Wolfhart Pannenberg has developed a similar view in his systematic theology. See Pannenberg, *Systematic Theology*, 2:363–88. See discussion of kenotic Christology in the nineteenth century in the following sources: Breidert, *Die kenotische Christologie*; D. Brown, *Divine Humanity*; T. Thompson, "Nineteenth-Century Kenotic Christology," 74–111; Welch, *God and Incarnation*; Welch, *Protestant Thought in the Nineteenth Century*, 1:233–40.

> As an example of such life [freedom of a Christian] the Apostle cites Christ, saying, "Have this mind among yourselves, which you have in Christ Jesus, . . . [etc.]." This salutary word of the Apostle has been obscured for us by those who have not at all understood his words, "form of God," "for of a servant," "human form," "likeness of men," and have applied them to the divine and human nature. Paul means this: Although Christ was filled with the form of God and rich in all good things, so that he needed no work and no suffering to make him righteous and saved (for he has all this eternally), yet he was not puffed up by them and did not exalt himself above us and assume power over us, although could rightly have done so; but, on the contrary, he so lived, labored, worked, suffered, and died that he might be like other men and in fashion and in actions be nothing else than a man, just as if he had need of all these things and had nothing of the form of God. But he did all this for our sake, that he might serve us and that all things which he accomplished in this form of a servant might become ours. So a Christian, like Christ is head, is filled and made rich by faith and should be content with this form of God which has obtained by faith . . . [and therefore] serve, help, and in every way deal with his neighbor as he sees that God through Christ has dealt and still deals with him.[49]

In a passage from *Two Kinds of Righteousness* (1518), Luther makes similar observation:

> This is what the text we are now considering says: "Let this mind be in you, which was also in Christ Jesus" [Phil. 2:5]. This means you should be as inclined and disposed toward one another as you see Christ was disposed to you. How? Thus, surely, that "though he was in the form of God, [he] did not count equality with God a thing to be grasped, but emptied himself, taking the form of a servant" [Phil 2:6–7]. The term "form of God" here does not mean the "essence of God" because Christ never emptied himself of this. Neither can the phrase "form of a servant" be said to mean "human essence." But the "form of God" is wisdom, power, righteousness, goodness—and freedom too; for Christ was a free, powerful, wise man, subject to none of the vices or sins to which all other men are subject. He was pre-eminent in such attributes as are particularly proper to the form of God. Yet he was not haughty in that form; he did not please himself (Rom 15:3); nor did he disdain and despise those who were enslaved and subjected to various evils.[50]

In this, Luther is clear that Christ's own royal freedom makes his servanthood possible. For Luther then, the Christian's own freedom is then derivative of Christ's freedom. As the glorious Lord, Christ unilaterally donates himself to humanity, giving them a share in his power, glory, and righteousness, while taking into himself sin and death (*der fröhlicher wechsel*). Therefore, the person of faith is free to engage in the same self-donation to his fellow creature, because finally being free of the need to self-justify he can truly and spontaneously fulfill the law. As a result, the *communicatio idiommatum* translates into not only an exchange of reality between Christ and the believer, but also a new relationship with the neighbor.

This interpretation of the second chapter of Philippians also agrees with the Christ's kenotic life-form as it is portrayed in the rest of the New Testament. For example, Mark

49. *AE* 31:366.

50. *AE* 31:301.

describes Jesus at his baptism as receiving the Word of God that he was "my Son" with whom "I am well pleased" (Mark 1:11). This is suggestive of two things. First, "Son" as we observed earlier is a royal title taken from Psalm 2:7. This is, as we have seen, not only a divine title, but it also denotes the royal addressee as the inheritor of all that is God's ("I will make the nations your heritage, and the ends of the earth your possession" v. 8). In this, we can observe a strong parallel between the idea of Christian freedom being based in becoming a co-heir and Christ's possession of the "form of God." Secondly, "with whom I am well pleased" presupposes that before any of his messianic activity Christ is pleasing to God, and for this reason does not need to fulfill the law. God is already pleased with him from eternity; he need not merit the Father's pleasure. Therefore, Christ is able to fulfill the Father's will because of his divine freedom from the law as a royal person with whom God is already "well pleased." Luke goes back earlier and describes the promise of royal dominion to Mary before Jesus's birth: "He . . . will be called the Son of the Most High. The Lord God will give him the throne of his father David, and . . . his kingdom will never end" (Luke 1:32 NIV). Luke describes Jesus as being conscious of this royal freedom from the beginning of his life. It was a motivating factor for his vocation: "Did you not know that I must be in my Father's house?" (2:49). This self-consciousness of his royal freedom allows Jesus to follow his Father's will even to death on the cross.

Returning to the New Testament epistles, Hebrews gives the same witness to Christ's kenotic life-form that we observed in the Synoptic Gospels and Paul: "Although he was a son, [i.e., a free royal person, Psalm 2 is also cited in 1:5] he learned obedience through what he suffered. And being made perfect, he became the source of eternal salvation to all who obey him" (Heb 5:8–9). Christ's freedom as a royal Son that allowed him to obediently fulfill the law is, according to the author of Hebrews, the archetype of our own faith. Part of this fulfillment of law was his suffering which involved the disuse of his divine attributes (such as the ability to avoid death, etc.). Christ could do this, because as a Son, he knew that he would be vindicated from his death on the cross and be exalted to the manifestation of the fullness of his glory. After a long list of those who were vindicated because of their trust in God, the author concludes with Jesus: "[We look] to Jesus, the founder and perfecter of our faith, who for the joy that was set before him endured the cross, despising the shame, and is seated at the right hand of the throne of God" (Heb 12:2). Again, as in Paul, the Christian possesses the same royal freedom of obedience as Christ did through faith.

In light of this exegesis, what are we to make of the Crypto-Kenotic controversy? First, it should be said that the Saxon-Kenotic theologians are to be preferred regarding the real suspension of Christ's use of some of his divine attributes in the state of humiliation.[51] If the gospel means the full self-giving of God, God in Christ must fully stand in solidarity with his people in a posture of service to them. Part of this service to them is Christ's temporary disuse of certain divine attributes communicated to his humanity,

---

51. See *AE* 12:127 where Luther speaks of Philippians 2: "He says that Christ emptied Himself of the divine form; that is, He did not use His divine might nor let His almighty power be seen, but withdrew it when he suffered."

such as deathlessness or in some cases omniscience (Mark 13:32).[52] Nevertheless, as the Gospels demonstrate, this does not mean that he ceased to use all of his divine attributes. Jesus certainly knew his mission and his identity. Moreover, he possessed the miraculous ability to read minds, and prophecy about the future. If such divine attributes were not used, his mission would ultimately be undermined.

For this reason, the difficulty with the idea of "concealment" or "secret use" is not that it contradicts Christ's full humanity. Obviously Christ fully uses his divine glory in his present state of exaltation, but yet has not ceased to be human. Rather positing a "secret use" misunderstands the exercise of divine glory and limits it to the exercise of force. God is of course to be feared in that he possesses absolute sovereignty over his creation.[53] Nevertheless, according God's Triune reality, revealed in the incarnation, death, and resurrection of the Son, the other side of his sovereignty is his ability to communicate himself and donate himself fully to the other. This ability is expressed in time through the historical *kenosis* of the Son and is eternally rooted in the divine being. Due to the infinity of his glory, God (as we have noted) is an eternal event of self-donation and self-communication in the form of begetting and procession. Therefore for God, the absolute demonstration of his power is his ability to fully give of himself and wholly donate himself to the other. In becoming incarnate and suffering the vicissitudes of human existence, God in Christ fully donates himself to the human situation after the Fall and thereby demonstrates his glory and power. This being said, we do not mean to suggest that this is the only way that God demonstrates his glory. Sovereign self-assertion (law) and self-donation (gospel) are both integral to God's character as God. One is not true at the expense of the other, and God exercises both aspects of his reality through the masks of his creatures (*larva Dei*) in the kingdoms of the left and the right.[54] These dual aspects of the divine character are mysteriously held together in the darkness of *Deus absconditus*, the full revelation of which cannot be known this side of the last judgment, as Luther notes.[55]

52. Luther writes concerning Mark 13:32:
   Argument: God knows all things. Christ does not know all things. Therefore Christ is not God. I prove the minor premise from Mark, where Christ says that he does not know the last day. Response: The solution is that Christ there speaks after a human manner, as he also says: "All things have been given to me by the Father." Often he speaks of himself as if simply of God, sometimes simply as of man. The Father does not will that the human nature should have to bear divine epithets [*ut humana natura debeat gerere dicta divina*], despite the union, and yet sometimes [Christ] speaks of himself as of God, when he says, "The Son of Man will be crucified." (Luther, "Disputation on the Divinity," in *WA* 39.2:92–121)

This has been the subsequent Lutheran tradition's reading of Mark 13:32. See Gerhard, *On Christ*, 284; Lenski, *St. Mark's Gospel*, 590–91; F. Pieper, *Christian Dogmatics*, 2:285. As an alternative to the historic Lutheran tradition's reading of this text, in a personal conversation, David Scaer has argued that one could interpret this statement to simply mean that Jesus committed the time of the last day to the Father, just as he committed his death to the Father's will and patiently awaited "the hour."

53. SC 1; *CT* 539. The explanation of the first commandment rightly begins: "We should fear, love, and trust in God above all things." Fear for scripture and Luther's exposition of it, is an essential characteristic of our regard for God and our obedience to him in the law.

54. *AE* 26:95. Luther writes in the Galatians commentary of 1531–1535: "the whole creation is a face or mask of God."

55. *AE* 33:292.

The Swabian-Cryptocist position seems to not comprehend this and insists that the only way to possess sovereignty is to exercise it in the form of raw power. In other words, if the human nature did not always assert its communicated divine glory at least in a concealed fashion, it would be divided and separated from the divine person's governance of the universe. But we must conclude that a Jesus who secretly used his raw power would be one that did not really possess it. He would be forced to assert it in order not to lose it. Nevertheless, the Crypoticists are correct that Christ exercised his universal dominion in his state of humiliation. He exercised his sovereignty by working out salvation for humanity. Paradoxically, he was able to suffer humiliation and suspend the direct use of much of his power because of the freedom of universal dominion that he possessed: *"No one takes it from me, but I lay it down of my own accord. I have authority to lay it down,* and I have authority to take it up again. This charge I have received from my Father"* (John 10:18, emphasis added). Therefore, Christ's suspension of his glory is his secret use of it. He is truly "servant of all," only because he is "Lord of all." Viewed from this perspective, both schools of thought are in fact correct.

This being said, it again must be emphasized that the divine glory that we are speaking of is that communicated to his humanity in the person of Christ. God's divinity (considered in the abstract) remains divine in the incarnation and does not cease to exercise itself in its fullest measure. Hence, we should of course also avoid the understanding of *kenosis* pursued by certain modern theologians since the time of Gottfried Thomasius.[56] According to this line of reasoning (existing in more and less extreme forms), *kenosis* means the loss of Christ's divine attributes (moral attributes are retained, but glorious attributes are lost according to both natures!), with only a gradual regaining of any sense of personal identity and mission. In an earlier chapter, we have already rejected such a view since it contradicts God's reality as God. God, in the incarnation does not cease being God. Otherwise, the incarnation would not be a real incarnation, but a transmutation. Since the finite is capable of the infinite, God in his glory can truly communicate himself to the finite without modifying his being.

Following a similar line of reasoning, many modern theologians would reject the loss of all divine attributes within the divine nature itself (contra Thomasius), while strongly implying a complete loss of divine self-understanding or at very least its tempering within Christ's humanity. It is of course relatively difficult to find theologians who will explicitly or systematically make such a claim.[57] Nevertheless, those modern theologians who accept the ability of the historical-critical method to pick apart the Gospel narratives and at the same time claim adherence to the basic claims of the creed, must necessarily hold to such a stance on some level. That is to say, if one accepts the

---

56. See comments in Thomasius, *Christi*, 1:333, 467–68. Thomasius allowed some consciousness of divinity on the part of the human Jesus. He tends to emphasize the development of Jesus's consciousness over time. This is better than later theologians who radicalized his position and suggested that Jesus had lost his consciousness of divinity and only regained it after his resurrection."

57. Karl Barth seems to suggest such a position here: *CD* 4.1.301–3. This understanding of *kenosis* seems to be very strongly implied in other modern Protestant theologians such as: Wolfhart Pannenberg, Jürgen Moltmann, Robert Jenson, Gerhard Forde, Carl Braaten, and Eberhard Jüngel (to name only a few!). Within Catholicism, Karl Rahner and Hans Urs von Balthasar provide more definite statements about Christ's kenotic self-consciousness, that we do not have the space to critique or discuss them here.

historical-critical method's ability to tell us what level of messianic self-consciousness that it was possible for the man Jesus to have (in light of his *sitz im leben*), one implicitly accepts that he could have no knowledge greater than any other ordinary human being and must therefore have suspended all his divine attributes in the state of humiliation.

Such a position is logically contradictory. If Christ is an omnipotent being, then the historical-critical method cannot test any of Jesus's statements found in the Gospels for their historical reliability. As God, it would in fact be his own prerogative as to which attributes (his divine knowledge included) he would suspend in his state of humiliation. Consequently, historical criticism could not predict the will of an omnipotent being in such matters. One would have to rely on the historical information in the Gospels themselves to determine this. Hence, such a position is presumptuous in that it claims that humans can know what God will do or not do before he acts, or, at very least, reveals how he will act.

Moreover, not only does taking such a stance totally contradict the Gospels and the witness of the New Testament in general, but it also makes Jesus into something of an aimless and clueless Messiah. Such a figure hardly could be viewed as the fulfillment of all divine revelation. Since it is clear (even to many secular scholars) that the prophets of the Old Testament were aware of their identities and mission, Christ would stand below them in their level of the comprehension of the truth of God's revelation.

Nevertheless, for many (particularly in popular seminary teaching among mainline Protestants and liberal Catholics) this is an appealing perspective. For them, Christ could not really experience what it meant to be *vere homo* if he were conscious of his divine reality and destiny. Doubtless, this assumption works from the all too modern supposition that a finite, centered self-consciousness is what makes one human (Descartes) and that that this consciousness is always determined by temporal historical forces operating within a causally closed system (Marxism, Positivism, etc.).

In response, we must suggest that these presuppositions contradict the biblical understanding of human life, wherein the prophets going back to Adam always had an understanding of their identity and mission. They were conscious of this because the Word of God determined their self-understanding. Contrary to the modernist supposition regarding the nature of human life, scripture teaches that humanity is determined by God's own effective narration of reality through his two words of law and gospel. All existence is ultimately grounded in the transcendental divine horizon of God's effective address in his Word in creation and redemption.

Through the Word of God, the Christian already understands their identity as a coheir with Christ and their destiny to share with him the resurrection of the dead. Thereby the Church lives out an authentic human existence as a creature of the Word. This is also true of Christ in his earthly existence and in fact made it possible for him to live out an authentic human existence in opposition to fallen humanity's phony and sinful existence. Arguing from lesser to greater, we cannot suppose that what was true for the prophets and for the Church, was not true for Christ. Indeed, if he did not know his own identity as one who shared all with the Father, he would have been incapable of the perfect royal freedom necessary to fulfill the Father's will and recapitulate true human existence. If he did not know the specific content of his mission, then he would not have been able to redeem us by his absolute obedience to the Father's will.

Of course, many might object that if Jesus was fully conscious of his identity and mission then he would not have really fully entered into the terror of human existence under sin and God's wrath. We must of course agree that the Messiah needed to enter into full solidarity with fallen humanity. As will be shown in the next chapter, theologians like Luther and Thomasius are correct that Jesus could not have redeemed humanity if he did not fully experience God's wrath against sin.[58] Nevertheless, for Jesus to fully enter into God's wrath, it was by no means necessary for him to lose the knowledge of his true identity. In fact, many passages in the New Testament suggest (notably Luke 12:49–50) that Jesus was able to fully enter into the terror of human existence because of his consciousness of his identity and mission. As God, Jesus knew the suffering that awaited him as a human being. This fact deepened his terror and suffering as he anticipated his death, as can particularly be observed in his prayers in Gethsemane.

Moreover, Christ's obedience as *vere homo* was, according to the Gospels, deepened by the fact that he knew that an alternative course of action was possible: "Do you think that I cannot appeal to my Father, and he will at once send me more than twelve legions of angels? But how then should the Scriptures be fulfilled, that it must be so?" (Matt 26:53–54). Whereas the first Adam had no alternative but to stand under God's law (whether in obedience or judgment), the second Adam, had no need to fulfill the law, yet was obedient to it even unto death on the cross. For this reason, the knowledge that Jesus had of his identity and mission both strengthened his solidarity with fallen human experience and the authenticity of his obedience.

Moreover, it should again be observed that contrary to what is commonly claimed, the historical-critical method cannot discredit the Gospels' portrayal of Christ's messianic self-consciousness. Historical critics frequently claim that the later Church created the New Testament's portrayals of self-conscious divinity and messianic identity after the fact.[59] Again, as stated earlier, such claims are largely rooted in the presupposition that supernatural revelation is impossible within the closed system of cosmic history. Not only is this mere conjecture and impossible to prove, but it should be noted that recent studies of the Gospel material have made convincing arguments that the theory of later communal inventions of these materials is false and that in fact the Gospels are products of eye-witness testimony.[60] Assuming such conjectures are in some sense scientific, modern theologians have unfortunately put too much stock in them and developed alternative explanations regarding the historicity of the Gospels' portrayal of Jesus's kenotic life-form. In particular, it is often asserted that after Jesus rose from the dead the later Church read the post-resurrection glory back into his earlier existence.[61]

---

58. See *AE* 5:219, 12:126–27, 26:277. Also see Thomasius, *Bekenntniss der Lutherischen Kirche*, 100–105.

59. This is largely the position taken by Bultmann and his disciples. See Bultmann, *Synoptic Tradition*.

60. For one excellent example see Richard Bauckham, *Jesus and the Eyewitnesses*.

61. As we observed earlier, this is implied by Karl Barth's *CD* 4.1.301–3. In general, this has been a position taken by modern theologians since the time of Martin Kähler. See Kähler, *So-Called Historical*

Two points should be made in response to this. First, as Martin Hengel notes, the resurrection and exaltation cannot have been the basis of the claims that Jesus was the divine Messiah, since the Jews of the Second Temple believed in many exalted Patriarchs (i.e., Enoch, among others) and martyrs to whom they never attributed any such role.[62] Even if Jesus was resurrected, nothing in his career apart from his own claims to be the Messiah would induce Second Temple Jews to believe he was the Messiah. None of the text that we have from that period suggests that the Jews believed in a suffering, dying, and rising Messiah, although much later rabbis would develop something approximating this belief (i.e., the Messiah Ben Joseph).[63]

That early Christian beliefs about Jesus's person were not a product of the resurrection alone is especially true with regard to the New Testament's claims of Christ's divinity. A resurrected man is nonetheless still a man.[64] To many Jews, a single resurrected man might indicate the beginning of the eschaton (as it doubtless did for Jewish-Christian

---

Jesus. Kähler's main distinction was between the "*historische*" (historical) and "*geschichtliche*" (historic) Jesus. The true object of belief of Christian faith is not the "*historische*" (historical) Jesus that can merely be reconstructed through historical science, but the Jesus who had an existential impact on the disciples ("*geschichtliche*" or "historic"). According to Kähler's conception, the messianic expectations of the disciples always colored their perception of Jesus and after the resurrection, the new experience of Jesus as resurrected Lord even more deeply shaped their whole perception of his earlier life. This line of reasoning was sharpened by Bultmann and his insistence on the "kerygmatic Christ" as the object of Christian belief in contradistinction to a historically reconstructed Jesus. The kerygmatic Christ was the Christ that was constructed by the Church after the resurrection experience and read back into the life of the earthly Christ to the point that it is impossible to discern what comes from the early Church and what comes from Christ himself. See Bultmann, *Jesus and the Word*. More recently, Marcus Borg has developed this contrast in a more extreme manner in his distinction between the "pre-Easter" and "post-Easter" Jesus. See Borg, *Meeting Jesus Again*. Joseph Ratzinger correctly observes that modern thought on this subject is essentially a return to the two main heresies of the early second century, Ebionism and Docetism. The historical critics wish to define Jesus in purely naturalistic terms and therefore reduc^ him to the level of a mere human (Ebionism), while at the same time spiritualizing his saving reality as an idea or an abstract concept of God's relationship with humans present in the kerygma (Docetism). Contemporary Christians must hold the two natures together by defending the supernatural saving reality of Jesus in his concrete historical life. See Ratzinger, *Introduction to Christianity*, 193–202.

62. Hengel, *Son of God*, 62. He writes:
    It should be noted here that the resurrection by itself is inadequate to explain the origin of Jesus' messiahship. The exaltation of a martyr to God was by no means indication of his eschatological and messianic, i.e. his unique status.

63. See brief discussion in Neill, *Who Did Jesus Think He Was?*, 40–41.

64. Against Pannenberg, *Jesus*, 68–69. Pannenberg imposes a metaphysic and concept of history on the New Testament material that the Second Temple Jews did not share. Namely Pannenberg is heavily influenced by the Heideggerian concept that the whole of one's life is comprehended only in death and therefore one acts anticipating the whole. This is also true of universal history for Pannenberg. Hence, Jesus is God because he reveals the whole of history in his eschatological resurrection and therefore universality of God's Lordship within history. Though it is of course true that Jesus's resurrection is an eschatological event (indeed a prolept eschaton as Pannenberg insists), it is not the case that Second Temple Jews or the authors of the New Testament would have shared Pannenberg's presuppositions about how knowledge of God's lordship is to be had. Neither would they have accepted the Heideggerian claim that the truth of any existence is comprehended in the whole or an anticipation there of. Whereas the interests of the early Church appear to be mainly soteriological, for Pannenberg, living within the post-Kantian environment of German Protestant dogmatics, the main goal is epistemic (i.e., how to get reliable knowledge of God apart from a theory of the divine inspiration of scripture).

heretics like the Ebionites), but it would not indicate divinity (again, as observed earlier, a conclusion that the Ebionites refused to reach). Indeed all humans would eventually be resurrected. Therefore, if we followed Pannenberg's line of reasoning, this would logically make all human beings divine in that by being resurrected they would reveal God's power in a new and definitive way. Since Second Temple Jews clearly did not believe this regarding the future general resurrection, it is difficult to see why early Christians would have come to believe that Jesus was divine because he revealed God's power in a definitive way by his resurrection. Hence, the resurrection could not have created the exalted claims regarding Jesus's identity we find in the New Testament, but rather vindicated ones that already existed (Rom 1:3–4).

Moreover, the claims of earlier generations of scholars that a high and descending Christology only gradually developed can no longer be taken seriously.[65] Much of the newer scholarship on the development of Christology demonstrates an early and very Jewish high Christology.[66] As we have seen, the Synoptic Gospels all hold high and descending Christologies, not simply John. Neither does there appear to be any trace of a lower Christology in the other books of the New Testament. The Apostle Paul is in fact the best evidence for early high Christology, as we have previously demonstrated. Since it is clear that the original disciples whom he knew validated Paul's ministry, it can hardly be doubted that they made the same claims about Jesus. Otherwise, they might very well have entered into a controversy with Paul about his exalted claims about Christ's nature in the manner they did regarding Jewish dietary laws and circumcision. Neither was the belief in Jesus's divinity the result of the early Christians taking on pagan beliefs, as some earlier twentieth-century interpreters argued.[67] As Jews and despisers of pagan polytheism (Rom 1:18–23), it was not the purpose of Paul or any of the other New Testament authors to turn Jesus into a pagan demi-god. We must therefore consequently conclude that if their belief that Jesus was the divine Messiah was not generated by the resurrection (as we have seen above it could not have been), then they must have based their belief on Jesus's claims about himself.

All this suggests that the disciples must have already believed in Jesus as the divine Messiah (an odd a claim as this might have been in the context of Second Temple Judaism) in some sense prior to the resurrection, as in fact the Gospels indicate. Furthermore, if they had this understanding, it cannot be doubted that the source was Jesus himself (as again the Gospels claim), since he very well could have discouraged overly exalted estimations of his person and mission in the space of three years of ministry.

It might be objected that the Gospels also indicate that the disciples frequently misunderstood Jesus's identity and mission. Nevertheless, as Peter's confession in the Synoptic Gospels demonstrates, it was not Jesus's identity that they misunderstood, but rather its implications for his mission. The paradox of one who is both God and Messiah but who will also suffer and die is something that was unacceptable to them and therefore

65. See an older version of this theory in Wilhelm Boussett, *Kyrios Christos*. A new and highly influential version of this thesis can be found in James D. G. Dunn, *Christology in the Making*.

66. See the arguments for early high Christology in the following: Bauckham, *God Crucified*; Gathercole, *Pre-Existent Son*; Hurtado, *Lord Jesus Christ*; Hurtado, *How On Earth?*

67. See for example the aforementioned Boussett, *Kyrios Christos*.

they willfully misunderstood Jesus in many instances. Peter's response of rebuke to Jesus's Passion predictions immediately following his confession of Jesus's identity clearly reveals this (Matt 16:21–28). In short, Jesus's exalted identity did not cause offense, since the disciples eagerly embraced it, thereby believing that they could gain a share in his power and glory (Mark 10:36–40; Luke 9:46–47). For this reason, it would appear that it was more Jesus's mission than his identity that caused misunderstanding and offense.

In summary, as God and Messiah, Jesus was aware of his identity and mission. This freed him to become a servant to all and to conduct the Father's apocalyptic war for creation against sin, death, the devil, and the law. As the Davidic Messiah, Christ fought this war through the means of his priestly and prophetic offices, to which we turn to now.

Chapter 12

The Mystery of the Work of Christ, Part 3

Christ's Office as High Priest

Offices of Christ: The Priestly Office

As we have seen, Jesus is the true king and therefore "Lord of all." For this reason he is capable of laying down his life in a priestly act as "servant of all."[1] His priestly office (*munus sacerdotale*) therefore proceeds from his kingly office and depends upon it. As the true Davidic king, Jesus is also the true Melchizedekian high priest (Ps 110) as the New Testament consistently interprets his messianic role.[2]

In light of the Jewish and Old Testament background of the New Testament, this aspect of Christ's identity is a very important marker for the early Christian understanding of the Messiah over and against other Jewish messianic expectations of the first century. Crispin Fletcher-Louis has noted that contrary to popular scholarly belief there are a very small number of documents written in the period of the Second Temple which posit a single royal Messiah.[3] By his reckoning, most Jews of this period seem to have either expected a single priestly Messiah, or possibly two Messiahs, one priestly and the other

---

1. Althaus, *Die Christliche Wahrheit*, 462–78; Johann Baier, *Compendium Theologiae Positivae*, 2:107–28; Hoenecke, *Evangelical Lutheran Dogmatics*, 3:179–215; L. Hütter, *Compendium Locorum Theologicorum*, 2:933–34; Gerhard, *On Christ*, 320; Graebner, *Outline of Doctrinal Theology*, 135–44; Koehler, *Summary of Christian Doctrine*, 110–18; Lindberg, *Christian Dogmatics*, 256–84; Luthardt, *Kompendium der Dogmatik*, 224–47; Martensen, *Christian Dogmatics*, 302–14; J. Mueller, *Christian Dogmatics*, 305–13; von Oettingen, *Lutherische Dogmatik*, 2.2:203–76; Philippi, *Kirchliche Glaubenslehre*, 4.2:24–344; F. Pieper, *Christian Dogmatics*, 2:342–384; Schaller, *Biblical Christology*, 142–89; H. Schmid, *Doctrinal Theology*, 342–70.

2. Psalm 110 is the most cited Psalm in the New Testament. See discussion in Bateman, "Psalm 110:1 and the New Testament," 438–53.

3. Fletcher-Louis, "Jesus and the High Priest," 8–9. See the following in which scholars describe the messianic expectations of Second Temple Judaism. Most claim that the Jews of Christ's time held a belief in a single Davidic Messiah: Charlesworth, "Concept of the Messiah," 188–218; Charlesworth, "Jewish Messianology to Christian Christology," 225–64; Charlesworth, *Messiah*; Charlesworth, *Qumran-Messianism*; Collins, *Scepter and the Star*; C. Evans and Flint, *Eschatology, Messianism*; Fitzmyer, *One Who is to Come*; W. Green, "Introduction: Messiah in Judaism," 1–13; Hess, *Israel's Messiah*; Lenowitz, *Jewish Messiahs*; Neusner, *Messiah in Context*; Neusner et al., *Judaisms and their Messiahs*; Zetterholm, *Messiah in Early Judaism and Christianity*.

kingly.[4] This was a logical expectation in light of the prophecy of 2 Samuel 7, which ties the temple and the Messiah together. According to this first-century Jewish expectation, while the kingly Messiah would defeat God's enemies, a priestly Messiah would work in tandem with him by restoring true worship. As we have seen from the Old Testament, God's enemies were necessarily idolaters and consequently their destruction and the establishment of true worship always went hand-in-hand. For this reason, Jesus would have been utterly unintelligible to his contemporaries had he not claimed a messianic priesthood based on Psalm 110.[5]

This observation possesses two interesting implications. First, this unification of the two offices stands not only in coherence with the New Testament witness, but also with Jesus's designation of himself as the "Son of Man." As we noted in earlier chapters on the scriptural witness, the "Son of Man" of Daniel 7 possesses both priestly and kingly attributes.[6] Secondly, the Epistle to the Hebrews, which might appear to many modern readers as revolving around a rather eccentric topic, is in fact an extremely important confessional document of early Christianity. If Fletcher-Louis is correct, in effect, Hebrews appears to have the highly necessary function of differentiating the Christian priest-king Messiah doctrine against the more common single priestly Messiah or dual Messiah expectations of late Second Temple Jews.

As the true heavenly high priest promised by Psalm 110, Christ fulfills all sacrifice. This is a major theme in the New Testament. Jesus is the true Temple (John 2:18) and all rituals and sacrifices of the Levitical cult are typological of his grace (Col 2:17, Heb 10:1). For this reason, the early Lutheran scholastic theologian David Chytraeus observed that "God instituted so many different kinds of sacrifice in order that . . . the variety of Christ's benefits and of spiritual sacrifices . . . [would be] foreshadowed by this diversity of sacrificial types."[7] Among these various sorts of sacrifice, we noted in earlier chapters that there are three main categories: sacrifices of praise, sacrifices of atonement, and sacrifices meant to ratify and enact testaments.

Christ fulfills all of these forms of sacrifice. To begin with, his life and death served as a sacrifice of praise, because possessing the fullness of divine glory he was not subject to the law. Therefore his actions of obedience were spontaneous acts of praise before God the Father. Secondly, his obedience and death served as an atoning sacrifice, in that by it he rendered both infinite obedience and suffered infinite retribution in a single theanthropic act on behalf of humanity to the Father. Finally, his death confirmed the testament of the gospel and thereby became a source of our true knowledge and true worship of God. For this reason, in the same way that his regal office is ordered to his priestly office, so Christ's priestly office is ordered to his prophetic office.

In examining Christ's sacrificial work, we begin first with his fulfillment of the sacrifice of praise. As the possessor of the fullness of divine glory, Christ was utterly free from the law and therefore the archetype of Christian freedom. For this reason, any obedience that he rendered to the Father is not a legal obligation, but rather a sacrifice

4. Fletcher-Louis, "Jesus and the High Priest," 9–17.

5. Ibid., 19–20.

6. Ibid., 24–28.

7. Chytraeus, *On Sacrifice*, 52.

of praise: "I glorified you on earth, having accomplished the work that you gave me to do" (John 17:4).[8] Indeed, Jesus's own "glorification" (the revelation of his divine power through his death on the cross) is a glorification of the Father. In dying under God's wrath and the most extreme opposition from sinful humanity, he still confesses God's goodness and grace and therefore trusts in his vindication and exaltation by the Father: "Father, glorify me in your own presence with the glory that I had with you before the world existed" (John 17:1). Therefore Jesus dies glorifying the Father and confessing his faithful goodness.

Even Jesus's lamentation on the cross (Mark 15:34) is itself a confession of faith in the goodness and grace of God. Jesus's dying words in Mark are, it must be remembered, a quotation from the prophecy of Psalm 22 and therefore cannot be separated from the liturgical function of lamentation. The Psalms were utilized as the liturgy of the temple and therefore are all concerned in a sense with the praise of God for his goodness.[9] Psalms of lamentation also assume the existence of and trust in divine goodness. One does not lament if they do not consider God to be gracious and good. Lamentation is faith's response to appearances that contradict its trust in God's goodness and graciousness. Those who do not believe God is good and gracious do not lament because the world is precisely as a non-existent or malevolent deity would have it. Therefore, Jesus in his lamentation maintains his faith in God's Word, in spite of divine hiddenness and condemnation.[10]

As the true human being, Jesus Christ displays perfect faith in God's goodness. Knowing himself to share all things in common with the Father and having this reconfirmed throughout his whole life through God's external Word (in the prophecy of the scriptures, spoken to his parents, at his baptism and at Tabor, etc.), he trusted with a victorious faith in his own vindication (Heb 12:1–2). Adam and Eve, being surrounded by all good things, doubted God's beneficence at the tree of the knowledge of good and evil. By contrast, Jesus on the tree of the cross experienced the most extreme opposition, abandonment, and condemnation in his death. Nevertheless, unlike our first parents, he praised God and did not doubt his word of grace: "you are my Son with whom I am well pleased" (Mark 1:11). It is for this reason that both Luther and Thomasius are correct, that Jesus could only redeem if he experienced the total abandonment and wrath of God.[11] Jesus's active righteousness is rooted in his perfect faith in the face of total abandonment.

The second category of sacrifice that Christ fulfills is that of atoning sacrifice. As our exegetical findings in previous chapters makes clear, the New Testament writings

8. H. Schmid, *Doctrinal Theology*, 353. Quenstedt writes: "The cause [of redemption] on account of which the Son of God was subject to the Law was not his own obligation; for Christ not only as God, but also according to His human nature, was in no way subject to the Law. . . . For Christ, with respect to Himself, was the Lord of the entire Law, and not its servant."

9. Mowinckel, *Psalms in Israel's Worship*, 2–3.

10. For a similar argument see Bayer, "Toward a Theology of Lament," 211–20. Gerhard also suggests that Jesus was a hero of faith who was not defeated even in death. See Gerhard, *History of the Suffering*, 265.

11. See *AE* 5:219, 12:126–27, 26:277. Also see Thomasius, *Bekenntniss der Lutherischen Kirche*, 100–105.

consistently and unambiguously teach that Jesus's death was a sacrifice for sin, in accordance with the types of the Levitical cult and the prophecies of the Old Testament (Ps 22, Isa 53, etc.). Nevertheless, in modern theology this aspect of Jesus's work has been frequently rejected. This is the case for two main reasons. First, it is often doubted by many New Testament scholars (and others) that Jesus actually regarded his death as the final sacrifice for sin.[12] Nevertheless, this objection lacks validity. Even if we did not possess an infallible witness in the New Testament writings (as we do, Luke 10:16, John 16:12–16), there are in fact very good historical reasons for believing that Jesus held his death to be a sacrifice for the sins.

To begin with, the earliest traditions that we possess regarding Jesus's death come to us from writings of St. Paul, dating from the 50s of the first century.[13] Paul delivers to his congregation the tradition that Jesus's death was a sacrifice for sins that he has clearly received from the earliest disciples. He states explicitly: "I delivered to you as of first importance *what I also received*: *that Christ died for our sins* in accordance with the Scriptures, that he was buried, that he was raised on the third day in accordance with the Scriptures" (1 Cor 15:3–4, emphasis added). In 1 Corinthians 15:1–11, Paul begins by referring again to the tradition that he has received that Christ died as a sacrifice for sin. After this, he proceeds to speak of it within a body of traditions that refer to Jesus's resurrection appearances to the apostles. Paul ends by affirming the unity of his proclamation with that of the original disciples of Jesus by stating: "Whether then it was I or they, so we preach and so you believed" (1 Cor 15:11). Hence Paul himself both testifies to this understanding of the death of Jesus as being the earliest tradition and as the one he directly received from the other apostles.

Not only does Paul attest that the earliest disciples understood Jesus's death as a sacrifice for sins (which strongly suggests that Jesus himself did as well), but he also more directly affirms that this was Jesus's own self-understanding by recounting the words of institution at the Last Supper. The words of institution clearly attest Jesus's understanding of his death as a sacrifice for sins in that it presents his flesh and blood as something separated.[14] As the Old Testament makes clear, atoning sacrifice for Israel was in fact the act of separating body from blood (Lev 17:11). Therefore, in the words of institution Jesus presented his physical substance as something sacrificed for sins by speaking of his flesh and blood as having been separated: "this is my body," "this is my blood," etc.

The veracity of Paul's own witness to these words and the narrative of institution in 1 Corinthians 11:23–26 cannot be doubted. According to the passages in 1 Corinthians (mentioned above), Galatians 1–2, and Acts, the apostle clearly knew Jesus's original followers and therefore those who had been in Jesus's own presence when he spoke the

---

12. See the following: Borg, *Meeting Jesus Again*, 128–33; Bultmann, *History of the Synoptic Tradition*, 144, 262–75; Crossan, *Historical Jesus*, 354–95; Fredriksen, *Jesus of Nazareth*, 241–59; Funk, *Honest to Jesus*, 219–41; Pannenberg, *Jesus*, 208–24; Theissen and Merz, *Historical Jesus*, 100, 571–72. Among English speakers of the era of the late Enlightenment, Thomas Paine played a pivotal role in popularizing the idea. See Paine, *Age of Reason*, 35.

13. Ehrman, *New Testament*, 262.

14. Jeremias, *Eucharistic Words of Jesus*, 222. Jeremias writes that Jesus "is applying to Himself terms from the language of sacrifice . . . each of the two nouns ['body' and 'blood'] presuppose a slaying that has separated flesh and blood. In other words: Jesus speaks of himself as a sacrifice."

words of institution. Unless we are to believe that they intentionally lied about what Jesus had said, the words must be understood as historical and therefore Jesus without a doubt understood his death to be a sacrifice for sins.

Beyond Paul's witness to the words of institution, there is also the attestation of them by the Synoptic tradition. The Synoptic Gospels record the words in a very nearly identical form. There is some variation, but this is not surprising. Such variation is doubtless due to how the words were translated differently from the original Aramaic and there was also probably some stylization of them due to liturgical usage. What is important though is that this dual witness to the words gives us multiple attestation of their veracity. Multiple attestation is generally one of the criterion used by liberal scholars to test the veracity of the words of Jesus.[15] Using even their own highly skeptical criteria, the data shows that the words of institution must be considered historical and therefore Jesus must have considered his death a priestly act of sacrifice for sin.[16]

The Gospels also give further historical evidence that Jesus intended his death to be a sacrifice for sin. As N. T. Wright has pointed out, it cannot credibly be believed that the early Church invented Jesus's prayer in Gethsemane that his vocation of dying might be changed (Matt 26:36–46, Mark 14:32–42, Luke 22:39–46).[17] Rather, it seems likely that they would have invented scenes where Jesus heroically and without visible fear embraced his death. In support of this, there is fairly good evidence that the Gospels' portrayal of Jesus stand in rather stark contrast to the images of heroic martyrdom found elsewhere in the immediate historical environment. For example, one might point to Josephus' description of the binding of Isaac in the *Antiquities of the Jews*.[18] One could also point to Eusebius's source for the martyrdom of St. Polycarp.[19] In both of these histories, the hero goes unflinchingly to his death and does not attempt to ask God for a reprieve. Josephus tells us that it "pleased" Isaac to hear of his impending death. Raymond Brown has made a similar comparison of Jesus to the brave and stoic martyrs of 2 Maccabees.[20]

Hence, it is highly implausible that the early Church invented Jesus's prayer that his vocation of death be changed. If they had, they would have for absolutely no discernible reason broken with the cultural ideal of heroic martyrdom in the surrounding environment. Likewise, they would have made Jesus look weak and un-heroic to many of their contemporaries. Furthermore, since this scene is therefore clearly historically accurate, it demonstrates that Jesus believed that it was his mission to die. Combined with the authenticity of the words of institutions, this data all appears to point to the fact that Jesus understood this death to be a sacrifice for sins.

Finally, it should be noted that Jesus's belief that it was his vocation to die as a sacrifice for sins was not unprecedented, but possesses close parallels in Second Temple Jewish apocalypticism. As Wright has shown, the idea of the necessity of Israel's eschatological suffering for sin as a prelude to the eschaton was a staple of apocalyptic Jewish

15. See good discussions in Meier, *Marginal Jew*, 174–75, 218–21.

16. Against Crossan, *Historical Jesus*, 360–67.

17. N. T. Wright, *Christian Origins*, 2:606.

18. *Antiquities of the Jews*, 1.13, in Josephus, *Works of Josephus*, 43–44.

19. *Church History*, 4.14–16, in Eusebius, *Church History*, 145–52.

20. R. Brown, *Death of the Messiah*, 218.

thought.[21] Furthermore, that this suffering could take on a vicarious and representative character has also been attested among a variety of Jewish apocalyptic texts, as well as the literature coming out of Qumran.[22] Both Ben Whitherington III and more recently Brant Pitre have demonstrated that Jesus's claim to be the bringer and embodiment of the kingdom was closely tied up with the idea of vicarious and representative suffering.[23] Within certain strands of the Jewish apocalyptic worldview, being the agent of the kingdom would have necessitated Jesus's suffering of what have been typically referred to as "the Messianic woes."[24] Pitre makes this judgment after surveying a large number of Second Temple Jewish eschatological texts that refer to representative and atoning suffering as a necessary perquisite to the kingdom.[25]

These insights from this recent scholarship are especially helpful because they shed light on the close connection between Jesus's belief that he was to be the final sacrifice for sins and the centrality of his message of the kingdom. In doing this, certain scholarly myths are dispelled. Specifically, it is frequentl asserted that Jesus proclaimed the kingdom whereas later Christianity proclaimed his death and atonement. In light of the facts presented above, it is clear that this is a false dichotomy. Since Jesus's death is the only thing that could bring the kingdom, atonement and the kingdom are mutually dependent on one another. Therefore, the proclamation of the Church and Jesus are simply two sides of the same coin.

The second objection to the atoning work of Christ is that it gives the Church an unpleasant understanding of who God is. According this interpretation, the theology of substitutionary atonement paints a picture of God as a vicious and arbitrary tyrant who needs Jesus's blood before he can forgive and be gracious.[26] The first major problem

21. N. T. Wright, *Christian Origins*, 1:277–79.

22. Witherington, *Christology of Jesus*, 252. Whitherington also discusses 4 Maccabees and does not consider its references to vicarious, salvific suffering to be a product of Hellenism. Wright also makes reference to this belief at Qumran. According his reading, the Essenes believed that the righteous suffering of the "Teacher of Righteousness" pointed ahead to the community's own eschatological suffering. Such suffering would be atoning for sin. See N. T. Wright, *Christian Origins*, 2:581–82.

23. See the aforementioned Pitre, *Jesus, the Tribulation*.

24. Witherington, *Christology of Jesus*, 123.

25. Pitre, *Jesus, the Tribulation*, 41–127.

26. See the following as contemporary examples of those critical of substitutionary atonement: Alison, *Raising Abel*; Brondos, *Salvation and the Cross*; Finlan, *Options on Atonement*; Finlan, *Problems with the Atonement*; Girard, *Scapegoat*; Girard, *Violence and the Sacred*; Heim, *Saved from Sacrifice*; Weaver, *Nonviolent Atonement*. Within Lutheran circles, the rejection of substitutionary atonement can be traced back to Johannes von Hofmann, a Neo-Lutheran Pietist who taught at Erlangen in the mid-nineteenth century. For scholarship on von Hofmann, see the following: M. Becker, *Self-Giving God and Salvation History*; M. Becker, "Life and Work of Johannes v. Hofmann," 177–98; M. Becker, "Hofmann as Ich-Theologie?, 265–93; M. Becker, "Hofmann's Revisionist Christology," 288–328; M. Becker, "Self-Giving God," 417–46; Forde, *Law-Gospel Debate*; L. Green, *Erlangen School of Theology*, 105–33. In a similar manner to Schleiermacher, von Hofmann saw Jesus's obedience as being his faithfulness to his calling under extreme opposition. See von Hofmann, *Encyclopädie der Theologie*, 85. Substitutionary atonement cannot properly interpret his work and is in fact alien to the Bible. See von Hofmann, *Der Schriftbeweis*, 2nd ed., 2.1:320–33. Throughout his biblical exegesis, von Hofmann makes the extremely bizarre argument that the statements of scripture that teach that Jesus died "for us" are really simply to be understood as suggesting that he suffered opposition from the human race and the devil (like all other martyrs)

with this interpretation is that it denies the stark reality of the exacting nature of God's law. All such attacks on God's law and the necessity of its fulfillment reveal themselves in light of the cross to be mere strategies of self-justification. Gerhard Forde (a critic of substitionary atonement) is correct to observe that antinomianism is the "impossible heresy."[27] No matter how badly people wish to remove the power the law, it cannot be removed without its fulfillment.

Because of this, those who reject substitutionary atonement and yet still wish to continue to stand within the tradition of Christian theology must explain why human beings need some form of reconciliation. If humans are unreconciled, implicitly the law and its exacting demands have been acknowledged. Without fail those who deny the exacting nature of God's law and the necessity of vicarious satisfaction, develop an alternative scheme of redemption. This typically involves fulfillment of the law in a more benign form by believers themselves. Jesus, we are told, influences humanity to be reconciled to God by either by his love (Abelard), or his moral example (Socinians) or perhaps through the demystification of social violence (Girard). The fact of the matter remains though that these critics still acknowledge that the law must be fulfilled, no matter how benign the law is described as being. Ultimately, either Christ or the believer will fulfil the law. If it is the believer and not Christ, then the fallen human pattern of self-justification and self-trust will remain unbroken.

Our second response to this criticism of substitution follows from the first. For Christ to redeem, he must deal with the problem of the law. As we have seen, the demands of the law are real and inescapable. They cannot be obfuscated or denied. This does not mean that divine grace is prompted by the law's fulfillment. God in Christ acts graciously prior to the fulfillment of the law by donating himself to humanity in the incarnation. That God can act in a gracious manner prior to the law's fulfillment is not at issue. Rather what is at issue is whether it is necessary for him in act of redemption to

---

on our behalf (von Hofmann, *Der Schriftbeweis*, 1st ed., 2.1:115–40). God in Christ simply endured opposition from sinful humanity and Satan, and thereby overcoming it with his love. Von Hofmann found himself opposed by Friedrich Philippi. See Philippi, *Dr. v. Hofmann gegenüber lutherischer Versöhnung—und Rechtfertigungslehre*. See Gottfried Thomasius, *Das Bekenntniss der lutherischen kirche von der Versöhnung und die Versöhnungslehre D. Chr. K. v. Hofmann's*, mainly on the legitimate grounds that his theory of atonement destroyed objective atonement and thereby forensic justification. Von Hofmann has found two major advocates in the twentieth century: Gustaf Aulén and Gerhard Forde. Aulén in the aforementioned *Christus Victor* (but also in his *Faith of the Christian Church*, 199–210) argues that substitution is an unnecessary and crass rationalization of the work of Christ. Atonement should be more thought of as an image of God struggling against sin and demonic forces in a *mirabile duellum*. In this struggle, he becomes victorious in a manner that transcends human dogmatic rationalization. Similarly, Gerhard Forde (see "Work of Christ," 2:5–104; Forde, "Caught in the Act," 85–97) argues that Jesus Christ represents a break on God's part with his activity of hiddenness, wrath, and law. By forgiving in spite of humanity's extreme opposition to his grace, he destroys humanity's previous existential configuration to law and self-justification, and thereby brings forth new creatures of faith. Having fulfilled the law by faith, human beings are now free from the accusation of the law. It is our judgment (based on our exegetical study above) that none of these descriptions of the work of Christ are faithful either to the scriptures or the tradition of the Lutheran Confessions. Ultimately, they make God untrustworthy by suggesting that it is possible for him simply to break with his faithfulness to his word of law (von Hofmann), or return human beings to their own self-trust and self-justification by suggesting that it is in fact they who fulfill the law (von Hofmann, Forde).

27. Forde, "Authority of the Church," 61.

deal with the problem of the law. God must deal with the problem of the law because he is as faithful to his word of law as he is to his word of the gospel. This recognition draws us to God's concrete activity in salvation history and away from an abstract concept of God's love as a general and disembodied ideal.

In the concrete reality of God's dealings with both Adam and Israel (*protevangelium*, Abrahamic and Sinaitic covenants, etc.), he is faithful to both his words of law and gospel. In fact, if he were not faithful to his word of law, his own faithfulness to the gospel word would ultimately come into question as well. If his promise to punish sin remained fulfillment (Deut 32:35), it would make his promise to forgive empty at best. In Romans, Paul states that prior to the coming of Jesus Christ, God "in his divine forbearance he had passed over former sins" (Rom 3:25). Nevertheless, God also finally remained faithful to both his mercy as well as his holiness in "Christ Jesus . . . [whom God put forth] as a propitiation by his blood, to be received by faith . . . to show his righteousness at the present time, so that *he might be just and the justifier* of the one who has faith in Jesus" (Rom 3:24–26, emphasis added).

By giving his words of law and gospel to our first parents God began to speak forth the new narrative of creation. The new narrative is constituted by the *kenosis* of the Son and his recapitulation of Adam. The new narrative of creation began in the history of the Old Testament by the giving of the divine presence through the Word. Being present in his word of promise, God subjected himself to Israel and humanity, and thereby entering into his kenotic existence.[28] As our exegesis has shown, Israel also experienced this divine presence within the cult as well. In this, the preincarnate Christ was always present with Israel in both Word and sacrament (i.e., the cult).

As the sin of humanity increased, God's self-donating grace manifested itself in greater degrees (Rom 5:20). Ezekiel tells us that when God sent Israel into exile, the *kavod* (the preincarnate Son) entered into exile with them (Ezek 10–11). The depth of the Son's *kenosis* intensified as the visible manifestations of divine wrath intensified. The final act of divine judgment coincides then with the final and overwhelming act of grace, as the prophets predicted and Christ confirmed (Mal 3:2; Isa 61:2, 63; Matt 3, Mark 1; Luke 3). The Son must finally enter into human existence and thereby also enter into the condemnation of the law (Gal 4:4). In acknowledgement of this, Hans Urs von Balthasar observes: "It is that wrath [the wrath of divine retribution against sin] which the Son must face in his Passion. The fearful, divinely grounded wrath which blazes up throughout the Old Testament and finally consumes faithless Jerusalem in the fire of divine glory (Ezek 10, 2), Jesus must bring to its eschatological end."[29]

---

28. Von Balthasar, *Theo-Drama*, 4:333. Von Balthasar writes: "It [*kenosis*] consists in the identification of the divine Logos with the man Jesus . . . an event that is itself in continuity with the antecedent *kenosis* of the Word of God in his covenant with Israel. (The latter continues the covenant with mankind as a whole, which is itself based on the prior creation of creatures endowed with freedom.) This *kenosis*, in all its *ever-intensifying and ever more concentrated stages, remains God's very own secret; he thereby reveals and communicates his own nature to the world*" (emphasis added). Also see See Jenson, *Systematic Theology*, 1:141. Jenson correctly remarks that Christ is already present as the "narrative pattern in the history of Israel."

29. Von Balthasar, *Mysterium Paschale*, 139.

For this reason theologians like I. A. Dorner and Wolfhart Pannenberg are in a sense correct to see the incarnation as the culmination of the process of the two natures coming together into a single theandric subject.[30] What they are mistaken about is that this does not happen in the life of Christ, who was always a single theandric subject from the moment of his conception. Rather, it is the history of Israel that is the arena for the process of the Word becoming flesh. The Old Testament is the story of God binding himself to Israel and humanity by his promise of redemption (Gen 3:15, 15, 17, 22, etc.). This bond manifests itself in greater and greater degrees, until it culminates in the total unity of the two in the incarnation.

Therefore, in entering into creation, Jesus does not merely become a human being, but fully identifies with sin itself and thereby God's eschatological judgment against it. This is because, as we have previously observed, Jesus's new narrative of creation *enhypostatizes* the old narrative of creation, just as the word of gospel incorporates within itself the word of the law. Christ is head of the new humanity and creation (Eph 1:22, 5:22; Col 1:15–20). He is the second Adam (Rom 5; 1 Cor 15) and hence also the head and representative of all (Rom 5:15–19). Therefore he actualizes the fulfillment of the law and lives out the life of the true humanity, while at the same time suffering the curse pronounced by God over the old creation. In effect, he unites both in himself. This fact is witnessed to by both the Old Testament prophets and the New Testament authors: "the Lord has laid on him the iniquity of us all" (Isa 53:6), "[he] was numbered with the transgressors; yet he bore the sin of many" (53:12), "for our sake he made him to be sin who knew no sin, so that in him we might become the righteousness of God" (2 Cor 5:21), "he himself bore our sins in his body on the tree" (1 Pet 2:24). In the Gospel histories themselves, this act of identification with sin and sinners can be observed everywhere. Jesus begins his life by being born to a sinner, the Virgin Mary. He identifies with sinners in his baptism and his ministry by his table fellowship. This identification finally culminates with his death on the cross, crucified between two sinners.[31]

As a result, Christ unites in himself the sins of the first Adam, while at the same representing in his person the righteousness of the second Adam. He indeed unites all things in himself (Eph 1:9–10). This is fitting, because just as the second born sons of the Old Testament were elect (Abel, Isaac, Jacob, David, etc.), so, Jesus, as Adam's younger brother is the true elected and righteous one, of whom they were a type.[32] At the same time as the "the firstborn of all creation" (Col 1:15) he is the older brother of Adam and therefore identifies with the condemned older brothers of the Old Testament as well (Cain, Ishmael, Esau, Saul, etc.). In his redemptive work, he brings together all things and redeems them in his person.[33] As we also observed in our earlier discussion regarding priesthood and sacrifice, the animals and the high priest of the old Levitical cult also

---

30. See Dorner, *System of Christian Doctrine*, 3:283–380; Pannenberg, *Systematic Theology*, 2:363–88.

31. Elert, *Christian Ethos*, 187–88. Elert writes:
> This man [Jesus] has become their [sinners] friend, he is one of them. By becoming like them, however, he also makes them his equals. As soon as he seats himself at the same table with them, the difference between the sinner and the Sinless One is wiped out.

32. Peter Leithart, personal conversation.

33. Karl Barth makes a similar argument. See *CD* 2.2.351–409.

stood as types of Christ as well, in that they symbolized the unity of sin and righteousness in themselves.

This unity of the righteousness and the imputation of sin in Christ, returns us to the categories of "active" and "passive" righteousness that we discussed in a previous chapter. Although, this particular theological nomenclature arose during the Osianderian controversy and became prominent in the period of Protestant scholasticism (both Reformed and Lutheran), the terms nevertheless correctly embody Luther's own understanding of the work of Christ. In contrast to Anselm, who as we observed thought of the death of Christ primarily as an act of supererogation, Luther from the time of his very earliest Psalm commentaries (1513–1515) taught that Jesus died identified with sin and sinners.[34]

In these Psalm commentaries, the Reformer interprets all the statements of the Psalmist to be the prayers of Christ. This is true even of the Psalms of sin and repentance.[35] Consequently, for Luther (in contrast to Anselm) it is proper to speak of Christ as one who identifies with sin and sinners: "He would have no punishments if it were not for our sins and our punishments. Thus the Psalm is speaking about Him and about us at the same time, and it must be read with the most devoted love for Christ. Let us, I say, understand our sins and His punishment at the same time, expressed in the same words."[36] Luther makes a similar description in his comment regarding Psalm 8:4: "Whoever heard of strength being destroyed by weakness? But this is what Christ did. In lowliness, weakness and shame He stripped the whole world of its strength, honor, and glory, and altogether annihilated it and transferred it to himself."[37] He goes on to observe: "Therefore Christ was stuck in our mud, namely, in the lust of our flesh, which leads Him into the deep and abyss."[38] It should of course be recognized that none of these statements reflect Luther's mature understanding of justification or atonement. Rather, they primarily embody his early theology of mystical humility.[39] Nevertheless, these statements seem to suggest that Luther was even at this time moving in a new and powerful direction regarding his understanding of Christ and his work.

---

34. Anselm, *Cur Deus Homo?*, 2.18, in *Scholastic Miscellany*, 179. We read:
Thus when the Lord Jesus willed to endure death (as we have said), because he had the right either to suffer or not to suffer, he ought to have done what he did, because he willed what ought to be done, and yet he was not obliged to do it, because there was no debt involved. For in his human nature (since he himself was God and man), from the time he became man, he received from the divine nature, which is different from the human, the right to claim as he had all that he possessed so completely from himself, and was so perfectly self-sufficient, *that he neither owed any recompense to anyone else nor needed to give in order to have something repaid to him.* (emphasis added)

35. Lienhard, *Luther*, 25. Also see Vogelsang, *Anfange von Luthers Christologie*.

36. *AE* 10:354.

37. *AE* 10:89.

38. *AE* 10:355.

39. Brecht, *Martin Luther*, 1:161–74; L. Green, *How Melanchthon Helped Luther*, 61–110; Kittelson, *Luther the Reformer*, 74–76; Köstlin, *Theology of Luther*, 1:79–227; Lohse, *Martin Luther's Theology*, 43–95; Marius, *Martin Luther*, 89–127; Oberman, *Luther*, 179–85; Saarnivaara, *Luther Discovers the Gospel*, 52–119; Yeago, "Catholic Luther," 37–41.

Later in his Galatians commentary of 1531–1535 (the content of which is endorsed by the Formula of Concord[40]) Luther describes Christ in much the same manner. Atonement for Luther constitutes a *duellum mirabile* between God's wrath and love, his law and his gospel: "Thus the curse, which is divine wrath against the whole world, has the same conflict with the blessing, that is, with eternal grace and mercy of God in Christ. Therefore the curse clashes with the blessing and wants to damn it and annihilate it. But it cannot."[41] Christ and his grace enter creation to identify with sinners. He becomes their righteousness and bears their guilt and punishment: "But because in the same Person, who is *the highest, the greatest, and the only sinner*, there is also *eternal and invincible righteousness*, therefore two converge: the highest, *greatest and only sin; and the highest, the greatest, and the only righteousness*."[42] From this, it is clear that Christ's justifying righteousness is both an active and passive one.[43] He is both the righteousness of the sinner in a positive sense and the one who absorbs the sin of the whole creation.

As a result, the Finnish Luther scholar Tuomo Mannermaa correctly observes: "to Luther . . . the *Logos* did not take upon himself merely human nature, in a 'neutral' form, but precisely the concrete and actual human nature. This means that Christ really has and bears the sins of all human beings in the human nature he has assumed."[44] In this regard Erich Seeberg rightly observes that Christ anticipates the *simul iustus et peccator* of the believer in that he unites in himself both blessedness and the curse, sin and death with life and righteousness. In fact, we should go further than Seeberg and suggest that for Luther in the Galatians commentary Christ truly is *simul iustus et peccator*.[45] Whereas the Christian is sinful and yet is imputed righteous, Christ is righteous, yet imputed a sinner. In this regard, Luther writes: "all the prophets saw this, that Christ was to become the greatest thief, murderer, adulterer, robber, desecrator, blasphemer, etc., there has ever been anywhere in the world. . . *He is a sinner*."[46] For the Reformer then, the depth of Christ's self-donation to sinners is so great that he does not merely become human, but also suffers the imputation of their sin. This of course does not mean that for Luther Jesus is literally sinful in himself. Rather he is such due to God's own imputation:

40. FC SD 3; *CT* 925.

41. *AE* 26:281.

42. *AE* 26:281 (emphasis added). Eduard Preuss also gives a good description of Christ's acceptance of the imputation of sin. See Preuss, *Justification of the Sinner*, 15–22.

43. See Hinlicky, *Luther and the Beloved Community*, 73–90. Hinlicky claims that Luther teaches that Christ only possesses passive righteousness, not active righteousness. He then attributes the idea of the dual righteousness to orthodoxy and Melanchthon. As the citation above shows, this is not correct since Christ both bears divine retribution against sin, while at the same time stands before God as the positive righteousness of the sinner. Insofar as the terminology of "active" and "passive" righteousness is concerned, it arose from the Osianderian controversy and was formulated in such a way as to safeguard the communication of attributes that Osiander denied. For this reason, the dual righteousness is essential to the confession of the communication of attributes within the hypostatic union.

44. Mannermaa, *Christ Present in Faith*, 13.

45. E. Seeberg, *Luthers Theologie*, 8. Also see an interesting discussion of Luther on these points in von Balthasar, *Theo-Drama*, 4:284–90.

46. *AE* 26:277 (emphasis added).

> Thus a magistrate regards someone as a criminal and punishes him if he catches
> him among thieves, even though the man has never committed anything evil or
> worthy of death. Christ was not found among sinners; but of His own free will
> and by the will of the Father He wanted to be an associate of sinners and thieves
> and those who were immersed in all sorts of sin. Therefore, when the Law found
> Him among thieves, it condemned and executed Him as a thief.[47]

From this it can yet again be observed that the *fröhlicher wechsel* stands in a direct
relationship with Luther's concept of the communication of attributes. Just as Luther
teaches that the incarnation represents an exchange of realities between humanity and
divinity, so too atonement means an exchange of human sin for Christ's theandric righteousness. As Mannermaa correctly observes above, the identification of the Second
Person of the Trinity with human nature involves identification with its miserable state
after the Fall. Such solidarity with sinful humanity logically leads to suffering the curse
of death that is the just due of sinners (Rom 6:23). Therefore, as we stated in an earlier
chapter, the work and person of Christ are in fact the same realities observed from two
different perspectives.

In the modern period, few theologians have followed a similar path to Luther with
the notable exceptions of the Reformed theologian Karl Barth and the Roman Catholic
theologian Hans Urs von Balthasar. This is true even in spite of their trepidations regarding Luther's understanding of the communication of attributes. Nevertheless both have
echoed similar (though of course not identical) themes in their own atonement theology.

In his *Theo-Drama*, von Balthasar describes Christ serving as a representative of
both what creation should be and of its actual alienation from God.[48] Creation's true
end is to be found in playing its role with the divine drama "in Christ." Embodying this
role means standing in a receptive relationship to God by echoing the Son's continuous
and eternal generation from the Father. To the extent that creation corresponds to this
role, it embodies true freedom.[49] Christ redeems because as the true creature he embodies this attitude of receptivity doing God's will as it is gradually revealed to him by the
Spirit. This is reflected in the Gospel histories' descriptions of his patiently awaiting the
coming of the "hour."[50] In the same way, he bears creation's alienation from God and
drinks the cup of divine wrath.[51] Having suffered God's rejection and overcome the
power of sin, he draws creation into fellowship with God's Triune life by the power of
his resurrection.[52]

Similarly, Karl Barth (true to his Reformed background) describes Jesus as embodying both the divine decrees of reprobation and election. As Barth correctly observes,
throughout the history of salvation the Bible exemplifies election and rejection in the
form of the contrast between accepted and rejected individuals (Cain and Abel, Ishmael
and Isaac, Esau and Jacob, Saul and David, etc.). The elder brother or person consistently

---

47. *AE* 26:277–78.

48. Von Balthasar, *Theo-Drama*, 4:332–38.

49. Ibid., 2:266–70. Also see his discussion in von Balthasar, *Theology of History*, 29–50.

50. Von Balthasar, *Theo-Drama*, 4:231–40.

51. Ibid., 4:332–51.

52. Ibid., 5:425–87.

resists God's grace and is condemned, whereas the younger does not and is redeemed.[53] For Barth, Jesus Christ is the basis and object of all electing grace. He therefore unites God's rejection of fallen humanity and the actualization of human fidelity to God as the perfect covenant partner.[54] In other words, he is both the object of divine rejection, as well as the election. As a result, he both bears God's condemnation of sin and nothingness, while at the same time serving as a righteous representative of the human race. In this, he becomes the archetype and sole basis of election.[55]

In light of our commitment to the Lutheran symbolic writings we cannot endorse every aspect of Barth and von Balthasar's accounts. Neither of course do we have the space here to dissect major areas of disagreement. There is nevertheless a basic agreement between them and the Lutheran confessional tradition that Christ's redemptive activity consists in bearing both all sins and actualizing redemptive righteousness.

Entering into a specific description of the priestly work of atonement, it should be understood that Christ's active and passive righteousness, though distinct, stands united in Christ's perfect faith manifested in his willing death on the cross. His active righteousness takes the form of obedience to the Father's will. The will of the Father is that Christ must take upon himself the guilt of humanity. By accepting the divine judgment, Christ transferred all guilt to himself, thereby fulfilling all passive righteousness as well. Unlike the habitual self-justification of sinful humanity, Christ is free from all self-justification. Being infinitely righteous and possessing a perfect faith, he is free to take upon himself all guilt (2 Cor 5:21; 1 John 2:2). Whereas when confronted with his sin the first Adam justified himself by casting the blame on his bride Eve (Gen 3:12), the second Adam refuses to justify himself and in fact takes upon himself the guilt of his bride the Church (Eph 5). Indeed, when accused, the Gospel histories repeatedly echo Isaiah's prophecy by reporting that Christ "opened not his mouth" (Isa 53:7). In this, he accepts the divine judgment of guilt pronounced against him, while at the same time believing the divine faithfulness (Heb 12:1–2; 1 Pet 2:23) proclaimed at his baptism and at the transfiguration: "you are my Son . . . in whom I am well pleased."

Jesus puts up no barriers against the wrath of God, but allows himself to be utterly stripped before the whole world (Matt 27:28). Whereas Adam hid his nakedness after sinning at the tree of the knowledge of good and evil (Gen 3:10–11), Christ allows his nakedness to be publically exposed on the tree of the cross. Christ's redemptive nudity was foreshadowed elsewhere in scripture. As we observed in an earlier chapter, after giving the *protevangelium*, God covered the nakedness of Adam and Eve with the sacrifice of an animal (Gen 3:21).[56] As self-justifiers, Adam and Eve attempted to cover their own nakedness with leaves. In covering their nakedness with a sacrifice which he himself provided, God showed that it is his own alien righteousness that must cover sin (Rom 1:17, Phil 3:9). After Noah had become intoxicated (on a kind of forbidden fruit, like Adam!),[57] Shem (the ancestor and type of Christ) covered his father's nakedness and

53. *CD* 2.2.351–410.

54. *CD* 2.2.94–195.

55. Ibid.

56. *AE* 1:221–22. Luther makes a similar, but different argument.

57. Leithart, *House for My Name*, 56. Leithart notes the garden parallel, but not the fact that the

therefore his sin (Gen 9:23). In the same manner, at the end of Genesis, Potiphar's wife (the new Eve, 39:15) uncovers Joseph's nakedness due to his unwillingness to engage in adultery (adultery being the type of all idolatry and apostasy in scripture).[58] It is also worth noting, that one of the possible meanings of the Hebrew word for atonement (*kap·pêr*) is to cover.[59] Therefore Paul bids us to "*put on* the Lord Jesus Christ" (Rom 13:14, emphasis added). By becoming uncovered, Christ thereby covers humanity with his righteousness.

Because Jesus willingly made himself the representative sinner, the governing authorities who sought to destroy him carried out their proper roles as masks of God's law and wrath (Rom 13:1–5). This makes the cross a public and visible manifestation of the exile, wherein Israel's disobedience (a representation of universal disobedience) was revealed fully through the suffering of its representative king under foreign domination as a punishment for sin. This domination echoes Adam's own loss of dominion and subjection to the power of Satan (Eph 2:2). In Jesus, the condemnation of the exile was concentrated and therefore eliminated through its judgment in the flesh (Rom 8:3). As true God and true man, he could both represent the human race, as well as pay the infinite debt of sin.[60] The cross therefore stands as a revelation of the infinity of divine wrath against sin. Because Christ's infinite theandric person was the only thing capable of paying for sin, the impotence of finite human effort was revealed.[61]

Insofar as he is also the representative righteous one, Jesus reveals human fallenness by suffering at the hands of sinners. In this role, he is accused and tried by the representatives of the whole of false humanity; both Jews and Gentiles.[62] Though von

fruit causes him to sin.

58. Ibid., 65.

59. Milgrom, *Leviticus 1–16*, 1079–84.

60. Chrytraeus, *Summary of the Christian Faith*, 37–38. Echoing Luther's theologic (and also Athanasius and Anselm's!), Chrytraeus writes:

Why was it necessary that there be a unity between the two natures, divine and human, in Christ our Mediator? . . . First, it was necessary that He be a man because man had sinned and the course of justice would demand that he pay the penalty. He had to be a man to be able to suffer and die on behalf of man. Again that was necessary in order for Him to show His love for people to people with the assumption of human nature, and to glorify that love for people (which the devil had terribly torn apart and crushed) by His being taken up and placed at the right hand of God the Father. Second, he had to be God to provide a ransom or payment for sins and to be a merit sufficient for new righteousness and life. He had to be God to be able to sustain the burden of the wrath of God and its punishments, to overcome death and the devil, and to restore righteousness and life. Again, He had to be God in order to enter into the Holy of Holies, to look into the heart of the Father, to be present to the hearts of those who call upon Him and everywhere in the Church, to listen to those who call upon Him and defend and preserve them, and to give the wisdom of God and His Holy Spirit to those who ask for such gifts. Because at the first creation the Logos, the Son of God, had given to people the life and light which was the image of God; it was fitting for divine wisdom that the image of God which had been corrupted be restored in us with the same Word with which it had been created.

61. Both Luther and the Formula agree on this point, as we observed in the last chapter. *AE* 26:33, 37:209–10, 41:103–4; FC SD 3; *CT* 935.

62. *CD* 1.2:110. Barth writes:

The co-operation of Jews and heathens at the crucifixion of Jesus is naturally not accidental, different though their respective shares in it are. In much the same way they also stand side by side in the first two chapters of Romans as concluded under the same judgment.

Hofmann was incorrect to suggest that Jesus faced the opposition of sinful humanity and the devil alone, he was correct to see Jesus's death as a culmination of the whole history of righteous suffering that began with Abel.[63] In agreement with this, Jesus himself testifies to this fact on many occasions (Matt 23:35; Luke 11:51, 13:32–35). His death is therefore a manifestation of universal fallenness. Christ, the true mediator, also reveals humanity's enthrallment with false mediators by dying in the hands of the same. He is accused by the Pharisees (false prophets), offered for sacrifice by the temple aristocracy (false priests), and finally excluded by the Romans (false kings).

Christ's truth and sinlessness exposes the sinfulness and falsehood of the whole of humanity. Fallen humanity refuses to hear his divine Word of law and promise, and therefore it must destroy him. As we have previously observed, the end point of self-justification is self-deification. Self-deification can only end with the elimination of the true God, against whose judgment it strives.[64] As the true God, Jesus's death at the hands of sinners reveals the ultimate end of self-justification.[65]

Self-justification and self-deification are an infinite task because God's being and justice are infinite. Those who suffer eschatological judgment will experience God's law and judgment infinitely (Isa 66:24; Dan 12:2; Matt 25:41, v. 46; Rev 20:10). Consequently, they will eternally persist in their self-justification. In the concrete experience of our temporal existence, the infinity of the law is clearly manifested by the fact that the human drive for self-justification is unending. The law never stops demanding and imputing us with guilt. Moreover, the nature of time itself will never allow us to do away with our guilt. No matter how many good works we do, our guilt is never expiated. It eternally stands over and against us, as does the full burden of our past. Even if somehow we were to succeed in being righteous by our own actions (which is of course impossible!), there would still never be an end in sight. We would have to maintain our righteousness by our actions forever and ever. Only in death would the question of our righteousness be settled. Nevertheless, because the "wages of sin is death" (Rom 6:23), the verdict could never be anything but negative.[66]

The infinity of the law and the infinity of our concupiscence are simply two manifestations of our self-deification. Our concupiscence is in fact born of the same desire to master God, which Paul calls "covetousness" (6:1–14).[67] At the root of all sinful desire is the will to master and possess the other. This is ultimately rooted in our unbelief, whose lack of trust manifests itself in the need to control. The ultimate object of this desire for

---

Also find similar observations in Pannenberg, *Systematic Theology*, 2:425–26.

63. Von Hofmann, *Der Schriftbeweis*, 1st ed., 2.1:115–40.

64. Forde, "Work of Christ," 2:68. Forde writes: "To put it bluntly, our so-called freedom cannot stop until it has done away with God altogether."

65. *CD* 1.2.92. Barth writes:
> Man unveils himself here as really and finally guilty. But that this did happen, that man really and finally revealed himself as guilty before God by killing God, had to happen thus and not otherwise in the event in which God asserted His real lordship.

66. Many of the insights in this section come from conversations with Steven Paulson.

67. Ernst Käsemann, *Commentary on Romans*, 194. Käsemann shows that many Jews of the Second Temple period described the whole law as summarized by the command not to covet and connected it to Adam's coveting of God's divinity. This is how Paul should be read here.

mastery is God and his uncontrollable judgment against us. My self-justification leads me to ultimately covet his divinity: "But sin, seizing an opportunity through the commandment, produced in me all kinds of covetousness. *For apart from the law, sin lies dead*" (8:7, emphasis added). Bound to sin, we have no other recourse but to try to master God, and his annihilating judgment.[68] God hidden in his majesty and active in his masks of the law cannot be trusted, but only opposed.

The only solution to these dual manifestations of our divine ambition (*ambition divinitatis*) is death and resurrection.[69] This occurs first with Christ and then within us (6:1–14).[70] Indeed as Gustaf Wingren correctly observes: "'law and grace' is 'death and resurrection.'"[71] Christ's death overcomes the infinity of divine law. By rejecting self-justification, Christ stands as infinitely just before God. By dying on the cross, Christ infinitely destroys our sinful status before God (*coram Deo*) by suffering the punishment that is its proper due: "I have been crucified with Christ. It is no longer I who live, but Christ who lives in me" (Gal 2:20). With the law ended (Rom 10:4), it no longer baits our sinful nature into the need for self-justification. As Paul observes:

> For a married woman is bound by law to her husband while he lives, but if her husband dies she is released from the law of marriage. Accordingly, she will be called an adulteress if she lives with another man while her husband is alive. But if her husband dies, she is free from that law, and if she marries another man she is not an adulteress. Likewise, my brothers, you also have died to the law through the body of Christ, so that you may belong to another, to him who has been raised from the dead, in order that we may bear fruit for God. For while we were living in the flesh, our sinful passions, *aroused by the law*, were at work in our members to bear fruit for death. But now we are *released from the law, having died to that which held us captive*, so that we serve in the new way of the Spirit and not in the old way of the written code. (7:2–6, emphasis added)

By eliminating our guilt Christ also ends our previous existence within the sphere of infinite desire and self-justification.[72] In utterly surrendering himself to us, there remains no room for us to try to master him by self-justification.

---

68. Forde does an excellent job describing this. See Forde, "The Work of Christ," 2:65–69.

69. See Luther's comments on divine ambition in *WA* 27:504. Also see observation in Jüngel, *Entsprechungen*, 190–92.

70. See Forde, *Justification by Faith*. Forde does a good job describing atonement and justification in terms of death and resurrection. Unfortunately he is not able to hold this together with penal substitution. Werner Elert does a fairly good job of this. See Elert, *Christian Ethos*, 182–94.

71. Wingren, *Living Word*, 137.

72. Elert, *Christian Ethos*, 194. Elert writes:
   Christ is the end of nomological existence and thereby also the originator of a new existence. Because God has accepted the atonement of the guilt of all, that guilt is now expiated. Henceforth there can be a guiltless existence which is no longer subject to retribution and to death.

Also see Elert, *Law and Gospel*, 29. Elert writes:
   [The] death of Christ is judgment. God is here administering justice according to the law of retribution. Here the nomological being of mankind is not only exposed in its falsehood, but because expiation must occur right here, it is mortally wounded.

Also see Pannenberg, *Systematic Theology*, 2:427:
   Those whom Jesus represents have the possibility in their death, by reason of its linking to the

Our passive existence of faith *coram Deo* participates in the proleptic eschaton of Jesus's Sabbath rest (Matt 11:28–30, Heb 4:9).[73] Becoming totally passive in the death of judgment, we are made ready to receive God's gift of new creation by faith. Jesus, the true Son of Man, reveals to us ahead of time God's own final judgment of justification through Word and sacrament. By this we receive in the present the benefits of his eternal rest through faith in the gospel. By resurrecting humanity through his omnipotent Word of promise, Christ enhypostatizes into the new creation the corpse of our desires and orientation to the law. As a result, the refuse of our old infinite drives are shrunk down into their proper finitude and molded into the dimensions of our earthly life within the orders of creation. Although *coram Deo*, the desire for self-justification is ended first by the imputation of righteousness and then by the sanctification of faith; *coram mundo* our old desires and configuration to the law are now harnessed in the service of the neighbor. Through the freedom of this sanctifying word of promise, our existence *coram mundo* recapitulates the pre-lapsarian existence of Adam and Eve by the exercise of righteous works.[74]

This brings us to the final aspect of Christ's fulfillment of all sacrifice: His death and resurrection confirms and enacts a testament. It is no accident that Jesus offered himself up on Golgotha, which is a hillock in the vicinity of Mount Moriah where both the Abrahmic (Gen 22) and the Davidic (2 Sam 24) testaments were confirmed by sacrifice.[75] Both acts of sacrifice prefigured Christ in different ways. In the first case, a father offered up his only son, whereas in the second a king offered himself up for the salvation of his people. Jesus is both the true Son of the Father and the true king of Israel. Also, in both cases, a substitute saved the originally intended victim. Christ fulfilled all these types in his substitutionary sacrifice on the altar of the cross. By his death he also fulfills the promises of universal dominion to a son of David and of universal blessing of all nations present in both the Abrahmic and Davidic testaments, which themselves are restatements and continuations of the *protevangelium*.

The new testament of forgiveness could only come through Christ's substitutionary death. As the book of Revelation makes clear, it is only because of his death that the "lamb slain from the foundation of the world" (1 Pet 1:18–20, Rev 13:8) is worthy to open the scroll of the testament (Rev 5:4–11).[76] We find a similar witness in Paul (Gal 3:15), where the gospel is described as a last will and testament.[77] The author of Hebrews

---

death of Jesus, of attaining to the hope of participation in the new resurrection life that has already become manifest in Jesus. Rom. 6.5)

73. Pannenberg's apt description. See Pannenberg, *Jesus*, 157; Pannenberg, *Systematic Theology*, 2:347–51.

74. *AE* 31:360. Luther writes:
Through his faith he [the believer] has been restored to Paradise and created anew, has no need of works that he may become or be righteous; but that he may not be idle and may provide for and keep his body, he must do such works freely only to please God.

75. See argument in Hahn, *Lamb's Supper*, 14–28.

76. See discussion of the seven seals in Zahn, *Introduction to the New Testament*, 393–94. Also see Chilton, *Days of Vengeance*, 166; Beasley-Murray, *Book of Revelation*, 121; Brighton, *Revelation*, 107; Court, *Myth and History*, 55–56.

77. See Lenski, *St. Paul's Epistles to the Galatians*, 157–58. Lenski rightly observes that *diatheke* is used here for an individual will or testament.

agrees and writes regarding Christ's death: "For a will takes effect only at death, since it is not in force as long as the one who made it is alive" (Heb 9:17).

In his death, Christ offered up his active and passive righteousness to the Father (Heb 9:14). In his resurrection and exaltation he received all in his inheritance from the Father (Phil 2:9–11). Possessing all, Christ may give all to both the Father and us. The infinity of his active and passive righteousness is held up to the Father as a sacrifice for sins and given to humanity as a testament of his alien righteousness through Word and sacrament. Charles Porterfield Krauth describes this well in his discussion of the relationship of the work of Christ to the sacrament of the altar:

> The idea of sacrifice under the Old Dispensation sheds light upon the nature of the Lord's Supper. . . . Sacrifice through the portion burnt, is received of God by the element of fire; the portion reserved is partaken of by men, is communicated to them, and received by them. The eating of the portion of the sacrifice, by the offerer, is as real a part of the whole sacred act as the burning of the other part is. Man offers to God; this is sacrifice. God gives back to man; this is sacrament. The oblation, or the thing offered, supplies both sacrifice and sacrament, but with the difference, that under the Old Dispensation God received part and man received part; but under the New, God receives all and gives back all: Jesus Christ, in His own divine person, makes that complete which was narrowed under the Old Covenant by the necessary limitations of mere matter.[78]

In giving his testament, Christ makes humanity his coheirs through faith (Rom 8:17). Just as in dying Christ actualized his objective righteousness before the Father, in rising he confirms and enacts his testament of alien righteousness through Word and sacrament: "[he] was delivered up for our trespasses and raised for our justification" (Rom 4:25). In rising, he reveals his conquest of death through his atonement of sin. Having overcome sin and death, he now lives to give humanity a share in his victory through his promise of justification.

Christ's testament, actualized in his death and resurrection, objectively justifies the whole world: "Therefore, as one trespass led to condemnation for all men, so one act of righteousness leads to justification and life for all men" (Rom 5:18, see also Rom 4:25; 2 Cor 5:19).[79] In regard to this fact, Luther comments in his sermon of John 3:19 (1538):

---

78. C. Krauth, *Conservative Reformation*, 591. Krauth nicely develops an authentic Lutheran understanding of the self-offering of Christ moving in both directions: both towards the Father as sacrifice and towards us as sacrament. This stands in contrast to Gerhard Forde's insistence that substitution represents only our own movement towards God or us buying God off with our good works as it comes to be embodied in Jesus. See Forde, *Where God Meets Man*, 32–44; Forde, *On Being a Theologian*, 12. As a divine subject, Christ is God fulfilling his own law. The Son's offering of himself up to the Father is God's own action in fulfilling his Word of both law and gospel. This does not mean that humans are capable of "buying God off," but rather that God himself remains faithful to us in law and gospel.

79. For discussions of objective justification, see Preuss, *Justification of the Sinner*, 22–28; Hoenecke, *Evangelical Lutheran Dogmatics*, 3:179–83; Koehler, *Summary of Christian Doctrine*, 146–47; J. Mueller, *Christian Dogmatics*, 310–11; F. Pieper, *Christian Dogmatics*, 2:321, 347–51. Also see Walther, "Christ's Resurrection," 233. Walther correctly observes:

> For God has already forgiven you your sins 1800 years ago when He in Christ absolved all men by raising Him after He first had gone into bitter death for them. Only one thing remains on your part so that you also possess the gift. This one thing is—faith. And this brings me to the second part of today's Easter message, in which I now would show you that every man who wants to be

[It is] as though Christ wished to say: "Whoever believes, does not go to hell; whoever does not believe, already has the sentence of death pronounced on him." Why? Well, because he does not believe in Christ. This is the judgment: that such an ineffably comforting doctrine of God's grace, procured for the world through Christ, is proclaimed, but that the world still wants to believe the devil rather than God and His beloved Son. And this despite the fact that God assures us: "Sin, hell, judgment, and God's *wrath have all been terminated by the Son."*... Now what is still lacking? *Why the judgment if all sin has been removed by the Son?* The answer is that the judgment is incurred by man's refusal to accept Christ, the Son of God. Of course, man's sin, both that inherited from Adam and that committed by man himself, is deserving of death. But this judgment results from man's unwillingness to hear, to tolerate, and to accept the Savior, who removed sin, bore it on His shoulders, and locked up the portals of hell . . . it is expressly *stated here that Christ came and removed the sin of the world so completely that it is entirely deleted, entirely forgiven.*[80]

As Luther observes, Christ's universal and objective justification is valid whether or not sinners believe it. Stated in another way, Christ's new narrative of creation incorporates all created beings and thereby determines their reality by way of their relationship to him. This makes the story of the old creation under sin and death a mere subplot whose ultimate determinative power is neutralized within Jesus's new narrative of universal and objective reconciliation. This new narrative of universal justification that Christ enacts begins from the moment that the *protevangelium* is spoken forth (Gen 3:15). The justification of Adam and Eve was actualized even prior to them having faith in the promise of the redemption by the "lamb slain from the foundation of the world" (1 Pet 1:18–20, Rev 13:8).

In light of this universal redemption, the only sin (as Luther remarks above) is the rejection of the promise of the gospel. Just as the originating sin was a rejection of the first commandment (disbelief in the fact that God would be their faithful and gracious God), so too the first commandment is now restated on the basis of Christ's redemption from sin, death, the law, and the devil.[81] Christ is the gracious and redeeming God, and therefore all sins can only be a manifestation of the rejection of this fact (Rom 14:23). Luther writes: "Yet every sin since the beginning of the world has been unbelief and ignorance of Christ, since the promise concerning the Seed of the woman was given

---

saved must accept by faith the general absolution, pronounced 1800 years ago, as an absolution spoken individually to him.

Again he writes in the same passage:
Christ's Glorious Resurrection from the Dead the Actual Absolution of the Entire Sinful World Here I would point out two things: 1. That this is certain and true, and 2. That therefore every man who wants to be saved must by faith accept this general absolution as applying also to him.

R. C. H. Lenski, as well as others in the Ohio and Iowa synods (probably due to Pietist influence) rejected this idea. See Lenski, *St. Paul's Epistle to the Romans*, 377–83; Lenski, *First and Second Epistle to the Corinthians*, 1042–49.

80. *AE* 22:382–83 (emphasis added).

81. *AE* 1:147. Luther writes: "Unbelief is the source of all sins; when Satan brought about this unbelief by driving out or corrupting the Word, the rest was easy for him."

right after the fall of Adam (Gen 3:15), which was made known throughout the houses of the fathers until the fullness of time (cf. Gal 4:4)."[82]

This does not of course mean that in the actual manifestation of sin in the form of individual deeds, people cannot still violate God's commandments in other ways. People certainly remain capable of committing adultery or stealing. Nevertheless, every time a sin is committed against God's commandments, it is ultimately a manifestation of unbelief in Christ's gracious redemption. After the advent of the gospel, all sins are simply expressions of unbelief and ingratitude for Christ's great work on behalf of sinners. For non-Christians, because all actions are performed in unbelief (irrespective of whether they are technically violating a commandment by their actions), every deed is a blasphemy against the grace of Christ. For believers, daily sins express the weakness and imperfection of faith, even if they remain covered because of Christ's imputation of righteousness.

In light of this situation, the author of the Epistle to the Hebrews describes people who sin as "trampling" on the Son of God (Heb 10:26–29). Jesus states clearly that although all are objectively forgiven, rejection of that forgiveness presented by the Holy Spirit in Word and sacrament is the unpardonable sin:

> Whoever is not with me is against me, and whoever does not gather with me scatters. Therefore I tell you, every sin and blasphemy will be forgiven people, but the blasphemy against the Spirit will not be forgiven. And whoever speaks a word against the Son of Man will be forgiven, but whoever speaks against the Holy Spirit will not be forgiven, either in this age or in the age to come. (Matt 12:30–32)

Hence, although Christ objectively pronounces his justification over the whole world through his death and resurrection, subjective reception of that justification only occurs where faith receives that promise in Word and sacrament. This does not mean that there are in fact two justifications. Rather, faith incorporates us redemptively into the single event of Christ's suffering the judgment of sin and his actualization of perfect righteous *coram Deo*. Through faith, we become in God's eyes a single subject with Christ, first by imputation and then by mystical union.[83]

For this reason we may say that the sinner's true being before God is externalized in the person of Christ.[84] This is not a legal fiction because Christ's new narrative of

---

82. Luther, *Only the Decalogue is Eternal*, 66–67.

83. FC SD 3; *CT* 933, 35. The Confessors write:
Likewise also the disputation concerning the indwelling in us of the essential righteousness of God must be correctly explained. For although in the elect, who are justified by Christ and reconciled with God, God the Father, Son, and Holy Ghost, who is the eternal and essential righteousness, dwells by faith (for all Christians are temples of God the Father, Son, and Holy Ghost, who also impels them to do right), yet this indwelling of God is not the righteousness of faith of which St. Paul treats and which he calls *iustitiam Dei*, that is, the righteousness of God, for the sake of which we are declared righteous before God; but it follows the preceding righteousness of faith, which is nothing else than the forgiveness of sins and the gracious adoption of the poor sinner, for the sake of Christ's obedience and merit alone.

84. See Bayer, *Theology the Lutheran Way*, 53. Bayer describes Christian existence as being "enhypostatized" by the Word of God addressed to us.

creation has become the ground of all reality.[85] In Jesus, the believer finds his or her true self. This true self has suffered the infinite judgment of sin and has actualized an omnipotent righteousness: "For you have died, and *your life is hidden with Christ in God*" (Col 3:3, emphasis added). As a result, the believer is radically de-centered. The believer finds the ground of its reality not in themselves, but external to itself in God's omnipotent address in Christ Jesus received by the passivity of faith. Christ's narrative of reconciliation objectively stands as the sinner's true reality before God. Justified sinners are "in Christ Jesus" (2 Cor 5:7) and "abide in him" (John 5:4 KJV) through faith. Indeed, as Luther says, believers are "baked into a single loaf" with Christ.[86] Conversely, just as in the original creation, Adam and Eve became alienated from God's gracious Word and therefore from their true essence, so too in the new creation, the sinner who persists in unbelief is alienated from their true self in Christ Jesus.[87]

As a result Christ's Word of redemption becomes a curse for those who reject it; it takes on the function of both law and gospel. It becomes condemning for those who reject Christ's testament and persist in the sin of unbelief, just as it becomes redeeming for those who receive it with faith.[88] Christ is both the cornerstone of the eschatological temple (Ps 118:22–23; Mark 12:10–12; Eph 2:19–22; 1 Pet 2:4–6) and the eschatological stone of destruction (Dan 2:35, Matt 21:42–44). When Christ the lamb opens his testament in the book of Revelation, it both redeems the Church and brings about eschatological judgment and destruction for the unbelieving world.

The fact of both the redeeming and destructive possibilities present in the testament of Christ is most dramatically illustrated in the giving of the testament of Christ's body and blood. As Christ's separated body and blood, the content of the sacrament is Christ's very redeeming sacrifice on the cross. For those who believe and therefore "discern" the body and blood of the Lord, life and salvation are received through the proclamation of his death *pro nobis* (1 Cor 11:25). Nevertheless, for those who reject the objective promise by failing to discern the body and blood, their expectation can only be one of condemnation (11:27–31).

For this reason, ultimately Christ's testament is able to function as both the killing word of law and the revivifying word of the gospel. In the last chapter, we will deal with the proclamation of Christ's testament in his prophetic office.

---

85. See good description in Thielicke, *Evangelical Faith*, 1:153–72.

86. *WA* 22:97.

87. In this sense, the claim of many of the Neo-Chalcedonians (rooted in an Ultra-Realist ontology) that Christ incorporated the total human nature (*pâsan tền anthrōpóēta*) into himself, has a certain element of truth. See Meyendorff, *Christ in Eastern Christian Thought*, 54. All our stories become subplots of Christ's story.

88. Commenting on Hebrew 9:15, John Chrysostom notes that the giving of a testament means the disinheritance of some who reject it. See Chrysostom, *Homily 16 on Hebrews*, 1; *NPNFa* 14:443. He writes:

> And a testament is of this character: It makes some heirs, and some disinherited. So in this case also: I will that where I am, Christ says, they also may be. John 17:24. And again of the disinherited, hear Him saying, I pray not for all, but for them that believe in Me through their word. John 17:20.

Chapter 13

The Mystery of the Work of Christ, Part 4

The Descensus *ad* Inferos *and Christ's Prophetic Office*

Descensus ad Inferos

HAVING DISCUSSED THE CONFIRMATION of Christ's testament actualized in his sacrifice on the altar of the cross, it is appropriate that we now begin to discuss the exercise of his prophetic office, particularly in his state of exaltation. As the Formula of Concord teaches, Christ's descent into hell is the first stage of his state of exaltation.[1] This stands in coherence with the fact that Christ's redemptive work is finished and completed on the cross. On the cross, Christ's actualization of his testament is complete and therefore it becomes incumbent that he proclaimed that testament first in the preternatural world (within which sin originated), and then the temporal world (to which Satan spread sin) as both Colossians 2:9–15 and 1 Peter 3:18–22 show.

---

1. Althaus, *Die Christliche Wahrheit*, 479–85; Baier, *Compendium Theologiae Positivae*, 2:90–97; Hoenecke, *Evangelical Lutheran Dogmatics*, 3:123–27; L. Hütter, *Compendium Locorum Theologicorum*, 2:1107; Graebner, *Outline of Doctrinal Theology*, 125–26; Koehler, *Summary of Christian Doctrine*, 100–101; Lindberg, *Christian Dogmatics*, 240–41; Luthardt, *Kompendium der Dogmatik*, 247–48; Martensen, *Christian Dogmatics*, 316–18; J. Mueller, *Christian Dogmatics*, 296–98; von Oettingen, *Lutherische Dogmatik*, 2.2:135–48; F. Pieper, *Christian Dogmatics*, 2:314–22; Schaller, *Biblical Christology*, 102–4; H. Schmid, *Doctrinal Theology*, 395–400.

FC SD 9; *CT* 1049–53. The Confessors write:

> And since even in the ancient Christian teachers of the Church, as well as in some among our teachers, dissimilar explanations of the article concerning the descent of Christ to hell are found, we abide in like manner by the simplicity of our Christian faith [comprised in the Creed], to which Dr. Luther in his sermon, which was delivered in the castle at Torgau in the year 1533, concerning the descent of Christ to hell, has pointed us, where we confess: I believe in the Lord Christ, God's Son, our Lord, dead, buried, and descended into hell. For in this [Confession] the burial and descent of Christ to hell are distinguished as different articles; and we simply believe that the entire person, God and man, after the burial descended into hell, conquered the devil, destroyed the power of hell, and took from the devil all his might. We should not, however, trouble ourselves with high and acute thoughts as to how this occurred; for with our reason and our five senses this article can be comprehended as little as the preceding one, how Christ is placed at the right hand of the almighty power and majesty of God; but we are simply to believe it and adhere to the Word [in such mysteries of faith]. Thus we retain the substance [sound doctrine] and [true] consolation that neither hell nor the devil can take captive or injure us and all who believe in Christ.

1 Peter 3:18–22 historically has been highly important *sedes* for the exposition of this doctrine within Lutheran dogmatics. The Apostle Peter tells us that:

> For *Christ* also suffered once for sins, the righteous for the unrighteous, that he might bring us to God, *being put to death in the flesh but made alive in the spirit,* in which *he went and proclaimed to the spirits in prison,* because they formerly did not obey, when God's patience waited in the days of Noah, while the ark was being prepared, in which a few, that is, eight persons, were brought safely through water. Baptism, which corresponds to this, now saves you, not as a removal of dirt from the body but as an appeal to God for a good conscience, through the *resurrection of Jesus Christ, who has gone into heaven and is at the right hand of God,* with angels, authorities, and powers having been subjected to him. (1 Pet 3:18–22, emphasis added)

In reading this passage, two important points should be observed. First is the sequence of death, revivification ("made alive in the spirit"), descent into hell, resurrection, and finally ascension. In particular, Peter describes Christ "being made alive in the spirit" as a separate event from the resurrection, the latter which he places after the descent into hell. To fill out this account, the New Testament elsewhere testifies that, prior to Christ's revivification, he enjoyed heavenly bliss in accordance with his promise to the thief: "Truly, I say to you, today you will be with me in Paradise" (Luke 23:43).

In interpreting 1 Peter 3:18–22, R. C. H. Lenski argues that "resurrection" is conceptually distinguishable in the New Testament from the notion of "revivification."[2] Whereas resurrection represents both the public announcement of Christ's coming back to life and the event of returning to life,[3] revivification refers more specifically to the reunification of Christ's body with his soul with the accompanying translation of his body into a glorified state.[4] This is exegetically justifiable not only on the grounds of the 1 Peter text above, but also on the basis of the fact that the apostles describe themselves as witnesses to the resurrection without having actually seen Jesus come back to life (see for example, Acts 2:21, etc.). Furthermore, since in the passage above Peter places the descent between revivification and resurrection, Lenski correctly suggests that the descent into hell is properly understood as transcending the normal boundaries of time and space. In some inscrutable manner, the event occurred on Easter Sunday between Jesus's return to life and his leaving the tomb in triumph.[5] Having won his victory over sin, death, the devil, and the law in the total substance of his humanity (body and soul), it was fitting that Christ announce that victory to the demonic forces of the old creation in that full human substance as well. This is a point also strongly emphasized by Luther.[6] The descent of Christ's total humanity into hell is possible because of his ability to be present when and where he chooses due to the full communication of divine glory (*genus majestaticum*).

---

2. H. Schmid, *Doctrinal Theology*, 395–400.

3. Lenski, *St. Peter, St. John, and St. Jude*, 161.

4. Ibid., 159–60.

5. Ibid., 161–62.

6. See Luther, "Martin Luther's Torgau Sermon," 245–55. This is taken originally from *WA* 37:62–67.

Moreover, there is an obvious theo-logic to this sequence. Just as Satan's false word brought about sin and destruction first in the preternatural world (Rev 12:4) and then the temporal (Gen 3), so too the announcement of Christ's victory in the word of his testament had to occur first in the spiritual realm and then the temporal.[7] Indeed, Christ's own movement immediately after his death parallels Satan's fall within the preternatural realm. Immediately after Christ's death occurred, he entered heaven (Luke 23:43), from which Satan fell (10:18). After the revivification he descended to hell into which Satan was caste (Rev 20:1–3). Subsequently, his resurrection victory is announced on earth, into which Satan spread his heavenly revolt.

In discussing the 1 Peter passage above, David Scaer correctly observes that there is also a threefold announcement of Christ's victory after the revivification.[8] Jesus first descended to announce his victory over Satan, was resurrected to announce his victory on earth, and finally ascended to stand before the Father as intercessor and ruler (note the "right hand of God" is a reference to the Melchizedekiah priest-king of Psalm 110). In this, he proclaimed his victory to the whole of creation. In all three locations, he shows his rule as Lord (kingly), and proclaims the power of his sacrifice (priestly, prophetic).

As is evident, the same sequence that Peter speaks of in the aforementioned passage is also reproduced in the Apostles' Creed. Regarding this subject, Scaer convincingly argues that Peter's didactic formula is the basis of the sequence presented in the creed.[9] St. Peter, states Scaer, is very likely drawing on a proto-creedal formula already familiar to his audience. In turn this text and the earlier proto-creedal formula regarding the *descensus* likely forms the basis of the Apostles' Creed.[10] Since both 1 Peter (see 1 Pet 5:13) and the *Romanum* (an early creed from circa AD 150 that probably served as a basis for the Apostles' Creed) originated in the Church of Rome, the connection seems plausible.[11] Although the *Romanum* does not mention the *descensus*, this does not necessarily mean that there is no connection between an earlier creedal formula mentioning it (possibly cited by Peter) and the Apostles' Creed. Either the *Romanum* was understood to be an abbreviated version of earlier creeds (it should be noted that there is no mention of the article of creation either!) or the *descensus* was Peter's later addition to the proto-creedal formula.[12] If this latter possibility is in fact the case, then the original creedal formula would be preserved for us in the *Romanum* and was later expanded (with the apostle's addition to it) in the form of the Apostles' Creed.

The second point to note is that the goal of Christ's descent is to preach to the condemned. As Scaer correctly observes, the description of those who are "in prison" makes it impossible for us to impute a redemptive role to this preaching. In the ancient world, a prison was a place where people were held to await further punishment, in this case, the Last Judgment.[13] Hence the medieval and patristic description of Christ rescuing

---

7. Scaer, "He Did Descend into Hell," 99.

8. Ibid.

9. Ibid., 94–95.

10. Ibid.

11. Ibid., 94.

12. Ibid., 94–95.

13. Ibid., 99.

the holy dead from *limbus patrum* is excluded.[14] In fact, the entire idea that people were unable to enter heaven prior to the crucifixion is contrary to scripture, which teaches that Christ is the "lamb slain from the foundation of the world" (1 Pet 1:18–20, Rev 13:8) and that Abraham was justified by faith before God in the coming of Christ (Gen 15:6, Rom 4).

Similarly, the idea that Christ entered hell to give persons the option of or perhaps a second chance at salvation[15] is excluded not only on the basis of the 1 Peter text, but also by Hebrews 9:27: "it is appointed for man to die once, and after that comes judgment." Some might point to the fact that Peter later tells us "the gospel was preached even to those who are dead" (1 Pet 4:6), but this refers to those who are spiritually dead in the temporal world, not in the preternatural world. In any case, as we have seen, Jesus's testament may function as either law or gospel depending upon the person being addressed. Christ's victory is not actually good news for the damned, since it shows them both their sins and rejection of God's promise of redemption that began with the *protevangelium*. Furthermore, the term "gospel" elsewhere in the New Testament may simply mean a summary of apostolic teaching (Rom 2:16), so in this case it need not exclusively mean a redemptive message. Hence, it must be clearly stated that for the damned and the demonic forces of the old creation, Christ's victory confirms their already actualized defeat and cannot be construed as a message of redemption.

There are other teachings that Lutheran dogmatics must also reject regarding the *descensus*. In light of the exegesis of 1 Peter 3:18–22 and its historical relation to the creed, the *descensus* cannot be construed as referring to the last stage of the state of humiliation as Reformed theologians have taught. The apostle clearly refers to Jesus's visit to a real realm of the damned. Furthermore, as we have seen, this text in all likelihood forms the basis for the creedal statement.[16] Therefore the creed must be interpreted on the basis of it. Nevertheless, according to Reformed teaching, the creed here refers to the psychological suffering of Christ in Gethsemane and on the cross. In light of the fact that the Father utterly abandons Christ to the fate of the damned, this experience of suffering is the *descensus*.[17] Considered on the basis of the creed alone, the teaching makes

14. See summary and description in Pitstick, *Light in the Darkness*, 7–86. This remains the modern Roman Catholic view. See *Catechism of the Catholic Church*, 164. We read:

> Scripture calls the abode of the dead, to which the dead Christ went down, "hell"—Sheol in Hebrew or Hades in Greek—because those who are there are deprived of the vision of God. Such is the case for all the dead, whether evil or righteous, while they await the Redeemer: which does not mean that their lot is identical, as Jesus shows through the parable of the poor man Lazarus who was received into "Abraham's bosom": "It is precisely these holy souls, who awaited their Saviour in Abraham's bosom, whom Christ the Lord delivered when he descended into hell." Jesus did not descend into hell to deliver the damned, nor to destroy the hell of damnation, but to free the just who had gone before him.

15. This has become a popular argument among some modern theologians. See the following: Braaten, "Person of Jesus Christ," 1:549; Burnfeind, "Harrowing of Hell," 5–14; Pannenberg, *Jesus*, 272–73.

16. Scaer, "He Did Descend into Hell," 94–95.

17. See various Reformed treatments in the following: Bavinck, *Reformed Dogmatics*, 2:550, 567–73, 576–79, 587–88; Berkhof, *Reformed Dogmatics*, 340–44; Buswell, *Systematic Theology*, 2:312; Bosma, *Reformed Doctrine*, 165–66; *ICR* 2.16.8–12, in Calvin, *Institutes of the Christian Religion* 1:512–20; van Genderen and Velema, *Concise Reformed Dogmatics*, 394–96; Grudem, *Systematic Theology*, 584–607;

little sense in that the phrase "he descended into hell" comes after the phrase "and he was buried" and not before it, as one would expect if the Reformed interpretation were correct. Neither can it (as many Reformed theologians argue) be viewed as a summary statement of the preceding sentences regarding Christ's passion. In early commentaries on the creed (notably that of Rufinius) there is no indication that anyone in the early Church understood the statement in this fashion.[18] On the other hand, it is not inaccurate to say that Christ was utterly abandoned by the Father and that he experienced damnation on the cross, as Luther himself states.[19] This being said, it is important to affirm that this is not what the creed is referring to and that there was a real descent to the damned after the revivification.

Lastly, we must also exclude the interpretation of the *descensus* by the previously mentioned Roman Catholic theologian Hans Urs von Balthasar. Put succinctly: according to von Balthasar, Christ descended into hell in order to continue to suffer in solidarity with fallen humanity and to thereby sanctify suffering. As a result of his redemptive suffering, he created purgatory, along with the possibilities of salvation in heaven or damnation in hell.[20] In fact despite rather fierce critiques of von Balthasar by persons within his own tradition,[21] the logic of his position nicely parallels the Roman Catholic distinction between temporal and eternal punishment. Roman Catholic teaching on this point implies (though many theologians of that communion would deny) that Christ's cross needs to be supplemented by the temporal punishment of believers through penance in this life and purgatory in the next.[22] In a parallel manner, von Balthasar's position

---

Grudem, "He Did Not Descend into Hell, 103–13; Heppe, *Reformed Dogmatics*, 490–94; Hoeksema, *Reformed Dogmatics*, 214–26; Hodge, *Systematic Theology*, 2:616–25, 407–12; Ursinus, *Commentary of Zacharias Ursinus*, 228–32; Witsius, *Sacred Dissertations*, 2:137–65.

18. Rufinius, *Commentary on the Apostles' Creed*, 28–30; *NPNFb* 3:553–55.

19. Luthardt, *Kompendium der Dogmatik*, 248–49. Also see *AE* 42:105, where Luther describes Christ's death in this way in "Sermon on Preparing to Die" (1519). He writes:

> So then, gaze at the heavenly picture of Christ, who descended into hell for your sake and was forsaken by God as one eternally damned when he spoke the words on the cross, "*Eli, Eli, lama sabachthani!*—My God, my God, why has thou forsaken me?" In that picture your hell is defeated and your uncertain election is made sure.

Also see discussion in Elert, *Structure of Lutheranism*, 249.

20. Von Balthasar, *Mysterium Paschale*, 148–88.

21. Pitstick, *Light in the Darkness*, 87–348; Pitstick, "Development of Doctrine, or Denial?," 129–45. Also see Pitstick and Oakes, "Balthasar, Hell, and Heresy," 25–29; Pitstick and Oakes, "More on Balthasar," 16–18.

22. The Catholic claim is that penance and purgatorial suffering does not so much supplement the work of Christ, but is rather an entry into it. In light of the fact that it is I who do the penance and I who suffer in purgatory, on a practical and existential level, this explanation is extremely unconvincing. See *Catechism of the Catholic Church*, 366–67. In regard to penance we read:

> The satisfaction that we make for our sins, however, is not so much ours as though it were not done through Jesus Christ. We who can do nothing ourselves, as if just by ourselves, can do all things with the cooperation of "him who strengthens" us. Thus man has nothing of which to boast, but all our boasting is in Christ . . . in whom we make satisfaction by bringing forth "fruits that befit repentance." These fruits have their efficacy from him, by him they are offered to the Father, and through him they are accepted by the Father.

Though it is not their intention to teach as such, descriptions like these give the impression that both merit and satisfaction augment the merit and satisfaction of Christ.

suggests that Christ must continue his suffering in a preternatural realm in order to supplement the cross in the temporal realm.

Von Balthasar's position is not unlike that which was held by Johannes Aepinus, an early Lutheran pastor at Hamburg, who also claimed that Christ completed his suffering not on the cross, but in hell.[23] The authors of the Formula of Concord rejected Aepinus's view in accordance with their understanding of the cross and justification. Christ's testament is clearly finished on the cross in that he himself states: "It is finished" (John 19:30). By his death, Christ ended the law "by canceling the record of debt that stood against us with its legal demands. This he set aside, *nailing it to the cross*" (Col 2:14, emphasis added). Therefore his work of redemption does not need to be supplemented by further suffering. In the same manner, the reception of Christ's testament through faith in the promises of Word and sacrament incorporates the believer into the finality of his proleptic eschaton. Believers are thereby freed from any future need to supplement the work of redemption with their own.

Offices of Christ: The Prophetic Office

Finally, we turn to Christ's prophetic office (*munus propheticum*).[24] As we have seen earlier, Adam as the protological minister of the Word, failed to trust in and properly apply the Word of God when faced with the challenge of Satan. By this, sin and death entered into the world (Rom 5:12). Jesus Christ reverses Adam's falsehood and introduction of death because he is "the faithful witness, the firstborn of the dead" (Rev 1:4). The exercise of all Christ's offices is ultimately ordered to his prophetic office. By actualizing a new testament in his blood, he establishes the Word of the gospel that destroys sin, death, the law, and the devil.

Because Jesus is the eternal Word of God and the true prophet, all divine revelation centers on him. According to Deuteronomy 18, truth of prophecy is predicated on whether the prophet speaks in the name of YHWH and whether that prophecy comes true. As the "yes" to all of God's promises (2 Cor 1:19–20) and as the true divine Name, Jesus Christ supremely embodies this criterion. By his incarnation, all of God's promises spoken by him in his preincarnate state through the prophets came true. He is both the source and object of revelation. Similarly, he does not just speak in the divine Name, but is the divine Name in person. Within Jesus's ministry, his own prophecy and that of all those who testify to him was validated by the supreme fulfillment of the resurrection.

---

23. Bente, *Historical Introductions*, 194–95; Hägglund, *History of Theology*, 283; Kolb, "Historical Background," 56–57; Schaff, *Creeds of Christendom*, 1:296–98.

24. Althaus, *Die Christliche Wahrheit*, 102–7, 507; Baier, *Compendium Theologiae Positivae*, 2:103–7; Hoenecke, *Evangelical Lutheran Dogmatics*, 3:169–77; L. Hütter, *Compendium Locorum Theologicorum*, 2:927–28; Gerhard, *On Christ*, 319; Graebner, *Outline of Doctrinal Theology*, 145–48; Koehler, *Summary of Christian Doctrine*, 107–10; Lindberg, *Christian Dogmatics*, 253–55; Luthardt, *Kompendium der Dogmatik*, 223–24; Martensen, *Christian Dogmatics*, 295–301; J. Mueller, *Christian Dogmatics*, 303–4; von Oettingen, *Lutherische Dogmatik*, 2.2:183–303; Philippi, *Kirchliche Glaubenslehre*, 4.2:11–23; F. Pieper, *Christian Dogmatics*, 2:334–41; Schaller, *Biblical Christology*, 123–41; H. Schmid, *Doctrinal Theology*, 340–42.

In his resurrection, Jesus confirmed his testament that he gave to the Church through apostolic word. As we have seen in our discussion of the book of Revelation, the opening of Christ's testament unleashes the power of the new creation that undoes the dominion of the devil. God's war for creation is a war between the word of Christ's testament and Satan's false word (John 8:44). As we saw earlier in texts such as the Genesis commentary[25] and the Smalcald Articles,[26] Luther understood this fact and juxtaposed faithfulness and truth of God's Word with Satan's corruption of the Word. Indeed, as John teaches the ultimate goal of Christ's work is to undo the falsehood of the devil: "The reason the Son of God appeared was to destroy the devil's work" (1 John 3:8).

Therefore Luther describes Christ's war with Satan as ultimately being a conflict between a false and true word. This is in many respects a novel understanding in the history of Christian thought.[27] Although the patristic theologians rightly took the devil very seriously, they did not comprehend the real source of Satan's power as primarily tied up in his corruption of and opposition to the Word of God. Instead, for many of the church fathers, the devil was represented as a malevolent force to be overpowered (Irenaeus, Athanasius) or tricked (Origen, Gregory of Nyssa, etc.) by a still more powerful and crafty supreme deity. Despite the element of biblical truth in their accounts, this often led to their descriptions of the work of Christ as something quasi-mythological.[28] God was pictured as striving with the devil as if he were a higher deity warring with a lesser one. Similarly, many theories of penal satisfaction make the devil the catalyst of the need for satisfaction, but little more. As we saw earlier, this has the tendency (particularly in the case of popular American Evangelicalism) of representing atonement as an abstract repayment of debt in a heavenly bank. Atonement with this scheme is almost completely severed from the concrete experience of slavery to demonic forces and the need for the living Word of God to break through that bondage. Lastly, theories of moral influence move even farther away from the biblical concept of Satan. For this group of thinkers, bondage to the devil eliminates the possibility of moral influence, because an enslaved person cannot be influenced to change their behavior. As a result, the concept of Satan becomes either superfluous or detrimental to human moral agency.

In contrast to all this, Luther properly defines the nature of the devil and his false mediation. For the Reformer, God not only opposes the devil, but the devil also functions as a mask of God's own wrath. This is the case because the "the whole creation is

---

25. *AE* 1:47–60.

26. SA 3:8; *CT* 495–96.

27. Beyond the Genesis commentary, see the following descriptions of the devil in Luther's writings: AE 12:374, 13:97, 27:146, 33:52, 175–76, 227, 37:18, 47:113–14. For sources regarding Luther's view of the devil see the following: Althaus, *Theology of Martin Luther*, 161–68; Bayer, *Martin Luther's Theology*, 194–95; Hinlicky, *Luther and the Beloved Community*, 379–85; Janz, *Westminster Handbook to Martin Luther*, 37–40; Kolb, *Martin Luther*, 121–23, 163–71; Kolb and Arand, *Genius of Luther's Theology*, 99, 119, 139; Lohse, *Martin Luther's Theology*, 66–67, 158–59, 251–56, 332–35.

28. Anselm correctly saw this. See Anselm, *Cur Deus Homo?*, 1.6, in *Scholastic Miscellany*, 107. He writes:

As for saying that he [Jesus] came to conquer the Devil for you, in what sense do you dare assert that? Does not the omnipotence of God reign everywhere? How then did God need to come down from heaven to defeat the Devil?

a face or mask of God," which includes the devil.[29] Thus Luther states: "Thus God wears the mask of the devil, and the devil wears the mask of God; God wants to be recognized under the mask of the devil, and He wants the devil to be condemned under the mask of God."[30] Satan distorts the Word of God (thereby taking the place of God)[31] and holds humans in his bondage.[32] Human belief in Satan's false word incurs God's wrath, while bondage to Satan is also a manifestation of this very same wrath. There is a great deal of biblical support for the vision of Satan's power. He is often pictured as an accuser of sinful humanity in the heavenly court (Job 1:6–8, 2:1–7; Zech 3:1–10; Rev. 12:10). In fact, the word "Satan" can mean "adversary" or even "accuser" in the original Hebrew.[33] All this suggests the devil functions as a channel for the condemnation of sinful humanity in their violation of the law. At the same time, God opposes the devil throughout scripture culminating in Jesus's defeat of him. In effect, the Bible pictures Satan as God's enemy who nonetheless maintains his power because he is a mask of God's wrath against sin.

Although God is just and faithful, unbelief in his graciousness leads humans to only perceive his law, hiddenness, and wrath (Rom 1:18–32). As a result of this ignorance of God's true heart, humans come to stand in self-justifying opposition to God's Word (6:7–25). Because of this, sinners only become more and more ensnared in the power of Satan's false word because they perceive God hidden in his wrath as untrustworthy. Therefore, God's war against the devil is both waged against his own activity of wrath, as well as against human unbelief. Fulfilling the law, Christ's testament of the gospel undoes God's wrath and thereby also his *opus alienum* that allows the devil to function as the "god of this world" (2 Cor 4:4).[34] This is why Jesus's healing miracles and exorcisms (i.e., acts of opposition to the manifestations of the reign of Satan) are always preceded by the forgiveness of sins. Through the forgiveness of sins, God both defeats the power of Satan and overcomes human unbelief. God does not wish to have a wrathful relationship with

29. *AE* 26:95.

30. *AE* 27:43.

31. *AE* 1:147. Luther writes:

> Satan imitates God. Just as God had preached to Adam, so he himself also preaches to Eve . . . Therefore just as from the true Word of God salvation results, so also from the corrupt Word of God damnation results.

One interesting discovery of recent research is that Luther's use of scatological language is connected to his understanding of the devil. The devil's feces (*teufelsdreck*) is his rhetoric of lying for Luther. This way of speaking about Satan stands in continuity with the medieval tradition and is not the result of a disturbed or psychologically abnormal mind. See Oberman, "Teufelsdreck," 51–68.

32. *AE* 33:115. Luther himself put it well in *Bondage of the Will*. The will is not a neutral thing but is determined by its relatedness to God:

> If God is within us and Satan absent, then on the one hand nothing but a good will is present; if God is absent and Satan present, on the other hand nothing but a bad will is within us. Neither God nor Satan allow a mere and pure will to exist in us.

33. J. Russell, *Devil*, 189.

34. This does not mean of course that God somehow prompts the devil to work destruction and evil. God is not the author of evil. CA 19; CT 53. We read:

> Of the Cause of Sin they teach that, although God does create and preserve nature, yet the cause of sin is the will of the wicked, that is, of the devil and ungodly men; which will, unaided of God, turns itself from God, as Christ says John 8:44: When he speaketh a lie, he speaketh of his own.

Rather his *opus alienum* uses the work of the devil to punish sin.

humanity, but rather one of grace and self-donation, wherein humans assume the role of passive receivers of his goodness. By defeating the devil, God in Christ reestablishes himself as a gracious giver and humans as grateful receivers.

This view of the history of salvation as a *duellum mirabile* between the word of Christ's grace and the power of Satan is dramatized well in Luther's most famous hymn *A Mighty Fortress is Our God* (1527–1528?). The hymn pictures the devil overpowering God's creation: "The old knavish foe/He means earnest now/ Force and cunning slay His horrid policy/ On earth there's nothing like him."[35] In order to prevail, Christ must utterly donate himself to human beings by entering into the battlefield of creation: "Ask'st though who is this?/ Jesus Christ it is/Lord of Host alone,/ *And God but him is none*/ So he must win the battle."[36] How does Luther describe Satan's defeat? Here he does not describe the crucifixion and resurrection, as he does in other hymns such as *Dear Christians One and All Rejoice*[37] and *Christ Jesus Lay in Death's Strong Bands*.[38] Rather, without excluding the work of sacrificial atonement as a necessary basis, he emphasizes in this hymn Christ's prophetic Word of grace as that which ultimately undoes Satan: "Let him [Satan] rage his worst/ No hurt brings about/ His doom it is gone out/ *One word can overturn him*.[39] / *The word they shall allow to stand*."[40] God's omnipotent Word of grace cannot be overturned. Indeed, even if "the world with devils swarm" and take "life/ Wealth, name, child and wife" the divine promise of grace cannot be abrogated.[41] God by his omnipotent Word has promised believers the kingdom of his glory: "Let everything go/ They have no profit so/ The kingdom ours remaineth."[42] In the end, all Christians are heirs of the kingdom and become "lords of all." They are thereby reestablished in their proper role as receivers of divine grace. In the same manner, God, by entering into the field of battle with Satan, reestablishes his relationship with humans as one of self-donation.

From all this it may be ascertained that the prophetic office of Christ is concerned with the defeat of the devil and the wrath of God by the word of the testament. This has two parts: the actualization (i.e., the work of substitutionary sacrifice) and the giving of the testament. The testament is received by faith brought about by Christ's prophetic Word active both in his own ministry and that of the prophets and apostles: "The one who hears you hears me" (Luke 10:16). The faith that receives this testament is a "conviction of things not seen" (Heb 11:1) and therefore Luther states in the Galatians commentary: "Thus faith is a sort of knowledge or *darkness that nothing can see*. Yet the Christ

35. *AE* 53:284.

36. *AE* 53:285 (emphasis added).

37. *AE* 53:217–20.

38. *AE* 53:249–51.

39. It is frequently reported in popular literature on this hymn that this little "word" is "liar." In a search of Luther's writings, I have been unable to confirm this. Even if one cannot directly confirm this, it works well with my point, namely, that the devil is a liar because he rejects the gospel. The gospel by being true makes Satan a liar. Furthermore, the truth is a person (Jesus!) and not a "something." Christ is the gospel and the gospel is Christ.

40. *AE* 53:285 (emphasis added).

41. *AE* 53:285.

42. Ibid.

of whom faith takes hold is sitting in this darkness as God sat in the midst of darkness on Sinai and in the temple."[43] For this reason, Christ's testament must be given in a concealed form in order to make room for faith.

This returns us to the contrast between the "theology of the cross" and the "theology of glory" spoken of in an earlier chapter.[44] As we previously observed, the theologian of glory believes that they may ascend to God in his majesty on the wings of their own self-created (*autopoesis*) similarity to him. The theologian of the cross is by contrast passive and trusts in God's promises over and against contrary vision (*sub contrario*). The theologian of the cross is therefore receptive rather than active in their relationship to God. Instead of relying on the vision of God in the glory of his works (Rom 1:18–20), he or she receptively hears God's Word. Abraham became receptive to the word of promise because he was put into a "deep sleep" and "great darkness fell upon him" (Gen 15:12). Only then did God appear and speak his promises of blessing to him.

The grace promised by the "word of the cross" (1 Cor 1:18) is contrary to vision because the cross is not only the culmination of divine grace, but also of divine judgment. For this reason the word of the cross functions at the same time as law and gospel. It gives the gift of the testament, as well as destroys any noetic or moral pretensions of the active creature: "I will destroy the wisdom of the wise; the intelligence of the intelligent I will frustrate" (1 Cor 1:19, Isa 29:14). The darkness of judgment wrought in the cross, and corresponding lack of vision, empties out all human pretensions. By "suffering God" (Bayer) in the word of the cross, we are made receptive to its offer of divine grace *extra nos*. Lacking any basis for self-justification, we finally justify God by believing his Word is true. By this address and the faith that it works, we are determined as *simul iustus et peccator*. By ceasing to justify ourselves and by justifying God in his Word, we become receptive to God's goodness and are restored to our proper role as creatures.

Christ's prophetic activity *sub contrario* did not begin with the incarnation and the cross, but was present in the history of salvation from the speaking forth of the *proevanglium* in the garden. As God's eternal Word, Christ was present and active in the garden of Eden in the condemnation of Adam and Eve, as well as in the giving of the promise of the savior. Every promise of God to humans after the Fall assumes their condemnation and fallenness. Consequently, every act of grace and self-donation is necessarily concealed under a corresponding act of judgment. To Adam and Eve, the audible promise of the savior conflicted with their visible situation of exile and condemnation under the law.

This dissonance between sight and hearing continued and deepened in the subsequent history of salvation. As Paul observed regarding Abraham: "He did not weaken in faith when he considered his own body, which was as good as dead (since he was about

---

43. *AE* 26:129–30 (emphasis added).

44. See the follow section in the *Heidelberg Disputation* in *AE* 31:52–58. See the following sources on the subject in Luther's writings: Althaus, *Die Christliche Wahrheit*, 126, 129–30; Althaus, *Theology of Martin Luther*, 25–35; Anthony, *Cross Narratives*, 1–105; Deutschlander, *Theology of the Cross*; Eckermann, "Luthers Kreuzestheologie," 306–17; Forde, *On Being a Theologian*; Koppperi, "Theology of the Cross," 155–72; Köstlin, *Theology of Luther*, 1:284–86; von Loewenich, *Luthers Theologia Crucis*; McGrath, *Luther's Theology of the Cross*; Modalsli, "Heidelberger Disputation," 33–39; Nestingen, "Luther's Heidelberg Disputation," 147–54; Ngien, *Suffering of God*; Prenter, *Luther's Theology of the Cross*; Sasse, "Theology of the Cross," 35–45; Vercruysse, "Luther's Theology of the Cross," 523–48.

a hundred years old), or when he considered the barrenness of Sarah's womb" (Rom 4:19). In the later history of Israel itself, this dissonance manifested primarily in the conflict between visible judgment of exile, based on the Sinaitic covenant, and the corresponding, continued, and audibly accessible assertion of the promise of the Abrahamic and Davidic testaments given by the prophets. This tension was simply a continuation and deepening of the original tension between the law and the gospel proclaimed to Adam and Eve.

With each manifestation of divine judgment, Israel entered deeper and deeper into the judgment of the exile. In each temporal judgment, God manifests in greater and greater degrees his fidelity to his word of law against the ever increasing manifestation of human sin. With this increasing manifestation of judgment, Israel simultaneously received from the prophets greater and greater promises of restoration. This is not to say that Isaiah (for example) prophesied anything that was not already implicitly present in the promises given to Adam and Eve, and the patriarchs. Rather, the same promises of redemption became more and more definite and concrete. For example, "with his stripes we are healed" and "his soul was made an offering for sin" (Isa 53) is far more exact regarding the form of redemption than is "you shall bruise his heel" (Gen 3:15). Nevertheless, both reflect the same reality of redemption through Christ.

Finally, the promise of the prophetic works of the exile (Ezekiel and Daniel) was that the end to cosmic exile was dawning and God's kingdom would finally be established (Ezek 37–48; Dan 2, 7, 12). As we have already noted, this took the form of ultimate eschatological manifestation of law and gospel: eternal exile (in hell) and the promise of eternal restoration (in the kingdom of God). All the promises of *protevanglium* would come true: sin would be judged, the dead would be restored to life, and YHWH would return in person. In this final climax of history, God's faithfulness to his Word as law and gospel would find its final fulfillment.

Jesus entered into the midst of Judaism's apocalyptic anticipation of this final eschatological fulfillment.[45] He brought to completion the Old Testament's prophecies of the ultimate fulfillment of both the law and the gospel. He united in himself both the maximal self-donation of God as an embodied promise (*genus majestaticum*) and divine hiddenness under sin, death, and retribution. This is because the total self-donation of God (gospel) presupposes the total divine eschatological judgment of sin (law). Forgiveness is meaningless if it does not stand juxtaposed to divine wrath and judgment. If there were no wrath and no sin was imputed, then there would be nothing to be forgiven. In this regard, Jesus claimed within his ministry that he had come to announce and bring about the kingdom of God, through a totalizing judgment and salvation (Isa 61).

Having entered into total solidarity with the sufferings of Israel and humanity under the law, Christ represents the ultimate dissonance between hearing and vision. Only in this manner could he end all the pretensions of sinful humanity, thereby establishing them in true receptivity to the Word of God. It is for this reason that he elects the poor and the morally degenerate. He is the mighty and righteous one hidden in the midst of sin and weakness.

---

45. See the following sources on the subject: Cohn, *Cosmos, Chaos*, 163–93; Collins, *Apocalyptic Imagination*; P. Hanson, *Dawn of Apocalyptic*; D. Russell, *Message and Method*; Sacchi, *Jewish Apocalyptic*; N. T. Wright, *Christian Origins*, 1:280–337.

The dissonance between visible manifestation and audible promise does not merely characterize Jesus's ministry among the outcasts, but is present at every stage of Jesus's life, death, and resurrection. Beginning with his birth to the Virgin Mary, Jesus gives the appearance of being conceived in a morally impure manner, even to his earthly father (Matt 1:19). Nevertheless, Joseph in his dream is given a promise of Mary's purity and Jesus's messianic identity through the word and promise of an angel. At his birth itself, though the shepherds see a glimpse of heavenly glory (Luke 2:8–14), they must nevertheless believe in the word of the angels in that the child in the poverty of a manager is the true king.

In being baptized in the Jordan with those confessing their sins, Jesus is attested by his Father's voice from heaven that he is not a sinner (contrary to appearance), but a "beloved Son" and is given the Holy Spirit hidden in the form of a dove. In the Transfiguration, Christ's true identity is revealed and attested by the law and prophets (represented by Moses and Elijah), but he immediately warns his inner circle to "tell no one what they had seen, until the Son of Man had risen from the dead" (Mark 9:9). Even faced with the direct revelation of his glory, the apostolic witness must remain veiled. When the event of the Transfiguration is revealed (after the resurrection), it is made manifest like the earlier revelations, with a word and witness, and with no immediate vision of glory.

Before the Sanhedrin, Jesus finally confesses his divinity directly to the high priest. He does this by claiming not only that he will be vindicated, but that he will ultimately share in YHWH's glory cloud and throne (Mark 14:62).[46] In both the Synoptic (Matt 26:65, Mark 16:64), and the Johannine (John 10:33, 19:7) witnesses he is charged with blasphemy because of his claims regarding his own divinity. To human vision, he is the greatest sinner. Whereas Adam merely wished to be God and grasped at divinity, Jesus directly claims to be God. Nevertheless, Jesus's appearance as a blasphemer stands in contradiction to the reality revealed audibly by the Father, his own self-testimony, and that of the prophets. Rather than being a human being who is exalting himself, he is God lowering himself in a kenotic act of self-donation and obedience to the Father's will (John 5:20). Rather than being one who grasps at divinity (Phil 2:6), he is in the midst his disciples as "one who serves" (Luke 22:26).

Hidden under the form of weakness, sin, and condemnation for the originating human sin, Jesus is witnessed to by the word of the Centurion: "Truly this man was the Son of God!" (Mark 15:39) and "Certainly this man was innocent!" (Luke 23:47). Christ is also witnessed to by the writing above the cross: "Jesus of Nazareth, The King of the Jews" (John 19:19). These words indicate that the Davidic testament is fulfilled in the cross by God's triumph over his enemies, even if such fulfillment is hidden. Indeed, in the cross Christ is "glorified," (12:23), even when it appears that he is being shamed.

Finally, even in the glory of his resurrection Christ again remains hidden. When both the women and the apostles reach the tomb, it is empty and the vision of the resurrection event itself is denied to them.[47] There is nonetheless an angelic word of prom-

---

46. See Gathercole, *Pre-Existent Son*, 60–61; N. T. Wright, *Christian Origins*, 2:551. Both assert that Jesus's claim to share the divine throne and glory cloud would have been viewed as a claim of divinity within the context of Second Temple Judaism.

47. Later apocryphal Gospels were not so restrained. See the "Gospel of Peter 9:1–4" in R. Miller,

ise: "He is not here, but has risen" (Luke 24:6). In his resurrection appearances, he is only perceived as the gardener until he addresses Mary Magdalene with his word (John 20:16). Though Thomas perceives his reality and confesses "my Lord and my God" upon seeing him, it is only because Jesus has enabled him to have this spiritual vision by first addressing him (20:27–29). On the road to Emmaus, he becomes visible to the travelers only when he "took bread" (Luke 24:30), a theological echo of the visible word of the sacrament of the altar.[48] The visionaries of the apostolic generation are not granted more. Although Paul was taken into the third heaven, he did not see but only "*heard things that cannot be told*, which man may not utter" (2 Cor 12:4, emphasis added). In order that he would remain receptive to grace, he was given a thorn in the flesh, for "My grace is sufficient for you, for my power is made perfect in weakness" (12:9). When John entered heaven he only saw the form of weakness in a "Lamb standing, as though it had been slain" (Rev 5:6) but contrary to vision heard "behold, the Lion of the tribe of Judah, the Root of David, has conquered" (5:5).

This condescending and concealing movement of the Son actualized in the narrative of Christ's life, death, and resurrection also unfolds the word of the testament as a specifically Trinitarian act of mutual concealment and revelation.[49] The dialectic of the hidden and revealed God is not properly understood as the unfolding of an essentially unitarian account of the deity (even though certain Lutheran theologians have given that impression![50]), but is rather shaped by the Trinitarian structure of the divine life and the taxis of its temporal manifestation.

At Christ's baptism, the Father testifies that he is his Son. As we noted above, Jesus does not appear to be God's Son in that he stands in solidarity of with sinners. Throughout his ministry, Christ testifies of the Father against the experience of condemnation suffered by Israel. The Father hides as *Deus absconditus* under wrath and law. He does so through the mask (*larva Dei*) of continuing exile and a decaying creation (Rom 8:22). In contradistinction to this mask, Jesus testifies that the Father is the gracious giver of

---

Complete Gospels, 405. This adds plausibility to the Gospel reports of the resurrection. If the canonical Gospel narrative of the resurrection were merely inventions they would likely have given more detail and possibly created a vision of the resurrection event itself.

48. See argument in Just, *Luke*, 2:972–1020; Just, *Ongoing Feast*.

49. See Gerrish, "Unknown God," 263–93. Gerrish helpfully distinguishes in Luther's thought between what he calls "Hiddenness 1" and "Hiddenness 2." Hiddenness 1 is God's hiddenness in revelation, wherein he conceals himself and makes himself known only by his Word. Hiddenness 2 is God's hiddenness in his majesty, relentlessly working all-in-all. Following Luther in this section, we describe the Father's hiddenness as primarily (though not exclusively) one of Hiddenness 2, and the Son's hiddenness as primarily (though not exclusively) one of Hiddenness 1.

50. See Helmer, *Trinity and Martin Luther*. Helmer is correct that previous Luther scholars (she notes Holl and Elert, among others) have downplayed the Trinitarian structure of divine agency and revelation in Luther's thought in favor of the dialectic of hidden-revealed. Though she is correct to highlight the necessity of understanding Luther in Trinitarian terms, she also does so at times at the expense of the hidden-revealed dialectic. In developing our own position in the tradition of Luther, we will conceive both models of divine agency through one another. Although we do not have time to argue Luther's perspective on this issue, the citations at the end of this section from the Large Catechism seem to suggest that this might also be a helpful way of reading Luther as well. Instead of reading the Catechisms and *Bondage of the Will* insolation (as often has been done), perhaps one should read them in light of one another!

every good. Jesus, as the true Son of the Father, is his very image (Col 1:15, Heb 1:3) in his ministry of compassion and forgiveness. He sees what the Father does and does it himself (John 5:20). Those who have seen him have seen the Father (14:9). Although the Father is hidden and no one has ever seen him (1:18), he reveals his grace by making the rain fall on the just and unjust (Matt 5:45) and loves those who abuse his grace (5:43–48). Indeed, only the Son knows the Father, just as the Father alone knows the Son (Matt 11:27, John 10:15). This is because Jesus and the Father are one (John 10:30), and Jesus is in Father and the Father is in Jesus (14:11). Nevertheless, this unity of the Father and the Son is hidden and only revealed by the power of the Spirit. This unity is both revealed and concealed at Jesus's baptism through Jesus's reception of the Spirit under the concealing form of a dove. In Jesus's ministry, the Spirit reveals the unity of the Father and the Son through the word that Jesus gives (Matt 11:27).

As Jesus's ministry persists, the *aporia* between his testimony regarding his unity with Father and the actual circumstances of his existence grows ever deeper. Jesus forgives sinners who are condemned by the Father's law by means other than those set down by the Pentateuch (i.e., temple and cultic sacrifice). Jesus is not opposed to the law (Matt 5:17), but rather claims that the law is ordered to the gospel (John 3:17). Jesus's identification with sinners and his eventual death along with them will therefore be an act of divine redemption, not a final condemnation of him as a mere messianic pretender. In fact, the Father's love for the Son lies in the fact that he bears this judgment (10:15). This judgment will not be an end in itself, but rather will serve the purpose of the Father's loving plan to redeem the whole world (3:16). His *opus alienum* is therefore ordered to his *opus proprium*. This truth is nevertheless not really accessible to vision. The Father, whom Jesus prays to and testifies of, finally reacts in silence to Jesus's cry of desperation in Gethsemane. The Father remains loving even though his benevolence is hidden when he actively abandons the Son and condemns him. In the same way, Jesus remains divine and righteous, though he dies under the veil of sin and weakness. On the cross, the visible rupture between the Father and the Son (as well as between vision and hearing!) is completed when we hear both: "My God, my God, why have you forsaken me?" (Matt 27:45–46) and "Truly this was the Son of God!" (Matt 27:54).

In the resurrection, the Spirit who raises Christ (Rom 8:11) resolves the *aporia* between the Son's testimony and the Father's action. Jesus's claim that the Father's wrath is ordered to his love is validated once and for all. Similarly, his claim of unity with the Father is reaffirmed in the unity of the Spirit, for: "In that day [that is, at the time of the receiving the Spirit after the resurrection] you will know that I am in my Father" (John 14:20).[51] This revelation is nevertheless hidden in that no one directly observes the event of resurrection. Jesus himself testifies to the disciples that he has been raised and gives them the Spirit (20:19). By receiving the Spirit, they will preserve and propagate Jesus's infallible testimony regarding the Father (14:16–26). The Spirit's activity is also hidden for believers in Word and sacrament. The audible word given by Jesus in his promises concerning the word of

---

51. See Jüngel, *God as the Mystery of the World*, 363–78. Jüngel rightly observes that the contours of God's Trinitarian life are manifested in the life of Jesus. The Son's obedience to the Father and his abandonment by him reveal the distinction of the Father and the Son. The resurrection by the Spirit reveals their unity.

the apostles and sacraments testifies to the Spirit's hidden work. In establishing the means of grace, Jesus testifies to the work of the Spirit against vision, in the same manner that the Father testified of him and he testified of the Father *sub contrario*.[52]

Faith holds to Jesus as the true revealed God over-against sinful human perceptions of the Father hidden in majesty. Faith also trusts in the Spirit and the Father's word of testimony regarding Jesus in opposition to his manifest form of weakness and condemnation. Through this testimony, faith recognizes that Jesus is a mirror of the Father's heart. Luther writes in the Large Catechism: "For (as explained above) we could never attain to the knowledge of the grace and favor of the Father except through the Lord Christ, *who is a mirror of the paternal heart*, outside of whom we see nothing but an angry and terrible Judge." Faith gains this knowledge through trust in the hidden work of the Spirit in Word and sacrament: "But of Christ we *could know nothing either*, unless it had been revealed by the Holy Ghost."[53] Therefore for Luther, the whole dialectic of the hidden and revealed God resolves itself for faith in the Trinitarian advent of Christ's life made accessible in Word and sacrament.[54] The mutual concealment and revelation of the divine being will only pass away at the eschaton when the hearing of faith gives way to the knowledge of vision (Matt 5:8; 1 Cor 13:12).

Conclusion: The Testament in the Proclamation of the Church

Christ's prophetic office finds fulfillment in his activity through the Church. As the omnipresent Lord of all, Jesus is present and active in the Word of God proclaimed wherever the true Church is gathered (Matt 18:20, 28:20). This redeeming presence is not only hidden in the proclamation of the Word, but also in the sacraments. Hidden in the waters of baptism, the promise of incorporation into Christ's death and resurrection is made manifest audibly. In the same manner, believers are sustained by the promise of the testament of Christ's body and blood. Being stripped of all he has to the point of even having his garment gambled away by the Roman soldiers (Ps 22:18, Matt 27:35), Jesus is left with nothing to will to humanity but his sacrificed body and blood.[55] Under the vision of bread we are given the audible promise "This is My Body . . . this is My Blood" (Matt 26:27–28). Just as Satan once brought about sin at the tree of the knowledge of good and evil through eating, so now Christ reestablishes humanity in relationship with God through eating. By his presence in the proclamation of the Church, God establishes his Word triumphantly in us against all false mediation and self-justification. The Word of promise is victorious and established forever. *Verbum Domini Manet in Aeternum!*

---

52. See Pannenberg, *Systematic Theology*, 1:339–41. Pannenberg correctly observes that for Luther the hidden-revealed dialectic cannot be uniformly applied to the Father and the Son. Rather, he characterizes Luther's understanding as suggesting that the unity of the persons of the Trinity will be only fully manifested eschatologically, something he finds somewhat problematic.

53. LC 2.3; *CT* 695.

54. See discussion in Arand, "Confessing the Trinitarian Gospel," 203–14; Arand, "Luther on the Creeds," 147–70.

55. I owe this observation to Rev. David Fleming.

Bibliography

Abelard, Peter. "Exposition of the Epistle to the Romans." In *A Scholastic Miscellany: Anselm to Ockham*, translated and edited by Eugene Fairweather, 276–87. Philadelphia: Westminster, 1966.

Achtemeier, Paul. *1 Peter: A Commentary on First Peter*. Minneapolis: Fortress, 1996.

Adams, David L. "The Present God: A Framework for Biblical Theology." *Concordia Journal* 22 (1996) 279–94.

Alexander, Joseph. *Commentary on Isaiah*. 2 vols. New York: Scribner, 1867.

———. *Commentary on the Gospel of Mark*. Grand Rapids: Zondervan, 1900.

Alexandria, Cyril of. *Commentary on the Gospel of Saint Luke*. Translated by R. Payne Smith. New York: Studion, 1983.

———. *On the Unity of Christ*. Translated by John McGuckin. Crestwood, NY: St. Vladimir's Seminary, 2000.

Alison, James. *Raising Abel: The Recovery of Eschatological Imagination*. New York: Crossroad, 1996.

Allen, Willoughby. *A Critical and Exegetical Commentary on the Gospel According to St. Matthew*. New York: Scribner's Sons, 1907.

Allbeck, Willard. *Studies in the Lutheran Confessions*. Philadelphia: Muhlenberg, 1952.

Allison, Dale. *The New Moses: A Matthew Typology*. Minneapolis: Fortress, 1994.

Allison, Dale, and W. D. Davies. *A Critical and Exegetical Commentary on the Gospel according to Saint Matthew*. 3 vols. Edinburgh: T. & T. Clark, 1988–1997.

Althaus, Paul. *Die Christliche Wahrheit: Lehrbuch der Dogmatik*. Gütersloh: C. Bertelsmann, 1952.

———. *Das Sogenannte Kerygma und der Historie Jesus: Zur Kritik der Heutigen Kerygma-Theologie*. Gütersloh: C. Bertelsmann, 1958.

———. *The Theology of Martin Luther*. Translated by Robert Schultz. Minneapolis: Augsburg, 1966.

Anderson, Bernhard. *Contours of Old Testament Theology*. Minneapolis: Fortress, 1999.

Anselm. *Cur Deus Homo?* In *A Scholastic Miscellany: Anselm to Ockham*, translated and edited by Eugene Fairweather, 100–183. Philadelphia: Westminster, 1966.

———. "The Virgin Conception and Original Sin." In *Why God Became Man and the Virgin Conception and Original Sin*, translated by Joseph Colleran, 165–211. Albany, NY: Magi, 1946.

Anthony, Neal. *Cross Narratives: Martin Luther's Christology and the Location of Redemption*. Eugene, OR: Wipf and Stock, 2010.

Aquinas, Thomas. *Commentary on the Epistle to the Hebrews*. South Bend, IN: St. Augustine's, 2006.

———. *Commentary on the Gospel of St. John*. Translated by James A. Weisheipl and Fabian R. Larcher. Albany, NY: Magi, 1980.

———. *Summa Theologiae*. 60 vols. Blackfriars ed. Cambridge: Blackfriars/New York: McGraw-Hill, 1964–1973.

Arand, Charles. "Confessing the Trinitarian Gospel." *Concordia Theological Quarterly* 67 (2003) 203–14.

———. "Luther on the Creeds." In *The Pastoral Luther: Essays in Luther's Practical Theology*, edited by Timothy Wengert, 147–70. Grand Rapids: Eerdmans, 2009.

———. "Two Kinds of Righteousness as a Framework for Law and Gospel in the Apology." *Lutheran Quarterly* 15, no. 4 (2001) 417–39.

Arand, Charles, Robert Kolb, and James Nestingen. *The Lutheran Confessions: History and Theology of the Book of Concord*. Minneapolis: Fortress, 2012.

Archer, Gleason. *A Survey of Old Testament Introduction*. Chicago: Moody, 1964.

Aristotle. *De Anima*. Translated by Hugh Lawson-Tancred. New York: Penguin, 1986.

———. *The Metaphysics*. Translated by David Bostock. New York: Oxford University Press, 1994.

———. *Nicomachean Ethics.* Translated by Terence Irwin. Indianapolis: Hackett, 1999.

Athanasius. *De Incarnatione Verbi Dei.* In *The Christology of the Later Fathers,* translated and edited by Archibald Robertson, 55–110. Philadelphia: Westminster, 1954.

Attridge, Harold. *The Epistle to the Hebrews.* Philadelphia: Fortress, 1989.

———. "Let Us Strive to Enter That Rest: The Logic of Hebrews 4:1–11." *Harvard Theological Review* 73, nos. 1–2 (1980) 279–88.

Aulén, Gustaf. *Christus Victor: An Historical Study of the Three Main Types of the Idea of Atonement.* Translated by A. G. Hebert. New York: Macmillan, 1969.

———. *The Faith of the Christian Church.* Translated by Eric Wahlstrom and G. Everett Arden. Philadelphia: Muhlenberg, 1948.

Ayres, Lewis. *Nicaea and Its Legacy: An Approach to Fourth-Century Trinitarian Theology.* Oxford: Oxford University Press, 2006.

Baier, Johann. *Compendium Theologiae Positivae.* Edited by C. F. W. Walther. 2 vols. Grand Rapids: Emmanuel, 2005–2006.

Baird, William. *Paul's Message and Mission.* New York: Abingdon, 1960.

Baker, Albert. *Saint Paul and his Gospel.* London: Eyre and Spottiswoode, 1940.

Balentine, Samuel. *Leviticus.* Louisville, KY: John Knox, 2002.

Balthasar, Hans Urs von. *Mysterium Paschale: The Mystery of Easter.* Translated by Aidan Nichols. Edinburgh: T. & T. Clark, 1990.

———. *Theo-Drama.* Translated by Graham Harrison. 5 vols. San Francisco: Ignatius, 1983–1998.

———. *A Theology of History.* San Francisco: Ignatius, 1994.

Baltzer, Karl. *The Covenant Formulary in Old Testament, Jewish, and Early Christian Writings.* Translated by D. E. Green. Philadelphia: Fortress, 1971.

Barclay, William. *Epistle to the Hebrews.* London: Lutterworth, 1965.

———. *The Letters of John and Jude.* Louisville, KY: Westminster John Knox, 2002.

Barnes, Michel Rene. "Veni Creator Spiritus." Online: http://www.marquette.edu/maqom/spiritus.pdf

Barrett, C. K. *A Commentary on the First Epistle to the Corinthians.* New York: Harper & Row, 1968.

Barth, Gerhard. "Matthew's Understanding of the Law." In Günther Bornkamm, Gerhard Barth, and Heinz Joachim Held, *Tradition and Interpretation in Matthew,* 58–164. Translated by Percy Scott. Philadelphia: Westminster, 1963.

Barth, Karl. *Church Dogmatics.* Translated by G. T. Thomason et al. 4 vols. Edinburgh: T. & T. Clark, 1936–77.

———. "Gospel and Law." In *Community, State and Church: Three Essays,* translated and edited by Will Herberg, 71–100. New York: Doubleday, 1960.

———. *The Theology of John Calvin.* Translated by Geoffrey Bromiley. Grand Rapids: Eerdmans, 1995.

Bateman, Herbert, IV. "Psalm 110:1 and the New Testament." *Bibliotheca Sacra* 149 (1992) 438–53.

Bauckham, Richard. *The Climax of Prophecy: Studies in the Book of Revelation.* Edinburgh: T. & T. Clark, 1993.

———. "For Whom Were the Gospels Written?" In *The Gospels for All Christians: Rethinking the Gospel Audiences,* edited by Richard Bauckham, 9–48. Grand Rapids: Eerdmans, 1998.

———. *God Crucified: Monotheism and Christology in the New Testament.* Grand Rapids: Eerdmans, 1998.

———. *Jesus and the Eyewitnesses: The Gospels as Eyewitness Testimony.* Grand Rapids: Eerdmans, 2007.

———. *Jude, 2 Peter.* Waco, TX: Word, 1983.

———. *The Theology of the Book of Revelation.* Cambridge, UK: Cambridge University Press, 1993.

Baur, August. *Zwinglis Theologie: Ihr Werden und Ihr System.* 2 vols. Zürich: Georg Olms Verlag, 1983–1984.

Bavinck, Herman. *Reformed Dogmatics.* 4 vols. Grand Rapids: Baker, 2003–2008.

Bayer, Oswald. "Creation as History." In *The Gift of Grace: The Future of Lutheran Theology,* edited by Niels Hendrik Gregersen, Bo Holm, Ted Peters, and Peter Widmann, 253–63. Minneapolis: Augsburg, 2005.

———. "God as Author of My Life History." *Lutheran Quarterly* 2 (1988) 437–56.

———. *Living By Faith: Justification and Sanctification.* Translated by Geoffrey Bromiley. Grand Rapids: Eerdmans, 2003.

———. *Martin Luther's Theology: A Contemporary Interpretation.* Translated by Thomas Trapp. Grand Rapids: Eerdmans, 2008.

———. "Poetological Doctrine of the Trinity." *Lutheran Quarterly* 15 (2001) 43–58.

———. *Promissio: Geschichte der reformatorischen Wende in Luthers Theologie.* Göttingen: Vandenhoeck & Ruprecht, 1971.

———. *Theology the Lutheran Way.* Translated and edited by Jeffrey Silcock and Mark Mattes. Grand Rapids: Eerdmans, 2007.

———. "Toward a Theology of Lament." In *Caritas et Reformatio: Essay on Church and Society in Honor of Carter Lindberg*, edited by David Whiford, 211–20. St. Louis: Concordia Academic, 2002.

———. "With Luther in the Present." *Lutheran Quarterly* 21 (2007) 1–16.

———. "Worship and Theology." In *Worship and Ethics: Lutherans and Anglicans in Dialogue*, edited by Oswald Bayer and Alan Suggate, 148–61. New York: Walter de Gruyter, 1996.

Beale, G. K. *The Book of Revelation: A Commentary on the Greek Text.* Grand Rapids: Eerdmans, 1999.

———. *The Temple and the Church's Mission: A Biblical Theology of the Dwelling Place of God.* Downer's Grove, IL: InterVarsity, 2004.

———. *We Become What We Worship: A Biblical Theology of Idolatry.* Downer's Grove, IL: InterVarsity, 2008.

Beasley-Murray, George. *The Book of Revelation.* London: Oliphants, 1974.

———. *John.* Nashville: Thomas Nelson, 1999.

Becker, Jürgen. *Das Evangelium nach Johannesm.* Würzburg: Echter Verlag, 1979.

Becker, Matthew. "Appreciating the Life and Work of Johannes v. Hofmann." *Lutheran Quarterly* 17 (2003) 177–98.

———. "Hofmann as Ich-Theologie? The Object of Theology in Johann von Hofmann's *Werk*." *Concordia Journal* 29 (2003) 265–93.

———. "Hofmann's Revisionist Christology." *Lutheran Quarterly* 17 (2003) 288–328.

———. *The Self-Giving God and Salvation History: The Trinitarian Theology of Johannes von Hofmann.* New York: T. & T. Clark, 2004.

———. "The Self-Giving God: The Trinity in Hofmann's Theology." *Pro Ecclesia* 12 (2003) 417–46.

Becker, Siegbert. *The Foolishness of God: The Place of Reason in the Theology of Martin Luther.* Milwaukee: Northwestern, 1982.

Beckwith, Carl. "Martin Chemnitz's Reading of the Fathers in *Oratio de Lectione Patrum*." *Concordia Theological Quarterly* 73 (2009) 231–56.

———. "Martin Chemnitz's Use of the Church Fathers in His Locus on Justification." *Concordia Theological Quarterly* 63 (2004) 271–90.

Beckwith, Isbon. *The Apocalypse of John.* New York: Macmillan, 1922.

Beker, Johan. *The Triumph of God: The Essence of Paul's Thought.* **Translated by** Loren T. Stuckenbruck. Minneapolis: Fortress, 1990.

Bell, Theo M. M. C. "Man is a Microcosmos: Adam and Eve in Luther's Lectures on Genesis 1535–1545." *Concordia Theological Quarterly* 69 (2005) 159–84.

Belleville, Linda. *Reflections of Glory: Paul's Polemical use of the Moses-Doxa tradition in II Corinthians 3:1–18.* Sheffield, UK: JSOT, 1991.

Bente, F. *Historical Introductions to the Book of Concord.* St. Louis: Concordia, 1965.

Bente, F., and W. H. T. Dau, eds. *Concordia Triglotta: The Symbolic Books of the Evangelical Lutheran Church: German-Latin-English.* St. Louis: Concordia, 1921.

Bergsma, John. *Jubilee from Leviticus to Qumran: A History of Interpretation.* Leiden: Brill, 2007.

Berkhof, Louis. *Reformed Dogmatics.* Grand Rapids: Eerdmans, 1941.

Berkouwer, G. C. *The Triumph of Grace in the Theology of Karl Barth.* Translated by Harry R. Boer. Grand Rapids: Eerdmans, 1956.

Bernard, J. H. *A Critical and Exegetical Commentary on the Gospel according to St. John.* Edinburgh: T. & T. Clark, 1928.

Berryman, Philip. *Liberation Theology.* Philadelphia: Temple University Press, 1987.

Betz, Hans Dieter. *Paulinische Studien.* Tübingen: Mohr Siebeck, 1994.

Beyschlag, Karlmann. *Die Erlanger Theologie.* Erlangen: Martin Luther Verlag, 1993.

Bianchi, Ugo. *Le Origini Dello Gnosticismo.* Leiden: Brill, 1967.

Bielfeldt, Dennis. "Luther's Late Trinitarian Disputations: Semantic Realism." In Dennis Bielfeldt, Mickey L. Mattox, and Paul R. Hinlicky, *The Substance of the Faith: Luther's Doctrinal Theology for Today*, 59–130. Minneapolis: Fortress, 2008.

Bigg, Charles. *A Critical and Exegetical Commentary on the Epistle of St. Peter and St. Jude.* Edinburgh: T. & T. Clark, 1901.

Block, D. I. "My Servant David: Ancient Israel's Vision of the Messiah." In *Israel's Messiah in the Bible and Dead Sea Scrolls,* edited by R. S. Hess and M. D.Carroll, 17–57. Grand Rapids: Baker, 2000.

Bock, Darrell. *Blasphemy and Exaltation in Judaism: The Charge against Jesus in Mark 14:53–65.* Grand Rapids: Baker, 2000.

———. *Luke.* Grand Rapids: Zondervan, 1996.

———. *Proclamation from Prophecy and Pattern: Lucan Old Testament Christology.* Sheffield, UK: Sheffield, 1997.

Bockmuehl, Markus. *The Epistle to the Philippians.* London: A and C Black, 1997.

Boer, Harry R. *The Book of Revelation.* Grand Rapids: Eerdmans, 1979.

Boice, James Montgomery. *Genesis, An Expositional Commentary: Genesis 12:1–36:43.* Vol. 2. Grand Rapids: Zondervan, 1985.

———. *Romans.* Vol. 1. Grand Rapids: Baker, 1991.

Bolliger, Daniel. *Infiniti Contemplatio: Grundzuge Der Scotus-Und Scotismusrezeption Im Werk Huldrych Zwinglis.* Leiden: Brill, 2003.

Bonar, Andrew. *A Commentary on the Book of Leviticus.* New York: Robert Carter & Brothers, 1851.

Bonhoeffer, Dietrich. *Christ the Center.* New York: Harper & Row, 1966.

Bonsirven, Joseph. *L'Apocalypse de Saint Jean: Traduction et Commentaire.* Paris: Beauchesne, 1951.

Boor, Werner de. *Das Evangelium des Johannes.* Wuppertal: Brockhaus, 1960.

Borg, Marcus. *Meeting Jesus Again for the First Time: The Historical Jesus and the Heart of Contemporary Faith.* San Francisco: HarperSanFrancisco, 1994.

Boring, M. Eugene. *1 Peter.* Nashville: Abingdon, 1999.

Borland, James A. *Christ in the Old Testament: A Comprehensive Study of Old Testament Appearances of Christ in Human Form.* Chicago: Moody, 1978.

Bornkamm, Günther. *Paulus.* Stuttgart: Kohlhammer, 1969.

Bornkamm, Heinrich. *Luther's World of Thought.* Translated by Martin Bertram. St. Louis: Concordia, 1965.

Borsch, Frederick. *The Christian and Gnostic Son of Man.* Naperville, IL: Alec R. Allenson, 1970.

———. *The Son of Man in Myth and History.* Philadelphia: Westminster, 1967.

Bosma, M. J. *Exposition of the Reformed Doctrine.* Grand Rapids: Zondervan, 1957.

Boussett, Wilhelm. *Kyrios Christos.* Göttingen: Vandenhoeck & Ruprecht, 1965.

Bovon, François. *Das Evangelium nach Lukas.* 4 vols. Zürich: Benziger Verlag, 1939–2009.

Boyd, Gregory. *God at War: The Bible and Spiritual Conflict.* Downer's Grove: InterVarsity, 1997.

———. *Is God to Blame?: Moving Beyond Pat Answers to the Problem of Suffering.* Downer's Grove, IL: InterVarsity, 2003.

———. *Satan and the Problem of Evil: Constructing a Trinitarian Warfare Theodicy.* Downer's Grove, IL: InterVarsity, 2001.

Braaten, Carl. "The Person of Jesus Christ." In *The Christian Dogmatics,* edited by Carl Braaten and Robert Jenson, 1:469–561. 2 vols. Philadelphia: Fortress, 1983.

Braun, Herbert. *An die Hebräer.* Tübingen: Mohr Siebeck, 1984.

Brawley, Robert. "Abrahamic Covenant Traditions and the Characterization of God in Luke-Acts." In *The Unity of Luke-Acts,* edited by Jozef Verheyden, 109–32. Louvain: Peeters, 1998.

Brecht, Martin. *Martin Luther.* Translated by James Schaaf. 3 vols. Minneapolis: Fortress, 1985–1993.

Breidert, Martin. *Die kenotische Christologie des 19. Jahrhunderts.* Gutersloher Verlagshaus: Mohn, 1977.

Brenz, Johannes. *De Personali Vnione Duarum Naturarum In Christo, Et Ascensu Christi In Coelum, Ac Sessione Eius Ad Dextram Dei Patris. Qua Vera Corporis Et Sanguinis Christi Praesentia in Coena explicata est, et confirmata.* Tübingen: Apud Viduam Vlrici Morhardi, 1561.

Brighton, Louis. *Revelation.* St. Louis: Concordia, 1999.

Broadus, John. *Commentary on the Gospel of Matthew.* Philadelphia: American Baptist, 1886.

Bromiley, Geoffrey. *Historical Theology: An Introduction.* Grand Rapids: Eerdmans, 1978.

———. *An Introduction to the Theology of Karl Barth.* Grand Rapids: Eerdmans, 1979.

Brondos, David. *Fortress Introduction to Salvation and the Cross.* Minneapolis: Fortress, 2007.

Brooks, Walter Edward. "The Perpetuity of Christ's Sacrifice in the Epistle to the Hebrews." *Journal of Biblical Literature* 89 (1970) 205–14.

Brosend, William, II. *James and Jude*. Cambridge, UK: Cambridge University Press, 2004.

Brown, David. *Divine Humanity: Kenosis Explored and Defended*. London: SCM, 2011.

Brown, John. *The Systematic Theology of John Brown of Haddington*. Grand Rapids: Reformation Heritage, 2002.

Brown, Raymond. *Christ Above All: The Message of Hebrews*. Downers Grove, IL: InterVarsity, 1982.

———. *The Death of the Messiah, From Gethsemane to the Grave: A Commentary on the Passion Narratives in the Four Gospels*. Vol. 1. New York: Doubleday, 1994.

———. *The Gospel According to John: I–XII*. New York: Doubleday, 1966.

———. *An Introduction to the Gospel of John*. New York: Doubleday, 2003.

———. *An Introduction to New Testament Christology*. New York: Paulist, 1994.

Brox, Nobert. *Understanding the Message of Paul*. Translated by Joseph Blenkinsopp. Notre Dame: University of Notre Dame Press, 1968.

Bruce, F. F. "The Davidic Messiah in Luke-Acts." In *Biblical and Near Eastern Studies: Festschrift in Honor of William Sanford LaSor*, 7–17. Edited by Gary A. Tuttle. Grand Rapids: Eerdmans, 1978.

———. *The Epistle of Paul to the Romans: An Introduction and Commentary*. Grand Rapids: Eerdmans, 1963.

———. *The Epistle to the Hebrews*. Grand Rapids: Eerdmans, 1990.

Bruce, F. F., I. Howard Marshall, and W. Ward Gasque. *The Epistle to the Galatians: A Commentary on the Greek Text*. Grand Rapids: Eerdmans, 1982.

Brueggemann, Walter. *The Covenanted Self: Explorations in Law and Covenant*. Minneapolis: Fortress, 1999.

———. *Theology of the Old Testament: Testimony, Dispute, Advocacy*. Minneapolis: Fortress, 1997.

Bruner, Frederick Dale. *Matthew: A Commentary*. 2 vols. Dallas: Word, 1987–1990.

Brunner, Peter. *Worship in the Name of Jesus*. Translated by M. H. Bertram. St. Louis: Concordia, 1968.

Brütsch, Charles. *La Clartéde l'Apocalypse*. Paris: Librairie Protestante, 1966.

Buchanan, George. *The Book of Revelation: Its Introduction and Prophecy*. Lewiston, NY: Mellen Biblical, 1993.

Büchsel, Friedrich. *Das Evangelium nach Johannes: Übersetzt und Erklärt*. Göttingen: Vandenhoeck & Ruprecht, 1946.

Bulgakov, Sergius. *The Lamb of God*. Translated by Boris Jakim. Grand Rapids: Eerdmans, 2008.

Bultmann, Rudolf. *Der Alte und der Neue Mensch in der Theologie des Paulus: Sonderausgpabe*. Darmstadt: Wissenschaftliche Buchgesellschaft, 1929.

———. *Begriff der Offenbarung im Neuen Testament*. Tübingen: Mohr, 1929.

———. *Beitrage zum Verstandnis der Jenseitigkeit Gottes im Neuen Testament*. Darmstadt: Wissenschaftliche Buchgesellschaft, 1965.

———. *Die Drei Johannesbrief*. Göttingen: Vandenhoeck & Ruprecht, 1969.

———. *Die Erforschung der Synoptischen Evangelien*. Berlin: Topelmann, 1960.

———. *Das Evangelium des Johannes*. Göttingen: Vandenhoeck & Ruprecht, 1950.

———. *Die Geschichte der Synoptischen Tradition*. Göttingen: Vandenhoeck & Ruprecht, 1957.

———. *The Gospel of John*. Translated by G. K. Beasley-Murray. Oxford: Basil Blackwell, 1971.

———. *History and Eschatology: The Presence of Eternity*. New York: Harper, 1962.

———. *History of the Synoptic Tradition*. Translated by John Marsh. New York: Harper and Row, 1968.

———. *Jesus and the Word*. Translated by Louise Pettibone Smith and Erminie Huntress Lantero. New York: Scribner, 1958.

———. *Jesus Christ and Mythology*. New York: Scribner, 1958.

———. *Primitive Christianity in Its Contemporary Setting*. Translated by R. H. Fuller. London: Thames and Hudson, 1956.

———. *The Second Letter to the Corinthians*. Translated by Roy A. Harrisville. Minneapolis: Augsburg, 1985.

———. *Theologie des Neuen Testaments*. 2 vols. Tübingen: Mohr, 1953.

Burger, Karl von. *Das Evangelium nach Johannes*. Nördlingen: Beck, 1868.

Burkett, Delbert. *The Son of Man: A History and Evaluation*. Cambridge, UK: Cambridge University Press 1999.

Burnfeind, Peter. "The Harrowing of Hell: Filling in the Blanks." *Logia* 18 (2009) 5–14.

Bibliography

Busch, Eberhard. *The Great Passion: An Introduction to Karl Barth's Theology.* Translated by Geoffrey Bromiley. Grand Rapids: Eerdmans, 2004.

Buswell, James. *A Systematic Theology of the Christian Religion.* 2 vols. Grand Rapids: Zondervan, 1962–1963.

Caird, G. B. *A Commentary on the Revelation of St. John the Divine.* New York: Harper & Row, 1966.

———. "The Glory of God in the Fourth Gospel: An Exercise in Biblical Semantics." *New Testament Studies* 15 (1969) 265–77.

———. *The Gospel of St. Luke.* Baltimore: Penguin, 1963.

Calvin, John. *Commentary on the Gospel according to John.* Translated by William Pringle. 2 vols. Grand Rapids: Eerdmans, 1949.

———. *The Harmony of Matthew, Mark and Luke.* 3 vols. Translated by William Pringle. Grand Rapids: Eerdmans, 1949.

———. *The Institutes of the Christian Religion (1559).* Translated and edited by John T. McNeill and Ford Lewis Battles. 2 vols. Philadelphia: Westminster, 1967.

Cantinat, Jean. *Les Épîtres de Saint Jacques et de Saint Jude.* Paris: J. Gabalda, 1973.

Carrington, Philip. *According to Mark: A Running Commentary on the Oldest Gospel.* Cambridge, UK: Cambridge University Press, 1960.

Carson, D. A. *The Gospel according to John.* Grand Rapids: Eerdmans, 1991.

Casel, Odo. *The Mystery of Christian Worship.* New York: Crossroads, 1999.

Catechism of the Catholic Church. Rome: Libereria Editric Vaticana, 2000.

Cedar, Paul. *James, 1, 2 Peter, Jude.* Waco, TX: Word, 1984.

Chapman, J. Arundel. *The Theology of Karl Barth: A Short Introduction.* London: Epworth, 1931.

Charles, R. H. *A Critical and Exegetical Commentary of the Revelation of St. John.* 2 vols. New York: Scribner's Sons, 1920.

Charlesworth, James. "The Concept of the Messiah in the Psedeupigrapha." In *Aufsteig und Niedergang der römanischen welt,* edited by Wolfgang Hasse and Hildegard Temporini, 188–218. New York: Walter de Gruyter, 1979.

———. "From Jewish Messianology to Christian Christology: Some Caveats and Perspectives." In *Judaism and their Messiahs at the Turn of the Christian Era,* edited by Jacob Neusner, W. S. Green, and E. Fredrichs, 225–64. Cambridge, UK: Cambridge University Press, 1987.

———, ed. *The Messiah: Developments in Earliest Judaism and Christianity.* Minneapolis: Fortress, 1992.

———. *Qumran-Messianism: Studies on the Messianic Expectations in the Dead Sea Scrolls.* Tübingen: Mohr Siebeck, 1998.

Chemnitz, Martin. *Examination of the Council of Trent: Part I.* Translated by Fred Kramer. St. Louis: Concordia, 1971.

———. *Loci Theologici.* Translated by J. A. O. Preus. 2 vols. St. Louis: Concordia, 1989.

———. *The Two Natures in Christ.* Translated by J. A. O. Preus. St. Louis: Concordia, 1971.

Chemnitz, Martin, Polycarp Leyser, and Johann Gerhard. *The Harmony of the Four Evangelists.* Translated by Richard Dinda. Vol. 1. Malone, TX: Repristination, 2009.

Chester, Andrew. *Messiah and Exaltation: Jewish Messianic and Visionary Traditions and the New Testament Christology.* Tübingen: Mohr Siebeck, 2007.

Chilton, David. *The Days of Vengeance: An Exposition of the Book of Revelation.* Ft. Worth, TX: Dominion, 1987.

———. *Paradise Restored: A Biblical Theology of Dominion.* Ft. Worth, TX: Dominion, 1987.

Churton, Tobias. *The Gnostics.* London: Weidenfeld and Nicolson, 1987.

Chytraeus, David. *Auslegung der Offenbarung Johanni.* Rostock: Gedruckt durch Jacobum Siebenbürger, 1568.

———. *On Sacrifice: A Reformation Treatise in Biblical Theology.* Translated by John Warwick Montgomery. St. Louis: Concordia, 1962.

———. *A Summary of the Christian Faith.* Translated by Jamse Heiser. Malone, TX: Repristination, 1994.

Clements, R. E. *God and Temple.* Oxford: Basil Blackwell, 1965.

Cohn, Norman. *Cosmos, Chaos, and the World to Come: The Ancient Roots of Apocalyptic Faith.* New Haven, CT: Yale University Press, 1995.

Cole, R. A. *The Epistle of Paul to the Galatians.* Grand Rapids: Eerdmans, 1965.

Collins, John. *The Apocalyptic Imagination: An Introduction to Jewish Apocalyptic Literature*. New York: Crossroads, 1998.

———. *Daniel: A Commentary*. Minneapolis: Fortress, 1993.

———. "Kabob." In *The New International Dictionary of Old Testament Theology and Exegesis*, edited by Willen VanGemeren, 2:577–87. 5 vols. Grand Rapids: Zondervan, 1997.

———. *The Scepter and the Star: Messianism in Light of the Dead Sea Scrolls*. Grand Rapids: Eerdmans, 2010.

Coloe, Mary L. *God Dwells With Us: Temple Symbolism in the Fourth Gospel*. Collegeville, MN: Liturgical, 2001.

Congar, Yves. *The Meaning of Tradition*. San Francisco: Ignatius, 2004.

———. *The Mystery of the Temple*. Translated by Reginald F. Trevett. Westminster, MD: Newman, 1962.

———. "Regards et réflexions sur la christologie de Luther." In *Das Konzil von Chalkedon: Geschichte und Gegenwart*, edited by Aloys Grillmeier and Heinrich Bacht, 3:457–86. 3 vols. Wurzburg: Echter Verlag, 1953–1954.

Conzelmann, Hans. *A Commentary on the First Epistle to the Corinthians*. Translated by James Leitch. Philadelphia: Fortress, 1975.

———. *The Theology of St. Luke*. Translated by Geoffrey Buswell. New York: Harper and Brothers, 1960.

Cook, W. Robert. "The 'Glory' Motif in the Johannine Corpus." *Journal of the Evangelical Theological Society* 27 (1984) 291–97.

Copleston, Fredrick. *A History of Philosophy: Greece and Rome*. Vol. 1. New York: Doubleday, 1993.

———. *A History of Philosophy: Medieval Philosophy*. Vol. 2. New York: Doubleday, 1993.

Corbin, Bruce. *The Book of Revelation*. Grand Rapids: Zondervan, 1938.

Cory, Catherine. *The Book of Revelation*. Collegeville, MN: Liturgical, 2006.

Couliano, Ioan. *The Tree of Gnosis: Gnostic Mythology from Early Christianity to Modern Nihilism*. Translated by H. S. Wiesner. San Francisco: HarperSanFrancisco, 1992.

Court, John. *Myth and History in the Book of Revelation*. London: SPCK, 1979.

Cox, Clyde. *Apocalyptic Commentary: An Exposition on the Book of Revelation*. Cleveland, TN: Pathway, 1959.

Craddock, Fred. *First and Second Peter and Jude*. Louisville, KY: Westminster John Knox, 1995.

———. *Luke*. Louisville, KY: John Knox, 1990.

Cranfield, C. E. B. *The Gospel according to Saint Mark: An Introduction and Commentary*. Cambridge, UK: Cambridge University Press, 1959.

———. *I and II Peter and Jude: Introduction and Commentary*. London: SCM, 1960.

———. *Romans: A Shorter Commentary*. Grand Rapids: Eerdmans, 1985.

Croken, Robert. *Luther's First Front: The Eucharist as Sacrifice*. Ottawa: University of Ottawa Press, 1990.

Cross, Frank Moore. *Canaanite Myth and Hebrew Epic: Essays in the History of the Religion of Israel*. Cambridge, MA: Harvard University Press, 1973.

———. "Kinship and Covenant in Ancient Israel." In *From Epic to Canon: History and Literature in Ancient Israel*, 3–21. Baltimore: Johns Hopkins University Press, 1998.

Crossan, John Dominic. "Anti-Semitism and the Gospel." *Theological Studies* 26 (1965) 189–214.

———. *The Historical Jesus: The Life of a Mediterranean Jewish Peasant*. San Francisco: HarperOne, 1993.

Crouzel, Henri. *Origen*. Translated by A. S. Worrall. San Francisco: Harper & Row, 1989.

Cullman, Oscar. *Early Christian Worship*. Translated by A. Steward Todd and James Torrance. London: SCM, 1953.

Daise, Michael. *Feast in John: Jewish Feastivals and Jesus' "Hour" in the Fourth Gospel*. Tübingen: Mohr Siebeck, 2007.

Daly, Mary. *Amazon Grace: Re-Calling the Courage to Sin Big*. New York: Macmillan, 2006.

———. *Beyond God the Father: Toward a Philosophy of Women's Liberation*. Boston: Beacon, 1973.

———. *The Church and the Second Sex*. San Francisco: Harper & Row, 1968.

———. *Gyn/Ecology: The Metaethics of Radical Feminism*. Boston: Beacon, 1978.

———. *Outercourse: The Bedazzling Voyage, Containing Recollections from My Logbook of a Radical Feminist Philosopher*. San Francisco: HarperSanFrancisco, 1992.

———. *Pure Lust: Elemental Feminist Philosophy*. Boston: Beacon, 1984.

———. *Quintessence: Realizing the Archaic Future: A Radical Elemental Feminist Manifesto*. Boston: Beacon, 1998.

Bibliography

Daly, Robert. *The Origins of the Christian Doctrine of Sacrifice*. Philadelphia: Fortress, 1978.

John of Damascus, St. *The Orthodox Faith*. In *Saint John of Damascus: Writings*, translated by Frederic H. Chase, Jr., 165–406. Fathers of the Church, 37. Washington, DC: Catholic University of America Press, 1958.

D'Angelo, M. R. *Moses in the Letter to the Hebrews*. Missoula, MT: Scholars, 1979.

Daniélou, Jean. *A History of Early Christian Doctrine Before the Council of Nicaea: The Origins of Latin Christianity*. Vol. 3. Philadelphia: Westminster, 1980.

———. *Origen*. Translated by Walter Mitchell. New York: Sheed and Ward, 1955.

Danker, Frederick. *Jesus and the New Age: A Commentary on St. Luke's Gospel*. Philadelphia: Fortress, 1988.

Dannhauer, Johann Konrad. *Hernenevtica Sacra*. Argentorati: Josiae Staedelii, 1654.

Davidson, Andrew. *The Epistle to the Hebrews*. Grand Rapids: Zondervan, 1952.

Davidson, Robert. *Genesis 12–50*. Cambridge, UK: Cambridge University Press, 1979.

Davies, Brian. *The Thought of Thomas Aquinas*. Oxford: Oxford University Press, 1992.

Davies, G. H. "Glory." In *The Interpreter's Dictionary of the Bible*. 4 vols. 2:401–3. Nashville: Abingdon, 1962.

Davies, Margaret. *Matthew*. Sheffield, UK: JSOT, 1993.

Davis, Leo Donald. *The First Seven Ecumenical Councils (325–787): Their History and Theology*. Collegeville, MN: Liturgical, 1990.

Dean, J. T. *The Book of Revelation*. Edinburgh: T. & T. Clark, 1930.

Delitzsch, Franz. *Biblical Commentary on the Prophecies of Isaiah*. 2 vols. Grand Rapids: Eerdmans, 1954.

———. *Commentar zum Briefe an die Hebräer*. Leipzig: Dörffling und Franke, 1857.

Deme, Daniel. *The Christology of Anselm of Canterbury*. Burlington, VT: Ashgate, 2003.

Dempster, Stephen G. *Dominion and Dynasty: A Biblical Theology of the Hebrew Bible* Downers Grove, IL: InterVarsity, 2003.

Denzinger, Heinrich. *The Sources of Catholic Dogma*. Translated by Roy Deferrari. St. Louis: B. Herder, 1957.

Deterding, Paul. *Colossians*. St. Louis: Concordia, 2003.

Deutschlander, Daniel. *The Theology of the Cross: Reflections on His Cross and Ours*. Milwaukee: Northwestern, 2008.

Deutz, Rupert of. *Commentaria in Evangelium Sancti Iohannis*. Edited by Rhabanus Haacke. Turnholte: Brepols, 1969.

DeVries, Dawn. *Jesus Christ in the Preaching of Calvin*. Louisville, KY: John Knox Westminster, 1996.

Dickson, David. *A Brief Exposition of the Evangel of Jesus Christ according to Matthew*. London: Ralph Smith, 1651.

Dodd, C. H. *The Interpretation of the Fourth Gospel*. Cambridge, UK: Cambridge University Press, 1953.

———. "ΙΛΑΣΚΕΣΘΑΙ: Its Cognates, Derivatives, and Synonyms in the Septuagint." *Journal of Theological Studies* 32 (1931) 352–60.

Dorner, I. A. *History of the Development of the Doctrine of the Person of Christ*. Translated by William Alexander, D. W. Simon, and Patrick Fairbairn. 5 vols. Edinburgh: T. & T. Clark, 1872–1882.

———. *History of Protestant Theology, Particularly in Germany*. Translated by George Robson and Sophia Taylor. 2 vols. Edinburgh: T. & T. Clark, 1871.

———. *A System of Christian Doctrine*. Translated by Alfred Cave and J. S. Banks. 4 vols. Edinburgh: T. & T. Clark, 1888.

Dozeman, Thomas. *Exodus*. Grand Rapids: Eerdmans, 2009.

Drane, John. *Introducing the Old Testament*. San Francisco: Harper & Row, 1987.

———. *Paul, Libertine or Legalist? A Study in the Theology of the Major Pauline Epistles*. London: SPCK, 1975.

Dubose, William. *The Gospel According to Saint Paul*. New York: Longman and Green, 1908.

Dumbrell, W. J. *Covenant and Creation: A Theology of the Old Testament Covenants*. Carlisle, UK: Paternoster, 1984.

Dunderberg, Ismo. *Beyond Gnosticism: Myth, Lifestyle, and Society in the School of Valentinus*. New York: Columbia University Press, 2008.

Dunn, James D. G. *Christology in the Making: A New Testament Inquiry into the Origins of the Doctrine of the Incarnation*. Grand Rapids: Eerdmans, 1996.

———. *The New Perspective on Paul: Collected Essays.* Tübingen: Mohr Siebeck, 2005.

———. *Romans 1–8.* Nashville: Thomas Nelson, 1988.

———. *The Theology of Paul the Apostle.* Grand Rapids: Eerdmans, 1998.

———. *Unity and Diversity in the New Testament.* Philadelphia: Westminster, 1977.

Dunnhill, John. *Covenant and Sacrifice in the Letter to the Hebrews.* New York: Cambridge University, 1992.

Durham, John I. *A Complete Commentary Upon the Book of the Revelation.* Falkirk: Robert Renny, 1799.

———. Durham, John I. *Exodus.* Waco, TX: Word, 1987.

Düsterdieck, Friedrich. *Critical and Exegetical Handbook to the Revelation of John.* Translated by Henry E. Jacobs. New York: Funk & Wagnalls, 1887.

Ebeling, Gerhard. *Dogmatik des Christlichen Glaubens.* 3 vols. Tübingen: Mohr, 1979.

———. *Einfuhrung in Theologische Sprachlehre.* Tübingen: Mohr, 1971.

———. *Evangelische Evangelienauslegung: Eine Untersuchung zu Luthers Hermeneutik.* München: Evangelischer Verlag Albert Lempp, 1942.

———. *Frei aus Glauben.* Tübingen: Mohr, 1968.

———. *Die Geschichtlichkeit der Kirche und Ihrer Verkundigung als Theologisches Problem: Drei Vorlesungen.* Tübingen: Mohr, 1954.

———. *Kirchengeschichte als Geschichte der Auslegung der Heiligen Schrift.* Tübingen: Mohr, 1947.

———. *Luther: Einfuhrung in Sein Denken.* Tübingen: Mohr, 1964.

———. *Luthers Seelsorge: Theologie in der Vielfalt der Lebenssituationen an Seine Briefen Dargestellt.* Tübingen: Mohr Siebeck, 1997.

———. *Lutherstudien.* 3 vols. Tübingen: Mohr Siebeck, 1971–1989.

———. *The Nature of Faith.* Translated by Ronald Smith. London: Collins, 1961.

———. *The Problem of Historicity in the Church and its Proclamation.* Translated by Grover Foley. Philadelphia: Fortress, 1967.

———. *Psalmenmeditationen.* Tübingen: Mohr, 1968.

———. *The Study of Theology.* Translated by Duane Priebe. Philadelphia: Fortress, 1978.

———. *Theologie und Verkündigung; ein Gesprach mit Rudolf Bultmann.* Tübingen: Mohr, 1962.

———. *The Truth of the Gospel: An Exposition of Galatians.* Translatd by David Green. Philadelphia: Fortress, 1985.

———. *Das Wesen des Christlichen Glaubens.* Tübingen: Mohr, 1959.

———. *Wort Gottes und Tradition; Studien zu einer Hermeneutik der Konfessionen.* Göttingen: Vandenhoeck & Ruprecht, 1964.

———. *Wort und Glaube.* Tübingen: Mohr, 1960.

Ebrand, Johann. *Der Brief an die Hebräer.* Königsberg: A. W. Unzer, 1850.

Eckermann, Willigis. "Die Aristoeleskritik Luthers: ihre Bedeutung für seine Theologie." *Catholica* 32 (1978) 114–30.

———. "Luthers Kreuzestheologie. Zur Frage nach ihrem Ursprung." *Catholica* 37 (1983) 306–17.

Eckhardt, Burnell. "Luther and Moltmann: The Theology of the Cross." *Concordia Theological Quarterly* 49 (1985) 19–28.

———. *The New Testament in His Blood: A Study of the Holy Liturgy of the Christian Church.* Kewanee, IL: Gottesdienst, 2010.

Edgar, William. "Ethics: The Christian Life and Good Works according to Calvin." In *Theological Guide to Calvin's Institutes: Essays and Analysis,* edited by David Hall and Peter Lillback, 320–46. Philipsburg, NJ: Presbyterian and Reformed Publishing, 2008.

Edmondson, Stephen. *Calvin's Christology.* Cambridge, UK: Cambridge University Press, 2004.

Edwards, James. *The Gospel according to Mark.* Grand Rapids: Eerdmans, 2002.

Edwards, Thomas. *A Commentary on the First Epistle to the Corinthians.* London: Hodder & Stoughton, 1885.

Ehrman, Bart. *The New Testament: A Historical Introduction to the Early Christian Writings.* New York: Oxford University Press, 1997.

Eichrodt, Walther. *Theology of the Old Testament.* Translated by J. A. Baker. 2 vols. Philadelphia: Westminster, 1961–1967.

Elert, Werner. *Der Ausgang der Altkirchlichen Christologie: Eine Untersuchung uber Theodor von Pharan und seine Zeit als Einfuhrung in die alte Dogmengeschichte.* Berlin: Lutherisches Verlagshaus, 1957.

———. *The Christian Ethos: The Foundation of the Christian Way of Life*. Translated by Carl Schindler. Philadelphia: Muhlenberg, 1957.

———. "The Christian Faith: An Outline of Lutheran Dogmatics." Translated by Martin Bertram and Walter Bouman. Unpublished manuscript, 1974.

———. *Law and Gospel*. Translated by Edward Shroeder. Philadelphia: Fortress, 1967.

———. *The Structure of Lutheranism*. Translated by Walter A. Hansen. Vol. 1. St. Louis: Concordia, 1962.

Ellingworth, Paul. *The Epistle to the Hebrews: A Commentary on the Greek Text*. Grand Rapids: Eerdmans, 1993.

Erdman, Charles. *The Epistle to the Hebrews: An Exposition*. Philadelphia: Westminster, 1934.

———. *The Gospel of Matthew: An Exposition*. Philadelphia: Westminster, 1920.

Eskola, Timo. *Messiah and the Throne: Jewish Merkabah Mysticism and Early Christian Exaltation Discourse*. Tübingen: Mohr Siebeck, 2001.

Eusebius. *The Church History: A New Translation with Commentary*. Translated by Paul Maier. Grand Rapids: Kregel, 1999.

Evans, Craig. *Saint Luke*. Philadelphia: Trinity, 1990.

Evans, Craig, and Peter Flint, eds. *Eschatology, Messianism, and the Dead Sea Scrolls*. Grand Rapids: Eerdmans, 1997.

Evans, G. R. "Anselm of Canterbury." In *The Medieval Theologians*, edited by G. R. Evans, 94–101. Oxford: Blackwell, 2001.

———. "Eutyches, Nestorius, and Chalcedon." In *The First Christian Theologians: An Introduction to Theology in the Early Church*, edited by G. R. Evans 243–48. Malden, MA: Blackwell, 2004.

Ezra, Daniel Stökl Ben. *The Impact of Yom Kippur on Early Christianity: The Day of Atonement from Second Temple Judaism to the Fifth Century*. Tübingen: Mohr Siebeck, 2003.

Fagerberg, Holsten. *A New Look at the Lutheran Confessions (1529–1537)*. Translated by Gene Lund. St. Louis: Concordia, 1972.

Faley, R. J. *Bonding with God: A Reflective Study of Biblical Covenant*. New York: Paulist, 1997.

Farrell, Walter. *A Companion to the Summa: The Way of Life*. Vol. 4. New York: Sheed and Ward, 1942.

Farrer, Austin. *The Triple Victory: Christ's Temptations According to Saint Matthew*. London: Faith Press, 1965.

Faye, Eugene de. *Origen and His Work*. Translated by Fred Rothwell. New York: Columbia University Press, 1929.

Fee, Gordon D. *Paul's Letter to the Philippians*. Grand Rapids: Eerdmans, 1995.

Feinberg, Charles. "The Scapegoat of Leviticus Sixteen." *Bibliotheca Sacra* 115 (1958) 320–33.

Feine, Paul. *Saint Paul as a Theologian*. New York: Eaton and Mains, 1908.

Fendt, Leonhard. *Der Christus der Gemeinde: Eine Einführung in das Evangelium nach Lukas*. Berlin: Furche Verlag, 1937.

Fenton, J. C. *The Gospel of Saint Matthew*. Baltimore: Penguin, 1963.

Fiedler, Peter. *Das Matthäusevangelium*. Stuttgart: W. Kohlhammer, 2006.

Filoramo, Giovanni. *A History of Gnosticism*. Translated by Anthony Alcock. Oxford: Basil Blackwell, 1990.

Filson, Floyd. *A Commentary on the Gospel according to Saint Matthew*. New York: Harper, 1961.

Finkelstein, Israel, and Neil Silberman. *The Bible Unearthed: Archaeology's New Vision of Israel's History and the Origin of its Sacred Texts*. New York: Free Press, 2002.

Finlan, Stephen. *Options on Atonement in Christian Thought*. Collegeville, MN: Liturgical, 2007.

———. *Problems with the Atonement: The Origins of, and Controversy about the Atonement Doctrine*. Collegeville, MN: Liturgical, 2005.

Fischer, George Park. "The Augustinian and Federal Theories of Original Sin Compared." In *History and Theology*, 355–409. New York: Scribner, 1880.

Fitzmyer, Joseph A. *According to Paul: Studies in the Theology of the Apostle*. New York: Paulist, 1993.

———. "Anti-Semitism and the Cry of 'All the People' (Mt 27:25)." *Theological Studies* 26 (1965) 667–71.

———. "Further Light on Melchizedek from Qumran Cave 11." In *Essays on the Semitic Background of the New Testament*, 245–67. Missoula, MT: Scholars, 1974.

———. "Melchizedek in the MT, LXX, and the NT." *Biblica* 81 (2000) 63–69.

———. "The New Testament Title 'Son of Man.'" In *A Wandering Aramean: Collected Aramaic Essays*, 143–60. Missoula, MT: Scholars, 1999.

——. "'Now This Melchizedek . . .' (Heb. 7:1)." In *Essays on the Semitic Background of the New Testament*, 221–43. Missoula, MT: Scholars, 1974.

——. *The One Who is to Come*. Grand Rapids: Eerdmans, 2007.

Fletcher-Louis, Crispin H. T. "God's Image, His Cosmic Temple and the High Priest: Towards an Historical and Theological Account of the Incarnation." In *Heaven on Earth: The Temple in Biblical Theology*, edited by T. Desmond Alexander and Simon Gathercole, 81–100. Carlisle, UK: Paternoster, 2004.

——. "The High Priest as Divine Mediator in the Hebrew Bible: Daniel 7:13 as a Test Case." *Society of Biblical Literature Seminar Papers* (1997) 161–75. Online: http://www.marquette.edu/maqom/dan1.

——. "Jesus and the High Priest." Online: http://www.marquette.edu/maqom/jesus.pdf.

Forde, Gerhard. "Authority of the Church: The Lutheran Reformation." In *A More Radical Gospel: Essays on Eschatology, Authority, Atonement, and Ecumenism*, edited by Mark Mattes and Steven Paulson, 53–67. Grand Rapids: Eerdmans, 2004.

——. *On Being a Theologian of the Cross: Reflections on Luther's Heidelberg Disputation 1518*. Grand Rapids: Eerdmans, 1997.

——. "Caught in the Act: Reflections on the Work of Christ." In *A More Radical Gospel: Essays on Eschatology, Authority, Atonement, and Ecumenism*, edited by Mark Mattes and Steven Paulson, 85–97. Grand Rapids: Eerdmans, 2004.

——. "Fake Theology: Reflections on Antinomianism Past and Present." In *The Preached God: Proclamation in Word and Sacrament*, edited by Steven Paulson and Mark Mattes, 214–25. Grand Rapids: Eerdmans, 2007.

——. *Justification by Faith: A Matter of Death and Life*. Mifflintown, PA: Sigler, 1991.

——. "Karl Barth on the Consequence of Lutheran Christology." In *The Preached God: Proclamation in Word and Sacrament*, edited by Steven Paulson and Mark Mattes, 69–88. Grand Rapids: Eerdmans, 2007.

——. *The Law-Gospel Debate: An Interpretation of Its Historical Development* Minneapolis: Augsburg, 1969.

——. "Radical Lutheranism." In *A More Radical Gospel: Essays in Eschatology, Authority, Atonement, and Ecumenism*, edited by Steven Paulson and Mark Mattes, 3–16. Grand Rapids: Eerdmans, 2004.

——. *Theology is for Proclamation*. Minneapolis: Fortress, 1990.

——. *Where God Meets Man: Luther's Down-To-Earth Approach to the Gospel*. Minneapolis: Fortress, 1972.

——. "The Work of Christ." In *The Christian Dogmatics*, edited by Robert Jenson and Carl Braaten, 2:5–104. 2 vols. Philadelphia: Fortress, 1984.

Fossum, Jarl. "Kyrios Jesus as the Angel of the Lord in Jude 5–7." *New Testament Studies* 33 (1987) 226–43.

Fraenkel, Peter. "Ten Questions concerning Melanchthon, the Fathers, and the Eucharist." In *Luther and Melanchthon in the History and Theology of the Reformation*, edited by Vilmos Vatja, 146–64. Philadelphia: Muhlenberg Press, 1961.

France, R. T. *The Gospel of Mark*. Grand Rapids: Eerdmans, 2002.

——. *The Gospel of Matthew: A Commentary on the Greek Text*. Grand Rapids: Eerdmans, 2007.

Franz, Wolfgang. *Commentarius in Leviticum in qvo leges Mosaicae, ceremoniales & rituales solide explicantur*. Leipzig: Johannis Christophori Weidneri, 1696.

Franzmann, Martin. *Commentary on Romans*. St. Louis: Concordia, 1968.

Fredrikson, Paula. *From Jesus to Christ: The Origins of the New Testament Images of Jesus* New Haven, CT: Yale University Press, 1988.

——. *Jesus of Nazareth, King of the Jews: A Jewish Life and the Emergence of Christianity*. New York: Alfred A. Knopf, 2000.

Freed, Edwin D. *The Apostle Paul and His Letters*. Oakville, CT: Equinox, 2005.

Frei, Hans. *The Eclipse of the Biblical Narrative: A Study in Eighteenth and Nineteenth Century Hermeneutics*. New Haven, CT: Yale University Press, 1974.

Fronmüller, G. F. C. *The Epistle General of Jude*. New York: Charles Scribner, 1868.

Fuchs, Eric, and Pierre Reymond. *La Deuxieme Epitre de Saint Pierre: L'Epitre de Saint Jude*. Neuchatel: Delachaux et Niestle, 1980.

Frühwald-König, Johannes. *Tempel und Kult: Ein Beitrag zur Christologie es Johannesevangeliums*. Regensburg: Friedrich Pustet, 1998.

Funk, Robert. *Honest to Jesus: Jesus for a New Millennium*. San Francisco: HarperSanFrancisco 1997.

Furnish, Victor Paul. *Theology and Ethics in Paul*. Louisville, KY: Westminster John Knox, 2009.

Gaetcher, Paul. *Das Matthäus Evangelium: Ein Kommentar*. Innsbruck: Tyrolia Verlag, 1963.

Gaffin, Richard. "Glory." In *The New Dictionary of Biblical Theology*, edited by T. Desmond Alexander and Brian Rosner, 507–11. Downer's Grove: InterVarsity, 2000.

Galtier, Paul. "Saint Cyrille d'Alexandrie et saint Léon Le Grand à Chalcédoine." In *Das Konzil von Chalkedon: Geschichte und Gegenwart*, edited by Aloys Grillmeier and Heinrich Bacht, 1:345–87. 3 vols. Wurzburg: Echter Verlag, 1953–1954.

Gathercole, Simon. *The Pre-Existent Son: Recovering the Christologies of Matthew, Mark, and Luke*. Grand Rapids: Eerdmans, 2006.

———. *Where is Boasting?: Early Jewish Soteriology and Paul's Response in Romans 1–5*. Grand Rapids: Eerdmans, 2002.

Gardiner, Frederic. "On *diatheke* in Hebrews 16, 17." *Journal of Biblical Literature* 5 (1885) 8–19.

———. *The Last of the Epistles: A Commentary upon the Epistle of Saint Jude*. Boston: J. P. Jewett, 1856.

Garvie, Alfred. *Studies of Paul and his Gospel*. New York: Hodder & Stoughton, 1911.

Gasper, Giles. *Anselm of Canterbury and His Theological Inheritance*. Burlington, VT: Ashgate, 2004.

Gaston, Lloyd. "The Messiah of Israel as the Teacher of the Gentiles: The Setting of Matthew's Christology." *Interpretation* 29 (1975) 24–40.

Gawrisch, Wilbert R. "On Christology: Brenz and the Question of Ubiquity." In *No Other Gospel: Essays in Commemoration of the 400th Anniversary of the Formula of Concord, 1580–1980*, edited by Arnold Koelpin, 229–54. Milwaukee: Northwestern, 1980.

Geldenhuys, Norval. *Commentary on the Gospel of Luke*. Grand Rapids: Eerdmans, 1951.

Genderen, J. van, and W. H. Velema. *Concise Reformed Dogmatics*. Translated by Gerrit Bilkes, edited by M. van der Maas. Philipsburg, NJ: Presbyterian and Reformed Publishing, 2008.

George, Timothy. *Theology of the Reformers*. Nashville: Broadman, 1988.

Gerhard, Johann. *Commentarius super Epistolam ad Ebraeos*. Jena, Saxon: 1641.

———. *An Explanation of the History of the Suffering and Death of Our Lord Jesus Christ*. Translated by Elmer Hohle. Malone, TX: Repristination Press, 1998.

———. "The Image of God." In *The Doctrine of Man in Classical Lutheran Theology*, 27–68. Translated and edited by Mario Colacci, Lowell Satre, J. A. O. Preus, Otto Stalke, and Ber Narverson. Minneapolis: Augsburg, 1962.

———. *Theological Commonplaces, Exegesis I: On the Nature of Scripture and Theology*. Translated by Richard Dinda. St. Louis: Concordia, 2005.

———. *Theological Commonplaces, Exegesis IV: On Christ*. Translated by Richard Dinda. St. Louis: Concordia, 2009.

———. *Theological Commonplaces: Exegesis XXV, On the Church*. Translated by Richard Dinda. St. Louis: Concordia, 2010.

Gerrish, B. A. *Grace and Gratitude: The Eucharistic Theology of John Calvin*. Minneapolis: Fortress, 1993.

———. *Grace and Reason: A Study in the Theology of Luther*. Eugene, OR: Wipf and Stock, 2005.

———. "To the Unknown God: Luther and Calvin on the Hiddenness of God." *Journal of Religion* 53 (1973) 263–93.

Gess, Wolfgang Friedrich. *Christi und Werk*. 3 vols. Basel: Bahnmaiers Buchhandlung, 1870–1887).

Gibbs, Jeffrey. *Matthew 1–11*. St. Louis: Concordia, 2006.

———. "The Son of God and the Father's Wrath: Atonement and Salvation in Matthew's Gospel." *Concordia Theological Quarterly* 72 (2008) 211–26.

Gieschen, Charles. *Angelomorphic Christology: Antecedents and Early Evidence*. Leiden: Brill, 1998.

———. "The Divine Name in Ante-Nicene Christianity." *Viliae Christianae* 57 (2003) 130–48.

———. "The Real Presence of the Son Before Christ: Revisiting an Old Approach to Old Testament Christology." *Concordia Theological Quarterly* 68 (2004) 105–26.

———. "The Name of the Son of Man in 1 Enoch." In *Enoch and Messiah Son of Man: Revisting the Book of Parables*, 238–49. Edited by Gabriele Boccaccini. Grand Rapids: Eerdmans, 2007.

Gielesser, Philip. "Appendix: Diatheke: Covenant or Testament?" In *The New Testament: God's Word to the Nations*, 531–40. Cleveland: Biblion, 1988.

Gill, John. *An Exposition of Genesis*. Springfield, MO: Particular Baptist, 2010.

———. *An Exposition of the Epistle of Paul the Apostle to the Romans*. Springfield, MO: Particular Baptist, 2002.

Girard, René. *The Scapegoat*. Baltimore: Johns Hopkins University Press, 1989.

———. *Violence and the Sacred*. Baltimore: Johns Hopkins University Press, 1979.

Glasgow, James. *The Apocalypse Translated and Expounded*. Edinburgh: T. & T. Clark, 1872.

Glenn, Paul. *A Tour of the Summa*. New York: Herder, 1960.

Gnilka, Joachim. *Das Evangelium nach Markus*. 2 vols. Zurich: Benziger, 1978–1979.

Godet, Johannis von F. *Commentary on St. Paul's Epistle to the Corinthians*. Edinburgh: T. & T. Clark, 1887.

———. *Commentar zu dem Evangelium Johannis*. Hannover: Carl Meyer, 1869.

Goldingay, John. *Old Testament Theology*. 3 vols. Downers Grove, IL: InterVarsity, 2006–2009.

Gollnick, James. *Flesh as Transformation Symbol in the Theology of Anselm of Canterbury: Historical and Transpersonal Perspectives*. Lewiston, NY: Mellen, 1985.

González, Justo. *A History of Christian Thought*. 3 vols. Nashville: Abingdon, 1987.

Gooding, David. *According to Luke: A New Exposition of the Third Gospel*. Grand Rapids: Eerdmans, 1987.

Goodspeed, Edger. *The Epistle to the Hebrews*. New York: Macmillan, 1908.

Gordon, Cyrus. "*Almah* in Isaiah 7:14." *Journal of Bible and Religion* 21 (1953) 106.

Gordon, Robert. *Christ as made known to the Ancient Church: An Exposition of the Revelation of Divine Grace, as unfolded in the Old Testament Scriptures*. 4 vols. Edinburgh: Johnstone and Hunter, 1854.

Gould, Ezra. *A Critical and Exegetical Commentary on the Gospel According to Saint Mark*. New York: Scribner, 1907.

Grabbe, Lester. *Introduction to First Century Judaism: Jewish History and Religion in the Second Temple Period*. New York: T. & T. Clark, 1995.

———. "The Scapegoat Tradition: A Study in Early Jewish Interpretation." *Journal for the Study of Judaism* 18 (1987) 152–67.

Graebner, A. L. *Outline of Doctrinal Theology*. St. Louis: Concordia, 1949.

Grane, Leif. *Die Confessio Augustana: Einführung in die Hauptgedanken der Lutheraischen Reformation*. Göttingen: Vandenhoeck & Rupreacht, 1970.

Grant, Robert. *Gnosticism and Early Christianity*. New York: Columbia University Press, 1959.

———. *Irenaeus of Lyons*. New York: Routledge, 1997.

Grässer, Erich. *An die Hebräer*. 3 vols. Zürich: Neukirchener Verlag, 1990–1997.

Gratsch, Edward J. *Aquinas' Summa: An Introduction and Interpretation*. New York: Alba, 1985.

Green, Gene. *Jude and 2 Peter*. Grand Rapids: Baker Academic, 2008.

Green, Joel. *The Gospel of Luke*. Grand Rapids: Eerdmans, 1997.

———. *1 Peter*. Grand Rapids: Eerdmans, 2007.

Green, Lowell. *The Erlangen School of Theology: Its History, Teaching, and Practice*. Ft. Wayne, IN: Lutheran Legacy, 2010.

———. *How Melanchthon Helped Luther Discover the Gospel: The Doctrine of Justification in the Reformation*. Greenwood, SC: Attic, 1980.

———. "Philosophical Presuppositions in the Reformed-Lutheran Debate on John 6." *Concordia Theological Quarterly* 56 (1992) 17–37.

Green, Oliver. *The Epistle of Paul the Apostle to the Hebrews*. Greenville: Gospel House, 1966.

Green, W. S. "Introduction: Messiah in Judaism: Rethinking the Question." In *Judaism and their Messiahs at the Turn of the Christian Era*, edited by Jacob Neusner, W. S. Green, and E. Fredrichs, 1–14. Cambridge, UK: Cambridge University Press, 1987.

Greggs, Tom. *Barth, Origen, and Universal Salvation: Restoring Particularity*. New York: Oxford University Press, 2009.

Greschat, Martin. *Martin Bucer: A Reformer and His Times*. Translated by Stephen E. Buckwalter. Louisville, KY: Westminster John Knox, 2004.

Griffith-Jones, Robin. *The Gospel According to Paul: The Creative Genius Who Brought Jesus to the World*. San Francsico: HarperOne, 2005.

Grillmeier, Aloys. *Christ in Christian Tradition*. Pt. 2, vol. 2. Louisville, KY: Westminster John Knox, 1995.

Gritsch, Eric. *A History of Lutheranism*. Minneapolis: Fortress, 2002.

———. *Martin: God's Court Jester: Luther in Retrospect*. Philadelphia: Fortress, 1983.

Grollenberg, Lucas. *Paul*. Philadelphia: Westminster, 1978.

Groningen, G. van. *First Century Gnosticism: Its Origin and Motifs*. Leiden: Brill, 1967.

Grosheide, F. W. *Commentary on the First Epistle to the Corinthians*. Grand Rapids: Eerdmans, 1956.

Grudem, Wayne. "He Did Not Descend into Hell: A Plea for Following Scripture Instead of the Apostles' Creed." *Journal of Evangelical Theological Studies* 34 (1991) 103–13.

———. *Systematic Theology: An Introduction to Biblical Doctrine*. Grand Rapids: Zondervan, 1995.

Grundman, Walter. *Das Evangelium nach Markus*. Berlin: Evangelische Verlagsanstalt, 1959.

———. *Das Evangelium nach Matthäus*. Berlin: Evangelische Verlagsanstalt, 1968.

Gundry, Robert H. *Matthew: A Commentary on his Literary and Theological Art*. Grand Rapids: Eerdmans, 1982.

Gunkel, Hermann. *Creation and Chaos in the Primeval Era and the Eschaton: A Religio-Historical Study of Genesis 1 and Revelations 12*. Translated by Peter Machinist. Grand Rapids: Eerdmans, 2006.

———. *Genesis*. Translated by Mark E. Biddle. Macon, GA: Mercer University Press, 1997.

Gunneweg, Antonius. *Biblische Theologie des Alten Testaments: Eine Religionsgeschichte Israels in Biblisch-Theologischer Sicht*. Stuttgart: Kohlhammer, 1993.

Gunton, Colin. *The Promise of Trinitarian Theology*. Edinburgh: T. & T. Clark, 2006.

Guthrie, George. "Hebrews' Use of the Old Testament: Recent Trends in Research." *Currents in Biblical Research* 1 (2003) 271–72.

Gutiérrez, Gustavo. *A Theology of Liberation: History, Politics and Salvation*. Maryknoll, NY: Orbis, 1988.

———. *We Drink from Our Own Wells: The Spiritual Journey of a People*. London: SCM, 1983.

Haar, Stephen. *Simon Magus: The First Gnostic?* New York: Walter de Gruyter, 2003.

Hafemann, Scott. *Paul, Moses, and the History of Israel: The Letter/Spirit Contrast and the Argument from Scripture in 2 Corinthians 3*. Waynesboro, GA: Paternoster, 2005.

Hagen, Kenneth. "Luther on Atonement-Reconfigured." *Concordia Theological Quarterly* 61 (1997) 251–76.

Hägglund, Bengt. *History of Theology*. Translated by Gene Lund. St. Louis: Concordia, 1968.

Hagner, Donald. *Hebrews*. Peabody, MA: Hendrickson, 1990.

———. *Matthew*. 2 vols. Dallas: Word, 1993–1995.

Hahn, Scott. "A Broken Covenant and the Curse of Death: A Study of Hebrews 9:15–22." *Catholic Biblical Quarterly* 66 (2004) 428–29.

———. "Christ, Kingdom, and Creation: Davidic Christology and Ecclesiology in Luke-Acts." *Letter and Spirit* 3 (2007) 113–38.

———. "Covenant in the Old and New Testaments: Some Current Research (1994–2004)." *Currents in Biblical Research* 3 (2005) 263–92.

———. *A Father Who Keeps His Promises: God's Covenant of Love in Scripture*. Ann Arbor, MI: Servant, 1998.

———. *Kinship by Covenant: A Canonical Approach to the Fulfillment of God's Saving Promises*. New Haven, CT: Yale University Press, 2009.

———. *The Lamb's Supper: The Mass as Heaven on Earth*. New York: Doubleday, 1999.

———. "Temple, Sign, and Sacrament: Towards a New Perspective on the Gospel of John." *Letter and Spirit* 4 (2008) 107–43.

Haikola, Lauri. *Gesetz und Evangelium bei Matthias Flacius Illyricus: Eine Untersuchung zur Lutherischen Theologies vor der Konkordienformel*. Lund: Gleerup, 1952.

———. *Studien zu Luther un zum Luthertum*. Uppsala: A. B. Lundquistika Bokhandeln, 1958.

Haldane, Robert. *Commentary on Romans*. Grand Rapids: Kregel, 1988.

Hamann, Henry. "The Righteousness of Faith before God." In *A Contemporary Look at the Formula of Concord*, edited by Robert Preus and Wilbert Rosin, 137–62. St. Louis: Concordia, 1978.

Hamilton, Victor. *The Book of Genesis: Chapters 1–17*. Grand Rapids: Eerdmans, 1990.

Hanratty, Gerald. *Studies in Gnosticism and in the Philosophy of Religion*. Dublin: Four Courts, 1997.

Hanson, K. C. "Blood and Purity in Leviticus and Revelation." *Journal of Religion and Culture* 28 (1993) 215–30.

Hanson, K. C., and Douglas Oakman. *Palestine in the Time of Jesus: Social Structures and Social Conflicts*. Minneapolis: Augsburg Fortress, 1998.

Hanson, Paul. *The Dawn of Apocalyptic: The Historical and Sociological Roots of Jewish Apocalyptic*. Philadelphia: Fortress, 1975.

Hanson, R. P. C. *The Search for the Christian Doctrine of God: The Arian Controversy*. Grand Rapids: Baker Academic, 2006.

Hanson, Tyrell. *Jesus Christ in the Old Testament*. London: SPCK, 1965.

Hare, Douglas. *The Son of Man Tradition*. Minneapolis: Fortress, 1990.

Harnack, Adolf von. *History of Dogma*. 7 vols. Translated by Neil Buchanan. New York: Dover, 1961.

———. *Marcion: Das Evangelium Vom Fremden Gott*. Berlin: Wissenschaftliche Buchgesellschaft, 1960.

———. *Das Wesen des Christentums*. Leipzig: J. C. Hinrichs, 1900.

Harnack, Theodosius. *Luthers Theologie besonderer Beziehung auf seine Versöhnung und Erlösunglehre*. 2 vols. Amsterdam: Rodopi, 1969.

Harold, Guy. *The Gospel of Matthew*. London: Macmillan, 1971.

Harrington, Daniel. *The Gospel of Matthew.* Collegeville, MN: Liturgical, 1991.

Harrison, Everett. "Glory." In *The International Standard Bible Encyclopedia*, edited by Geoffrey Bromiley, 4 vols., 2:477–83. Grand Rapids: Eerdmans, 1982.

Harrison, R. K. *Introduction to the Old Testament*. Peabody, MA: Hendrickson, 2004.

Harrisville, Roy. *Fracture: The Cross as Irreconcilable in the Language and Thought of the Biblical Writers*. Grand Rapids: Eerdmans, 2006.

Harrisville, Roy, and Walter Sundberg. *The Bible in Modern Culture: Baruch Spinoza to Brevard Childs*. Grand Rapids: Eerdmans, 2002.

Harstad, Adolph. *Joshua*. St. Louis: Concordia, 2005.

Hart, David Bentley. *The Beauty of the Infinite: The Aesthetics of Christian Truth*. Grand Rapids: Eerdmans, 2003.

Hartin, Patrick. *James, First Peter, Jude, Second Peter*. Collegeville, MN: Liturgical, 2006.

Hartley, John E. *Leviticus*. Nashville: Thomas Nelson, 1992.

Harvey, Robert, and Philip H. Towner. *2 Peter and Jude*. Downers Grove, IL: InterVarsity, 2009.

Hasel, G. F. "The Meaning of the Animal Rite in Gen. 15." *Journal for the Study of the Old Testament* 19 (1980) 61–78.

Hastings, Rashdall. *The Idea of Atonement in Christian Theology*. London: Macmillan, 1919.

Hauck, Friedrich. *Das Evangelium des Markus*. Leipzig: A. Deichertsche Verlagsbuchhandlung, 1931.

Hawthorne, Gerald F. *Philippians*. Nashville: Thomas Nelson, 2004.

Hefner, Philip. "The Creation." In *The Christian Dogmatics*, edited by Carl Braaten and Robert Jenson, 2 vols., 1:269–362. Philadelphia: Fortress, 1983.

Hegermann, Harald. *Der Brief an die Hebräer*. Berlin: Evangelische Verlagsanstalt, 1988.

Heidt, William. *The Book of the Apocalypse. Introduction and Commentary*. Collegeville, MN: Liturgical, 1962.

Heim, S. Mark. *Saved from Sacrifice: A Theology of the Cross*. Grand Rapids: Eerdmans, 2006.

Heliso, Desta. *Pistis and the Righteous One*. Tübingen: Mohr Siebeck, 2007.

Helm, Paul. *John Calvin's Ideas*. Oxford: Oxford University Press, 2004.

Helm, Robert. "Azazel in Early Jewish Tradition." *Andrews University Seminary Studies* 32 (1994) 217–26.

Helmer, Christine. *The Trinity and Martin Luther: A Study on the Relationship between Genre, Language, and the Trinity in Luther's Works (1523–1546)*. Mainz: P. von Zabern Verlag, 1999.

Hendriksen, William. *Exposition of Philippians*. Grand Rapids: Baker, 1962.

Hengel, Martin. *The Four Gospels and the One Gospel of Jesus Christ: An Investigation of the Collection and Origin of the Canonical Gospels*. Harrisburg, PA: Trinity Press, 2000.

———. *The Son of God: The Origins of Christology and the History Jewish-Hellenistic Religion*. Philadelphia: Fortress, 1976.

Hengstenberg, E. W. *Christology of the Old Testament*. Translated by Theodore Meyer and James Martin. 4 vols. Grand Rapids: Kregel, 1956.

Heppe, Heinrich. *Reformed Dogmatics Set Out and Illustrated From the Sources*. Translated by G. T. Thomson. London: George Allen and Unwin, 1950.

Hérings, Jean. *L' Epitre aux Hebreux*. Neuchatel: Delachaux and Niestle, 1954.

Hess, Richard S., ed. *Israel's Messiah in the Bible and the Dead Sea Scrolls*. Grand Rapids: Baker Academic, 2003.

Hewitt, Thomas. *The Epistle to the Hebrews: An Introduction and Commentary*. London: Tyndale, 1960.

Hillmann, Wilibrord. *Der Brief an die Hebräre*. Düsseldorf: Patmos Verlag, 1965.

Hillyer, Norman. *1 and 2 Peter, Jude*. Peabody, MA: Hendrickson, 1992.

Hindson, E. E. *Isaiah's Immanuel*. Philipsburg, NJ: Presbyterian & Reformed Publishing, 1978.

Hinlicky, Paul. *Paths Not Taken: Fates of Theology from Luther through Leibniz*. Grand Rapids: Eerdmans, 2009.

———. *Luther and the Beloved Community: A Path for Christian Theology after Christendom*. Grand Rapids: Eerdmans, 2010.

Hirsch, Emmanuel. *Die Theologie von Andreas Osiander und ihre Geschtlichen Voraussetzugen*. Göttingen: Vanderhoeck und Ruprecht, 1919.

Hobbs, Herschel. *The Cosmic Drama: An Exposition of the Book of Revelation*. Waco, TX: Word, 1971.

———. *An Exposition of the Gospel of Luke*. Grand Rapids: Baker, 1966.

———. An Exposition of the Gospel of Mark. Grand Rapids: Baker, 1970.

Hodd, J. E. "A Note on Two Points in Aaron's Headdress." *Journal of Theological Studies* 26 (1925) 74–75.

Hodge, Charles. *Commentary on the Epistle to the Romans*. Philadelphia: James Claxton, 1866.

———. *An Exposition of the First Epistle to the Corinthians*. Grand Rapids: Eerdmans, 1956.

———. *Systematic Theology*. 3 vols. New York: Scribner, Armstrong and Co., 1873.

Hoeksema, Herman. *Behold, He Cometh: An Exposition of the Book of Revelation*. Grand Rapids: Reformed Free Publishing, 1969.

———. *Reformed Dogmatics*. Grand Rapids: Reformed Free Publishing, 1966.

Hoenecke, Adolf. *Evangelical Lutheran Dogmatics*. Translated by Joel Fredrich, James L. Langebartels, Paul Prange, and Bill Tackmier. 4 vols. Milwaukee: Northwestern, 1999–2009.

Hofmann, Johannes von. *Biblische Hermeneutik*. Nördlingen: Beck, 1880.

———. *Encyclopädie der Theologie*. Nördlingen: Beck, 1879.

———. *Der Schriftbeweis*. 1st ed., 2 vols. Nördlingen: Beck, 1852–1855.

———. *Der Schriftbeweis*. 2nd ed., 2 vols. Nördlingen: Beck, 1857–1860.

Hogg, Charles. "The Ever-Virgin Mary: Johann Gerhard to the Present." *Lutheran Forum* 39 (2005) 36–39.

Hogg, David. *Anselm of Canterbury: The Beauty of Theology*. Burlington, VT: Ashgate, 2004.

Holl, Karl. *Gesammelte Aufsätze*. 3 vols. Tübingen: Mohr, 1928.

Holladay, Carl. *The First Letter of Paul to the Corinthians*. Austin, TX: Sweet, 1979.

Hooker, Morna. *The Son of Man in Mark: A Study of the Background of the Term "Son of Man" and Its Use in St. Mark's Gospel*. London: SPCK, 1967.

Horne, Mark. *The Victory According to Mark: An Exposition of the Second Gospel*. Moscow, ID: Canon, 2003.

Horrell, David. *The Epistles of Peter and Jude*. Peterborough: Epworth, 1998.

Horton, Fred. *The Melchizedek Tradition: A Critical Examination of the Sources to the Fifth Century A. D. and in the Epistle to the Hebrews*. Cambridge, UK: Cambridge University Press, 2005.

Hoskins, Paul. *Jesus as the Fulfillment of the Temple in the Gospel of John*. Carlisle, UK: Paternoster, 2006.

Houtman, Cornelis. *Exodus: Chapters 20–40*. Vol. 3. Translated by Sierd Woudstra. Leuven: Peeters, 2000.

Huby, Joseph. *Evangile selon Saint Marc: Traduction et Commentaire*. Paris: Beauchesne, 1924.

Hughes, John. "Hebrews 9:15ff. and Galatians 3:15ff.: a Study in Covenant Practice and Procedure." *Novum Testarnentum* 21 (January 1979) 27–96.

Hughes, Philip. *The Book of the Revelation: A Commentary*. Grand Rapids: Eerdmans, 1990.

———. *A Commentary on the Epistle to the Hebrews*. Grand Rapids: Eerdmans, 1977.

Hultgren, Arland. *Paul's Gospel and Mission: The Outlook from his Letter to the Romans*. Philadelphia: Fortress, 1985.

Hummel, Horace. *Ezekiel*. 2 vols. St. Louis: Concordia, 2005–2007.

———. *The Word becoming Flesh: An Introduction to the Origin, Purpose, and Meaning of the Old Testament*. St. Louis: Concordia, 1979.

Hunnius, Nicolaus. *Epitome Credendorum*. Translated by Paul Gottheil. Nuremberg: U. E. Sebald, 1847.

Hunsinger, George. *Disruptive Grace: Studies in the Theology of Karl Barth*. Grand Rapids: Eerdmans, 2000.

———. *How to Read Karl Barth: The Shape of His Theology*. New York: Oxford University Press, 1993.

Hunter, Archibald. *The Gospel according to Saint Mark*. London: SCM, 1948.

Hurst, L. D. *The Epistle to the Hebrews: Its Background of Thought*. Cambridge, UK: Cambridge University Press, 2005.

Hurtado, Larry. *How On Earth Did Jesus Become A God?: Historical Questions About Earliest Devotion to Jesus*. Grand Rapids: Eerdmans, 2005.

———. *Lord Jesus Christ: Devotion to Jesus in Earliest Christianity*. Grand Rapids: Eerdmans, 2005.

Huttar, David. "Glory." In *The Evangelical Dictionary of Biblical Theology*, edited by Walter Elwell, 287–88. Grand Rapids: Baker Academic, 1996.

Hütter, Leonard. *Compendium Locorum Theologicorum Ex Scripturis Sacris et Libro Concordiae: Lateinisch-Deutsch-Englisch*. Translated by Henry Jacobs. 2 vols. Stuttgart-Bad Cannstatt: Friedrich Frommann Verlag, 2006.

Hütter, Reinhard. "(Re–) Forming Freedom: Reflections 'After Veritatis splendor' on Freedom's Fate in Modernity and Protestantism's Antinomian Captivity." *Modern Theology* 17 (2001) 117– 61.

Illyricus, Matthias Flacius. *How to Understand the Sacred Scriptures*. Translated by Wade Johnston. Saginaw, MI: Magdeburg Press, 2011.

Ireneaus. *On Apostolic Preaching*. Translated by John Behr. New York: St. Vladimir Press, 1997.

Jacob, Edmond. *Grundfragen Alttestamentlicher Theologie*. Mainz: Kohlhammer, 1970.

Jansen, John. *Calvin's Doctrine of the Work of Christ*. London: James Clark and Co., 1956.

Janz, Denis. *The Westminster Handbook to Martin Luther*. Louisville, KY: Westminster John Knox, 2010.

Jenson, Robert. *Alpha and Omega: A Study in the Theology of Karl Barth*. New York: Thomas Nelson and Sons, 1963.

———. "The Bible and the Trinity." *Pro Ecclesia* 11 (2002) 329–39.

———. "Can We Have a Story?" *First Things* 11 (March 2000) 16–17.

———. "How the World Lost Its Story." *First Things* 4 (October 1993) 19–24.

———. "Luther's Contemporary Theological Significance." In *The Cambridge Companion to Martin Luther*, edited by Donald K. McKim, 272–88. Cambridge: Cambridge University Press, 2003.

———. *Story and Promise: A Brief Theology of the Gospel about Jesus*. Philadelphia: Fortress, 1973.

———. *Systematic Theology*. 2 vols. New York: Oxford University Press, 1997–1999.

———. "You Wonder Where the Body Went." In *Essays in the Theology of Culture*, 216–24. Grand Rapids: Eerdmans, 1995.

Jeremias, Johannes. *Das Evangelium nach Markus*. Chemnitz: M. Müller, 1928.

———. *The Eucharistic Words of Jesus*. London: SCM, 1966.

———. *Schlüssel zur Theologie des Apostels Paulus*. Stuttgart: Calwer Verlag, 1971.

Jerome. *Commentary on Matthew*. Translated by Thomas Scheck. Washington, DC: Catholic University of America Press, 2008.

Jewett, Robert. *Romans: A Commentary*. Minneapolis: Fortress, 2007.

Johnson, Elizabeth. *The Church Women Want: Catholic Women in Dialogue*. New York: Continuum, 2002.

———. *Consider Jesus: Waves of Renewal in Christology*. New York: Crossroad, 1990.

———. *Friends of God and Prophets: A Feminist Theological Reading of the Communion of Saints*. New York: Continuum, 1998.

———. *Quest for the Living God: Mapping Frontiers in the Theology of God*. New York: Continuum, 2007.

———. *She Who Is: The Mystery of God in Feminist Theological Discourse*. New York: Crossroad, 1992.

———. *Truly Our Sister: A Theology of Mary in the Communion of Saints*. New York: Continuum, 2003.

———. *Who Do You Say that I Am?: Introducing Contemporary Christology*. Pietermaritzburg, South Africa: Cluster, 1997.

———. *Women, Earth, and Creator Spirit*. New York: Paulist, 1993.

Johnson, Luke Timothy. *The Gospel of Luke*. Collegeville, MN: Liturgical, 1991.

Johnson, Robert. *The Letter of Paul to the Galatians*. Austin, TX: Sweet, 1969.

Johnson, Sherman. *A Commentary on the Gospel According to Saint Mark*. New York: Harper, 1960.

Jonas, Hans. *The Gnostic Religion: The Message of the Alien God and the Beginnings of Christianity*. Boston: Beacon, 1963.

Jones, Paul. *The Humanity of Christ: Christology in Karl Barth's Church Dogmatics*. Edinburgh: T. & T. Clark, 2008.

Josephus. *The Works of Josephus*. Translated by William Whiston. Peabody, MA: Hendrickson, 1995.

Juel, Donald H. *Mark*. Minneapolis: Augsburg Fortress, 1990.

Jüngel, Eberhard. *Barth-Studien*. Zürich-Köln: Benziger Verlag, 1982.

———. *Entsprechungen: Gott-Wahrheit-Mensch*. Tübingen: Mohr Siebeck, 2002.

———. *God as the Mystery of the World: On the Foundation of the Theology of the Crucified One in the Dispute between Theism and Atheism*. Translated by Darrell Guder. Grand Rapids: Eerdmans, 1983.

———. *Justification: The Heart of the Christian Faith: A Theological Study with an Ecumenical Purpose*. Translated by Jeffrey Cayzer. New York: T. & T. Clark, 2001.

Juntunen, Sammeli. "Christ." In *Engaging Luther: A (New) Theological Assessment*, edited by Olli-Pekka Vainio, 59–79. Eugene, OR: Cascade, 2011.

Just, Arthur. *Heaven on Earth: The Gifts of Christ in the Divine Service.* St. Louis: Concordia, 2008.

———. *Luke.* 2 vols. St. Louis: Concordia, 1996–1997.

———. *The Ongoing Feast.* Collegeville, **MN: Liturgical, 1993.**

Kähler, Martin. *So-Called Historical Jesus and the Historic-Biblical Christ.* Philadelphia: Fortress, 1988.

Kahnis, Karl. *Die Lutherische Dogmatik, Historisch-Genetisch Dargestellt.* 3 vols. Leipzig: Dörffling und Franke, 1861–1868.

Kaiser, Denis. *The Doctrine of the Atonement According to Peter Lombard: A Literary and Historical Analysis.* Norderstedt: GRIN Verlag, 2008.

Kant, Immanuel. *Critique of Pure Reason.* Translated by Norman Kemp Smith. New York: St. Martin's Press, 1958.

Kantzer, Kenneth. "The Christology of Karl Barth." *Bulletin of Evangelical Theology* 1 (1958) 25–28.

Karlberg, Mark. "The Mosaic Covenant and the Concept of Work in Reformed Hermeneutics: A Historical-Critical Analysis with Particular Attention to Early Covenant Eschatology." PhD diss., Westminster Theological Seminary, 1980.

———. "Reformed Interpretation of the Mosaic Covenant." *Westminster Theological Journal* 43 (1980) 1–57.

Käsemann, Ernst. *Commentary on Romans.* Translated by Geoffrey W. Bromily. Grand Rapids: Eerdmans, 1980.

Kass, Leon. *The Beginning of Wisdom: Reading Genesis.* New York: Free Press, 2003.

Kearney, P. J. "Liturgy and Creation: The P Redaction of Exodus 25–40." *Zeitschrift fur Alttestamentliche Zeitscrift* 89 (1977) 375–87.

Keegan, Terence. *A Commentary on the Gospel of Mark.* New York: Paulist, 1981.

Keener, Craig. *A Commentary on the Gospel of Matthew.* Grand Rapids: Eerdmans, 1999.

Keil, Carl. *Biblical Commentary on Daniel.* Grand Rapids: Eerdmans, 1955.

———. *Bibelsk Commentar uber Genesis.* Christiania: Cammermeyer, 1870.

———. *Commentar über den Brief an die Hebräer.* Leipzig: Dörffling und Franke, 1885.

———. *Commentar über das Evangelium des Johannes.* Leipzig: Dörffling und Franke, 1881.

———. *Commentar über die Evangelien des Markus und Lukas.* Leipzig: Dörffling und Franke, 1879.

———. *Commentar über das Evangelium des Matthäus.* Leipzig: Dörffling und Franke, 1877.

———. *Commentar über die Briefe des Petrus und Judas.* Leipzig: Dörffling und Franke, 1883.

Keil, Carl, and Franz Delitzsch. *The Pentateuch.* Translated by James Martin. Vol. 2. Grand Rapids: Eerdmans, 1956.

Keller, Werner. *The Bible as History.* New York: Bantam, 1983.

Kelly, J. N. D. *A Commentary on the Epistles of Peter and Jude.* New York: Harper & Row, 1969.

———. *Early Christian Doctrines.* New York: Harper and Brothers, 1958.

Kelly, Thomas M. *Theology at the Void: The Retrieval of Experience.* Notre Dame: Notre Dame University Press, 2002.

Kent, Homer. *The Epistle to the Hebrews: A Commentary.* Grand Rapids: Baker, 1972.

Kerr, Alan. *The Temple of Jesus' Body: The Temple Theme in the Gospel of John.* Sheffield, UK: Sheffield Academic, 2002.

Ketter, Peter. *Die Apokalypse: Übers und Erklärt.* Freiburg: Herder, 1953.

Kilcrease, Jack. "Creation's Praise: A Short Liturgical Reading of Genesis 1–2 and the Book of Revelation." *Pro Ecclesia* 21 (Summer 2012) 314–25.

———. "Kenosis and Vocation: Christ as the Author and Exemplar of Christian Freedom." *Logia* 19, no. 4 (Reformation, 2010) 21–34.

Kilgallen, John. *A Brief Commentary on the Gospel of Mark.* New York: Paulist, 1989.

King, C. W. *The Gnostics and Their Remains, Ancient and Mediaeval.* Minneapolis: Wizards Bookshelf, 1973.

Kitchen, K. A. *On the Reliability of the Old Testament.* Grand Rapids: Eerdmans, 2006.

Kittel, Rudolf. *Handbuch der Alttestamentlichen Theologie.* Leipzig: S. Hirzel, 1895.

Kittelson, James. *Luther the Reformer: The Story of the Man and His Career.* Minneapolis: Augsburg, 1986.

Kiuchi, Nobuyoshi. *Leviticus.* Downers Grove, IL: InterVarsity, 2007.

———. *The Purification Offering in the Priestly Literature: Its Meaning and Function.* Sheffield, UK: JSOT, 1987.

Klann, Richard. "Original Sin," in *A Contemporary Look at the Formula of Concord,* ed. Robert Preus and Wilbert Rosin, 103–21. St. Louis: Concordia Publishing, 1978.

Klein, Hans. *Das Lukasevangelium: Übersetzt und Erklärt*. Göttingen: Vandenhoeck & Ruprecht, 2006.

Klein, R. W., and T. Krüger. *1 Chronicles: A Commentary*. Minneapolis: Fortress, 2006.

Kleinig, John. *Grace Upon Grace: Spirituality for Today*. St. Louis: Concordia, 2008.

———. *Leviticus*. St. Louis: Concordia, 2003.

Knox, Ronald. *Saint Paul's Gospel*. New York: Sheed and Ward, 1953.

Koehler, Edward. *A Summary of Christian Doctrine: A Popular Presentation of the Teachings of the Bible*. St. Louis: Concordia, 2006.

Koester, Craig R. *Hebrews*. New Haven: Yale University Press, 2001.

———. *Symbolism in the Fourth Gospel: Meaning, Mystery, Community*. Minneapolis: Fortress, 1995.

Kolb, Robert. *Bound Choice, Election, and the Wittenberg Theological Method: From Martin Luther to the Formula of Concord*. Grand Rapids: Eerdmans, 2005.

———. "Historical Background of the Formula of Concord." In *A Contemporary Look at the Formula of Concord*, edited by Robert Preus and Wilbert Rosin, 12–87. St. Louis: Concordia, 1978.

———. *Martin Luther: Confessor of the Faith*. Oxford: Oxford University Press, 2009.

Kolb, Robert, and Charles Arand. *The Genius of Luther's Theology: A Wittenberg Way of Thinking for the Contemporary Church*. Grand Rapids: Eerdmans, 2008.

Koppperi, Kari. "Theology of the Cross." In *Engaging Luther: A (New) Theological Assessment*, edited by Olli-Pekka Vainio, 155–72. Eugene, OR: Cascade, 2011.

Kordić, Ivan. "Croatian Philosophers IV: Matija Vlaèiæ Ilirik—Mathias Flacius Illyricus." *Prolegomena* 4 (2005) 219–33.

Köstlin, Julius. *The Theology of Luther in Its Historical Development and Inner Harmony*. Translated by Charles Hay. 2 vols. Philadelphia: Lutheran Publication Society, 1897.

Kraftchick, Steven. *Jude, 2 Peter*. Nashville: Abingdon, 2002.

Kraus, Hans-Joachim. *Psalms 1–59: A Commentary*. Translated by Hilton C. Oswald. Minneapolis: Augsburg, 1988.

———. *Psalms 60–150: A Commentary*. Translated by Hilton C. Oswald. Minneapolis: Augsburg, 1989.

Krauth, Charles Porterfield. *The Conservative Reformation and Its Theology*. St. Louis: Concordia, 2007.

Küng, Hans. *Great Christian Thinkers: Paul, Origen, Augustine, Aquinas, Luther, Schleiermacher, Barth*. London: Continuum, 1994.

Kurtz, Johann. *Der brief an die Hebräer*. Mitau: Aug. Neumann's Verlag, 1869.

———. *Der Mosaische Opfer ein Beitrag zur Symbolik des Mosaischen Cultus*. Mitau: Friedrich Lucas, 1842.

Kuss, Otto. *Der Brief an die Hebräer*. Regensburg: F. Pustet, 1966.

———. *Paulus: Die Rolle des Apostels in der theologischen Entwicklung der Urkirche*. Regensburg: F. Pustet, 1971.

Lacarriere, Jacques. *The Gnostics*. Translated by Nina Rootes. London: Peter Owen, 1977.

Ladd, George. *A Commentary on the Revelation of John*. Grand Rapids: Eerdmans, 1972.

Lagrange, Marie-Joseph. *Evangile selon Saint Jean*. Paris: J. Gabalda, 1936.

———. *Evangile selon Saint Luc*. Paris: J. Gabalda, 1948.

———. *Evangile selon Saint Marc*. Paris: J. Gabalda, 1911.

———. *Evangile selon Saint Matthieu*. Paris: J. Gabalda, 1948.

Lamarche, Paul. *Evangile de Marc: Commentaire*. Paris: J. Gabalda, 1996.

Laubach, Fritz. *Der Brief an die Hebräer*. Wuppertal: R. Brockhaus, 1967.

LaVerdiere, Eugene. *The Beginning of the Gospel: Introducing the Gospel according to Mark*. 2 vols. Collegeville, MN: Liturgical, 1999.

———. *Luke*. Wilmington, DE: Michael Glazier, 1980.

Lawrenz, Carl. "On Justification, Osiander's Doctrine of the Indwelling of Christ." In *No Other Gospel: Essays in Commemoration of the 400th Anniversay of the Formula of Concord, 1580–1980*, edited by Arnold Koelpin, 149–74. Milwaukee: Northwestern, 1980.

Lawson, John. *The Biblical Theology of Saint Irenaeus*. London: Epworth, 1948.

Leaney, A. R. C. *A Commentary on the Gospel according to Saint Luke*. New York: Harper, 1958.

Lehmann, Karl, and Horst Georg Pöhlmann. "Gott, Jesus Christus, Wiederkunft Christi." In *Confessio Augustana Bekenntnis Des Einen Glaubens: Gemeinsame Untersuchung Lutherischer und Katholischer Theologen*, 57–63. Frankfurt: Verlag Otto Lembeck, 1980.

Leithart, Peter. *Deep Comedy: Trinity, Tragedy and Hope in Western Literature*. Moscow, ID: Canon, 2006.

———. *1 and 2 Kings*. Grand Rapids: Brazos, 2006.

———. *The Four: A Survey of the Gospels*. Moscow, ID: Canon, 2010.

———. *A House for My Name: A Survey of the Old Testament*. Moscow, ID: Canon, 2000.

———. *A Son to Me: An Exposition of 1 and 2 Samuel*. Moscow, ID: Canon, 2003.

Lems, Shane. "The Covenant of Works in Dutch Reformed Orthodoxy." *Outlook* 57 (2007) 13–18.

Lenowitz, Harris. *The Jewish Messiahs: From the Galilee to Crown Heights*. New York: Oxford University Press, 1998.

Lenski, R. C. H. *The Interpretation of Matthew's Gospel*. Peabody, MA: Hendrickson, 1998.

———. *The Interpretation of Paul's Epistle to the Romans*. Peabody, MA: Hendrickson, 1998.

———. *The Interpretation of St. Luke's Gospel*. Peabody, MA: Hendrickson, 1998.

———. *The Interpretation of St. Mark's Gospel*. Peabody, MA: Hendrickson, 1998.

———. *The Interpretation of St. Paul's Epistles to the Galatians, to the Ephesians, and to the Philippians*. Peabody, MA: Hendrickson, 1998.

———. *The Interpretation of St. Paul's Epistles to the Colossians, to the Thessalonians, to Timothy, to Titus, and to Philemon*. Peabody, MA: Hendrickson, 1998.

———. *The Interpretation of St. Paul's First and Second Epistles to the Corinthians*. Peabody, MA: Hendrickson, 1998.

———. *The Interpretation of the Epistle to the Hebrews and the Epistle of James*. Peabody, MA: Hendrickson, 1998.

———. *The Interpretation of the Epistles of St. Peter, St. John, and St. Jude*. Peabody, MA: Hendrickson, 1998.

Leupold, Herbert. *Exposition of Daniel*. Minneapolis: Augsburg, 1961.

———. *Exposition of Genesis*. 2 vols. Grand Rapids: Baker, 1958–1959.

———. *Exposition of Isaiah*. 2 vols. Grand Rapids: Baker, 1968–1971.

———. *Exposition of the Psalms*. Columbus, OH: Wartberg, 1959.

———. *Exposition of Zechariah*. Grand Rapids: Baker, 1971.

Levenson, Jon. *Creation and the Persistence of Evil: The Jewish Drama of Divine Omnipotence*. San Francisco: Harper & Row, 1988.

———. *The Death and Resurrection of the Beloved Son: The Transformation of Child Sacrifice in Judaism and Christianity*. New Haven, CT: Yale University Press, 1993.

Levine, Baruch. *Leviticus*. New York: Jewish Publication Society, 1989.

Lienhard, Marc. *Luther: Witness to Jesus Christ: Stages and Themes of the Reformer's Christology*. Translated by Edwin H. Robertson. Minneapolis: Fortress, 1982.

Lieu, Judith. *The Gospel of Luke*. London: Epworth, 1997.

Lightfoot, J. B. *The Epistle of St. Paul to the Galatians*. Grand Rapids: Zondervan, 1969.

———. *St. Paul's Epistle to the Philippians*. Peabody, MA: Hendrikson's, 1987.

Lilje, Hanns. *Die Petrusbriefe und der Judasbrief*. Kassel: Oncken Verlag, 1954.

Lillback, Peter. "Ursinus' Development of the Covenant of Creation: A Debt to Melanchthon or Calvin?" *Westminster Theological Journal* 43 (1981) 247–88.

Lincoln, Andrew T. *The Gospel according to Saint John*. Peabody, MA: Hendrickson, 2005.

Lindbeck, George. *The Nature of Doctrine: Religion and Theology in a Post-Liberal Age*. Philadelphia: Westminster, 1984.

Lindberg, Conrad Emil. *Christian Dogmatics and Notes on the History of Dogma*. Translated by C. E. Hoffsten. Rock Island, IL: Augustana Book Concern, 1922.

Lindemann, Andreas. *Paulus, Apostel und Lehrer der Kirche: Studien zu Paulus und zu frühen Paulusverständnis*. Tübingen: Mohr Siebeck, 1999.

Little, C. H. *Lutheran Confessional Theology: A Presentation of the Doctrines of the Augsburg Confession and the Formula of Concord*. St. Louis: Concordia, 1943.

Locher, Gottfried. *Zwingli's Thought: New Perspectives*. Leiden: Brill, 1981.

Lockwood, Gregory. *1 Corinthians*. St. Louis: Concordia Publishing, 2000.

Loenertz, R. J. *The Apocalypse of Saint John*. London: Catholic Book Club, 1948.

Loewenich, Walther von. *Luthers Theologia Crucis*. München: Kaiser Verlag, 1954.

Logan, Alastair. *Gnostic Truth and Christian Heresy: A Study in the History of Gnosticism*. Peabody: Hendrickson, 1996.

———. *The Gnostics: Identifying an Early Christian Cult*. London: T. & T. Clark, 2006.

Lohmeyer, Ernst. *Das Evangelium des Markus: Übersetzt und Erklärt*. Göttingen: Vandenhoeck & Ruprecht, 1951.

Löhr, Max. *Alttestamentliche Religions Geschichte*. Leipzig: G. J. Göschen, 1906.

Lohse, Bernhard. *Martin Luther's Theology: Its Historical and Systematic Development*. Translated by Roy Harrisville. Minneapolis: Fortress, 1999.

Lombard, Peter. *The Sentences*. Translated by Giulio Silano. 4 vols. Toronto: Pontifical Institute of Medieval Studies, 2007–2010.

Long, Thomas. *Hebrews*. Louisville, KY: John Knox Westminster, 1997.

Longenecker, Richard. *Studies in Paul, Exegetical and Theological*. Sheffield, UK: Sheffield Phoenix Press, 2004.

———. *Studies on Hermeneutics, Christology and Discipleship*. Sheffield, UK: Sheffield Phoenix Press, 2004.

Louth, Andrew. *Maximus the Confessor*. New York: Routledge, 1996.

———. *St. John Damascene: Tradition and Originality in Byzantine Theology*. New York: Oxford University Press, 2002.

Lubac, Henri de. *Medieval Exegesis: The Four Senses of Scripture*. Translated by Marc Sebanc. 3 vols. Grand Rapids: Eerdmans, 1999–2009.

Lücke, Friedrich. *Commentar Über das Evangelium des Johannes*. 2 vols. Bonn: Eduard Weber, 1833–1834.

Lupieri, Edmondo. *A Commentary on the Apocalypse of John*. Translated by Maria Poggi Johnson and Adam Kamesar. Grand Rapids: Eerdmans, 2006.

Luthardt, Christoph. *Das Evangelium nach Johannes und die Apostelgeschichte*. München: Beck, 1894.

———. *Kompendium der Dogmatik*. Leipzig: Döffling und Franke, 1893.

Luther, Martin. *American Edition of Luther's Works*. Edited by Jaroslav Pelikan and Helmut Lehmann. 55 vols. Philadelphia and St. Louis: Fortress Press and Concordia Publishing, 1957–1986.

———. *D. Martin Luthers Werke: Kritische Gesammtausgabe*. 120 vols. Weimar: Hermann Böhlau and H. Böhlaus Nachfolg, 1883–2009.

———. "Disputation on the Divinity and Humanity of Christ, February 27, 1540." Translated by Christopher B. Brown. In WA 39.2: 92–121. Online: http://www.iclnet.org/pub/resources/text/wittenberg/luther/luther-divinity.txt.

———. "Easter Sunday Afternoon—March 28, 1529: The Resurrection of Christ as Proclamation." In *The 1529 Holy Week and Easter Sermons of Dr. Martin Luther,* translated by Irving Sandberg, 129–137. St. Louis: Concordia Academic, 1999.

———. "Martin Luther's Torgau Sermon on Christ's Descent into Hell and Resurrection." In *Sources and Contexts of the Book of Concord*, translated by Robert Kolb, edited by Robert Kolb and James Nestingen, 245–55. Minneapolis: Augsburg Fortress, 2001.

———. *Only the Decalogue is Eternal: Martin Luther's Complete Antinomian Theses and Disputations*. Translated and edited by Holger Sontag. Minneapolis: Lutheran Press, 2008.

Luttikhuizen, Gerard. *Gnostic Revisions of Genesis Stories and Early Jesus Traditions*. Leiden: Brill, 2006.

Luz, Ulrich. *Das Evangelium nach Matthäus*. 4 vols. Zürich: Neukirchener Verlag, 1985–2002.

Maccoby, H. Z. "Jesus and Barabbas." *New Testament Studies* 16 (1969) 55–60.

MacIntyre, Alister. *Whose Justice? Which Rationality?* Notre Dame: Notre Dame University Press, 1989.

Mahan, Brian, and L. Dale Richesin. *The Challenge of Liberation Theology: A First World Response*. Maryknoll, NY: Orbis Books, 1981.

Maher, Michael. *Genesis*. Wilmington, DE: Michael Glazier, 1982.

Maier, Paul. *In the Fullness of Time: A Historian Looks at Christmas, Easter, and the Early Church*. Grand Rapids: Kregel, 1997.

Maimela, Simon. "The Atonement in the Context of Liberation Theology." *International Review of Mission* 75 (1986) 261–69.

Mangina, Joseph. *Karl Barth: Theologian of Christian Witness*. Louisville, KY: Westminster John Knox Press, 2004.

Mannermaa, Tuomo. *Christ Present in Faith: Luther's View of Justification*. Translated and edited by Kirsi Sjerna. Minneapolis: Fortress Press, 2005.

Manschreck, Clyde. *Melanchthon: The Quiet Reformer*. New York: Abingdon, 1958.

Mansel, Henry Longueville. *The Gnostic Heresies of the First and Second Centuries*. London: J. Murray, 1875.

Manson, William. *The Gospel of Luke*. London: Hodder & Stoughton, 1948.

Manton, Thomas. *An Exposition on the Epistle of Jude*. London: Banner of Truth Trust, 1962.

Maritain, Jacques. *Integral Humanism*. Translated by J. Evans. Notre Dame: University of Notre Dame Press, 1968.

Marius, Richard. *Martin Luther: The Christian between God and Death*. Cambridge, MA: Harvard University Press, 1999.

Marjanen, Antti, ed. *Was there a Gnostic Religion?* Göttingen: Vandenhoeck & Ruprecht, 2005.

Marquart, Kurt. *Anatomy of an Explosion: Missouri in Lutheran Perspective*. Ft. Wayne, IN: Concordia Theological Seminary Press, 1977.

———. *The Church and Her Fellowship, Ministry, and Governance*. Confessional Lutheran Dogmatics. Vol. 9. St. Louis: Luther Academy, 1990.

———. "Luther and Theosis." *Concordia Theological Quarterly* 64 (2000) 183–205.

Marshall, I. Howard. *Luke: Theologian and Historian*. Downer's Grove, IL: InterVarsity, 1998.

Marshall, J. L. "Melchizedek in Hebrews, Philo, and Justin Martyr." *Studia Evangelica* 7 (1982) 339–42.

Martens, Elmer A. *God's Design: A Focus on Old Testament Theology*. Grand Rapids: Baker, 1994.

Martensen, H. *Christian Dogmatics: A Compendium of the Doctrines of Christianity*. Translated by William Urwick. Edinburgh: T. & T. Clark, 1866.

Martin, G. George. *The Gospel according to Mark: Meaning and Message*. Chicago: Loyola, 2005.

Martin, Ralph. *Reconciliation: A Study of Paul's Theology*. Altanta: John Knox, 1981.

Martyn, J. Louis. *Theological Issues in the Letters of Paul*. Nashville: Abingdon, 1997.

Mason, Eric. *You are a Priest Forever: Second Temple Jewish Messianism and the Priestly Christology of the Epistle to the Hebrews*. Leiden: Brill, 2008.

Mattes, Mark. "Beyond the Impasse: Reexamining the Third Use of the Law." *Concordia Theological Quarterly* 69, nos. 3–4 (2005) 271–91.

———. *The Role of Justification in Contemporary Theology*. Grand Rapids: Eerdmans, 2004.

Mattox, Mickey. *"Defender of the Holy Matriarchs": Luther's Interpretation of the Women of Genesis in the Eranationes of Genesin 1535–1545*. Leiden: Brill, 2003.

Maurer, Wilhelm. *Kirche und Geschichte*. 2 vols. Göttingen: Vanderhoeck & Ruprecht, 1970.

McBride, S. Dean. "The Deuteronomic Name Theology." PhD diss., Harvard University, 2008.

McCarthy, D. J. *Old Testament Covenant: A Survey of Current Opinions*. Richmond: John Knox, 1972.

———. *Treaty and Covenant*. Rome: Pontifical Biblical Institute, 1963.

McConnell, John. *The Epistle to the Hebrews: Introduction and Commentary*. Collegeville, MN: Liturgical, 1960.

McConville, J. Gordon. "God's Name and God's Glory." *Tyndale Bulletin* 30 (1979) 149–63.

McDonald, William. *The Epistle to the Hebrews: From Ritual to Reality*. Neptun ., NJ: Loizeaux Bros., 1971.

McDonnell, Kilian. *John Calvin: the Church, and the Eucharist*. Princeton, NJ: Princeton University Press, 1967.

McFadyen, John. *The Epistle to the Corinthians*. London: Hodder & Stoughton, 1911.

McFague, Sallie. *The Body of God: An Ecological Theology*. Minneapolis: Fortress, 1993.

———. *Life Abundant: Rethinking Theology and Economy for a Planet in Peril* Minneapolis: Augsburg Fortress, 2000.

———. *Metaphorical Theology: Models of God in Religious Language*. Philadelphia: Fortress, 1982.

———. *Models of God: Theology for an Ecological, Nuclear Age*. Philadelphia: Fortress, 1987.

———. *A New Climate for Theology: God, the World and Global Warming*. Minneapolis: Augsburg Fortress, 2008.

———. *Speaking in Parables: A Study in Metaphor and Theology*. Philadelphia: Fortress, 1975.

———. *Super, Natural Christians: How We Should Love Nature*. London: SCM, 1997.

McGiffert, Michael. "From Moses to Adam: The Making of the Covenant of Works." *Sixteenth Century Journal* 19 (1988) 131–55.

McGrath, Alister. *Iustitia Dei: A History of the Christian Doctrine of Justification*. Cambridge, UK: Cambridge University Press, 1998.

———. *Luther's Theology of the Cross: Martin Luther's Theological Breakthrough*. New York: Basil Blackwell, 1985.

———. *A Scientific Theology*. 3 vols. Grand Rapids: Eerdmans, 2002–2003.

McGuckin, John Anthony. *St. Cyril of Alexandria: The Christological Controversy: Its History, Theology, and Texts*. Crestwood, NY: St. Vladimir's Seminary Press, 2000.

———. *The Westminster Handbook to Origen*. Louisville, KY: Westminster John Knox, 2004.

McKenzie, S. L. *Covenant*. St. Louis: Chalice, 2000.

McKnight, Scott. *1 Peter*. Grand Rapids: Zondervan, 1996.

McLean, Bradley. "On the Revision of Scapegoat Terminology." *Numen* 37 (1990) 168–73.

McNamara, Martin. "Melchizedek: Gen 14,17–20 in the Targums, in Rabbinic and Early Christian Literature." *Biblica* 81 (2000) 1–31.

Meier, John P. *A Marginal Jew, Rethinking the Historical Jesus: Roots of the Problem and the Person*. Vol. 1. New York: Doubleday, 1991.

———. *Matthew*. Wilmington: Michael Glazier, 1980.

Meinhold, Peter. *Die Genesisvorlesung Luthers und ihre Herausgeber*. Stuttgart: W. Kohlhammer, 1936.

Melanchthon, Philipp. *Melanchthon on Christian Doctrine: Loci Communes 1555*. Translated by Clyde L. Manschreck. New York: Oxford University Press, 1965.

Mendenhall, George. *Law and Covenant in Israel and the Ancient Near East*. Pittsburgh: Biblical Colloquium, 1955.

Menzies, Allan. *The Earliest Gospel: A Historical Study of the Gospel according to Mark*. New York: Macmillan, 1901.

Metzger, Bruce. *A Textual Commentary on the Greek New Testament*. London: United Bible Societies, 1971.

Meyendorff, John. *Christ in Eastern Christian Thought*. Washington, DC: Corpus, 1969.

Meyer, Heinrich. *Critical and Exegetical Handbook to the Gospel of John*. Translated by William Urwick. New York: Funk and Wagnalls, 1884.

Meyer, Marvin. *The Gnostic Discoveries: The Impact of the Nag Hammadi Library*. San Francisco: HarperSanFrancisco, 2005.

Michael, Johannes. *Am Tisch der Sünder: das Evangelium nach Markus*. Recklinghausen: Paulus Verlag, 1960.

Michaelis, Wilhelm. *Das Evangelium nach Matthäus*. Zürich: Zwingli Verlag, 1948.

Michaels, J. Ramsey "The Centurion's Confession and the Spear's Thrust." *Catholic Biblical Quarterly* 29 (1967) 102–9.

———. *I Peter*. Waco, TX: Word, 1988.

Michel, Otto. *Der Brief an die Hebräer, Übersetzt und Erklärt*. Göttingen, Vandenhoeck & Ruprecht, 1966.

Milbank, John. *Theology and Social Theory: Beyond Secular Reason*. Malden, MA: Blackwell, 2006.

Milgrom, Jacob. *Leviticus 1–16: A New Translation and Commentary*. New York: Doubleday, 1991.

Miller, Donald. *The Gospel according to Luke*. Richmond: John Knox, 1959.

Miller, Robert, ed. *The Complete Gospels*. San Francisco: Harper Collins, 1994.

Milligan, William. *The Book of Revelation*. New York: George H. Doran, 1889.

Minns, Denis. *Irenaeus*. Washington, DC: Georgetown University Press, 1994.

Mitchell, Christopher. *Song of Songs*. St. Louis: Concordia, 2003.

Mlakushyil, George. *The Christocentric Literary Structure of the Fourth Gospel*. Rome: Pontifical Biblical Institute, 1987.

Modalsli, Ole. "Die Heidelberger Disputation im Lichte der evangelischen Neuentdeckung Luthers." *Lutherjahrbuch* 47 (1980) 33–39.

Moe, Olaf. *The Apostle Paul*. 2 vols. Translated by L. A. Vigness. Minneapolis: Augsburg, 1950–1954.

Moffatt, James. *A Critical and Exegetical Commentary on the Epistle to the Hebrews*. New York: Scribner, 1924.

Moll, Carl. *The Epistle to the Hebrews*. New York: Scribner, 1896.

Möller, Hans. *Biblische Theologie des Alten Testaments*. Zwickau: J. Hermann, 1937.

Moltmann, Jürgen. *The Crucified God: The Cross of Christ as the Foundation and Criticism of Christian Theology*. Translated by R. A. Wilson and John Bowden. Minneapolis: Fortress, 1993.

Moms, Leon. "The Use of ilaskesthai etc. in Biblical Greek." *Expository Times* 62 (1951) 227–33.

Montefiore, Hugh. *A Commentary on the Epistle to the Hebrews*. New York: Harper & Row, 1964.

Moo, Douglas. *The Epistle to the Romans*. Grand Rapids: Erdmans, 1996.

———. *2 Peter and Jude*. Grand Rapids: Zondervan, 1996.

Mopsuestia, Theodore of. *Commentary on the Gospel of John*. Translated by Marco Conti. Downers Grove, IL: InterVarsity Press Academic, 2010.

Morgan, G. Campbell. *The Gospel according to Luke*. New York: Revell, 1931.

———. *The Gospel according to Mark*. Chicago: Fleming H. Revell, 1927.

Morris, Leon. "Propiatiate; Propiation." In *The International Standard Bible Encyclopedia*, 3:1004–5. Grand Rapids: Eerdmans, 1986.

Moses, Stuart, and Ebenezer Henderson. *A Commentary on the Epistle to the Hebrews*. London: William Tegg, 1864.

Motyer, S. "The Rendering of the Veil: A Markan Pentecost." *New Testament Studies* 33 (1987) 155–57.

Moule, David. *The Gospel According to Mark*. Cambridge, UK: Cambridge University Press, 1965.

Mounce, Robert. *The Book of Revelation*. Grand Rapids: Eerdmans, 1998.

Mowinckel, Sigmund. *He That Cometh*. Oxford: Blackwell, 1956.

———. *The Psalms in Israel's Worship*. Translated by D. R. Ap-Thomas. Grand Rapids: Eerdmans, 2004.

Mueller, David. *Foundation of Karl Barth's Doctrine of Reconciliation: Jesus Christ Crucified and Risen*. Lewiston, NY: Edwin Mellen Press, 1990.

———. *Karl Barth*. Waco, TX: Word, 1972.

Mueller, John Theodore. *Christian Dogmatics*. St. Louis: Concordia, 2003.

Mühlen, Karl-Heinz zur. "Luther's Kritik am scholastischen Aristotelismus in der 25. These der Heidelberger Disputation von 1518." In *Reformatorisches Profil: Studien zum Weg Martin Luthers und der Reformation*, edited by Johannes Brosseder and Athina Lexutt, 40–65. Göttingen: Vandernhoeck & Ruprecht, 1995.

Müller, Paul-Gerhard. *Lukas-Evangelium*. Stuttgart: Verlag Katholisches Bibelwerk, 1984.

Muller, Richard. *Christ and the Decree: Christology and Predestination in the Reformed Theology from Calvin to Perkins*. Grand Rapids: Baker Academic, 2008.

———. "The Covenant of Works and the Stability of Divine Law in Seventeenth-Century Reformed Orthodoxy: A Study in the Theology of Herman Witsius and Wilhelmus á Brakel." In *After Calvin: Studies in the Development of a Theological Tradition*, 175–89. Oxford: Oxford University Press, 2003.

———. *Post-Reformation Reformed Dogmatics: The Rise and Development of Reformed Orthodoxy ca. 1520 to ca. 1725*. 4 vols. Grand Rapids: Baker Academic, 2003.

Müller-Jurgens, Wilhelm. *Apokalypse: Die Geheime Offenbarung des Johannes: Textgestaltung und Kommentar*. Nürnberg: Glock und Lutz Verlag, 1962.

Murphy, Francesca Aran. *God is Not a Story: Realism Revisited*. New York: Oxford University Press, 2007.

Murphy, Fredrick. *Fallen is Babylon: The Revelation of John*. Harrisburg, PA: Trinity Press, 1998.

Murray, John. *The Epistle to the Romans*. Grand Rapids: Eerdmans, 1997.

Murray, Scott. "The Concept of *diatheke* in the Letter to the Hebrews." *Concordia Theological Quarterly* 66 (2002) 41–60.

Neil, William. *The Epistle to the Hebrews: Introduction and Commentary*. London: SCM, 1955.

Neill, J. C. *Who Did Jesus Think He Was?* Leiden: Brill, 1995.

Nestingen, James. "The End of the End: The Role of Apocalyptic in the Lutheran Reform." *Word and World* 15 (1995) 195–205.

———. "Luther in Front of the Text: The Genesis Commentary." *Word and World* 14 (1994) 186–94.

———. "Luther's Heidelberg Disputation: An Analysis of the Argument." *Word and World*, Supplement Series 1 (1992) 147–54.

Neusner, Jacob. *Messiah in Context: Israel's History and Destiny in Formative Judaism*. Philadelphia: Fortress, 1984.

———, ed. and trans. *The Mishnah: A New Translation*. New Haven, CT: Yale University Press, 1988.

Neusner, Jacob, William Scott Green, and Ernest Frerichs, eds. *Judaisms and the Messiahs at the Turn of the Christian Era*. New York: Cambridge University Press, 1987.

Neve, J. L. *A History of Christian Thought*. Vol. 1. Philadelphia: Muhlenberg, 1946.

Nevin, John. *The Mystical Presence*. Hamden, CT: Achon, 1963.

Newbolt, M. R. *The Book of Unveiling: A Study of the Revelation of St. John*. London: SPCK, 1952.

Newell, William. *The Book of the Revelation*. Chicago: Moody, 1935.

Newman, John Henry. *An Essay on the Development of Christian Doctrine*. New York: Cosimo Classics, 2007.

Neyrey, Jerome. *2 Peter, Jude: A New Translation with Introduction and Commentary*. New York: Doubleday, 1993.

Ngien, Dennis. *The Suffering of God According to Martin Luther's 'Theologia Crucis.'* Vancouver, BC: Regent College, 2005.

Nicholson, E. W. *God and His People: Covenant and Theology in the Old Testament*. Oxford: Clarendon, 1986.

Nicole, Roger. "C. H. Dodd and the Doctrine of Propitiation." *Westminster Theological Journal* 17 (1955) 117–57.

———. "Hilaskesthai Revisited." *Evangelical Quarterly* 49, no. 3 (1977) 173–77.

Niditch, Susan. *Ancient Israelite Religion.* New York: Oxford University Press, 1997.

Nielsen, J. T. *Adam and Christ in the Theology of Irenaeus of Lyons: An Examination of the Function of the Adam-Christ typology in the Adversus Haereses of Irenaeus, against the Background of the Gnosticism of His Time.* Assen: Van Gorcum, 1968.

Niesel, Wilhelm. *The Theology of Calvin.* Translated by Harold Knight. Philadelphia: Westminster, 1956.

Niessen, Richard. "The Virginity of the 'Almah in Isaiah 7:14." *Bibliotheca Sacra* 137 (1980) 133–50.

Nineham, D. E. *Saint Mark.* Baltimore, MD: Penguin, 1964.

Nolland, John. *The Gospel of Matthew: A Commentary on the Greek Text.* Grand Rapids: Eerdmans, 2005.

Norris, Richard. *The Christological Controversy.* Philadelphia: Fortress, 1980.

Noth, Martin. *Exodus: A Commentary.* Translated by J. S. Bowden. Philadelphia: Westminster, 1962.

———. *Leviticus: A Commentary.* Translated by J. E. Anderson. Philadelphia: Westminster, 1965.

Nygren, Anders. *Agape and Eros.* Translated by Philip Watson. New York: Harper & Row, 1969.

———. *Commentary on Romans.* Philadelphia: Fortress, 1978.

Oberholtzer, Thomas. "The Kingdom Rest in Hebrews 3:1–4:13." *Biblia Sacra* 145 (1988) 185–96.

Oberman, Heiko. "The 'Extra' Dimension in the Theology of Calvin." In *The Dawn of the Reformation,* 234–58. Edinburgh: T. & T. Clark, 1992.

———. *The Harvest of Medieval Theology: Gabriel Biel and Later Medieval Nominalism.* Grand Rapids: Baker Academic, 2000.

———. *Luther: Man between God and the Devil.* Translated by Eileen Walliser- Schwarzbart. New Haven, CT: Yale University Press, 1989.

———. "Teufelsdreck: Eschatology and Scatology in the 'Old' Luther." In *The Impact of the Reformation,* 51–65. Grand Rapids: Eerdmans, 1994.

O'Brien, Peter. *The Epistle to the Philippians: A Commentary on the Greek Text.* Grand Rapids: Eerdmans, 1991.

Oettingen, Alexander von. *Lutherische Dogmatik: System der Christlichen Heilswahrheit.* 2 vols. München: Beck, 1897–1902.

Omanson, Roger. "A Superior Covenant: Hebrews 8:1–10:18." *Review & Expositor* 82 (1985) 361–73.

Olson, Oliver. "Contemporary Trends in Liturgy Viewed from the Perspective of Classical Lutheran Theology." *Lutheran Quarterly* 25 (1974) 110–57.

———. "Liturgy as Action." *Dialog* 14 (1975) 108–13.

———. "Matthias Flacius." In *The Reformation Theologians: An Introduction to Theology in the Early Modern Period,* edited by Carter Lindberg, 83–93. Malden, MA: Blackwell, 2002.

Olson, Roger. *The Story of Christian Theology: Twenty Centuries of Tradition and Reform.* Downers Grove, IL: InterVarsity, 1999.

Orback, Robert, and Albert Kirk. *A Commentary on the Gospel of John.* New York: Paulist, 1981.

Origen. *On First Principles.* Translated by Henri De Lubac. Glouster: Peter Smith, 1973.

Osborn, Eric. *Irenaeus of Lyons.* New York: Cambridge University Press, 2001.

———. "Irenaeus of Lyons." In *The First Christian Theologians: An Introduction to Theology in the Early Church,* edited by G. R. Evans, 121–26. Malden, MA: Blackwell Publishing, 2004.

Osborne, Grant. *Romans.* Downer's Grove, IL: InterVarsity, 2004.

Osiander, Andreas. *Von dem Einigen Mittler Jhesu Christo un Rechtfertigung des Glaubens Benkenntnus.* Königsberg: 1551.

Osiander, Johann Adam. *Commentarii in Pentateuchum Pars Tertia. Sive Commentarius in Leviticum.* Tübingen: Bibliopolae Stutgard, 1677.

Ostrogorski, George. *History of the Byzantine State.* New Brunswick, NJ: Rutgers University Press, 1969.

Overman, J. Andrew. *Church and Community in Crisis: The Gospel according to Matthew.* Valley Forge, PA: Trinity Press International, 1996.

Pagels, Elaine. *The Gnostic Gospels.* New York: Random House, 1979.

Paine, Thomas. *The Age of Reason: Being an Investigation of the True and Fabulous Theology.* Los Angeles: Indo-European Publishing, 2011.

Pannenberg, Wolfhart. "Dogmatic Theses on the Doctrine of Revelation." In *Revelation as History*, edited by Wolfhart Pannenberg, Rolf Rendtorff, Trutz Rendtorff, and Ulrich Wilkens, translated by David Granskou, 123–58. New York: MacMillan, 1968.

———. *Jesus: God and Man*. Translated by Lewis Wilkins and Duane Priebe. Philadelphia: Westminster, 1968.

———. *Systematic Theology*. Translated by Geoffrey Bromiley. 3 vols. Grand Rapids: Eerdmans, 1991–1998.

Parker, T. H. L. *Calvin: An Introduction to His Thought*. Louisville, KY: Westminster John Knox Press, 1995.

Patterson, Alexander. *A Commentary, Expository and Practical, on the Epistle to the Hebrews*. Edinburgh: T. & T. Clark, 1856.

Paulson, Steven. *Luther for Armchair Theologians*. Louisville, KY: Westminster John Knox, 2004.

———. *Lutheran Theology*. Edinburgh: T. & T. Clark, 2011.

Pelikan, Jaroslav. *The Christian Tradition: A History of the Development of Doctrine*. 5 vols. Chicago: University of Chicago Press, 1971–1989.

Penna, Romano. *Paul the Apostle: A Theological and Exegetical Study*. 2 vols. Collegeville, MN: Liturgical, 1996.

Perdue, Leo. *The Collapse of History: Reconstructing Old Testament Theology*. Minneapolis: Fortress, 1994.

Perkins, Pheme. *First and Second Peter, James, and Jude*. Louisville, KY: John Knox, 1995.

———. *The Gnostic Dialogue: The Early Church and the Crisis of Gnosticism*. New York: Paulist, 1980.

———. *Gnosticism and the New Testament*. Minneapolis: Fortress, 1993.

Perlitt, L. *Bundestheologie im Alten Testament*. Neukirchen–Vluyn: Neukirchener Verlag, 1987.

Peterson, Robert. *Calvin's Doctrine of the Atonement*. Philipsburg, NJ: Presbyterian and Reformed Publishing, 1983.

Petrella, Ivan. *The Future of Liberation Theology: An Argument and Manifesto*. Aldershot: Ashgate, 2004.

Petrement, Simone. *A Separate God: The Christian Origins of Gnosticism*. Translated by Carol Harrison. San Francisco: Harper & Row, 1990.

Pfeiffer, Charles. *The Epistle to the Hebrews*. Chicago: Moody, 1962.

Pfitzner, Victor. *Hebrews*. Nashville: Abingdon, 1997.

Philip, Lee. *Against the Protestant Gnostics*. Oxford: Oxford University Press, 1987.

Philippi, Friedrich. *Dr. v. Hofmann gegenüber lutherischer Versöhnung—und Rechtfertigungslehre*. Erlangen: Theodor Bläsing, 1856.

———. *Kirchliche Glaubenslehre*. 6 vols. Gütersloh: Drud und Berlag von G. Bertelsmann, 1870–1901.

Phythian-Adams, W. J. *The People and the Presence*. London: Oxford University Press, 1942.

Pieper, August. *An Exposition of Isaiah 40–66*. Translated by Erwin Kowalke. Milwaukee: Northwestern, 1979.

———. "The Law is not made for the Righteous Man." In *The Wauwatosa Theology*, edited by Curtis Jahn, 3 vols., 2:73–100. Milwaukee: Northwestern, 1997.

Pieper, Francis. *Christian Dogmatics*. 3 vols. St. Louis: Concordia, 1950–1953.

Pinomaa, Lennart. *Faith Victorious: An Introduction to Luther's Theology*. Translated by Walter J. Kokkonen. Philadelphia: Fortress, 1963.

Pitre, Brant. *Jesus, the Tribulation, and the End of Exile*. Grand Rapids: Baker Academic, 2005.

Pitstick, Alyssa Lyra. "Development of Doctrine, or Denial? Balthasar's Holy Saturday and Newman's Essay." *International Journal of Systematic Theology* 11 (2009) 129–45.

———. *Light in the Darkness: Hans Urs von Balthasar and the Catholic Doctrine of Christ's Descent into Hell*. Grand Rapids: Eerdmans, 2007.

Pitstick, Alyssa Lyra, and Edward T. Oakes. "Balthasar, Hell, and Heresy: An Exchange." *First Things* (2006) 25–29.

———. "More on Balthasar, Hell, and Heresy." *First Things* **(January 2007) 16–18.**

Placher, William. *A History of Christian Theology: An Introduction*. Philadelphia: Westminster, 1983.

Plantinga, Alvin. *Faith and Philosophy: Philosophical Studies in Religion and Ethics*. Grand Rapids: Eerdmans, 1964.

———. *God and Other Minds: A Study of the Rational Justification of Belief in God*. Ithaca: Cornell University Press, 1967.

———. *God, Freedom, and Evil*. New York: Harper & Row, 1974.

———. "Is Naturalism Irrational?" In *The Analytic Theist: An Alvin Plantinga Reader*, edited by James Sennett, 72–96. Grand Rapids: Eerdmans, 1998.

———. *The Nature of Necessity*. Oxford: Clarendon, 1974.

———. "Sheehan's Shenanigans: How Theology becomes Tomfoolery." In *The Analytic Theist: An Alvin Plantinga Reader*, edited by James Sennett, 316–27. Grand Rapids: Eerdmans, 1998.

———. *Warrant and Proper Function*. New York: Oxford University Press, 1993.

———. *Warrant: The Current Debate*. New York: Oxford University Press, 1993.

———. *Warranted Christian Belief*. New York: Oxford University Press, 2000.

Plumer, William. *Commentary on Paul's Epistle to the Romans*. Edinburgh: W. Oliphant, 1871.

———. *Commentary on the Epistle of Paul, the Apostle, to the Hebrews*. New York: A. D. F. Randolph, 1872.

Plummer, Alfred. *A Critical and Exegetical Commentary on the Gospel according to St. Luke*. Edinburgh: T. & T. Clark, 1922.

Plumptre, E. H. *The General Epistles of Saint Peter and Saint Jude*. Cambridge: Cambridge University Press, 1879.

Potter, G. R. *Zwingli*. Cambridge, UK: Cambridge University Press, 1976.

Prat, Ferdinand. *The Theology of Saint Paul*. Translated by John Stoddard. 2 vols. Westminster, MD: Newman Bookshop, 1958.

Preger, Wilhelm. *Matthias Flacius Illyricus und seine Zeit*. 2 vols. Erlangen: Blassing, 1859–1861.

Prenter, Regin. *Creation and Redemption*. Translated by Theodor Jensen. Philadelphia: Fortress, 1967.

———. *Luther's Theology of the Cross*. Phildelphia: Fortress, 1971.

———. *Spiritus Creator: Luther's Concept of the Holy Spirit*. Translated by John Jensen. Philadelphia: Muhlenberg, 1953.

Preus, J. A. O. *The Second Martin: The Life and Theology of Martin Chemnitz*. St. Louis: Concordia, 1994.

Preus, Robert. *Getting into the Theology of Concord: A Study of the Book of Concord*. St. Louis: Concordia, 1977.

———. "The Hermeneutics of the Formula of Concord." In *Doctrine is Life: Essays on Scripture*, edited by Klement Preus, 215–42. St. Louis: Concordia, 2006.

———. "How is the Lutheran Church to Interpret the Old and New Testaments?" In *Doctrine is Life: Essays on Scripture*, edited by Klement Preus, 179–214. St. Louis: Concordia, 2006.

———. *The Inspiration of Scripture: A Study of the Theology of the Seventeenth Century Lutheran Dogmaticians*. Edinburgh: Oliver and Boud, 1955.

———. "Notes on the Inerrancy of Scripture." *Bulletin of the Evangelical Theological Society* 8, no. 4 (1965) 127–38.

———. *Post-Reformation Lutheran Dogmatics*. 2 vols. St. Louis: Concordia, 1970–1972.

———. *The Theology of Post Reformation Lutheranism: A Study of Theological Prolegomena*. St. Louis: Concordia, 1970.

———. "Vicarious Atonement in John Quenstedt." *Concordia Theological Monthly* 32 (1961) 78–97.

Preus, Samuel. *From Shadow to Promise: Old Testament Interpretation from Augustine to the Young Luther*. Cambridge, MA: Harvard University Press, 1969.

———. *Spinoza and the Irrelevance of Biblical Authority*. Cambridge, UK: Cambridge University Press, 2009.

Preuss, Eduard. *The Justification of the Sinner Before God*. Translated by J. A. Friedrich. Ft. Wayne, IN: Lutheran Legacy, 2011.

Prigent, Pierre. *L'Apocalypse de Saint Jean*. Paris: Delachaux et Niestle, 1981.

Quasten, Johannes. *Patrology*. Translated by Placis Solari. 4 vols. Allen, TX: Christian Classics, 1995.

Quell, Gottfried. "Diatheke." In *Theological Dictionary of the New Testament*, edited by Gerhard Kittel, translated by G. W. Bromiley, 2:107–20. Grand Rapids: Eerdmans, 1964.

Quere, Ralph. *Christum Cognescere: Christ's Efficacious Presence in the Eucharistic Theology of Melanchthon*. Nieuwkoop: de Graaf, 1977.

Rad, Gerhard von. *Old Testament Theology: Single Volume Edition*. Translated by D. M. G. Stalker. Peabody, MA: Prince, 2005.

———. *Genesis: A Comentary*. Translated by John Marks. Philadelphia: Westminster, 1972.

Radner, Ephraim. *Leviticus*. Grand Rapids: Brazos, 2008.

Rahner, Hugo. "Leo der Große, der Papst des Konzils." In *Das Konzil von Chalkedon: Geshichte und Gegenwart*, edited by Aloys Grillmeier and Heinrich Bacht, 1:323–39. Wurzburg: Echter Verlag, 1953–1954.

Rahner, Karl. *Foundations of Christian Faith: An Introduction to the Idea of Christianity*. Translated by William Dyvh. New York: Seabury, 1978.

———. *The Trinity*. London: Continuum, 1986.

Rasmusson, Arne. "A Century of Swedish Theology." *Lutheran Quarterly* 21 (2007) 131–38.

Ratzinger, Joseph. *Introduction to Christianity*. Translated by J. R. Foster. San Francisco: Ignatius, 2004.

———. *Principles of Catholic Theology: Building Stones for Fundamental Theology*. Translated by Mary Frances McCarthy. San Francisco: Ignatius, 1987.

Redford, Donald. *Egypt, Canaan, and Israel in Ancient Times*. Princeton: Princeton University Press, 1993.

Reid, Thomas. *Essays on the Powers of the Human Mind; to which are prefixed, an Essay on Quantity, and an Analysis of Aristotle's Logic*. 3 vols. Edinburgh: Bell and Bradfute, 1812.

———. *An Inquiry into the Human Mind, on the Principles of Common Sense*. Edinburgh: Bell and Bradfute, 1810.

———. *Thomas Reid's Lectures on Natural Theology (1780)*. Washington, DC: University Press of America, 1981.

Rendall, Frederic. *The Epistle to the Hebrews*. New York: Macmillan, 1888.

Rendtorff, Rolf. *The Canonical Hebrew Bible: A Theology of the Old Testament*. Translated by David E. Orton. Leiden: Deo, 2005.

———. *Die Bundesformel*. Stuttgart: Verlag Katholisches Bibelwerk, 1995.

Rengstorf, Karl. *Das Evangelium nach Lukas*. Göttingen: Vandenhoeck & Ruprecht, 1967.

Rhodes, Ron. *Christ Before the Manger: The Life and Times of the Preincamate Christ*. Grand Rapids: Baker, 1992.

Richard, Earl. *Reading 1 Peter, Jude, and 2 Peter: A Literary and Theological Commentary*. Macon, GA: Smyth and Helwys, 2000.

Richard, James W. *Philip Melanchthon: The Protestant Preceptor of Germany 1497–1560*. New York: Burt Franklin, 1974.

Ridderbos, Herman. *The Epistle of Paul to the Churches at Galatia*. Grand Rapids: Eerdmans, 1953.

Riddle, Matthew. *The Gospel According to Mark*. New York: C. Scribner's sons, 1881.

Riehm, Eduard. *Alttestamentliche Theologie*. Halle: Verlag von Eugen Strien, 1889.

Rienecker, Fritz. *Das Evangelium des Lukas*. Wuppertal: R. Brockhaus, 1959.

———. *Das Evangelium des Matthäus*. Wuppertal: R. Brockhaus, 1953.

Rigg, H. A. "Barabbas." *Journal of Biblical Literature* 66 (1945) 417–56.

Rigg, J. M. *St. Anselm of Canterbury: A Chapter in the History of Religion*. London: Methuen, 1896.

Riggenbach, Eduard. *Der Brief an die Hebräer*. Leipzig: A. Deichewrt, 1922.

Rilliet, Jean. *Zwingli: Third Man of the Reformation*. Translated by Harold Knight. Philadelphia: Westminster, 1959.

Ringe, Sharon. *Luke*. Louisville, KY: Westminster John Knox, 1995.

Risisi, Mathias. *Alpha und Omega; eine Deutung der Johannes-Offenbarung*. Basel: Friedrich Reinhardt, 1966.

Ritschl, Albrecht. *A Critical History of the Christian Doctrine of Justification and Reconciliation*. Translated by John Black. Edinburgh: Edmonton and Douglas, 1872.

———. *Die Christliche Lehre von der Rechtfertigung und Versohnung*. 3 vols. Bonn: A. Marcus, 1895–1903.

Ritschl, Otto. *Dogmengeschichte des Protestantismus*. 4 vols. Göttingen and Leipzig: Vandenhoeck & Ruprecht, 1908–1927.

Roberts, Alexander, and James Donaldson, eds. *Ante-Nicene Fathers*. 10 vols. Peabody, MA: Hendrickson, 2004.

Robinson, John A. T. *Redating the New Testament*. Philadelphia: Westminster, 1976.

Robinson, Theodore. *The Epistle to the Hebrews*. London: Hodder & Stoughton, 1948.

———. *The Gospel of Matthew*. London: Hodder & Stoughton, 1947.

Rodriguez, Angel. "Leviticus 16: Its Literary Structure." *Andrews University Seminary Studies* 34 (Autumn 1996) 269–86.

Rogness, Michael. *Melanchthon: Reformer without Honor*. Minneapolis: Augsburg, 1969.

Rohls, Jan. *Reformed Confessions: From Zurich to Barmen.* Translated by John Hoffmeyer. Louisville, KY: John Knox Westminster, 1998.

Rohnert, Wilhelm. *Die Dogmatik der Evangelisch-Lutherischen Kirche.* Braunschweig: H. Wollermann, 1902.

Roo, Jacqueline C. R. De. "Was the Goat for Azazel Destined for the Wrath of God?" *Biblica* 81 (2000) 233–42.

Rooke, Deborah W. "Jesus as Royal Priest: Reflections on the Interpretation of the Melchizedek Tradition in Heb 7." *Biblica* 81 (2000) 81–94.

Rooker, Mark. *Leviticus.* Nashville: Broadman & Holman, 2000.

Roos, Magnus Friedrich. *Kurze Erklärung der Zween Briefe des Apostels Petrus und des Briefs des Apostels Judas.* Tübingen: Ludwig Friedrich Fues, 1798.

Roseman, Philipp. *Peter Lombard.* New York: Oxford University Press, 2004.

Rothschild, Clare. *Hebrews as Pseudepigraphon: The History & Significance of the Pauline Attribution of Hebrews.* Tübingen: Mohr Siebeck, 2009.

Roukema, Riemer. *Gnosis and Faith in Early Christianity: An Introduction to Gnosticism.* Translated by John Bowden. Harrisburg, PA: Trinity, 1999.

Rowe, J. Nigel. *Origen's Doctrine of Subordination: A Study in Origen's Christology.* New York: Peter Lang, 1987.

Royster, Dmitri. *The Epistle to the Hebrews: A Commentary.* Crestwood, NY: St. Vladimir's Seminary Press, 2003.

Rudolph, Kurt. *Gnosis: The Nature and History of Gnosticism.* Translated by Robert Mclachlan Wilson. San Francisco: Harper Collins, 1987.

Ruether, Rosmary Radford. *America, Amerikkka: Elect Nation and Imperial Violence.* New York: Equinox, 2007.

———. *Gaia and God: An Ecofeminist Theology of Earth Healing.* San Francisco: HarperCollins, 1994.

———. *The Church Against Itself.* New York: Herder and Herder, 1967.

———. *Goddesses and the Divine Feminine: A Western Religious History.* Berkeley: University of California Press, 2005.

———. *Integrating Ecofeminism Globalization and World Religions.* Lanham, MD: Rowman and Littlefield, 2005.

———. *Sexism and God-Talk: Toward a Feminist Theology.* Boston: Beacon, 1993.

———. *The Wrath of Jonah: The Crisis of Religious Nationalism in the Israeli-Palestinian Conflict.* Minneapolis: Augsburg Fortress, 2002.

Rushdoony, Rousas John. *Systematic Theology.* 2 vols. Vallecito, CA: Ross, 1994.

Rushton, G. H. *First Peter.* London: Epworth, 1968.

Russell, Bertram. *A History of Western Philosophy.* New York: Touchstone, 1967.

Russell, David. *The Message and Method of Jewish Apocalyptic: 200 B. C. to 100 A. D.* Philadelphia: Westminster, 1964.

Russell, Jeffrey Burton. *The Devil: Perceptions of Evil from Antiquity to Primitive Christianity.* Ithaca: Cornell University Press, 1977.

Russell, Norman. *Cyril of Alexandria.* New York: Routledge, 2000.

Rydelnik, Michael. *The Messianic Hope: Is the Hebrew Bible Really Messianic?* Nashville: B & H Publishing, 2010.

Saarinen, Risto. *The Pastoral Epistles with Philemon and Jude.* Grand Rapids: Brazos, 2008.

Saarnivaara, Uuras. *Luther Discovers the Gospel: New Light upon Luther's Way from Medieval Catholicism to Evangelical Faith.* St. Louis: Concordia Publishing, 1951.

Sabin, Marie Noonan. *The Gospel According to Mark.* Collegeville, MN: Liturgical, 2006.

Sabourin, Leopold. *The Gospel according to St. Matthew.* Bombay: St. Paul Publications, 1982.

Sacchi, Paolo. *Jewish Apocalyptic and Its History.* Sheffield, UK: Sheffield Academic Press, 1990.

Sand, Alexander. *Das Evangelium nach Matthäus: Übersetzt und Erklärt.* Regensburg: Pustet, 1986.

Sanders, E. P. *Judaism: Practice and Belief 63 BCE–66 CE.* London: SCM, 1998.

———. *Paul and Palestinian Judaism: A Comparison of Patterns of Religion.* Philadelphia: Fortress, 1977.

———. *Paul, the Law and the Jewish People.* Philadelphia: Fortress, 1983.

Sanders, J. N. *A Commentary on the Gospel according to Saint John.* London: Black, 1968.

Sasse, Hermann. "Liturgy and Confession: A Brotherly Warning Against the 'High Church' Danger." In *The Lonely Way: Selected Essays and Letters*, 1941–1976, translated by Matthew Harrison, Paul Anderson, Charles Evanson, John Klenig, and Norman Nagel, 299–316. St. Louis: Concordia, 2002.

———. "The Theology of the Cross." In *We Confess Anthology*, translated by Norman Nagel, 35–45. St. Louis: Concordia, 1998.

———. *This is My Body: Luther's Contention for the Real Presence in the Sacrament of the Altar*. Minneapolis: Augsburg, 1959.

Scaer, David P. "Baptism and the Lord's Supper in the Life of the Church." *Concordia Theological Quarterly* 45 (1981) 37–59.

———. *Christology*. Confessional Lutheran Dogmatics. Vol. 6. St. Louis: Luther Academy, 1989.

———. *Discourses in Matthew: Jesus Teaches the Church*. St. Louis: Concordia, 2004.

———. "The Doctrine of the Trinity in Biblical Perspective." *Concordia Theological Quarterly* 67 (2003) 323–34.

———. "Flights from the Atonement." *Concordia Theological Quarterly* 72 (2008) 195–210.

———. "He Did Descend into Hell: In Defense of the Apostles' Creed." *Journal of the Evangelical Theology Society* 35 (1992) 91–99.

———. *James, The Apostle of Faith: A Primary Christological Epistle for the Persecuted Church*. St. Louis: Concordia, 1994.

———. "The Law Gospel Debate in the Missouri Synod." *Springfielder* 36 (1972) 156–71.

———. "The Law Gospel Debate in the Missouri Synod Continued." *Springfielder* 40 (1976) 107–18.

———. "Law and Gospel in Lutheran Theology." *Logia* 3 (1994) 27–34.

———. "Lutheran Viewpoints on the Challenge of Fundamentalism: Eschatology." *Concordia Journal* 10 (1984) 4–11.

———. "Man Made in the Image of God and Its Relationship to the First Promise." *Concordia Theological Quarterly* 41 (1977) 20–35.

———, ed. *Nicene and Post-Nicene Fathers*. 14 vols. First Series. Peabody, MA: Hendrickson, 2004.

———. "Ordaining Women: Has the Time Come?" *Logia* 4 (1995) 83–85.

———. "Problems of Inerrancy and Historicity in Connection with Genesis 1–3." *Concordia Theological Quarterly* 41 (1977) 21–25.

———. "Sacraments as an Affirmation of Creation." *Concordia Theological Quarterly* 57 (1993) 241–63.

———. "Semper Virgo: A Doctrine." *Logia* 19 (2010) 15–19.

———. "Semper Virgo: Pushing the Envelope." *Lutheran Forum* 41 (2007) 24–28.

———. *The Sermon on the Mount: The Church's First Statement of the Gospel*. St. Louis: Concordia, 2000.

———. *What Do You Think of Jesus?* St. Louis: Concordia, 1973.

Schaberg, Jane. *The Illegitimacy of Jesus: A Feminist Theological Interpretation of the Infancy Narratives*. San Francisco: Harper & Row, 1987.

Schaff, Philip. *The Creeds of Christendom*. 3 vols. New York: Harper and Brothers, 1881.

Schaff, Philip, and William Wace, eds. *Nicene and Post-Nicene Fathers*. 14 vols. Second Series. Peabody, MA: Hendrickson, 2004.

Schaller, John. *Biblical Christology: A Study in Lutheran Dogmatics*. Milwaukee: Northwestern, 1981.

Schanz, Paul. *Commentar über das Evangelium des Heiligen Johannes*. Tübingen: Franz Fues, 1885.

———. *Commentar über das Evangelium des Heiligen Lucas*. Tübingen: Franz Fues, 1883.

———. *Commentar über das Evangelium des Heiligen Marcus*. Freiburg: Herder Verlag, 1881.

———. *Commentar über das Evangelium des Heiligen Matthäus*. Freiburg: Herder, 1879.

Schelkle, Karl. *Die Petrusbriefe und der Judasbrief*. Freiburg: Herder, 1961.

———. *Paulus: Leben, Briefe, Theologie*. Darmstadt: Wissenschaftliche Buchgesellschaft, 1981.

Schick, Eduard. *Das Evangelium nach Johannes*. Würzburg: Echter Verlag, 1956.

———. *Die Apokalypse*. Würzburg: Echter Verlag, 1952.

Schierse, Franz. *Der Brief an die Hebräer*. Düsseldorf: Patmos Verlag, 1968.

Schlatter, Adolf. *Der Evangelist Johannes, Wie er Spricht, Denkt und Glaubt*. Stuttgart: Calwer, 1948.

———. *Der Evangelist Matthäus*. Stuttgart: Calwer Verlag, 1948.

———. *Evangelium des Lukas aus seinen Quellen Erklärt*. Stuttgart: Calwer Vereinsbuchhandlung, 1960.

Schleiermacher, Friedrich. *Brief Outline of the Study of Theology*. Translated by Terrence Tice. Richmond: John Knox, 1966.

———. *Christmas Eve: Dialogue on the Incarnation*. Translated by Terrence Tice. San Francisco: EM Texts, 1990.

———. *The Christian Faith*. Translated by H. R. Mackintosh and J. S. Stewart. New York: T. & T. Clark, 1999.

———. *Introduction to Christian Ethics*. Translated by John Shelley. Nashville: Abingdon, 1989.

———. *On Religion: Speeches to Its Cultured Despisers*. Translated by Richard Crouter. New York: Cambridge University Press, 1988.

Schlink, Edmund. *Theology of the Lutheran Confessions*. Translated by Paul Koehneke and Herbert J. A. Bouman. Philadelphia: Fortress, 1961.

Schmauk, Theodore, and C. Theodore Benze. *The Confessional Princinple and the Confessions of the Lutheran Church*. St. Louis: Concordia, 2005.

Schmid, Heinrich. *The Doctrinal Theology of the Evangelical Lutheran Church*. Translated by Charles Hay and Henry Jacobs. Minneapolis: Augsburg, 1961.

Schmid, Josef. *Das Evangelium nach Markus*. Regensburg: F. Pustet, 1958.

———. *Das Evangelium nach Matthäus*. Regensburg: F. Pustet, 1959.

Schmidt, Werner. *Altes Testament*. Stuttgart: Kohlhammer, 1989.

Schmucker, Samuel. "The Person and Work of Christ." In *Lectures on the Augsburg Confession*, 68–106. Philadelphia: Lutheran Publication Society, 1888.

Schnackenburg, Rudolf. *Das Evangelium nach Markus Erläutert*. 2 vols. Düsseldorf: Patmos Verlag, 1966–1971.

———. *The Gospel According to St. John*. Translated by David Smith and G. A. Kon. Vol. 1. New York: Herder and Herder, 1968.

———. *The Gospel According to St. John*. Translated by Kevin Smith. Vol. 3. New York: Crossroads, 1975.

Schneider, Gerhard. *Das Evangelium nach Lukas*. Würzburg: Echter Verlag, 1977.

Schneider, Johannes. *Das Evangelium nach Johannes*. Berlin: Evangelische Verlagsanstalt, 1978.

Schnelle, Udo. *Apostle Paul: His Life and Theology*. Translated by M. Eugene Boring. Grand Rapids: Baker Academic, 2005.

———. *Das Evangelium nach Johannes*. Leipzig: Evangelische Verlagsanstalt, 1998.

Schniewind, Julius. *Das Evangelium nach Matthäus*. Göttingen: Vandenhoeck & Ruprecht, 1964.

Schoeps, Joachim. *Paulus: Die Theologie des Apostels im Lichte der Jüdischen Religionsgeschichte*. Tübingen: J. C. B. Mohr, 1959.

Schofield, J. N. *Introducing Old Testament Theology*. Philadelphia: Westminster, 1964.

Schreiner, Thomas. *Paul, Apostle of God's Glory in Christ: A Pauline Theology*. Downer's Grove, IL: InterVarsity, 2006.

———. *Romans*. Grand Rapids: Baker, 1998.

Schreiner, Thomas, and James Buchanan. *Exegetical Commentary on Galatians*. Grand Rapids: Zondervan, 2010.

Schultz, Hermann. *Die Offenbarungsreligion auf ihrer Vorchristlichen Entwickelungsstufe Dargestellt*. Göttingen: Vandenhoeck & Ruprecht, 1896.

Schultz, Robert. *Gesetz und Evangelium in der Lutherischen Theologie des 19. Jahrhunderts*. Berlin: Lutherisches Verlagshaus, 1958.

Schulz, Siegfried. *Das Evangelium nach Johannes: Übersetzt und Erklärt*. Göttingen: Vandenhoeck & Ruprecht, 1987.

Schwarz, Reinhard. "The Last Supper: The Testament of Jesus." In *The Pastoral Luther: Essays in Luther's Practical Theology*, edited by TimothyWengert, 198–210. Grand Rapids: Eerdmans, 2009.

Schweitzer, Albert. *The Quest for the Historical Jesus*. Edited by John Bowden. Minneapolis: Fortress, 2001.

Schweizer, Eduard. *Das Evangelium nach Lukas: Übersetzt und Erklärt*. Göttingen: Vandenhoeck & Ruprecht, 1982.

———. *Das Evangelium nach Matthäus*. Göttingen: Vandenhoeck & Ruprecht, 1973.

———. *The Good News According to Mark*. Translated by Donald H. Madvig. Richmond: John Knox, 1970.

Schwiebert, E. G. *Luther and His Times: The Reformation from a New Perspective*. St. Louis: Concordia, 1950.

Seeberg, Alfred. *Der Brief an die Hebräer*. Leipzig: Quelle und Meyer, 1912.

Seeberg, Erich. *Luthers Theologie: Christus, Wirklichkeit und Urbild*. Vol. 2. Stuttgart: W. Kohlhammer Verlag, 1937.

Seeberg, Reinhold. *Text-Book of the History of Doctrines.* Translated by Charles Hay. 2 vols. Grand Rapids: Baker, 1977.

Segal, Alan. *The Two Powers in Heaven: Early Rabbinical Reports about Christianity and Gnosticism.* Leiden: Brill, 1977.

Sena, Patrick. *The Apocalypse: Biblical Revelation Explained.* New York: Alba, 1983.

Senior, Donald, and Daniel J. Harrington. *1 Peter, 2 Peter, and Jude.* Collegeville, MN: Liturgical, 2003.

Sherman, Robert. *King, Priest, and Prophet: A Trinitarian Theology of Atonement.* New York: T. & T. Clark, 2004.

Siggins, Ian D. Kingston. *Martin Luther's Doctrine of Christ.* New Haven, CT: Yale University Press, 1970.

Sigmund, P. E. *Liberation Theology at the Crossroads: Democracy or Revolution?* Oxford: Oxford University Press, 1990.

Simar, Huber. *Theologie des Heiligen Paulus.* Freiburg: Herder, 1883.

The Sixteen Documents of Vatican II and the Instruction on the Liturgy. Boston: St. Paul, 1965.

Sloan, Robert. *The Favorable Year of the Lord: A Study in the Jubilary Theology in the Gospel of Luke.* Austin, TX: Schola, 1997.

Smith, Carl. *No Longer Jews: The Search for Gnostic Origins.* Peabody, MA: Hendrickson, 2004.

Smith, Christian. *The Emergence of Liberation Theology: Radical Religion and the Social Movement Theory.* Chicago: University of Chicago Press, 1991.

Socinus, Faustus. *The Racovian Catechism.* Translated by Thomas Rees. London: Paternoster Row, 1818.

Söf̈ding, Thomas. *Das Wort vom Kreuz: Studien zur Paulinischen Theologie.* Tübingen: Mohr Siebeck, 1997.

Spong, John Shelby. *Born of a Woman.* San Francisco: HarperOne, 1994.

Sri, Edward. "Release from the Debt of Sin: Jesus' Jubilee Mission in the Gospel of Luke." *Nova et Vetera* 9 (2011) 183–94.

St. John, Harold. *An Analysis of the Gospel of Mark: The Son of God as Mark Portrayed Him.* London: Pickering and Inglis, 1956.

Staab, Karl. *Das Evangelium nach Matthäus.* Würzburg: Echter Verlag, 1951.

Stade, Berhard. *Biblische Theologie des Alten Testaments.* 2 vols. Tübingen: Mohr, 1905–1911.

Stanton, Graham. *A Gospel for a New People of God: Studies in Matthew.* Louisville, KY: Westminster John Knox, 1992.

Steenberg, M. C. *Irenaeus on Creation: The Cosmic Christ and the Saga of Redemption.* Leiden: Brill, 2008.

Steiger, Johan Anselm. "The Communicatio Idiomatum as the Axle and Motor of Luther's Theology." *Lutheran Quarterly* 14 (2000) 125–58.

Steiner, George. *Real Presences.* Chicago: University of Chicago Press, 1991.

Steinmann, Andrew. *Daniel.* St. Louis: Concordia, 2008.

Steinmetz, David. "Miss Marple Reads the Bible: Detective Fiction and the Art of Biblical Interpretation." In *Taking the Long View: Christian Theology in Historical Perspective,* 15-26. Oxford: Oxford University Press, 2011.

Stendahl, Krister. *Paul among Jews and Gentiles, and Other Essays.* Philadelphia: Fortress, 1976.

Stephens, W. P. *The Theology of Huldrych Zwingli.* Oxford: Clarendon, 1986.

Strack, H. L., and P. Billerbeck. *Kommentar zum Neuen Testament aus Talmud und Midrach.* 4 vols. München: Beck, 1922–1928.

Strathmann, Hermann. *Das Evangelium nach Johannes: Übersetzt und Erklärt.* Göttingen: Vandenhoeck & Ruprecht, 1963.

Strauss, Mark. *The Davidic Messiah in Luke-Acts: The Promise and Its Fulfillment in Lukan Christology.* Sheffield, UK: Sheffield Academic Press, 1995.

Strehle, Stephen. *The Catholic Roots of the Protestant Gospel: Encounter Between the Middle Ages and the Reformation.* Leiden: Brill, 1995.

Strobel, August. *Der Brief an die Hebräer.* Göttingen: Vandenhoeck & Ruprecht, 1991.

Stott, John. *Romans: Good News for God's World.* Downer's Grove, IL: InterVarsity, 1994.

Stott, W. "The Conception of 'Offering' in the Epistle to the Hebrews." *New Testament Studies* 9 (1962/1963) 62–66.

Stuart, Moses. *A Commentary on the Apocalypse.* Edinburgh: Maclachlan, 1847.

Stuhlmacher, Peter. *Paul's Letter to the Romans: A Commentary.* Translated by Scott J. Hafemann. Louisville, KY: Westminster John Knox, 1994.

Stuhlmueller, Carroll. *The Gospel of St. Luke: Introduction and Commentary.* Collegeville, MN: Liturgical, 1964.

Summers, Ray. *Commentary on Luke: Jesus, The Universal Savior.* Waco, TX: Word, 1972.

Swetnam, James. "Sacrifice and Revelation in the Epistle to the Hebrews: Observations and Surmises on Hebrews 9, 26." *Catholic Biblical Quarterly* 30 (1968) 227–34.

———. "A Suggested Interpretation of Hebrews 9,15–18." *Catholic Biblical Quarterly* 27 (October 1965) 373–90.

Tabor, James. *The Jesus Dynasty: The Hidden History of Jesus, His Royal Family, and the Birth of Christianity.* New York: Simon and Schuster, 2007.

Tannehill, Robert. *Luke.* Nashville: Abingdon, 1996.

Taylor, Vincent. *The Gospel according to Mark.* Grand Rapids: Baker, 1981.

Terrien, Samuel. *The Elusive Presence: Toward a New Biblical Theology.* New York: Harper & Row, 1978.

Tertullian. *On Exhortation to Chastity.* Translated by William Le Saint. New York: Fathers of the Church, 1978.

———. *Treatises on Penance and Purity.* Translated and edited by William Le Saint. Westminster: Newman, 1959.

Thielicke, Helmut. *The Evangelical Faith.* Translated by Geoffrey Bromiley. 3 vols. Grand Rapids: Eerdmans, 1974–1982.

Theissen, Gerd. *The Religion of the Earliest Churches: Creating a Symbolic World.* Minneapolis: Fortress, 1999.

Theissen, Gerd, and Annette Merz. *The Historical Jesus: A Comprehensive Guide.* Minneapolis: Fortress, 1998.

Tholuck, August. *Commentar zum Evangelio Johannis.* Gotha: Perthes, 1857.

———. *Commentarie öfwer Brefwer till Hebreerna.* Lund: C. W. K. Gleerup, 1838.

———. *Exposition of the Epistle to the Romans.* Translated by Robert Menzies. Philadelphia: Sorin and Ball, 1844.

Thomas, Derek. "The Mediator of the Covenant." In *Theological Guide to Calvin's Institutes: Essays and Analysis,* edited by David Hall and Peter Lillback, 205–25. Philipsburg, NJ: Presbyterian and Reformed Publishing, 2008.

Thomasius, Gottfried. *Das Bekenntniss der Lutherischen Kirche von der Versöhnung und die Versöhnungslehre D. Chr. K. v. Hofmann's: Mit einem Nachwort von Th. Harnack.* Erlangen: Theodor Bläsing, 1857.

———. *Christi: Person und Werk: Darstellung der Evangelisch-Lutherischen Dogmatik vom Mittpunkte Christologie aus.* 2 vols. Erlangen: Andreas Deichert Verlag, 1886–1888.

Thompson, James. „Hebrews 9 and Hellenistic Concepts of Sacrifice." *Journal of Biblical Literature* 98 (1979) 567–78.

Thompson, Thomas. "Nineteenth-Century Kenotic Christology: The Waxing, Waning, and Weighing of a Quest for a Coherent Orthodoxy." In *Exploring Kenotic Christology: The Self-Emptying of God,* edited by Stephan C. Evans, 74–11. New York: Oxford University Press, 2006.

Thunberg, Lars. *Microcosm and Mediator: The Theological Anthropology of Maximus the Confessor.* Chicago: Open Court, 1995.

Thurston, Bonnie B., and Judith M. Ryan. *Philippians and Philemon.* Collegeville, MN: Liturgical, 2005.

Thurston, R. W. "**Midrash** and 'Magnet' Words in the New Testament." *Evangelical Quarterly* 5 (1979) 22–39.

Tiede, David. *Luke.* Minneapolis: Augsburg, 1988.

Tillich, Paul. *A History of Christian Thought: From its Judaic and Hellenistic Origins to Existentialism.* Edited by Carl Braaten. New York: Simon and Schuster, 1968.

———. *Systematic Theology.* 3 vols. Chicago: University of Chicago Press, 1951–1963.

Tödt, H. E. *The Son of Man in the Synoptic Tradition.* Translated by Dorothea Barton. Philadelphia: Westminster, 1965.

Torrence, T. F. *Karl Barth, Biblical and Evangelical Theologian.* Edinburgh: T. & T. Clark, 1990.

Torres, Miguel De La. *Handbook on U.S. Theologies of Liberation.* Atlanta: Chalice, 2004.

Torrey, Charles. *The Apocalypse of John.* New Haven, CT: Yale University Press, 1958.

Trigg, Joseph W. *Origen.* New York: Routledge, 1998.

Trocmé, Etienne. *L'Evangile selon Saint Marc.* Geneva: Labor et Fides, 2000.

Tuckett, Christopher Mark. *Christology and the New Testament: Jesus and his Earliest Followers*. Louisville, KY: Westminster John Knox, 2001.

Turner, J. David. *Matthew*. Grand Rapids: Baker, 2008.

Turner, J. David, Ellis Deibler, and Janet L. Turner. *Jude: A Structural Commentary*. Lewiston, NY: Mellen Biblical Press, 1996.

Twesten, August Detlev. *Matthias Flacius Illyricus, eine Verlesung. Mit Autobiorgraphischen Beilagen und einer Abhandlung über Melanchthons Verhalten zum Interim von Hermann Rössel*. Berlin: Bethage, 1844.

Tylanda, Joseph. "Christ the Mediator: Calvin versus Stancaro." *Calvin Theological Journal* 7 (1972) 5–16.

———. "The Controversy on Christ the Mediator: Calvin's Second Reply to Stancaro." *Calvin Theological Journal* 8 (1972) 131–57.

Tzamalikos, P. *Origen: Philosophy of History and Eschatology*. Leiden: Brill, 2007.

Um, Stephen T. *The Theme of Temple Christology in John's Gospel*. New York: T. & T. Clark, 2006.

Urban, Linwood. *A Short History of Christian Thought*. New York: Oxford University Press, 1995.

Ursinus, Zacharias. *The Commentary of Zacharias Ursinus on the Heidelberg Catechism*. Translated by G. W. Williard. Grand Rapids: Eerdmans, 1956.

Vainio, Okki-Pekka. *Justification and Participation in Christ: The Development of the Lutheran Doctrine of Justification from Luther to the Formula of Concord (1580)*. Leiden: Brill, 2008.

Vajta, Vilmos. *Luther on Worship: An Interpretation*. Philadelphia: Muhlenberg, 1958.

Van Buren, Paul. *Christ in Our Place: The Substitutionary Character of Calvin's Doctrine of Reconciliation*. Edinburgh: Oliver and Boyd, 1957.

Van den Eynde, Sabine. "Children of the Promise: On the Διαθηκη-Promise Abraham in Luke 1:72 and Acts 3:25." In *The Unity of Luke–Acts*, edited by Jozef Verheyden, 470–82. Louvain: Peeters, 1998.

Van Seters, John. *Abraham in History and Tradition*. New Haven, CT: Yale University Press, 1975.

Vanhoye, Albert. "Esprit éternel et feu du sacrifice en He 9,14." *Biblica* 64 (1983) 263–74.

———. *Our Priest is Christ: The Doctrine of the Epistle to the Hebrews*. Rome: Pontifical Biblical Institute, 1977.

Vanier, Jean. *Drawn into the Mystery of Jesus through the Gospel of John*. New York: Paulist, 2004.

Vercruysse, Joseph. "Luther's Theology of the Cross in the Time of the Heidelberg Disputation." *Gregorianum* 57 (1976) 523–48.

Vermes, Geza. *Jesus the Jew*. Philadelphia: Fortress, 1981.

Vinson, Richard. *Luke*. Macon, GA: Smyth and Helwys, 2008.

Vogel, Heinrich. "On Original Sin, The Flacian Aberration." In *No Other Gospel: Essays in Commemoration of the 400th Anniversay of the Formula of Concord, 1580–1980,* edited by Arnold Koelpin, 126–31. Milwaukee: Northwestern, 1980.

Vogelsang, Erich. *Die Anfange von Luthers Christologie: Nach der Ersten Psalmenvorlesung, Insbesondere in Ihren Exegetischen und Systematischen Zusammenhangen mit Augustin und der Scholastik Dargestellt*. Berlin: Walter **de Gruyter, 1929.**

Vögtle, Anton. *Der Judasbrief, der 2. Petrusbrief*. Solothurn: Benziger, 1994.

Vos, Geerhardos. *The Teaching of the Epistle to the Hebrews*. Grand Rapids: Eerdmans, 1956.

Waldrop, Charles. *Karl Barth's Christology: Its Basic Alexandrian Character*. Berlin: de Gruyter, 1984.

Walther, C. F. W. "Christ's Resurrection—The World's Absolution." In *The Word of His Grace: Occasional and Festival Sermons,* 225–36. Lake Mills: Graphic, 1978.

———. *Church and Ministry*. Translated by J. T. Mueller. St. Louis: Concordia, 1987.

Walton, J. H. *Covenant: God's Purpose, God's Plan*. Grand Rapids: Zondervan, 1994.

Wannenwetsch, Bernd. "Luther's Moral Theology." In *The Cambridge Companion to Martin Luther,* edited by Donald K. McKim, 120–36. Cambridge: Cambridge University Press, 2003.

Wansbrough, Henry. *Theology in Saint Paul*. Notre Dame, IN: Fides, 1970.

Watson, Philip S. *Let God Be God!: An Interpretation of the Theology of Martin Luther*. Philadelphia: Fortress, 1970.

Watts, John D. W. *Basic Patterns in Old Testament Religion*. New York: Vantage, 1971.

Wawrykow, Joseph. "Grace." In *The Theology of Thomas Aquinas,* edited by Rik Van Nieuwenhove and Joseph Wawrykow, 192–222. Nortre Dame: University of Notre Dame Press, 2005.

Weaver, J. Denny. *The Nonviolent Atonement*. Grand Rapids: Eerdmans, 2001.

Weidner, Franklin. *Annotations on the Revelation of St. John the Divine.* New York: Christian Literature, 1898.

———. *Commentary on the Gospel of Mark.* Allentown, PA: Diehl, 1881.

Weinfeld, Moshe. "The Covenant of Grant in the Old Testament and in the Ancient Near East." *Journal of the American Oriental Society* 90 (1970) 184–203.

Weiss, Hans-Friedrich. *Der Brief an die Hebräer: Übersetzt und Erklärt.* Göttingen: Vandenhoeck & Ruprecht, 1991.

Welch, Claude. *God and Incarnation in Mid-Nineteenth century German Theology: G. Thomasius, I. A. Dorner, A. E. Biedermann.* New York: Oxford University Press, 1965.

———. *Protestant Thought in the Nineteenth Century.* 2 vols. New Haven, CT: Yale University Press, 1972–1985.

Wellhausen, Julius. *Das Evangelium Lucae: Übersetzt und Erklärt.* Berlin: G. Reimer, 1904.

———. *Das Evangelium Marci.* Berlin: Reimer, 1909.

———. *Prolegomena to the History of Israel.* Whitefish, MT: Kessinger, 2004.

Wenham, Gordon *Genesis 1–15.* Waco, TX: Word, 1987.

———. "Sanctuary Symbolism in the Garden of Eden Story." In *Proceeding in the Ninth World Congress of Jewish Studies,* edited by Moshe Goshen-Gottstein, 19–25. Jerusalem: World Union of Jewish Studies: Magnes Press, Hebrew University, 1988.

Westbrook, Raymond, and Theodore J. Lewis. "Who Led the Scapegoat in Leviticus 16:21?" *Journal of Biblical Literature* 127 (2008) 417–22.

Westcott, Brooke. *The Epistle to the Hebrews.* Grand Rapids: Eerdmans, 1892.

Westermann, Claus. *Elements of Old Testament Theology.* Translated by Douglas Stott. Atlanta: John Knox, 1982.

———. *Genesis 12–36: A Commentary.* Translated by John Scullion. Minneapolis: Augsburg, 1995.

White, Graham. *Luther as Nominalist: A Study in the Logical Methods Used in Martin Luther's Disputations in Light of Their Medieval Background.* Helsinki: Luther-Agricola-Society, 1994.

Whiteley, D. E. H. *The Theology of Saint Paul.* Philadelphia: Fortress, 1964.

Wiefel, Wolfgang. *Das Evangelium nach Lukas.* Berlin: Evangelische Verlagsanstalt, 1988.

———. *Das Evangelium nach Matthäus.* Leipzig: Evangelische Verlagsanstalt, 1998.

Wikenhauser, Alfred. *Das Evangelium nach Johannes.* Regensburg: F. Pustet, 1961.

Wilckens, Ulrich. *Das Evangelium nach Johannes: Übersetzt und Erklärt.* Göttingen: Vandenhoeck & Ruprecht, 1998.

Wilkens, Robert Louis. "The Church's Way of Speaking." *First Things* (August/September 2005) 27–31.

Williams, George Huntston. *The Radical Reformation.* Ann Arbor, MI: Edwards Brothers, 1992.

Williams, Janet P. "Pseudo-Dionysius and Maximus the Confessor." In *The First Christian Theologians: An Introduction to Theology in the Early Church,* edited by G. R. Evans, 193–99. Malden, MA: Blackwell, 2004.

Williams, Rowan. *On Christian Theology.* Oxford: Blackwell, 2000.

———. "Origen." In *The First Christian Theologians: An Introduction to Theology in the Early Church,* edited by G. R. Evans, 132–42. Malden, MA: Blackwell, 2004.

Williamson, P. R. *Abraham, Israel and the Nations: The Patriarchal Promise and Its Covenantal Development in Genesis.* Sheffield, UK: Sheffield Academic, 2000.

Williamson, Ronald. *The Epistle to the Hebrews.* London: Epworth, 1965.

Willis, David. *Calvin's Catholic Christology: The Function of the So-called "Extra-Calvinisticum."* Leiden: Brill, 1966.

Willis, John. *A History of Christian Thought.* 3 vols. Hicksville, NY; Pamona, FL: Exposition, 1976–1985.

Wilson, Robert McLachlan. *The Gnostic Problem: A Study of the Relations between Hellenistic Judaism and the Gnostic Heresy.* London: A. R. Mowbray, 1958.

Wingren, Gustaf. *Creation and Law.* Translated by Ross McKenzie. Philadelphia: Muhlenberg, 1961.

———. *Gospel and Church.* Translated by Ross McKenzie. Philadelphia: Fortress, 1964.

———. *The Living Word.* Translated by Victor Pogue. Philadelphia: Fortress, 1960.

———. *Man and the Incarnation: A Study in the Biblical Theology of Irenaeus.* Translated by Ross Mackenzie. Edinburgh: Oliver and Boyd, 1959.

———. *Theology of Conflict: Nygren, Barth, Bultmann.* Translated by Eric Wahlstrom. Edinburgh: Oliver and Boyd, 1958.

Witherington, Ben, III. *The Christology of Jesus*. Minneapolis: Fortress, 1990.

———. *The Gospel of Mark: A Socio-Rhetorical Commentary*. Grand Rapids: Eerdmans, 2001.

———. *Letters and Homilies for Jewish Christians: A Socio-Rhetorical Commentary on Hebrews, James and Jude*. Nottingham, UK: Apollos, 2007.

———. *Matthew*. Macon, GA: Smyth and Helwys, 2006.

———. *Paul's Narrative Thought World: The Tapestry of Tragedy and Triumph*. Louisville, KY: Westminster John Knox, 1994.

Witsius, Herman. *Sacred Dissertations on What is Commonly Called the Apostles Creed*. Translated by Donald Fraser. 2 vols. Glasgow: Khull, Blackie and Company, 1823.

Witte, Johannes. "Die Christologie Calvins." In *Das Konzil von Chalkedon: Geshichte und Gegenwart*, edited by Aloys Grillmeier and Heinrich Bacht, 3:487–529. 3 vols. Wurzburg: Echter Verlag, 1953–1954.

Wohlenberg, Gustav. *Das Evangelium des Markus*. Leipzig: A. Deichert, 1910.

———. *Der Erste und Zweite Petrusbrief und der Judasbrief*. Leipzig: A. Deichert, 1915.

Wolff, Richard. *A Commentary on the Epistle of Jude*. Grand Rapids: Zondervan, 1960.

———. *The Gospel According to Mark*. Wheaton, IL: Tyndale, 1969.

Wright, J. Stafford. "The Virgin Birth." In *The New International Dictionary of New Testament Theology*, edited by Colin Brown. 3 vols. Grand Rapids: Zondervan, 1975.

Wright, N. T. "Born of a Virgin?" In *The Meaning of Jesus: Two Visions*, edited by N. T. Wright and Marcus Borg, 171–78. San Francisco: HarperCollins, 1999.

———. *Christian Origins and the Question of God*. 3 vols. Minneapolis: Fortress, 1992–2003.

———. *The Climax of the Covenant: Christ and the Law in Pauline Theology*. Edinburgh: T. & T. Clark, 1991.

———. "Harpagmos and the Meaning of Philippians 2:5–11." *Journal of Theological Studies* 37 (1986) 321–52.

———. *John for Everyone: Chapters 11–21*. Vol. 2. Louisville, KY: Westminster John Knox, 2004.

———. *Who Was Jesus?* Grand Rapids: Eerdmans, 1992.

Yeago, David. "The Bread of Life: Patristic Christology and Evangelical Soteriology in Martin Luther's Sermons on John 6." *St. Vladimir's Theological Quarterly* 39 (1995) 257–79.

———. "The Catholic Luther." *First Things* (March, 1996) 37–41.

Yee, Gale. A. *Jewish Feasts and the Gospel of John*. Wilmington, DE: Michael Glazier, 1989.

Young, Edward. "The Immanuel Prophecy: Isaiah 7:14–16." *Westminster Theological Journal* 15 (1953) 97–124.

Young, Norman. "The Gospel according to Hebrews 9." *New Testament Studies* 27 (1981) 208–9.

Youngblood, Ronald. *The Heart of the Old Testament: A Survey of Key Theological Themes*. Grand Rapids: Baker, 1998.

Zachman, Randall. "Jesus Christ as the Image of God in Calvin's Theology." *Calvin Theological Journal* 25 (1990) 46–52.

Zahn, Theodor. *Das Evangelium des Johannes*. Leipzig: A. Deichert, 1921.

———. *Das Evangelium des Lucas*. Leipzig: A. Deichert, 1920.

———. *Das Evangelium des Matthäus*. Leipzig: A. Deichert, 1922.

———. *Introduction to the New Testament*. Translated by John Moore Trout, William Arnot Mather, Louis Hodous, Edward Strong Worcerter, William Hoyt Worrell, and Rowland Backus Dodge. Vol. 3. Grand Rapids: Kregel, 1953.

Zetterholm, Magnus, ed. *The Messiah in Early Judaism and Christianity*. Minneapolis: Fortress, 2007.

Ziegler, Roland. "The New English Translation of The Book of Concord (Augsburg/Fortress 2000): Locking the Barn Door After . . . " *Concordia Theological Quarterly* 66 (2002): 145–65.

Zummerli, Walther. *Grundriss der Alttestamentlichen Theologie*. Stuttgart: W. Kohlhammer, 1972.

Zwingli, Huldrych. "Friendly Exegesis, that is, Exposition of the Matter of the Eucharist to Martin Luther, February 1527." In *Huldrych Zwingli Writings*, translated and edited by H. Wayne Pipkin, 2:238–369. 2 vols. New York: Pickwick, 1984.